INTERNATIONAL FINANCIAL REPORTING STANDARDS: CONTEXT, ANALYSIS AND COMMENT

Consumer Behaviour Analysis
Edited by Gordon Foxall
3 volume set

Technology, Organizations and Innovation
Edited by Patrick Dawson
4 volume set

Marketing
Edited by Michael Baker
5 volume set

Organizational Studies
Edited by University of Warwick's Organizational Behaviour Staff
4 volume set

Industrial Relations
Edited by John Kelly
5 volume set

Public Management
Edited by Stephen P. Osborne
5 volume set

Corporate Governance
Edited by Thomas Clarke
5 volume set

Knowledge Management
Edited by Nonaka Ikujiro
3 volume set

Accounting Ethics
Edited by J. Edward Ketz
4 volume set

Forthcoming:

Supply Chain Management
Edited with an introduction by Steve New
4 volume set

Brands and Brand Management
Edited by Richard Elliott
4 volume set

Cross-Cultural Management
Edited by Tim G. Andrews & Richard Mead
4 volume set

Marketing Research
Edited by David F. Birks & Tim Macer
4 volume set

INTERNATIONAL FINANCIAL REPORTING STANDARDS: CONTEXT, ANALYSIS AND COMMENT

Critical Perspectives in Business and Management

Edited by

David Alexander and Christopher Nobes

Volume I
Context: The need for international standardisation of accounting

Routledge
Taylor & Francis Group

LONDON AND NEW YORK

First published 2008
by Routledge
2 Park Square, Milton Park, Abingdon, Oxon, OX14 4RN, UK

Simultaneously published in the USA and Canada
by Routledge
270 Madison Avenue, New York, NY 10016

Routledge is an imprint of the Taylor & Francis Group, an informa business

Typeset in 10/12pt Times NR MT by Graphicraft Limited, Hong Kong
Printed and bound in Great Britain by
MPG Books Ltd, Bodmin, Cornwall

British Library Cataloguing in Publication Data
A catalogue record for this book is available from the British Library

Library of Congress Cataloging in Publication Data

International financial reporting standards : context, analysis and comment /
edited by David Alexander and Christopher Nobes.
p. cm. – (Critical perspectives on business and management)
Includes bibliographical references and index.
ISBN 978-0-415-38097-3 (set) – ISBN 978-0-415-38098-0 (cloth : alk. paper)
1. International Accounting Standards Board.   2. International Accounting Standards
Committee.   3. Financial statements – Standards.   4. Accounting –
Standards.   I. Alexander, David, 1941–   II. Nobes, Christopher.
HF5626.I58376   2007
657′.30218–dc22   2007045142

ISBN10: 0-415-38097-9 (Set)
ISBN10: 0-415-38098-7 (Volume I)

ISBN13: 978-0-415-38097-3 (Set)
ISBN13: 978-0-415-38098-0 (Volume I)

Publisher's Note

References within each chapter are as they appear in the original
complete work.

CONTENTS

CONTENTS

CONTENTS

CONTENTS

CONTENTS

CONTENTS

A series of eye-witness reports on IASC Board meetings, published
in *Accounting and Business*, written by Christopher Nobes

VOLUME IV THE IASB: THE STANDARDS AND THEIR WIDESPREAD ADOPTION

CONTENTS

XV

CONTENTS

CONTENTS

ACKNOWLEDGEMENTS

The publishers would like to thank the following for permission to reprint their material:

Blackwell Publishing for permission to reprint R. H. Parker, 'Some International Aspects of Accounting', *Journal of Business Finance*, 3, 4, Winter 1971, pp. 29–36. Reprinted by permission of Blackwell Publishing.

American Accounting Association for permission to reprint Frederick D. S. Choi and Richard M. Levich, 'Behavioral Effects of International Accounting Diversity', *Accounting Horizons*, June 1991, pp. 1–13. Reproduced by kind permission of the American Accounting Association and the authors.

Frederick D. S. Choi and Richard M. Levich for permission to reprint their 'Behavioral Effects of International Accounting Diversity', *Accounting Horizon*, June 1991, pp. 1–13.

Elsevier for permission to reprint Ray Ball, S. P. Kothari and Ashok Robin, 'The Effect of International Institutional Factors on Properties of Accounting Earnings'. This article was published in *Journal of Accounting and Economics*, 29, 2000, pp. 1–51. Copyright Elsevier 2000. Reprinted with permission.

Blackwell Publishers for permission to reprint Ole-Kristian Hope, 'Disclosure Practices, Enforcement of Accounting Standards, and Analysts' Forecast Accuracy: An International Study', *Journal of Accounting Research*, 41, 2, 2003, pp. 235–272. Reprinted by permission of Blackwell Publishing.

Robert H. Parker, 'Importing and Exporting Accounting: The British Experience', in Anthony G. Hopwood, ed., *International Pressures for Accounting Change* (Prentice-Hall, 1989), pp. 7–29.

Blackwell Publishing for permission to reprint S. J. Gray, 'Towards a Theory of Cultural Influence on the Development of Accounting Systems Internationally', *Abacus*, 24, 1, March 1988, pp. 1–15. Reprinted by permission of Blackwell Publishing.

Elsevier for permission to reprint S. Chanchani and R. Willett, 'An Empirical Assessment of Gray's Accounting Value Constructs'. This article was published in *International Journal of Accounting*, 39, 2, 2004, pp. 125–154. Copyright Elsevier 2004. Reprinted with permission.

Elsevier for permission to reprint Timothy S. Doupnik and Stephen B. Salter, 'External Environment, Culture, and Accounting Practice: A Preliminary Test of a General Model of International Accounting Development'. This article was published in *International Journal of Accounting*, 30, 3, pp. 189–207. Copyright Elsevier 1995. Reprinted with permission.

Blackwell Publishing for permission to reprint Christopher Nobes, 'Towards a General Model of the Reasons for International Differences in Financial Reporting', *Abacus*, 34, 2, September 1998, pp. 162–187. Reprinted by kind permission of Blackwell Publishing.

Elsevier for permission to reprint Richard Briston, 'The Evolution of Accounting in Developing Countries'. This article was published in *International Journal of Accounting, Education and Research*, Fall 1978, pp. 105–120. Copyright Elsevier 1978. Reprinted with permission.

Blackwell Publishing for permission to reprint Nabil Baydoun and Roger Willett, 'Cultural Relevance of Western Accounting Systems to Developing Countries', *Abacus*, 31, 1, March 1995, pp. 67–92. Reprinted by permission of Blackwell Publishing.

Blackwell Publishing for permission to reprint H. R. Hatfield, 'Some Variations in Accounting Practice in England, France, Germany and the United States', *Journal of Accounting Research*, Autumn 1966, pp. 169–182. Reprinted by permission of Blackwell Publishing.

Elsevier for permission to reprint G. G. Mueller, 'Accounting Principles Generally Accepted in the United States Versus Those Generally Accepted Elsewhere'. This article was published in *International Journal of Accounting*, 3, 1, 1968, pp. 91–103. Copyright Elsevier 1968. Reprinted with permission.

American Accounting Association for permission to reprint R. D. Nair and Werner G. Frank, 'The Impact of Disclosure and Measurement Practices on International Accounting Classifications', *Accounting Review*, LV, 3, July 1980, pp. 426–450. Reproduced by kind permission of the American Accounting Association and the authors.

R. D. Nair for permission to reprint R. D. Nair and Werner G. Frank, 'The Impact of Disclosure and Measurement Practices on International Accounting Classifications', *Accounting Review*, LV, 3, July 1980, pp. 426–450.

Blackwell Publishing for permission to reprint C. W. Nobes, 'An Empirical Analysis of International Accounting Principles: A Comment', *Journal of*

Accounting Research, 19, 1, Spring 1981, pp. 268–270. Reprinted by kind permission of Blackwell Publishing.

Blackwell Publishing for permission to reprint C. W. Nobes, 'A Judgemental International Classification of Financial Reporting Practices', *Journal of Business Finance and Accounting*, 10, 1, Spring 1983, pp. 1–19. Reprinted by kind permission of Blackwell Publishing.

Accounting and Business Research for permission to reprint Leo G. van der Tas, 'Measuring Harmonisation of Financial Reporting Practice', *Accounting, and Business Research*, 18, 70, Spring 1988, pp. 157–169. Reprinted by permission of CCH Magazines.

Blackwell for permission to reprint J. S. W. Tay and R. H. Parker, 'Measuring International Harmonization and Standardization'. *Abacus*, 26, 1, March 1990, pp. 71–88. Reprinted by permission of Blackwell Publishing.

Blackwell for permission to reprint Leo G. van der Tas, 'Measuring International Harmonization and Standardization: A Comment, *Abacus*, 28, 2, September 1992, pp. 211–216. Reprinted by permission of Blackwell Publishing.

Blackwell for permission to reprint J. S. W. Tay and R. H. Parker, 'Measuring International Harmonization and Standardization: A Reply', *Abacus*, 28, 2, September 1992, pp. 217–220. Reprinted by permission of Blackwell Publishing.

Blackwell for permission to reprint Simon Archer, Pascale Delvaille and Stuart McLeay, 'A Statistical Model of International Accounting Harmonization', *Abacus*, 32, 1, March 1996, pp. 1–29. Reprinted by permission of Blackwell Publishing.

Taylor & Francis for permission to reprint Vera M. Krisement, 'An Approach for Measuring the Degree of Comparability of Financial Accounting Information', *European Accounting Review*, 6, 3, 1997, pp. 465–485 (Taylor & Francis Ltd, http://www.informaworld.com) reprinted by permission of the publisher and Vera M. Krisement.

Accounting and Business Research for permission to reprint Richard D. Morris and R. H. Parker, 'International Harmony Measures of Accounting Policy: Comparative Statistical Properties', *Accounting and Business Research*, 29, 1, Winter 1998, pp. 73–86. Reprinted by permission of CCH Magazines.

Taylor & Francis for permission to reprint Leandro Cañibano and Araceli Mora, 'Evaluating the Statistical Significance of *De Facto* Accounting Harmonization: A Study of European Global Players', *European Accounting Review*, 9, 3, 2000, pp. 349–369 (Taylor & Francis Ltd, http://www.informaworld.com) reprinted by permission of the publisher and authors.

Disclaimer

The publishers have made every effort to contact authors/copyright holders of works reprinted in *International Financial Reporting Standards: Context, Analysis and Comment (Critical Perspectives in Business and Management)*. This has not been possible in every case, however, and we would welcome correspondence from those individuals/companies whom we have been unable to trace.

Chronological table of reprinted articles and chapters

Date	Author	Article/chapter	References	Vol.	Chap.
1966	Henry Rand Hatfield	Some variations in accounting practice in England, France, Germany and the United States	*Journal of Accounting Research* (Autumn): 169–82	I	12
1968	G. G. Mueller	Accounting principles generally accepted in the United States versus those generally accepted elsewhere	*International Journal of Accounting* 3(1): 91–103	I	13
1971	R. H. Parker	Some international aspects of accounting	*Journal of Business Finance* 3(4): 29–36	I	1
1973	ICAEW (and others)	An agreement to establish an international accounting standards committee	London: ICAEW etc., 6pp.	II	31
1976	Sir Henry Benson	The story of international accounting standards: a personal record	*Accountancy* (July): 34–9	II	26
1978	Richard J. Briston	The evolution of accounting in developing countries	*International Journal of Accounting* (Fall): 105–20	I	10
1979	John A. Hepworth	International Accounting Standards Committee – the future	W. J. Brennan (ed.) *The Internationalization of the Accountancy Profession*, Toronto: CICA, pp. 49–57	II	29
1980	R. D. Nair and Werner G. Frank	The impact of disclosure and measurement practices on international accounting classifications	*Accounting Review* 55(3): 426–50	I	14
1981	R. D. Nair and Werner G. Frank	The harmonization of international accounting standards, 1973–1979	*International Journal of Accounting* (Fall): 61–77	II	40
1981	C. W. Nobes	An empirical analysis of international accounting principles: a comment	*Journal of Accounting Research* 19(1): 268–70	I	15
1982	J. A. Burggraaff	IASC developments: an update	*Journal of Accountancy* (September): 104–10	II	30
1982	Thomas G. Evans and Martin E. Taylor	"Bottom line compliance" with the IASC: a comparative analysis	*International Journal of Accounting* (Fall): 115–28	II	42

Chronological Table continued

Date	Author	Article/chapter	References	Vol.	Chap.
1982	W. E. Olson	The establishment of international organizations	W. E. Olson, *The Accounting Profession – Years of Trial: 1969–1980*, New York: AICPA, pp. 223–43	II	28
1983	IASC	Preface to Statements of International Accounting Standards	London: IASC, 5pp.	II	32
1983	C. W. Nobes	A judgemental international classification of financial reporting practices	*Journal of Business Finance and Accounting* 10(1): 1–19	I	16
1983	William J. Violet	The development of international accounting standards: an anthropological perspective	*International Journal of Accounting* (Spring): 1–12	II	34
1984	S. M. McKinnon and Paul Janell	The International Accounting Standards Committee: a performance evaluation	*International Journal of Accounting* (Spring): 19–34	II	41
1988	S. J. Gray	Towards a theory of cultural influence on the development of accounting systems internationally	*Abacus* 24(1): 1–15	I	6
1988	Leo G. van der Tas	Measuring harmonisation of financial reporting practice	*Accounting and Business Research* 18(70): 157–69	I	17
1989	Sir Henry Benson	Accounting standards	Sir H. Benson, *Accounting For Life*, London: Kogan Page, pp. 102–14	II	25
1989	Robert H. Parker	Importing and exporting accounting: the British experience	Anthony G. Hopwood (ed.) *International Pressures for Accounting Change*, Englewood Cliffs, NJ: Prentice-Hall, pp. 7–29	I	5
1989	Juan M. Rivera	The internationalization of accounting standards: past problems and current prospects	*International Journal of Accounting* 24(4): 320–41	II	35
1990	J. S. W. Tay and R. H. Parker	Measuring international harmonization and standardization	*Abacus* 26(1): 71–88	I	18

Year	Author(s)	Title	Source	Part	No.
1990	R. S. Olusegun Wallace	Survival strategies of a global organization: the case of the International Accounting Standards Committee	*Accounting Horizons* 4(2): 1–22	II	36
1991	Rudolf Brunovs and Robert J. Kirsch	Goodwill accounting in selected countries and the harmonization of international accounting standards	*Abacus* 27(2): 135–61	II	43
1991	Frederick D. S. Choi and Richard M. Levich	Behavioral effects of international accounting diversity	*Accounting Horizons* (June): 1–13	I	2
1991	Richard Karl Goeltz	International accounting harmonization: the impossible (and unnecessary?) dream	*Accounting Horizons* 5(1): 85–8	II	37
1991	S. E. C. Purvis, Helen Gernon and Michael A. Diamond	The ISAC and its comparability project: prerequisites for success	*Accounting Horizons* (June): 25–44	II	38
1992	IASC	ISAC Constitution	London: IASC, 5pp.	II	33
1992	J. S. W. Tay and R. H. Parker	Measuring international harmonization and standardization: a reply	*Abacus* 28(2): 217–20	I	20
1992	Leo G. van der Tas	Measuring international harmonization and standardization: a comment	*Abacus* 28(2): 211–16	I	19
1993	Sara York Kenny and Robert K. Larson	Lobbying behaviour and the development of international accounting standards: the case of the IASC's joint venture project	*European Accounting Review* 3: 531–54	II	39
1995	Nabil Baydoun and Roger Willett	Cultural relevance of Western accounting systems to developing countries	*Abacus* 31(1): 67–92	I	11
1995	Timothy S. Doupnik and Stephen B. Salter	External environment, culture, and accounting practice: a preliminary test of a general model of international accounting development	*International Journal of Accounting* 30(3): 189–207	I	8
1996	Simon Archer, Pascale Delvaille and Stuart McLeay	A statistical model of international accounting harmonization	*Abacus* 32(1): 1–29	I	21

Chronological Table continued

Date	Author	Article/chapter	References	Vol.	Chap.
1996	Sir Bryan Carsberg	The role and future plans of the International Accounting Standards Committee	I. Lapsley (ed.) *Essays in Accounting Thought*, Edinburgh: Institute of Chartered Accountants of Scotland, pp. 68–84	III	45
1996	Peter Walton	Accountancy – the most exciting profession in the world	*Accounting and Business* (June): 12–13	II	27
1997	John Flower	The future shape of harmonization; the EU versus the IASC versus the SEC	*European Accounting Review* 6(2): 281–303	III	47
1997	Vera M. Krisement	An approach for measuring the degree of comparability of financial accounting information	*European Accounting Review* 6(3): 465–85	I	22
1998	Sir Bryan Carsberg	The future of the IASC	*Accounting and Business* (January): 8–9	III	46
1998	John Flower	The future shape of harmonization: a reply	*European Accounting Review* 7(2): 331–3	III	49
1998	Richard D. Morris and R. H. Parker	International harmony measures of accounting policy: comparative statistical properties	*Accounting and Business Research* 29(1): 73–86	I	23
1998	Christopher Nobes	Towards a general model of the reasons for international differences in financial reporting	*Abacus* 34(2): 162–87	I	9
1998	Christopher Nobes	The future shape of harmonization: some responses	*European Accounting Review* 7(2): 323–30	III	48
1998	Christopher Nobes	Prospects for world standards by 2000?	*Accounting and Business* (January): 10–11	III	55
1998	Christopher Nobes	IASC's brave new world	*Accounting and Business* (March): 22–3	III	56
1998	Christopher Nobes	Life is definitely not a beach at the IASC	*Accounting and Business* (June): 18–19	III	57
1998	Christopher Nobes	IASC ties up loose ends	*Accounting and Business* (September): 26–7	III	58
1998	Donna L. Street and Kimberley A. Shaughnessy	The evolution of the G4 + 1 and its impact on international harmonization of accounting standards	*Journal of International Accounting, Auditing and Taxation* 7(2): 131–61	III	50

Chronological Table continued

Date	Author	Article/chapter	References	Vol.	Chap.
2000	Donna L. Street and Sidney J. Gray	IAS adopters respond to cherry-picking ban	*Accounting and Business* (April): 40–1	III	72
2000	Donna L. Street, Nancy B. Nichols and Sidney J. Gray	Assessing the acceptability of international accounting standards in the US: an empirical study of the materiality of US GAAP reconciliations by non-US companies complying with IASC standards	*International Journal of Accounting* 35(1): 27–63	III	73
2000	Wayne B. Thomas	The value-relevance of geographic segment earnings disclosures under SFAS 14	*Journal of International Financial Management and Accounting* 11(3): 133–55	III	68
2001	Peter H. Collett, Jayne M. Godfrey and Sue L. Hrasky	International harmonization: cautions from the Australian experience	*Accounting Horizons* 15(2): 171–82	III	53
2001	Ronald A. Dye and Shyam Sunder	Why not allow FASB and IASB standards to compete in the U.S.?	*Accounting Horizons* 15(3): 257–71	IV	78
2001	Hervé Stolowy, Axel Haller and Volker Klockhaus	Accounting for brands in France and Germany compared with IAS 38 (intangible assets): an illustration of the difficulty of international harmonization	*International Journal of Accounting* 36: 147–67	III	67
2002	Bruce K. Behn, Nancy B. Nichols and Donna L. Street	The predictive ability of geographic segment disclosures by U.S. companies: SFAS No. 131 vs. SFAS No. 14	*Journal of International Accounting Research* 1: 31–44	III	69
2002	Stephen A. Zeff	"Political" lobbying on proposed standards: a challenge to the IASB	*Accounting Horizons* 16(1): 43–54	IV	81
2003	Martin Glaum and Donna L. Street	Compliance with the disclosure requirements of Germany's New Market: IAS versus US GAAP	*Journal of International Financial Management and Accounting* 14(1): 64–100	III	74

Chronological Table continued

Year	Author	Title	Source		No.
2005	Karel van Hulle	From accounting directives to international accounting standards	C. Leuz, D. Pfaff and A. Hopwood (eds) *The Economics and Politics of Accounting: International Perspectives on Research Trends, Policy and Practice*, Oxford: Oxford University Press, pp. 349–75	IV	89
2005	Brenda Van Tendeloo and Ann Vanstraelen	Earnings management under German GAAP versus IFRS	*European Accounting Review* 14(1): 155–80	IV	95
2005	Jens Wüstemann and Sonja Kierzek	Revenue recognition under IFRS revisited: conceptual models, current proposals and practical consequences	*Accounting in Europe* 2: 69–106	IV	85
2006	David Alexander	Legal certainty, European-ness and *realpolitik*	*Accounting in Europe* 3: 65–80	IV	86
2006	Christopher W. Nobes	Revenue recognition and EU endorsement of IFRS	*Accounting in Europe* 3: 81–9	IV	87
2006	Christopher Nobes	The survival of international differences under IFRS: towards a research agenda	*Accounting and Business Research* 36(3): 233–45	IV	100
2006	Christopher Nobes and Hans Robert Schwencke	Modelling the links between tax and financial reporting: a longitudinal examination of Norway over 30 years up to IFRS adoption	*European Accounting Review* 15(1): 63–87	IV	99
2006	Jens Wüstemann and Sonja Kierzek	True and fair view revisited – a reply to Alexander and Nobes	*Accounting in Europe* 3: 91–116	IV	88

INTRODUCTION

This volume is the first in a series of four concerned with published papers on the background, life and works of the International Accounting Standards Committee (IASC) and its successor, the International Accounting Standards Board (IASB).

The content of the four volumes can be summarised as follows:

Volume I   Context: The Need for International Standardisation of Accounting

Volume II   The Early Years of the International Accounting Standards Committee

Volume III   The Later Years of the International Accounting Standards Committee

Volume IV   The IASB: The Standards and their Widespread Adoption

Big ideas, such as standardised financial reporting for the whole world, do not spring fully formed from barren desert. There must be fertile ground; seeds need to be planted. Turning the ideas into action requires that weak original growth must be encouraged and protected; effort and energy need to be put into it.

This first volume (of four) looks at the context of the birth of the International Accounting Standards Committee (IASC) and its successor. The volume is divided into four parts, which are briefly outlined below.

The field of study is so large that we have been able to reproduce only a small sample of relevant papers here. Good surveys of the field are provided by Meek and Saudagaran (1990), Wallace and Gernon (1991) and Saudagaran and Meek (1997).

Diversity and its effects

One key contextual issue is the degree to which accounting is different internationally. If it were not different, standardisation would not be needed. Part 1 of this volume is concerned with diversity and its effects. Robert Parker (Chapter 1), in an early paper in the field, gives examples of international differences and why they are interesting. The latter was not obvious at the time.

1

Gray (1980) introduced a measure of conservatism that uses data from companies' reconciliations to US accounting numbers. The measure was later used by several researchers, including Weetman and Gray (1991), Cooke (1993), Hellman (1993), Norton (1995), Adams *et al.* (1999) and Whittington (2000). Chapters 2–5 are examples of research on the size and effects of international differences.

Frederick Choi and Richard Levich (Chapter 2) examine how analysts and investors respond to international accounting diversity. A more extensive work on the subject is Choi and Levich (1990). Choi *et al.* (1983) had earlier looked at the dangers of ratio analysis based on unadjusted accounting numbers from different countries. Choi & Lee (1991) and Lee & Choi (1992) look at the effects of goodwill on international differences in merger premia. However, Nobes and Norton (1997) suggest that the tax effects reported by Lee and Choi cannot be correct because goodwill on consolidation was not relevant for tax. Later, Miles and Nobes (1998) found that analysts still do not adjust for international differences.

Chapters 3 and 4 are empirical. In Chapter 3 Ray Ball, S. P. Kothari and Ashok Robin compare code law countries with common law countries (see also, Chapters 8 and 9). They find that companies in code law countries report bad news more slowly. Ole-Kristian Hope (Chapter 4) shows that increased disclosures by companies lead to greater accuracy of analysts' forecasts. Elsewhere, Pope and Walker (1999) look at earnings measures in the UK and the US. They examine delays in reporting good news and bad news, and the degree to which bad news is shown as extraordinary.

Influences on accounting

A topic related to diversity is the study of the reasons for international similarities or differences in accounting. This is the topic of Part 2. A grasp of this may help one to understand how to standardise and, indeed, whether to standardise.

In Chapter 5 Robert Parker examines the spread of accounting technology across borders, using the British case to show examples of both importing and exporting. A subsequent major strand of research looks at the influence of culture on accounting; and culture can be exported or imported. S. J. Gray (Chapter 6) sets out the theory of cultural influence, and Shalin Chanchani and Roger Willett (Chapter 7) and elsewhere Salter and Niswander (1995) attempt to empirically assess the theory, with some difficulty and with mixed results. Chanchani and MacGregor (1999) synthesise the studies on culture.

In Chapter 8 Timothy Doupnik and Stephen Salter incorporate cultural and other variables into a general model of the causes of international accounting differences, and then generate data to test the model. However, Christopher Nobes (Chapter 9) suggests that this mixture of variables amounts to double counting, and proposes elimination of the cultural variables, except where a country is dominated culturally from outside (in which case, culture is the only independent variable needed). For independent countries, Nobes suggests that the key variable is the nature of the financing system. In Volume III, a paper by Jason Zezhong Xiao *et al.* provides empirical support for that hypothesis (see Chapter 54).

A particular issue of importing/exporting is whether an accounting system designed for one type of country should be imported by another. This subject is examined by Richard Briston (Chapter 10) and by Nabil Baydoun and Roger Willett (Chapter 11) (see also Hove, 1986). They all see problems with such imports. Richard Goeltz takes up the theme in relation to the spread of international standards in Volume II (see Chapter 37).

Classification

The classification of accounting systems is discussed in Part 3. This is an old field of study, dating back to Henry Hatfield's paper of 1911 (Chapter 12). However, only a few other publications appeared prior to the 1980s. Gerhard Mueller (1967) investigated classification, but the result was a whole book that cannot be reproduced here. A summary can be found in Choi and Mueller (1992, pp. 43–8). However, Mueller's connected paper on the classification of differing environments for accounting is reproduced as Chapter 13. The American Accounting Association's early work (AAA, 1977) in this area deals with some criteria that should be obeyed for good classification.

In Chapter 14, by R. D. Nair and Werner Frank, Price Waterhouse (PW) data is used to prepare a classification of countries by accounting. This is perhaps the best of several studies based on PW data. It separates measurement from disclosure practices. Other studies are available by da Costa *et al.* (1978) and Frank (1979). In Chapter 15 Christopher Nobes criticises all of them by suggesting that the data has many faults and was not designed for the purpose of classification.

A new approach is suggested by Nobes (Chapter 16), introducing a hierarchy and purpose-built data. This approach has been tested by Doupnik and Salter (1993). Roberts (1995) looked critically at classification studies, and his warnings have been heeded by Nobes (see Chapter 9).

The issue of whether there is an Anglo-American cluster of accounting systems has been the subject of much discussion, in particular whether the IASC was dominated by this alleged cluster. Alexander and Archer (2000) note many differences between the UK and the US accounting systems (broadly defined to include regulatory issues). However, Nobes (2003) suggests that UK and US financial reporting practices are sufficiently similar (compared to those of other countries) to comprise a family. D'Arcy (2001) uses *de jure* data to suggest that there is no Anglo-American cluster, but Nobes (2004) casts doubt on the reliability of the data.

Measuring standardisation

The fourth and final part of this volume contains papers on the measurement of standardisation or harmonisation. Leo van der Tas (Chapter 17) broke new ground by applying statistical methods concerned with concentration to the subject of accounting. J. S. W. Tay and Robert Parker (Chapter 18) defined a series of terms (e.g. harmony, harmonisation) and then made some suggestions for improving the techniques of van der Tas. The subsequent exchange between the authors is reproduced in Chapters 19 and 20.

Following on from this, there were many papers on statistical techniques, generally used to measure standardisation for a few practices for a few countries. Chapters 21–23 by Simon Archer *et al.*, Vera Krisement, and Richard Morris and Robert Parker are examples. Other papers include van der Tas (1992), Emenyonu and Gray (1992, 1996), Hermann and Thomas (1995), Archer *et al.* (1995), Rahman *et al.* (1996) and Aisbitt (2001).

Taplin (2004) synthesises the debate, and in Chapter 24 Leandro Cañibano and Araceli Mora apply the techniques to the measurement of standardisation of accounting among a particular group of companies: 'European global players'. They suggest that, to a certain degree, harmonisation is 'spontaneous' rather than being driven by standard-setters. This point was suggested earlier for disclosure by Zarzeski (1996).

References

AAA (1977) 'Report of the American Accounting Association Committee on International Operations and Education, 1975–1976', *Accounting Review*, Supplement to Vol. 5(2): 67–101.

Adams, C. A., P. Weetman, E. A. E. Jones and S. J. Gray (1999) 'Reducing the Burden of US GAAP Reconciliations by Foreign Companies Limited in the United States: The Key Question of Materiality', *European Accounting Review* 8(1): 1–22.

Aisbitt, Sally (2001) 'Measurement of Harmony of Financial Reporting Within and Between Countries: The Case of the Nordic Countries', *European Accounting Review* 10(1): 51–72.

Alexander, D. and S. Archer (2000) 'On the Myth of "Anglo-Saxon" Financial Accounting', *International Journal of Accounting* 35(4): 539–57.

Archer, Simon, Pascale Delvaille and Stuart McLeay (1995) 'The Measurement of Harmonisation and the Comparability of Financial Statement Items: Within-Country and Between-Country Effects', *Accounting and Business Research* 25(98) (Spring): 67–80.

Chanchani, Shalin and Alan MacGregor (1999) 'A Synthesis of Cultural Studies in Accounting', *Journal of Accounting Literature* 18: 1–30.

Choi, F. D. S., H. Hino, S. K. Min, S. O. Nam, J. Ujiie and A. Stonehill (1983) 'Analyzing Foreign Financial Statements: The Use and Misuse of International Ratio Analysis', *Journal of International Business Studies* (Spring/Summer).

Choi, Frederick D. S. and Changwoo Lee (1991) 'Merger Premia and National Differences in Accounting for Goodwill', *Journal of International Financial Management & Accounting* 3(3) (Autumn): 219–40.

Choi, F. D. S. and R. M. Levich (1990) *The Capital Market Effects of International Accounting Diversity*, Homewood: Dow-Jones Irwin.

Choi, F. D. S. and G. G. Mueller (1992) *International Accounting*, Englewood Cliffs, NJ: Prentice-Hall, Chapter 2.

Cooke, T. E. (1993) 'The Impact of Accounting Principles on Profits: The US Versus Japan', *Accounting and Business Research* 23(92) (Autumn): 460–76.

da Costa, R. C., J. C. Bourgeois and W. M. Lawson (1978) 'A Classification of International Financial Accounting Practices', *International Journal of Accounting* (Spring).

d'Arcy, A. (2001) 'Accounting Classification and the International Harmonisation Debate – An Empirical Investigation', *Accounting, Organizations and Society* 26: 327–49.

Doupnik, T. S. and S. B. Salter (1993) 'An Empirical Test of a Judgmental International Classification of Financial Reporting Practices', *Journal of International Business Studies* 24(1): 41–60.

Emenyonu, Emmanuel N. and Sidney J. Gray (1992) 'EC Accounting Harmonisation: An Empirical Study of Measurement Practices in France, Germany and the UK', *Accounting and Business Research* 23(89) (Winter): 49–58.

Emenyonu, Emmanuel N. and Sidney J. Gray (1996) 'International Accounting Harmonization and the Major Developed Stock Market Countries: An Empirical Study', *International Journal of Accounting* 31(3): 269–79.

Frank, W. G. (1979) 'An Empirical Analysis of International Accounting Principles', *Journal of Accounting Research* (Autumn): 593–605.

Gray, S. J. (1980) 'The Impact of International Accounting Differences from a Security-Analysis Perspective: Some European Evidence', *Journal of Accounting Research* 18(1) (Spring): 64–76.

Hellman, Niclas (1993) 'A Comparative Analysis of the Impact of Accounting Differences on Profits and Return on Equity: Differences between Swedish Practice and US GAAP', *European Accounting Review* 2(3) (December): 495–530.

Herrmann, Don and Wayne Thomas (1995) 'Harmonisation of Accounting Measurement Practices in the European Community', *Accounting and Business Research* 25(100) (Autumn): 253–65.

Hove, Mfandaidza R. (1986) 'Accounting Practices in Developing Countries: Colonialism's Legacy of Inappropriate Technologies', *International Journal of Accounting, Education and Research* (Fall): 81–100.

Lee, Changwoo and Frederick D. S. Choi (1992) 'Effects of Alternative Goodwill Treatments on Merger Premia: Further Empirical Evidence', *Journal of International Financial Management & Accounting* 4(3) (Autumn): 220–36.

Meek, G. K. and S. M. Saudagaran (1990) 'A Survey of Research on Financial Reporting in a Transnational Context', *Journal of Accounting Literature* 9.

Miles, Samantha and Christopher Nobes (1998) 'The Use of Foreign Accounting Data in UK Financial Institutions', *Journal of Business Finance and Accounting* 25(3 and 4) (April/May): 309–28.

Mueller, G. G. (1967) *International Accounting, Part I*, London: Macmillan.

Nobes, C. W. (2003) 'On the Myth of "Anglo-Saxon" Financial Accounting: A Comment', *International Journal of Accounting* 38(1): 95–104.

Nobes, C. W. (2004) 'On Accounting Classification and the International Harmonisation Debate', *Accounting, Organizations and Society* 29(2): 189–200.

Nobes, Christopher and Julie Norton (1997) 'Effects of Alternative Goodwill Treatments on Merger Premia: A Comment', *Journal of International Financial Management and Accounting* 8(2).

Norton, Julie (1995) 'The Impact of Financial Accounting Practices on the Measurement of Profit and Equity: Australia Versus the United States', *Abacus* 31(2) (September): 178–200.

Pope, Peter F. and Martin Walker (1999) 'International Differences in the Timeliness, Conservatism, and Classification of Earnings', *Journal of Accounting Research* 37 (Supplement): 53–87.

Rahman, A., P. Perera and S. Ganeshanandam (1996) 'Measurement of Formal Harmonisation in Accounting: An Exploratory Study', *Accounting and Business Research* 26(41) (Autumn).

Roberts, A. (1995) 'The Very Idea of Classification in International Accounting', *Accounting, Organisations and Society* 20(7/8): 639–64.

Salter, S. B. and F. Niswander (1995) 'Cultural Influence on the Development of Accounting Systems Internationally: A Test of Gray's [1988] Theory', *Journal of International Business Studies* 26(2): 379–97.

Saudagaran, S. M. and G. K. Meek (1997) 'A Review of Research on the Relationship Between International Capital Markets and Financial Reporting by Multinational Firms', *Journal of Accounting Literature* 6: 127–59.

Taplin, R. (2004) 'A Unified Approach to the Measurement of International Accounting Harmony', *Accounting and Business Research* 34(1): 57–73.

van der Tas, Leo G. (1992) 'Evidence of EC Financial Reporting Practice Harmonization: The Case of Deferred Taxation', *European Accounting Review* 1(1) (May): 69–104.

Wallace, R. S. O. and H. Gernon (1991) 'Frameworks for International Comparative Accounting', *Journal of Accounting Literature* 10: 209–64.

Weetman, Pauline and Sidney J. Gray (1991) 'A Comparative International Analysis of the Impact of Accounting Principles on Profits: The USA Versus the UK, Sweden and The Netherlands', *Accounting and Business Research* 21(84), (Autumn): 363–79.

Whittington, M. (2000) 'Problems in Comparing Financial Performance Across International Boundaries: A Case Study Approach', *International Journal of Accounting* 35(3): 399–413.

Zarzeski, Marilyn Taylor (1996) 'Spontaneous Harmonization Effects of Culture and Market Forces on Accounting Disclosure Practices', *Accounting Horizons* 10(1) (March): 18–37.

Part 1

DIVERSITY AND
ITS EFFECTS

1

SOME INTERNATIONAL ASPECTS OF ACCOUNTING[1]

R. H. Parker

Source: *Journal of Business Finance* 3(4) (1971): 29–36.

The theme of this lecture is the growing importance of the international aspects of accounting. The paper is divided into four parts since one can, I think, distinguish four different reasons why we in Britain should be interested in international accounting. I shall call them the historical reason, the multinational reason, the comparative reason and the European reason.

I

The *historical* reason is the least important, but it is worth remembering that modern accounting is not the invention of any one country. A number of countries have made important contributions.

Not surprisingly leadership in accounting and financial affairs has tended to coincide with leadership in trade and industry. In so far as we can fix a date at all, modern accounting began in the Italian city states round about the year 1300. The Italians remained the leaders for over two centuries and it was as the "Italian method of bookkeeping" that the techniques of double entry accounting spread slowly throughout Europe. The direction of the flow is neatly summed up in the second half of the title of the English edition (1547) of Jan Ympyn's *Nieuwe Instructie* (New Instruction):

> A Notable and very excellente woorke, expressyng and declaryng the maner and forme how to kepe a boke of accomptes or reconynges. . . . Translated with greate Diligence out of the Italian toung into Dutche, and out of Dutche, into French, and now out of Frenche into Englishe.

By the 16th century commercial supremacy had in fact moved to Flanders and the Netherlands, and in the writings of Simon Stevin of Bruges we find the beginnings of discounted cash flow and investment analysis. In an appendix to his Tables of Interest (Antwerp, 1582) he describes "a general rule for finding which is the most profitable of two or more conditions, and by how much it is more profitable than the other". The rule is to find the present value of each proposed condition in respect to a given rate of interest, the difference between these present values showing by how much one condition is better than the other [1].

By the 19th century Britain had become the leader and it was, of course, in Scotland that the accountancy profession as we know it today first began. During the first half of the century, Scottish accountants were active as trustees of sequestrated and deceased estates. They were also engaged in the winding up of partnerships, and in the keeping and balancing of merchants' account books. The close links with the legal profession are apparent and Sir Walter Scott in a letter written in 1820 described accountancy as one of the "branches of our legal practice" [2]. It soon became rather more than that and lawyers were no doubt no more numerate then than they are today. In any case, a Society of Accountants in Edinburgh was granted a royal charter in 1854. The Glasgow accountants followed in 1855 and the Aberdeen accountants in 1867. The English were slower [3]. Societies of accountants were formed in Liverpool and London in 1870, in Manchester in 1871 and in Sheffield in 1877. In 1880 they came together as The Institute of Chartered Accountants in England and Wales. Like the Scots their main work at first was in the field of bankruptcies, liquidations and trusteeships.

As the century progressed there was an increased emphasis on auditing, the first important text being Pixley's *Auditors. Their Duties and Responsibilities* published in London in 1881. In 1905 Richard Brown, a leading Scottish accountant, asked: "Why should not the adjustment of an Income Tax Return of profits, where a difficulty has arisen, be left to an accountant?" [4] and during the First World War taxation replaced bankruptcy as the most important branch of work, after auditing, in most accountants' offices.

At the same time there was a growing interest in accounting as an aid to management. The most important early British work on costing, Garcke and Fells' *Factory Accounts*, written jointly by an engineer and an accountant, was first published in 1887. After the War, in 1919, associations of cost accountants were established both in Britain (the Institute of Cost and Works Accountants) and in the United States (the National Association of Cost Accountants). It was in fact to the United States that accounting as well as commercial leadership was now passing. The American accountancy profession was at first very much an offshoot of the British one [5], but it grew very quickly, especially in the fields of cost accounting and education. Richard Brown, though describing (in 1905) the U.S. accounting profession as only about twenty years old, could yet state that:

> Withal a good deal may be learned from our American cousins in matters of Accounting, more especially in the working of costing systems and in the devising of methods of bookkeeping by which the results of the trading of huge concerns are shown with a frequency and a rapidity which would astonish accountants or book-keepers of the old-fashioned school [6].

The world owes both standard costing and direct costing mainly to the Americans [7]. The phrase "direct costing" is used in both the French and German languages to describe the technique known in Britain by the equally misleading name of "marginal costing".

When the first American business school—the Wharton School of Finance and Commerce at the University of Pennsylvania—was founded in 1881, it included a professor of accounting on its staff and today there are almost certainly more university teachers of accounting and allied subjects in the United States than in the rest of the world put together.

II

Accounting has thus always been international in scope. My second reason, the *multinational* reason, is ensuring that it will become even more so.

Companies have traded outside their own national boundaries for centuries but it is only comparatively recently that the term "multinational company" has come into common use. It is difficult to provide a precise definition of the term. A broad definition is that a multinational company is any firm which performs its main operations, either manufacture or the provision of a service, in at least two countries [8].

As soon as companies begin to trade and manufacture outside their home country accounting and financial problems arise. Some of the problems are peculiar to international operations, others are simply new versions of ones already existing at home.

The most obvious accounting problem peculiar to international activity is that of foreign currencies. Rules of "translating" from one currency to another have had to be established. In general, one can distinguish between the "closing rate" method in which all amounts in foreign currencies are translated at the rate ruling at the date of the balance sheet; and the "historic rate" method in which fixed assets, depreciation, permanent investments, long-term receivables, long-term liabilities and share capital are translated at acquisition rates, current assets at closing rates, remittances at "actual", and revenue and expenses other than depreciation at average rates.

It is interesting to note that whilst the former method appears to be growing in popularity among British companies, it has made little headway among American ones. I have suggested elsewhere the reasons for this [9]. The historic rate method is only satisfactory for major currency devaluations and revaluations at infrequent intervals if we make rather heroic assumptions about changes in local replacement costs. British companies increasingly hold their foreign assets in North America and Western Europe, where periodic rather than continual devaluation and revaluation is the norm. On the other hand, the closing rate method works very badly—and the historic rate method reasonably well—where the home country is one like the United States and the foreign country one in which inflation and devaluation are continual, as they are in those Latin American countries which invariably provide the American text-book examples.

This is an example of accounting principles being influenced by the local environment. A more universal approach, the combining of the use of current replacement costs with closing exchange rates, has been adopted by the Philips company of the Netherlands [10] and also, I suspect, less systematically by some British companies using the closing rate method.

An example of a national accounting problem made more difficult by international operations is the setting of transfer prices. A great deal has been written about the problems of setting such prices within national firms. Some writers have stressed an approach based on marginal analysis; others have thought behavioural considerations to be more important [11]. At the international level, with the foreign subsidiary replacing the national division, new factors are added [12].

First, and most obviously, transfer prices can be used to minimize taxes on a world-wide basis. For example, the Report of the Committee of Enquiry into the Relationship of the Pharmaceutical Industry with the National Health Service (the "Sainsbury Report") includes the following paragraph:

> The second difficulty about foreign-owned firms, the transfer price of raw materials or intermediates procured from foreign affiliates, is likewise an intricate one and we have reason to believe from the results of our financial questionnaire that it is of considerable importance. Foreign firms reported a much higher cost of materials as a percentage of the total cost of manufacture than did British firms and we believe that the propriety of such costs should be investigated. We are aware that the United Kingdom tax authorities have a right to investigate these transfer prices in order to ensure that foreign-owned manufacturing or distributing companies in this country (no matter in what industry) are not improperly reducing the apparent amount of their profits in the United Kingdom by inflating the transfer prices that they pay to their foreign parents. The tax authorities of other countries have and operate similar powers. We recommend that the attention of the British tax authorities should be drawn to the transfer prices of pharmaceutical raw materials or intermediates, and that the Ministry, in assessing

the Standard Cost Returns of foreign-owned manufacturing companies, should make use of the ability of chemical engineers to form reasonable assessments of the production costs of chemical materials. They should be unwilling to accept the prices noted on Standard Cost Returns unless the foreign-owned firm offers confirmation of the reasonableness of its transfer prices, and the Ministry's own professional staff consider them reasonable.

Tables in the financial appendix to the report showed that British companies imported 21.6% of their materials in 1965, subsidiaries of American companies 39.0%, subsidiaries of Swiss companies 74.1% and subsidiaries of other European companies 47.1%. Materials consumed were 49.2% of the total cost of manufacture for British companies, 57.7% for American subsidiaries, 85.5% for Swiss subsidiaries and 60.0% for other European subsidiaries. For British companies profits before interest and taxation were 22.5% of sales, royalties, service charges and other trading income, for American subsidiaries 23.2%, for Swiss subsidiaries 8.7% and for other European subsidiaries 15.3% [13].

One disadvantage of relatively high transfer prices is that the larger the transfer price, the larger the import duty payable. The holding company's net gain may not therefore be very great, especially as there is a tendency, at least among the advanced industrial countries of Western Europe and North America, for tax differentials to narrow.

Secondly, transfer prices can be used to reduce exchange losses. A country suffering from balance of payments difficulties may restrict remittances of dividends, but not remittances in payment of materials or machinery imported by the subsidiary. Brooke and Remmers give the example of a financial director who explained that no dividend had been received from a couple of subsidiaries for a number of years, "but do they ever pay through the nose when they have a mechanical breakdown!" [14].

Thirdly, transfer prices may be deliberately set low in order to provide finance for a subsidiary.

Fourthly, transfer prices can be used to shift profits, for political just as much as for tax reasons, from country to country.

The opportunities mentioned above have their drawbacks: the expense of administration; possible trouble with tax and customs authorities; and, very importantly, adverse repercussions on the company's control system.

Arbitrary transfer prices combined with inter-country differences in accounting principles may make the reported profits of foreign subsidiaries meaningless:

The truth is that profitability exercises in [the pharmaceutical] industry are meaningless. More than anything else profitability tends to reflect accounting practice. . . .

What does the rapid fall in foreign subsidiary profits since 1954 tell us? Simply that firms have begun to realize (rather late in life in some instances) that the British M.P. is extremely badly informed. He is happier with large remissions of royalties, inflated raw material costs (which effectively cheat the Exchequer) and transfer of profits to the parent represented as cost items, than he is with high profits here, with 50% going into the Exchequer and 25% going into capital investments in Britain's future [15].

III

The third reason for studying international accounting is the *comparative* one. We can learn by observing how others have reacted to accounting problems which, especially in industrial nations, often do not differ very markedly from our own. To take just three examples:

(a) It is sometimes suggested in Britain that accounting principles and valuation methods should be written into the Companies Act or that companies should follow exactly the same rules in reporting to shareholders as they do in reporting to the Inland Revenue.

The former suggestion has already been put into practice in the German Federal Republic where the Companies Act (*Aktiengesetz*) of 1965 sets out in legal terms the familiar accounting philosophy of historical cost modified by conservatism. Section 153, for example, provides that fixed and financial assets shall be carried at the cost of acquisition or construction less depreciation or diminution in value. Section 155 prescribes the valuation of current assets at the costs of acquisition or manufacture or a lower valuation if the latter

(i) is necessary in accordance with reasonable business judgment in order to prevent the valuation of these assets from being changed in the near future as a result of fluctuations of values, or

(ii) is held permissible for purposes of taxation.

It is expressly stated that such lower valuation may be retained even if the reasons for it have ceased to exist! [16]

The influence of taxation law on the accounts prepared for shareholders varies from country to country. In France the rule that all deductions claimed for tax purposes must be similarly recorded in the accounts has meant that there is almost no difference between the financial statements prepared for the shareholders and those prepared for tax purposes. German law, on the other hand, makes a clear distinction between a commercial balance sheet (*Handelsbilanz*) and a tax balance sheet (*Steuerbilanz*). A freer choice of valuation methods is permitted by commercial law than by tax law.

In the United States, the last-in first-out method of inventory valuation can be used for tax purposes only if it is also used in the published financial statements, whilst the Canadian *Anaconda* case [17] has had the effect of ruling out LIFO for shareholders as well as for tax not only in Canada but also in Britain. The omission of *all* overheads when valuing stock-in-trade is not an accepted accounting practice in North America but it is in Britain where its use for tax purposes was approved by the House of Lords in the *Duple Motor Bodies* case [18].

(*b*) In the current debate in Britain about comparability of financial statements and uniformity of accounting principles, suggestions of reform are sometimes made which could lead to some kind of national plan or chart of accounts.

Writing in 1946, Professor Lauzel, a leading promoter of the French national accounting plan, stated that "if one wants accounting to be a valid instrument for measuring and making comparisons over time and in space, it has to fulfil a certain number of conditions and, especially, the following:

> it must use a *terminology* based on precise definitions;
> it must *classify* facts logically according to well defined criteria;
> it must supply a general method for the recording of *movements* between classes of accounts;
> it must state rules as general as possible for determining the *values* to be recorded" [19].

A national accounting plan drawn up on lines such as these would clearly be rather more than just an exercise in bookkeeping.

The French Accounting Plan was first published in 1947 and revised in 1957. Its requirements are imposed by law on the nationalized industries and on state-controlled or subsidized firms and organizations. Decrees of 28 December 1959 and 13 April 1962 prescribe the eventual extension of its field of application to all industrial and commercial enterprises. A *guide comptable professionel* will be drawn up for each industry [20].

I shall not attempt to argue here whether or not we in Britain should move towards such a national accounting plan. It is worth pointing out, however, as an illustration that uniformity by itself is not enough, some of the weaknesses of French accounting.

First, as has already been noted, the influence of taxation on French accounts is much too strong. To quote Lauzel once more:

> From this point of view it can appear regrettable, for example, that the accounts must obligatorily record 'fiscal' depreciation ... that is either too low or too high in relation to standards reasonably taking account of the real factors of the wearing out of the plant and equipment. There is a similar problem for stocks, which, it

15

must be admitted, are sometimes undervalued, sometimes overvalued, in the tax return, in relation to the principles which seem to flow from rational management concepts [21].

Secondly, uniformity has been stressed at the expense of disclosure. French balance sheets have remained very conservative documents, and consolidated financial statements were very rare until quite recently.

Thirdly, there has tended to be uniformity of method rather than of principle. For example the Plan provides, without explanation, for stocks to be valued at the lower of weighted average cost and net selling price. (But this is not always observed in practice.)

(c) Methods of showing the effects of inflation on financial statements are receiving renewed attention in Britain, although the current situation is unfortunately still well summarized in the following quotation from the booklet *Accounting for Stewardship in a period of Inflation* published by the Research Foundation of the Institute of Chartered Accountants in England and Wales:

> ... the majority of companies in the United Kingdom have made no attempt in their published annual statements to measure the extent to which their reported profits have been attributable to the progressive decline in the value of the currency in which they are measured, and those few which have done so have generally confined their calculations to one aspect only of this change, namely its bearing on charges against profits for the amortisation of long-term expenditure on fixed assets [22].

Inflation is ignored for tax purposes, but accelerated capital allowances and the recently abolished investment grants have to some extent mitigated the situation.

The position in other countries has been different, especially in those that have suffered much more extreme inflation than we have yet experienced in Britain. Both the German [23] and French [24] examples are instructive in that they demonstrate the tendency to return to historical cost accounting after the inflationary blizzard has passed.

At the end of the Second World War the German economy had collapsed completely and the then existing monetary unit, the Reichsmark (RM), was virtually worthless. It continued, however, to be used in financial statements and departure from historical cost was legally impossible. In 1948 the currency was reformed and a new monetary unit, the Deutsche Mark (DM) was introduced. It was followed by the *DM Eröffnungsbilanzgesetz* (literally the DM opening balance sheet law) which gave every German company a fresh start from a valuation point of view. The basic objective of the law was to restate all assets at amounts approximating current replacement cost as closely as possible. After the reform had been achieved German financial reporting reverted to the system of historical cost modified by conservatism already described. Holzer and Schönfeld comment as follows on one result of the law:

> It made possible tax deductible depreciation on the basis of revalued assets; ie, expenses could be deducted which had never been cash outlays. The resulting tax savings (the corporate tax rate was 50%) produced substantial benefits for industry and were more effective and of a more permanent nature than those accruing from accelerated depreciation measures. It goes without saying that businesses with relatively large capital investments were the main beneficiaries [25].

In France from 1945–59 companies were permitted (but not compelled) for tax purposes to revalue most fixed assets and also receivables and payables in foreign currencies. The revaluation had to be achieved through the use of revaluation coefficients published in the *Journal officiel*. Depreciation was based on the restated book values and was fully deductible for tax purposes. Stocks could not be revalued but a tax-free reserve for stock replacement could be established. During the 1960s French financial statements reverted to historical cost, the rise in the price level having slowed down.

In contrast to Germany and France, the main influence on Dutch accounting is economic theory rather than legislation. Replacement cost rather than historical cost concepts are used by a number of important companies [26].

IV

These remarks lead to my fourth reason for looking at international aspects of accounting: the *European* reason. Whether or not Britain joins the European Economic Community, we shall be increasingly affected by the progress in Europe towards harmonization of tax law and company law. There is no doubt, for example, that the Government's recent decision to replace the purchase tax and selective employment tax by a value-added tax was greatly influenced by the European example [27]. The Government has also announced that it intends to reform the structure of corporation tax so as to remove the present discrimination against distributed profits, on which tax is currently paid twice, once by the company and once by the shareholder. The choice is between the German "two-rate system", under which the company pays a lower rate of tax on distributed than on undistributed profits, and the French "imputation system", under which the shareholder receives a credit for part of the tax paid by the company. In making the choice regard will have to be paid, as the Government Green Paper points out, to "the timing and direction of developments in company taxation within the European Economic Community" [28].

Rather less well-known but also of great interest to accountants is the progress being made within the European Economic Community towards the harmonization of financial reports to shareholders. The Council of the Community approved a first directive on company law harmonization on 9 March 1968 [29]. The first section of the directive dealt with publicity and provided, *inter alia*, for the publication of a balance sheet and a profit and loss account for each financial period. Harmonization of the contents of these documents was, however, postponed. A draft directive on these matters was prepared and published in 1969 by a Study Group under the chairmanship of Dr. W. Elmendorff of the German Federal Republic [30].

The Study Group considered that its task was not to work out completely new regulations but rather to investigate the extent to which the various national legislations could be harmonized. Their proposals follow the German pattern of stating expressly the methods of asset valuation to be used and of favouring historical cost modified by conservatism. The details for each item are set out in articles 26 to 34. Article 25, however, permits other methods so long as these are in accord with "normal accounting practices" and so long as the notes to the balance sheet and profit and loss account provide information of the differences arising thereby. Article 2 provides that the accounts must conform to "normal accounting procedures". The Institute of Chartered Accountants in England and Wales has pointed out that these terms need to be defined:

> To achieve uniformity and consistency in practice it will undoubtedly prove necessary to make available authoritative statements in clarification of what may be regarded as normally accepted procedures. At present these may differ not only between states, but even within national boundaries. We believe it should be the task of the Community's recognized accountancy organizations to cooperate with the object of progressively narrowing such differences, in the same way as it is the policy of this Institute to do so in the United Kingdom [31].

The Study Group's proposals on audit also follow the German rather than the British pattern. The auditor "must check whether the bookkeeping and the annual accounts are in accordance with legal requirements, the articles of association and normal accounting practice" (article 43) and he "must also report when, in carrying out his work, he unearths elsewhere than in the annual accounting documents facts which either place the existence of the company in peril or could have a profound effect on its progress or which reveal serious acts on the part of the directors contrary to the articles of association" (article 46).

The Study Group's proposals were submitted to the *Direction générale du marché intérieur* of the European Commission which, after consulting mainly legal advisers, has sent a revised draft to member states for consideration. A version of the proposals is included in the recently published draft statute for a "Societas Europea" (SE), ie, a European Company which would co-exist in each country of the EEC alongside the existing companies created under the separate national laws [32]. An interesting new feature is that the use of a replacement cost basis is now expressly permitted [33].

It is in my opinion a pity that Britain has so far had very little influence on the harmonization of legislation in Western Europe. No doubt this will change rapidly if we become a full member of the European Communities. So far as accounting is concerned there is, the value-added tax apart, still plenty of time. No firm decisions have yet been made in the fields of direct taxation and financial reporting.

V

I have tried in this paper to give some idea of the scope of the international aspects of accounting. I have not been comprehensive. If I have left the reader with the impression of a new, exciting and relatively unexplored field of great practical importance and much academic interest, then I have succeeded in what I set out to achieve.

Note

1 An Inaugural Lecture delivered at the University of Dundee on 20 April 1971.

References

[1] Stevin Simon, *Tafalen van Interest*, Antwerp: Christoffel Plantijn, 1582. The original is reprinted with a facing translation in D. J. Struik (ed.), *The Principal Works of Simon Stevin*, Vol. 11A, Mathematics, Amsterdam: C. V. Swets & Zeitlinger, 1958, pp. 25–117. The passage quoted is on p. 107 of the translation.

[2] Brown, R. (ed.), *A History of Accounting and Accountants*, Edinburgh: Jack, 1905, p. 197.

[3] Partly because the law of bankruptcy was more advanced in Scotland than in England. See A. C. Littleton, *Accounting Evolution to 1900*, New York: American Institute Publishing Co., 1933, pp. 285–6.

[4] Brown, *op. cit.*, pp. 339–40.

[5] Murphy, M. E., *Advanced Public Accounting Practice*, Homewood, Ill.: Irwin, 1966, chapters 1 and 2.

[6] Brown, *op. cit.*, pp. 271, 279–80.

[7] Solomons, D., "The Historical Development of Costing" in his *Studies in Cost Analysis*, London: Sweet & Maxwell, 2nd ed. 1968; C. Weber, *The Evolution of Direct Costing*, Urbana, Ill.: Center for International Education and Research in Accounting, 1966.

[8] Brooke, M. Z. and Remmers, H. L., *The Strategy of Multinational Enterprise*, London: Longman, 1970, p. 5.

[9] Parker, R. H., "Principles and Practice in Translating Foreign Currencies", *Abacus*, Vol. 6, No. 2, December 1970.

[10] Breek, P. C., "Accounting Problems Peculiar to International Enterprises", *The New Horizons of Accounting*, Proceedings of 9th International Congress of Accountants, Paris, 1967.

[11] See, for example, the papers by Hirschleifer and Shillinglaw in C. P. Bonini, R. K. Jaedicke and H. M. Wagner (eds), *Management Controls*, New York: McGraw-Hill, 1964.

[12] Brooke and Remmers, *op. cit.*, especially pp. 172–6.

[13] Report of the Committee of Enquiry into the Relationship of the Pharmaceutical Industry with the National Health Service 1965–1967 (London: HMSO, 1967), Cmnd. 3410. Paragraph 301, p. 84; Appendix I, Tables 6, 8, 16, pp. 102–3, 108.

[14] Brooke and Remmers, *op. cit.*, p. 173.

[15] Cooper, M. H., *Prices and Profits in the Pharmaceutical Industry*, Oxford: Pergamon, 1966, pp. 39–40.

[16] The text of the Act in German and English can be found in R. Mueller and E. G. Galbraith (editors and translators), *The German Stock Corporation Law*. Bilingual edition with Introduction, Frankfurt am Main: Fritz Knapp Verlag, 1966.

[17] *Minister of National Revenue v. Anaconda American Brass, Ltd.* [1956] A.C. 85 (P.C.).

[18] *Ostime v. Duple Motor Bodies, Ltd.* [1961] 1 W.L.R. 739 (H.L.).

[19] Conseil national de la comptabilité, *Plan comptable général*, Paris: Imprimerie nationale, 1965, Introduction, p. 11; also, P. Lauzel, *Le plan comptable français*, Paris: Presses Universitaires de France, 2nd edition, 1967, pp. 15–16.

[20] The text of the decrees is given in 1965 printing of the Plan. See also Lauzel, *op. cit.*, chapter 4.

[21] Lauzel, *op. cit.*, pp. 103–4.

[22] Research Foundation of the Institute of Chartered Accountants in England and Wales, *Accounting for Stewardship in a Period of Inflation*, London, 1968, p. 5.

[23] See H. P. Holzer and H.-M. Shönfeld, "The German Solution of the Post-War Price Level Problem", *Accounting Review*, April 1963, reprinted in Berg, Mueller and Walker, *Readings in International Accounting*, Boston: Houghton Mifflin, 1969.

[24] See, for example, L. Petit, *Le bilan dans les entreprises*, Paris: Presses Universitaires de France, 5th edition, 1967, ch. 2.

[25] Berg, Mueller and Walker, *op. cit.*, p. 251.

[26] Notably Philips. See A. Goudeket, "An Application of Replacement Value Theory", *Journal of Accountancy*, July 1960, reprinted in Berg, Mueller and Walker, *op. cit.*

[27] *Value-added Tax*, Cmnd. 4621, 1971.

[28] *Reform of Corporation Tax*, Cmnd. 4630, 1971, para. 10.

[29] *Journal officiel* No. L65, 14 March 1968.

[30] Proposal for a directive to coordinate, with a view to making them equivalent, the guarantees demanded in the Member-States from companies within the meaning of article 58, 2nd paragraph, of the Treaty of Rome for the purpose of protecting the interests both of the members of such companies and of third

parties. Annual financial reports (form and valuation); contents of the notes and the report of management; audit by an accountant and publication. (Dusseldorf: Verlagsbuchhandlung des Instituts der Wirtschaftsprüfer GmbH., 1969). See also Elmendorff's article, "Coordination of the legal accounting requirements in the various countries of the European Economic Community", *Journal UEC*, October 1967.

[31] Uniform Code for Contents, Form and Audit of Financial Statements of Companies within the European Community. Comments made on behalf of the Institute of Chartered Accountants in England and Wales on the proposals of the Groupe d'Elmendorff. Paragraph 4.

[32] Commission of the European Communities, Secretariat, *Proposal for a Council Regulation embodying a Statute for European Companies* (Brussels, 24 June 1970). See also D. Thompson, *The Proposal for a European Company*, London: Chatham House and PEP, 1969.

[33] Article 181 of the draft S.E. statute; W. Schattinga, "The Harmonisation of European Practices in the Presentation of External Financial Accounts", *Accountant's Magazine*, April 1971.

2

BEHAVIORAL EFFECTS OF INTERNATIONAL ACCOUNTING DIVERSITY

Frederick D. S. Choi and Richard M. Levich

Source: *Accounting Horizons* (June 1991): 1–13.

Owing to international linkages of commodity prices, interest rates and currency values, governments around the globe are supporting initiatives to coordinate national policies. In recent years these initiatives have included such areas as trade policy, fiscal and monetary policy, banking regulation, and rules governing the operation and structure of financial markets.

A closely related development in the world of finance is the desire to harmonize international accounting standards. With the rapid growth in international capital markets, cross border mergers and acquisitions and international commerce, financial decisions are increasingly international in scope.[1] Financial statements, on the other hand, are typically prepared according to local accounting standards and regulations. When accounting reports retain a nationalistic character, it is reasonable to fear that problems of understanding and interpretation may develop outside the country in which the reports are prepared.[2] Apparent differences in financial measures of enterprise risk and return characteristics could be due as much to differences in accounting measurement practices as they are to real differences in the attributes being measured.

In response to these and related concerns, international efforts are underway to reduce the number of accounting alternatives that now exist. The major private-sector vehicle for articulating international standards of accounting and reporting is the International Accounting Standards Committee (IASC). Representing more than 95 accountancy organizations worldwide, its principal objectives are to promulgate international accounting standards and seek their worldwide acceptance.[3]

22

The work of the IASC has recently been given additional impetus by the growing interest among national security market regulators in international accounting standards. As a consequence of significant cross-border financing, the recently-formed International Organization of Securities Commissions (IOSCO) has endorsed international accounting standards as desired minima to be used in multinational securities offerings, listings, and other foreign issues of equity and debt securities.[4]

The quest for harmonized accounting standards is also supported by the European Community. In attempting to eliminate barriers to the harmonization of product, factor and financial markets within the EC by the end of 1992, the European Commission now feels that any new European accounting requirements should be developed in the context of international accounting standards and that Europe should play an active role in the process of establishing such uniform standards.[5]

Motivation

Some might take the case for accounting harmony to be irrefutable. Like apple pie and motherhood, harmony and coordination of national accounting policies, they argue, can only promote economic welfare. This extreme apple pie view misses several critical points. First, while accounting diversity exists,[6] investors may have developed adequate coping mechanisms so that their financial decisions are not impeded. Second, while investors prefer more information as opposed to less, corporations incur information preparation costs that can be substantial. Disclosure of additional information might result in competitive costs and alternative accounting principles might have real cash flow effects, neither of which would be selected voluntarily by corporations. Finally, national business environments may embody substantial differences—in tax policy, fiscal policy, regulatory objectives, managerial systems, performance incentives and other cultural factors. Strictly harmonized international accounting standards may result in unlike business operations being made to produce accounting statements that are alike. Clearly, this outcome would not benefit statement readers.

These observations suggest that policy choices regarding international accounting standards entail both costs and benefits. As such, policy prescriptions in the area must be based on empirical evidence. Unfortunately, little is known as to whether accounting diversity is actually a problem. The data suggest that accounting diversity has not been an insurmountable barrier—despite accounting diversity, the international dimensions of capital markets have experienced tremendous growth.[7] Still, accounting diversity may have reduced the amount of international financial transactions or adversely affected pricing relative to some ideal system.

In this article, we summarize the main findings of an interview survey of major capital market participants.[8] Through this survey, we collected

23

empirical evidence regarding several aspects of accounting diversity. First, is accounting diversity perceived to be a problem, and if so, why? Second, are attempts made to cope with national accounting differences and are these coping mechanisms successful? And third, do problems associated with accounting diversity lead to capital market effects.

Our main finding is that approximately one-half of those in our survey feel that accounting diversity affects their capital market decisions. The remaining half responded that accounting diversity had no such effect, in many cases because successful coping mechanisms were used or because accounting diversity was not deemed to be an important factor in the first instance. This roughly even split between those who feel that accounting diversity affects their decisions and those investors who are able to cope or firms who elect to depart from U.S. or IASC practices suggests that it will be difficult to reach a consensus on uniform international accounting policies.

The remainder of this article is organized as follows. In the first section, we describe our survey sample design and methodology. We then report the survey findings for the entire sample, and sub-groupings of institutional investors, corporate issuers, underwriters and regulators. We follow this with a discussion of the overall conclusions and implications of the survey. The article concludes with a short offering of suggestions for future research.

Sample design and methodology

As our primary focus is on respondent attitudes, behavior and reasons behind such, we utilized personal interviews as our method of gathering data. To arrive at a representative sample for these interviews, we stratified the universe of accounting statement readers and preparers into several dimensions—geographic location, user group and size.

To be sure the information we gathered from market participants had a direct bearing on our research questions, we sampled participants domiciled in countries whose accounting and reporting practices depart quite significantly from international norms; i.e. those of the United States and United Kingdom. Hence, we decided to include statement users in Japan, Switzerland and West Germany. We also wanted to include financial markets whose investment institutions have a significant stake in foreign securities and which are active in trading. In the interest of time and resources, we narrowed our choice to Frankfurt, London, New York, Tokyo and Zurich.

We identified institutional investors, corporate issuers, investment underwriters and market regulators as the primary audience-of-interest for international accounting statements. To uncover issues that might not be captured by interviewing direct users or preparers of accounting information, we also interviewed representatives of rating agencies, an international financial data service and an organization working towards international accounting harmony. Individuals queried had to be high enough in the management hierarchy to have decision responsibilities; i.e., actually make international investment, funding, underwriting and regulatory decisions. And, as organizational size may affect the degree of sophistication that is brought to bear on dealing with international accounting differences, we decided to interview representatives of both large and less large organizations.

Reasoning that accounting differences would have a greater impact on the valuation of international equity as opposed to debt securities, we focussed more attention on equity investments, issues and listings as opposed to bonds.

Our sample design produced a total of 52 institutions, distributed across various categories as shown in Table 1. The names of the institutions are listed in Table 2.

Owing to the expense associated with the interview method (especially in an international context), our sample is not large. However, survey respondents were selected in largely random fashion and, hence, our findings should be fairly representative. To assist with our interviews, we constructed a questionnaire which included factual and behavioral questions relating to decision processes, information requirements, nature of accounting diversity, coping mechanisms and capital market effects.[9] In addition to responses

Table 1 Matrix of interview candidates.

	Location					
Groups	*New York*	*London*	*Zurich*	*Frankfurt*	*Tokyo*	*Total*
Buyers of Securities						
Large	3[a]	2	2	N.A.	2	9
Less Large	2	1	3[b]	N.A.	2	8
Sellers of Securities						
Large	2	2	1	2	2	9
Less Large	2	2	N.A.	1	1	6
Underwriters	2[c]	2	N.A.	2	2	8
Others						
—Regulators/Standards Board	1	1	1		1	4
—Exchange Officials	1	1	1	1	1	5
—Ratings Agencies/ Data Services	2				1	3
Total	15	12	8	6	11	52

Note: (a) One interviewed in Tokyo office;
(b) One interviewed in New York and Zurich offices;
(c) One interviewed in London office.

25

Table 2 List of organizations interviewed.

B.A.T. Industries, plc	Nippon Life Insurance Co.
Bank Julius Baer	Nissan Motor Company, Ltd.
Bear Sterns & Co., Inc.	Pfizer Inc.
BHF-Bank	Prudential-Bache
Brown Brothers Harriman & Co.	Prudential Portfolio Managers Limited
Cadbury Schweppes, plc	Reckitt & Colman, plc
Canon Inc.	SANYO Electric Co., Ltd.
Capital Research Co.	Schering
Deutsche Bank	Joseph E. Seagram & Sons, Inc.
Exxon Corporation	Security Pacific Hoare Govett Ltd.
Federation of German Stock Exchanges	Siemens AG
The Fuji Bank, Ltd.	Standard & Poor's Ratings Group
General Electric Company	Swiss Bank Corporation
International Accounting Standards	Swiss National Bank
Board	Teachers Insurance Annuity Association
Kleinwort Benson Ltd.	—College Retireme Equity Fund
Lombard Odier & Cie.	Tokyo Stock Exchange
London Stock Exchange	Union Bank of Switzerland
Merrill Lynch Asset Management	Volkswagen AG
The Mitsubishi Trust and Banking	S. G. Warburg & Co., Ltd.
Corp.	WPP Group, plc
Moody's Investors Service	Yamaichi Securities Company
Morgan Grenfell Group, plc	Yamaichi Investment Trust
Morval & Cie., S. A.	Management
Nihon Keizai Shimbun Inc. (Data Bank	Zurich Stock Exchange
Bureau)	In addition, four organizations that
Nestle, S. A.	wished to remain anonymous were
New York Stock Exchange	interviewed.

of the "yes/no" variety, most questions were left open-ended to enable us to learn more about why a particular response was given and the nature of such response.[10]

Interviews ranged from one to four hours in length, averaging about two hours. Nearly all of the interviews were conducted by two individuals to minimize bias and misrepresentation of responses.[11] A language translator accompanied the interviewers in those instances where the interview subject requested one. All interview subjects were sent a sample of the interview questions in advance and some institutions prepared written responses ahead of time. All interview subjects were promised that their remarks would be kept confidential.

To condense the information contained in these often wide-ranging discussions, we prepared a second form coding 23 key items from each interview. These 23 items are listed in Table 3. We gathered descriptive information on each institution interviewed to allow us to test whether the response patterns were correlated with specific user characteristics.

Table 3 23 Coded items from each interview.

A. Descriptive
    1. Country
    2. User Group
    3. Size
    4. Scope of international operations
    5. Organization structure
    6. Length of international financial experience
B. Definition of Accounting Diversity
    7. Is it principles?
    8. Is it disclosure?
    9. Is it auditing?
C. Are your measurements hindered by diversity
    10. In GAAP?
    11. In disclosure?
    12. In auditing?
D. Does accounting diversity
    13. Affect your capital market decisions?
E. Do you cope with diversity
    14. In GAAP?
    15. In disclosure?
    16. In auditing?
F. Are there capital market impacts relating to
    17. Geography
    18. Security types
    19. Company types
    20. Information processing costs
    21. Security valuation
G. Regarding the future
    22. Do you plan to become more active in international financial markets?
    23. Do you favor harmonizing international accounting standards along the lines proposed by the IASC?

Survey findings

A summary of answers to the question of whether international accounting diversity affects capital market decisions appears in Table 4.[12] Overall approximately one-half of those in our sample (24 "yes," 26 "no") feel that their capital market decisions are affected by accounting diversity. This finding is conservative as it does not include second-order behavioral effects; i.e., it does not include users who changed the way in which they analyze foreign investments as a result of the accounting diversity problem. Therefore, we must reject the hypothesis that accounting diversity has no effect on capital market decisions.

We cross tabulated the results using five descriptive categories—nationality, size, extent of international investing/funding experience, scope of international investing/funding activities and organization structure. The results are shown in Table 5.

Table 4 Summary findings for investors, issuers, underwriters, regulators and others.
Key Question: "Does accounting diversity affect your capital market decisions?"

	Yes	*No*	*N.A.*	*Total*
Investors	9	7	1	17
Issuers	6	9		15
Underwriters	7	1		8
Regulators	0	8		8
Raters & Others	2	1	—	3
Total	24	26	1	51

Table 5 Summary findings by country, size, experience, scope of activity, and organizational structure.
Key Question: "Does accounting diversity affect your capital market decisions?"

Country	*Yes*	*No*	*N.A.*	*Total*
U.S.	6	9	1	16
Germany	4	2		6
Japan	6	5		11
Switzerland	3	5		8
U.K.	5	5	—	10
Total	24	26	1	51

Size	*Yes*	*No*	*N.A.*	*Total*
Large	15	12		27
Less Large	9	6	1	16
N.A.	0	8	—	8
Total	24	26	1	51

Experience	*Yes*	*No*	*N.A.*	*Total*
Long	15	17		32
Short	9	8	1	18
N.A.	—	1	—	1
Total	24	26	1	51

Scope	*Yes*	*No*	*N.A.*	*Total*
Limited	9	12	1	22
Extensive	15	14		29
Total	24	26	1	51

Org. Structure	*Yes*	*No*	*N.A.*	*Total*
Centralized	13	15		28
Decentralized	10	11	1	22
N.A.	1	—	—	1
Total	24	26	1	51

For each cross tabulation, we constructed a chi-square statistic to test for independence of "Yes" and "No" responses within each category. In each case, we could not reject the hypothesis that the "Yes" and "No" responses split proportionately regardless of country, size, experience, scope or organizational structure.[13]

As can be seen in Table 4, responses on the effects of accounting diversity on capital market decisions were not uniform either within respondent groups or between respondent groups. Hence, we examine each response group in more detail.

Institutional investors

More than half (9 out of 17) of the investors we interviewed stated that accounting differences make it more difficult for them to measure their decision variables and ultimately affect their investment decisions. Seven did not feel hindered by accounting differences. Those not hampered by accounting differences tended to focus on the economics of a foreign operation, rely on local financial statements, utilize the services of local brokers and research institutes, or ignore accounting differences altogether because of their top-down investment approach.[14]

Countries or regions whose accounting principles were mentioned as a source of concern for analysts when investing outside the home country are, in alphabetical order, Australia, Continental Europe, France, Hong Kong, Japan, Korea, Latin America, Luxembourg, Norway, Portugal, Switzerland, the United States and West Germany. Of this set, countries most frequently mentioned were Japan, Switzerland and West Germany.

Industries identified as posing analysts with similar difficulties include banking, insurance, financial services in general, semiconductors and mining.

Differences in generally accepted accounting principles (GAAP) which are troublesome to those interviewed relate to multinational consolidations, valuation of fixed assets, deferred taxes, pensions, marketable securities, discretionary reserves, foreign currency transactions and translation, leases, goodwill, depreciation, long-term construction contracts, inventory valuation and provisions.

Similar country and industry responses were noted with respect to financial disclosure differences. Half of the respondents reported being hindered by the absence of comparable disclosure standards. Disclosure items most frequently mentioned were segmental information, methods of asset valuation, foreign operations disclosures, frequency and completeness of interim information, description of capital expenditures, hidden reserves, and off-balance sheet items.

Our analysis revealed no apparent correlation of these results with either investor size, country-of-domicile, organization structure, length of experience in international investing, scope of international investments or investment approach.

All investors interviewed attempt to cope with accounting diversity in some fashion. For the nine investors responding that accounting measurement differences is a problem, the "yes group," seven coped by restating foreign accounts to an accounting framework more familiar to the user. Two of the nine coped by adopting different investment strategies. One institutional investor chose to limit its foreign investments to government bonds. Investments in equities (very small) were limited to countries whose accounting principles were similar to its own. The other coped by adopting a top-down approach to foreign investments; i.e., it first selected promising countries, then diversified within countries.

For the seven investors responding that accounting diversity is not a problem that affects their capital market decisions, four coped by developing a multiple principles capability (MPC); i.e., undertaking to familiarize themselves with foreign accounting principles and adopt a local perspective when analyzing foreign financial statements. Three of the seven investors coped by relying on information less sensitive to corporate accounting treatment. Specifically, one institutional investor utilizes a dividend discount model as opposed to a discounted earnings framework as a basis for its investment decisions. Another investor copes successfully with accounting diversity by relying solely on macroeconomic variables in making asset allocations by country and then investing in a diversified portfolio of securities within each country. Finally, one investor circumvents the problem of accounting differences by relying primarily on "sociological trends" in making investment picks. This involves first seeing in what direction consumer preferences are moving and then investing in industry leaders which are expected to capitalize on such trends.

Investors were evenly divided on the question of whether their decisions are affected by differences in financial disclosure practices. For the "No" group, coping generally took the form of company visitations to secure added information. Coping with differential disclosures sometimes takes the form of assigning firms into investment versus speculative grades. Firms providing full disclosure are classified into the former category while firms that are less forthcoming are put into the latter.

Investors who say that disclosure differences impact their investment decisions generally cope in similar fashion as the "no effect" group. Corporate visitations are a frequently mentioned coping mechanism.

For the "yes group," accounting diversity is associated with capital market effects. These effects, reported separately for GAAP differences and disclosure differences, are summarized in Table 6. These effects relate to the location of market activity, the types of companies invested in and the pricing of international securities. Owing to the size of the institutions we surveyed, information processing costs associated with accounting

30

Table 6 Capital market effects of accounting diversity: investors.

	From GAAP Differences	From Disclosure Differences
Geographic spread of investments	3	3
Types of companies/securities selected	6	7
Information processing costs	5*	2*
Assessment of security returns or valuation	8	8

*Two reported these costs were significant.

differences were generally not considered significant. However, this was not the case for all investors.

Corporate issuers

In contrast to investor responses, most of the issuers, nine out of 15 in our sample, report that accounting differences (GAAP differences) have no impact on their funding decisions. Reasons for the non-effect include company funding strategies which insulate the company from reporting to foreign investors (internal funding, borrowing or private placements), management's focus on economic fundamentals, management's confidence in investors' abilities to deal with accounting differences, the value of name recognition which minimizes the need to focus on accounting considerations, and various other coping strategies which have proved effective.

Concern over accounting differences expressed by six of the nine issuers relates to financial statement effects. As one issuer quipped:

> Our accounting treatment for certain intangibles significantly affects our reported net worth. As a consequence, we have not been ale to get a credit rating from the major rating agencies. Thus far, we have not attempted to raise funds in the U.S. but have floated commercial paper in Europe instead.

Differences in disclosure requirements, on the other hand, appear to have an impact on funding decisions, especially for issuers domiciled in Japan and West Germany. This suggests that accounting and regulatory diversity are closely linked issues from the standpoint of corporate issuers.[15] Disclosure items mentioned most frequently in this regard include preparation of consolidated statements, provision of information on business segments, reporting quarterly results, and explaining the nature of various reserves to foreign analysts.

Firms who report they are not affected by accounting differences tend to be from North America, are large in size, have had long experience in international financial markets and have engaged in extensive international funding arrangements. But there are exceptions.

Corporate issuers who said that accounting differences had no effect on their funding decisions, nine of 16, cope in a variety of ways. One non-U.S. issuer copes by restating its accounts to a U.S. basis. In this instance, switching to U.S. GAAP has the effect of casting their statements in a more positive light. Two issuers coped by partially restating to U.S. GAAP. In one case, the company had been grandfathered in the United States and does not have to fully conform to U.S. GAAP restatements. In the other case, partial restatement to U.S. GAAP makes the company's operating income appear more favorable but does not affect its bottom line one way or the other. Three of the nine cope by going on road shows and hosting analysts' meetings. Three cope by essentially doing nothing. In the latter case, all three companies happen to be North American firms who enjoy reciprocity when raising funds in foreign markets. Non-U.S. regulators generally respect the accounting principles of the issuer's home country.

There are additional reasons which appear to explain the immunity of this segment of the issuing sample to accounting effects. Five of the nine issuers had previously floated new equity issues in the United States. Two had issued ADR's in the U.S. market and had been grandfathered from having to meet more stringent U.S. reporting requirements. Finally, two were large, cash rich firms who were not dependent on external sourcing for their funding needs. Capital market effects were negligible for this group.

Corporate issuers who say their funding decisions are affected by accounting differences also attempt to cope with such differences. Accounting coping takes the form of partial GAAP restatements for three of the six members of this issuer segment. In these cases, full restatement would have made one issuer appear to be less well-off than before. The other two would look much better under full restatement, given the conservative reporting practices in their home countries. However, both were unwilling to go the full route as full restatements would increase their competitive costs. The other three members of this group used road shows or hosted analysts meetings to answer questions relating to accounting or disclosure issues. For two of the three issuers, restatement to U.S. GAAP would make them look better but reveal privileged information to competitors. Restatement for the third issuer would have made it look less profitable.

The six issuers comprising our "yes, accounting diversity is a problem" group also cope in a financial sense. All have avoided raising funds or listing their shares in the U.S. market by either (1) by-passing the U.S. market for the Eurobond market (two companies), (2) relying on domestic bank financing as opposed to floating commercial paper in the United States (one company), (3) encouraging foreign investors to come to their financial market to buy their shares locally (one company), (4) offering sponsored but unlisted

Table 7 Capital market effects of accounting diversity: issuers.

	From GAAP Differences	From Disclosure Differences
Geographic location of funding/listing activity	3	6
Types of securities issued/investors courted	3	1
Information processing costs	5*	4*
Issuing costs/share valuation	7	3

*Three reported these costs were significant.

ADR's in the United States (two companies), and (5) undertaking a U.S. private placement (one company).

For the six companies described above, accounting differences, particularly disclosure differences, are associated with capital market effects (see Table 7). These effects range from the geographic location of funding/listing activities to their cost of capital. The issuers were either unwilling or unable to quantify the magnitude of the effect, but as the following quotes indicate, accounting differences can produce both positive and negative market effects.[16]

> Several years ago we pioneered the practice of disclosing a condensed balance sheet in the regular financial section of the balance sheet, and in an appendix, a more detailed balance sheet in which the accounting is essentially equivalent to U.S. norms. . . . Our P/E ratio is currently more than twice that of our major competitor and we feel it is due to our accounting and investor relations policy. (A)

> We have probably paid more to obtain external capital in the international markets owing to our reluctance to disclose certain items of information which we view as proprietary. However, in terms of the history of corporate practices in our country, this is not considered a major concern. (B)

Underwriters

Accounting diversity is regarded as a problem by most of the underwriters (7 of 8) in our sample. This is a problem, in turn, that is associated with capital market effects ranging from the geographic scope of their underwriting activities to the pricing of international issues (see Table 8).

Underwriters cope with accounting diversity, both accounting principles and disclosure, in a variety of ways. The respondent who is not bothered by accounting differences copes by (1) soliciting only the top-tier firms in the industry, (2) relying on credit ratings, and (3) accessing foreign capital via

Table 8 Capital market effects of accounting diversity: underwriters.

	From GAAP Differences	From Disclosure Differences
Geographic spread of underwriting activities	3	7
Types of companies/securities selected	2	5
Information processing costs	6*	5*
Assessment of security returns or valuation	4	2

*Five respondents say this costs is significant.

private placements. Underwriters who are concerned with accounting differences cope in both an accounting and non-accounting sense. Coping with accounting principles differences takes the form of (1) restating foreign accounts to local GAAP (five respondents), (2) restating to both local and U.S. GAAP (one), or (3) examining rates of change in original accounting data (one).

Coping with disclosure differences manifests itself in the form of (1) requests for additional information (five underwriters), (2) obtaining guarantees from the parent company or some third party (one), or (3) avoiding the U.S. market in favor of a less demanding one (two).

Regulators

Market regulators ultimately decide on whether or not to approve an application for a public offering or security exchange listing. As regulators in our sample receive applications from corporate entities around the world, they might be expected to find coping with accounting and reporting differences difficult. Contrary to what we expected, none of the eight regulators we interviewed reported being hindered by accounting principles differences in making their determinations. Most regulators coped with accounting differences by adopting an MPC posture when dealing with foreign companies; one, in particular, coped by restating foreign accounts to domestic GAAP. Owing to the nature of their organizations, most regulators coped with disclosure differences simply by requesting additional information. Second audit opinions were requested in those instances where auditor qualifications or audit procedures were in doubt.

While accounting measurement differences did impose additional information processing costs on market regulators, this cost was not considered significant. Two regulators indicated, however, that disclosure differences had some adverse effect on the volume of foreign issuing or listing activities conducted in their national jurisdictions. One acknowledged the loss of foreign issuers or listers to markets requiring less extensive disclosure practices. The second, on the other hand, expressed concern that excessive leniency produced similar capital market effects by reducing investor confidence in its market.

Other respondents

Responses from other users we sampled confirm our findings with respect to the investor group. Those who restate financial statements from one set of accounting principles to another report that their decisions are affected by accounting differences. On the other hand, the decisions of those embracing local accounting norms; i.e., those whom we have labeled MPC'ers, are not affected by accounting diversity.

Conclusions and implications

A major implication of our findings is that accounting differences *are* important and affect the capital market decisions of a significant number of market participants we surveyed regardless of nationality, size, experience, scope of international activity and organization structure. Based on the responses we have received from active market participants, the presumption that accounting diversity does not interfere with international capital market efficiency is not a foregone conclusion.

All investors in our sample who attempt to restate foreign accounting information as a coping mechanism report that accounting diversity affects their investment decisions. In other words, restatement is not sufficient to remove the problem of accounting diversity.

This finding suggests that either (a) existing restatement algorithms are still at a very crude stage of development, (b) existing algorithms are not being applied effectively, or (c) no algorithm is capable of producing a proper and meaningful restatement. If restatement fails to be an effective coping mechanism because of (a) or (b), then more effort in restatement may result in a payoff. If the true answer is (c), then investors may be right in developing their skills to read and interpret foreign financial statements in their original form.

In our sample, only four of 17 investors relied on original unrestated accounting information for their investment decisions (MPC'ers). Interestingly, but perhaps not surprisingly, none of these respondents reported that accounting diversity poses a problem as far as their investment decisions are concerned. Based on our survey, investors who make the effort to understand the firms in a foreign country on their own terms; i.e., familiarize themselves with local environmental norms and develop skills in interpreting foreign accounts in their original form, are least likely to encounter problems caused by accounting differences.

Large issuers with extensive experience in international finance appear to be less associated with problems caused by accounting differences than otherwise. While there are exceptions, it appears that firms who are venturing into the international capital markets or who are relatively inexperienced stand to benefit from advice on how to effectively deal with such differences.

Nationality also seems to play a role in explaining issuer behavior. U.S. and U.K. firms whose standards of accounting and financial disclosure tend to be relatively high appear to have greater flexibility in accessing international capital markets. On the other hand, German, Japanese and Swiss firms, whose financial statements are less transparent; e.g., in the areas of segmental disclosures and hidden reserves, appear to have less flexibility in assessing certain capital markets.[17]

This phenomenon, however, may also be related to the asymmetry we observe between the United States and other countries in our sample with regard to financial market regulation. Other countries practice reciprocity in accepting the accounting and reporting practices of the issuer's mother country. In contrast, the United States requires restatement or reconciliation to U.S. GAAP and U.S.-style disclosure for public issues or listed securities. This posture imposes additional costs on non-U.S. issuers and some are not willing to bear these costs. Despite this asymmetry, however, it appears that greater corporate transparency is an important ingredient in affording firms access to certain capital markets.

To better understand corporate funding and coping behavior, we find it useful to model a firm's cost of capital as a function of (1) financial costs, (2) information preparation costs, and (3) competitive costs. In communicating with foreign readers who are used to a different accounting and reporting framework, firms can restate local GAAP statements into the accounting principles of the reader's country-of-domicile, supply additional disclosures, and/or have the audit report reflect an enhanced set of auditing standards. At the margin, additional information should lower the financial costs to the firm. But, additional information is costly to prepare and may also increase the competitive costs to the firm. Thus, the firm will provide that amount of information that optimizes the trade-off between competitive costs and financial costs.

We find this framework helpful in explaining the corporate decision effects of accounting diversity and coping behavior that we observed. For example, it helps to explain why some firms were willing to restate to another set of GAAP but not disclose certain items of information, while others were willing to disclose more but unwilling to undertake GAAP restatements. It also helps to rationalize corporate behavior which avoids any form of accounting coping in favor of purely financial strategies; e.g., firms using firm-specific advantages (such as the value of name recognition) to seek to avoid compliance with costly regulation by going to the Euromarkets.

Country of origin plays a role in our model of "total cost minimization." Issuers from a country with substantial accounting disclosure (e.g., the United

Kingdom) tend to be more concerned about the impact of GAAP differences on their competitive costs. Issuers from a country with limited disclosures (e.g., Germany and Japan) tend to be more concerned about the competitive costs of additional disclosure.

One implication of our findings is that firms face the choice of how much they wish to accommodate the information needs of investors and other readers of their financial statements. One option is to restate their reported numbers to the accounting framework of the reader's country-of-domicile. In doing so, firms must be careful to avoid "losing something in the translation." Supplementary disclosures which enable investors to understand the company and its operating environment seem called for. Alternatively, issuers can provide investors with their original financial statements. The text and currency framework may be translated but strictly for the reader's convenience. To avoid the risk of misunderstanding by readers who are not familiar with the reporting firm's accounting procedures, periodic road shows in which management meets with analysts to resolve accounting and other questions is useful.

The positive correlation between length of international experience, frequency of exposure to international markets and the lesser importance attributed to accounting diversity as a decision problem highlights the channels through which diversity may pose a barrier to capital market entry abroad. It also suggests that a key coping mechanism for issuers may simply be perserverence and selective accommodation of investor information needs. If the investor's optimal coping mechanism is to be an MPC'er, then the issuer's best coping mechanism may be to help the investor to implement an MPC approach.

Being financial intermediaries between corporate issuers and investors, the responses of underwriters more than likely reflect those of their clients. Issuers adopt different financial disclosure policies based on the trade-offs we modeled with respect to financial and competitive costs. Given their financial disclosure decisions, some firms will be excluded from issuing in certain markets or face unfavorable financial terms. For these corporations, the effect on geographical location for raising long-term capital represents an ongoing cost.

Underwriters also deal with a heterogeneous investor clientele, many of whom are non-MPC'ers. As intermediaries, underwriters must adapt to the decision needs of their clientele. For investors who are non-MPC'ers, restatement of foreign accounting numbers to a set of principles that are more meaningful to potential investors is a legitimate service activity. For clients which have developed a multiple principles capability, specific advice on local accounting, financial and cultural norms is an important service to provide.

It appears that national regulators are not hindered by accounting diversity in making their regulatory decisions. All have adopted coping mechanisms that may reflect the historical structure of a country's regulatory environment, the relationship that each regulatory body has with its constituencies and other capital market norms unique to each country.

However, extremes in regulatory disclosure requirements can have adverse effects on the location of market activity and, therefore, market growth. Accordingly, the issue of identifying an optimum disclosure framework for international corporate issuers or listers in an important consideration among some regulators.

The demand for harmonized accounting standards does not seem to be emanating from most of the market regulators we surveyed. Many regulators seem to prefer alternatives to those being advanced by the International Accounting Standards Committee. It appears that support for international accounting standards stems not so much from the adverse effects of accounting diversity on regulatory decision processes as it does from the competitive market for regulation; i.e., the desire among regulators to find acceptable accounting principles and disclosure levels that, when adopted by all regulators, will not disadvantage one national capital market to any other in its competitive bid to attract foreign issuers or listers.

To conclude, users of international accounting information face a choice problem—to restate from one accounting framework to another; or to develop a facility for relying on local accounting norms—with benefits and costs associated with each. Users of international accounting data appear to have done the decision calculus and each has concluded that its posture is optimum.

Suggestions for future research

While we have identified an association between accounting diversity and capital market effects, many questions remain. What, for example, is the quantitative impact of accounting diversity on investors? Do investors who rely on original accounting statements of foreign reporting entities outperform investors who rely on accounting numbers that have been restated to the accounting principles of the reader's country? Does the release of restated accounting figures lead to a share price reaction? Does accounting diversity affect the prices paid in international mergers and acquisitions?

Unanswered questions also relate to the impact of accounting differences on corporate issuers. Thus, do issuers who provide additional accounting information enjoy an improvement in their cost of capital or price-earnings ratio? Do issuers who list their shares in foreign markets, in any of the forms now available, see any impact on share prices? On the negative side, do foreign issuers in a highly regulated market such as the United States experience a higher cost of raising funds than that of a comparable U.S. counterpart owing to lower corporate transparency?

In the area of accounting policy, perhaps the overriding question in the realm of international accounting and capital markets is whether initiatives toward greater harmony in national accounting standards are warranted. In this investigation, we provide limited evidence that the present level of coping with accounting diversity by market agents is considered effective. Obviously, quantitative measures of coping effectiveness are needed and offer a promising area of future inquiry. Nevertheless, the evidence presented here, together with the existence of numerous cost-benefit tradeoffs, suggests that policy prescriptions regarding international accounting must be based on empirical evidence. A broad range of empirical studies will help achieve a more rational approach to policy making in this area.

Acknowledgements

The authors gratefully acknowledge the comments of John Bildersee, Ernest Bloch, Michael Frinquelli, Philip Peller, Joshua Ronen, Arnold Sametz, J. Matthew Singleton, Roy Smith and Ingo Walter on earlier drafts of this manuscripts.

This article is based on a two-year research project sponsored by the Arthur Andersen Foundation and Salomon Brothers, Inc. The complete study, *The Capital Market Effects of International Accounting Diversity* will be published by Dow Jones-Irwin.

Notes

1 In 1988, for example, U.S. gross purchases and sales of foreign stocks exceeded $140 billion, a nine-fold increase over the flows reported in 1982. Foreigner gross purchases and sales of U.S. stocks exceeded $380 billion, a five-fold increase over the same time span. See, U.S. Government Accounting Office, 1989, pp. 9–10.
2 Dean Foust, "The SEC Is Relaxing—So Investors Should Be Nervous," *Business Week*, July 2, 1990, p. 32.
3 International Accounting Standards Committee, *Objectives and Procedures* (London: IASC, January 1983), pars. 8(a) and 8(b).
4 Arthur Wyatt, "International Accounting Standards: A New Perspective," *Accounting Horizons*, September 1989, p. 107.
5 "Funding IASC's Work Programme," *IASC News*, April 1990, p. 1.
6 The term "accounting diversity" encompasses national differences in accounting measurement, financial disclosure and auditing standards/practices.
7 We observe, for example, that many investors perform security analysis on foreign companies, suggesting that accounting diversity has not been an insurmountable barrier to investing internationally. It is currently estimated that, worldwide, at least one equity trade in nine has a foreign investor on the other side. As of year-end 1988, 6.7 percent of world equity market capitalization was held by cross-border investors (see Howell and Cozzini, 1989). Similarly, many firms comply with regulatory accounting requirements of other countries and some companies exceed such requirements (see Meek and Gray, 1989). In those cases where companies decide against a U.S. listing (Biddle and Saudagaran,

1989), many of these firms do not feel disadvantaged by being closed out of the U.S. public market. They cope by assessing the Euromarkets, secure private placements, engage in swaps, etc. In this sense, accounting diversity does not appear to have been an insurmountable barrier to the achievement of low cost funding through international markets.

8 Frederick D. S. Choi and Richard M. Levich. *The Capital Market Effects of International Accounting Diversity*, 1990.

9 The questionnaire is available from the authors upon request.

10 The questionnaire was pre-tested including circulation among academic colleagues specializing in accounting, finance, economics and behavioral science.

11 All interviews were tape recorded and a written transcript prepared.

12 Of the 52 institutions we surveyed, one was an agency charged with promoting accounting harmony. We omitted this institution as it was not itself a preparer or direct user of accounting statements and did not make capital market decisions itself.

13 We decided that "size" was not a relevant category for regulators and they were excluded from the calculation, resulting in a 24 and 18 split.

14 In a "top-down" investment approach, institutional investors rely on macro-economic data and information on market parameters for their asset allocation decisions and country-weightings. Once countries are selected, investment managers typically diversify their stock selections within a country eliminating the need to engage in cross-country comparisons.

15 Most firms outside the United States view the Financial Accounting Standards Board (FASB) and the U.S. Securities and Exchange Commission (SEC) as parts of the same regulatory apparatus.

16 Quotes from different individuals that appear in a series are labeled (A), (B), and so forth.

17 These findings are consistent with some of the findings of Biddle and Saudagaran (1989).

3

THE EFFECT OF INTERNATIONAL INSTITUTIONAL FACTORS ON PROPERTIES OF ACCOUNTING EARNINGS

Ray Ball, S. P. Kothari and Ashok Robin

Source: *Journal of Accounting and Economics* 29 (2000): 1–51.

Abstract

International differences in the demand for accounting income predictably affect the way it incorporates economic income (change in market value) over time. We characterize the 'shareholder' and 'stakeholder' corporate governance models of common and code law countries respectively as resolving information asymmetry by public disclosure and private communication. Also, code law directly links accounting income to current payouts (to employees, managers, shareholders and governments). Consequently, code law accounting income is less timely, particularly in incorporating economic losses. Regulation, taxation and litigation cause variation among common law countries. The results have implications for security analysts, standard-setters, regulators, and corporate governance. © 2000 Elsevier Science B.V. All rights reserved.

1. Introduction

We show that differences in the demand for accounting income in different institutional contexts cause its properties to vary internationally. The properties of accounting income we study are timeliness and conservatism. Timeliness is defined as the extent to which current-period accounting income incorporates current-period economic income, our proxy for which is change in market value of stockholders' equity. Conservatism is defined in the Basu (1997) sense as the extent to which current-period accounting

41

income asymmetrically incorporates economic losses, relative to economic gains.

A central result is that accounting income in common-law countries is significantly more timely than in code-law countries, due entirely to quicker incorporation of economic losses (income conservatism). Conversely, information asymmetry more likely is resolved in code-law countries by institutional features other than timely and conservative public financial statements, notably by closer relations with major stakeholders. In contrast with Roe (1994), we conclude that enhanced common-law disclosure standards reduce the agency costs of monitoring managers, thus countering the advantage of closer shareholder–manager contact in code-law countries.

We believe that timeliness and conservatism together capture much of the commonly used concept of financial statement 'transparency.' In comparison with a system that allows economic losses to be reflected in accounting income gradually over time, timely incorporation of economic losses in accounting income incents managers to stem the losses more quickly. Because accounting income flows into balance sheet accounts, conservatism as we define it also makes leverage and dividend restrictions binding more quickly. It makes optimistic non-accounting information released by managers less credible to uninformed users. Conservative accounting thus facilitates monitoring of managers and of debt and other contracts, and is an important feature of corporate governance.

The principal institutional variable we study is the extent of political influence on accounting. Our simplest proxy for political influence is a dichotomous classification of countries into code law systems with high political influence versus common law systems in which accounting practices are determined primarily in the private sector. We hypothesize that politicization of accounting standard setting and enforcement weakens the demand for timely and conservative accounting income, and conversely increases the demand for an income variable with low volatility. In our sample, Australia, Canada, UK and USA are classified as common-law countries (they comprise a group known as G4 + 1, exclusive of New Zealand) and France, Germany and Japan are classified as code-law.

In code-law countries, the comparatively strong political influence on accounting occurs at national and firm levels. Governments establish and enforce national accounting standards, typically with representation from major political groups such as labor unions, banks and business associations. At the firm level, politicization typically leads to a 'stakeholder' governance model, involving agents for major groups contracting with the firm. Current-period accounting income then tends to be viewed as the pie to be divided among groups, as dividends to shareholders, taxes to governments, and bonuses to managers and perhaps also employees. Compared to common-law countries, the demand for accounting income under code law is influenced more by the payout preferences of agents for labor, capital and government, and less by the demand for public disclosure. Conversely, because these groups' agents are represented in corporate governance, insider communication solves the information asymmetry between managers and stakeholders. We hypothesize that their preferences penalize volatility in payouts and thus in income. Thus, code-law accounting standards give greater discretion to managers in deciding when economic gains and losses are incorporated in accounting income. Managers reduce income volatility by varying the application of accounting standards or by influencing operating, financing and investment decisions (for example, by deferring discretionary expenditures such as R&D in bad earnings years).

Under the 'shareholder' governance model that is typical of common-law countries, shareholders alone elect members of the governing board, payouts are less closely linked to current-period accounting income, and public disclosure is a more likely solution for the information asymmetry problem. In comparison with the more political process in code-law countries, the desirable properties of accounting income in common law countries are determined primarily in the disclosure market. We hypothesize those properties include timeliness in incorporating negative economic income (i.e., asymmetric conservatism).

We caution that the code/common classes are by no means homogeneous, with financial reporting in no country being determined in a purely market or planning system. Notable historical examples of overlapping include the codification imposed on a predominantly common-law reporting system by the Companies Acts in the UK and by the Securities and Exchange Acts in the US, and the enactment of French and German legislation to permit consolidated financial statements prepared under common-law accounting standards. Despite these limitations, our results indicate the code/common classification is a valid proxy for the extent of political relative to market determination of financial reporting. Nevertheless, we develop finer hypotheses based on tax and regulatory differences across individual countries.

We also caution that institutional determinants of financial reporting vary over time. As a coarse test, we divide the sample into two sub-periods, and observe an increase in asymmetric conservatism of accounting income in most countries. One interpretation is that timely incorporation of economic losses in accounting income is an efficient corporate governance mechanism, providing better incentives to attend to losses and hence maximize value, which increased international product market competition has created incentives for even code-law corporations to adopt.

The sample studied is more than 40,000 firm-year accounting incomes reported during 1985–95, under the accounting rules of seven countries. Code-law income in this sample is substantially less timely and less conservative on average than common-law income. It does not even exhibit more timeliness than dividends. Within the common-law group, there is less asymmetric conservatism in accounting income in the United Kingdom, a country we characterize in terms of lower political involvement in accounting, lower litigation costs and less issuance of public debt. In addition to a detailed analysis of seven countries, we also study properties of accounting income in a sample of eighteen other countries. The results are consistent with our general thesis, that important properties of accounting income (conservatism in particular) around the world are a function of the varying demands that accounting income satisfies under different institutional arrangements.

Our research design addresses the incorporation of economic income in accounting income over time, under different international institutions. This has several advantages over simply studying international variation in accounting standards. First, much accounting practice is not determined by accounting standards, for reasons that include: practice is more detailed than standards; standards lag innovations in practice; and companies do not invariably implement standards.[1] Second, the extent to which accounting practice is determined by formal standards varies internationally, and the incentive to follow accounting standards depends on penalties under different enforcement institutions, so studying accounting standards per se is incomplete and potentially misleading in an international context. Third, reported income is influenced by managers' operating, financing and investment decisions, as well as by accounting standards. For example, managers can reduce volatility in accounting income by deferring discretionary expenditures (such as R&D) in bad years. Because the use of accounting income in corporate governance varies internationally, we expect managers' operating, financing and investment decisions to affect accounting income differentially across countries, and report evidence consistent with that expectation. For both these reasons, we study international variation in properties *of the actually reported income numbers*, inferred from the way they incorporate economic income over time.

Our research design's validity depends on two measures. First, we study the flow of *market-valued* economic income into *book-valued* accounting income, using the fiscal-year change in market value of equity (adjusted for dividends and capital transactions) as a proxy for economic income. A major concern is that the accuracy of this proxy is correlated with the institutional independent variables in the study, and in particular that code-law countries have endogen-ously lower market liquidity and public disclosure standards. Second, the research design requires us to infer independent variables, such as the degree of political versus market determination of reported income, from our characterization of salient institutional facts. While our characterization is based on surveying a wide range of sources, it undoubtedly is subject to error. In the concluding section, we argue that both types of measurement error create a bias *against* our hypotheses.

We contribute to a growing literature on the effects of international accounting differences, including Jacobsen and Aaker (1993), Alford *et al.*

(1993), Amir *et al.* (1993), Bandyopadhyay *et al.* (1994), Harris *et al.* (1994), Joos and Lang (1994), Barth and Clinch (1996), and Pope and Walker (1999). We also contribute to the literature on international corporate governance, including Baums *et al.* (1994) and La Porta *et al.* (1997).

The following section outlines the model used to test the timeliness and conservatism of accounting income. The third section describes the data. Section four surveys the salient institutional facts used to develop and then test hypotheses on properties of income internationally. Section five extends these tests to a comparison of income with dividends and cash flows. The sixth section reports specification tests and the concluding section discusses the research design and the implications of the results.

2. A model of incorporation of economic income in accounting income

The research design infers timeliness and conservatism from the way firms' accounting incomes incorporate their economic incomes over time. We therefore specify accounting income as the dependent variable. We measure firms' economic incomes as fiscal-year changes in market values of equity, adjusted for dividends and capital contributions (Hicks, 1946).

'Clean surplus' accounting (Ohlson, 1988) implies two relevant identities for all firms. First, accounting income equals fiscal-year change in book value of equity, adjusted for dividends and capital contributions. Second, a firm's accounting and economic incomes summed over its lifetime are identical.[2] We investigate the temporal process of the incorporation of economic income in accounting income, i.e., the accounting model of income determination, and how it is affected by international institutional factors. Our research design allows for three fundamental features of the accounting model of income determination: accounting 'recognition' principles that generally reduce the timeliness of accounting income by smoothing its incorporation of economic income over time; the effectiveness of accounting accruals in ameliorating serial correlation in operating cash flows; and accounting income-statement conservatism.

The most fundamental feature of accounting determining the incorporation of economic income in accounting income over time is the accounting 'recognition' principles (FASB, 1985, Paras 78–89), including the Revenue Realization and Expense Matching principles. Whereas economic income immediately incorporates changes in expectations of the present values of future cash flows, the recognition principles incorporate such changes in accounting income gradually over time, generally at points close to when the actual cash flow realizations occur. Hence, accounting income systematically lags economic income (Ball and Brown, 1968) and the lag extends over multiple periods (Beaver *et al.*, 1980; Easton *et al.*, 1992; Kothari and Sloan, 1992). The recognition principles therefore cause economic income to be incorporated in accounting income in a lagged and 'smoothed' fashion over time.

This feature of accounting income arises because there is demand for an income variable with properties additional to timeliness. While timeliness per se is desirable, information asymmetry between managers and users creates a demand for an income variable that is observable independently of managers. Accounting income thus incorporates only the subset of available value-relevant information that is independently observable, whereas economic income incorporates information that is not independent of managers, such as plans and forecasts (our proxy for economic income incorporates the sharemarket reaction to managers' forward-looking statements). In other words, accounting income does not attempt to anticipate future cash flows to the same extent as economic income. The first-order effect of the recognition principles thus is to make accounting income a complex moving average of past economic incomes.

The second fundamental feature of the accounting income-determination model is that accounting accruals imperfectly ameliorate serial correlation in operating cash flows. The accounting model provides for some anticipation of future cash flows through accrual accounting. For example, if managers pay an account for inventory early, then there is a decrease in current-period operating cash flow and, ceteris paribus, an offsetting increase in subsequent periods. Accrual accounting rules attempt to insulate income from the effect of the early payment, by expensing an amount in both periods that is based on inventory usage, not payments. In general, short term variation in firms' operational financing and investment decisions (such as changes in inventories, accounts payable and accounts receivable) causes negative serial correlation in operating cash flows, which accrual accounting attempts to remove from accounting income (Dechow et al., 1998). Hence, operating cash flow can be viewed as a noisier and less timely version of accounting income. However, accrual accounting is imperfect, because it is costly, so anticipation of future cash flows via accruals does not completely remove the noise in the cash flow time series.

The first two features of the accounting model of income determination together imply:

$$Y_{it} = f_j(\Delta V_{it}, \Delta V_{it-1}, \Delta V_{it-2}, \Delta V_{it-3}, \ldots, V_{it}) \tag{1}$$

where Y and ΔV, respectively, denote accounting and economic income, and V denotes noise due to imperfect accounting accruals. Economic income, ΔV, is fiscal-year change in the market capitalization of equity plus dividends and minus capital contributions during the year (Hicks, 1946). We hypothesize that the accounting model is applied differently across countries, and assume the model's parameters hold for all firms i that report under the accounting systems of country j. Assuming that ΔV is independent over time, this simplifies to

$$Y_{it} = g_j(\Delta V_{it}, \eta_{it}) \tag{2}$$

The disturbance η_{it} incorporates lagged changes in market values (ΔV_{it-1}, ΔV_{it-2}, ΔV_{it-3}, ...) as well as noise due to the residual serial correlation in cash flows not removed by accounting accruals (V_{it}). Both components of the disturbance term affect the R^2 of regression (2), which is used as a proxy for the timeliness property of accounting income. After scaling by opening market value, V_{it-1}, the dependent and independent variables are annual rate of return ($R_{it} \equiv \Delta V_{it}/V_{it-1}$) and earnings yield ($NI_{it} \equiv Y_{it}/V_{it-1}$), and a linear specification gives

$$NI_{it} = \alpha_{0j} + \alpha_{1j}R_{it} + \xi_{it} \tag{3}$$

The third fundamental feature of the accounting income model we study is conservatism. A longstanding example of income conservatism is the 'lower of cost or market' inventory rule, which incorporates inventory losses more quickly in income than gains. A topical example is new information about future cash flows from long-term assets. The recognition principles normally incorporate this information in accounting income at or near the point when the actual cash flow realizations occur. However, a variety of accounting rules and practices cause immediate write-offs against income when expected future cash flows *decrease*, without waiting for the cash flow decreases to be realized. In the US, SFAS 121 recently formalized long-standing write-off practices for long-lived assets in the form of asset impairment rules.[3] Upward revaluation is comparatively rare in the US: it has not been practiced since the Securities and Exchange Commission (SEC) was established in 1934, though it is practiced in some countries. Consequently, unrealized increases in asset values generally do not flow into income until approximately when the underlying cash flow increases occur, but unrealized decreases are more likely to be incorporated quickly.[4]

Following Basu (1997), we incorporate conservative asymmetry in accounting income timeliness by modifying (3) for asymmetric incorporation of negative economic income:

$$NI_{it} = \beta_{0j} + \beta_{1j}RD_{it} + \beta_{2j}R_{it} + \beta_{3j}R_{it}RD_{it} + \varepsilon_{it} \tag{4}$$

The dummy variable RD_t assumes its value based on the sign of stock return, not earnings: one if return R_t is negative, and zero otherwise. β_{2j} and ($\beta_{2j} + \beta_{3j}$) capture the incorporation in current-year accounting income of positive and negative economic income respectively, in country j.

This specification has several attractive features. One advantage of specifying accounting income as the dependent variable is avoiding the need for a noisy earnings expectations model. Here, the independent variable (annual stock return) is relatively free of short-term microstructure, liquidity or mispricing effects. An additional advantage of the specification is that it incorporates the fundamental tenets of accounting income recognition. In particular, it incorporates lags that arise from the demand for an independent income measure, and piecewise linearity allows us to study international differences in asymmetric timeliness, or conservatism.

Initially, we estimate separate individual-country relations for each country j, pooling all firms i reporting under the country's accounting standards and all years t. International differences in income timeliness, for positive and negative economic income combined, are reflected in the R^2's of individual-country regressions (4).

3. Data

Accounting income, cash flow, and dividends over 1985–95 are from the Global Vantage Industrial/Commercial (IC) file. Accounting income NI_t is net income before extraordinary items (IC data 32).[5] Dividends (DIV) is dividends paid (IC data 36). Operating cashflow (OCF) is net income before extraordinary items (IC data 32) plus depreciation (IC data 11), minus the change in non-cash current assets (IC data 75 minus data 60), plus the change in current liabilities other than the current portion of long-term debt (IC data 104 minus data 94). All variables are scaled by market value of equity, calculated from the Global Vantage Issue file as price times number of outstanding shares, adjusted for stock splits and dividends using the Global Vantage adjustment factor. Change in accounting income ΔNI_t is $NI_t - NI_{t-1}$. Stock return R is the holding-period return, including dividends, over the firm's fiscal accounting year. Each firm/year observation is assigned to a country based on Periodic Descriptor Array 13 on the IC file, indicating the accounting standards used in preparing its financial statements that year (normally the country of the firm's home exchange).[6]

We exclude the two extreme percentiles of each variable $(NI, \Delta NI, DIV, OCF$ and $R)$.[7] Next, we exclude each firm/year with a missing value for any variable, giving the same observation set for the various variables and models estimated. Finally, we exclude countries with less than 1000 firm/year observations over the thirteen years. This leaves us with a final sample of 40,359 firm/year observations in eleven years from seven countries: Australia, Canada, UK and USA (common law countries) and France, Germany and Japan (code law countries). We also summarize results for a secondary sample of 18 countries with at least 100 firm-year observations.

Table 1 contains sample descriptive statistics. Individual-country samples are pooled firm-years, ranging in size from 1054 (France) to 21,225 (US). In

Table 1 Sample characteristics[a].

Panel A: descriptive statistics

	N	R			NI			DIV			OCF		
		μ	Med	σ	μ	Med	σ	μ	Med	σ	μ	Med	σ
Australia	1,321	17.3	9.9	52.6	2.6	6.7	19.0	3.5	3.6	3.3	11.6	10.9	33.3
Canada	2,901	12.1	6.0	46.8	3.2	5.3	15.4	2.0	1.4	2.4	15.1	12.2	28.9
US	21,225	12.7	8.1	42.8	3.1	6.2	14.4	1.9	1.0	2.4	11.7	10.3	21.4
UK	5,758	13.5	9.8	38.0	6.6	7.2	8.8	3.4	3.3	2.0	12.7	10.4	18.8
France	1,054	14.9	6.6	43.0	6.1	6.6	10.8	2.3	2.1	1.9	22.1	15.7	36.2
Germany	1,245	8.9	4.2	31.5	3.7	4.2	9.0	2.0	2.0	1.7	18.4	14.3	26.8
Japan	6,855	3.7	-2.8	33.4	1.7	1.8	2.1	0.7	0.7	0.4	4.7	4.2	7.8

Panel B: Observations by fiscal year end (month)

	1	2	3	4	5	6	7	8	9	10	11	12	Total
Australia	5	0	32	4	30	964	32	2	45	0	6	201	1,321
Canada	113	26	131	51	21	105	47	144	155	72	31	2,005	2,901
US	964	405	872	401	446	2,094	562	506	1,666	700	425	12,184	21,225
UK	297	119	1,222	333	119	344	121	143	590	164	66	2,240	5,758
France	0	2	23	0	0	3	0	12	24	5	0	985	1,054
Germany	0	19	4	0	0	75	9	0	183	7	3	945	1,245
Japan	94	363	5,341	39	68	29	9	14	150	67	144	537	6,855
Total	1,473	934	7,625	828	684	3,614	780	821	2,813	1,015	675	19,097	40,359

Table 1 (cont'd)

Panel C: Observations by year

	85	86	87	88	89	90	91	92	93	94	95	Total
Australia	11	29	88	91	116	165	160	164	181	178	138	1,321
Canada	189	221	277	276	306	325	306	311	317	325	48	2,901
US	1,586	1,661	2,234	2,240	2,159	2,098	2,006	2,111	2,153	2,189	788	21,225
UK	98	314	438	508	621	703	722	751	756	733	114	5,758
France	9	66	74	72	98	147	155	151	131	146	5	1,054
Germany	20	74	83	76	90	145	180	189	170	192	26	1,245
Japan	3	328	668	739	841	881	850	857	874	814	0	6,855
Total	1,916	2,693	3,862	4,002	4,231	4,464	4,379	4,534	4,582	4,577	1,119	40,359

[a] *Sample* consists of 40,359 firm-year observations selected from the Global Vantage Industrial/Commercial and Issue files over 1985–95, using the following procedure. First, for each variable (see below) we eliminate the two extreme percentiles of firm-year observations. Second, we eliminate all firm-year observations with missing values for one or more variables, to facilitate comparability with results in previous tables. Third, we eliminate all firm-year observations from countries with less than 1,000 observations, leaving seven countries represented. Australia, Canada, United States, and the United Kingdom are the common-law countries, the rest are code-law countries.

R = buy-and-hold security return inclusive of dividends over the fiscal year;

NI = annual earnings per share before extraordinary items deflated by beginning of period price;

DIV = annual dividends per share deflated by beginning of period price;

OCF = annual operating cash flow per share deflated by beginning of period price;

N = the number of firm/year observations.

Panel A, mean fiscal-year returns range from 3.7% (Japan) to 17.3% (Australia). Mean *NI* ranges from 1.7% (Japan) to 6.6% (UK). All countries' mean and median *OCF* (from which capital investments are not deducted) exceed *NI* (from which depreciation, a weighted average of past capital investments, is deducted).

Consistent with asymmetric conservatism, accounting income is negatively skewed (all medians exceed means), which contrasts with the positive skew of stock returns (all means exceed medians). That is, conservative accounting tends to incorporate economic losses as larger but transitory, capitalized amounts, and to incorporate economic gains as smaller but persistent flows over time, thus generating the negative skew of accounting income. The differential skew of earnings relative to returns calls into question the traditional linear earnings-returns specification, and supports the Basu (1997) piecewise linear version.

Also consistent with our model, in all seven countries the rank order of volatilities across variables is (highest first): *R*, *OCF*, *NI* and *DIV*. Our interpretation is: (i) accounting income is a lagged function of present and past years' returns (a type of moving average), and hence has lower volatility than individual-year stock returns; (ii) cash flow from operations is noisier than income, and hence is more volatile; and (iii) dividends is a further lagged function of accounting income, and hence is the least volatile variable. We comment on the relative magnitudes of the *R* and *NI* volatilities below.

Panel B reports the distribution of ending months for companies' fiscal years. December is the norm in Canada, France, Germany and US. March is the norm in Japan and June is the norm in Australia. Code law countries exhibit more conformity with their norm, presumably due to the greater influence of regulation and tax accounting in those countries, discussed below. UK, which we categorize below as the least regulated country in the sample, exhibits the greatest dispersion in fiscal year-ends. Panel C reports the sample distribution by calendar year.

4. Hypotheses and tests: international timeliness and conservatism of accounting income

We develop hypotheses concerning the influence of institutional variables on the two properties of accounting income captured by our model: timeliness and conservatism (or asymmetric timeliness). There have been numerous attempts to classify nations' accounting systems, based on a variety of institutional variables, but little empirical research has been directed at determining which variables explain differences in important properties of accounting income.[8]

4.1 Demand for timely accounting income in code and common law governance

Perhaps the most fundamental institutional variable causing accounting income to differ internationally is the extent of political influence on both standard setting and enforcement. An admittedly imperfect proxy for political influence – but a proxy our results legitimate – is whether standard setting and enforcement occur under codified law (a governmental process) or common law (a market process).[9] We hypothesize that the demand for timely incorporation of economic income in accounting income is lower under the code-law 'stakeholder' model of corporate governance than under the common-law 'shareholder' model. Below we describe the origins of and salient features of code- and common-law institutional environments. The discussion highlights the differences between the two systems and their differential implications for properties of accounting income. However, there is overlap between the code- and common-law institutions and accounting standard setting, which likely weakens empirical support for the hypotheses we develop.

Common law arises from individual action in the private sector. It emphasizes following legal procedure over rules (David and Brierley, 1985, p. 24; Posner, 1996). Common laws – including accounting standards – evolve by becoming commonly accepted in practice. While it might be efficient for private-sector bodies to codify generally accepted accounting rules and make them binding on their members, such standards arise in an accounting market, not in government. Common law enforcement is a private matter, involving civil litigation. Common law originated in England and it is now found in UK and many former British colonies. The common-law countries in our sample are Australia, Canada, UK and US.

Common law historically has evolved to meet the demands of contracting in markets. The 'shareholder' model of corporate governance, in which shareholders alone elect the governing board, predominates in common-law countries. Alchian and Demsetz (1972) argue this is efficient due to the additional incentive of residual claimants to effectively monitor managers. Compared to code-law governance, board members are less likely to hold large blocks, there is more monitoring of managers by external debt and equity markets (including analysts), and lenders and employees seldom have board representation. We hypothesize that, because parties contracting with the firm operate at greater 'arm's length' from managers, information asymmetry in common-law countries is more likely to be resolved by timely public disclosure.

Code-law originates from collective planning in the public sector. Governments or quasi-governmental bodies, such as France's *Conseil National de la Comptabilité* or Japan's Business Accounting Deliberation Council (which advises the Ministry of Finance) establish code-law accounting standards.[10]

The code prescribes regulations ranging from abstract principles (e.g., 'prudence') to detailed procedures (e.g., the format of financial statements). Code-law enforcement is a governmental function, involving administrative bodies undertaking criminal prosecution for code violation. Code-law countries in our sample are France, Germany and Japan.

The code- and common-law common classes overlap in practice, in that financial reporting in no country is determined in a purely market or planning system. The UK Companies Acts imposed codification on a predominantly common-law system during the 19th century. In the US, the Securities and Exchange Acts played a similar role in the 1930s, among other things creating the SEC as a US government agency with responsibility for regulation of accounting standards. We acknowledge that the code- and common-law separation is not watertight and that there is some overlap in the nature of standard setting in the two categories of countries. Nevertheless, we believe the distinction is informative because, after reviewing the institutional details, we conclude it captures differences in the extent of political influence on accounting standard-setting (versus private contracting in the markets).

An important difference between common-law and code-law countries is the manner of resolving information asymmetry between managers and potential users of accounting income, including debt and equity investors, employees, suppliers and customers. Code-law corporate governance tends to be conducted by elected or appointed agents for these parties.[11] These agents tend to be informed by private 'inside' access to information. Thus, employees and stockholders each elect 50% of the supervisory board of German *Aktiengesellschaft* (stock corporations). Banks typically dominate stock voting due to their largeblock holdings and due to the German practice of banks voting individuals' stocks as agents (Köndgen, 1994). The supervisory board appoints and monitors the managerial board, and approves the financial statements. For the system to be tractable, the number of contracting parties must be small, so managers have close relations with intermediaries: notably, banks, other financial institutions, labor unions, governments, major customers and suppliers. There is no presumption that parties operate at a distance. Consequently, the demand for timely public disclosure in code-law countries is not as great as in common-law countries.[12] We propose that this reduces the demand for timely incorporation of economic income in code-law accounting income.

Conversely, we propose that code-law accounting income meets other demands. The stakeholder model views accounting income as a common 'pie' divided among stakeholders, as dividends to shareholders, taxes to governments, and bonuses to managers and perhaps employees. The portfolio weights of managers and employees typically are skewed toward their employer firms, so their incentive is to reduce volatility in payouts. Regulation of bank leverage ratios penalizes volatility in bank income and thus in the accounting income and/or dividends on their equity investments. Code-law banking systems typically are hierarchical, so bank representatives are well aware of governments' incentives to reduce volatility of tax receipts. Employee representatives typically are re-elected annually. While incentives to reduce volatility in accounting income exist in common-law countries (Healy, 1985), we hypothesize that code-law governance amplifies them.

Volatility can be reduced, at the expense of timeliness, through accounting methods that 'smooth' accounting income over time, incorporating economic income gradually over several periods. The Recognition Rules inherently smooth accounting income in all countries (though we also argue they frequently are overridden in the case of negative economic income). Nevertheless, code-law accounting gives managers considerably more latitude in timing income recognition. In good years, income can be reduced by asset write-downs (e.g., excessive allowances for bad debts), by provisions (e.g., excessive provisions for future losses or future expenses) and by transfers to reserves. In bad years, accounting income can be increased by reversing these adjustments.[13] We predict that code-law accounting income incorporates a lower proportion of current-period economic income, 'smoothing' its incorporation to a greater extent over time.

H$_1$:   *Code-law countries' accounting incomes are more 'smoothed' and less timely in incorporating current-period changes in market value than common-law countries'.*

The summary statistics reported in panel A of Table 1 are broadly consistent with this hypothesis, in that code-law countries exhibit a lower ratio of *NI* volatility to *R* volatility.[14] We formally test the hypothesis using a variety of Basu regressions (4): individual-country regressions with observations pooled across time; annual Fama/MacBeth cross-sectional regressions for individual countries; a secondary sample of eighteen other countries; and (in Section 4.3) a pooled-countries regression that allows formal tests of differences among countries.

4.1.1 Evidence from country regressions with observations pooled across time

Initially, we test Hypothesis 1 by comparing the adjusted R^2's of the individual country, each estimated from pooled time series and cross-section data. While we make a distinction between common- and code-law countries, the categories are by no means homogeneous. For example, in Section 4.4 we argue that the UK is different from the remaining three common-law countries due to differences in the extent of accounting regulation, litigation environment, and the existence of public versus private debt. The empirical

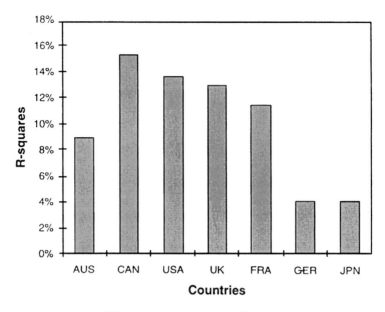

Figure 1 International differences in earnings timeliness R-squares from individual country regressions of earnings on (a) annual return and (b) annual return times negative return dummy.

analysis therefore reports results separately for the common-law countries excluding the UK, for the UK, and for the code-law countries.

The left-hand side of panel A of Table 2 reports the results and Fig. 1 graphs them. With the possible exception of France, there is a clear difference between individual code-law country R^2s (ranging from 4.2% to 12.6%) and common- law country R^2's (from 9.1% to 17.0%), consistent with the hypothesis. When countries are grouped, the R^2 for the pooled code-law sample is 5.2%, approximately one-third the common-law equivalent of 14.4% (excluding UK). The international differences in the degree of income-return association we document are similar to those in Alford *et al.* (1993), despite slightly different time periods and models.

To assess whether the differences in R^2's are statistically significant, we estimate the standard deviation of estimated R^2's, which Cramer (1987) shows is a function of sample size, the number of independent variables and the true R^2. For four independent variables including intercepts, a true R^2 of 5%, and sample size 1,000 (5,000, 20,000), the standard deviation of the estimate is 1.3% (0.6%, 0.3%). For a true R^2 of 15%, it is 2.0% (0.8%, 0.5%). Assuming independence across countries, differences in the order of 5% between our sample countries are significant, and the pooled common-law sample R^2 of 14.4% significantly exceeds the code-law R^2 of 5.2%. Since independence likely is violated, we report alternative tests below.

Table 2 Contemporaneous association between earnings and returns. Statistics based on pooled cross-section and time-series regressions and annual cross-sectional regressions using firm-year observations for each country. Intercepts are not reported[a].

Panel A: $NI = \beta_0 + \beta_1 RD + \beta_2 R + \beta_3 R*RD + \epsilon$

	Pooled regressions						Annual cross-sectional regressions					
	β_2	$t(\beta_2)$	β_3	$t(\beta_3)$	Adj. R^2(%)	N	Avg. β_2	$t(\beta_2)$	Avg. β_3	$t(\beta_3)$	Adj. R^2(%)	$t(R^2)$
Australia	−0.01	−0.53	0.37	8.63	9.1	1,321	0.02	0.99	0.33	6.12	11.15	3.68
Canada	0.00	0.12	0.40	17.21	17.0	2,901	0.01	0.51	0.39	6.82	18.19	5.59
USA	0.03	8.57	0.29	34.02	14.7	21,225	0.03	3.43	0.33	14.34	17.15	13.82
UK	0.04	10.14	0.15	13.32	13.8	5,758	0.05	4.23	0.14	5.41	16.76	8.81
France	0.08	7.30	0.07	2.30	12.6	1,054	0.06	2.95	0.14	2.71	17.59	4.52
Germany	0.05	4.28	0.10	3.27	5.4	1,245	0.04	2.01	−0.01	−0.06	7.47	4.85
Japan	0.01	5.95	0.01	2.58	4.2	6,855	0.00	0.55	0.02	3.26	6.88	4.07
Common	0.02	7.07	0.31	39.10	14.4	25,447	0.02	2.36	0.34	15.31	16.74	12.85
UK	0.04	10.14	0.15	13.32	13.8	5,758	0.05	4.23	0.14	5.41	16.76	8.81
Code	0.04	13.27	0.01	2.19	5.2	9,154	0.04	4.55	0.04	1.91	7.00	6.07

Panel B:

	R = $\beta_0 + \beta_1$ NI + ε			R = $\beta_0 + \beta_1$ NI + $\beta_2 \Delta$NI + ε					
	β_1	t(β_1)	Adj. R^2(%)	β_1	t(β_1)	β_2	t(β_2)	Adj. R^2(%)	N
Australia	0.47	6.30	2.9	0.44	5.75	0.12	2.84	3.4	1,321
Canada	0.79	14.49	6.7	0.72	13.06	0.26	6.44	8.0	2,901
USA	0.90	46.08	9.1	0.76	36.52	0.37	18.58	10.5	21,225
UK	1.44	26.67	11.0	1.21	20.40	0.46	9.07	12.2	5,758
France	1.40	12.22	12.3	1.28	10.86	0.46	4.23	13.7	1,054
Germany	0.76	7.84	4.6	0.71	6.78	0.13	1.30	4.7	1,245
Japan	3.16	16.82	4.0	2.23	11.04	2.85	11.83	5.9	6,855
Common	0.85	47.52	8.2	0.74	39.71	0.30	18.92	9.4	25,447
UK	1.44	26.67	11.0	1.21	20.40	0.46	9.07	12.2	5,758
Code	1.44	22.44	5.2	1.29	19.10	0.47	7.04	5.7	9,154

[a]*Sample* consists of 40,359 firm-year observations selected from the Global Vantage industrial/Commercial and Issue files over 1985–95, using the following procedure. First, for each variable (see below) we eliminate the two extreme percentiles of firm-year observations. Second, we eliminate all firm-year observations with missing values for one or more variables, to facilitate comparability with results in previous tables. Third, we eliminate all firm-year observations from countries with less than 1,000 observations, leaving seven countries represented. Australia, Canada, United States, and the United Kingdom are the common-law countries, the rest are code-law countries.

  R = buy-and-hold security return inclusive of dividends over the fiscal year;

  RD = equals one if return R is negative and zero otherwise.

  NI = annual earning per share before extraordinary item deflected by beginning of period price;

  ΔNI = change in NI per share, adjusted for stock splits and stock dividends, deflated by beginning of period price;

  N = the number of firm/year observations.

  In panel A, the reported *t*-statistics for the average of the slope coefficients from annual cross-sectional regressions for each country are the ratios of the mean estimated coefficients to the standard deviation of the distribution of 11 annual estimated slope coefficients, divided by the square root of 11 (see Fama and MacBeth, 1973).

4.1.2 Annual cross-sectional regressions

An alternative test, due to Fama and MacBeth (1973), estimates separate annual cross-sectional Basu regressions (4), using observations for each country as well as for each of three pooled country groups (code-law, common-law and UK). We exclude the 6 of 77 country-years with fewer than 20 firm observations. For each country and each country-group, the right-hand side of panel A of Table 2 reports the time-series average of the estimated annual slope coefficients and the average of the annual regression R^2's and their t-statistics. The t-statistic is the ratio of the sample mean to the standard deviation of the time-series distribution of the estimated coefficients or R^2's, divided by the square root of the number of annual cross-sections (= 11 or 10 depending on the availability of 20 or more observations). From this test, the mean R^2 for the common-law group is 16.7% (t-statistic = 12.85) compared to 7.0% (t-statistic = 6.07) for the code-law group and 16.8% (t-statistic = 8.81) for the UK. The common-law countries' average R^2 is significantly greater than that for the code-law countries at the 0.01 level.

4.1.3. Secondary sample of eighteen countries

A secondary sample of eighteen countries with between 100 and 1000 firm-year observations provides similar results. We use the Mueller *et al.* (1997, pp. 11–12, Exhibits 1–4) classifications of countries as following a British–American or a Continental accounting model to proxy for our private-sector common-law and public-sector code law categories. We thereby classify eight additional countries as common-law (Hong Kong, India, Ireland, Malaysia, Netherlands, New Zealand, Singapore, and South Africa), nine as code-law (Austria, Belgium, Denmark, Finland, Italy, Norway, Spain, Sweden, and Switzerland), and add Thailand as a code-law country based on our own assessment. While the Mueller *et al.* classifications agree with ours for each of the seven countries in our primary sample, we are less confident of the eighteen additional country classifications. Specifically, we suspect that many countries following British-American accounting rules nevertheless lack common-law litigation enforcement and exhibit reduced demand for timely accounting income. Classification errors are expected to reduce the significance of the secondary sample results.

For each of the eight common-law and ten code-law countries, we estimate a pooled Basu regression (4). Annual cross-sectional regressions for each country are not feasible due to insufficient observations. In the interest of parsimony, we summarize the main results. Detailed results in tabulated form are available to interested readers upon request. The average R^2 for the code-law countries is 6.5%, the median is 7.0%, the minimum is 1%, and the maximum is 14.6%. In comparison, the average R^2 for the common-law countries is 15.3%, the median is 12.4%, the minimum is 9.8%, and the maximum is 22.5%. The difference in mean R^2's of the common and code-law countries is statistically significant. The results are consistent with those reported for the seven countries in Table 2 and provide an independent confirmation of H_1.

4.2 Universal demand for conservative accounting income

In this section we argue that conservatism, defined as asymmetric timeliness in incorporating economic gains and losses (Basu, 1997), is a general property of accounting income.[15] This section serves as a lead-in to Section 4.3, which focuses on the effect of code- and common-law institutional differences on the degree of accounting conservatism.

Accountants contract to supply users with asymmetrically conservative income (i.e., to incorporate economic losses in a more timely fashion than gains) due to three properties of the accounting information market. First, managers possess specific information (Alchian, 1984) that is costly for external users to produce themselves (is not independently verifiable). Because managers have asymmetric incentives to disclose positive and negative specific information, information of negative innovations in expected future cash flows (economic losses) is more credible than positive innovations, and accountants are more likely to incorporate it in income. Second, lenders are important users of accounting information, including income and book value (a function of income), and they are asymmetrically affected by economic gains and losses (Watts and Zimmerman, 1986). Third, we propose that timely disclosure of economic losses is an important corporate governance mechanism. We assume that reversing bad investment decisions and strategies is personally more costly to managers than continuing good ones, and that informed monitoring by boards, analysts, investors and lenders is a mechanism to force them to undertake the cost. For these reasons, accountants supply income and book values that incorporate economic losses in a more timely fashion than economic gains.

The above properties of the market for accounting information are universal (though we argue below that they vary in degree internationally). We therefore expect accounting income to be asymmetrically conservative in all countries. Empirically, accounting income should exhibit higher R^2's for bad news (i.e., negative fiscal-year return) observations than for positive. Table 3 reports that negative-return R^2's exceed their positive-return counterparts in all commonlaw countries and in Germany.[16] The exceptions are the code-law countries France and Japan, discussed below.

Table 3 and Fig. 2 show that in all seven countries the coefficient on negative returns exceeds its counterpart on positive returns. Accounting income in the US is approximately ten times as sensitive to negative as to positive returns (estimated slopes of 0.32 and 0.03). The median country in terms of relative sensitivity to negative versus positive returns is the UK,

Table 3 Contemporaneous association between earnings and returns separately in good and bad news years. Statistics from pooled cross-section and time-series regressions using firm-year observations for each country. Intercepts are not reported[a].

| | Good news: $NI = \beta_0 + \beta_1 R + \varepsilon(R \geq 0)$ | | | Bad news: $NI = \beta_0 + \beta_1 R + \varepsilon(R < 0)$ | | |
	β_1	Adj. $R^2(\%)$	N	β_1	Adj. $R^2(\%)$	N
Australia	−0.01	−0.1	813	0.36	10.1	508
Canada	0.00	−0.1	1,688	0.40	17.9	1,213
USA	0.03	0.8	12,721	0.32	11.7	8,504
UK	0.04	3.2	3,612	0.19	11.6	2,146
France	0.08	9.0	611	0.16	4.7	443
Germany	0.05	2.4	712	0.16	4.9	533
Japan	0.01	1.1	3,141	0.02	0.8	3,714
Common	0.02	0.4	15,222	0.33	12.2	10,225
UK	0.04	3.2	3,612	0.19	11.6	2,146
Code	0.04	3.3	4,464	0.05	1.7	4,690

[a]*Sample* consists of 40,359 firm-year observations selected from the Global Vantage industrial/ Commercial and Issue files over 1985–95, using the following procedure. First, for each variable (see below) we eliminate the two extreme percentiles of firm-year observations. Second, we eliminate all firm-year observations with missing values for one or more variables, to facilitate comparability with results in previous tables. Third, we eliminate all firm-year observations from countries with less than 1,000 observations, leaving seven countries represented. Australia, Canada, United States, and the United Kingdom are the common-law countries, the rest are code-law countries.

R = buy-and-hold security return inclusive of dividends over the fiscal year;

NI = annual earnings per share before extraordinary items deflated by beginning of period price;

N = the number of firm/year observations.

with a ratio of approximately five (0.19: 0.04). A formal test of the asymmetry is provided in Table 2, panel A. The incremental slope β_3 on negative fiscal-year returns (i.e. return interacted with the return dummy variable, $R*RD$) is significantly positive for all seven countries. A Fama-MacBeth test, with the β_3 coefficients estimated from separate annual cross-sectional country regressions, also is reported in Table 2, panel A. The average incremental slope is significant for all countries except Germany.

Unreported results for the secondary sample of 10 code-law and 8 common-law countries also are consistent with asymmetric timeliness being a universal property of accounting income. The incremental slope on negative returns is positive in 12 of the 18 countries.

4.3 Demand for greater income conservatism under common-law governance

We propose that common-law accounting income is more asymmetrically conservative than code-law, due to greater demand for timely disclosure of

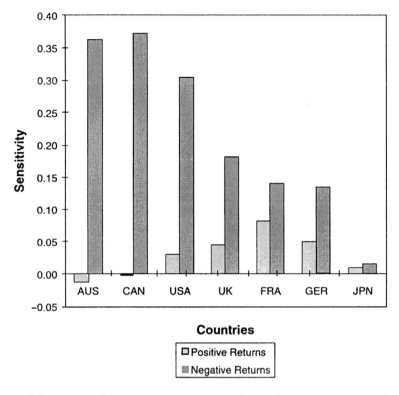

Figure 2 International differences in asymmetry in earnings response to good and bad news; sensitivity to positive and negative returns from pooled regression of earnings on (a) annual return and (b) annual return times negative return dummy.

economic losses. Each of the three properties of the market for accounting information described above is qualitatively weaker in code-law governance. First, the closer code-law relation between managers and agents for contracting groups (banks, labor unions) reduces information asymmetry. Second, banks and other financial institutions tend to supply both debt and equity capital, making their loss function more symmetric. Third, there is less reliance on external monitoring of managers. Consistent with lower demand for timely incorporation of economic losses, the expected litigation cost of untimely incorporation is lower. Conversely, in code-law countries there is a demand for a low-volatility income variable, due to the more direct relation between current-year accounting income and short-term payouts such as dividends and bonuses. Reluctance to cut dividends (Lintner, 1956) leads to a preference for gradually incorporating an economic loss in income over time, for example by waiting for the reduced underlying cash flow realizations to occur, as distinct from recognizing it as a large, capitalized, transitory amount.

H_2:   *Common-law accounting income is more asymmetrically conservative than code-law.*

The separate positive and negative return samples in Table 3 reveal that the greater *overall* timeliness of common-law accounting income reported above is due entirely to years with economic losses. For the common-law group, the 12.2% negative-return year R^2 significantly exceeds the 0.4% in positive-return years. In all common-law countries, R^2's in negative-return years exceed those in positive-return years. Accounting income in Australia, Canada and the US over the sample period essentially ignores current-year economic gains. Common-law accounting income seems directed primarily toward incorporation of economic losses. With the exception of Germany, the same cannot be said of code-law accounting. For the code-law sample, the negative-return year R^2 of 1.7% actually is lower than 3.3% for the positive-return years. These results are consistent with the hypothesis that, relative to code-law countries, the common-law demand for accounting income originates more in arm's length corporate governance, debt contracts, and investor litigation, and less in determining short-term payouts.

As another test of a differential degree of conservatism in code- and common-law countries, we focus on the slope coefficients from the Basu regression (4) results in Table 2 and Fig. 2. The β_{2j} slopes 2 show that accounting income in every common-law country exhibits *less* sensitivity to positive returns than in France and Germany (accounting income in Japan exhibits the least timeliness for both return samples). In contrast, the incremental negative-return slopes β_{3j} for common-law countries range from 0.15 to 0.40, considerably larger than the code-law range of 0.01–0.10. The pooled incremental slopes are 0.31 for the common-law group as a whole (excluding UK) and 0.01 for the code-law group. The difference is statistically significant at the 0.01 level.[17]

The incremental β_{3j} slope of 0.01 for Japan is the lowest in the sample (due to relative sample sizes it dominates the code-law group slope). Low income conservatism is consistent with the stylized institutional facts for Japan, in which one-time accounting write-offs are rare, economic losses reputedly are dribbled slowly into reported income over time (the banking sector being a notorious case), there is no provision for under-funded pension liabilities or other post-retirement liabilities, and the 'lower of cost or market' rule is not even used for inventories.[18]

4.3.1 Pooled sample

To formally test for international differences in the degree of conservatism, we estimate (4) using data pooled across countries:

$$NI = \beta_0 + \sum_j \beta_{0j} \, CD_j + \beta_1 \, RD + \sum_j \beta_{1j} \, RD \, CD_j + \beta_2 R$$

$$+ \sum_j \beta_{2j} R \, CD_j + \beta_3 R \, RD + \sum_j \beta_{3j} R \, RD \, CD_j. \qquad (5)$$

Six dummy variables identify the country of the accounting standards used for each firm/year, with $CD_j = 1$ for firm/years under country j and $= 0$ otherwise. US is the 'base country,' with zero values for all country dummy variables. The coefficient β_2 on return measures the incorporation of current economic income into US firms' accounting incomes. The coefficient β_{2j} on the product of return and the country j dummy variable measures the country's *incremental* incorporation, relative to the US. The coefficients β_3 and β_{3j} measure the asymmetric conservatism of accounting income under US standards and the incremental conservatism under other countries' standards. Thus, $\beta_2 + \beta_{2j} + \beta_3 + \beta_{3j}$ measures the incorporation of negative economic income in country j. Table 4 reports results of the pooled country-dummy regression Eq. (5). Accounting income in all sample code-law countries (France, Germany and Japan) exhibits significantly less incremental sensitivity to negative economic income than under US standards.

4.4 Regulation, litigation and debt differences among common-law countries

The distinction between common-law and code-law countries provides useful insights, but as we observe above the categories are by no means homogeneous. We consider two important institutional differences within the class of common-law countries: the method and extent of their regulation of accounting; and the extent to which their securities litigation rules favor plaintiffs.

4.4.1 Regulation

We propose that, among common-law countries, income conservatism increases with regulation of accounting standard setting and enforcement. Building on Peltzman (1976), Watts and Zimmerman (1986, pp. 229–231) argue that the political process and the SEC as its agent have an incentive to avoid perceived responsibility for investor losses. We argue that responsibility is attributed more to managers, and less to the political process, if losses are disclosed in financial statements in a more timely fashion. Consequently, regulation adds criminal penalties to the common-law civil remedy of damages for untimely disclosure of material bad news. Accounting is regulated to varying degrees in all common-law countries. For reasons summarized below, we characterize UK as the least regulated accounting market among our sample common-law countries.

63

Table 4 Comparative asymmetry in the contemporaneous returns-earnings relation: pooled regressions with individual-country effects[a].

Reported statistics are for the following model using the pooled cross-section and time-series of firm/year observations for all countries:

$$NI = \beta_0 + \sum_j \beta_{0j} \, CD_j + \beta_1 \, RD + \sum_j \beta_{1j} \, RD \, CD_j + \beta_2 R + \sum_j \beta_{2j} R \, CD_j$$

$$+ \beta_3 R \, RD + \sum_j \beta_{3j} R \, RD \, CD_j + \varepsilon$$

Results are not reported for the intercept, the negative-return intercept, and their respective country dummies. The country category models use the common law countries of Australia, Canada and the US as the base category; dummies are used for (1) the UK and (2) the code law countries of France, Germany and Japan.

	Coeff.	t-Stat.
Panel A: country dummies model		
Earnings 'good news' sensitivity		
β_2 (*Return*)	0.03	9.88
β_{2j} (*Return*Country Dummies*):		
Australia	−0.03	−3.95
Canada	−0.03	−3.80
UK	0.02	2.40
France	0.05	4.16
Germany	0.03	1.57
Japan	−0.02	−2.64
F-stat. for country return dummies		11.35
		p < 0.01
Incremental 'bad news' sensitivity		
β_3 (*Return Dummy*Return*)	0.29	39.21
β_{3j} (*Return Dummy*Return*Country Dummies*)		
Australia	0.07	2.64
Canada	0.11	5.28
UK	−0.14	−8.26
France	−0.22	−5.81
Germany	−0.19	−4.41
Japan	−0.29	−15.74
F-stat.: Country Negative Ret Dummies		67.44
		p < 0.01
Regression		
N		40,359
Adj. R^2		15.4%
F		272.98

Table 4 (cont'd)

Panel B: country category dummies model

Earnings 'good news' sensitivity	Coeff.	t-stat.
β_2 (*Return*)	0.02	8.36
β_{2j} (*Return*Country Category Dummy*):		
UK	0.02	3.52
Code	0.01	2.37

F-stat. for country category return dummies	7.94
	p < 0.01

Incremental 'bad news' sensitivity

β_3 (*Return Dummy*Return*)	0.31	46.23
β_{3j} (*Return Dummy*Return*Country Category Dummy*):		
UK	−0.16	−9.50
Code	−0.30	−19.00

F-stat.: Country Category Negative Return	200.92
Dummy	p < 0.01

Regression

N	40,359
Adj. R^2	14.9%
F	642.07

---

[a]*Sample* consists of 40,359 firm-year observations selected from the Global Vantage industrial/ Commericial and Issue files over 1985–95, using the following procedure. First, for each variable (see below) we eliminate the two extreme percentiles of firm-year observations. Second, we eliminate all firm-year observations with missing values for one or more variables, to facilitate comparability with results in previous tables. Third, we eliminate all firm-year observations from countries with less than 1,000 observations, leaving seven countries represented. Australia, Canada, United States, and the United Kingdom are the common-law countries, the rest are code-law countries.

R = buy-and-hold security return inclusive of dividends over the fiscal year;

NI = annual earnings per share before extraordinary items deflated by beginning of period price;

RD = the proxy for bad news = 1 if $R < 0$ and = 0 otherwise;

CD_j = country identifier = 1 for firm/years in country j and = 0 otherwise. USA is the 'base country' with $CD_j = 0 \ \forall j$.

The Securities Exchange Act of 1934 created the SEC as a US Government agency authorized to mandate and administer accounting standards. The SEC by-and-large has accepted the standards of the accounting profession, but nevertheless has retained a close supervisory role. It has intervened in standard setting on several occasions, as has Congress on occasions (e.g., in the debate on mark-to-market accounting, and by examining some firms' in-process R&D write-offs). We conclude that the US operates a closely regulated common-law system.

The effect is to compound the civil and criminal penalties for non-disclosure of material bad news. It has become a violation of both the common-law obligation to disclose (the civil law penalty for which is remedial damages awarded in private litigation) and a similar and some-times stronger statutory obligation (the criminal law penalty for which is a fine, incarceration and/or prohibition from practice). We conjecture that this dual system of penalties creates additional incentives to recognize eco-nomic losses in regulated common-law countries.

Australia and Canada are widely viewed as having evolved from the loosely regulated UK model (described below) to the US regulatory model. Both commenced with a largely self-regulating profession, initially adopted provincial (rather than federal) regulation, and then moved to a system in which governmental or semi-governmental bodies set national accounting standards. Australia created a regulatory body (now constituted as the Australian Securities Commission) 'obviously modeled on the SEC' (Nobes and Parker, 1995, p. 106). It also removed standard setting from the private sector, assigning it in 1984 to a government-appointed authority (now the Australian Accounting Standards Board), whose accounting standards can be overturned only by the Australian Parliament. These changes predate our sample period, so we characterize Australian accounting as highly regulated (see Choi and Mueller, 1992, p. 86).

Canada has evolved to a regulated federal model in a similar fashion. Accounting was increasingly regulated with the establishment of the provin-cial securities commissions, and the enactment of provincial and federal securities laws. Various revisions of the Ontario Companies Act have been particularly influential. In 1975, federal regulations required financial state-ments to comply with the accounting standards promulgated in the Canadian Institute of Chartered Accountants' *CICA Handbook*, thereby giving them statutory status. The SEC has indirectly influenced Canadian accounting, due to large Canadian corporations listing in New York.

Among the common-law countries in our sample, we classify the UK as having the least regulated accounting market over our sample period. There is no UK regulatory body comparable to the SEC in the US. UK financial markets (the City of London) have historically been viewed as primarily 'self-regulating,' and the UK parliament has seldom intervened in account-ing matters (Choi and Mueller, 1992, Chapter 3; Nobes and Parker, 1995, Chapter 6; Radebaugh and Gray, 1997, Chapter 5). In 1990, UK established the Accounting Standards Board (ASB), modeled on the US FASB and accountable to a newly created Financial Reporting Council. The ASB was authorized to issue Financial Reporting Standards (FRSs) that are backed by law (Radebaugh and Gray, 1997, pp. 91–92; Choi and Mueller, 1992, pp. 116–118). Nevertheless, the law allows a company to deviate from FRSs if it discloses the effect on its accounts. Even these changes did not take place until near the end of our sample period, 1985–95. We therefore treat UK accounting as less regulated than other sample common-law countries (Australia, Canada and US).

4.4.2 Litigation

Among common-law countries, we also propose that income conservatism increases in the expected costs to accounting firms and their clients from securities litigation. Expected litigation costs affect managers' and auditors' disclosure decisions (Kothari et al., 1988). The expected costs are a function of lawsuit probability, award size and legal fees. Securities lawsuits induce a demand for conservatism because the payoff function is asymmetric: they almost invariably allege investor losses arising from insufficiently conservative disclosures. We expect countries with higher expected litigation cost of non-disclosure are more likely to demand accounting income that incorporates economic losses in a timely fashion.

Our assumption is that expected litigation costs are lower in the UK than in Australia, Canada and US. Relevant UK institutional facts include: punitive damages are more difficult to obtain; juries are seldom used in civil litigation; absence of class action suits; and the so-called 'English rule,' under which losing plaintiffs pay part of defendants' costs.[19] In code-law countries, civil litigation is comparatively rare and the size of awards is comparatively small.

4.4.3 Private debt

UK corporate debt is predominantly private. We conjecture there is less information asymmetry between managers and private lenders than in the case of public debt, thus reducing the demand for timely incorporation of economic losses in UK accounting income.

4.4.4 Regulation, litigation and private debt considered jointly

Overall, we classify UK as having lower regulatory and litigation costs and predominantly private debt, so we predict less conservatism in UK accounting income than in other common-law countries. Nevertheless, relative to code-law countries, UK is expected to be more income conservative.

H₃: *U.K. accounting income is less conservative than in other common-law countries and more conservative than in code-law countries.*

The data weakly support this hypothesis. The UK negative-return R^2 of 11.6% in Table 3 falls between that of the common-law group (12.2%) and the code-law group (1.7%). The incremental negative-return slope β_3 of 0.15 in panel A of Table 2 is significantly smaller than those for the other common-law countries (β_3 from 0.29 to 0.40), and it is marginally significantly greater than those for the code-law countries (β_3 from 0.01 to 0.10).[20]

4.5 Advantage of the Basu (1997) piecewise linear model

The misspecification in linear models for the common-law countries is seen from their generally lower R^2's in panel B of Table 2, compared with the Basu piecewise linear regressions in panel A, which is graphically depicted in Fig. 3. Code-law countries exhibit considerably less asymmetry, and hence their R^2's differ little between the specifications. In contrast, the asymmetry is sufficiently strong in Australia, Canada and US to cause R^2's from the Basu model to be approximately 1.6 to 3.2 times their linear model equivalents. Thus, linear earnings-returns models are potentially misleading in a common-law context and in international comparisons, due to substantial international differences in timing of economic loss incorporation.

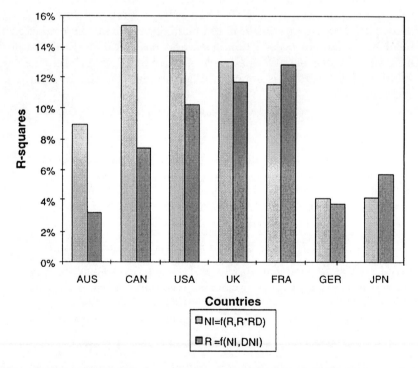

Figure 3 International differences in the contemporaneous relation between earnings and returns; R-squares from (1) the pooled reverse regressions of earnings against (a) annual return and (b) Annual return times negative return dummy and (2) annual return against NI and ΔNI.

5. Hypotheses and tests: accounting income versus dividends and cash flows

In this section, we compare accounting income with dividends and cash flows internationally. We argue that code-law institutional links between current-year income and dividends imply they incorporate similar information. Consistent with this hypothesis, we report that accounting income is timelier than dividends in common-law countries but not in code-law countries. Income is *less* timely than dividends in Germany and Japan. In contrast, accounting income is timelier than cash flows from operations in all countries.

5.1 Laws and practices linking current-period income and dividends

Accounting income is influenced, in varying degrees across countries, by firms' current dividend decisions. One influence results from laws on the taxation of corporate income and of dividend distributions.[21] We address these linkages in code and common-law countries separately.

5.1.1 Code-law links between dividends and accounting income

In the code-law 'stakeholder' corporate governance model, governments frequently are viewed as stakeholders, and tax payments are viewed as government's share of the same income 'pie' from which dividends and bonuses are paid. Politics requires reported and taxable incomes to converge, particularly since the government is responsible for both tax and accounting codes. Tax rules in the three sample code-law countries allow a deduction against taxable income only if also taken against reported accounting income (Choi and Mueller, 1992, p. 104). In code-law countries generally, it thus is considered imprudent to report income in excess of that required to justify dividends and bonuses, to minimize corporate tax. The consequence is that accounting income is influenced by short-term dividend policy.

The influence is particularly strong in Germany, where (Nobes and Parker 1995, pp. 269–272) the *Handelsgesetzbuch* ('commercial code') includes the *Massgeblichkeitsprinzip* ('authoritative principle') that tax accounting be based on the firm's *Handelsbilanz* ('commercial balance sheet'). Choi and Mueller (1992, p. 96) conclude of Germany: 'The dominance of tax accounting rules means that there is literally no difference between financial statements prepared for tax purposes and financial statements published in financial reports. . . . Financial reports reflect tax laws – not primarily the information needs of investors and other financial market participants.' The relation between income and dividends is tightened in Germany by two additional institutional factors. First, Federal law forbids management from paying dividends less than 50% of income without stockholders voting approval.

Second, undistributed profits are taxed at a higher rate than distributed profits (currently 45% versus 30%, excluding the 'solidarity surcharge').

These code-law institutional factors impose an additional role on the (already reduced) public-disclosure role of accounting income: corporate policy on current payouts to 'stakeholders,' including governments (via taxation), shareholders (via dividends), and managers and employees (via bonuses). If these distributions per se are uninformative, then the testable implication is that code-law accounting income is noisier and less oriented to incorporating current economic income, relative to dividends, than common-law income.

H_4: *Code-law accounting income is less timely relative to dividends than common-law.*

Table 5 reports the contemporaneous association between returns and dividends, for the same sample of firm-years as for accounting income in Table 2. Fig. 4 depicts comparative R^2's for income and dividends. Results generally support the hypothesis that common-law accounting income is more timely relative to dividends than code-law. In the last column of panel A, the ratio of the returns/income R^2 to the returns/dividends R^2 exceeds unity for three of the four common-law countries. For the pooled common-law countries, the ratio is 170%. In contrast, dividends are *more* timely than income in two of the three code-law countries (Germany and Japan). In Germany, where there are particularly binding institutional links between them, accounting income captures only 56% as much current value relevant information as dividends. The equivalent ratio for Japan is 78%. For the pooled code-law group, the ratio is 96%, meaning current-year income and

Table 5 Contemporaneous association between dividends and returns[a].

Statistics are from regressions using the pooled cross-section and time-series of firm/year observations for each country. Intercepts are not reported.

Panel A: $DIV = \beta_0 + \beta_1 RD + \beta_2 R + \beta_3 R*RD + \varepsilon$

	β_2	$t(\beta_2)$	β_3	$t(\beta_3)$	Adj.R^2(%)	N	Ratio
Australia	0.00	−1.85	0.06	8.67	11.1	1,321	0.82
Canada	−0.01	−9.06	0.04	11.26	7.3	2,901	2.34
USA	−0.02	−26.54	0.05	34.24	9.2	21,225	1.60
UK	0.01	8.69	0.02	9.25	9.7	5,758	1.42
France	0.01	4.22	0.02	3.90	8.8	1,054	1.43
Germany	0.02	6.66	0.01	0.99	9.6	1,245	0.56
Japan	0.00	2.28	0.01	9.72	5.5	6,855	0.78
Common	−0.01	−25.23	0.05	35.67	8.4	25,447	1.70
UK	0.01	8.69	0.02	9.25	9.7	5,758	1.42
Code	0.01	10.08	0.01	3.78	5.5	9,154	0.96

Table 5 *(cont'd)*

Panel B:	DIV = $\beta_0 + \beta_1 R + \varepsilon (R \geq 0)$					DIV = $\beta_0 + \beta_1 R + \varepsilon (R < 0)$				
	β_1	Adj. R²(%)	N	Ratio	Vuong	β_1	Adj. R²(%)	N	Ratio	Vuong
Australia	0.00	0.2	813	-0.36	0.65	0.06	18.3	508	0.55	2.41
Canada	-0.01	3.8	1,688	-0.02	5.22	0.03	7.9	1,213	2.26	-3.69
USA	-0.02	4.4	12,721	0.18	9.67	0.04	10.4	8,504	1.12	-1.48
UK	0.01	1.9	3,612	1.73	-1.74	0.03	9.3	2,146	1.24	-1.48
France	0.01	2.2	611	4.12	-2.46	0.03	9.5	443	0.49	1.88
Germany	0.02	4.8	712	0.50	1.43	0.02	3.8	533	1.31	-0.6
Japan	0.00	0.1	3,141	11.00	-2.74	0.01	4.5	3,714	0.19	6.06
Common	-0.01	3.4	15,222	0.13	8.71	0.04	10.3	10,225	1.19	-2.45
UK	0.01	1.9	3,612	1.73	-1.74	0.03	9.3	2,146	1.24	-1.48
Code	0.01	1.5	4,464	2.17	-2.87	0.01	2.7	4,690	0.62	1.89

[a]*Sample* consists of 40,359 firm-year observations selected from the Global Vantage industrial/Commercial and Issue files over 1985–95, using the following procedure. First, for each variable (see below) we eliminate the two extreme percentiles of firm-year observations. Second, we eliminate all firm-year observations with missing values for one or more variables, to facilitate comparability with results in previous tables. Third, we eliminate all firm-year observations from countries with less than 1,000 observations, leaving seven countries represented. Australia, Canada, United States, and the United Kingdom are the common-law countries, the rest are code-law countries. However, the common law country category in the third row from the bottom excludes the UK.

R = buy-and-hold security return inclusive of dividends over the fiscal year;

RD = 1 if $R = 0$ and $RD = 0$ if $R > 0$;

DIV = annual dividends per share deflated by beginning of period price;

N = the number of firm/year observations.

$Ratio$ = in panel A, the ratio of the R²s of the equivalent earnings (Table 2) and dividends (this table) regressions, in panel B, the ratio of the R²s of the equivalent earnings (Table 3) and dividends (this table) regressions.

Vuong statistic is a likelihood ratio statistic that compares the fit of the return/dividend model in this table in panel B against the return/earnings model in Table 3, both estimated separately using the good news and bad news return observations. The Vuong statistic is distributed unit-Normal, i.e., a Z-statistic.

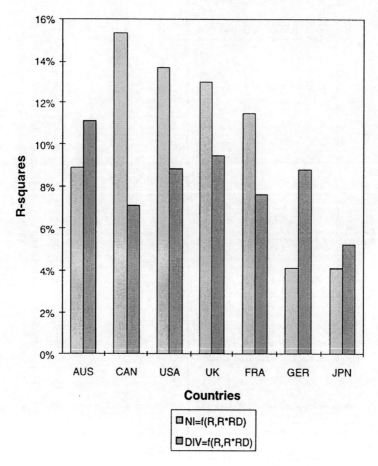

Figure 4 Earnings versus dividends; R-squares from the individual country reverse
regressions of (1) NI and (2) DIV against (a) annual return and (b) annual
return times negative return dummy.

dividends capture approximately the same amount of current-year economic
income. These results are consistent with the timeliness of code-law accounting income being constrained by its direct role in determining current-year
dividend payouts.

Panel B of Table 5 reports separate dividend/return relations in positive
and negative return years, comparable to Table 3 for accounting income.
Since these are univariate regressions, we can report Vuong's (1989)
likelihood ratio statistic for selection among non-nested models in which
the dependent variable is the same, but the independent variables differ. We
calculate the Vuong statistic with a common dependent variable (returns)
but competing independent variables (accounting income and dividends).

The results from the Vuong test in panel B of Table 5 are weakly consistent with Hypothesis 4. For example, for the bad news or negative returns sample, the Vuong test statistic (distributed as unit-Normal, i.e., a Z-statistic) shows that common-law accounting income explains returns significantly more than dividends, but that the opposite is true for code-law countries. We also estimate, but do not report, a linear relation model with dividends levels and changes, comparable to panel B of Table 2. These results also support Hypothesis 4.

5.1.2 Common-law tax imputation link between dividends and accounting income

Among common-law countries, there is considerable variation in the taxation of dividend distributions. We focus on 'imputation,' which penalizes corporations for reporting taxable income in excess of distributed dividends. There is an incentive to structure transactions and use accounting standards that make taxable income conform to dividend policy, which affects accounting income because it is correlated with taxable income. Australia, Canada and the UK operate imputation systems (Coopers & Lybrand, 1982–95), but not the US.[22] Provided dividends per se are uninformative, the testable implication is that accounting income in the US exhibits greater timeliness relative to dividends than it does in Australia and Canada.[23]

H$_5$: *The differential timeliness of accounting income relative to dividends is greater in the US than in common-law countries with dividend imputation (Australia, Canada, UK).*

There are mixed results for this hypothesis as seen from the 'ratio' reported in the last column of panel A of Table 5. The results for Australia and UK reported are consistent with the hypothesis (the ratios are less than that for USA), but those for Canada are not. One conjecture is that the marginal investor in Canada is a US resident and does not receive imputation credits, so that Canada effectively is in the same tax category as the US.

5.2 Accounting income and cash flows from operations

We propose that cash flows are noisier than accounting income in reflecting contemporaneous value-relevant information (Dechow, 1994) in all countries. Provided there is no new information in managers' current financing and investment decisions, accruals are expected to make accounting income incorporate economic income in a more timely basis than cash flows. This logic holds under the accrual-accounting systems of all countries.

Table 6 Contemporaneous association between cashflows and returns[a].

Statistics are from regressions using the pooled cross-section and time-series of firm/year observations for each country. Intercepts are not reported.

Panel A: OCF = $\beta_0 + \beta_1$ RD + β_2R + β_3R*RD + ε

	β_2	$t(\beta_2)$	β_3	$t(\beta_3)$	Adj. R^2(%)	N	Ratio
Australia	0.07	*2.74*	0.16	*2.11*	2.4	1,321	3.80
Canada	0.02	*1.07*	0.25	*5.28*	3.6	2,901	4.75
USA	0.04	*7.81*	0.10	*7.39*	3.1	21,225	4.78
UK	0.11	*11.40*	−0.02	*−0.87*	3.7	5,758	3.69
France	0.19	*4.78*	−0.16	*−1.39*	3.3	1,054	3.79
Germany	0.16	*4.28*	−0.04	*−0.37*	2.6	1,245	2.10
Japan	0.01	*1.17*	0.08	*7.18*	1.7	6,855	2.49
Common	0.04	*8.04*	0.12	*9.19*	3.0	25,447	4.79
UK	0.11	*11.40*	−0.02	*−0.87*	3.7	5,758	3.69
Code	0.08	*8.92*	0.00	*−0.04*	2.2	9,154	2.34

Table 6 and Fig. 5 report results for the contemporaneous association between returns and operating cash flow, for the same sample of firm/years as for income and dividends in Tables 2, 3 and 5. In all countries, the income R^2's are higher than those of operating cash flow, the ratio ranging from 2.10 (Germany) to 4.78 (US). This result would be obtained in less than 1% of cases by chance, assuming independence across the seven countries. The Vuong statistic and the ratio of explanatory powers of the income/ return and cash flow/return relations reported in panel B indicate that the greater timeliness of accounting income than operating cash flow is due largely to bad news years. These findings generalize well-known US results on timeliness of accounting income compared to cash flow (Ball and Brown, 1968; Dechow, 1994; Basu, 1997), and contrast sharply with results reported above for dividends.

The incremental timeliness of accounting income (relative to cash flows) measures the extent to which accruals under a particular country's accounting rules are oriented toward timely incorporation of economic income. We hypothesize that common-law accruals reflect a greater demand for timely accounting income, and hence predict that common-law accounting income has more incremental timeliness (relative to cash flows) than code-law accounting income.

H$_6$: *Common-law accounting income is more timely relative to operating cash flows.*

Results generally support Hypothesis 6. In panel A of Table 6, three of the top four ratios of return/income R^2 to return/cash flow R^2 are common-law countries. Accounting income in Germany and Japan incorporates the least amount of current-period economic income, relative to cash flows.

Table 6 (cont'd)

Panel B:	OCF = $\beta_0 + \beta_1 R + \varepsilon (R \geq 0)$					OCF = $\beta_0 + \beta_1 R + \varepsilon (R < 0)$				
	β_1	Adj. R^2(%)	N	Ratio	Vuong	β_1	Adj. R^2(%)	N	Ratio	Vuong
Australia	0.07	0.9	813	0.25	0.92	0.23	1.4	508	12.88	-3.38
Canada	0.02	0.0	1,688	384.00	0.42	0.27	2.8	1,213	2.82	-6.23
USA	0.04	0.5	12,721	9.34	-1.51	0.14	1.4	8,504	7.31	-12.88
UK	0.11	3.4	3,612	0.55	0.18	0.09	0.7	2,146	13.85	-6.93
France	0.19	2.9	611	0.76	-2.12	0.03	-0.2	443	-47.40	-1.67
Germany	0.16	2.2	712	2.22	-0.16	0.13	0.3	533	13.96	-2.18
Japan	0.01	0.0	3,141	10.00	-2.79	0.09	2.2	3,714	2.07	2.61
Common	0.04	0.4	15,222	8.12	-0.13	0.16	1.6	10,225	6.45	-14.62
UK	0.11	3.4	3,612	0.55	0.18	0.09	0.7	2,146	13.85	-6.93
Code	0.08	1.3	4,464	1.20	-3.10	0.08	0.5	4,690	5.49	-2.18

[a]*Sample* consists of 40,359 firm-year observations selected from the Global Vantage industrial/Commercial and Issue files over 1985–95, using the following procedure. First, for each variable (see below) we eliminate the two extreme percentiles of firm-year observations. Second, we eliminate all firm-year observations with missing values for one or more variables, to facilitate comparability with results in previous tables. Third, we eliminate all firm-year observations from countries with less than 1,000 observations, leaving seven countries represented. Australia, Canada, United States, and the United Kingdom are the common-law countries, the rest are code-law countries. However, the common law country category in the third row from the bottom excludes the UK.

R = buy-and-hold security return inclusive of dividends over the fiscal year;

RD = 1 if $R \leq 0$ and $RD = 0$ if $R > 0$;

OCF = annual operating cash flow per share, where operating cashflow is defined as earnings plus decrease in non-cash current assets plus increase in non-debt current liabilities plus depreciation;

N = the number of firm/year observations.

Ratio = in panel A, the ratio of the R^2s of the equivalent earnings (Table 2) and operating cash flow (this table) regressions, in panel B, the ratio of the R^2s of the equivalent earnings (Table 3) and operating cash flow (this table) regressions.

Vuong statistic is a likelihood ratio statistic comparing the fit of the return/operating cash flow model in this table with the return/earnings model in Table 3, both estimated separately from the good news and bad news observations in panel B.

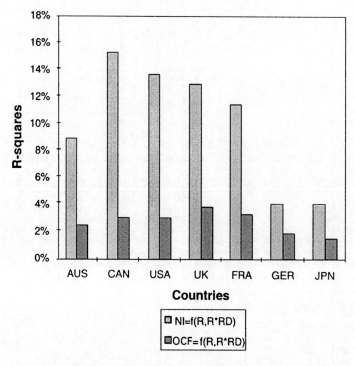

Figure 5 Earnings versus cashflows R-squares from the individual country reverse regressions of (1) NI and (2) OCF against (a) annual return and (b) annual return times negative return dummy.

Thus, the greater timeliness of common-law income is not due entirely to underlying transactions.

6. Specification tests: income and returns

The relation between accounting income and stock returns is robust with respect to a variety of specification tests, reported in Tables 7 and 8.

6.1 Variation in expected returns

When economic income is the independent variable, a possible misspecification arises from variation in expected returns (across time, countries and firms). Assume the true model for accounting income incorporates only the component of ΔV_t due to information about future cash flows a, and not due to variation in expected returns r. Assume these components are independent, both of each other and over time. Our model (2) then can be simplified as

76

$$NI_t = h(a_t, \zeta_t) \tag{6}$$

where the disturbance term ζ_t now incorporates expected return effects, in addition to lagged information about cash flows and accounting noise. Using ΔV_t as a proxy for a_t then would introduce measurement error in the independent variable, due to variation in expected returns.

Table 7 reports pooled regressions with two alternative controls for marketwide expected return effects. In column (2) the independent variable, annual return, is defined relative to the mean return for the firm's country/ year. In column (3) the dependent variable, accounting income, is scaled by the country/year long-term interest rate. In both cases, results are similar to those in column (1), which repeats the results from Table 4 for comparison. We conclude market-wide effects do not substantially influence our results.

6.2 Consolidated versus parent income and control for special items

In countries where parent companies are not required to 'equity account' their share of affiliated-company income, their accounting income omits a component that accrues to their stockholders. This could be viewed as introducing measurement error that likely is positively correlated with parent-company income, thereby biasing the regression slopes downward. A counter-argument is that we are interested in properties of accounting income *as reported* under different countries' accounting rules, including any omission of affiliate income. Nevertheless, we replicate column (1) results for the 33,441 total firm/years for which Periodic Descriptor Array No. 13 on Global Vantage specifically labels income as 'fully consolid-ated,' thus including parent companies' proportional shares of affiliates' incomes. The sample size reduction is due almost entirely to Japan, which loses most of its observations.[24] Results (unreported) are almost identical except for Japan (due to the small sample size).

The reported results in the paper are based on using accounting income before extraordinary items. Special items, which are included in calculating accounting income, have characteristics similar to extraordinary items, in that they tend to be negative and transitory (e.g., Collins *et al.*, 1997). We repeat the analysis using accounting income net of special items and obtain qualitatively similar results.

6.3 Extending the lag in accounting income

Column (4) of Table 7 reports results with the dependent variable $NI2_{yr} = NI_t + NI_{t+1}$, allowing an additional year to incorporate economic income in accounting income. As expected, the coefficients generally increase: the median two-year coefficient is 1.6 times its one-year equivalent.[25] Accounting

Table 7 Comparative asymmetry in the contemporaneous returns-earnings relation: alternative specifications[a].
Reported statistics are for the following model using the pooled cross-section and time-series of firm/year observations for all countries:

$$NI = \beta_0 + \sum_j \beta_{0j}\, CD_j + \beta_1\, RD + \sum_j \beta_{1j}\, RD\, CD_j + \beta_2 R + \sum_j \beta_{2j} R\, CD_j + \beta_3 R\, RD + \sum_j \beta_{3j} R\, RD\, CD_j$$

Results are not reported for the intercept, the negative return intercept, and their respective country dummies. The country category models use the common law countries of Australia, Canada and the US as the base category; dummies are used for (1) the UK and (2) the code law countries of France, Germany and Japan.

Model Y Control	(1) NI Coeff.	t-Stat.	(2) NI R_{it} Coeff.	t-Stat.	(3) NI/R_F Coeff.	t-Stat.	(4) NI2yr Coeff.	t-Stat.	(5) NI SIC Coeff.	t-Stat.
Panel A: country dummies model										
Earnings 'good news' sensitivity										
β_2 (Return)	0.03	9.88	0.01	3.96	0.36	9.88	−0.05	−84.24	0.04	10.25
β_{2j} (Return*Cntry Dums):										
Australia	−0.03	−3.95	−0.04	−3.17	−0.48	−4.24	−0.02	−3.02	−0.04	−4.15
Canada	−0.03	−3.80	−0.01	−1.63	−0.32	−3.54	0.06	10.03	−0.02	−3.28
UK	0.02	2.40	0.03	3.74	0.14	1.57	0.09	2.92	0.01	1.57
France	0.05	4.16	0.06	3.48	0.65	3.86	0.55	21.28	0.05	3.69
Germany	0.03	1.57	0.04	1.81	0.55	2.54	0.21	19.32	0.02	1.42
Japan	−0.02	−2.64	0.00	−0.51	−0.17	−1.69	0.07	6.82	−0.02	−3.12
F-stat for Country Return Dummies	11.35 $p < 0.01$		7.73 $p < 0.01$		10.28 $p < 0.01$		164.13 $p < 0.01$		9.75 $p < 0.01$	

Incremental 'bad news' sensitivity

β₃ (Rdum*Return)	0.29	39.21	0.29	47.25	3.66	38.11	0.43	26.13	0.29	31.04
β₃ⱼ (Rdum*Ret*Cntry Dums):										
Australia	0.07	2.64	0.01	0.37	0.19	0.50	0.12	1.85	0.08	2.89
Canada	0.11	5.28	0.05	2.92	0.45	1.70	0.12	2.43	0.11	5.25
UK	−0.14	−8.26	−0.17	−11.11	−2.05	−9.10	−0.24	−2.47	−0.14	−7.96
France	−0.22	−5.81	−0.14	−4.40	−2.87	−5.99	−0.68	−7.40	−0.21	−5.54
Germany	−0.19	−4.41	−0.24	−5.74	−2.49	−4.55	−0.31	−7.48	−0.20	−4.73
Japan	−0.29	−15.74	−0.29	−16.80	−3.43	−14.90	−0.42	−10.70	−0.28	−15.16
F-stat: Country Negative Ret Dums	67.44 p < 0.01		72.74 p < 0.01		54.55 p < 0.01		37.81 p < 0.01		63.43 p < 0.01	

Regression

N	40,359		40,359		39,240		33,082		40,359	
Adj. R²	15.4%		16.8%		13.8%		22.5%		16.2%	
F	272.98		303.32		234.19		410.56		117.16	

Panel B: country category dummies model

Earnings 'good news' sensitivity

β₂ (Return)	0.02	8.36	0.01	2.82	0.26	8.22	−0.05	−83.70	0.03	8.99
β₂ⱼ (Return*Cntry Dums):										
UK	0.02	3.52	0.04	4.35	0.23	2.75	0.20	19.12	0.02	2.58
Code	0.01	2.37	0.02	2.87	0.24	2.99	0.15	15.26	0.01	1.53
F-stat for Cntry Cat Return Dums	7.94 p < 0.01		12.24 p < 0.01		7.20 p < 0.01		297.97 p < 0.01		3.98 p < 0.01	

Table 7 (cont'd)
Incremental 'bad news' sensitivity[a]

Model Y Control	(1) NI Coeff.	t-Stat.	(2) NI R_{it} Coeff.	t-Stat.	(3) NI/R_F Coeff.	t-Stat.	(4) NI2yr Coeff.	t-Stat.	(5) NI SIC Coeff.	t-Stat.
β_3 (RDum*Return)	0.31	46.23	0.30	53.64	3.76	43.28	0.46	30.27	0.31	36.68
β_{3j} (RDum*Ret* Cntry Cat Dums):										
UK	−0.16	−9.50	−0.17	−11.72	−2.14	−9.69	−0.34	−8.14	−0.16	−9.25
Code	−0.30	−19.00	−0.28	−18.82	−3.47	−17.41	−0.48	−13.65	−0.29	−18.31
F-stat: Cntry Cat Negative Ret Dums	200.92 $p < 0.01$		218.66 $p < 0.01$		174.82 $p < 0.01$		111.56 $p < 0.01$		187.17 $p < 0.01$	
Regression										
N	40,359		40,359		39,240		33,082		40,359	
Adj. R^2	14.9%		16.2%		13.5%		21.3%		15.7%	
F	642.07		711.90		557.84		938.83		148.07	

[a]Sample consists of 40,359 firm-year observations selected from the Global Vantage industrial/Commercial and Issue files over 1985–95, using the following procedure. First, for each variable (see below) we eliminate the two extreme percentiles of firm-year observations. Second, we eliminate all firm-year observations with missing values for one or more variables, to facilitate comparability with results in previous tables. Third, we eliminate all firm-year observations from countries with less than 1,000 observations, leaving seven countries represented. Australia, Canada, United States, and the United Kingdom are the common-law countries, the rest are code-law countries. The sample sizes for model (3) that uses NI/R_F as the dependent variable and model (4) that uses only the two-year NI values are 39,240 and 33,082 respectively.

R = buy-and-hold security return inclusive of dividends over the fiscal year;

NI = annual earnings per share before extraordinary items deflated by beginning of period price;

NI/R_F = earnings deflated by the long-term interest rate;

$NI2yr$ = the sum of net income over the two years t and $t + 1$;

RD = the proxy for bad news = 1 if $R < 0$ and = 0 otherwise;

CD_j = country identifier = 1 for firm/years in country j and = 0 otherwise. USA is the 'base country' with $CD_j = 0$ $\forall j$.

In model (2) the regression is controlled for mean annual country return by scaling NI and by redefining RD; in model (5) the regression is controlled for the 10 most prevalent 2-digit SIC code by creating the appropriate dummy variables based on these SIC codes.

Interest rates: R_F is measured as the longest term bond yield available in the IMF's International Financial Statistics for the calendar year most coincident with the firm's fiscal year [−11, 0]. Rates for the individual countries are for: treasury bonds 2 years (Australia); govt. bond yield > 10 yr (Canada); govt. bond yield (Germany); govt. bond yield, moyens (France); long term govt. bond yield (UK); govt. bond yield (Japan); govt. bond yield 10 yr (USA).

income thus incorporates economic income over time (it is 'smoothed,' and has 'momentum' or 'persistence').

6.4 Control for industry composition

Another concern is correlated omitted variables. For example, if the proportion of growth options relative to assets in place varies across countries, then common application of the *revenue realization rule* will cause accounting income to vary internationally in timeliness, due to 'real' rather than 'accounting' effects. This concern is reduced by our result that international differences in timeliness are due in part to accounting accruals and not entirely to differences in timeliness of cash flows. A related concern is that our sample contains only listed corporations. Public corporations are less prevalent under code-law systems probably because the latter do not facilitate public disclosure and public capital markets (see La Porta *et al.*, 1997) to the same extent as common-law systems. For example, UK has approximately four times as many listed corporations as Germany. To alleviate concern that our results are due to different sample composition across countries, column (5) reports results after controlling for industry effects, in the form of interactive dummy variables for the ten most prevalent 2-digit SIC codes. Little change is apparent. The regression adjusted R^2 rises slightly and the F-statistic falls. The F-statistics for the countries' dummy slopes fall slightly. All remain significant at the 0.01 level. There is little change in the coefficients for both individual countries and country groups.

6.5 Subperiod results

Splitting the sample into two subperiods, 1985–90 and 1991–95, reveals three interesting results, reported in Table 8. First, the incremental coefficients on negative economic income increase in the second subperiod for six of the seven individual-country regressions (4), the exception being Japan. Several countries exhibit statistically significant increases, including Australia (0.48 versus 0.26), UK (0.19 versus 0.09), France (0.22 versus 0.04) and Germany (0.19 versus 0.05). The coefficient on negative economic income for US increases, but not significantly (0.33 versus 0.28). These results suggest Basu (1997) might have erred in attributing increased asymmetry over time in US accounting income to changes in US litigation rules, since similar increases have occurred in France and Germany. An intriguing possibility is that timely incorporation of economic losses has become a more important corporate governance mechanism over time worldwide (if not in Japan), and that pressure to adopt it has come from increased international product market competition (if not from changes in the policies of standard-setters around the world). Under this explanation, timely incorporation of economic losses in accounting income is an efficient

Table 8 Contemporaneous association between earnings, dividends, cash flows and returns sub-period analysis[a].

Analysis: Statistics are from regressions using the pooled cross-section and time-series of firm/year observations for each country. Intercepts are not reported.

Panel A: $NI = \beta_0 + \beta_1 RD + \beta_2 R + \beta_3 R*RD + \varepsilon$

	1985–90						1991–95					
	β_2	$t(\beta_2)$	β_3	$t(\beta_3)$	Adj. R^2(%)	N	β_2	$t(\beta_2)$	β_3	$t(\beta_3)$	Adj. R^2(%)	N
Australia	0.02	1.04	0.26	5.31	13.0	500	−0.02	−0.99	0.48	7.55	9.4	1,821
Canada	0.00	−0.23	0.38	12.94	19.8	1,594	0.01	1.30	0.44	11.63	15.8	1,307
USA	0.03	6.14	0.28	26.79	17.3	11,978	0.03	6.54	0.33	22.14	12.9	9,247
UK	0.04	7.49	0.09	6.92	13.7	2,682	0.06	9.02	0.19	11.64	17.4	3,076
France	0.09	5.96	0.04	1.09	19.1	466	0.06	3.15	0.22	4.24	10.5	588
Germany	0.05	3.86	0.04	0.97	6.1	488	0.04	1.95	0.19	4.08	5.3	757
Japan	0.01	5.21	0.02	4.96	7.0	3,460	0.00	0.16	0.01	1.56	1.0	3,395
Common	0.02	5.64	0.29	30.12	17.3	14,071	0.02	5.32	0.36	26.22	12.7	11,374
UK	0.04	7.49	0.09	6.92	13.7	2,682	0.06	9.02	0.19	11.64	17.4	3,076
Code	0.03	10.97	0.00	0.42	5.3	4,413	0.05	8.05	0.01	1.38	4.4	4,739

Panel B: $DIV = \beta_0 + \beta_1 RD + \beta_2 R + \beta_3 R*RD + \varepsilon$

	1985–90						1991–95					
	β_2	$t(\beta_2)$	β_3	$t(\beta_3)$	Adj. R^2(%)	N	β_2	$t(\beta_2)$	β_3	$t(\beta_3)$	Adj. R^2(%)	N
Australia	0.00	−0.36	0.06	5.09	14.4	500	−0.01	−1.89	0.07	7.30	10.3	821
Canada	−0.01	−5.37	0.04	8.12	7.4	1,594	−0.01	−6.60	0.05	7.69	7.0	1,307
USA	−0.02	−18.02	0.05	25.51	9.8	11,978	−0.01	−19.45	0.05	23.09	8.9	9,247
UK	0.00	2.40	0.03	7.80	8.1	2,682	0.01	8.64	0.02	5.99	11.3	3,076
France	0.01	4.03	0.02	2.02	13.7	466	0.01	1.42	0.04	4.24	6.7	588
Germany	0.02	5.40	0.01	1.00	10.7	488	0.01	3.69	0.01	1.34	8.2	757
Japan	0.00	6.61	0.00	5.16	9.2	3,460	0.00	−0.61	0.01	7.81	7.2	3,395
Common	−0.01	−17.25	0.05	26.29	9.2	14,071	−0.01	−18.40	0.05	24.33	8.0	11,374
UK	0.00	2.40	0.03	7.80	8.1	2,682	0.01	8.64	0.02	5.99	11.3	3,076
Code	0.01	9.31	0.00	−0.51	4.2	4,413	0.01	9.99	0.00	1.88	9.7	4,739

Panel C: $OCF = \beta_0 + \beta_1 RD + \beta_2 R + \beta_3 R*RD + \epsilon$

Australia	0.01	*0.21*	0.14	*1.31*	1.0	500	0.09	*3.02*	0.23	*2.07*	3.3	821
Canada	-0.02	*-0.73*	0.29	*4.62*	3.4	1,594	0.04	*2.07*	0.22	*3.03*	3.9	1,307
USA	0.03	*3.82*	0.09	*5.13*	2.5	11,978	0.05	*7.15*	0.13	*5.99*	3.8	9,247
UK	0.11	*7.24*	-0.02	*-0.55*	3.1	2,682	0.12	*9.05*	-0.03	*-0.78*	4.5	3,076
France	0.20	*3.42*	-0.15	*-0.96*	2.6	466	0.23	*3.95*	-0.17	*-1.00*	4.3	588
Germany	0.12	*2.40*	0.12	*0.87*	2.4	488	0.25	*4.08*	-0.19	*-1.40*	3.0	757
Japan	0.03	*4.99*	0.03	*1.54*	1.9	3,460	-0.01	*-0.75*	0.12	*6.72*	3.8	3,395
Common	0.02	*2.87*	0.12	*6.88*	2.5	14,071	0.05	*8.13*	0.15	*6.98*	3.7	11,374
UK	0.11	*7.24*	-0.02	*-0.55*	3.1	2,682	0.12	*9.05*	-0.03	*-0.78*	4.5	3,076
Code	0.08	*7.30*	-0.07	*-2.34*	1.6	4,413	0.21	*11.49*	-0.08	*-2.39*	6.3	4,739

[a]*Sample* consists of 40,359 firm-year observations selected from the Global Vantage industrial/Commercial and Issue files over 1985–95, using the following procedure. First, for each variable (see below) we eliminate the two extreme percentiles of firm-year observations. Second, we eliminate all firm-year observations with missing values for one or more variables, to facilitate comparability with results in previous tables. Third, we eliminate all firm-year observations from countries with less than 1,000 observations, leaving seven countries represented. Australia, Canada, United States, and the United Kingdom are the common-law countries, the rest are code-law countries. However, the common law country category in the third row from the bottom in each panel excludes the UK.

R = buy-and-hold security return inclusive of dividends over the fiscal year;

$RD = 1$ if $R \leq 0$ and $RD = 0$ if $R > 0$;

NI = annual earnings per share before extraordinary items deflated by beginning of period price;

DIV = annual dividends per share deflated by beginning of period price;

OCF = annual operating cash flow per share deflated by beginning of period price, where operating cashflow is defined as earnings plus decrease in non-cash current assets plus increase in non-debt current liabilities plus depreciation;

N = the number of firm/year observations.

governance mechanism that reduces managers' incentives to continue with loss-making investments and strategies, thereby reducing agency-related negative NPVs. We believe this phenomenon is worthy of further study.

Second, despite increased sensitivity to economic losses, the R^2's in six of seven country regressions (4) decreased between subperiods, generalizing the US result (Ramesh and Thiagarajan, 1995; Lev, 1997). Third, the results for cash flow from operations, reported in panel C, contrast unexpectedly with those for accounting income. Between subperiods, the point estimates of the slopes on positive returns *increased* for six of seven countries, the incremental slopes on negative returns show no systematic change, and the R^2's in all of the individual-country cash flow regressions *increase*. We have no explanation for these apparently systematic cash flow changes.

7. Conclusions, implications, and limitations

The worldwide trend toward 'internationalization' of markets, especially capital markets, in which accounting information is used has rekindled academic and professional interest in different national accounting models. The properties of accounting information prepared under common-law accounting standards are of particular contemporary interest because the International Accounting Standards Committee (IASC) recently completed a set of 'international' accounting standards widely viewed as reflecting a largely common-law approach of 'transparent,' timely disclosure.

We show that common-law accounting income does indeed exhibit significantly greater timeliness than code-law accounting income, but that this is due entirely to greater sensitivity to economic losses (income conservatism). This result has important implications for corporate governance. We conjecture that early incorporation of economic losses, as distinct from gradual incorporation over time, increases managers' incentives to attend to the sources of losses more quickly. It brings more and quicker pressure from security analysts, makes leverage and dividend restrictions binding more quickly, and affects current managers' and employees' bonuses. It also makes excessively optimistic statements by managers less credible. Conservative accounting thus facilitates monitoring of managers and is an important feature of common-law corporate governance. In contrast with Roe (1994), we conclude that enhanced common-law disclosure standards reduce the agency costs of monitoring managers, thus countering the advantages of closer shareholder-manager contact in code-law countries.

Our results suggest an explanation for the emergence of a largely common-law model in international transacting, and in particular for the IASC adoption of a more 'transparent' common-law approach to disclosure. The cost of cross-border transacting by parties who are geographically, culturally and linguistically separated from the firm's management presumably is greater in a system that assumes they are informed insiders than in one with more timely public disclosure. Timely disclosure of economic losses is particularly important to cross-border lenders. Whether this model will prevail in international transacting depends on whether high disclosure-quality firms (i.e., firms known a priori as likely to recognize economic losses in a timely fashion) can signal their quality effectively to users, or equivalently on whether low-quality firms can be excluded from false signaling. In the absence of common-law penalties to false signaling, it is difficult to see how high-quality firms in code-law countries will be able to reduce contracting costs through improved financial reporting, other than by listing in a common-law jurisdiction and exposing themselves to common-law penalties for low-quality disclosure.

Greater common-law income conservatism should be no surprise, considering the use of accounting income in common-law arm's-length debt and equity markets, and especially considering common-law litigation. Nevertheless, German accounting in particular is widely presumed to be more conservative, because German managers have unusual discretion to reduce reported income during good years. However, they also have unusual discretion to delay recognition of economic losses, and thus to increase reported income in bad years. This was a common UK practice at the beginning of the twentieth century (Yamey, 1962), but effectively was extinguished in common-law countries by the Royal Mail case.[26] Similar observations can be made about accounting in Japan.

Our research design is subject to several limitations. The most obvious concern is the validity of stock returns as a proxy for economic income, particularly in code-law countries, which have endogenously lower liquidity and public disclosure standards. 'Noise' in annual stock returns as a measure of market-valued income could be a correlated omitted variable. We counter with three observations. First, poor public disclosure does not necessarily impede the flow of information into stock prices, since the information flow can occur instead via the trading of informed insiders. In the absence of effectively enforced insider-trading laws, which in many ways are fundamentally incompatible with code-law governance, corporate insiders' incentives are to trade on information and thereby incorporate it into prices. This, Ramseyer (1993) conjectures, explains the practice of Japanese banks trading in their clients' stock. To some degree, equating poor public disclosure with uninformed stock prices involves projecting common-law precepts onto code-law institutions, which are more likely to solve information asymmetry by private rather than public communication. Second, our results seem inconsistent with the hypothesis that stock returns reflect poor information flows in code law countries, which would imply less anticipation of accounting income, a stronger income 'surprise' effect, and a stronger return-income association. We observe the opposite. Third, we study stock returns over intervals of one and two years, not over short 'event windows,' which is long enough for international differences in liquidity, market microstructure and disclosure timing effects to have minimal impact.

Correlated omitted variables are another obvious concern. For example, if the proportion of growth options relative to assets in place varies across countries, then common application of the revenue realization rule will cause income to vary internationally in timeliness, due to 'real' rather than 'accounting' effects. Similarly, our results hold only for listed corporations. The number of listed code-law corporations is endogenously small compared with common-law countries, in part because code-law systems are not designed for the demands of public disclosure, so private corporations are comparatively more efficient and consequently more prevalent. Thus, our sample is less representative of code-law accounting in general. This concern is addressed to a degree in the Table 7 control for SIC codes. Another concern is whether the sample period is representative. Japan, for example, went through boom and bust during 1985–95. Specification tests in Table 7 address this concern, where the results change little when annual firm return is defined relative to the mean return for that country/year, and when income is scaled by the country/year interest rate.

Another concern is our characterization of the relevant institutional features of the seven countries in our primary sample. In particular, the code/common law categorization is a proxy for an underlying economic construct, the extent to which accounting is determined by market supply and demand relative to political forces. The categories overlap, as is obvious from the roles of the Companies Acts in the UK and the SEC in the US. To some degree, this concern is alleviated by the consistent evidence we report from our primary sample. In addition, we report consistent evidence from a secondary sample of eighteen countries, suggesting that our results are generalizable.

A final concern is that institutional determinants of financial reporting vary over time. For example, shareholder lawsuits are reported as rising in Japan (*Wall Street Journal*, January 7, 2000, p. A13), which could signal a change in governance or incentives of financial statement preparers. While we have mechanically divided the 1985–95 period into approximately equal sub-periods and have thereby observed a systematic increase in conservatism, a finer partitioning based on changes in institutional determinants of accounting might obtain clearer results.

The research design also has its strengths. It studies the incorporation of economic income into accounting income over time, under different international institutions, using a model of accounting income determination that is based on fundamental properties of accounting. We believe the results to be of interest to accountants, analysts, standard-setters, regulators and students of corporate governance.

Acknowledgements

We gratefully acknowledge the helpful comments of David Alexander, Eli Bartov, Sudipta Basu, Gary Biddle, Sir Bryan Carsberg, Dan Collins, Peter Easton, Bob Holthausen (the editor), Scott Keating, Christian Leuz, Gerhard Mueller, Christopher Nobes, the late Dieter Ordelheide, Peter Pope, Abbie Smith, Peter Taylor, Ross Watts, Greg Waymire, Steve Zeff, Jerry Zimmerman, the referee, and seminar participants at: Carnegie Mellon University, University of California at Berkeley, University of California at Los Angeles, CUNY Baruch College, EIASM Workshop in European Accounting in Krakow, 1999 Financial Accounting and Auditing Conference of the Institute of Chartered Accountants in England & Wales, Universität Frankfurt am Main, Hong Kong University of Science and Technology 1998 Summer Symposium, IAAER/CIERA 1998 Conference, Inquire Europe Autumn 1998 Seminar, University of Iowa, Harvard Business School, KPMG-AAA International 1999 Accounting Conference, London Business School, London School of Economics, Massachusetts Institute of Technology, Melbourne Business School, New York University, Ohio State University, University of New South Wales, University of Technology in Sydney, and Washington University in St Louis. The paper has received a Vernon K. Zimmerman Award and an Inquire Europe Prize. Ball and Kothari received financial assistance from the John M. Olin Foundation and the Bradley Policy Research Center, and Kothari acknowledges financial assistance from the New Economy Value Research Lab at the MIT Sloan School of Management.

Notes

1 Asset impairment standards such as SFAS 121 in the US are an important example of accounting standards linking accounting and economic incomes. Information asymmetry implies that implementation of impairment standards depends on the incentive of financial statement preparers (managers and auditors) to disclose information about economic losses, which varies internationally (compare US and Japan).

2 We use clean surplus accounting as a concept to motivate the research design. We assume the degree of violation of clean surplus accounting is not systematically related to the international institutional factors we investigate. Research on the return-earnings relation typically exacerbates clean-surplus violation by excluding extraordinary items.

3 This 1995 accounting standard formalized what already had become common practice. Elliott and Hanna (1996) report an increase in negative 'one time' charges against income for US firms around 1970, rising to 20% of firms annually by the early 1990s. Collins et al. (1997) report a similar increase, and that by the early 1980s 25–30% of US firms reported negative incomes *before* one-time charges. These data are consistent with our view that formalized common-law accounting standards primarily arise endogenously from common practice in the market for accounting.

4 Asset revaluations occur for acquisitions accounted under the purchase method, but do not flow through income.

5 German companies do not deduct minority interest from consolidated net income, but Global Vantage alters their numbers to comply with US practice. We therefore define German Y as IC data 32+ data 27, which reconciles to the numbers actually reported. The adjustment has only a trivial effect on the results.

6 In correspondence, Christian Leuz and the late Dieter Ordelheide note that some French and German firms recently have issued consolidated financial statements prepared under International Accounting Standards. This practice largely post-dates our sample. If Global Vantage classifies these observations as 'German,' the errors create a potential bias against our hypotheses.

7 The rationale is to eliminate observations potentially with errors or with extreme values due to scaling. The disadvantage is that potentially informative observations are deleted and there is the danger of an incorrect inference.

8 American Accounting Association (1977) classifies accounting systems using eight variables: political system (traditional oligarchy, totalitarian oligarchy, modernizing oligarchy, tutelary democracy, political democracy), economic system, stage of political development, financial reporting objectives, source of accounting standards, education and licensing of accountants, mechanism to enforce standards, and accounting client (public or private). Nobes (1992) and Nobes and Parker (1995, Chapter 4) survey classification schemes. How these variables affect important properties of accounting information internationally is largely untested. International accounting texts typically list variables to justify classifications, without correlating them with the national accounting standards listed in subsequent chapters, let alone with properties of the financial statements actually prepared under those standards.

9 David and Brierley (1985) provide a survey.

10 Romans implanted code-law (also referred to as civil law, La Porta *et al.*, 1997) in many continental European countries. The most detailed accounting code is the French *Plan comptable général*, adapted under occupation from Germany's 1937 standardization of accounting for war planning (Standish, 1997, p. 60). Japan has a code-law system, derived from the German legal and French accounting systems during the Meiji Era (1868–1910). Scandinavian law is another code-law category with origins in Roman law (David and Brierley, 1985 and La Porta *et al.*, 1997).

11 See Nobes and Parker (1995, Chapter 12), Roe (1994) and Miwa (1996).

12 La Porta *et al.* (1997) predict that, in addition to differences in legal systems, differences in the extent of law enforcement affects the development of capital markets across countries. It is possible that variation in law enforcement has predictive power with respect to the demand and supply of accounting information that we ignore.

13 Daimler-Benz reported 1993 German-rule income of DM615 million, but subsequent US GAAP disclosure revealed that a loss of DM1839 million had been hidden by various accounting adjustments (Ball, 1998).

14 The code-law ratio range is 0.06–0.29; common-law is 0.33–0.36 (excluding 0.23 for UK, discussed below).

15 We describe asymmetric timeliness in incorporating economic losses as 'income conservatism.' The concept is related to, but different from, balance sheet conservatism (reporting low book value of equity by under-stating assets and/or over-stating liabilities). Income conservatism implies balance sheet conservatism, but not vice versa: while code-law companies typically report conservative book values, they also are more likely to boost income in bad years. This *reduces* the

asymmetric timeliness of accounting income and is difficult to describe as 'conservative' in its effect *on income*. Asymmetric timeliness is different from, but related to, Gray's (1980) concept of conservatism.

16 For the separate positive and negative return regressions, we examined plots of the residuals against returns, and found no evidence of non-linearity (which was a concern for the negative-return sample in particular).

17 Unreported incremental negative return slopes in the additional 18-country sample are inconsistent with our hypothesis. While the R^2's are consistent with greater conservatism in common-law countries and the slopes are consistent with universal conservatism, the slopes do not suggest greater conservatism in common-law countries. However, due to small sample sizes many of the positive code-law country incremental slopes are not significant.

18 Nobes and Parker (1995, pp. 298–300).

19 The English rule is applied in UK, Australia, and most of Western Europe (Posner, 1986, p. 537), though not uniformly. It affects expected litigation costs via the frequency of litigation and the legal costs of the defendant, but not the size of awards, with unclear net effect. Katz (1987) argues: 'While it is conceivable that the English rule would lower the total number of cases brought to trial, it would likely increase the average expenditure per case. . . . Even if the number of cases were to fall by as much as 30 percent, total expenditure could rise by more than 50 percent under the English rule.' Katz' analysis does not take account of one institutional detail, however: English courts award only *reasonable* costs of successful defendants, thus reducing the incentive to spend. See also Shavell (1982), Posner (1986, pp. 534–540), Hughes and Snyder (1995), Posner (1996) and Miceli (1997).

20 In response to a prior draft of this paper, Pope and Walker (1999) claim that the UK income before extraordinary items appears less conservative than US because UK firms enjoy greater discretion in reporting economic losses as extraordinary items. They use data from *Datastream* whereas we use the Compustat Global Vantage database. Reconciliation of the differences between the two studies is beyond the scope of our research.

21 Except as indicated, taxation facts are from annual editions of Coopers & Lybrand *International Tax Summaries*.

22 The Australian imputation system is described in Hamson and Ziegler (1990). The Canadian system is dividend credits, not full imputation; and the marginal Canadian investor could pay US tax and thus not receive credits.

23 We expect this to be reinforced in US by stock repurchases to distribute cash to investors. Repurchases contain information about future income (Dann *et al.*, 1991), likely reducing information in dividends.

24 Excluding these observations is not clearly necessary because Japanese rules require equity accounting in the parent's books (Nobes and Parker, 1995, Chapter 13). Few observations are excluded for Germany where public companies have issued consolidated income since the European Union's Seventh Directive.

25 The exception is the positive-return slopes for the US and Australia. The sample size decreases, due mainly to losing one year. Results are for overlapping samples.

26 *Rex v. Lord Kylsant* 1932 1 KB 442. This case-law was codified in the 1948 UK Companies Act, which required companies to distinguish reserves from provisions, 'making the creation of secret reserves more difficult.' (Nobes and Parker, 1995, p. 103). The case can lay claim to be the legal genesis of the Rule 10b-5 in the US. US German practice is exemplified by the notorious Daimler-Benz case (Ball, 1998).

References

Alchian, A., 1984. Specificity, specialization, and coalitions. Journal of Institutional and Theoretical Economics 140, 34–49.

Alchian, A., Demsetz, H., 1972. Production, information costs and economic organization. American Economic Review 62, 777–795.

Alford, A., Jones, J., Leftwich, R., Zmijewski, M., 1993. The relative informativeness of accounting disclosures in different countries. Journal of Accounting Research 31 (Suppl.), 183–223.

American Accounting Association, 1977. Report of the Committee on International Accounting. Supplement to Accounting Review 52.

Amir, E., Harris, T., Venuti, E., 1993. A comparison of the value-relevance of U.S. versus non-U.S. GAAP accounting measures using form 20-F reconciliations. Journal of Accounting Research 31 (Suppl.), 230–264.

Ball, R., 1998. Daimler-Benz AG: evolution of corporate governance from a code-law 'stakeholder' to a common-law 'shareholder value' system. Unpublished manuscript, University of Rochester.

Ball, R., Brown, P., 1968. An empirical evaluation of accounting income numbers. Journal of Accounting Research 6, 159–178.

Bandyopadhyay, S., Hanna, D., Richardson, G., 1994. Capital market effects of U.S.-Canada GAAP differences. Journal of Accounting Research 32, 262–277.

Barth, M., Clinch, G., 1996. International accounting differences and their relation to share prices: evidence from U.K., Australian, and Canadian firms. Contemporary Accounting Research 13, 135–170.

Basu, S., 1997. The conservatism principle and the asymmetric timeliness of earnings. Journal of Accounting and Economics 24, 3–37.

Baums, T., Buxbaum, R., Hopt, K. (Eds.), 1994. Institutional Investors and Corporate Governance Walter de Gruyter, Berlin.

Beaver, W., Lambert, R., Morse, D., 1980. The information content of security prices. Journal of Accounting and Economics 2, 3–28.

Choi, F., Mueller, G., 1992. International Accounting. Prentice-Hall, Englewood Cliffs, NJ.

Coopers & Lybrand, 1982–95. International Tax Summaries, Annual Editions. Wiley, New York.

Collins, D., Maydew, E., Weiss, I., 1997. Changes in the value-relevance of earnings and book values over the past forty years. Journal of Accounting and Economics 24, 39–67.

Cramer, J., 1987. Mean and variance of R^2 in small and moderate samples. Journal of Econometrics 35, 253–166.

Dann, L., Masulis, R., Mayers, D., 1991. Repurchase tender offers and earnings information. Journal of Accounting and Economics 14, 217–251.

David, R., Brierley, J., 1985. Major Legal Systems in the World Today. Stevens & Sons, London.

Dechow, P., 1994. Accounting earnings and cash flows as measures of firm performance: the role of accounting accruals. Journal of Accounting and Economics 18, 3–42.

Dechow, P., Kothari, S., Watts, R., 1998. The relation between earnings and cash flows. Journal of Accounting and Economics 25, 133–168.

Easton, P., Harris, T., Ohlson, J., 1992. Aggregate accounting earnings can explain most of security returns. Journal of Accounting and Economics 15, 119–142.

Elliott, J., Hanna, J., 1996. Repeated write-offs and the information content of earnings. Journal of Accounting Research 34, 135–155.

Fama, E., MacBeth, J., 1973. Risk, return, and equilibrium: empirical tests. Journal of Political Economy 81, 607–636.

Financial Accounting Standards Board (FASB), 1985. Statement of financial accounting concepts no. 6. FASB, Stamford, Connecticut.

Gray, S., 1980. International accounting differences from a security analysis perspective. Journal of Accounting Research 18, 64–76.

Hamson, D., Ziegler, P., 1990. The impact of dividend imputation on firms' financial decisions. Accounting and Finance 30, 29–53.

Harris, T., Lang, M., Möller, H., 1994. The value relevance of German accounting measures: an empirical analysis. Journal of Accounting Research 32, 187–209.

Healy, P., 1985. The effect of bonus schemes on accounting decisions. Journal of Accounting and Economics 7, 85–107.

Hicks, J. R., 1946. Value and Capital 2nd edition. Clarendon Press, Oxford.

Hughes, J., Snyder, E., 1995. Litigation and settlement under the English and American rules: theory and evidence. Journal of Law and Economics 38, 225–250.

Jacobsen, R., Aaker, D., 1993. Myopic management behavior with efficient, but imperfect, financial markets. Journal of Accounting and Economics 16, 383–405.

Joos, P., Lang, M., 1994. The effects of accounting diversity: evidence from the European Union. Journal of Accounting Research 32 (Suppl.), 141–168.

Katz, A., 1987. Measuring the demand for litigation. Journal of Law, Economics, & Organization 3, 143–176.

Köndgen, J., 1994. Duties of banks in voting their clients' stock. In: Baums, Buxbaum, Hopt (Eds.), (Chapter 18). Institutional Investors and Corporate Governance Walter de Gruyter, Berlin.

Kothari, S., Lys, T., Smith, C., Watts, R., 1988. Auditor liability and information disclosure. Journal of Accounting, Auditing and Finance 3, 307–339.

Kothari, S., Sloan, R., 1992. Information in earnings about future earnings: implications for earnings response coefficients. Journal of Accounting and Economics 15, 143–171.

La Porta, L., Lopez-de-Silanes, F., Shleifer, A., Vishny, R., 1997. Legal determinants of external finance. Journal of Finance 52, 1131–1150.

Lintner, J., 1956. Distribution of incomes of corporations among dividends, retained earnings, and taxes. American Economic Review 46, 97–113.

Miceli, T., 1997. Economics of the Law. Oxford University Press, Oxford.

Miwa, Y., 1996. Firms and Industrial Organization in Japan. New York University Press, New York.

Mueller, G., Gernon, H., Meek, G., 1997. Accounting: An International Perspective. Richard D. Irwin, Chicago, IL.

Nobes, C., 1992. International Classification of Financial Reporting. Routledge, London.

Nobes, C., Parker, R., 1995. Comparative International Accounting 4th Edition. Prentice-Hall, Englewood Cliffs, NJ.

Ohlson, J., 1988. Accounting earnings, book value and dividends: the theory of the clean surplus equation. Unpublished manuscript, Columbia University.

Peltzman, S., 1976. Toward a more general theory of regulation. Journal of Law and Economics 19, 211–240.

Pope, P., Walker, M., 1999. International differences in the timeliness, conservatism, and classification of earnings. Journal of Accounting Research 37 (Suppl.), 53–87.

Posner, R. A., 1986. Economic Analysis of Law, 3rd Edition. Little, Brown, Boston, MA.

Posner, R. A., 1996. Law and Legal Theory in the UK and USA. Clarendon Press, Oxford.

Radebaugh, L., Gray, S., 1997. International Accounting and Multinational Enterprises, 4th Edition. Wiley, New York.

Ramesh, K., Thiagarajan, R., 1995. Inter-temporal decline in earnings response coefficients. Unpublished manuscript, Northwestern University.

Ramseyer, J., 1993. Columbian cartel launches bid for Japanese firms. Yale Law Journal 102, 2005–2020.

Roe, M., 1994. Some differences in corporate governance in Germany, Japan and America. In: Baums, Buxbaum, Hopt (Eds.), (Chapter 2). Institutional Investors and Corporate Governance Walter de Gruyter, Berlin.

Shavell, S., 1982. Suit, settlement and trial: a theoretical analysis under alternative methods for the allocation of legal costs. Journal of Legal Studies 11, 55–81.

Standish, P., 1997. The French Plan Comptable. Expert Comptable Média, Paris.

Vuong, Q., 1989. Likelihood ratio tests for model selection and non-nested hypotheses. Econometrica 57, 307–333.

Watts, R., Zimmerman, J., 1986. Positive Accounting Theory. Prentice-Hall, Englewood Cliffs, NJ.

Yamey, B., 1962. Some topics in the history of financial accounting in England, 1500–1900. In: Baxter, W. T., Davidson, S. (Eds.), Studies in Accounting Theory. Sweet & Maxwell, London.

4

DISCLOSURE PRACTICES, ENFORCEMENT OF ACCOUNTING STANDARDS, AND ANALYSTS' FORECAST ACCURACY

An international study

Ole-Kristian Hope

Source: *Journal of Accounting Research* 41(2) (2003): 235–72.

Abstract

Using a sample from 22 countries, I investigate the relations between the accuracy of analysts' earnings forecasts and the level of annual report disclosure, and between forecast accuracy and the degree of enforcement of accounting standards. I document that firm-level disclosures are positively related to forecast accuracy, suggesting that such disclosures provide useful information to analysts. I construct a comprehensive measure of enforcement and find that strong enforcement is associated with higher forecast accuracy. This finding is consistent with the hypothesis that enforcement encourages managers to follow prescribed accounting rules, which, in turn, reduces analysts' uncertainty about future earnings. I also find evidence consistent with disclosures being more important when analyst following is low and with enforcement being more important when more choice among accounting methods is allowed.

1. Introduction

Although differences in accounting rules across countries have diminished significantly in recent years, owing to the harmonization efforts of the International Accounting Standards Committee/Board (IASC/IASB) and other organizations, there has not been a corresponding trend in the enforcement of accounting standards internationally (e.g., FEE [1999]). This is of concern to standard setters, regulators, and investors (e.g., SEC [2000]). Firms also vary widely in their disclosure practices. In this article, I examine the associations between the accuracy of financial analysts' earnings forecasts and variations in firms' disclosures and enforcement of accounting standards.

I focus on professional financial analysts as they are among the most important users of financial reports, and researchers have long been interested in learning about their use of accounting information (Schipper [1991]). Recently, accounting researchers show increased interest in the work of financial analysts outside the United States. Their research documents that both in the United States and elsewhere investors incorporate analysts' earnings forecasts in their firm valuations and respond to revisions in those forecasts, (e.g., Capstaff, Paudyal, and Rees [2000], Bercel [1994]).

This article contributes to the literature on determinants of analysts' earnings forecast accuracy and the international accounting literature. Few, if any, studies have investigated the potentially important role of enforcement of accounting standards internationally. Considerable variation persists in enforcement worldwide, even as cross-country differences in accounting measurement have diminished. In contrast to previous research, I examine effects of variations in *firm*-level disclosures in a cross-country setting. Given managers' discretion over how much information to disclose in annual reports, I also explore the possibility that disclosure levels and forecast accuracy are jointly determined.

Controlling for firm- and country-level factors, I document that the accuracy of analysts' earnings forecasts is positively associated with firm-level annual report disclosure quantity both in the United States and elsewhere. This finding is consistent with analysts' finding such information useful for forecasting. My comprehensive proxy for enforcement is significantly and positively related to forecast accuracy. This result suggests that strong enforcement encourages managers to follow the accounting standards that are in place, hence reducing analysts' uncertainty about managers' accounting choices. These results are subjected to a number of robustness tests, including a test of potential simultaneity between firms' disclosure choices and forecast accuracy.

I further hypothesize that disclosures are less positively correlated with forecast accuracy when a firm's analyst following is high (where analyst following is used as a proxy for the information environment). Multivariate results support this hypothesis. This finding is consistent with the contention that annual reports play a greater role in the communication process for firms followed by few analysts. Finally, I investigate and find evidence consistent with the benefits of enforcement being greater in environments that allow for greater choice among accounting methods.

The article is organized as follows. Section 2 provides background on disclosures and enforcement. Section 3 develops hypotheses and section 4 describes how disclosures, enforcement, and forecast accuracy are measured. Sections 5 and 6 present the control variables and empirical analysis, respectively. Conclusions and discussions of future research possibilities are presented in section 7. The Appendix contains details on the disclosure scores used.

2. Background on disclosures and enforcement

2.1 Disclosures

Many practitioners and researchers advocate enhanced firm disclosures (e.g., the Jenkins Committee, AICPA [1994]). Internationally, both the IASC/IASB and groups such as the International Organization of Securities Commissions (IOSCO) and International Federation of Stock Exchanges (FIBV/WFE) have actively promoted greater disclosure by firms and transparency of financial information. These groups assert that there are benefits to expanded disclosures. One such alleged benefit is reduced information asymmetry. Although accounting researchers extensively explain variations in disclosure levels among firms and countries, research on the effects of differences in disclosure levels is more limited, especially in international settings (Saudagaran and Meek [1997]).

Financial analysts employ several information sources to arrive at their evaluations of firm prospects. In this study I investigate the amount of information in annual reports. Lang and Lundholm [1993] find a high, significant, and positive correlation between annual report disclosures and other forms of disclosure (see also Holland [1998]). Surveys and other research evidence document that the annual report is a vital, though not sufficient, source of information to analysts both in the United States and elsewhere (e.g., AIMR [2000], Vergoossen [1993], Chang and Most [1985]).

Research investigating whether properties of analysts' forecasts are associated with firm disclosure follows either a within-country, firm-level approach or an across-country, country-level approach. For U.S. firms, Lang and Lundholm [1996] find ratings of annual report disclosures (a subset of the overall AIMR ratings) to be significantly negatively associated with forecast dispersion but *not* significantly related to forecast accuracy. Similarly, for firms domiciled in Sweden, Adrem [1999] finds no significant relationship between an active and informative disclosure strategy and forecast accuracy. For Singaporean firms, Eng and Teo [2000] report that, if earnings changes are controlled for, the amount of annual report disclosure is not significantly related to forecast accuracy.

Basu, Hwang, and Jan [1998] document that country-average disclosure levels are positively associated with forecast accuracy in a sample of seven countries. Using only country-level data from 37 countries, Khanna, Palepu, and Chang [2000] find a significant and positive relation between forecast accuracy and an annual report disclosure metric (country averages from CIFAR [1990]). Thus, there is mixed evidence from single- and multicountry studies that level of disclosure is related to the accuracy of analysts' earnings forecasts.

A limitation of using country-level disclosure scores is that the within-country variation in firm disclosures can be as great as between-country variation.[1] This is the case in my study. This article, in contrast to previous research, examines *firm-level* disclosures in an *across-country* setting. Moreover, I recognize that disclosures are not likely to be exogenous and consequently examine determinants of disclosure quantity (see section 6.4).

2.2 Enforcement of accounting standards

The subject of enforcement of accounting standards has attracted increased attention in recent years. Although we have observed diminishing differences in accounting recognition and measurement internationally, enforcement continues to differ significantly across countries, even being nonexistent in some countries (FEE [1999]).

Many scholars argue that the extent to which standards are enforced and violations prosecuted is as important as the standards themselves (e.g., Sunder [1997, p. 167]). In particular, the quality of financial information is a function of both the quality of accounting standards and the regulatory enforcement or corporate application of the standards (Kothari [2000, p. 92]). Absent adequate enforcement, even the best accounting standards will be inconsequential. If nobody takes action when rules are breached, the rules remain requirements only on paper. In some environments, for example, firms behave toward "mandatory" requirements as if they were voluntary (Marston and Shrives [1996]). To illustrate, even though accounting policy disclosures are required in most countries as well as by IAS 1 (e.g., Saudagaran and Diga [1997]), Frost and Ramin [1997] document considerable variation in accounting policy disclosures within and across countries.

Although academics and practitioners agree on the importance of enforcement as an essential element of the financial reporting infrastructure, there is little, if any, research on enforcement in an international setting. One potential explanation for this is that it is not easy to measure enforcement across countries. I discuss in section 4 how to operationalize enforcement.

3. Hypotheses

3.1 How variations in disclosures affect analysts' forecasts

Holland [1998] argues that an overall aim of a firm's disclosure activities is to increase investors' understanding of the firm's performance and future outlook, and to ensure that participants interpret firm-provided information in an informed and similar manner.

In forecasting future earnings, analysts face uncertainties related to understanding both the firm's economic situation and the accounting alternatives it uses. Annual report disclosures, as measured in this article (see section 4.1 and the Appendix), can aid analysts in forecasting earnings in several specific ways.

With respect to the economics of the firm, analysts can gain insight into future plans and firm strategy through the management discussion and analysis. Furthermore, the detail provided about product and market segments can be relevant for forecasting if some segments grow faster than others or have different risk profiles. Disclosures of subsequent events and investments in capital assets have potential to provide information on future earnings that is not reflected in the basic audited financial statements. The level of detail in the basic financial statements (income statement, balance sheet, and statement of cash flows) can assist in assessing the sustainability of earnings.

In addition to understanding firm strategy and prospects, analysts also need to have a solid understanding of the firm's accounting practices. Disclosures of the main accounting policies followed (typically in the first note) help analysts understand firms' financial reporting at a general level (Hope [2003a]). More detailed information can be acquired through the specific notes to the accounts.

To the extent that annual report disclosures are informative about firms' prospects and accounting practices (and to the extent that analysts actually rely on disclosures in the annual report), enhanced disclosure should be associated with greater earnings forecast accuracy. This leads to the following hypothesis, which is an extension of single-country studies to an across-country setting using firm-level disclosure data:

> *H1:* The quantity of annual report disclosure is positively associated with the accuracy of analysts' earnings forecasts.[2]

In general, the extent of disclosure in annual reports varies with several factors. In particular, it is possible that the demand for disclosure is endogenous and decreases with forecast accuracy. In section 6.4 I investigate determinants of disclosure quantity and test whether results are sensitive to the simultaneous testing of disclosures and forecast accuracy.

3.2 How variations in enforcement influence managers and analysts

I expect managers to follow prescribed accounting and disclosure rules to a greater extent when enforcement is stronger. For example, if the accounting standards prescribe that firms must use the percentage-of-completion method for recognizing revenue from long-term contracts, firms will actually do this.

In addition, I expect strong enforcement to reduce instances of financial reporting-related fraud. Reducing fraud increases the reliability of the financial reports (Ball [2001, p. 145]). Greater adherence to rules and regulations should reduce financial analysts' uncertainty about the accounting methods used and how they are applied (accounting uncertainty), in turn making the task of forecasting earnings relatively easier. The second hypothesis is then:

> *H2:* The level of enforcement of accounting standards is positively associated with the accuracy of analysts' earnings forecasts.

This hypothesis assumes that enforcement of accounting policies makes managers' reporting strategies more predictable. Alternatively, it could be that enforcement is stronger in environments in which accounting and disclosure practices are of the lowest quality or the least consistent. Said another way, the need for strong "policing" of accounting standards might be less in environments in which practice is satisfactory because of cultural or other reasons. This possibility, however, is not consistent with the country variations in enforcement noted in section 6.2. In environments in which enforcement is lax, moreover, it might be that analysts scrutinize managers' financial reporting choices more closely. Finally, lack of enforcement could enable managers to meet more easily analysts' forecasts by manipulation, as by smoothing earnings over time. As smooth earnings are likely to be associated with easier earnings forecasting, strong enforcement could be related to more variable earnings and, hence, lower forecast accuracy.[3]

3.3 Disclosures and analyst following

Disclosures provided in annual reports represent one part of firms' overall information environment. One proxy for a firm's information environment is its analyst following. I expect the importance of annual report disclosures in explaining forecast accuracy to vary with the number of analysts who follow the firm.[4] From a theoretical perspective it is not obvious whether disclosures and analyst following are substitutes or complements (e.g., see Bushman and Smith [2001]).[5] However, prior empirical research finds forecast accuracy to increase with the number of analysts (e.g., Lys and Soo [1995]). Similarly, Botosan [1997] finds annual report disclosure levels to be negatively associated with cost of equity capital, but only for firms followed by few analysts. These empirical findings are consistent with the importance of the annual report in the communication process being greater for firms with fewer analysts. From this follows hypothesis 3:

> *H3:* The quantity of annual report disclosure is less positively associated with forecast accuracy for firms that attract many analysts.

3.4 Enforcement and the extent of choice
among accounting methods

As discussed, I expect strong enforcement of accounting standards to make reporting decisions more predictable. In turn, this reduced uncertainty about firms' reporting choices makes forecasting easier. The impact of enforcement may, however, differ with other aspects of the financial reporting environment. I examine whether enforcement is particularly useful to analysts when firms are able to choose from a larger set of allowable accounting methods.

If accounting standards strictly limit the choice among accounting methods, analysts should face less uncertainty about which accounting methods are used in arriving at reported earnings numbers. Also, to the extent that a large number of allowable accounting methods contributes to higher task complexity for analysts (e.g., Ashbaugh and Pincus [2001]), strong enforcement should help ensure that consistent methods are employed over time, easing some of the forecasting complexity. Both of these arguments support the idea that enforcement of accounting standards is more useful (in explaining forecast accuracy) when there is greater choice among accounting methods, and lead to hypothesis 4:

H4: Enforcement is more positively related to forecast accuracy when firms can choose among a larger set of accounting methods.

The relation between enforcement and the number of allowable accounting methods is, however, likely to be complex.[6] For example, if enforcement is weak, the allowable number of accounting methods may not mean much, as managers have significant reporting discretion in such environments. Strong enforcement can presumably constrain potential abuse or manipulation of the flexibility stemming from being able to choose from several accounting methods.[7] It may also be that choice in accounting per se may make analysts' tasks more difficult because of higher task complexity (Ashbaugh and Pincus [2001]), regardless of enforcement level.

4. Measurement of test and dependent variables[8]

4.1 Annual report disclosures

In this study I use the Center for International Financial Analysis and Research (CIFAR [1993, 1995]) evaluations of corporate disclosure levels for leading nonfinancial companies in several countries. Using this source, I can, unlike previous research, investigate effects of variations in *firm*-level disclosures in an across-country setting. I use the total CIFAR disclosure score, which is constructed from 85 annual report variables. The Appendix gives details of the CIFAR scores and reports the results of extensive validity tests.

4.2 Enforcement

There is no straightforward and uncontroversial way to measure the strength of enforcement of accounting standards.[9] I construct a comprehensive measure of enforcement based on five country-level factors: audit spending, insider trading laws, judicial efficiency, rule of law, and shareholder protection. For each of these variables, a higher score denotes stronger enforcement. I aggregate the factors into one score by factor analysis. Consistent results obtain when I assign equal weights to each variable. I also present results with an alternative measure of enforcement (that excludes audit spending but includes two firm-level variables: audit firm type and stock exchange listings).

A country's commitment to enforcement can be partially gleaned by assessing how much it spends on audit services relative to the economy as a whole. More spending on external auditing is expected to be associated with stronger audit firms and closer compliance with accounting standards. Audit spending is measured as the total fees of a country's 10 largest auditing firms as a percentage of gross domestic produce (GDP) for 1990 (Mueller, Gernon, and Meek [1994]). This is not a perfect measure of the role of auditing because it covers only the top 10 audit firms[10] and, to a lesser extent, because it scales audit fees by GDP rather than by some measure of the size of listed firms. In addition, audit fees can reflect factors other than audit quality, such as cost drivers and litigation risk (e.g., Simunic [1980], Seetharaman, Gul, and Lynn [2002]). This metric is nevertheless used in previous research with results as predicted (e.g., Ali and Hwang [2000]).

Insider trading laws may deter managers from manipulating earnings to profit from trading in the firm's stock. Beneish and Vargus [2000] provide evidence that insider trading is related to earnings management. Bhattacharya and Daouk [2002] document that insider trading laws exist in 87 of the 103 countries in their sample, but enforcement (i.e., prosecutions) occurs in only 38 countries. Consistent with Bhattacharya and Daouk, I assign a score of 1 if a country had a law prohibiting insider trading, and 0 otherwise. Similarly, I assign a score of 1 if a country had prosecuted against insider trading, and 0 otherwise. The score included in the enforcement metric is the sum of the existence and enforcement of insider trading laws.

The third component of enforcement, judicial efficiency, measures the "efficiency and integrity of the legal environment as it affects business" (La Porta et al. [1998, p. 1124]). A country's judicial system might be functioning well but enforcement of accounting regulations lacking. It is difficult, however, to think of a situation in which the judicial system in general works poorly but enforcement of accounting standards is strong. The assessments of judicial efficiency produced by the country-risk rating agency Business International Corporation "may be taken to represent investors' assessments of conditions in the country in question" (La Porta *et al.* [1998, p. 1124]).

The fourth component of enforcement, rule of law, assesses a country's law and order tradition (La Porta *et al.* [1998, p. 1124]). If no one cares, regulations covering the content of financial reports are not likely to be effective. Assessments of law and order tradition are produced by the country-risk rating agency International Country Risk. Both judicial efficiency and rule of law are on a scale from 0 to 10, with lower scores for lower efficiency levels and less tradition for law and order, respectively.

Finally, Hung [2000] and Ball [2001] argue that strong shareholder protection should attenuate management opportunism in financial reporting. Managers in weak shareholder protection environments are more likely than managers in strong shareholder protection environments to manipulate earnings. For example, mechanisms by which shareholders might sue directors for losses incurred because of manipulated financial reports are more plentiful in the United States than in Germany (Hung [2000], La Porta *et al.* [1998]). Hence, the higher anticipated cost to managers of engaging in manipulation in the United States might be expected to deter such behavior.[11] I employ the same La Porta *et al.* [1998] measure of shareholder protection (or antidirector rights) as Hung.[12]

Because of the limitations of country-level audit spending in capturing the quality of the auditing regime noted earlier, I also present results with an alternative measure that excludes audit spending. This alternative model is augmented with audit firm type and stock exchange listings. As previously discussed, this measure is based on factor analysis of the six components. Equally weighting the components yields similar empirical results.

I expect Big 6 auditors to be better enforcers of accounting standards, both because of their greater expertise and the value of their brand-name reputations (e.g., Francis, Maydew, and Sparks [1999], Becker *et al.* [1998]). In defining auditor type, I distinguish between Big 6 and other auditors.[13] I include stock exchange listings because in some jurisdictions the stock exchange serves as the primary enforcer of accounting standards. A firm from a country with weak insider trading laws or other judicial weaknesses may be subjected to strong enforcement if it is listed on exchanges that exert such controls. For example, an Italian firm may list on the New York Stock Exchange (NYSE) to lower its cost of equity capital (or for other reasons). Listing on NYSE subjects the firm to scrutiny by the Securities and Exchange Commission (SEC), and any sanctions imposed by the SEC for improper reporting could endanger the firm's listing status and, hence, be very costly. In fact, Ball [2001, p. 167] argues that listing on a prestigious exchange is a more credible signal of information quality than adopting other accounting standards (e.g., U.S. GAAP or IAS), in part because such a listing exposes the firm to greater litigation. I include a detailed variable measuring the number of stock exchanges on which a firm is listed.[14] Including audit firm type and stock exchange listings comes at a cost, however, in that these variables may be viewed as managerial choice variables.

4.3 Accounting choice and analyst following

To measure the extent of choice between accounting methods allowed by domestic GAAP, I use the country-level variable constructed by Basu, Hwang, and Jan [1998], who assign a score between 0 (no choice) and 2 for each accounting area, sum the scores across all dimensions, and assign ranks to countries.[15] The areas they include are the accounting for corporate acquisitions, amortization of goodwill, inventory, research and development, deferred taxes, investment in securities, foreign currency translation, fixed-asset revaluation in excess of cost, and marketable debt securities. Analyst following is the number of analysts reporting to IBES, averaged over fiscal months 4–12.

4.4 Dependent variable

Following Lang and Lundholm [1996], forecast accuracy is defined as:

$$\frac{-|Actual\ EPS - Forecasted\ EPS|}{Beginning\text{-}of\text{-}fiscal\text{-}year\ stock\ price}$$

Both forecasted and actual earnings per share are from IBES Domestic and International Summary Files. Forecast accuracy is computed as the simple average of the measure across the months included in the testing window (see Lang and Lundholm [1996, p. 477]). I deflate by stock price to facilitate comparisons across firms.[16]

Because the annual report information needs to be available to analysts at the time their forecasts are issued, I examine the accuracy of forecasts issued after the release of the annual reports. CIFAR [1995, vol. II] has countrywide statistics on the timing of the publication of the annual reports relative to the fiscal year-end. These statistics are based on the same firms for which it provides annual report disclosure scores. Based on these statistics, which are corroborated by Frost and Ramin [1997], I use consensus forecasts of annual earnings made in months 4–12 following the fiscal year-end. In section 6.5 I test whether results are sensitive to this choice of forecast horizon.

5. Control variables

Table 1 summarizes and defines the control variables. I control for variations in GAAP regimes and earnings predictability. I also control for other

Table 1 Variables Used.

Variable	Explanation	Data Source(s)
Forecast accuracy	The negative of the absolute difference between actual EPS and analysts' forecasts (averaged over fiscal months 4–12) scaled by stock price. (Winsorized at −1.)	IBES
Disclosures	Firm-level total annual report disclosure scores. See the Appendix.	CIFAR [1993, 1995]
Enforcement	Degree of enforcement of accounting standards. Measure based on factor analysis of (1) country-level audit spending, (2) judicial efficiency, (3) rule of law, (4) insider trading laws (existence and enforcement), and (5) shareholder protection (antidirector rights). Alternative measure excludes (1) but includes two firm-level variables: stock exchange listings and audit firm type (see below).	La Porta *et al.* [1998], Mueller, Gernon, and Meek [1994], Bhattacharya and Daouk [2002], CIFAR [1995]; see Note
Stock exchange listings	Summary of all the major stock exchanges on which a firm was listed during the sample period. Listings on domestic exchanges as well as European (other than London), London, Asian, and U.S. listings are recorded. For U.S. firms, listings on the London Stock Exchange and Tokyo Stock Exchange have been recorded in addition to domestic listings. Listings on U.S. exchanges are given a weight of 1.5, all other listings, including ADRs (without exchange listing) are given a weight of 1, and the scores for each firm are summed.	See Note; various Web-based sources; direct contact with firms
Analyst following	The number of analysts averaged over fiscal months 4–12.	IBES
Extent of choice among accounting methods	Country ranking of number of accounting methods allowed in nine areas: investment in securities, corporate acquisitions, amortization of goodwill, inventory, deferred taxes, research and development, marketable debt securities, fixed asset revaluation in excess of cost, and foreign currency translation. A higher score means more choice (i.e., the scale has been inverted from the Basu, Hwang, and Jan [1998] scale).	Basu, Hwang, and Jan [1998]; self-scored for Nordic countries; Austria and Switzerland assumed equal Germany, New Zealand equal Australia and Belgium equal France (see Hope [2001]).
Firm size	Market value of equity in 1993 U.S.\$ millions.	See Note

Table 1 (cont'd)

Variable	Explanation	Data Source(s)
Earnings change	The absolute value of the change in earnings over the previous year scaled by the previous year's earnings.	IBES
Negative earnings	Indicator variable for loss firms.	See Note
Industry	Nine indicator variables for IBES industry sectors.	IBES
Uncertainty avoidance	The degree to which people feel uncomfortable with ambiguity and an uncertain future.	Hofstede [1980]
Individualism	A preference for a loosely knit social fabric or an independent, tightly knit fabric.	Hofstede [1980]
Domestic listed firms	The number of domestic listed firms divided by population in 1995. A measure of the importance of the stock market.	La Porta *et al.* [1997]
Earnings surprise management	Country scores of earnings management for the first half of the 1990s. Computed as the ratio of small (5%) positive earnings surprises to small negative earnings surprises.	Brown and Higgins [2001]
Common law	Indicator variable equal to 1 for common law legal origin, and 0 otherwise.	La Porta *et al.* [1997]
French, German, and Nordic legal system	Indicator variables for French, German, and Nordic code law systems (with common law as the reference group)	La Porta *et al.* [1997]
Concentration	Country-level measure of ownership concentration. Measured as the mean fraction of the firms' voting rights owned by the controlling shareholder.	La Porta, Lopez-de-Silanes, and Schleifer [1999]
Leverage	Total liabilities divided by total assets.	See Note
ROE	Net income divided by shareholders' equity.	See Note
Parent only	Indicator variable for firms that issue only parent financial statements.	See Note
Auditor	Indicator variable for Big 6 (/Big 8) auditor.	See Note

Firm-level data are from Datastream, Global Vantage, Compustat/CRSP, Moody's International, Global Access/ISI, S&P, CIFAR Global Company Handbook, various stock exchanges, Bank of New York, IBES, ETLA, and other sources.

firm- and country-level factors that may affect the accuracy of analysts' earnings forecasts.

5.1 GAAP regimes and earnings predictability

Earnings may not be equally predictable across all countries and firms (even with identical information sets). One way of classifying earnings predictability is: lines of business and/or economic circumstances differ across countries, and the GAAP regime under which the firm reports.[17] I include control variables that attempt to capture variation due to this heterogeneity.

To the extent that firms within a given country are similar, the inclusion of country indicator variables controls for cross-country variation in economic circumstances. Therefore, country indicators are included in one of the models presented. Similarly, to the extent that firms within a given industry are similar, including an indicator variable for industry membership controls for line-of-business differences in the compositions of country samples. Some industries are more stable than others and, hence, more amenable to earnings forecasting. IBES industry indicator variables are included in all models.

With respect to differences in GAAP regimes, the issues relate to variations in earnings management and variations in legal environment that affect the timeliness of earnings. Cross-country variations in earnings forecasts likely reflect variations in management incentives and ability to manage earnings. Ball, Kothari, and Robin [2000] and Leuz, Nanda, and Wysocki [2001] argue that income smoothing is more prevalent in code law than in common law countries because of differences in accounting rules, corporate governance, and legal environment. Both studies present evidence consistent with this hypothesis. Several studies (e.g., Barth, Elliott, and Finn [1999]), however, find that investors reward U.S. firms for reporting smooth earnings, and examples abound of earnings management by firms in the United States and other common law countries (e.g., Peasnell, Pope, and Young [2000], Healy and Whalen [1999], Black, Sellers, and Manly [1998]). Brown and Higgins [2001] report that U.S. managers are more likely than managers in other countries to engage in earnings management. In light of the foregoing, I include a country-level measure of earnings surprise management from Brown and Higgins and expect this variable to be positively associated with forecast accuracy.[18]

Building on Basu [1997], Ball, Kothari, and Robin [2000] investigate the way accounting incorporates economic income over time using a sample of companies from common law (Australia, Canada, United Kingdom, and United States) and code law (France, Germany, and Japan) countries. They argue that the demand for accounting income varies with "shareholder" and "stakeholder" corporate governance models. Specifically, the authors find evidence consistent with international differences in the asymmetric timeliness of earnings.[19] Of particular relevance to the present study, Ball, Kothari, and Robin find that firms in common law countries are more likely to reflect economic losses in earnings in a timely manner, introducing large negative transitory components in earnings of some firms. Such components may make earnings less predictable (unless analysts in these environments are especially attuned to this possibility). Based on the evidence in Ball, Kothari, and Robin, it would be desirable to condition on the likelihood that firms experience current or past good or bad news, for example, based on stock returns. Unfortunately, data limitations preclude the inclusion of such a control variable. Instead, I include the following control variables for variations in timeliness of earnings: corporate governance model, the existence of losses, and earnings variability. As a proxy for international variations in corporate governance, I include a country-level metric of the relative importance of the stock market, namely, the number of domestic firms divided by population (from La Porta *et al.* [1997]).[20] I expect a positive relation to forecast accuracy. To provide an alternative measure, I also present results with common law legal system as a control variable, where common law is an indicator variable equal to 1 if the firm is from a common law country, and 0 otherwise. Similarly, losses equal 1 if earnings are negative, and 0 otherwise. I also include a measure of earnings variability, measured as the scaled change in earnings from the previous year.[21] As proxies for analysts' task complexity, I expect losses and earnings variability to be negatively correlated with forecast accuracy.

5.2 Other control variables

In addition to the control variables for GAAP regimes and earnings predictability, I include controls for stock exchange listings, analyst following and firm size at the firm level, and culture at the country level.

I control for stock exchange listings for several reasons. Firms that are listed on several (and more "prestigious") exchanges are likely to be subjected to more pressure from capital markets. There is greater investor interest in such firms and typically more information than other annual report disclosures available about these firms. Stock exchange listings are also reasonable proxies for the use of non-domestic accounting standards (e.g., IAS or U.S. GAAP).

Lys and Soo [1995] argue that the number of analysts proxies for the intensity of competition in the market. Consequently, the number of analysts per firm is included to control for incentives to forecast accurately. I expect a positive relation between analyst following and forecast accuracy. In my sample, average forecasts in all countries are positively biased but not significantly different from 0, consistent with analysts' facing similar incentives across the sample countries. Both stock exchanges and financial analysts could be viewed as elements of the overall enforcement mechanism for accounting standards.[22] Including these two control variables means I am testing whether enforcement, beyond stock exchanges and analysts, matters in explaining variations in forecast accuracy.

I also control for firm size, which is used in the literature as a proxy for several factors. To the extent that size reflects information availability about a firm (other than through annual reports), a positive relation to forecast accuracy is expected. However, firm size can also proxy for a host of other factors, such as managers' incentives, for which predictions for the relation with forecast accuracy are unclear.

Variations in national cultures are shown to affect managers' financial reporting behavior (e.g., Salter [1998], Hope [2003c]) and could influence financial analysts' earnings forecasting (e.g., Rees, Swanson, and Clement [2000]).[23] I include uncertainty avoidance and individualism, two of Hofstede's [1980] constructs that are widely used in accounting research (e.g., Gray [1988]).[24] I do not have predictions for the signs of these two variables.[25]

6. Empirical analysis

The hypotheses are tested in the following general empirical model:

Forecast accuracy = *f*(*Disclosures, Enforcement,*
Interaction effects, Control variables)

This model is referred to as "the traditional cross-country regression" by Bushman and Smith [2001], augmented with firm-level variables. An advantage of a cross-country design is that it allows for sufficient in-sample variation, as there are considerable, quantifiable cross-country differences in financial accounting regimes (Bushman and Smith [2001]). That previous research documents significant cross-country differences in analysts' earnings forecast accuracy suggests that meaningful economic variations might be attributable to variations in disclosure practices and to the infrastructure of financial reporting.

Table 1 summarizes definitions and data sources of the variables used. In what follows, I explain sample selection and present descriptive statistics. I then follow with univariate and multivariate analyses. Finally, I report the results of robustness tests.

6.1 Sample

Panel A of table 2 summarizes the sample selection. The main constraint on sample size is the availability of annual report disclosure scores. There are 1,992 observations (from 1,434 firms) in CIFAR (1993, 1995).[26] CIFAR (1993, 1995) covers fiscal years 1991 and 1993 (see the Appendix for details).

Table 2 Sample and Descriptive Statistics.

Panel A: Sample

Observations for which annual report scores are available in CIFAR [1993, 1995]	1,992
Less: Missing analyst forecast data	439
Observations for which disclosure scores and forecast data are available	1,553
Less: Missing control variables	244
Number of observations in pooled sample	1,309
Number of observations in sample with only one observation per firm	890

Panel B: Descriptive statistics

				Percentiles	
	Mean	*Std. Dev.*	*25*	*50*	*75*
Forecast accuracy	−0.035	0.110	−0.019	−0.006	−0.002
Disclosure scores	74.7	7.9	70	75	80
Enforcement	0.17	1.39	−0.25	0.70	1.21
Stock exchange listings	1.8	1.1	1	1	2
Analyst following	18.1	9.5	11.0	17.2	24.3
Firm size (in millions, 1993 dollars)	6,243	10,240	968	2,869	7,224
Extent of choice in accounting	5.4	2.9	2	6	7.5
Earnings change	0.36	0.36	0.10	0.22	0.60
Negative earnings	0.16	0.36	0	0	0
Earnings surprise management	1.54	0.42	1.18	1.62	1.99

Panel C: Descriptive statistics, by country[a]

	Accuracy	*Disclosure*	*Analysts*	*Size*	*N*
Australia	−0.008	80.6	13.3	2,734	45
Austria	−0.084	60.7	7.3	365	15
Belgium	−0.024	69.5	12.6	2,608	14
Canada	−0.024	76.7	17.8	4,778	19
Denmark	−0.053	72.9	13.2	966	15
Finland	−0.098	81.0	10.5	662	18
France	−0.041	77.0	22.8	3,890	74
Germany	−0.074	67.8	28.5	4,301	55
Hong Kong	−0.049	73.0	22.9	3,930	24
Ireland	−0.018	80.6	5.0	388	10
Italy[b]	−0.083	68.0	17.3	1,374	18
Japan	−0.013	70.9	10.8	8,828	190
Netherlands	−0.089	73.2	30.2	6,069	29
New Zealand	−0.049	78.2	9.2	746	11
Norway	−0.089	78.0	16.1	942	23
Portugal[b]	−0.175	58.1	5.5	220	7
South Africa[b]	−0.046	75.9	3.9	1,053	32
Spain[b]	−0.180	69.7	23.0	3,166	24
Sweden	−0.044	83.0	17.3	1,488	27
Switzerland	−0.151	76.1	25.1	3,308	25
United Kingdom	−0.040	83.1	16.8	7,124	141
United States	−0.011	73.8	20.7	8,459	493

Table 2 (cont'd)

Panel D: Descriptive statistics for enforcement (and its components) and choice[c]

Country	Enforce	AudSp	ITLs	Jud	Rule	Anti	Choice
Australia	−0.25	0.48	1	10.00	8.52	4	5
Austria	−1.65	0.14	0.5	9.50	10.00	2	7
Belgium	−1.89	0.18	1	9.50	10.00	0	8
Canada	0.98	0.41	2	9.25	10.00	5	3.5
Denmark	−0.56	0.43	1	10.00	10.00	2	7.5
Finland	−0.22	0.12	1.5	10.00	10.00	3	7.5
France	−0.99	0.20	2	8.00	8.98	3	8
Germany	−2.92	0.15	0	9.00	9.23	1	7
Hong Kong[d]	0.10	0.54	1	10.00	8.22	5	3.5
Ireland	−0.78	0.70	1	8.75	7.80	4	6
Italy	−3.55	0.10	1	6.75	8.33	1	.
Japan	0.16	0.07	2	10.00	8.98	4	10
Netherlands	−0.19	0.68	1	10.00	10.00	2	9
New Zealand	0.24	0.48	1	10.00	10.00	4	5
Norway	0.70	0.21	2	10.00	10.00	4	7.5
Portugal	−3.21	0.18	1	5.50	8.68	3	.
South Africa	−3.39	0.35	1	6.00	4.42	5	.
Spain	−3.65	0.16	0	6.25	7.80	4	.
Sweden	0.55	0.36	2	10.00	10.00	3	7.5
Switzerland	−0.39	0.55	1	10.00	10.00	2	7
United Kingdom	1.16	0.60	2	10.00	8.57	5	6
United States	1.21	0.31	2	10.00	10.00	5	2

Panel E: Details of enforcement variable[e]

	Enforcement	Alternative Measure of Enforcement
Audit spending	0.25	
Insider trading	0.54	0.46
Judicial efficiency	0.52	0.53
Rule of law	0.36	0.49
Antidirector rights	0.49	0.38
Audit firm type		0.30
Stock exchange listings		0.18

[a]See table 1 for definitions of variables. Means per country are reported.

[b]Data on choice among accounting methods are not available for these countries. Tests involving choice are based on the remaining sample countries.

[c]Enforce = enforcement (see table 1); AudSp = audit spending (Mueller, Gernon, and Meek [1994]); ITLs = sum of existence and enforcement of insider trading laws (Bhattacharya and Daouk [2002]); Jud = judicial efficiency (La Porta *et al.* [1998]); Rule = rule of law (La Porta *et al.* [1998]); Anti = antidirector rights (a measure of shareholder protection; La Porta *et al.* [1998]); Choice = choice among accounting methods (see table 1).

[d]Data are not available on country-level audit spending for Hong Kong in Mueller, Gernon, and Meek [1994]. For Hong Kong, country-level audit spending is derived from CIFAR [1995; tables 3–6: Audit fees percentage]. Similar results obtain regardless of whether Hong Kong is included based on this measure. (Data are available for Singapore for all factors except country-level audit spending. Results are consistent with those reported when Singapore is included using an enforcement variable that excludes audit spending.)

[e]Scoring coefficients of first factor of unrotated principal components factor analysis.

Not all of these firms had IBES coverage during the sample period. Consequently, there are 1,553 observations (1,100 firms) for which disclosure scores and forecast data are available. Requiring data on enforcement reduces the sample to 1,351 observations with data available for ordinary least squares (OLS) tests. Finally, requiring data on control variables reduces the sample to 1,309 observations. Some of the firms have data for two years, and I report results both for the pooled sample and for the sample of 890 firms.

6.2 Descriptive statistics

Panel B of table 2 presents descriptive statistics for analyst data, test variables, and control variables. For tests that require data on the extent of choice among accounting methods, I lose observations from Italy, Portugal, South Africa, and Spain. The mean absolute forecast error (i.e., the negative of forecast accuracy as defined in section 4.3) for the overall sample is 3.5% of stock price, with a standard deviation of 11%. The mean forecast accuracy is highest in Australia and the United States and lowest in Spain, Portugal, and Switzerland (panel C of table 2).

CIFAR's scores are on a 0 to 100 scale, and the in-sample range of country averages is from 58.1 for Portugal to 83 for the United Kingdom. Sample firms from the United Kingdom, Sweden, and Finland have the highest mean total disclosure scores, and Portugal, Austria, and Germany have the lowest scores (broadly consistent with the rankings in Meek, Roberts, and Gray [1995]).

The United States, United Kingdom, and Canada have the highest enforcement scores; Spain and Italy have the lowest (see table 2, panel D). For the sample with data available on choice among accounting methods, Germany and Austria have the lowest enforcement scores. These rankings seem consistent with Gebhardt [2000], who concludes that sanctions against noncompliance with accounting standards are weak in Germany.[27] Panel D also shows the country-by-country data for the components of the enforcement variable (as well as descriptive statistics on choice among accounting methods). Panel E shows the details of the factors included in the enforcement measure and the alternative measure.

Dutch and German firms have the highest number of analysts (consistent with Basu, Hwang, andJan [1998]). The CIFAR sample firms are among the largest from each sample country (see the Appendix).[28] There is nevertheless considerable variation in firm size as measured by market capitalization (see panels B and C of table 2). U.S. firms are, on average, significantly larger than non-U.S. firms. On average, earnings changes for U.S. firms are smaller than non-U.S. firms (not shown), which could be due to a more stable economic environment in the United States, but it is also consistent with evidence in Brown and Higgins [2001] that U.S. managers are more likely to engage in income smoothing.

6.3 Univariate relations

Table 3 reports that the extent of annual report disclosures is significantly and positively correlated with forecast accuracy (0.14), consistent with H1 that annual report disclosures are useful to financial analysts in forecasting earnings. Consistent with H2, enforcement is positively correlated with forecast accuracy (0.21). Also, note the positive correlation between disclosure scores and enforcement (0.31). This is consistent with the intuition that enforcement should be associated with higher financial disclosure, at least for mandatory items.

Of the control variables, earnings change has the highest correlation with forecast accuracy (−0.24). Large earnings changes due to, for example, sudden changes in competitive environments or accounting choices such as "big baths" complicate earnings forecasting. Alternatively, large (negative) earnings changes reflect the asymmetric accounting recognition of gains and losses (Basu [1997]). Negative earnings firms are also associated with lower forecast accuracy (−0.13), consistent with the findings of Hwang, Jan, and Basu [1996]. Incorporating these two variables in the regression thus also partially controls for international variations in the timeliness of earnings (Ball, Kothari, and Robin [2000]). The proxy for earnings surprise management is negatively correlated with earnings change (−0.18). This suggests that the earnings change variable captures what it is intended to, as managed earnings streams should be associated with smaller earnings changes. Earnings surprise management is significantly and positively correlated with accuracy (0.19), consistent with managed earnings being easier to forecast. Uncertainty avoidance (individualism) is negatively (positively) correlated with forecast accuracy. As predicted, my proxy for capital market pressure, domestic listed firms, is positively related to forecast accuracy. Because of the high correlations among some of the country-level variables, I report regression results both with and without country-level controls.

6.4 Multivariate tests

6.4.1. OLS results

Table 4 provides OLS regression results for the relations between forecast accuracy and disclosures and enforcement. Based on the arguments in Bushman and Smith [2001] that the choice of country-level control variables can affect regression results in cross-country studies, I report results with different sets of control variables. Model 1 is the benchmark regression. Model 2 uses the alternative measure of enforcement. Model 3 uses an indicator for common law instead of the number of domestic listed firms as a proxy for corporate governance models. Model 4 replaces country-level control variables with country indicators. Model 5 includes only firm-level

Table 3 Correlations.

	Accur.	Disc.	Enforce	Exch.	An. foll.	Choice	Size	ΔEarn.	Loss	Unc. Av.	Indiv.	Listed
Disclosures	0.14											
Enforcement	0.21	0.31										
Stock exchange listings	0.09	0.38	0.07									
Analyst following	0.14	0.18	*0.04*	0.26								
Extent of choice	-0.12	*-0.04*	-0.55	0.14	-0.24							
Firm size	0.12	0.14	0.18	0.17	0.41	-0.08						
Earnings change	-0.24	-0.12	-0.12	0.03	-0.17	0.25	-0.15					
Negative earnings	-0.13	-0.12	*-0.01*	-0.03	-0.05	-0.03	-0.08	0.36				
Uncertainty avoidance	-0.05	-0.24	-0.38	0.05	0.00	0.75	0.00	0.19	-0.05			
Individualism	0.11	0.36	0.51	0.05	0.00	-0.56	0.14	-0.19	0.05	-0.65		
Domestic listed firms	0.11	0.26	0.42	0.15	*0.00*	-0.41	*0.02*	-0.17	-0.06	-0.32	0.17	
Earnings surprise mgmt	0.19	0.05	0.60	-0.07	0.18	-0.76	0.20	-0.18	*0.02*	-0.50	0.64	0.20

See table 1 for explanations of variables. Accur. is the accuracy of analysts' earnings forecasts. All Pearson correlations are significant at the 5% level (two-tailed) or better except for those in italics. Spearman correlations (not shown for brevity) are consistent with Pearson correlations.

Table 4 OLS Regression Results for the Relation Between Forecast Accuraty and Disclosure Quantity and Enforcement.

Panel A: Models 1 through 3

	Pred.	Model 1			Model 2			Model 3		
		Coef.	t	P > |t|	Coef.	t	P > |t|	Coef.	t	P > |t|
Disclosures	+	0.129	2.20	0.02	0.123	2.51	<0.01	0.130	2.20	0.02
Enforcement	+	1.231	3.03	<0.01	1.298	2.76	<0.01	1.081	2.58	<0.01
Stock exchange listings	+	0.617	2.97	<0.01				0.603	2.99	<0.01
Analyst following	+	0.128	2.93	<0.01	0.147	3.27	<0.01	0.130	2.97	<0.01
Firm size	?	-0.001	-2.00	0.05	-0.001	-2.15	0.03	-0.001	-1.94	0.05
Earnings change	-	-6.489	-4.57	<0.01	-6.414	-4.60	<0.01	-6.296	-4.57	<0.01
Negative earnings	-	-1.451	-1.10	0.14	-1.357	-1.04	0.15	-1.390	-1.03	0.15
Uncertainty avoidance	?	0.071	3.06	<0.01	0.059	2.86	<0.01	0.081	3.18	<0.01
Individualism	?	0.042	0.98	0.33	-0.003	-0.08	0.93	0.047	1.00	0.32
Domestic listed firms	+	-0.017	-0.70	0.24	-0.017	-0.71	0.24			
Common law	?							0.723	0.46	0.65
Earnings surprise management	+	3.088	2.50	<0.01	4.163	3.07	<0.01	2.962	2.09	0.02
Intercept		-13.73	-3.16	<0.01	-19.74	-3.50	<0.01	-15.33	-3.19	<0.01
N		1,309			1,323			1,309		
F		10			11			10		
Adj. R^2		0.12			0.12			0.12		

Table 4 (cont'd)

Panel B: Models 4 through 6

	Pred.	Model 4			Model 5			Model 6		
		Coef.	t	P > |t|	Coef.	t	P > |t|	Coef.	t	P > |t|
Disclosures	+	0.141	2.46	<0.01	0.122	2.05	0.02	0.131	2.29	0.01
Enforcement	+	1.212	2.29	0.01	1.443	4.33	<0.01	1.215	2.51	<0.01
Stock exchange listings	+	0.688	2.57	<0.01	0.434	2.19	0.02	0.382	1.78	0.04
Analyst following	+	0.124	2.97	<0.01	0.115	2.66	<0.01	0.177	3.08	<0.01
Firm size	?	−0.001	−2.30	0.02	−0.001	−0.16	0.88	−0.001	−2.04	0.04
Earnings change	−	−6.413	−4.60	<0.01	−6.169	−4.42	<0.01	−4.862	−2.52	<0.01
Negative earnings	−	−1.535	−1.18	0.12	−1.594	−1.21	0.12	−2.113	−1.25	0.11
Uncertainty avoidance	?							0.052	1.93	0.05
Individualism	?							0.011	0.21	0.84
Domestic listed firms	+							−0.029	−1.00	0.32
Earnings surprise management	+							3.440	1.96	0.03
Intercept		−0.676	−0.60	0.55	−2.459	−3.78	<0.01	−20.20	−3.14	<0.01
N		1,309			1,309			890		
F		8			11			7		
Adj. R^2		0.17			0.11			0.12		

See table 1 for explanations of variables. The dependent variable is financial analysts' earnings forecast accuracy. Nine industry indicator variables are included in all three models but not reported. The t-statistics are based on White [1980]. The p-values are one-sided for variables with predicted sign, two-sided otherwise. The coefficients have been multiplied by 100 and are thus expressed as percentages. Model 2 uses the alternative measure of enforcement that excludes country-level audit spending but includes stock exchange listings and audit firm type. Model 3 uses an alternative measure of corporate governance models: an indicator variable for common law (as opposed to code law) instead of the number of domestic listed firms. Model 4 includes 21 country indicator variables (with the U.S. as reference). Model 5 includes only firm-level control variables. Whereas models 1–5 are pooled regressions (i.e., with some firms represented twice), model 6 includes only one observation per firm.

controls. Model 6 presents results with only one observation per firm.[29] One-sided *p*-values are reported for variables with predicted signs; otherwise, two-sided *p*-values are used. Standard errors are based on White [1980].

Consistent with H1 and the univariate results, model 1 shows that annual report disclosures are significantly and positively related to forecast accuracy, with a *p*-value of .02. Unreported results show that disclosures are significantly positive in both the U.S. and non-U.S. subsamples.[30] These findings suggest that analysts find such disclosures useful.

To compare these results with those of prior studies that investigate disclosures at the country level only (e.g., Basu, Hwang, and Jane [1998], Khanna, Palepu, and Chang [2000]), I include the CIFAR country-average disclosure score as well as the firm-level variable. The estimated coefficient on the country-level variable is not significant, whereas the firm-level variable is significant and positive. Similarly, when I substitute the country-average score for the firm-level score, the coefficient is not significant (not tabulated). These results are consistent with there being significant variation in disclosures beyond country-level variation.

Recall that Adrem [1999] and Engand Teo [2000] do not find a significant association between disclosure level and forecast accuracy using firm-level disclosure measures. Similarly, Lang and Lundholm [1996] do not find a significant relation between annual report information and forecast accuracy.[31] One possible reason for the stronger results in this study is that there is greater variation in disclosure scores in a multicountry sample.

H2 predicts that enforcement will be positively associated with forecast accuracy. Model 1 in table 4 shows that this hypothesis holds at better than the 1% level. The result is consistent with strong enforcement encouraging (or forcing) managers to follow the accounting rules that are in place, thereby reducing analysts' "accounting uncertainty" and, in turn, the task complexity of forecasting future earnings. This finding adds to the limited prior research on the effects of variations in enforcement of accounting standards internationally. Model 2 shows that the result for enforcement holds when the alternative measure of enforcement is used.

As expected, the percentage change in earnings over the previous year, "earnings change," is significantly and negatively related to forecast accuracy. Firms listed on more (and more "prestigious") stock exchanges have higher forecast accuracy. This is both consistent with such firms being more forthcoming to the investment community (e.g., by having investor relations departments) and with stock exchanges acting as enforcers of accounting standards. It is not surprising that firms that are followed by more analysts also have significantly higher forecast accuracy. Contrary to the univariate results, firm size is negatively related and uncertainty avoidance is positively related to forecast accuracy. As predicted, the estimated coefficient on earnings surprise management is significant and positive.

In model 3 an indicator for common law legal system replaces the number of domestic firms as a proxy for cross-country variations in corporate governance models (Ball, Kothari, and Robin [2000]).[32] In model 4 country indicators are used instead of country-level control variables. Model 5 includes only firm-level controls. In model 6 there is only one observation per firm (i.e., the most recent observation). All these specifications yield results similar to those of model 1.

6.4.2. Simultaneous test of disclosure quantity and forecast accuracy

Whereas accounting and disclosure standards specify minimum standards for disclosure, actual disclosure is likely to vary with a number of factors. Consistent with this, significant variation in disclosure levels is found in both within- and across-country studies (e.g., Meek, Roberts, and Gray [1995]). Thus, it is important to test whether the potential endogeneity of disclosures affects the relation between analysts' forecast accuracy and disclosure levels. As the Hausman [1978] test rejects exogeneity of disclosures at the 5% level, I test both the determinants of disclosure quantity and the effects of these on forecast accuracy in a system of equations.

The literature on determinants of disclosure levels is extensive and not reviewed here (e.g., see Adrem [1999], Saudagaran and Meek [1997], Marston and Shrives [1996]). The firm-level factors I consider for explaining disclosure quantity are (see table 1): stock exchange listings, size, profitability, leverage, analyst following, industry membership, auditor type, and forecast accuracy. In addition, I include an indicator variable for whether the firm issues only parent-company financial statements rather than consolidated group statements. At the country level I include variables that proxy for variations in legal systems, as these are shown to be associated with variations in disclosure levels (e.g., La Porta et al. [1998], Jaggi and Low [2000]). Specifically, I use indicator variables for French, German, and Nordic code law regimes, with common law countries as the reference group. I also include a measure of average firm ownership concentration. Ownership concentration varies considerably across countries, and I expect high concentration to be associated with reduced public disclosure.[33]

Table 5 reports the results of three-stage least squares (3SLS) analysis. Models 1 and 2 present results excluding and including interaction terms, respectively. In model 1, both annual report disclosure scores and degree of enforcement of accounting standards are positively associated with forecast accuracy at less than the 1% level, supporting the OLS findings.[34] Results for the control variables are generally similar to those reported in table 4.

It is not surprising that the extent of annual report disclosures is strongly and positively associated with the number and type of stock exchange listings. Disclosures are also positively related to firm size and negatively related to

Table 5 Simultaneous Equations Analysis (3SLS) of Forecast Accuracy and Annual Report Disclosure Quantity.

| | Model 1 | | | | | | | | Model 2 | | |
| | Equation (1): Forecast Accuracy | | | | Equation (2): Disclosures | | | | Forecast Accuracy | | |
	Pred.	Coef.	z	P > |z|	Pred.	Coef.	z	P > |z|	Coef.	z	P > |z|
Disclosures	+	0.293	2.82	<0.01					0.313	2.38	0.01
Enforcement	+	1.163	2.73	<0.01					0.781	1.84	0.04
Disclosures*Analyst foll.	−								−0.274	−2.21	0.02
Enforcement*Choice	+								0.900	1.47	0.07
Choice	?								−4.594	−4.36	<0.01
Stock exchange listings	+	0.301	0.95	0.17	+	1.863	10.11	<0.01	0.810	2.67	<0.01
Analyst following	+	0.111	2.38	0.01	+	0.035	1.21	0.12	21.133	2.28	0.01
Firm size	?	−0.001	−1.27	0.20	+	0.001	1.91	0.03	0.001	0.08	0.94
Earnings change	−	−6.834	−7.11	<0.01					−6.727	−7.24	<0.01
Negative earnings	−	−0.613	−0.72	0.24					−0.537	−0.64	0.26
Uncertainty avoidance	?	0.090	4.10	<0.01					0.092	3.98	<0.01
Individualism	?	0.025	0.63	0.53					−0.008	0.19	0.85
Domestic listed firms	+	−0.031	−1.38	0.09					−0.078	−2.97	<0.01
Earnings surprise mgmt	+	4.077	2.69	<0.01					1.435	0.92	0.18
ROE					?	0.393	0.35	0.73			
Leverage					?	2.058	1.63	0.10			
Auditor					+	−0.011	−0.02	0.99			
Parent company					−	−10.80	−3.88	<0.01			
Forecast accuracy					?	0.030	0.52	0.60			
French code law					−	−3.436	−4.80	<0.01			
German code law					−	−6.647	−9.32	<0.01			
Nordic code law					+	1.864	2.18	0.02			
Concentration					−	0.541	0.23	0.82			
Intercept		−35.87	−3.92	<0.01		71.16	48.23	<0.01	−29.23	−2.89	<0.01
N		1,251				1,251			1,251		
Chi-squared		224				771			213		
R²		0.13				0.38			0.14		

Hausman's [1978] test rejects exogeneity of disclosure quantity at the 5% level. See table 1 for explanations of variables. Nine industry indicator variables are included in all equations but not reported. Z-values are one-sided for variables with predicted sign, two-sided otherwise. The coefficients for the forecast accuracy equation have been multiplied by 100 and are thus expressed as percentages. For model 2, *only* the forecast accuracy equation is shown for brevity. In model 2, Analyst following and Choice are indicator variables that take the value 1 if above median, and 0 otherwise.

the issuance of only parent company financials. Forecast accuracy is not a significant determinant of disclosure quantity. There is thus no evidence that managers consider the accuracy of analysts' forecasts when making disclosure decisions. Consistent with prior research, Nordic code law is associated with increased disclosure whereas French and German code law is associated with reduced financial disclosure (relative to common law countries).

For the tests of H3 and H4, in model 2 of table 5 I add interaction terms, Disclosures * Analyst Following and Enforcement * Choice, to the regression tests in tables 4 and 5.[35] OLS tests yield similar results as 3SLS, and for brevity I present results only with 3SLS. H3 predicts that annual report disclosures are relatively less important for explaining variations in forecast accuracy for firms with a large analyst following, where analyst following is used as a proxy for a firm's information environment. The interaction between disclosure and analyst following is negative as hypothesized, with a p-value of .02.[36] This result supports H3 and suggests that annual report disclosures are more important for firms followed by relatively few analysts. Furthermore, it is consistent with the notion that the information environment of firms that have a high analyst following are different from those of other firms. The result also complements Botosan's [1997] finding that annual report disclosure levels are only significantly (negatively) related to cost of equity capital for firms that attract a low analyst following.

H4 predicts that enforcement is relatively more important when firms operate in environments in which they can choose among a larger set of accounting methods. The interaction is positive, consistent with the contention that enforcement is particularly useful in explaining forecast accuracy when firms can choose among a larger set of accounting methods. This finding supports H4 and suggests that strong enforcement reduces managerial flexibility when managers can choose among a larger set of acceptable accounting methods. For example, strong enforcement could make managers adhere more closely to the consistency principle. This, in turn, reduces analysts' uncertainty about the basis on which earnings are computed. However, the estimated coefficient is only significant at the 7% level. I interpret this result as implying that there is some support (albeit not very strong) for the notion that enforcement of accounting standards may be especially relevant when there is "more to enforce."[37, 38]

6.5 Additional robustness and specification tests

Earlier, I concluded that results are not affected by the choice of scaling factor for the dependent variable, the inclusion or exclusion of the country-level control variables, endogeneity of disclosures, or dependence among observations. In this section, I report results of additional robustness tests.

To assess the sensitivity of the results to the underlying functional form assumption made by OLS, I reestimate the models using rank regression techniques. Similarly, given that the dependent variable has a highly skewed distribution with analyst following truncated at 0, I reestimate using Tobit. The results using rank and Tobit regressions support the reported results (not tabulated). I also assess the robustness of the findings to the presence of outliers. Excluding observations for which the absolute value of studentized residuals exceeds three results in a significantly higher R^2 and yields stronger results than those reported in tables 4 and 5.

As noted earlier, forecast accuracy is computed as the simple average of the measure based on forecasts of next year's earnings issued 4 to 12 months following the prior fiscal year-end. I test whether the choice of this forecast horizon affects the results by performing the tests again using forecasts issued in months 7 to 12 and month 12 only. I also perform the tests again using forecasts issued one or two months following the release of the annual report, where the release date differs by country as described in section 4.3. The results are not materially affected by these specifications.[39]

Bushman and Smith [2001] discuss how the set of control variables can affect the results of cross-country regressions. Removing country-level controls one at a time or altogether (compare model 5 in table 4) from the regressions does not affect results for disclosures and enforcement.

In summary, tests indicate that the findings are not driven by endogeneity of disclosures, functional form assumptions, outliers, forecast horizon, scaling factor, dependence among observations, or the set of control variables included.

7. Conclusions

In this study I investigate the effects of variations in annual report disclosure quantity and enforcement of accounting standards on the accuracy of financial analysts' earnings forecasts. Controlling for firm- and country-level factors, I document that firm-level annual report disclosure level is positively associated with forecast accuracy, which suggests that firm-level disclosures provide useful information to analysts. Prior international evidence on the relation between disclosures and forecast accuracy is inconclusive. I also add to the existing literature by using a firm-level measure of disclosures in an across-country sample, and by testing whether the result holds after controlling for the potential simultaneity between firms' disclosure choices and forecast accuracy.

I use a multicountry sample to take advantage of differences in the reporting infrastructure that go well beyond within-country variations. In particular, although accounting measurement and recognition rules have been significantly harmonized over time, there is still considerable variation in the enforcement of accounting standards across jurisdictions internationally. This lack of comparability in enforcement is of concern to national and international accounting standard setters, regulators, auditors, and financial

119

statement users. Notwithstanding this interest, there has been limited prior research on enforcement of accounting standards, particularly in an international setting.

My comprehensive proxy for enforcement, constructed from five underlying variables, is significantly and positively related to forecast accuracy. This is consistent with the argument that strong enforcement encourages (or forces) managers to follow the rules that are in place and thereby reduces analysts' accounting uncertainty. This, in turn, diminishes the task complexity of forecasting future earnings.

I further document that annual report disclosures are more positively related to forecast accuracy when a firm is followed by few analysts, consistent with my hypothesis that the annual report constitutes a relatively larger part of a firm's overall communication process when analyst following is low. I also find evidence consistent with the usefulness of enforcement being greater in environments in which firms are allowed to choose among a larger set of accounting methods.

The findings in this article are subject to certain limitations. A potential disadvantage of using an international sample is that test results are more likely to be affected by omitted correlated variables. This study, however, includes controls for a number of firm- and country-level variables, and the results are not sensitive to the set of control variables included. Also, the potential to test for causality rather than mere associations is limited. Nevertheless, according to Levine and Zervos [1993] cross-country studies can be "very useful" as long as results are interpreted as suggestive of the hypothesized relations. Bushman and Smith [2001, p. 299] state that "as long as researchers interpret the results of cross-country studies with their 'eyes wide open,' there is much to learn from this type of inquiry." Finally, the sample period of the first half of the 1990s might not be representative of today's environment, although efforts to improve enforcement internationally have mostly been a recent phenomenon.

In related research, I investigate relations between specific elements of annual report disclosures and analysts' earnings forecasts (and analyst coverage). Future research can address other implications of variations in enforcement. For example, researchers can investigate the effects of differential enforcement (broadly defined) on earnings management, value relevance of accounting data, or corporate governance issues. Such studies have the potential to be relevant to academics and practitioners alike.

Appendix: CIFAR disclosure scores and validity tests

CIFAR disclosure scores[40]

CIFAR conducted evaluations of corporate annual report disclosures in the first half of the 1990s. Firms from 42 countries are included in their 1993 and 1995 evaluations, covering fiscal years 1991 and 1993, respectively. CIFAR studied annual reports of about 1,000 industrial companies for both years, for a total of 1,992 observations.[41] Company selection was based on sales and assets within the country. Countrywide proportions were based on quantitative factors such as market capitalization and gross national product and on factors such as growth patterns and the importance and relative position of a country in the global economic scenario. The companies selected represent a cross section of various industry groups. According to CIFAR, most of the "leading" industrial companies from each country are included.

Eighty-five annual report variables were used to construct the overall annual report score.[42] Data for all of the variables were extracted directly from annual reports. CIFAR's annual report variables are divided into seven broad groups: general information, income statement, balance sheet, funds/cash flow statement, accounting policies, stockholders' information, and supplementary information (see the following discussion). Within each group, the percentage availability of the variable in the annual report of the company was computed. If a particular company did not disclose data, it was given 0 points for a given variable. If the disclosure of a particular item was not applicable (e.g., disclosing exports is not required if there are no exports), CIFAR reduced the denominator for percentage purposes by 1. Similarly, for companies with no share capital, such as government-owned companies or mutually held companies, stockholders' information was not considered for ranking and analysis. Thus, a given company was *not penalized for not disclosing nonapplicable items.*

Not all seven disclosure subgroups or detailed disclosure items are likely to be equally important to analysts in forecasting earnings.[43] For example, it is plausible that analysts care less about the comprehensiveness of the income statement than extensive note disclosures.[44] Similarly, detailed items such as address or fiscal year-end are likely not as important as segment information or MD&A (all in General information). Including these potentially less relevant disclosures reduces the power of the tests reported in the article.

Quality and reliability of CIFAR data

Cooke and Wallace [1989] discuss the challenges in measuring financial disclosure. According to these authors, the quality of indexes depends on their reliability (whether the results can be replicated by other researchers) and validity (whether the index scores have any meaning as a measure of information disclosure). Healy and Palepu [2001] argue that although "self-constructed" measures of disclosures such as CIFAR's increase the confidence that the measure truly captures what is intended, there is necessarily judgment involved, and hence, findings may be difficult to replicate. It is thus important to test the quality and reliability of the CIFAR disclosure data used in this study.

Several studies use CIFAR data and several others rely on CIFAR's descriptions of accounting practices in various countries (e.g., Blaine [1994], Salter and Niswander [1995]). Cooke and Wallace [1989] audit the CIFAR database and conclude that no biases or errors were present in the data. Recently, the CIFAR index is used extensively in the finance and economics literature (e.g., Rajan and Zingales [1998], Carlin and Mayer [Forthcoming], La Porta *et al.* [1997]). Bushman and Smith [2001, p. 312] describe the CIFAR index as an "obvious candidate for the quality of the

List of CIFAR Annual Report Variables

A: General information
Address/Telephone/Fax/Telex
Product Segment
Geographic Segment
Management Information
Subsidiaries Information
Future Plans/Chairman or CEO's
Statement
Number of Employees
Fiscal Year-End

B: Income statement
Consolidated Income Statement
Cost of Goods Sold
Complete Income Statement
Sales
Selling, General and Administrative
Expenses
Operating Income
Foreign Exchange Gains/Losses
Extraordinary Gains/Losses
Income Tax Expense
Minority Interest
Net Income Reported

C: Balance sheet
Complete Balance Sheet
Current Assets Separated from
Fixed Assets
Current Liability Separated from
LT Liability
Owners' Equity Separated from
Liability
Separation of Non-Equity
Reserves and
Retained Earnings
Cash and Cash Equivalents
Accounts Receivable
Inventories
Current Assets
Fixed Assets on Asset Side
Goodwill and Other Intangibles
Total Assets Can Be Derived
Shareholders' Equity Changes
Appropriation of Retained
Earnings

D: Funds flow/cash flow
Funds Flow Statement
Complete Funds Flow Statement
Funds from Operations
Funds Definition
Cash Flow Statement

E: Accounting policies
Accounting Standards
Financial Statements Cost Basis
50% Long-Term Investments
Starting Point for Funds Statement
Research & Development Costs
Pension Costs
Reasons for Extraordinary Items
Inventory Costing Method
20% Long-Term Investments
21–50% Long-Term Investments
Acquisition Method
Accounting for Goodwill
Deferred Taxes
Outside Manager of Pension Funds
Long-Term Financial Leases
Foreign Currency Translation Method
Foreign Currency Translation
Gains/Losses
Discretionary Reserves
Minority Interest
Contingent Liabilities

F: Stockholders' information
Dividends per Share
Earnings per Share
Number of Shares Outstanding
Multiple Shares
Par Value
Total Dividends
Stock Split/Dividend/Rights Issues
Stock Price
Stock Exchange Listing
Volume Traded
Diluted Earnings Per Share
Quarterly/Interim Dividends
Changes in Capital
Different Div. for Multiple Classes
of Shares
EPS for Multiple Classes of Shares
Significant Shareholders
Composition of Shareholdings

G: Supplementary information
Earnings per Share Numerator
Earnings per Share Denominator
Notes to Accounts
Disclosure of Subsequent Events
Remuneration of Directors and Officers
Research & Development Costs
Capital Expenditure
List of Board Members and Their
Affiliations
Exports; Financial Summary

financial accounting regime." According to Salter [1998], the strengths of the CIFAR data are (1) it is based on actual annual reports, (2) the data have been audited by external sources, (3) the information is clearly provided, and (4) the data are available for three periods (1991, 1993, and 1995), although firm-level data are only included in the two most recent reports.[45] In addition to relying on these sources, I have attempted to verify further the validity of the disclosure scores.

I conduct extensive validity tests of the CIFAR data (see Hope [2001]). For example, I compare rankings by country with country-specific sources. For the United States, I compare the overall CIFAR scores against Botosan's [1997] annual report scores. Our samples contain only 23 firms in common, and Botosan's sample is from a slightly earlier period. The correlation between Botosan's scores and CIFAR's supplementary information index is 0.45 (with a p-value of .03).[46] For 21 Swiss firms, the correlation between CIFAR's total disclosure scores and the annual report ratings by the Swiss Financial Analyst Federation for the same sample period (Caramanolis-Cotelli et al. [1999]) is 0.65 (with a p-value of .001). As further anecdotal evidence based on the Norwegian firms in the sample, all of the 1990–1995 winners of the Best Annual Report (*Farmandprisen*) are above the mean and median for CIFAR's total annual report disclosure scores.[47]

I also conduct validity tests of subcomponents of the CIFAR scores. Frost and Ramin [1997] investigate disclosures of accounting policies in five countries: France, Germany, Japan, United Kingdom, and United States. The rankings of the five countries by CIFAR and Frost and Ramin are identical with one exception. In addition, I obtain 21 annual reports of Norwegian firms from the Norwegian Corporate Registry and compare my scoring of accounting policy disclosures against CIFAR's. For most of the companies the difference in assigned score is small. Although my median and mean scores are higher than CIFAR's, the differences are not significant. The correlation between the two sets of scores is 0.82 (significant at less than the 1% level).

Although CIFAR employed analysts from several countries, they would arguably be better able to consistently compare disclosure levels *within* a country than across countries. Because of this possibility, in an earlier version of this article I used disclosure scores from which country means had been subtracted. Results similar to those reported obtain with this alternative specification. I conclude from the foregoing tests that the quality and reliability of the CIFAR data are satisfactory.

Acknowledgements

I appreciate the helpful comments on various versions of this paper by Joel Amernic, Hollis Ashbaugh, Ray Ball (editor), Sudipta Basu, Jeff Callen, Bjørn Joørgensen, Peter Pope (referee), Beverly Walther, and participants at the 2001 EIASM Workshop on Accounting and Regulation, 2002 European Accounting Association Meeting, 2002 *Journal of Accounting Research* conference, 2002 Canadian Academic Accounting Association meeting, and 2002 American Accounting Association annual meeting. All errors are my own. I gratefully acknowledge the financial support of the Norwegian School of Economics and Business Administration. I thank IBES International Inc. for providing earnings forecast data.

Notes

1 The benefit of using country-level rather than firm-level disclosure scores is that it can increase the sample size significantly and potentially eliminate some noise in firm-level measures.

2 As discussed in section 5, earnings timeliness should be negatively related to earnings predictability. The hypotheses in this paper are thus conditional on timeliness (and other factors) as described in section 5.

3 However, I attempt to control for country-level variations in earnings surprise management (see section 5).

4 Lang and Lundholm [1996, p. 486] find only limited (no) evidence that changes in firms' disclosure policies (analyst following) cause changes in analyst following (firms' disclosure policies).

5 Analyst services have both a demand and a supply side. On the one hand, expanded disclosure, such as more refined segment disclosure, potentially enables analysts to create valuable new information and hence increases the demand for analyst services. On the other hand, disclosure could preempt analysts' ability to distribute managers' private information to investors, leading to a decline in demand (e.g., Healy and Palepu [2001], Hope [2003]). The net effect of these (and other) forces is theoretically ambiguous.

6 Basu, Hwang, and Jan [1998] and Hope [2001] discuss the relation between forecast accuracy and extent of choice in accounting in detail.

7 The effect of such manipulation on forecast accuracy depends on the nature of the manipulation. Manipulation that involves smoothing earnings is likely to be positively related to forecast accuracy, whereas other types of manipulation (such as switching between methods to maximize bonus payments) have unclear relations with forecast accuracy.

8 Table 1 summarizes the variables used in the paper.

9 The difficulty in measuring enforcement arises in part because enforcement takes different forms in different countries. As Ball [2001, p. 128] puts it, "The accounting infrastructure complements the overall economic, legal and political infrastructure in all countries."

10 According to Ali and Hwang [2000], data on audit fees for *all* accounting firms are not available.

11 However, the potential payoffs from engaging in such behavior can also vary across countries.

12 La Porta *et al.* [1998] form their index by adding one point when each of the following is true: (1) shareholders can vote by mail, (2) shareholders are not required to deposit their shares before shareholder meetings, (3) cumulative voting is allowed, (4) the minimum percentage of share capital that entitles a shareholder to call an extraordinary shareholder meeting is less than 5%, and (5) minority shareholders are allowed to make legal claims against the directors (La Porta *et al.* [1998, pp. 1127–28]).

13 I also have finer partitionings of audit firm type, but using these does not affect the reported results. Today's Big 4 audit firms were the Big 8 and then Big 6 during the sample period.

14 The stock exchange variable summarizes all the major stock exchanges on which a firm was listed during the sample period. Listings on domestic exchanges, European (other than London), London, Asian, and American listings are recorded. For U.S. firms, listings on London Stock Exchange and Tokyo Stock Exchange have been recorded in addition to domestic listings. Listings on U.S. exchanges are given weight of 1.5, whereas all other listings, including ADRs (without exchange listing) are given weight 1, and the scores for each firm are summed.

15 I have inverted Basu *et al.*'s [1998] scoring so that a higher value means greater choice among accounting methods.

16 Using mean EPS (rather than stock price) as a scaling factor does not materially affect results.

17 I thank Peter Pope for suggesting this characterization of earnings predictability.

18 Brown and Higgins [2001] compute earnings surprise management as the ratio of small (5%) positive earnings surprises to small negative earnings surprises.

19 Pope and Walker [1999] formally model asymmetric timeliness and empirically examine delayed recognition of good and bad news. They show that the results in Ball, Kothari, and Robin [2000] may be sensitive to the choice of earnings number used. Specifically, Pope and Walker find that the difference in timeliness of earnings between U.S. and U.K firms reported by Ball, Kothari, and Robin depends on whether earnings are measured before or after extraordinary items.

20 Similar to Ball, Kothari, and Robin [2000], Nobes [1998, pp. 19–21] argues that the distinction between creditor/insider and equity/outsider countries is a key cause of international differences in financial reporting.

21 There is a mechanical relationship between earnings change and forecast accuracy because of the way they are defined. Excluding earnings change reduces the overall explanatory power of the tests but does not affect the significance of the test variables. Because of data limitations I cannot compute a time-series standard deviation of return on equity.

22 Financial analysts with proper training and experience may contribute to more effective enforcement of accounting standards by detecting irregularities and discussing these with management, writing about them in their investment reports, or both.

23 For example, Rees, Swanson, and Clement [2000] argue that some societies view employer-employee relationships like a family link. As a result, employees (such as financial analysts) may not have to demonstrate superior performance to keep their jobs.

24 Hofstede [1980], in a massive cross-cultural study of employees at a large multinational firm, finds significant national differences in work-related values. Hofstede defines four dimensions of culture that differ across countries. Uncertainty avoidance measures the degree to which a society feels uncomfortable with ambiguity and an uncertain future. Individualism (vs. collectivism) expresses a preference for a loosely knit social fabric or an independent, tightly knit fabric. Including either or both of Hofstede's other work-related values, power distance and masculinity, does not affect reported results.

25 Analysts' abilities might vary across countries and individuals. I include control variables (such as analyst following, firm size, industry, culture measures, and country dummies) that may pick up some of this variation. An implicit assumption in the paper is that any remaining variation in ability is not correlated with disclosures or enforcement. One source of variation in ability could be the nationality or location of the analysts making the forecasts, on which I do not have data. However, Capstaff, Paudyal, and Rees [1998] and Larran and Rees [1996] find no substantive differences in the behavior of the forecasts produced by local and foreign analysts for German and Spanish firms, respectively. Based on these findings, I assume that the location of the analyst providing the forecast is not important for this study.

26 Using a large number of sources (see note to table 1), I have been able to find firm-level financial data for all but 18 firms.

27 The enforcement index is significantly negatively correlated (−0.71 and −0.64) with measures of earnings discretion and income smoothing from Leuz, Nanda, and Wysocki [2001, table 2], suggesting that earnings management is more pervasive

in countries where the enforcement is low. Table 3 shows, however, that enforcement is positively correlated (0.60) with earnings surprise management from Brown and Higgins [2001]. I use the latter measure as a control variable as it (Leuz, Nanda, and Wysocki [2001]) is significantly negatively (positively) correlated with earnings change and positively correlated (negatively) with forecast accuracy, suggesting that the Brown and Higgins measure better captures the essence of managed earnings in my sample. Using either or both of Leuz, Nanda, and Wysocki's measures as controls does not affect any inferences in this paper.

28 CIFAR selected the "leading industrial companies" in each country (see Appendix). Consistent with its claim, mean (median) market capitalization of U.S. sample firms in 1993 was $9.5 billion (4.6 billion), compared with $6.6 billion (3.4 billion) for the S&P 500 and $0.9 billion (86 million) for all Compustat firms. Mean (median) return on equity was 0.07 (0.11) for U.S. sample firms, 0.13 (0.13) for the S&P 500, and 0.00 (0.08) for all Compustat firms. Mean (median) leverage (i.e., total liabilities divided by total assets) was 0.66 (0.66) for U.S. sample firms, 0.63 (0.63) for the S&P 500, and 0.54 (0.55) for all Compustat firms. Hence, U.S. sample firms are comparable with S&P 500 firms, but not necessarily with the universe of U.S. firms. Because of data limitations, it is difficult to make similar comparisons for non-U.S. firms.

29 Specifically, if two observations for a given firm are available, I use only the most recent observation (from CIFAR [1995]). The results are similar when only the oldest observations are included.

30 Similarly, when estimating the regression separately for common law and code law countries, disclosures are significant in both regressions with p-values of 1% and 4%, respectively.

31 Lang and Lundholm [1996] find a significant and positive association between total AIMR ratings and forecast accuracy for a sample of U.S. firms. They do not find a significant association between annual report ratings and forecast accuracy when they also include other publications and investor relations. Because I use CIFAR rather than AIMR, I do not have data on the latter two variables.

32 Previous research investigates the roles of the legal environment (e.g., Ball, Kothari, and Robin [2000]). Model 3 shows that the estimated coefficient on common law is not significant, whereas enforcement remains significant. Similarly, when I replace my aggregate enforcement measure with an indicator variable for common law, the estimated coefficient on legal system is insignificant (p-value of .85). These results suggest that my enforcement measure captures more than mere variations in legal environment.

33 I have also considered richer models for explaining variations in disclosure levels, with both more firm-level and more country-level variables. I choose to present the more parsimonious model as results are not affected by the inclusion or exclusion of the additional explanatory variables.

34 As with OLS (model 4), the 3SLS results are robust to only including one observation per firm.

35 In model 2, Analyst following and Choice are indicator variables that take the value 1 if above median, and 0 otherwise.

36 Panel C of table 2 shows that analyst following varies by country. Consistent results obtain when analyst following is country-mean adjusted.

37 In a previous version of this paper, I reported univariate tests of H3 and H4. The univariate tests support both the hypotheses at the 1% level.

38 In his discussion of this paper, Pope asserts that the association between enforcement and accuracy is "largely due to the interaction between enforcement

and choice." As can be seen from tables 4 and 5, however, enforcement is positive and significant both with and without choice included.

39 As expected, the significance of the disclosure variable is reduced when only month 12 forecasts are considered (with a one-sided p-value of 0.04 compared with 0.02 for months 4–12). The reduction in significance is consistent with annual report information being relatively less important to analysts when the release of the next period's earnings is closer.

40 Source: CIFAR [1993, 1995], particularly CIFAR [1995, pp. 357–60].

41 Specifically, in the CIFAR 1993 and 1995 editions, 986 and 1,006 firms were included, respectively, and 558 firms were included in both years, for a total of 1,992 firm-years (1,434 firms).

42 For fiscal year 1991, the index was based on 90 annual report variables.

43 Hope [2003b] explores the CIFAR subgroups whether the subgroups of CIFAR disclosures are equally important to analysts (as reflected in analyst following).

44 Consistent with this contention, income statement disclosures have the lowest correlation with forecast accuracy of the seven CIFAR groups. Results are stronger than those reported when the disclosure metric excludes income statement disclosure.

45 CD-ROM PROFESSIONAL [1992] has the following comment on the quality of data provided by CIFAR: "The quality and care given to the data is of a high standard."

46 Of the various categories of CIFAR disclosure scores, the supplementary information index (the average of general information, accounting policies, stock-holders' information, and supplementary information) corresponds most closely to Botosan's index. The correlation between CIFAR total scores and Botosan's scores is positive but not significant at conventional levels (correlation of 0.26, p-value of 0.23).

47 In addition, Frost, Gordon, and Hayes [2002] report that their country-level disclosure scores from 1998 (based on 12 measures) are significantly and positively correlated (0.32) with CIFAR country-level scores from 1993 (i.e., from CIFAR [1995]).

References

ADREM, A. H. "Essays on Disclosure Practices in Sweden—Causes and Effects." Unpubilshed doctoral dissertation, Lund University, Sweden, 1999.

AIMR CORPORATE DISCLOSURE SURVEY. A report to AIMR. St. Louis, MO: Fleishman-Hillard Research, 2000.

ALI, A., AND L.-S. HWANG. "Country-Specific Factors Related to Financial Reporting and the Value Relevance of Accounting Data." *Journal of Accounting Research* 38 (2000): 1–22.

AMERICAN INSTITUTE OF CERTIFIED PUBLIC ACCOUNTANTS (AICPA), SPECIAL COMMITTEE ON FINANCIAL REPORTING (A.K.A. JENKINS COMMITTEE REPORT). *Improving Business Reporting—A Customer Focus. Meeting the Information needs of Investors and Creditors.* New York: AICPA, 1994.

ASHBAUGH, H., AND M. PINCUS. "Domestic Accounting Standards, International Accounting Standards, and the Predictability of Earnings." *Journal of Accounting Research* 39(2001):417–34.

BALL, R. "Infrastructure Requirements for an Economically Efficient System of Public Financial Reporting and Disclosure." *Brookings-Wharton Papers on Financial Services* (2001): 127–69.

BALL, R.; S. P. KOTHARI; AND A. ROBIN. "The Effect of International Institutional Factors on Properties of Accounting Earnings." *Journal of Accounting and Economics* 29 (2000): 1–51.

BARTH, M. E.; J. A. ELLIOTT, AND M. W. FINN. "Market Rewards Associated with Patterns of Increasing Earnings." *Journal of Accounting Research* 37 (1999): 387–413.

BASU, S. "The Conservatism Principle and the Asymmetric Timeliness of Earnings." *Journal of Accounting and Economics* 24 (1997): 3–37.

BASU, S.; L. HWANG; AND C. L. JAN. "International Variation in Accounting Measurement Rules and Analysts' Earnings Forecast Errors." *Journal of Business Finance and Accounting* 25 (1998): 1207–47.

BECKER, C. L.; M. L. DEFOND; J. JIAMBALVO; AND K. R. SUBRAMANYAM. "The Effect of Audit Quality on Earnings Management." *Contemporary Accounting Research* 15 (1998): 1–24.

BENEISH, M. D., AND M. E. VARGUS. "Insider Trading, Earnings Management and Earnings Quality." Working paper, Indiana University and University of Southern California, 2000.

BERCEL, A. "Consensus Expectations and International Equity Returns." *Financial Analysts Journal* 50 (1994): 76–80.

BHATTACHARYA, U., AND H. DAOUK. "The World Pricing of Insider Trading." *Journal of Finance* 57 (2002): 75–108.

BLACK, E. L.; K. F. SELLERS; AND T. S. MANLY. "Earnings Management Using Asset Sales: An International Study of Countries Allowing Noncurrent Asset Revaluation." *Journal of Business Finance and Accounting* 25 (1998): 1287–1317.

BLAINE, M. Comparing the Profitability of Firms in Germany, Japan, and the United States. *Management International Review* 34 (1994): 125–48.

BOTOSAN, C. A. "Disclosure Level and the Cost of Equity Capital." *Accounting Review* 72 (1997): 323–49.

BROWN, L. D., AND H. N. HIGGINS. "Managing Earnings Surprises in the U.S. Versus 12 Other Countries." *Journal of Accounting and Public Policy* 20 (2001): 371–98.

BUSHMAN, R. M., AND A. J. SMITH. "Financial Accounting Information and Corporate Governance." *Journal of Accounting and Economics* 32 (2001): 237–333.

CAPSTAFF, J.; K. PAUDYAL; AND W. REES. "Analysts' Forecasts of German Firms' Earnings: A Comparative Analysis." *Journal of International Financial Management and Accounting* 9 (1998): 83–116.

CAPSTAFF, J.; K. PAUDYAL; AND W. REES. "Revisions of Earnings Forecasts and Security Returns: Evidence from Three Countries." Working paper, University of Strathclyde, University of Durham, and University of Glasgow, 2000.

CARLIN, W., AND C. MAYER. "Finance, Investment and Growth." *Journal of Financial Economics* (Forthcoming).

CENTER FOR INTERNATIONAL FINANCIAL ANALYSIS & RESEARCH (CIFAR). *Global Company Handbook.* All volumes. Princeton, NJ: CIFAR Publications, 1993.

CENTER FOR INTERNATIONAL FINANCIAL ANALYSIS & RESEARCH (CIFAR). *International Accounting and Auditing Trends.* Volumes I and II. Princeton, NJ: CIFAR Publications, 1990, 1993, and 1995.

CHANG, L. S., AND K. S. MOST. *The Perceived Usefulness of Financial Statements for Investors' Decisions.* Gainesville: University Presses of Florida, 1985.

COOKE, T. E., AND R. S. O. WALLACE. Global Surveys of Corporate Disclosure Practices and Audit Firms: A Review Essay. *Accounting and Business Research* 20 (1989): 47–58.

ENG, L. L., AND H. K. TEO. "The Relation Between Annual Report Disclosures, Analysts' Earnings Forecasts and Analyst Following: Evidence from Singapore." *Pacific Accounting Review* 11 (2000): 219–39.

FEDERATION DES EXPERTS COMPTABLES EUROPEENS (FEE). Discussion paper on a financial reporting strategy within Europe, 1999.

FRANCIS, J. R.; E. L. MAYDEW; AND H. C. SPARKS. "The role of Big 6 Auditors in the Credible Reporting of Accruals." *Auditing: A Journal of Practice and Theory* 18 (1999): 17–34.

FROST, C. A.; E. GORDON; AND A. HAYES. "Stock Exchange Disclosure and Market Liquidity: An Analysis of 50 International Exchanges." Working paper, Rutgers University and Ohio State University, 2002.

FROST, C. A., AND K. P. RAMIN. "Corporate Financial Disclosure: A Global Assessment" in *International Accounting and Finance Handbook*, Second edition, edited by F. D. S. CHOI. New York: Wiley, 1997: 18.1–18.33.

GEBHARDT, G. "The Evolution of Global Standards in Accounting" in *Brookings-Wharton Papers on Financial Services*, edited by R. Litan and A. Santomero. Brookings Institution Press, 2000: Washington, D.C.: 341–68.

GRAY, S. J. "Towards a Theory of Cultural Influence on the Development of Accounting Systems Internationally." *Abacus* 24 (1988): 1–15.

HAUSMAN, J. "Specification Tests in Econometrics." *Econometrica* 46 (1978): 1251–73.

HEALY, P. M., AND K. G. PALEPU. "Information Asymmetry, Corporate Disclosure and the Capital Markets: A Review of the Empirical Disclosure Literature." *Journal of Accounting and Economics* 31 (2001): 405–40.

HEALY, P. M., AND J. M. WHALEN. "A Review of the Earnings Management Literature and Its Implications for Standard Setting." *Accounting Horizons* 13 (1999): 365–83.

HOFSTEDE, G. *Cultur's Consequences: International Differences in Work Related Values.* Beverly Hills, CA: Sage, 1980.

HOLLAND, J. "Private Disclosure and Financial Reporting." *Accounting and Business Research* 28 (1998): 255–69.

HOPE, O.-K. "A Study of International Variations in the Financial Reporting Environment, Disclosure Practices and Analysts' Forecasts." Unpublished doctoral dissertation, Northwestern University, 2001.

HOPE, O.-K. "Disclosure Practices, Enforcement of Accounting Standards, and Analysts' Forecast Accuracy: An International Study." *Journal of Accounting Researcch* (Supplement 2003).

HOPE, O.-K. "Accounting Policy Disclosures and Analysts' Forecasts." *Contemporary Accounting Research* 20 (Forthcoming, 2003a).

HOPE, O.-K. "Analyst Following and the Influence of Disclosure Components, IPOs and Ownership Concentration." *Asia-Pacific Journal of Accounting and Economics* (Forthcoming, 2003b).

HOPE, O.-K. "Firm-Level Disclosures and the Relative Roles of Culture and Legal Origin." *Journal of International Financial Management and Accounting* 14 (Forthcoming, 2003c).

HUNG, M. "Accounting Standards and Value Relevance of Earnings: An International Analysis." *Journal of Accounting and Economics* 30 (2000): 401–20.

HWANG, L. S.; C. L. JAN; AND S. BASU. "Loss Firms and Analysts' Earnings Forecast Errors." *Journal of Financial Statement Analysis* 1 (1996): 18–30.

JACCARD, J.; R. TURRISI; AND C. K. WAN. *Interaction Effects in Multiple Regression.* Newbury Park, CA: Sage, 1990.

JAGGI, B., AND P. Y. LOW. "Impact of Culture, Market Forces, and Legal System on Financial Disclosures." *International Journal of Accounting* 35 (2000): 495–519.

KHANNA, T.; K. G. PALEPU; AND J. J. CHANG. "Analyst Activity Around the World." Working paper, Harvard University, 2000.

KOTHARI, S. P. "The Role of Financial Reporting in Reducing Financial Risks in the Market" in *Building an Infrastructure for Financial Stability*, edited by E. S. Rosengren and J. S. Jordan. Federal Reserve Bank of Boston Conference Series No. 44, 2000: 89–102.

LANG, M. H., AND R. J. LUNDHOLM. "Cross-Sectional Determinants of Analyst Ratings of Corporate Disclosures." *Journal of Accounting Research* 31 (1993): 246–71.

LANG, M. H., AND R. J. LUNDHOLM. "Corporate Disclosure Policy and Analyst Behavior." *Accounting Review* 71 (1996): 467–92.

LA PORTA, R.; F. LOPEZ-DE-SILANES; AND A. SCHLEIFER. "Corporate Ownership Around the World." *Journal of Finance* 54 (1999): 471–517.

LA PORTA, R.; F. LOPEZ-DE-SILANES; A. SHLEIFER; AND R. W. VISHNY. "Legal Determinants of External Finance." *Journal of Finance* 52 (1997): 1131–50.

LA PORTA, R.; F. LOPEZ-DE-SILANES; A. SHLEIFER; AND R. W. VISHNY. "Law and Finance." *Journal of Political Economy* 106 (1998): 1113–55.

LARRAN, J. M., AND W. REES. "Un analysis empirico de los pronosticos de los analistas financieros en el caso espanol." Working paper, University of Cadiz, 1996.

LEUZ, C.; D. NANDA; AND P. WYSOCKI. "Investor Protection and Earnings Management: An International Comparison." Working paper, University of Pennsylvania, University of Michigan, and MIT, 2001.

LEVINE, R., AND S. ZERVOS. "What Have We Learned About Policy and Growth from Cross-Country Regressions?" *American Economic Review* 83 (1993): 426–43.

LYS, T., AND L. SOO. "Analysts' Forecast Precision as a Response to Competition." *Journal of Accounting, Auditing and Finance* 10 (1995): 751–65.

MARSTON, C., AND P. SHRIVES. "A Review of Empirical Research into Financial Disclosure." Working paper, University of Northumbria at Newcastle, 1996.

MEEK, G. K.; C. B. ROBERTS; AND S. J. GRAY. "Factors Influencing Voluntary Annual Report Disclosures by U.S., U.K. and Continental European Multinational Corporations." *Journal of International Business Studies* 26 (1995): 555–72.

MUELLER, G. G.; H. GERNON; AND G. MEEK. *Accounting: An International Perspective*, Third edition. New York: Business One Irwin, 1994.

NOBES, C. "Causes of International Differences." In *Comparative International Accounting*, edited by C. Nobes and R. Parker. Prentice Hall Europe, 1998, London: 15–29.

PEASNELL, K. V.; P. F. POPE; AND S. YOUNG. "Accrual Management to Meet Earnings Targets: U.K. Evidence Pre- and Post-Cadbury." *British Accounting Review* 32 (2000): 415–45.

Pope, P. F., and M. Walker. "International Differences in the Timeliness, Conservatism, and Classification of Earnings." *Journal of Accounting Research* 37 (1999): 53–87.

Rajan, R., and L. Zingales. "Financial Dependence and Growth." *American Economic Review* 88 (1998): 559–86.

Rees, L.; E. P. Swanson; and M. Clement. "The Influence of Corporate Governance, Culture, and Income Predictability on the Characteristics that Distinguish Superior Analysts." Working paper, Texas A&M University and University of Texas, 2000.

Salter, S. B. "Corporate Financial Disclosure in Emerging Markets: Does Economic Development Matter?" *International Journal of Accounting* 33 (1998): 211–34.

Salter, S. B., and F. Niswander. Cultural Influence on the Development of Accounting Systems Internationally: A Test of Gray's (1988) Theory. *Journal of International Business Studies* 26 (1995): 379–97.

Saudagaran, S. M., and J. G. Diga. "Financial Reporting in Emerging Capital Markets: Characteristics and Policy Issues." *Accounting Horizons* 11 (1997): 41–64.

Saudagaran, S. M., and G. K. Meek. "A Review of Research on the Relationship Between International Capital Markets and Financial Reporting by Multinational Firms." *Journal of Accounting Literature* 16 (1997): 127–59.

Schipper, K. "Commentary on Analysts' Forecasts." *Accounting Horizons* 5 (1991): 105–21.

Securities and Exchange Commission (SEC). *SEC Concept Release on International Accounting Standards.* SEC, 2000, Washington, D.C..

Seetharaman, A.; F. A. Gul; and S. G. Lynn. "Litigation Risk and Audit Fees: Evidence from UK Firms Cross-Listed on US Markets." *Journal of Accounting and Economics* 33 (2002): 91–115.

Simunic, D. A. "The Pricing of Financial Audit Services—Theory and Evidence." *Journal of Accounting Research* 18 (1980): 161–90.

Sunder, S. *Theory of Accounting and Control.* Cincinnati, OH: South-Western Publishing, 1997.

Vergoossen, R. G. A. "The Use and Perceived Importance of Annual Reports by Investment Analysts in the Netherlands." *European Accounting Review* 2/3 (1993): 219–44.

White, H. "A Heteroskedasticity-Consistent Covariance Matrix Estimator and a Direct Test for Heteroskedasticity." *Econometrica* 48 (1980): 817–38.

Part 2

INFLUENCES ON ACCOUNTING

5

IMPORTING AND EXPORTING ACCOUNTING

The British experience[1]

Robert H. Parker

Source: Anthony G. Hopwood (ed.) *International Pressures for Accounting Change*, Englewood Cliffs, NJ: Prentice-Hall, 1989, pp. 7–29.

Accounting techniques, institutions and concepts are all capable of being imported and exported from one country to another. The following discussion considers, by way of three case studies, the British experience of such imports and exports and in particular the way in which the British have imported double entry bookkeeping (a technique) and have exported professional accountancy (an institution) and a 'true and fair view' (a concept).

The analysis focusses on the British experience for two reasons. First, it is the one with which the writer is most familiar. Secondly, and more importantly, British accounting history is not just of parochial interest. From being, in the sixteenth century, distinctly underdeveloped in mercantile accounting, Britain became in the nineteenth the pioneer of modern professional accountancy. In the twentieth century, however, the United States has become the pace-setter in many aspects of accounting.

The scope of the discussion has been limited as follows. First, there is no consideration of which accounting techniques, institutions or concepts *ought* to be transferred from one country to another and how this can best be done (Seidler, 1969; Needles, 1976). There is no assumption that one set of techniques, institutions or concepts is inherently better than another.

Secondly, countries are taken as a whole, with no attempt to distinguish between early and late adopters of an import. This means that the emphasis is placed on economic rather than sociological variables (cf. Griliches, 1960 in Rosenberg, 1971, page 266). Thirdly, the analysis is not concerned with imports which may be regarded as choices among accounting policies and analysed as part of a contracting process between managers and owners. (The literature in this area is summarized in Watts and Zimmerman, 1986).

The discussion is concerned with the international transfer of accounting technology (AT) in its widest sense. AT differs from physical productive technology in that it is non-proprietary (Taylor and Turley, 1985, page 3) and more specific to particular countries (Seidler, 1969, pages 36–7).

Each case study is built around the following questions:

1   What was available for import?
2   Who were the importers and exporters? Were they active or passive?
3   How did the importers find out about the potential import?
4   How did importers and exporters assess the costs and benefits?
5   How, if at all, were imports adapted, i.e. made appropriate to an environment different from that of the exporter?
6   How were problems of terminology dealt with?

Double entry bookkeeping

Double entry bookkeeping is a technique of recording economic events which was evolved by merchants in the Italian city states from the end of the thirteenth century onwards. It is not the only such technique and until about the year 1500 it was not used outside Italy except by Italian merchants who had established branches of their firms in other countries, including England (de Roover, 1956).

In principle, techniques are easier to import than institutions or concepts since there are presumably no cultural, social or political costs or benefits attached to them, but British merchants, the potential importers, did not start to adopt double entry until the sixteenth century.

To adopt a technique one must first find out about it. This was relatively easy since Italian merchants made no attempt to keep double entry a trade secret. On the other hand they were not active exporters. Italian cultural influence was strong throughout Europe, including England, during this period (as the settings of many of Shakespeare's plays attest) but both England and Scotland were influenced more by France and the Low Countries. The main commercial link with continental Europe was Antwerp, the port through which most English exports passed in the sixteenth and seventeenth centuries (Davis, 1973).

The ways in which British merchants could obtain a knowledge of double entry can be listed as follows:

1   Reading a manuscript or book
    (a) in a language other than English
    (b) in English

2   Learning from a native teacher in Britain
3   Learning from a foreign merchant or teacher resident in Britain
4   Learning abroad from a foreign merchant or teacher.

There is evidence that all these sources were used. Textbooks on double entry were published in Italy from 1494 (Pacioli's *Summa*) and in the Netherlands, France and Britain from 1543 onwards. A book which illustrates the way in which knowledge of doubt entry spread from country to country is Jan Ympyn's *Nieuwe Instructie . . .* published in Antwerp in Flemish (Dutch) and French (as the *Nouvelle Instruction . . .*) in 1543 and in London in 1547 (as *A Notable and Very Excellente Woorke . . .*). In his Prologue the author states that his book is based on a translation of a work in Italian by one Juan Paulo di Bianchi. No published work by an author of this name is known and there has been much speculation about the existence of a manuscript which may have been used not only by Ympyn but also by Pacioli (Yamey, 1967). Appended to Ympyn's work, unlike Pacioli's or Oldcastle's, is an illustrative set of books which, it has been plausibly suggested, may have been based on Ympyn's own business. The long title of the English version states that the book has been:

> Translated with great diligence out of the Italian toung into Dutche, and out of Dutche, into French, and now out of French into Englishe.

It is clear from this (and other similar evidence) that knowledge of double entry was made available throughout sixteenth century Europe through both books and manuscripts; that these were translated into various languages; and that they often contained illustrative sets of books (the first to do so was an Italian work by Tagliente published in 1525).

For merchants and their apprentices who needed oral as well as written instruction, teachers were available, many of whom were also textbook writers. Sixteenth century English examples (with the dates of their books in brackets) include Hugh Oldcastle (1543), James Peele (1553, 1569) and John Mellis (1588).

It is also possible that some British merchants learned double entry from foreign merchants or teachers resident in Britain. The earliest double entry or near double entry record written up in England which has survived is an account book (1305–8) of the London branch of the Gallerani company of Siena. There is no evidence, however, that the Gallerani had any influence on indigenous English accounting records (Nobes, 1982). More interesting in the history of *English* accounting are the four ledgers (1436–9) bound together in one volume of the London branch of the Borromei, a firm of merchant bankers with its main office in Milan. According to Kats (1926) the textbooks of James Peele have a number of features to be found in the

Borromei ledgers but not in Pacioli. Kojima (1980, page 63) has suggested that Oldcastle, a citizen and shearman (i.e. draper) acquainted with wool merchants, might have worked in an Italian firm or might have learnt the Italian language or Italian bookkeeping from contacts with Italian merchants. This, while plausible, is, of course, no more than conjecture.

It is possible that many British accountants learned more accounting from practical experience than they learned from books and teachers. The double entry or near double entry records of the sixteenth century which have survived suggest that English merchants may have gained such experience overseas (Ramsey, 1956). These account books include the ledger of Thomas Howell, a member of the Drapers' Company resident and trading in Spain; the ledger of John Smythe, a leading merchant of Bristol; the journal of Sir Thomas Gresham; the ledger of John Johnson, a merchant of the Staple at Calais (a French port which was an English possession from 1347 to 1558); and ledgers and a journal of Thomas Laurence, a Merchant Adventurer. Howell's ledger was written up in Spain; Smythe also had strong Spanish connections (Vanes, 1974). Gresham spent much of his career in the Netherlands. Johnson's business was in Calais; Laurence traded overseas.

One of the earliest English language texts, John Weddington's *A Breffe Instruction* . . . (1567) was even published in Antwerp rather than London. Weddington was an English merchant resident in Antwerp and at one time an agent of Gresham. His book differs in many ways from others of the time and it 'is highly probable that Weddington encountered the particular arrangement of the records, as taught by him in his book, in some business firm or firms in Antwerp' (Yamey, 1958, page 124).

There is no record of the use of double entry in Scotland before the seventeenth century, the first text of double entry, Colinson's *Idea Rationaria*, being published as late as 1683. The books (1696–1707) of the ill-fated Darien Scheme ('The company of Scotland trading to Africa and the Indies') were, it has been said, kept 'in exact concordance with the methods . . . in the schoolmasters' lesson-books' by a 'clerk who might have been Pacioli himself' (Row Fogo in Brown, 1905, page 157). In Scotland, textbooks were, of course readily available from England, but Dutch influence was also important. Colinson had lived and traded in the Netherlands, includes a Dutch quotation in his book, and dedicates it to the 'Lord Conservator of the Privileges of the Scots Nation in the 17 Provinces of the Netherlands . . .' (Parker, 1974).

It is clear from the above that British merchants in the sixteenth and seventeenth centuries had every opportunity to adopt double entry if they wished to do so. In fact it appears that double entry made slow headway and was not in widespread use until the nineteenth century (Yamey, 1977, page 17). It was only in that century that it ceased to be generally known as the 'Italian method' of bookkeeping: an indication perhaps that the import had been completed.

Such a slow adoption presumably reflects British merchants' assessment of the costs and benefits. It can be argued that Britain's stage of commercial development when double entry was first available for import was such that double entry was not an 'appropriate technique'. At the beginning of the sixteenth century, and for some time afterwards, England and Wales was 'a small poor country with a single-crop economy [wool]' (Kenyon, 1978, page 15). Scotland was even smaller and poorer. Nearly two centuries later, however, (about 1780) London had become the commercial centre of Europe.

There is little direct evidence of how British merchants perceived the benefits of double entry. The textbook writers who, in order to sell their books were more likely to overestimate than to underestimate – saw double entry as creating order from chaos by providing complete, integrated and interlocking records within a self-correcting system; better knowledge of, and hence control of, amounts owed and owing and of merchandise; and better profit calculations on individual ventures. They placed little emphasis on profit calculations and measures of wealth related to the whole enterprise (Winjum, 1972, pages 239–40). Yamey (1977, page 17) finds little evidence in pre-nineteenth century British accounting practice of systematic income measurement and asset valuation. Balancing was highly irregular and merchants more usually prepared inventories of their fortunes at irregular intervals. The profit and loss account was used as a place to which detailed but unwanted information could be removed. Winjum (1972, Chapter 11) concludes that double entry was valued more for its ability to provide systematic and comprehensive recording than for its ability to provide accurate income determination.

It would appear that most British merchants did not, until the nineteenth century, require much of what double entry had to offer. Orderliness and control were of course worth having but could often be achieved without double entry. Interlocking and self-correcting records were not always regarded as worth the effort. Annual profit calculation and asset valuation were of little use in the absence of sophisticated capital markets and income tax collectors, neither of which, so far as most business enterprises were concerned, were present until the late nineteenth century. It was only then that the benefits of double entry were generally perceived to exceed the costs.

One problem that any importers of a technique, institution or concept must face is that of terminology, especially when importer and exporter do not share a common language. The importer has a number of options (Parker, 1984, page 119). He can: treat the foreign words as native words; change them into native words; invent new words in his native language; or use already existing native words. English writers on double entry mainly chose the second option, taking and adapting from Italian such words as journal, folio, capital (replacing stock), cash (replacing money) and bank. It is also possible that the word bookkeeping is an adaptation of the equivalent Dutch word (Parker, 1984, pages 114–16).

What can we conclude about the import of double entry into Britain? Double entry was a technique which reached British merchants without any active exporting on the part of its Italian inventors. It was adopted because of its merits but only to the extent that it was thought to be an appropriate technology and it thus spread only slowly. Although it was close trading ties with the Netherlands that first made British merchants aware of the technique, its Italian origins have left a lasting mark on English accounting terminology.

Professional accountancy

We turn next to professional accountancy. We may note first of all that this is a more difficult import or export than double entry because it is an institution rather than a technique. Acceptance of the existence of self-regulating professional organisations, especially when they act as qualifying associations independent of any government control, implies acceptance of a particular form of economic and social structure.

There was little need for professional accountancy in Britain before the nineteenth century. Previously, accounting was regarded simply as one of the necessary skills of a merchant. In the nineteenth century, however, the growth of large-scale organisations and in particular of the railways, the development of the limited liability company, the high rate of insolvencies, and the introduction of income taxation produced demands for insolvency, auditing, costing and tax services. These demands led to the emergence of specialist experts who came together to discuss common problems, to distinguish competent and honourable practitioners from incompetent and dishonourable ones, to raise their status and to protect their material interests. They endeavoured to achieve these aims by formal association (Parker, 1986).

The way in which this took place (the 'British model' of professional accountancy) can be deduced from Table 1 which lists the numerous professional accountancy bodies established during the period 1853 to 1919. Three characteristics of these bodies may be discerned:

1. Many were formed on a regional basis and there are indeed still three separate Institutes of Chartered Accountants in the British Isles: of Scotland, in England and Wales, and in Ireland (covering both the Republic of Ireland and Northern Ireland).
2. If, in the absence of government regulation, the founders of an association are allowed to decide who is to be allowed to join and who is not, those who are excluded are likely to consider themselves harshly treated and to go out and form their own association (which explains the present existence of a Chartered Association of Certified Accountants).

Table 1 Accountancy bodies formed in the British Isles: 1853–1919.

1853	Society of Accountants in Edinburgh (Royal charter 1854)[1]
1853	Institute of Accountants and Actuaries in Glasgow (royal charter 1855)
1867	Society of Accountants in Aberdeen[1]
1870	Incorporated Society of Liverpool Accountants[2]
1870	Institute of Accountants in London[2]
1871	Manchester Institute of Accountants[2]
1872	Society of Accountants in England[2]
1877	Sheffield Institute of Accountants[2]
1880	Institute of Chartered Accountants in England and Wales
1880	Scottish Institute of Accountants[3]
1885	Society of Accountants and Auditors[4]
1885	Corporate Treasurers' and Accountants' Institute[5]
1888	Institute of Chartered Accountants in Ireland
1891	Corporation of Accountants in Scotland[6]
1903	Institute of Certified Public Accountants[7]
1904	London Association of Accountants[6]
1905	Central Association of Accountants[8]
1919	Institute of Cost and Works Accountants[9]

Notes to Table 1
1 Merged to form Institute of Chartered Accountants of Scotland, 1951
2 Merged to form Institute of Chartered Accountants in England and Wales, 1880
3 Absorbed by the Society of Accountants and Auditors, 1899
4 Name changed to Society of Incorporated Accountants and Auditors, 1908; to Society of Incorporated Accountants, 1954; integrated into the English, Scottish and Irish Chartered Institutes, 1957.
5 Name changed to Institute of Municipal Treasurers and Accountants, 1901; to Chartered Institute of Public Finance and Accountancy, 1973.
6 Amalgamated in 1939 to form the Association of Certified and Corporate Accountants.
7 Amalgamated in 1941 with the Association of Certified and Corporate Accountants (from 1971 the Association of Certified Accountants and from 1984 the Chartered Association of Certified Accountants).
8 Absorbed by the Institute of Certified Public Accountants, 1933.
9 Name changed to Institute of Cost and Management Accountants, 1972; to Chartered Institute of Management Accountants, 1986.

3. Since accountants practise not one technique but a related set of techniques, specialized associations may be formed, as happened with local government accountants in 1885 and cost accountants in 1919.

Professional accountancy can be imported and exported in a variety of ways, which may be listed as follows:

1. The *idea* of professional accountancy is exported, i.e. local accountants form their own association on:
   (a) the British model, or
   (b) some other model.
2. British accounting *qualifications* are exported, i.e. local accountants either:

    (a) form a local branch of a British body, or
    (b) become full members of a British body, by
        (i) qualifying in Britain, or
        (ii) qualifying in their own country

The combination of British political and economic dominance and technological advances meant that knowledge of professional accountancy developments in Britain could spread rapidly. By the end of the nineteenth century, the British Empire covered Canada, the Australian continent and New Zealand, much of southern, central, east and west Africa, India, Ceylon, parts of South East Asia, and numerous islands in the Mediterranean, Caribbean, Atlantic, Indian and Pacific Oceans. Moreover, Britain's 'informal empire' (Gallagher and Robinson, 1953) of overseas trade and investment spread well beyond these, notably to the United States, Argentina and Brazil. Many 'local accountants' were in fact British accountants (not necessarily members of a formal association) who had emigrated overseas. Steamships and the telegraph gave even remote Australia reliable and fast links with Britain and helped to defeat the 'tyranny of distance' (Blainey, 1966, Chapter 9).

The formation of associations on the British model, but independent of British bodies, was most common in Canada, Australia, New Zealand and South Africa, as is demonstrated in Table 2. The merits of such associations were expressed by a pioneer accountant in Melbourne, Thomas Brentnall, as follows:

> It was gradually borne in upon a few of us that if those who were holding themselves out as public practitioners were to gain the confidence and support of the public, there must be a standard fixedwhich would connote the possession of the necessary qualifications for this special work. To that end a meeting was held [in Melbourne] on April 12, 1886, at which thirty practising accountants met to consider the propriety of establishing an 'Association of those having kindred interests in their common calling, and a desire to place their profession on a higher plane that it had previously occupied in public esteem'. We knew the position attained by the Institute of Chartered Accountants in England and Wales, which had been incorporated by Royal Charter in 1880, by the Society of Accountants and Auditors in 1885, as well as the three Scottish Institutes which had come into existence some years previously. With these examples before us, we had no difficulty in arriving at the conclusion that our object could best be attained by following in their footsteps.
>
> (Brentnall, 1938, page 64)

As we shall see later, the accountants of Melbourne consciously rejected the alternative of constituting themselves a branch of a British body.

Table 2 Accountancy bodies formed in Canada, Australia, New Zealand and
South Africa: 1880–1904.

1880	The Association of Accountants in Montreal
1883	The Institute of Chartered Accountants of Ontario
1885	The Adelaide Society of Accountants (renamed The Institute of Accountants in South Australia, 1889)
1886	The Chartered Accountants' Association of Manitoba
1887	The Incorporated Institute of Accountants of Victoria (renamed Commonwealth Institute of Accountants, 1921)
1891	The Queensland Institute of Accountants
1894	The Sydney Institute of Public Accountants
1894	The Incorporated Institute of Accountants of New Zealand
1894	The Federal Institute of Accountants and Auditors in the South African Republic (became Transvaal branch of the [British] Society of Accountants and Auditors, 1902)
1895	The Institute of Accountants in Natal
1897	The Tasmanian Institute of Accountants
1898	The New Zealand Accountants' and Auditors' Association
1899	The Corporation of Accountants of Australia (Sydney)
1900	The Institute of Accountants and Auditors of Western Australia
1900	The Society of Accountants and Auditors of Victoria
1900	The Institute of Chartered Accountants of Nova Scotia
1902	The Dominion Association of Chartered Accountants (Canada)
1903	The Institute of Chartered Accountants in South Africa
1904	The Institute of Accountants of British Columbia
1904	The Transvaal Society of Accountants

Table 2 clearly shows the inheritance of both regionalism (e.g. by 1904 there was a separate professional body in every Australian state) and duplication (e.g. the larger Australian states had more than one body). Later (and thus not shown in the table), specialised bodies were also formed.

American accountants also formed their own associations but they adapted the British model to their own needs. The right to practise public accountancy came to depend upon a licensing authority (normally one of the States) with not all public accountants so certified considering it necessary to join a professional body. Unlike Britain, Canada and Australia, the United States managed to avoid a multiplicity of competing professional bodies. In the first comprehensive survey of accountancy bodies round the world, made on the occasion of the fiftieth anniversary of the Edinburgh Society of Accountants, Brown (1905, page 274) compared the advantages of the two models:

> The American plan prevents more effectively the misuse of the title adopted, while the British insures the benefits of association. There is greater freedom and elasticity under the British system, which is, however, accompanied by some liability to abuse.

Brown could also have pointed out that the British model lends itself more easily to the export of professional qualifications, since the barrier of a home-based licensing authority does not exist (Seidler 1969, page 44). British accountants have in fact been active exporters of professional accountancy qualifications. By the 1900s there were about 400 members of British accountancy bodies around the British Empire, forming 6 per cent of a total membership of about 7,000. In round terms 200 of the 400 were in Africa (mainly South Africa) and 100 in Australasia. Of the 400 over 70 per cent were incorporated accountants (Johnson and Caygill, 1971).

The attitudes of the various British bodies to accountancy overseas differed in interesting ways. The English Institute insisted that English chartered accountants could only be trained in England and Wales; the Scottish bodies, with their small home base, allowed training in England and Wales as well as in Scotland. The smaller home base also meant a greater migration of Scots CAs not only to England and Wales but also to the Empire and Commonwealth. In the 1960s, 4 per cent of them were located there; in the 1920s, 1940s and 1960s, 11 per cent (Johnson and Caygill, 1971, Table 1 page 158); in the 1970s and 1980s 7 per cent. Unlike certified accountants (see below) they were and are mainly to be found in the 'old' Commonwealth.

The Society of Incorporated Accountants and Auditors, however, kept in second place by the chartered bodies in the United Kingdom, made, under the indefatigable leadership of James Martin, determined efforts to expand through the British Empire. The historian of the Society (Garrett, 1961, page 14) reports that 'At an early stage the Society claimed for itself a "British Empire" policy'. The success of this varied from country to country.

In Australia it was unsuccessful. A commissioner for Australia (a Mr Charles A. Cooper) appointed in 1886 established a Committee in Victoria but was not able to make the Society the nucleus of a nascent profession in Australia. The first annual report of The Incorporated Institute of Accountants of Victoria (the body of which Brentnall was a founding member) records that 'Mr Cooper's proposals were, after careful consideration, set aside in favour of a local independent body'. Martin was, however, appointed in 1888 as a corresponding member of the Institute in London (Commonwealth Institute of Accountants, 1936, pages 8, 17). Nevertheless Martin complained at the First International Congress of Accountants in St Louis that Australia was 'dominated very largely by the working classes, and the working classes of Australia have nothing in common with professional men, and they brought our efforts to naught' (Official Record, 1904, page 105). Local practitioners in each colony formed their own accountancy bodies which after many vicissitudes were merged into the Institute of Chartered Accountants in Australia (1928) and the Australian Society of Accountants (1958).

What it failed to do in Australia, the Society was successful in achieving in South Africa (Garrett, 1961, pages 14, 55–9) – perhaps because Martin was able to go to South Africa personally (yet another example of the 'tyranny of distance' so important in Australian history); perhaps because South African governments were not dominated by the working classes; but also perhaps because accountants in Johannesburg 'having regard to the wide ramifications and finance of the mining industry . . . preferred to become part of a British Society with world-wide connexions, rather than remaining members of a body with local limitations' (Garrett, 1961, page 57). A mining industry also existed in Australia but its links with Britain were rather less. The South African arrangement lasted until the late 1950s.

Apart from Australia and South Africa, the Society established branches in Canada (Montreal, 1905), India (Bombay, 1931; Bengal, 1933) and Central Africa (Salisbury, 1954). A president of the Society, Harry L. Price, has even been claimed as the 'unlikely father' of the present organisational form of chartered accountancy in Canada. It was under Price's chairmanship during the 1908 conference in Atlantic City, New Jersey, of the American Association of Public Accountants, that the Dominion Association of Chartered Accountants and the Institute of Chartered Accountants of Ontario were reconciled. The event has a symbolic significance and according to the historian of the Ontario Institute is 'so beautifully and typically Canadian it is hard to imagine how it could be improved' (Creighton, 1984, page 63).

As the Society became stronger in the United Kingdom, its overseas activities became less important, and it underwent a 'loss of enthusiasm for Empire glory once it had fully established its position at home' (Johnson and Caygill, 1971, page 159).

By 1957, when the Society merged with the Chartered Institutes, the Association was already playing the leading role in this area which it has retained ever since. Between 1913 and 1967 the Association established branches in South Africa, India, Malaya, Jamaica, Trinidad, Hong Kong, Central Africa, Cyprus, British Guiana, Nigeria, the Bahamas, Canada and Tanzania (Johnson and Caygill, 1971). The Chartered Association, as it has now become, remains the world's largest exporter of accountancy qualifications. Six per cent of the Association's members were in the Commonwealth in the 1920s, rising to 11 per cent in the 1960s and 33 per cent in the 1980s. As already noted, overseas certified accountants, unlike overseas Scots CAs, are to be found in the 'new' Commonwealth rather than the 'old'. The Institute of Cost and Management Accountants has also built up a significant overseas membership in the last two decades (Banyard, 1985, pages 56, 79, 89).

As was the case with incorporated accountants in South Africa, many of the overseas members of the Association are also members of their own local accountancy bodies. It is a measure of the prestige value attaching to a word that most of these are 'chartered' rather than 'certified'. The historian of the English Institute (Howitt, 1966, pages 194–5) noted that 'chartered' bodies had been formed outside the United Kingdom as follows: Canada (1902, earlier in some provinces), Australia (1928, the only one based on a royal charter), Rhodesia (now Zimbabwe) (1928), South Africa (1946, earlier in some provinces), India (1949), Ceylon (now Sri Lanka) (1959), Pakistan (1961), Ghana (1963), Jamaica (1965) and Nigeria (1965). Since that date may be added the Bahamas, Bangladesh, Barbados, and Trinidad and Tobago.

What can we conclude about the British experience as an exporter of the institution of professional accountancy? Professional accountancy was both actively exported and actively imported. On the exporting side, some British bodies have been much more active than others, the difference being explainable in terms of their relative strengths in the *home* market. On the importing side, the United States actively imported the idea of professional accountancy (but not on the British model); Canada, Australia and New Zealand actively imported the British model but preferred to form their own local bodies rather than import British accounting qualifications; the countries of the 'new' Commonwealth have been twentieth century importers of British qualifications and have formed local bodies only recently; South African accountants until the 1950s were willing to hold both local and British qualifications.

How can these differences be explained? The active *nineteenth century* importers were in general located in those temperate regions of recent settlement which were recipients of British overseas investment; which had experienced British colonial rule but attained independence or a considerable measure of self-government; and where British cultural influence was strong and the English language dominant.

It is important to note the complex pattern of influences. Professional accountancy on the British model did not simply follow the direction of British investment which appears to have been a necessary but not a sufficient condition. Thus, the British model was *not* adopted in those areas (the United States and South America) to which British investment was directed most (see Table 3). Nor was it adopted first in those areas where British political power was the strongest but, on the contrary, succeeded best in those parts of the Empire which had achieved most self-government. In the *twentieth century* professional accountancy bodies have developed most rapidly *after* the achievement of independence. Under colonial rule development was sometimes slowed down by, for example, restricting public company audits to members of British bodies (Johnson and Caygill, 1971, page 170; Kapadia, 1973). On the other hand professional accountancy made little headway in areas such as South America where Britain had considerable investments but no political power.

For local professional bodies to develop on the British model, the further factor of strong British cultural influence (as in Australia, New Zealand,

Table 3 Direction of new British portfolio investment 1865–1914.

		%
By continent	North America	34
	South America	17
	Asia	14
	Europe	13
	Australasia	11
	Africa	11
		100
By political status	Independent	59
	British Empire	40
	Foreign Dependencies	1
		100
By climatic-ethnic category:	Temperate Regions of recent European settlement	68
	Tropics	27
	Non-tropical Asia	5
		100

Source: Simon (1967).

Canada, and to a lesser extent South Africa) was needed. British investment alone was not sufficient. 'In neither [the United States nor Argentina]', a distinguished economic historian has concluded, 'did the British create the social structure they encountered. Their [economic] activity aided and abetted the tendencies that were already there . . .' (Jenks, 1951, page 388). These conclusions can be extended to professional accountancy.

True and fair view

We turn finally to a discussion of an accounting concept, that of a true and fair view. In principle, just as an institution should be more difficult to export or import than a technique, a concept should be more difficult than an institution, since what is being transferred is part of a culture and a culture cannot easily be transferred piecemeal. On the other hand, concepts are expressed as forms of words rather than as actions or physical things, so apparent exports or imports may be easier.

The concept of a true and fair view received its first legal formulation in the British Companies Act 1947 but its origins can be traced back to the mid-nineteenth century (Chastney, 1975). It represents an amalgam of the previous Acts (see Table 4). The provisions of the 1947 Act (reenacted in the 1948 Act) followed the recommendations of the Cohen Committee on

Table 4 Extracts from British Companies Acts.

1844   ... the Directors ... shall cause ... a full and fair Balance Sheet to be made up ... (s.35)

1862   The Auditors shall make a Report to the Members upon the Balance Sheet and Accounts, and in every such Report they shall state whether, in their Opinion, the Balance Sheet is a full and fair Balance Sheet, containing the Particulars required by these Regulations, and properly drawn up so as to exhibit a true and correct View of the State of the Company's Affairs ... (para.94, Table A).

1879   (Banking Companies) The auditor or auditors ... shall state whether, in his or their opinion, the balance sheet ... is a full and fair balance sheet properly drawn up so as to exhibit a true and correct view of the state of the company's affairs, as shown by the books of the company ... (s.7)

1900   ... the auditors ... shall state whether, in their opinion, the balance sheet ... is properly drawn up so as to exhibit a true and correct view of the state of the company's affairs as shown by the books of the company ... (s.23)

1948   (1) Every balance sheet of a company shall give a true and fair view of the state of affairs of the company as at the end of its financial year, and every profit and loss account of a company shall give a true and fair view of the profit or loss for the financial year.
(3) ... the [detailed] requirements of [the 8th Schedule] shall be without prejudice either to the general requirements of subsection (1) of this section or to any other requirements of this Act (s.149, re-enacting s.13, Companies Act 1947).

1985   (2) The balance sheet shall give a true and fair view of the state of affairs of the company as at the end of the financial year; and the profit and loss account shall give a true and fair view of the profit or loss of the company for the financial year.
(3) Subsection (2) overrides –
(a) the requirements of Schedule 4, and
(b) all other requirements of this Act as to the matters to be included in a company's accounts or in notes to those accounts:
and accordingly the following two subsections have effect.
(4) If the balance sheet or profit and loss account drawn up in accordance with those requirements would not provide sufficient information to comply with subsection (2), any necessary additional information must be provided in that balance sheet or profit and loss account, or in a note to the accounts.
(5) If, owing to special circumstances, in the case of any company, compliance with any such requirement in relation to the balance sheet or profit and loss account would prevent compliance with subsection (2) (even if additional information were provided in accordance with subsection (4)), the directors shall depart from that requirement in preparing the balance sheet or profit and loss account (so far as necessary in order to comply with subsection (2)).
(6) If the directors depart from any such requirement, particulars of the departure, the reasons for it and its effect shall be given in a note to the accounts (s.228 = re-enactment of s.149 of 1948 Act as amended by 1981 Act; s.230 provides similarly for group accounts).

Company Law Amendment (1945) which in turn followed the memorandum submitted to it by the Institute of Chartered Accountants in England and Wales.

It is much less easy than in the previous sections of this chapter to state what was available for import, for British accountants have never defined very clearly what a true and fair view is or how to make it operational. An authoritative view of one of the accountant members of the Cohen Committee (Kettle, 1950, page 117) was that:

> A true and fair view implies that all statutory and other essential information is not only available but is presented in a form in which it can be properly and readily appreciated.

Asked for an explanation by continental Europeans when the Fourth Directive was under discussion in the 1970s, British accountants referred to 'fairness of presentation (i.e. unbiased as between the different users of financial information) and frank[ness] in the recognition of economic substance rather than mere legal form'. (Rutteman, 1984, page 8). One British commentator has concluded that 'True and fair is what you make it' (Chastney, 1975, page 92).

The potential importers of the concept in the 1950s were those countries which were accustomed, when amending their company legislation, to give great weight to British law, i.e. most of the member countries of the British Commonwealth. Australia may be taken as an example.

The legislation of the Australian States echoed the requirements of United Kingdom legislation fairly closely until the 1970s (NCSC, 1984, pages 8–9). There were originally good reasons for this which were expressed by parliamentarians and lawyers as follows:

> Investors at Home [i.e. in the United Kingdom] were shy about investing in a State whose company law they did not understand.
> (Manifold, quoted Gibson, 1971, page 48)

> ... uniformity would give to Victoria the guidance of English decisions and English textbooks on the Act would continuously furnish precedents and illustrations. Divergence would mean uncertainty ... access to a wide range of experience is vital, and ... this the narrow limits of a small community cannot furnish.
> (Moore, 1934, page 182)

These views prevailed into the 1950s and 1960s and the Victorian Act of 1955 and the Uniform Companies Acts based on it all included the phrase 'true and fair view'. The requirement remains in the present Australian Companies Act and Codes.

By the 1960s, however, the United States was replacing Britain as Australia's main trading partner and source of investment, and knowledge of American accounting was spreading. Australian accountants began to define a true and fair view in an American as well as a British way.

Recommendation on Accounting Principles No.1 (1963) of the Australian Institute, for example, stated that a true and fair view 'implies appropriate classification and grouping of the items . . . [and] also implies the consistent application of generally accepted principles'. In 1984 the Auditing Standards Board (AuSB) of the Australian Accounting Research Foundation (AARF) issued Statement of Auditing Practice AUP3, 'The Auditor's Report on Financial Statements' (Pound, 1984), which sought to introduce a reporting format in which the auditor's opinion was formed and expressed in the context of whether financial statements 'present fairly the financial position and results in accordance with Australian Accounting Standards'.

However, a consultative document of the Australian National Companies and Securities Commission (written by Professor R.G. Walker of the University of New South Wales) rejected suggestions that a true and fair view should be stated to be in accord with generally accepted accounting principles or approved accounting standards and proposed the following addition to the Australian Act:

> Without affecting the generality of the meaning of the term, *'true and fair view,'* a 'true and fair view' in relation to accounts or group accounts means a representation which affords those who might reasonably be expected to refer to those accounts (including holders or prospective purchasers of shares, debentures, notes or other interests, and creditors or prospective creditors) information which is relevant to the decisions which may be made by those persons in relation to the purchase, sale or other action in connection with their securities or interests.
>
> (NCSC, 1984, page 3)

The Auditing Standards Board reacted strongly against this recommendation which it regarded as placing 'an impossible responsibility on accountants, auditors and directors' and recommended instead the phrase 'present fairly . . . in accordance with approved accounting standards and comply with the Companies Code' (Edwards, 1985).

Whilst Australian accountants have begun to doubt the wisdom of their import, continental Europeans have been persuaded to write the concept of a true and fair view into their legislation. Table 5 shows how the wording of the relevant clause, which at first closely followed German law, was changed during the discussions of the various drafts. The changes were made at the suggestion of the United Kingdom negotiators but at the same time a minute of the Council of Ministers was recorded to the effect that in

Table 5 'True and Fair' in the Fourth Directive.

1971 Draft	1. The annual accounts shall comprise the balance sheet, the profit and loss account and the notes on the accounts. These documents shall constitute a composite whole. 2. The annual accounts shall conform to the principles of regular and proper accounting. 3. They shall be drawn up clearly and, in the context of the provisions regarding the valuation of assets and liabilities and the lay-out of accounts, shall reflect as accurately as possible the company's assets, liabilities, financial position and results.
1974 Draft (Art 2)	1. (as 1971 Draft) 2. The annual accounts shall give a true and fair view of the company's assets, liabilities, financial position and results. 3. They shall be drawn up clearly and in accordance with the provisions of this Directive.
1978 Final	1. (as 1971 Draft) 2. They shall be drawn up clearly and in accordance with the provisions of this Directive. 3. The annual accounts shall give a true and fair view of the company's assets, liabilities, financial position and profit or loss. 4. Where the application of the provisions of this Directive would not be sufficient to give a true and fair view within the meaning of paragraph 3 additional information must be given. 5. Where in exceptional cases the application of a provision of this Directive is incompatible with the obligation laid down in paragraph 3, that provision must be departed from in order to give a true and fair view within the meaning of paragraph 3. Any such departure must be disclosed in the notes on the accounts together with an explanation of the reasons for it and a statement of its effect on the assets, liabilities, financial position and profit or loss. The Member States may define the exceptional cases in question and lay down the relevant special rules.

Source: Nobes and Parker, 1984, page 84.

general following the provisions of the directive would be sufficient to achieve a true and fair view of a company's economic situation (Rutteman, 1984, page 8).

British accountants were keener to export the concept of a true and fair view than accountants of other EEC member states such as France and Germany were to import it. Whilst British accountants genuinely believe in the importance of the concept and its general applicability, the export took place in order to protect its role in British accounting rather than in the expectation of other countries making radical changes in their own accounting styles. It may be doubted whether a concept developed in a country where the main users of financial statements are investors is appropriate to countries where the main users are government (as tax collectors), creditors and trade unions. This may not matter, however, if the concept is interpreted in such a way as to fit its new environment.

This is quite likely to happen. In France, for example, there was, before the Fourth Directive, already a requirement for financial statements to be *régulier* (in accordance with the letter of the regulations) and *sincère* (in accordance with the spirit of the regulations). French law now requires that the statements be not only *régulier et sincère* but also show a true and fair view (*une image fidèle*). What this means has led to considerable debate (Pham, 1984) but the most probable result is that the concept will have no effect on the balance sheet and profit and loss account but will lead to additional disclosures in the notes to the accounts (which have assumed a new importance in France as a result of the Directive). It is not expected that German financial statements will change their nature unless the underlying economic and social structures do so first (Busse Von Colbe, 1984). The general idea of a true and fair v-iew existed in Dutch law before the Fourth Directive, although not in so many words. The law (as now stated in the Civil Code, article 362) has not been substantially changed in this respect and there is, for instance, no explicit reference to a true and fair view in Moret and Limperg's (1984) commentary on the new Dutch legislation on annual reports.

The phrase 'true and fair view' is Britain's contribution to twentieth century accounting terminology. Those importers for whom English is a native language have not had to translate it. Continental European importers on the other hand have had the task of translating the phrase into their own language (Rutherford, 1983). In French a true and fair view becomes *une image fidèle*, in Italian *un quadro fedele*, in Dutch *een getrouw beeld*. German speakers have had difficulty in finding the right translation. The more or less literal *ein den tatsachlichen Verhaltnissen entsprechendes Bild* may be translated as 'a picture corresponding to actual conditions'.

It is interesting to note that all four languages prefer a 'picture' to a 'view' and (except the 1978 German) express 'true and fair' by one word whose most literal translation is 'faithful'. This at least avoids the British and Australasian discussions about financial statements which are true but not fair. An American accountant unaware of the original English might translate the continental phrases as 'representational faithfulness' or 'faithful representation'. Whilst it is at first sight surprising that the Continental European countries have accepted such a concept it is clear that what they have really imported is a form of words which they are translating and applying so as not to disturb unduly what already exists. Perhaps this is the fate of all indefinable concepts.

Some conclusions

An analysis of the case studies presented in the preceding sections suggests two sets of conclusions. First, both exporters and importers must be considered and there is an important distinction between active exporters and importers on the one hand and passive exporters and importers on the other. Secondly, in assessing costs and benefits the position of exporters in their home markets is important, whilst it makes a difference to the importer whether it is a technique, an institution or a concept that is being imported.

The relationship between exporters and importers can be set out as follows:

A Active exporter	Active importer	
B Active exporter	Passive importer	
C Passive exporter	Active importer	
D Passive exporter	Passive importer	

Clearly, an import and export is likely to take place most quickly and effectively when an active exporter is faced with an active importer (situation A) and is least likely to be quick and effective when a passive exporter is faced with a passive importer (situation D).

Active exporters and importers are those who have made an assessment of the costs and benefits of importing or exporting a technique, institution or concept, have decided that the benefits outweigh the costs and are eager to go ahead. Examples of active exporters in this chapter are British accountancy bodies interested in expanding overseas and the United Kingdom negotiators keen to get the EEC to accept the concept of a true and fair view.

Success has for such exporters depended in part upon what importers were willing to accept. British accountancy bodies have regarded the British Empire and Commonwealth as a legitimate market and have used appropriate economic, political and cultural influence. The more advanced countries politically and economically have, however, preferred, and been able, to set up their own bodies rather than accept membership of British bodies. Continental Europeans have been willing to accept the concept of a true and fair view in the knowledge that they could adapt it to their own needs and also because they could successfully export standardized formats and valuation rules to Britain.

Examples of active importers are the Australian and Canadian accountants of the nineteenth century who formed accountancy bodies on the British model. They were also for a time active importers of British company accounting (including, in the case of Australia, the concept of a true and fair view).

Passive exporters and importers are those who have either not made an assessment of costs and benefits (perhaps through lack of knowledge) or have made the assessment and decided that the costs outweigh the benefits.

Table 6 Importing and Exporting Options.

EXPORTER	IMPORTER	
	Active	**Passive**
Active	Professional Accountancy	True and Fair View
Passive	–	Double Entry

An example of a passive exporter in this chapter is the early Italian practitioner of double entry. An example of a passive importer is a continental European negotiator who accepted the British concept of a true and fair view.

The three cases studied in this discussion can thus be entered in a matrix shown in Table 6.

The position of the exporter in the home market has been seen to be important both in the spread of professional accountancy throughout the British Empire and Commonwealth and in the export of the true and fair view to continental Europe. The former would probably have happened anyway, given the existence of active importers, but the latter would not have taken place if British practitioners had not been concerned to make sure that the concept survived in *British* law and practice.

It is easier to import a technique than an institution or a concept. Double entry has spread from Italy not just to Britain but to the whole world. Professional accountancy has spread more selectively. We have already noted Brown's (1905) findings for the United States and for Canada, Australia, South Africa and New Zealand. In other British colonies Brown found accountants but not, at that date, professional bodies. In continental Europe he noted the existence of bodies in Italy, Holland (from 1895) and Sweden (from 1899) but found none in any other European country. Where professional accountancy developed late in Europe it did so with more government intervention than in Britain or the United States and the bodies so created are less influential. They have not been created on either the British or American model and can hardly be regarded as imports from the United Kingdom or the United States.

Until recently, the concept of a true and fair view had spread even more selectively than professional accountancy, being confined to the United Kingdom and members of the British Commonwealth such as Australia, New Zealand, Nigeria and Singapore. It was not found in Canada or the USA. How real its export to continental Europe will be remains to be seen.

Note

1 Earlier drafts of this chapter were presented in 1985 at an EIASM workshop on 'Accounting and Culture' at the Free University of Amsterdam, at a number of Australian universities and at the national University of Singapore. I have benefited greatly from comments received.

References

Banyard, C. W., *The Institute of Cost and Management Accountants – A History* (London: The Institute of Cost and Management Accountants, 1985).

Blainey, G., *The Tyranny of Distance* (Melbourne: Sun Books, 1966).

Brentnall, T., *My Memories* (Melbourne: Robertson and Mullins, 1938).

Brown, R., *A History of Accounting and Accountants* (Edinburgh: Jack, 1905).

Busse von Colbe, W., A True and Fair View: A German Perspective, in S. S. J. Gray and A. G. Coenenberg (eds), *EEC Accounting Harmonisation: Implementation and Impact of the Fourth Directive* (Amsterdam: North-Holland, 1984)

Chastney, J. G., *True and Fair View – History, Meaning and the Impact of the Fourth Directive* (London: Institute of Chartered Accountants in England and Wales, 1975).

Commonwealth Institute of Accountants, Historical Survey 1886–1936, in *Commonwealth Accountants' Year Book 1936* (Melbourne Commonwealth Institute of Accountants, 1936).

Creighton, P., *Sum of Yesterdays* (Toronto: The Institute of Chartered Accountants of Ontario, 1984).

Davis, R., *English Overseas Trade 1500–1700* (London: MacMillan, 1973).

de Roover, R., The Development of Accounting Prior to Luca Pacioli According to the Account-Books of Medieval Merchants, in A. C. Littleton and B. S. Yamey, *Studies in the History of Accounting* (London: Sweet & Maxwell, 1956).

Edwards, B., 'True and Fair' – Not Just An Academic Debate, *Chartered Accountant in Australia*, March 1985.

Gallagher, J, and Robinson, R., The Imperialism of Free Trade, *Economic History Review*, 2nd ser., vol. VI, 1953, reprinted in W. R. Louis (ed.), *Imperialism* (New York: New Viewpoints, 1976).

Garrett, A. A., *History of the Society of Incorporated Accountants 1885–1957* (Oxford: The University Press, 1961).

Gibson, R. W., *Disclosure by Australian Companies* (Melbourne: Melbourne University Press, 1971).

Griliches, Z., Hybrid Corn and the Economics of Innovation, *Science*, 29 July 1960, reprinted in N. Rosenberg (ed.), *The Economics of Technological Change* (Harmondsworth: Penguin Books, 1971).

Howitt, (Sir) H. G., *The History of The Institute of Chartered Accountants in England and Wales 1880–1965 and of its Founder Accountancy Bodies 1870–1880* (London: Heinemann, 1966).

Jenks, L. H., Britain and American Railway Development, *Journal of Economic History*, Fall 1951.

Johnson, T. J. and Caygill, M., The Development of Accountancy Links in the Commonwealth, *Accounting and Business Research*, Spring 1971.

Kapadia, G. P., *History of the Accountancy Profession in India* (New Delhi: The Institute of Chartered Accountants of India, 1973).

Kats, P., Double Entry Book-keeping in England before Hugh Oldcastle, *Accountant*, V.74, 1926.

Kenyon, J. P., *Stuart England* (Harmondsworth: Penguin Books, 1978).

Kettle, R., Balance Sheets and Accounts under the Companies Act, 1948, in W. T. Baxter, *Studies in Accounting* (London: Sweet & Maxwell, 1950).

Kojima, O., James Peele and his Works, essay appended to 1980 reproduction of *The Pathe waye to perfectnes in th' accomptes of Debtour and Creditour* by James Peele 1569.

Harrison Moore, W., A Century of Victorian Law, *Journal of Comparative Legislation and International Law*, 3rd ser., vol.16, 1934.

Moret and Limperg, *New Dutch Legislation on Annual Reports* (Rotterdam, 1984).

National Companies and Securities Commission, *'A True and Fair View' and the Reporting Obligations of Directors and Auditors* (Canberra: Australian Government Publishing Service, 1984).

Needles, B. E., Implementing a Framework for the International Transfer of Accounting Technology, *International Journal of Accounting*, Fall 1976.

Nobes, C. W., The Gallerani Account Book of 1305–1308, *Accounting Review*, April 1982.

Nobes, C. W. and Parker, R. H., The Fourth Directive and the United Kingdom, in S. J. Gray and A. G. Coenenberg, *EEC Accounting Harmonisation: Implementation and Impact of the Fourth Directive* (Amsterdam: North-Holland, 1984).

Official Record of the Proceedings of the Congress of Accountants . . . 1904 (New York: Arno Press, 1978).

Parker, R. H., The First Scottish Book on Accounting: Robert Colinson's *Idea Rationaria* (1683), *Accountants Magazine*, September 1974.

Parker, R. H., Reckoning, Merchants' Accounts, Bookkeeping, Accounting or Accountancy? The Evidence of the Long Titles of Books on Accounting in English, in B. Carsberg and S. Dev, *External Financial Reporting* (London: Prentice Hall International, 1984).

Parker, R. H., *The Development of the Accountancy Profession in Britain to the Early Twentieth Century* (The Academy of Accounting Historians, Monograph Five, 1986).

Pham, D., A True and Fair View: A French Perspective, in S. J. Gray and A. G. Coenenberg (eds), *EEC Accounting Harmonisation: Implementation and Impact of the Fourth Directive* (Amsterdam: North-Holland, 1984).

Pound, G., New Statement of Auditing Practice – AUP 3, *Chartered Accountant in Australia*, May 1984.

Ramsey, P., Some Tudor Merchants' Accounts, in A. C. Littleton and B. S. Yamey, *Studies in the History of Accounting* (London: Sweet & Maxwell, 1956).

Rutherford, B. A., Spoilt Beauty: The True and Fair Doctrine in Translation, *AUTA Review*, Spring 1983.

Rutteman, P., *The EEC Accounting Directives and their Effects* (Cardiff: University College Cardiff Press, 1984).

Seidler, L. J., Nationalism and the International Transfer of Accounting Skills, *International Journal of Accounting*, Fall 1969.

Simon, N., The Pattern of New British Portfolio Foreign Investment, 1865–1914, in J. H. Adler, *Capital Movements and Economic Development* (London: Macmillan, 1967).

Taylor, P. and Turley, S., The International Transfer of Accounting Technology, University of Manchester Working Paper Series No. 8502, 1985.

Vanes, J. (ed.), *The Ledger of John Smythe* 1538–1550 (Bristol Record Society's Publications, vol. 28, 1974).

Watts, R. L. and Zimmerman, J. L., *Positive Accounting Theory* (Englewood Cliffs, N.J.: Prentice-Hall, 1986).

Winjum, J. O., *The Role of Accounting in the Economic Development of England: 1500–1750* (Centre for International Education and Research in Accounting, University of Illinois, 1972).

Yamey, B. S., John Weddington's *A Breffe Instruction*, 1567, *Accounting Research*, April 1958.

Yamey, B. S., Fifteenth and Sixteenth Century Manuscripts on the Art of Bookkeeping, *Journal of Accounting Research*, Spring 1967.

Yamey, B. S., Some Topics in the History of Financial Accounting in England 1500–1900, in W. T. Baxter and S. Davidson (eds), *Studies in Accounting* (London: Institute of Chartered Accountants in England and Wales 1977).

6

TOWARDS A THEORY OF CULTURAL INFLUENCE ON THE DEVELOPMENT OF ACCOUNTING SYSTEMS INTERNATIONALLY

S. J. Gray

Source: *Abacus* 24(1) (1988): 1–15.

Research has shown that accounting follows different patterns in different parts of the world. There have been claims that national systems are determined by environmental factors. In this context, cultural factors have not been fully considered. This paper proposes four hypotheses on the relationship between identified cultural characteristics and the development of accounting systems, the regulation of the accounting profession and attitudes towards financial management and disclosure. The hypotheses are not operationalized, and empirical tests have not been carried out. They are proposed here as a first step in the development of a theory of cultural influence on the development of accounting systems.

This paper explores the extent to which international differences in accounting, with specific reference to corporate financial reporting systems, may be explained and predicted by differences in cultural factors.

While prior research has shown that there are different patterns of accounting internationally and that the development of national systems tends to be a function of environmental factors, it is a matter of some controversy as to the identification of the patterns and influential factors involved (Mueller, 1967; Zeff, 1971; Radebaugh, 1975; Nair and Frank, 1980; Nobes, 1983). In this context the significance of culture does not appear to have been fully appreciated and thus the purpose of this paper is to propose a framework which links culture with the development of accounting systems internationally.

The first section of the paper reviews prior research on international classification and the influence of environmental factors. The second section addresses the significance of the cultural dimension and its application to accounting. The third section proposes a framework and develops hypotheses linking culture with the development of accounting attitudes and systems internationally, based on the cross-cultural work of Hofstede (1980, 1983). In the fourth section some culture area classifications are proposed. They have been developed on a judgmental basis, in the context of combinations of accounting attitudes or 'values' which determine (a) the authority for and enforcement of accounting systems, and (b) the measurement and disclosure characteristics of accounting systems.

International classification and environmental factors

Comparative accounting research has provided an enhanced awareness of the influence of environmental factors on accounting development (e.g., Mueller, 1967; Zeff, 1971; Radebaugh, 1975; Choi and Mueller, 1984; Nobes, 1984; Arpan and Radebaugh, 1985; Nobes and Parker, 1985). This research has contributed to a growing realization that fundamentally different accounting patterns exist as a result of environmental differences and that international classification differences may have significant implications for international harmonization and the promotion of economic integration. In this regard it has also been suggested that the identification of patterns may be useful in permitting a better understanding of the potential for change, given any change in environmental factors; and that policy-makers may be in a better position to predict problems that a country may be likely to face and identify solutions that may be feasible, given the experience of countries with similar development patterns (e.g., Nobes, 1984).

Research efforts in this area have tended to approach the international classification of accounting systems from two major directions. First, there is the deductive approach whereby relevant environmental factors are identified and, by linking these to national accounting practices, international classifications or development patterns are proposed (e.g., Mueller, 1967, 1968; Nobes, 1983, 1984). Second, there is the inductive approach whereby accounting practices are analysed, development patterns identified, and explanations proposed with reference to a variety of economic, social, political, and cultural factors (e.g., Frank, 1979; Nair and Frank 1980).

As regards the deductive approach to accounting classification, the environmental analysis by Mueller (1967) provides a useful starting point. Mueller identified four distinct approaches to accounting development in western nations with market-orientated economic systems. These were:

1. the macroeconomic pattern – where business accounting interrelates closely with national economic policies;
2. the microeconomic pattern – where accounting is viewed as a branch of business economics;
3. the independent discipline approach – where accounting is viewed as a service function and derived from business practice; and
4. the uniform accounting approach – where accounting is viewed as an efficient means of administration and control.

While all of these approaches were perceived to be closely linked to economic or business factors, a wider set of influences, for example, legal system, political system, social climate were recognized as being relevant, though without precise specification, to accounting development (Mueller, 1968; Choi and Mueller, 1984). Cultural factors received no explicit recognition, however, and were presumably subsumed in the set of environmental factors identified.

Mueller's analysis was adapted and extended by Nobes (1983, 1984) who based his classification on an evolutionary approach to the identification of measurement practices in developed Western nations. Nobes adopted a hierarchical scheme of classification in an endeavour to provide more subtlety and discrimination to the assessment of country differences. However, similarly to Mueller, no explicit mention was made of cultural factors. A basic distinction between microeconomic and macroeconomic systems was made together with a disaggregation between business economics and business practice orientations under a micro-based classification, and between Government/tax/legal and Government/economics orientations under a macro-uniform based classification. Further disaggregations were then made between U.K. and U.S. influences under the business practices orientation and between tax-based and law-based systems under the Government/tax/legal orientation. This classification system was then tested by means of a judgmental analysis of national financial reporting systems in fourteen countries.

A structural approach to the identification of accounting practices was adopted whereby major features were assessed, such as, the importance of tax rules, the use of prudent/conservative valuation procedures, the strictness of application of historical cost, the making of replacement cost adjustments, the use of consolidation techniques, the generous use of provisions, and the uniformity between companies in the application of rules. The results of the statistical analysis did not, however, go much beyond providing support for the classification of countries as either micro-based or macro-based. Thus the disaggregated elements of the classification scheme, though plausible, remain hypothetical accounting patterns subject to further empirical analysis.

By way of contrast, the inductive approach to identifying accounting patterns begins with an analysis of accounting practices. Perhaps the most important contribution of this type was by Nair and Frank (1980), who carried out a statistical analysis of accounting practices in fourty-four countries. An empirical distinction was made between measurement and disclosure practices as these were seen to have different patterns of development.

The empirical results, using factor analysis applied to individual practices, showed that in respect of the Price Waterhouse (1975) data it was possible to identify five groupings of countries, with Chile as a single-country 'group', in terms of measurement practices. The number of groupings increased to seven when disclosure practices were considered. The measurement groupings were characterized broadly, following the 'spheres-of-influence' classification suggested by Seidler (1967), as the British Commonwealth, Latin America/South European, Northern and Central European, and United States models. The disclosure groupings, on the other hand, could not be described plausibly on a similar 'spheres-of-influence' classification on account of their apparent diversity.

Subsequent to the identification of groupings, Nair and Frank attempted to assess the relationships of these groupings with a number of explanatory variables. While relationships were established in respect of some of the variables which included language (as a proxy for culture), various aspects of economic structure and trading ties, it was clear that there were differences as between the measurement and disclosure groupings. However, the hypotheses that (a) cultural and economic variables might be more closely associated with disclosure practices, and (b) trading variables might be more closely associated with measurement practices were not supported. It is curious to note here that the language variable, as a proxy for culture, was perceived to be a means of capturing similarities in legal systems which were thought to be particularly important in the determination of disclosure patterns. This is questionable in itself, but in any event no justification was given for the use of language as a proxy for culture.

From this brief review of some of the major studies in international classification it seems clear that to date only very broad country groupings or accounting patterns have been identified. At the same time, only very general relationships between environmental factors and accounting patterns have been established.

The significance of culture in the context of prior classification research is far from clear. It may be that cultural influences have been generally subsumed in the predominant concern with economic factors but this has not been made explicit. Accordingly, the influence of culture on accounting would seem to have been largely neglected in the development of ideas about international classifications.

The cultural dimension

The significance of culture in influencing and explaining behaviour in social systems has been recognized and explored in a wide range of literatures but especially the anthropology, sociology and psychology literatures, (e.g., Parsons and Shils, 1951; Kluckhohn and Strodtbeck, 1961; Inkeles and Levinson, 1969; Douglas, 1977; Hofstede, 1980).

Culture has been defined as 'the collective programming of the mind which distinguishes the members of one human group from another' (Hofstede, 1980, p. 25). The word 'culture' is reserved for societies as a whole, or nations, whereas 'subculture' is used for the level of an organization, profession or family. While the degree of cultural integration varies between societies, most subcultures within a society share common characteristics with other subcultures (Hofstede, 1980, p. 26).

An essential feature of social systems is perceived to be the inclusion of a system of societal norms, consisting of the value systems shared by major groups within a nation. Values have been defined as 'a broad tendency to prefer certain states of affairs over others' (Hofstede, 1980, p. 19). Values at the collective level, as opposed to the individual level, represent culture; thus culture describes a system of societal or collectively held values.

In the accounting literature, however, the importance of culture and its historical roots is only just beginning to be recognized. While there has been a lack of attention to this dimension in the international classification literature, Harrison and McKinnon (1986) and McKinnon (1986) have recently proposed a methodological framework incorporating culture for analysing changes in corporate financial reporting regulation at the nation specific level. The use of this framework to assess the impact of culture on the form and functioning of accounting is demonstrated with reference to the system in Japan. Culture is considered an essential element in the framework for understanding how social systems change because 'culture influences: (1) the norms and values of such systems; and (2) the behaviour of groups in their interactions within and across systems' (Harrison and McKinnon, 1986, p. 239).

Complementing Harrison and McKinnon's approach is the suggestion here that a methodological framework incorporating culture may be used to explain and predict international differences in accounting systems and patterns of accounting development internationally. More specifically, it is proposed here to explore the extent to which cultural differences identified by Hofstede's cross-cultural research (1980, 1983) may explain international differences in accounting systems.

Culture, societal values and the accounting subculture

Hofstede's (1980, 1983) research was aimed at detecting the structural elements of culture and particularly those which most strongly affect known behaviour in work situations in organizations and institutions. In what is probably one of the most extensive cross-cultural surveys ever conducted, psychologists collected data about 'values' from the employees of a multinational corporation located in more than fifty countries. Subsequent statistical analysis and reasoning revealed four underlying societal value dimensions along which countries could be positioned. These dimensions, with substantial support from prior work in the field, were labelled Individualism, Power Distance, Uncertainty Avoidance, and Masculinity. Such dimensions, which are examined further below, were perceived to represent elements of a common structure in cultural systems. It was also shown how countries could be grouped into culture areas, on the basis of their scores on the four value dimensions, using cluster analysis and taking into account geographical and historical factors. Figure 1 shows the culture areas identified and within each group any identifiable sub-groups.

The point of reviewing Hofstede's research here is that if societal value orientations are related to the development of accounting systems at the subcultural level, given that such values permeate a nation's social system,

More developed Latin	Less developed Latin	More developed Asian
Belgium	Colombia	Japan
France	Ecuador	
———	Mexico	
Argentina	Venezuela	
Brazil	———	
Spain	Costa Rica	
———	Chile	
Italy	Guatemala	
	Panama	*African*
	Peru	East Africa
	Portugal	West Africa
	Salvador	
	Uruguay	
Less Developed Asian	*Near Eastern*	
Indonesia	Arab countries	
Pakistan	Greece	
Taiwan	Iran	
Thailand	Turkey	*Asian-Colonial*
———	Yugoslavia	Hong Kong
India		Singapore
Malaysia		
Philippines		
Germanic	*Anglo*	*Nordic*
Austria	Australia	Denmark
Israel	Canada	Finland
———	Ireland	Netherlands
Germany	New Zealand	Norway
Switzerland	U.K.	Sweden
	U.S.A.	
	———	
	South Africa	

Figure 1 Culture Areas (Hofstede).

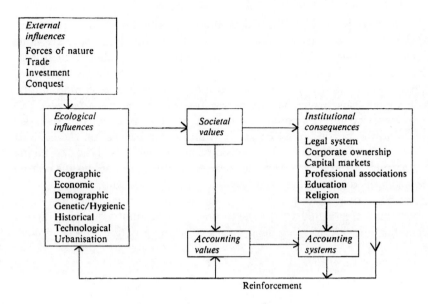

Figure 2 Culture, Societal Values and the Accounting Sub-Culture.

then it may be hypothesized that there should be a close match between culture areas and patterns of accounting systems internationally.

In order to explore further the relationship between culture and accounting systems in an international context it is necessary to identify the mechanism by which values at the societal level are linked to values at the accounting subcultural level as it is these latter values which are likely to influence directly the development of accounting systems in practice.

A model of this process is proposed in Figure 2. This is an adaptation and extension of the model relating to the formation and stabilizing of societal culture patterns proposed by Hofstede (1980, p. 27). In this model, societal values are determined by ecological influences modified by external factors such as international trade and investment, conquest, and the forces of nature. In turn, societal values have institutional consequences in the form of the legal system, political system, nature of capital markets, pattern of corporate ownership and so on. These institutions reinforce both ecological influences and societal values.

An extension of this model is proposed here whereby societal values are expressed at the level of the accounting subculture. Accordingly, the value systems or attitudes of accountants may be expected to be related to and derived from societal values with special reference to work-related values. Accounting 'values' will, in turn, impact on accounting systems.

If Hofstede has correctly identified Individualism, Power Distance, Uncertainty Avoidance, and Masculinity as significant cultural value dimensions then it should be possible to establish their relationship to accounting values. If such a relationship exists then a link between societal values and accounting systems can be established and the influence of culture assessed.

Before an attempt can be made to identify significant accounting values which may be related to societal values it is important to understand the meaning of the four value dimensions identified by Hofstede (1980, 1983) and referred to earlier. These dimensions are well expressed in Hofstede (1984, pp. 83–4) as follows:

Individualism versus Collectivism
Individualism stands for a preference for a loosely knit social frame-work in society wherein individuals are supposed to take care of themselves and their immediate families only. Its opposite, Collectivism, stands for a preference for a tightly knit social framework in which individuals can expect their relatives, clan, or other in-group to look after them in exchange for unquestioning loyalty (it will be clear that the word 'collectivism' is not used here to describe any particular political system). The fundamental issue addressed by this dimension is the degree of interdependence a society maintains among individuals. It relates to people's self-concept: 'I' or 'we'.

Large versus Small Power Distance
Power Distance is the extent to which the members of a society accept that power in institutions and organisations is distributed unequally. This affects the behaviour of the less powerful as well as of the more powerful members of society. People in Large Power Distance societies accept a hierarchical order in which everybody has a place which needs no further justification. People in Small Power Distance societies strive for power equalisation and demand justification for power inequalities. The fundamental issue addressed by this dimension is how a society handles inequalities among people when they occur. This has obvious consequence for the way people build their institutions and organisations.

Strong versus Weak Uncertainty Avoidance
Uncertainty Avoidance is the degree to which the members of a society feel uncomfortable with uncertainty and ambiguity. This feeling leads them to beliefs promising certainty and to maintaining institutions pro-tecting conformity. Strong Uncertainty Avoidance societies maintain rigid codes of belief and behaviour and are intolerant towards deviant persons and ideas. Weak Uncertainty Avoidance societies maintain a more relaxed atmosphere in which practice counts more than principles

165

and deviance is more easily tolerated. The fundamental issue addressed by this dimension is how a society reacts on the fact that time only runs one way and that the future is unknown: whether it tries to control the future or to let it happen. Like Power Distance, Uncertainty Avoidance has consequences for the way people build their institutions and organizations.

Masculinity versus Femininity
Masculinity stands for a preference in society for achievement, heroism, assertiveness, and material success. Its opposite, Femininity, stands for a preference for relationships, modesty, caring for the weak, and the quality of life. The fundamental issue addressed by this dimension is the way in which a society allocates social (as opposed to biological) roles to the sexes.

Having identified societal values is it possible then to identify significantly related accounting values at the level of the accounting subculture?

The following 'accounting' values, derived from a review of accounting literature and practice, are offered for consideration:

Professionalism versus Statutory Control – a preference for the exercise of individual professional judgment and the maintenance of professional self-regulation as opposed to compliance with prescriptive legal requirements and statutory control.

Uniformity versus Flexibility – a preference for the enforcement of uniform accounting practices between companies and for the consistent use of such practices over time as opposed to flexibility in accordance with the perceived circumstances of individual companies.

Conservatism versus Optimism – a preference for a cautious approach to measurement so as to cope with the uncertainty of future events as opposed to a more optimistic, laissez-faire, risk-taking approach.

Secrecy versus Transparency – a preference for confidentiality and the restriction of disclosure of information about the business only to those who are closely involved with its management and financing as opposed to a more transparent, open and publicly accountable approach.

It should be emphasized that there is no suggestion that these 'values' are necessarily the only values involved. What they do represent, however, is an attempt to identify value dimensions which appear to be widely recognized.

What arguments are there to support these accounting value dimensions? How do they relate to societal values? How are they likely to impact on the development of national accounting systems?

Professionalism versus statutory control

This is proposed as a significant accounting value dimension because accountants are perceived to adopt independent attitudes and to exercise their individual professional judgments to a greater or lesser extent everywhere in the world.

A major controversy in many Western countries, for example, surrounds the issue of the extent to which the accounting profession should be subject to public regulation/statutory control or be permitted to retain control over accounting standards as a matter for private self-regulation (e.g., Taylor and Turley, 1986).

The development of professional associations has a long history but they are much more firmly established in countries such as the U.S.A. and the U.K. than in some of the Continental European countries and in many of the less developed countries (e.g., Holzer, 1984; Nobes and Parker, 1985).

In the U.K., for example, the concept of presenting 'a true and fair view' of a company's financial position and results depends heavily on the judgment of the accountant as an independent professional. This is so to the extent that accounting information disclosures additional to, and sometimes contrary to, what is specifically required by law may be necessary. This may be contrasted with the traditional position in France and Germany where the professional accountant's role has been concerned primarily with the implementation of relatively prescriptive and detailed legal requirements (e.g., Gray and Coenenberg, 1984). With the implementation of the EEC directives this situation is now changing to the extent that there is some movement, if not convergence, along the professionalism spectrum.

To what extent then can professionalism be linked to the societal values of Individualism, Power Distance, Uncertainty Avoidance, and Masculinity? It is argued here that professionalism can be linked most closely with the individualism and uncertainty-avoidance dimensions. A preference for independent professional judgment is consistent with a preference for a loosely knit social framework where there is more emphasis on independence, a belief in individual decisions and respect for individual endeavour. This is also consistent with weak uncertainty avoidance where practice is all important, where there is a belief in fair play and as few rules as possible, and where a variety of professional judgments will tend to be more easily tolerated. There would also seem to be a link, if less strong, between professionalism and power distance in that professionalism is more likely to be accepted in a small power-distance society where there is more concern for equal rights, where people at various power levels feel less threatened and more prepared to trust people, and where there is a belief in the need to justify the imposition of laws and codes. As regards masculinity, however, there does not appear to be any significant link with professionalism.

Following from this analysis it may be hypothesized that:

H1: The higher a country ranks in terms of individualism and the lower it ranks in terms of uncertainty avoidance and power distance then the more likely it is to rank highly in terms of professionalism.

Uniformity versus flexibility

This would seem to be a significant accounting value dimension because attitudes about uniformity, consistency or comparability are incorporated as a fundamental feature of accounting principles world-wide (e.g., Choi and Mueller, 1984; Arpan and Radebaugh, 1985; Nobes and Parker, 1985).

This is a value which is open to different interpretations ranging from a relatively strict inter-company and inter-temporal uniformity, to consistency within companies over time and some concern for comparability between companies, to relative flexibility of accounting practices to suit the circumstances of individual companies.

In countries such as France, for example, a uniform accounting plan has long been in operation, together with the imposition of tax rules for measurement purposes, where there is a concern to facilitate national planning and the pursuit of macroeconomic goals. In contrast, in the U.K. and U.S.A. there is more concern with inter-temporal consistency together with some degree of inter-company comparability subject to a perceived need for flexibility (e.g., Choi and Mueller, 1984; Holzer, 1984; Arpan and Radebaugh, 1985).

To what extent then can uniformity be linked to societal value dimensions? It is argued here that uniformity can be linked most closely with the uncertainty-avoidance and individualism dimensions. A preference for uniformity is consistent with a preference for strong uncertainty avoidance leading to a concern for law and order and rigid codes of behaviour, a need for written rules and regulations, a respect for conformity and the search for ultimate, absolute truths and values. This value dimension is also consistent with a preference for collectivism, as opposed to individualism, with its tightly knit social framework, a belief in organization and order, and respect for group norms. There would also seem to be a link, if less strong, between uniformity and power distance in that uniformity is more easily facilitated in a large power-distance society in that the imposition of laws and codes of a uniform character are more likely to be accepted. As regards masculinity, however, there does not appear to be any significant link with uniformity. Following from this analysis it may be hypothesized that:

H2: The higher a country ranks in terms of uncertainty avoidance and power distance and the lower it ranks in terms of individualism then the more likely it is to rank highly in terms of uniformity.

Conservatism versus optimism

This would seem to be a significant accounting value dimension because it is arguably 'the most ancient and probably the most pervasive principle of accounting valuation' (Sterling, 1967, p. 110).

Conservatism or prudence in asset measurement and the reporting of profits is perceived as a fundamental attitude of accountants the world over. Moreover, conservatism varies according to country, ranging from a strongly conservative approach in the Continental European countries, such as France and Germany, to the much less conservative attitudes of accountants in the U.S.A. and U.K. (e.g., Beeny, 1975, 1976; Nobes, 1984; Choi and Mueller, 1984; Arpan and Radebaugh, 1985).

The differential impact of conservatism on accounting measurement practices internationally has also been demonstrated empirically (e.g., Gray, 1980; Choi and Mueller, 1984). Such differences would seem to be reinforced by the relative development of capital markets, the differing pressures of user interests, and the influence of tax laws on accountants in the countries concerned.

To what extent then can conservatism be linked to societal value dimensions? It is argued here that conservatism can be linked most closely with the uncertainty avoidance dimension. A preference for more conservative measures of profits is consistent with strong uncertainty avoidance following from a concern with security and a perceived need to adopt a cautious approach to cope with the uncertainty of future events. There would also seem to be a link, if less strong, between high levels of individualism and masculinity on the one hand, and weak uncertainty avoidance on the other, to the extent that an emphasis on individual achievement and performance is likely to foster a less conservative approach to measurement. As regards the power distance dimension there does not, however, appear to be any significant link with conservatism.

Following from this analysis it may be hypothesized that:

> H3:   The higher a country ranks in terms of uncertainty avoidance and the lower it ranks in terms of individualism and masculinity then the more likely it is to rank highly in terms of conservatism.

Secrecy versus transparency

This would seem to be a significant accounting value dimension which stems as much from management as it does from the accountant owing to the influence of management on the quantity of information disclosed to outsiders (e.g., Jaggi, 1975). Secrecy, or confidentiality, in business relationships is, nevertheless, a fundamental accounting attitude (Arpan and Radebaugh, 1985).

Secrecy would also seem to be closely related to conservatism in that both values imply a cautious approach to corporate financial reporting in general; but with secrecy relating to the disclosure dimension and conservatism relating to the measurement dimension. The extent of secrecy would seem to vary across countries with lower levels of disclosure, including instances of secret reserves, evident in the Continental European countries, for example, compared to the U.S.A. and U.K. (e.g., Barrett, 1976; Choi and Mueller, 1984; Arpan and Radebaugh, 1985). These differences would also seem to be reinforced by the differential development of capital markets and the nature of share ownership which may provide incentives for the voluntary disclosure of information (e.g., Watts, 1977).

To what extent, then, can secrecy be linked to societal value dimensions? It is argued here that secrecy can be linked most closely with the uncertainty-avoidance, power-distance and individualism dimensions. A preference for secrecy is consistent with strong uncertainty avoidance following from a need to restrict information disclosures so as to avoid conflict and competition and to preserve security. A close relationship with power distance also seems likely in that high power-distance societies are likely to be characterized by the restriction of information to preserve power inequalities. Secrecy is also consistent with a preference for collectivism, as opposed to individualism, with its concern for those closely involved with the firm rather than external parties. A significant but less important link with masculinity also seems likely to the extent that more caring societies where more emphasis is given to the quality of life, people and the environment, will tend to be more open especially as regards socially related information.

Following from this analysis it may be hypothesized that:

H4: The higher a country ranks in terms of uncertainty avoidance and power distance and the lower it ranks in terms of individualism and masculinity then the more likely it is to rank highly in terms of secrecy.

Accounting values and culture area classifications

Having formulated hypotheses relating societal values to accounting values internationally, it is evident that the most important societal values at the level of the accounting subculture would seem to be uncertainty avoidance and individualism. While power distance and masculinity are also significant to some extent, masculinity appears to be of somewhat lesser importance in the system of accounting values.

It is now proposed to hypothesize culture area classifications in the context of combinations of accounting values. For this purpose it is argued here that a useful distinction can be made between the authority for accounting systems, that is, the extent to which they are determined and enforced by

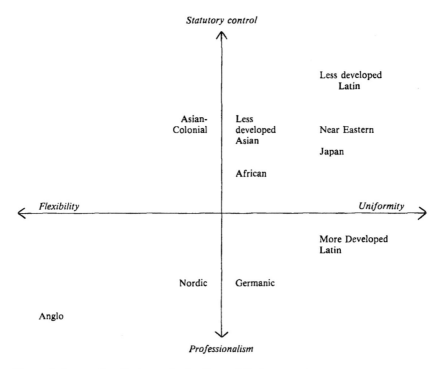

Figure 3 Accounting Systems: Authority and Enforcement.

statutory control or professional means on the one hand, and the measurement and disclosure characteristics of accounting systems on the other.

Accounting values most relevant to the professional or statutory authority for accounting systems and their enforcement would seem to be the professionalism and uniformity dimensions in that they are concerned with regulation and the extent of enforcement or conformity. Accordingly, these can be combined and the classification of culture areas hypothesized on a judgmental basis as shown in Figure 3. In making these judgments reference has been made to the relevant correlations between value dimensions and the resultant clusters of countries identified from the statistical analysis carried out by Hofstede (1980, pp. 223, 316). From this classification it seems clear that the Anglo and Nordic culture areas may be contrasted with the Germanic and more developed Latin culture areas on the one hand, and the Japanese, Near Eastern, less developed Latin, less developed Asian and African culture areas on the other. The Colonial Asian countries are separately classified, representing a mixture of influences.

Accounting values most relevant to the measurement practices used and the extent of information disclosed are self-evidently the conservatism

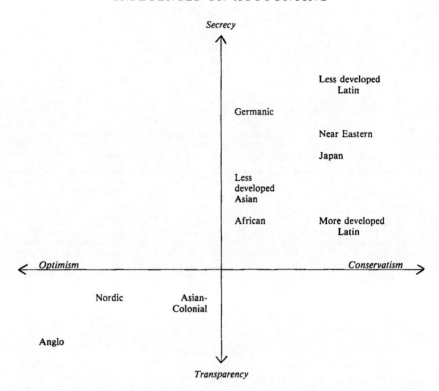

Figure 4 Accounting Systems: Measurement and Disclosure.

and secrecy dimensions. Accordingly, these can be combined and the classification of culture areas hypothesized on a judgmental basis as shown in Figure 4. In making judgments in respect of these classifications reference has also been made to the relevant correlations between value dimensions and the resultant clusters of countries identified from the statistical analysis carried out by Hofstede (1980, pp. 316, 324). Here there would appear to be a sharper division of culture area groupings with the Colonial Asian group relating more closely with the Anglo and Nordic groupings in contrast with the Germanic and more developed Latin groupings which appear to relate more closely to the Japanese, less developed Asian, African, less developed Latin, and Near Eastern area groupings.

Summary and conclusions

While prior research has shown that there are different patterns of accounting and that the development of national systems of corporate financial reporting is related to environmental factors, identification of the patterns and the influential factors involved remains controversial. The significance of culture in this context is far from clear and has been a relatively neglected issue in the development of ideas about international classification.

In this paper, a framework for analysing the impact of culture on the development of accounting systems internationally has been proposed. Value dimensions at the accounting subculture level have been identified, that is, professionalism, uniformity, conservatism and secrecy. These have been linked to cultural value dimensions at the societal level and hypotheses have been formulated for testing. Classifications of country groupings by culture area have also been hypothesized as a basis for testing the relationship between culture and accounting systems in the context of systems authority and enforcement characteristics on the one hand, and measurement and disclosure characteristics on the other.

Following this analysis, empirical research now needs to be carried out to assess the extent to which there is in fact a match between (a) societal values and accounting values, and (b) the proposed classification of country groupings, based on cultural influence, and the groupings derived from an analysis of accounting practices related to the value dimensions of the accounting subculture. However, for this to be feasible, further work to operationalize the link between accounting practices and accounting values will be necessary, and the relevant cross-cultural data assembled and organized.

In interpreting the results of empirical research relating to culture, the influence of any change factors will also need to be taken into account, bearing in mind the existence of external influences arising from colonization, war, and foreign investment, including the activities of multinational companies and large international accounting firms.

While much work lies ahead, this paper is offered as a contribution towards a theory of cultural influence on the development of accounting systems internationally. In doing so it is fully recognized that the ideas advanced are exploratory and subject to empirical testing and verification.

References

Arpan, J. S., and L. H. Radebaugh, *International Accounting and Multinational Enterprises*, Wiley, 1985.

Barrett, M. E., 'Financial Reporting Practices: Disclosure and Comprehensiveness in an International Setting', *Journal of Accounting Research*, Spring 1976.

Beeny, J. H., *European Financial Reporting – West Germany*, ICAEW, 1975.

——, *European Financial Reporting – France*, ICAEW, 1976.

Choi, F. D. S., and G. G. Mueller, *International Accounting*, Prentice-Hall, 1984.

Douglas, M., *Cosmology: An Enquiry into Cultural Bias*, Royal Anthropological Institute, 1977.

Frank, W. G., 'An Empirical Analysis of International Accounting Principles', *Journal of Accounting Research*, Autumn 1979.

Gray, S. J., 'The Impact of International Accounting Differences from a Security Analysis Perspective: Some European Evidence', *Journal of Accounting Research*, Spring 1980.

Gray, S. J. and A. G. Coenenberg (eds), *EEC Accounting Harmonisation: Implementation and Impact of the Fourth Directive*, North Holland, 1984.

Harrison, G. L., and J. L. McKinnon, 'Cultural and Accounting Change: A New Perspective on Corporate Reporting Regulation and Accounting Policy Formulation', *Accounting, Organizations and Society*, Vol. 11, No. 3, 1986.

Hofstede, G., *Culture's Consequences*, Sage Publications, 1980.

——, 'Dimensions of National Cultures in Fifty Countries and Three Regions', in J. B. Deregowski, S. Dziurawiec and R. Annis (eds), *Expiscations in Cross-Cultural Psychology*, Swets and Zeitlinger, 1983.

——, 'Cultural Dimensions in Management and Planning', *Asia Pacific Journal of Management*, January 1984.

Holzer, H. P. (ed.), *International Accounting*, Harper & Row, 1984.

Inkeles, A., and P. J. Levinson, 'National Character: The Study of Modal Personality and Sociocultural Systems', in G. Lindsey and E. Aronson (eds), *The Handbook of Social Psychology*, (2nd edn), Addison-Wesley, 1969.

Jaggi, B. L., 'The Impact of the Cultural Environment on Financial Disclosures', *International Journal of Accounting*, Spring 1975.

Kluckhohn, F. R., and F. L. Strodtbeck, *Variations in Value Orientations*, Greenwood Press, 1961.

McKinnon, J. L., *The Historical Development and Operational Form of Corporate Reporting Regulation in Japan*, Garland, 1986.

Mueller, G. G., *International Accounting*, Macmillan, 1967.

——, 'Accounting Principles Generally Accepted in the United States Versus those Generally Accepted Elsewhere', *International Journal of Accounting Education and Research*, Spring 1968.

Nair, R. D., and W. G. Frank, 'The Impact of Disclosure and Measurement Practices on International Accounting Classifications', *The Accounting Review*, July 1980.

Nobes, C. W., 'A Judgemental International Classification of Financial Reporting Practices', *Journal of Business Finance and Accounting*, Spring 1983.

——, *International Classification of Financial Reporting*, Croom Helm, 1984.

Nobes, C. W., and R. H. Parker, (eds), *Comparative International Accounting*, Philip Allan, 1985.

Parsons, T., and E. A. Shils, *Toward a General Theory of Action*, Harvard University Press, 1951.

Price Waterhouse International, *International Survey of Accounting Principles and Reporting Practices*, 1975.

Radebaugh, L. H., 'Environmental Factors Influencing the Development of Accounting Objectives, Standards and Practices in Peru', *International Journal of Accounting Education and Research*, Fall, 1975.

Seidler, L. J., 'International Accounting – the Ultimate Theory Course', *The Accounting Review*, October 1967.

Sterling, R. R., 'Conservatism: The Fundamental Principle of Valuation in Traditional Accounting', *Abacus*, December 1967.

Taylor, P., and S. Turley, *The Regulation of Accounting*, Blackwell, 1986.

Watts, R. L., 'Corporate Financial Statements: A Product of the Market and Political Processes', *Australian Journal of Management*, April 1977.

Zeff, S. A., *Forging Accounting Principles in Five Countries: A History and an Analysis of Trends*, Stipes, 1971.

7

AN EMPIRICAL ASSESSMENT OF GRAY'S ACCOUNTING VALUE CONSTRUCTS

Shalin Chanchani and Roger Willett

Source: *International Journal of Accounting* 39(2) (2004): 125–54.

Abstract

Gray [*Abacus* (1988) 1] proposed a framework for a theory of cultural relevance in accounting. This renewed an interest in culture-related studies in international accounting. To date, much of this literature has been theoretical or subjectively descriptive because the elements constituting Gray's framework lack an operational foundation. This paper addresses this shortcoming by presenting research that operationalizes and evaluates the empirical usefulness of Gray's accounting subcultural value constructs of professionalism, uniformity, conservatism, and secrecy.

The paper presents the results from an accounting values survey (AVS) administered to a sample of users and preparers of financial statements in New Zealand and India. The data are subjected to multivariate analysis, and the results provide some support for the usefulness of Gray's accounting values as empirically based classificatory constructs, although they may require some adaptation and reinterpretation. Professionalism appears as the most clearly defined construct and the elements of the uniformity construct also hold together well, although appearing to attract elements of the construct of secrecy. The part of the secrecy construct concerned with the level of detail in financial statements appears to be reasonably well defined by respondents to the survey and conservatism seems to fragment into two subdimensions, perhaps representing measurement and the disclosure aspects of that construct. A question arises as to the possible existence of other, as yet unrecognized, accounting-value constructs. The findings suggest the importance of further quantitative survey research of this type to investigate the relevance of cultural factors in understanding international accounting practices.

1. Introduction and motivation

Gray's (1988) article in *Abacus* entitled "Towards a Theory of Cultural Influence in the Development of Accounting Systems Internationally" was a pioneering paper in the development of the idea that culture might influence accounting practices. Gray proposed a theory linking societal and accounting values that bring together constructs from the social sciences (specifically, Hofstede, 1983, 1997, 2001) and international accounting literature. The literature has since seen a renewed interest in this area, but the discussion remains largely theoretical, as few empirical studies have tested Gray's theory in a rigorous manner. Any systematic test of the Hofstede–Gray framework should presumably be preceded by a rigorous examination of the elements comprising the framework; that is, are the theoretical constructs operational and empirically measurable? This paper is motivated by that question. The study reported in the paper examines Gray's subcultural accounting-value constructs, which are fundamental to the Hofstede–Gray framework. The analysis is based upon an approach that tests for the existence of Gray's value constructs as factors explaining the responses of a large sample of users and preparers of accounting information in India and New Zealand.

Section 2 outlines Gray's theory of cultural relevance, which is central to this paper. This section also reviews the literature that was produced in the wake of Gray's theory. Section 3 details the selection of the sample and methods of analysis. Section 4 presents the analysis of the survey results using reliability, factor, and cluster analyses. Section 5 contains a discussion of the results and the conclusions of the paper, its limitations, and some suggestions for future research.

2. Background and relevant prior research

Gray's argument that culture influences accounting rests on the framework shown in Fig. 1. The framework identifies a variety of factors supposedly affecting cultural or societal values. Societal values lead to the development and maintenance of institutions within a society including educational, social, and political systems and legal, financial, and corporate structures. Once in place, these systems should reflect and reinforce societal values, as depicted in the loop at the bottom of Fig. 1. This structure is supposed to remain stable, and changes at the national level are mainly due to major external factors. International trade, investment, multinational companies, and colonization are examples of the latter.

Drawing upon Hofstede's (1980, Chap. 1) framework, Gray incorporated accounting to it by depicting how accounting practices might influence and reinforce societal values. Gray's theory presents societal values at the level of the accounting subculture. Cultural or societal values at the national level permeate through to occupational subcultures, including the accounting

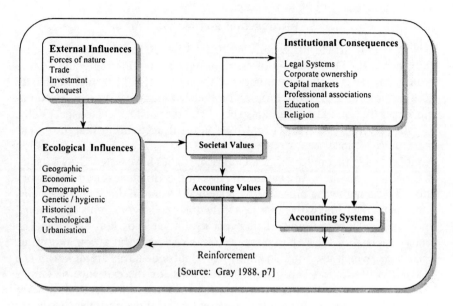

Figure 1 Culture, societal values and the accounting subculture.

profession, with varying degrees of integration. The value systems of accountants are derived from societal values, with specific reference to work-related values. Accounting values, in turn, influence accounting practices, including the reporting and disclosure of information. Thus, depending on the varying degrees of external and ecological forces shaping societal values, different accounting systems develop, reflect, and reinforce these values. Gray proposed that this framework might be used to explain international differences in accounting practices.

Gray went on to suggest that there should be a close match between cultural areas and patterns of accounting systems. This appears to be the basic argument supporting the contention that each culture should develop its own accounting systems to serve its own distinct requirements (e.g., Jaggi, 1975) and is the basis upon which Gray rests his theory of cultural relevance to accounting. Gray stated the following four hypotheses as part of his theory:

H1. The higher a country ranks in terms of individualism and the lower it ranks in terms of uncertainty avoidance and power distance, the more likely it is to rank highly in terms of professionalism.

H2. The higher a country ranks in terms of uncertainty avoidance and power distance and the lower it ranks in terms of individualism, the more likely it is to rank highly in terms of uniformity.

H3. The higher a country ranks in terms of uncertainty avoidance and the lower it ranks in terms of individualism and masculinity, the more likely it is to rank highly in terms of conservatism.

H4. The higher a country ranks in terms of uncertainty avoidance and power distance and the lower it ranks in terms of individualism and masculinity, the more likely it is to rank highly in terms of secrecy.

Empirical testing of the cultural relevance hypothesis requires operational definitions of societal values, but not necessarily of Gray's accounting-value constructs. For example, Salter and Niswander (1995) conducted a regression analysis of the relationship between the observable attributes of financial statements and the measurements based upon Hofstede's cultural values. Such direct tests of the cultural relevance hypothesis, using Gray's constructs only as *theoretical* intervening or moderating variables, are often claimed to test Gray's theory. Lanis (2001) has argued that such an approach is not an appropriate way to test Gray's theory and has proposed a revised Hofstedian theoretical framework to avoid what he criticizes as a "black box" approach to assessing the cultural relevance hypothesis. Little or no attempt seems to have been made to confirm the empirical meaningfulness of Gray's accounting value constructs directly or to measure them objectively. Some studies that otherwise give the appearance of doing so actually use subjective judgment to measure the relevant constructs in a manner that depends upon the undemonstrated assumption that Gray's accounting values are, in fact, meaningful, empirical constructs. Examples of such studies are Eddie (1991) and Gerhardy (1990).

The study reported in this paper specifically addresses this issue. It attempts to operationalize Gray's accounting value constructs, by interpreting responses to a questionnaire survey, and to assess if these value constructs are plausible, empirically, in the sense that they reveal systematic patterns in the respondent's recorded attitudes to the questionnaire items.

The questionnaire instrument for this study was designed from scratch, given that there was no prior study to inform its content and that the literature provided no advice about the manner in which Gray's accounting constructs should be operationalized. In constructing the questionnaire, we used three main sources as guides: the general principles of questionnaire design, the format of Hofstede's value-survey module (VSM) and the objectives of the Hofstede–Gray theoretical framework, and the implications of previous theoretical and empirical work on the Hofstede–Gray framework. The literature relating to the second and third sources are discussed in the following two subsections. The general principles of the design considered in choosing questionnaire items are discussed in Section 3.

179

2.1 The VSM and the Hofstede–Gray framework

Hofstede's VSM questionnaire was designed for a large–scale study of work–related attitudes of 116,000 IBM employees in over 40 countries in the 1960s. The details underlying the design are discussed at length in Hofstede (1980, 2001). On the basis of a factor analysis of responses to the survey, Hofstede initially proposed four dimensions and introduced a fifth dimension in a later study reported in *Culture and Organizations: Software of the Mind* (1997). These were described by Hofstede as "individualism versus collectivism," "large versus small power distance," "strong versus weak uncertainty avoidance," "masculinity versus femininity," and "long- versus short-term orientation." A discussion of the precise meaning of these terms is not necessary for present purposes; it is sufficient to state that Hofstede related the first four of these constructs to the basic sociological concepts of; the self, relationship to authority, control of aggression, and gender role differentiation, respectively (Hofstede, 1980). The fifth construct was distinctly related to "Confucianism" in oriental society.[1]

Gray's conceptualization of accounting subcultural values was influenced by Hofstede's societal value constructs. More than Hofstede did, Gray based his ideas on a priori reasoning and the general (and wide) experience of international accounting regimes, as opposed to an empirically based technique such as the factor analysis of survey data. Much less has been done to test Gray's accounting value constructs, the operationalization of which is the core of this paper. Gray's accounting values are summarized in the following subsections.

2.1.1 Professionalism versus statutory control

Gray (1988, p. 8) defined professionalism as a preference for the exercise of individual professional judgment and the maintenance of professional self-regulation, as opposed to compliance with prescriptive legal requirements and statutory control. As identified by Gray, professionalism may be identified at two levels: the level of the individual making professional judgments and the statutory level, possibly concerning self-governing, professional, regulatory institutions. Professionalism is considered a core dimension of accounting values because accountants are required to make professional judgments regarding valuation and various aspects of disclosure in financial information. Such judgments are made by accountants to a lesser or greater extent in different parts of the world, depending on various factors including legal and statutory requirements and prevalent professional practice (Belkaoui, 1990, 1995). At an organisational level, the development of accounting bodies in various parts of the world reflects differing degrees of self-regulation with professional bodies in the United States and United Kingdom possessing a larger degree of autonomy and self-regulation than those in continental Europe and developing countries. Writers such as Gray and Coenenberg (1984), Holzer (1984), Nobes and Parker (1995), and Taylor and Turley (1986) support the above arguments for professionalism, and there is little disagreement that this is a significant concept in accounting.

2.1.2 Uniformity versus flexibility

Gray (1988, p. 8) defined uniformity as a preference for the enforcement of similar accounting practices between companies and for the consistent use of such practices over time, as opposed to flexibility in accordance with the perceived circumstances of individual companies. This dimension thus consists of at least two components: inter-temporal consistency in accounting practices and uniformity in the application of accounting policies and rules across companies. There has been a wide variation in the application of accounting principles across firms and between countries. In France, for instance, where, traditionally, there has been a concern with facilitating national planning, a uniform accounting plan has been followed. This is in contrast to practices in the United Kingdom and the United States, where there is a perceived need for flexibility in adopting and following accounting policies. Writers such as Arpan and Radebaugh (1985), Choi and Mueller (1984), Holzer (1984), and Nobes and Parker (1995) have provided arguments in support of treating uniformity as a central notion underlying accounting practice.

2.1.3 Conservatism versus optimism

Gray (1988, p. 8) defined conservatism as a preference for a cautious approach to measurement, to cope with the uncertainty of future events as opposed to a more optimistic, laissez-faire, risk-taking approach. Conservatism here fundamentally means prudence or the use of caution and implies that accountants who are conservative should anticipate losses but not gains. It is considered by many as one of the most fundamental accounting concepts, even being "the most ancient and probably the most pervasive principle in accounting valuation" (Sterling, 1967, p. 110). Conservatism is usually thought to contrast widely in different parts of the world, ranging from a strongly conservative approach in Continental Europe to much less conservative attitudes among accountants in the United Kingdom and the United States. Gray suggested that such differences are reinforced by the relative development of capital markets, the differing pressures of users' interests, and the influence of tax laws on accountants in the countries concerned. In addition to Arpan and Radebaugh (1985), Beeny (1975, 1976), Choi and Mueller (1984), Gray (1980), Nobes (1992), and Sterling (1967) have noted the importance of the concept of conservatism in the practice of accounting.

2.1.4 Secrecy versus transparency

Gray defined secrecy as a preference for a cautious approach to disclosure, considering it a fundamental accounting attribute that stems from the influence of management on the quantity of information disclosed to outsiders. Jaggi (1975) had also previously attributed this dimension to management because firms often disclose minimal information in financial statements. Some research has claimed that secrecy varies considerably among countries, especially between continental Europe and the United States (Arpan & Radebaugh, 1985; Barrett, 1976; Choi & Mueller, 1984). These differences may also be reinforced by the differential development of capital markets and the nature of share ownership, which provide incentives for disclosure (Watts, 1977).

Gray (1988) was presented as being "the first step" towards a theory of cultural relevance, but with much empirical work to follow. It is appropriate to operationalize Gray's accounting values as empirical constructs if the usefulness of the hypotheses stated earlier are to be assessed objectively. To facilitate this objective, the following subsection reviews some research that has attempted to extend, apply, and critique the Hofstede–Gray framework that developed from Gray's thesis.

2.2 Theoretical developments and empirical assessments of the Hofstede–Gray framework

2.2.1 Theoretical developments

Perera (1989) and Perera and Matthews (1990) adapted Gray's theory, the former with special reference to developing countries,[2] in an attempt to trace the impact of accounting values upon different aspects of accounting practice. Fechner and Kilgore (1994) and Radebaugh and Gray (1993) also developed Gray's 1988 theory to try to relate accounting values more specifically to accounting practices. The idea behind these theories is illustrated by the framework of Radebaugh and Gray in Fig. 2. The key issue with frameworks such as those identified in Fig. 2 is that these are at an abstract level and are not readily amenable to empirical testing. To the extent that these aspects of accounting practice are validly related to accounting values, they may act as a guide in operationalizing the latter concepts through appropriately chosen items in a questionnaire instrument. However, this task requires further theoretical developments.

Baydoun and Willett (1995) and Willett, Nishimura, and Baydoun (1997), in a critical evaluation of Gray's theory, attempted to operationalize Gray's accounting values in terms of GAAP qualitative characteristics of good measurement and reporting practices (see Table 1) by questioning whether Gray's accounting values really served any useful purpose as intervening

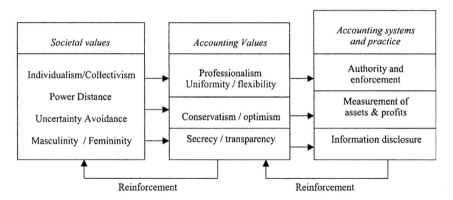

Figure 2 Gray's accounting dimensions and measurement and disclosure
Source: Radebaugh & Gray, 1993.

Table 1 Gray's dimensions and the qualitative characteristics of financial statements.

Accounting dimensions – technical aspects	Qualitative characteristics relating to disclosure	Examples of issues relating form & content of corporate reports
Uniformity	*Uniform content & presentation* Consistency Comparability	Standardised accounts Accounting policies
Conservatism	*Quality of information:* Timeliness Materiality Objectivity Verifiability Reliability Neutrality Substance over form	Normal publication date Cost versus market values Cash flow accounting Lower of cost and market
Secrecy	*Amount of information:* Accountability Decision usefulness	*Extent of disaggregated data:* Number of items disclosed Group accounts Supplementary statements

Source: Baydoun & Willett, 1995.

variables between Hofstede's dimensions of culture and the characteristics of accounting. One way of establishing if this is the case would be to see if Gray's accounting values could be operationalized as informative empirical constructs. This is an essential motivating point for the research reported in this paper.

Willett *et al.* (1997) reasoned that culture most clearly affects those parts of the accounting environment that are essentially social, such as the management structures of firms or the abilities, rights, and powers of different user groups to use or demand information. In particular, it was argued that culture influences disclosure practices more than measurement practices. If this analysis has validity, its implication for our current purposes is that a questionnaire should endeavor to cover both the social and technological aspects and, with regard to the latter, to include instances of both measurement and disclosure practices.

2.2.2 Empirical assessments of the cultural relevance hypothesis

A number of recent studies provide overviews of the cultural relevance literature in accounting. The cultural relevance hypothesis underpins much current work in comparative management control and environmental accounting. In a detailed review of cross-cultural research in management-control systems, Harrison and McKinnon (1999) identified several weaknesses in the literature, including what they saw as an excessive reliance on cultural value dimensions. Related to these matters, Bhimani (1999) provided a critique of cultural studies in managerial accounting, and Chow, Shields, and Wu (1999), Lau and Buckland (2000), and Tsui (2001) reported cross-cultural research in management-control systems. Chanchani and MacGregor (1999) particularly noted the lack of primary data in cultural relevance literature.

Eddie (1991) and Gehardy (1990) are examples of the informal use and testing of Gray's theory. Gerhardy applied the theory selectively and subjectively to analyze the accounting systems of West Germany. The study of Eddie of 13 countries of the Asia-Pacific region found support for Gray's theory, confirming all the predicted signs of association between societal and accounting values. However, as with the study of Gerhardy, the study of Eddie suffered from the possibility of bias because the factors comprising each of the accounting subcultural value indices and the weights assigned to the factors comprising the index were determined subjectively.

A variety of approaches to using Gray's theory are evident in the literature. In a normative analysis, Chow, Chau, and Gray (1995) applied Gray's model to study the impact of the accounting reforms in China since 1980, concluding that the reform process would be constrained by cultural imperatives but the empirical import of the paper is unclear. The Spanish study of Amat, Blake, Wraith, and Oliveras (1999) was based on Gray (1988) but is mainly descriptive and anecdotal. Willett et al. (1997) used a subjective assessment of Gray's accounting values, similar with the fashion adopted in Eddie (1991), to analyze the nature of accounting practices in the Asia-Pacific region finding that although the Hofstede–Gray analysis was consistent with the facts, a simpler explanation of the situation could be given in terms of colonialism and the institutional needs of users. A similar point was made in Nobes (1998).

The study by Salter and Niswander (1995), referred to earlier, is probably the most objective, published account relating to Gary's theory to date. It was based upon data from 29 countries, utilizing Gray's accounting values as theoretical terms and defining those values directly as elements of accounting practice. It was concluded that Gray's model was successful at explaining actual financial-reporting practices but relatively weak in explaining extant professional and regulatory structures. It was further suggested that both the development of financial markets and levels of taxation enhance the explanations offered by Gray. The present study is probably best seen as an attempt to support studies such as that of Salter and Niswander in their use of Gray's theory in international accounting research.

Gray's theory continues to be either referred to or relied upon in ongoing research. A number of recent studies have related accounting judgments on various matters to cultural influences. Schultz and Lopez (2001) found that judgments among accountants in France, Germany, and the United States vary significantly. Arnold, Bernardi, and Neidermeyer (2001) found that as uncertainty avoidance increases, materiality estimates increase. Other instances of relevant research include the investigation of cross-national issues in voluntary disclosure and foreign listing requirements (Meek, Roberts, & Gray, 1995), earnings measurement (Cooke, 1993; Gray, 1980; Weetman & Gray, 1991), cultural influence of financial reporting in translation and legal contexts (Jaggi & Low, 2000), uniformity as a cultural or economic phenomena (Roberts & Salter, 1999), cultural impact on project-evaluation decisions (Harrison, Chow, Wu, & Harrell, 1999), cultural differences in behavioral consequences of performance evaluation and reward systems (Aswasthi, Chow, & Wu, 2001), the effect of national culture on intellectual capital and knowledge management (Chow, Deng, & Ho, 2000; Lynn, 1999) and cultural issues relating to harmonization and regulation (Dyball & Valcarcel, 1999; Farrell & Cobbin, 2001). For a broad review and commentary see Radebaugh and Gray (2001).

In summary, as may be seen from this brief review, there continues to be a strong interest in cultural relevance research in accounting and in the application of Gray's (1988) theory to a variety of issues. The impact of this literature is probably more far-reaching than may at first appear. For instance, Gray's values have recently been referred to in a medical teaching journal, which discusses cultural relevance of patient-centered interviews (Nestle, 2001). Work to date that has attempted to validate the fundamental basis of the Hofstede–Gray framework has, however, been unsystematic, limited by the availability of data or lacking a convincing operationalization of the fundamental accounting value constructs. One way to address this deficiency is to develop a direct method of assessing Gray's constructs for validity and reliability, to begin the process of accumulating data to answer the question: What is the empirical status of Gray's accounting values as cultural constructs? The following section describes the method of operationalizing Gray's accounting value constructs through a question-naire instrument, as it was used in this research and based upon the considerations flowing from the preceding literature review.

3. Method

3.1 Operationalizing the variables

The design of the questionnaire instrument for this study was informed from a number of sources that we briefly discuss, partly to leave a trail of our reasoning and partly to refer to later in our analysis of the survey results.[3] A copy of the questionnaire instrument is found in Appendix A. The covering letter accompanying the questionnaire was brief and general, explaining the purpose of the research, obtaining informed consent, and assuring anonymity of response. It did not attempt to provide additional context to the questionnaire, such as whether the items related to public or private companies. It is acknowledged that some of the items are imprecise in nature and are open to alternative interpretations. The results reported later suggest some modification of the reasoning used in the first instance in the design of the questionnaire instrument. These are discussed in the concluding section.

The basic form and content of the instrument followed Hofstede's VSM and is referred to below as the accounting values survey (AVS). The reason for following Hofstede in this respect is that the design considerations under-lying the VSM are closely related to this study by the needs of testing the Hofstede–Gray cultural relevance hypothesis. Considerable effort has gone into the theoretical development of the VSM and it has been tested and used in many different empirical contexts (see Hofstede, 1980, pp. 13–39). Just as Hofstede's VSM uses four questionnaire items to capture each cultural value construct, so each of Gray's accounting values is captured in the AVS by four items on a seven-point, equally spaced Likert-type scale.[4] Our question-naire thus contained 16 content items in all.

The choice of each item and its wording was informed by general principles relating to the best practice of questionnaire design. The "disagree–agree" format is discussed in Backstrom and Hursch (1963, pp. 77–79) and Ticehurst and Veal (2000, p. 147). The items were designed to be comprehensive, simple, short, understandable, and unequivocal (Sekaran, 1992, pp. 202–209). In an attempt to prevent the possibility of the items merely reflecting obvious or linguistic similarities and lazy anchoring, the items relating to each accounting value were spread through the questionnaire instrument, four items apart. One issue of a theoretical nature that is still unclear at the present time is the need for "orthogonality" of the items. This matter generally relates to the exclusivity of the questionnaire items and, in this instance, it is complicated by the possible overlap of some of the underlying accounting value constructs implied in the literature cited earlier. Ideally, the questionnaire items should give comprehensive coverage to all accounting values, which should divide into statistically recognizable factors. In the design of the instrument, importance was placed upon simplicity and brevity to reduce the risk of a low response rate. At the time the survey was developed, we were not aware (and are not as yet aware) of any other questionnaire study that attempts to test for the existence of accounting values using primary data, and the questionnaire instrument was therefore designed, more or less, from scratch. The specific subject matter of each item was guided by the theoretical considerations described in the literature review. The departure point in this regard was the classificatory scheme implied by the analysis of Baydoun and Willett (1995) and Willett *et al.* (1997) of the potential differential impact of cultural values on the measurement, disclosure, and social aspects of the accounting environment. The questionnaire was designed to give comprehensive coverage of these aspects of accounting.

In the final questionnaire distributed to respondents, two items relating to each of the conservatism and uniformity constructs concerned the measurement dimension and two concerned disclosure. All the secrecy items related to disclosure issues. All the professionalism items were related to the social dimension of the accounting environment. The specific content of the items in each construct is discussed below.

3.1.1 Conservatism

Items 1, 5, 9, and 13 attempted to capture the construct of conservatism. Items 1 and 13 were taken to relate to measurement and Items 5 and 9 to disclosure. Most prior theoretical work appears to take the view, based upon statements by Gray (e.g., Radebaugh & Gray, 1993), that this accounting value pertains solely to issues of measurement. Despite this, the construct is discussed here as having both measurement and disclosure aspects. For example, the idea that historic costs are more relevant than market values are for decision making, or should be used for decision making, may be interpreted as a preference for conservatism, but these are, strictly speaking, preferences concerning disclosure, not measurement, issues. Measurement issues concern what numbers represent and what their statistical or other properties are. Questions of relevance and usefulness for decision making concern judgments that determine what information to disclose and whether time should be wasted measuring something at all, not how it should be measured. Two preparers may disagree about whether to disclose market values or historic costs (because one may be more "conservative" than the other, although not necessarily more "secretive"), but they may still agree on the proper way to measure both concepts. This is probably a moot point in the context of this paper because, if Questions 5 and 9 are considered to be about measurement rather than disclosure, it makes little difference to the findings of the study, as long as it is agreed that the questions do tap the construct of conservatism.

Item 1 required respondents to state the extent of their agreement as to whether profits and assets should be valued downwards in case of doubt. Item 13 asked the respondents to indicate the extent of their agreement to the statement that in times of rising prices LIFO instead of FIFO should be used in calculations as estimates. The stronger the agreement to these statements, the greater the extent to which the respondents were judged to adopt conservative valuation approaches. Items 5 and 9 asked whether market values are more relevant than historic costs are and whether they should be used in preference to historic costs, respectively. To the extent that respondents indicated a preference towards historic costs, they would be considered conservative.

3.1.2 Uniformity

Items 2, 6, 10, and 14 relate to the uniformity construct. Items 2 and 10 were designed to relate to the measurement dimension, Items 6 and 14 to the disclosure dimension. Item two required respondents to indicate their level of uniformity by providing a specific measurement context. Agreement to externally set depreciation rates was taken to indicate higher uniformity. Item 6 approached the disclosure dimension from a cross-sectional viewpoint, eliciting degrees of agreement to a standardized format for the purpose of reporting information. The stronger the extent of the respondent's agreement with this item, the stronger the inclination towards uniformity was taken to be. Item 10 approached the measurement issue in a time (consistency) context, asking respondents for their level of agreement to the statement that accounting policies, once chosen, should not be subsequently changed. Agreement on this question implied that the respondent degree of uniformity was high. Item 14 asked respondents about the extent of their agreement to a statement that the level of detailed standardization disclosed within financial statements should be increased. The extent to which the respondents agreed with the statement was taken to indicate their level of preference for uniform accounting disclosure practices.

3.1.3 Secrecy

The secrecy construct is represented by questionnaire Items 3, 7, 11, and 15. All 4 items were classified as being related to disclosure issues. Item 3 required a response to the statement that financial statements should be available to the general public rather than just to shareholders and managers. This was designed to capture the "external spread of user" aspect of secrecy noted in Baydoun and Willett (1995). Item 7 measured the respondent's attitude regarding the amount of detailed information disclosed in financial statements capturing an "information quantity" aspect of secrecy. Item 11 required respondents to indicate their agreement to the statement that information about management and owners should not be included in financial statements. As with Item 7, Item 11 relates to the information quantity and level of detail aspect of secrecy, with agreement to the item indicating higher secrecy. Item 15 was intended to capture the aspects of secrecy relating to managerial intentions. It was deliberately framed in an opposite manner to Item 11. To the extent that the respondents agreed to this statement, they were considered to hold transparency values, opposed to secrecy. Items 3 and 15 both relate to a transparency aspect of secrecy.

3.1.4 Professionalism

Items 4, 8, 12, and 16 relate to professionalism. The classification of all these items, as relating to the social dimension of accounting, is consistent with the theoretical literature and the interpretation given to this value in previous research. In general, this construct refers to the attributes of those who perform the accounting function rather than the characteristics of financial statements. Item 4 is a general and direct regulatory-framework question asking if the accounting profession should be self-regulated. The higher the agreement to this item, the higher the level of professionalism is taken to be. This is consistent with Gray's suggestion that professionalism is correlated with self-regulation and firmly established professional associations. Items 8 and 12, while being concerned with the attributes of accountants, attempt to relate these to the separate issues of measurement and disclosure. In both cases, agreement to assertions that accountants are the best judges of how to measure something and what should be disclosed was taken as indicating high professionalism. The last item (16) queried respondents' agreement to a statement about the standards of ethical conduct of the accountant. This was an attempt to tap into aspects of professionalism that may have been missed in the other items. As will be seen later, it became apparent that this was probably not the case.

3.2 Pilot test

In a pilot study of the survey instrument, the questionnaire, along with a cover letter, was distributed to members of staff in a university accounting department and selected international accounting academics in New Zealand, Australia, United Kingdom, the Netherlands, Hong Kong, and India to assess the instrument for biases and to elicit comments. Only 12 usable responses were received. These were subject to factor analysis to ascertain the construct validity of the questions capturing Gray's accounting values. The questions relating to each of Gray's four accounting values were factor analyzed separately. Two of the four accounting values appeared to have subfactors: uniformity over time and across firms, professionalism at the level of the practicing accountant and at the level of governing professional body. It was also noted that in the case of conservatism and secrecy, one question accounted for about 56% of the variation, and the other three together accounted for 44% of the variation. A number of changes to the form of the final questionnaire resulted from this analysis: the wording of seven questions was altered for clarity, the introduction to the questionnaire was altered to eliminate biases, and the wording of the cover letter was altered slightly.

3.3 Sample

The sample for this study consisted of users and preparers of financial statements in two countries: New Zealand and India. The reason for choosing the sampled countries was driven by pragmatic, as well as conceptual, considerations in the context of the larger study of which this research was a part (i.e., to provide a general assessment of the usefulness of Hofstede–Gray theory). Conceptually, including as many diverse subgroups in the sample as possible is desirable from the point of view of the question dealt with in this paper because the *same* value dimensions should emerge from the data, whatever the nature of the subgroups, if Grays' constructs represent robust, subcultural features of societies. There were two preparer groups and a number of user groups, so that with the two different source countries, the sample data should provide for a reasonably reliable assessment of the empirical usefulness of the constructs. In addition to this, the pragmatic considerations of information, access to support in the target countries, and language (eliminating the problems involved in translating the questionnaire instrument) were also considerations in selecting the sample countries.

Users were identified as financial analysts and bank loan officers, and preparers were identified as practicing and nonpracticing accountants. The objective in adopting such a sampling strategy was to achieve a balance in respondents who shared professional subcultural values but who were also capable of being selected from publicly available national lists distributed across each country. A criticism of Hofstede's original 1968 study has been the use of a narrow sample: employees of a large multinational corporation (IBM), with a possibly very strong corporate culture. The sample selected for this study attempts to overcome the problem of narrowness, while preserving the benefits of functional equivalence.

It is possible that the responses of lending officers and managers to questions directly focused on measurement and disclosure issues in accounting might not be based on considerations that are important in professional accounting work. However, as noted above, because Gray's accounting values are meant to represent a set of subcultural values or preferences, applicable across the entire accounting profession of a given country, this should probably not be seen as a weakness. To obtain an accurate, country-wide view of a county's accounting values, it is necessary to survey both the users and preparers of financial statements. The user–preparer distinction, of course, has a long tradition in accounting research that uses survey techniques to enquire into the usefulness of financial information (e.g., Buzby, 1979; Jones, Romano, & Smyrnios, 1995). In any event, as subsequent analysis demonstrates, the factor-analysis patterns remained broadly consistent across all groups of respondents, although perhaps, with some potentially interesting minor differences.[5]

The sampling strategy that was adopted is summarized in the Tables below. In both Tables 2 and 3, the first column identifies the source organisation, the second column indicates the specific group surveyed, the third column categorizes the sample as either users or preparers, the fourth column indicates the number of questionnaires mailed, and the fifth column describes the sampling method deployed.[6]

Table 2 Survey sample: New Zealand.

Organisation	Survey group	Category	Mailout	Sampling frame
NZ Society of Accountants	Practicing accountants	Preparers	300	Random
	Nonpracticing accountants	Preparers	300	Random
NZ Society of Financial Analysts	Financial analysts	Users	280	Population
Banks	Lending officers	Users	320	All branches
Total			1200	

Table 3 Survey sample: India.

Organisation	Survey Group	Category	Mailout	Sampling frame
Institute of Company Secretaries	Company secretaries	Preparers	2000	Random
Institute of Chartered Accountants in India	Chartered accountants	Preparers	1500	Random
Chartered and Financial Analysts	Financial analysts	Users	500	Population
Bombay Management Association	Financial analysts	Users	500	Population
Banks	Lending officers	Users	500	Restricted
Total			5000	

Table 4 Summary of responses.

Survey group	New Zealand			India		
	Out	In	Response rate (%)	Out	In	Response rate (%)
Users	600	246	41	1500	474	31.6
Preparers	600	264	44	3500	630	18
Total	1200	510	42.5	5000	1104	22.8

In total, 6200 questionnaires were administered to users and preparers of financial statements, and 1614 useable responses were received. Of these, 510 were from New Zealand and 1104 were from Indian respondents. The overall return rate was just over 26%, the response rate from New Zealand was 42.5% and that for the Indian sample was 22.8%. The users and preparers in New Zealand responded in almost equal proportion (41% and 44%, respectively), there was a greater variation in the Indian responses (31% and 18%, respectively). Table 4 provides a summary of response rates. The respondents for both the Indian and New Zealand sample are spread from a variety of sources with practicing accountants accounting for the largest contribution of responses overall (21% and 40% for India and New Zealand, respectively).

The overall response rate of 26% is comparable with the Melbourne Institute Social Science Survey, which conducts a monthly telephone survey of about 1200 households across Australia and achieves a response rate of 25%. The nature and causes of nonresponse, particularly within the Indian sample, is discussed below, and again, as a limitation of the study's findings, in the Conclusion. Table 5 presents an overview of the sample demographics.

In terms of gender, respondents in both countries were male dominated. Ninety-five percent of all Indian respondents were males, as opposed to 79% in New Zealand. With regard to age, the respondents in the two countries fell into roughly the same percentage in the different categories. The demographic regarding formal education showed the most disparity, with the Indian respondents reporting having had more formal education than the New Zealand respondents had. The extent of respondent's overseas experience also reveals differences in that, whereas only 22% of Indian respondents had any overseas experience, over one half of all New Zealand respondents had more than 1 year's experience working overseas.

It is not known why the Indian survey had a significantly lower response rate than the New Zealand survey. The way in which responses were received made statistical testing of any nonresponse bias ineffective. Dozens of survey returns from India carrying wildly varying dates were routinely received each day. For example, a response mailed on the 1st day of the month, was received on the 25th day of the same month. Other responses,

Table 5 Sample characteristics.

	India	*New Zealand*
Response rate (%)	22.8	42.5
Number of respondents	1104	510
Practicing accountants	234 (21.3%)	208 (40.8%)
Bank loan officers	34 (3.1%)	125 (24.6%)
Nonpracticing accountants	72 (6.5%)	59 (11.6%)
Financial analysts	137 (12.4%)	35 (6.9%)
Company secretaries	140 (12.7%)	–
Managers	354 (32.2%)	58 (11.4%)
Others	133 (10.9%)	25 (3.9%)
Number of male respondents	1055 (95.6%)	401 (79.4%)
Number of female respondents	48 (4.3%)	105 (20.6%)
Age of respondents		
Under 29 years	200 (18.2%)	112 (22%)
30–34 years	240 (21.7%)	86 (16.9%)
35–39 years	218 (19.7%)	105 (20.6%)
40–49 years	251 (22.7%)	120 (23.6%)
50 years and over	194 (17.5%)	86 (16.9%)
Overseas experience		
None	866 (78.4%)	247 (48.4%)
Up to 12 months	107 (9.7%)	87 (17.1%)
2 Years or more	130 (12.3%)	174 (34.0%)

completed and mailed out on the 15th were received on the 20th. Yet, others had no date. This, as with the problem of selecting a representative sample of Indian bank loan officers, is one of the many problems of eliciting survey data from a large number of respondents in a developing country.[7] In this respect, the study reported here offers some additional experiences that may help to inform future work in this area.

4. Results

The AVS data are analyzed by means of three statistical techniques: reliability, factor, and cluster analyses. This section describes the analysis of the returned survey data under each of these headings.

4.1 Reliability analysis

This subsection discusses within-construct reliability, the sensitivity of the items composing each construct, and the relative reliability of the constructs based on Cronbach's alpha. In Table 6, the first column displays the construct and the second column lists the set of items measuring the construct. Columns 3, 4, and 5 display the reliability coefficient for New Zealand, India, and the combined data, respectively. Analysis of various combinations of

Table 6 Reliability analysis.

Construct	Items	New Zealand (510)	India (1104)	Total (1614)
Uniformity	2, 6, 10, 14	.58	.35	.56
Uniformity	2, 6, 14	.60	.41	.59
Professionalism	4, 8, 12, 16	.51	.53	.55
Professionalism	4, 8, 12	.57	.57	.60
Secrecy	3, 7, 11, 15	.38	.31	.34
Secrecy	3, 11, 15	.36	.24	.31
Conservatism	1, 5, 9, 13	.23	.18	.21
Conservatism	1, 5, 9	.29	.21	.23
Conservatism	5, 9, 13	.33	.20	.23

This table shows the results of the reliability analysis for the conservatism, uniformity, secrecy and professionalism constructs, as operationalized by the AVS.

items was conducted to examine the sensitivity of the alpha scores to each of the items. The split-half method of measuring reliability was used. The results were consistent with those presented here.

Table 6 indicates scores of .56, .55, .34, and .21 for the constructs of uniformity, professionalism, secrecy, and conservatism, respectively, based on all four items operationalizing each of the constructs. These scores are less than the recommended threshold of .70 of Nunnally (1978). The scores for uniformity and professionalism are highest at around .60.

In the case of uniformity, there is a consistent (but probably insignificant)[8] effect on the Cronbach alpha from dropping Item 10, that is, the item concerning the consistency principle, that once accounting policies are determined, they should not be changed. In the case of professionalism, dropping Item 16 appeared to lead to more significantly increased reliability scores. A similar effect is evident in the factor and cluster analysis results reported below.

The highest Cronbach score for the secrecy construct (as defined here) was .38. Excluding Item 15, the item concerning whether management forecasts should be included in financial statements, rather than Item 7 reduces the reliability score to .34.

The conservatism construct performed most poorly in terms of Cronbach's alpha. Excluding Item 1, on the downward revaluation of assets and profits in the presence of uncertainty, seemed to increase the reliability score, although only marginally in the case of the total sample. A comparison of the reliability scores between the Indian and New Zealand sample shows that Indian scores are lower than those for New Zealand for almost all categories, which may be due to the larger degree of variation in the demographics and the different response percentages across groups of the former. It is difficult to judge, with any confidence, the import of the reliability scores for the validity of Gray's accounting value constructs, compared with their use elsewhere (e.g., as in Eddie, 1991). Cross-cultural studies, such as Hofstede (1980, 1997) and O'Connor (1995), did not report reliability scores. These reliability scores are a limitation on this study's conclusions but may nevertheless provide a useful benchmark for use in future research.

4.2 Factor analysis

This subsection discusses the results of factor analysis of the AVS data. Theoretically, if Gray's framework is correct and the AVS constructs have been operationalized accurately, the factor analysis of the AVS responses should reveal four factors, each loading the four items associated with the corresponding accounting value. The same pattern should be evident for subsets of the data (e.g., when split by country and user–preparer groups) if the constructs represent empirically meaningful, subcultural accounting values. The results presented in this and the following subsections give some support to this proposition. They are similarly supportive of Gray's hypotheses. The detailed analysis reported here is for the combined data (1614 cases). The analysis for the subsets of data split by country and user–preparer groups present similar results, although with some additional features referred to below.

Various extraction methods and rotations were applied to the data, all showing similar factor patterns. Table 7 details the results.

Only factors with eigenvalues greater than unity were extracted. This limits identified factors to those that explain more of the variation in the data than do individual variables. The scree plot shown in Fig. 3 indicates that five factors had an eigenvalue of one or above. The Kaiser–Meyer–Olkin (KMO) measure of sampling adequacy for the factor analysis of the AVS was just under 0.7, which would be classified as "middling" by Kaiser (1974). Bartlett's sphericity test statistic was highly significant, suggesting that factor analysis is an appropriate way of analyzing the data. The five factors explained 49% of the variation in the data using the principle-components method. The first, second, third, fourth, and fifth factors explained 16.3%, 11.2%, 7.7%, 7.4%, and 6.4% of the variance, respectively.

For purpose of reference here and later in the paper, it is convenient to use the following codes to refer to the combinations of items that appear in the factor analysis: C_1 = Items 1 and 13 (measurement aspect of conservatism); C_2 = Items 5 and 9 (disclosure aspect of conservatism); U_1 = Items 2 and 10 (measurement aspect of uniformity); U_2 = Items 6 and 14 (disclosure aspect of uniformity); P_1 = Items 4, 8, and 12 (regulatory and technical judgment aspect of professionalism, excluding the ethical aspect contained in Item 16); S_1 = Items 3 and 15 (transparency aspect of secrecy); and S_2 = Items 7 and 11 (level of detail aspect of secrecy). These codes allow the factors identified in Table 7 and the cluster analysis reported later to be

Table 7 Factor patterns.

No.	Item description	Factor 1	Factor 2	Factor 3	Factor 4	Factor 5
6	Financial statements of all companies should have standardized formats.	.725	.035	-.012	.025	.125
14	The level of detailed standardization in financial statements should be increased	.653	.054	-.098	.009	.255
10	Accounting policies once chosen should not be changed	.529	.153	.247	-.087	-.087
2	Depreciation rules should be set externally specifically for separate group of assets	.423	.001	.128	.062	.456
3	Financial statements should be available to general public rather than just shareholders and managers	.477	.107	-.355	.032	-.050
15	Management forecasts should be included in financial statements	.419	.030	-.183	.371	-.024
12	Professional accountants are the best judges of what to disclose in financial statements	.050	.798	.183	.038	.014
8	Professional accountants should be the best judges of how to measure a firm's financial position and performance	.183	.775	.161	-.029	.025
4	Accounting profession should be self-regulated	.022	.612	-.150	-.071	.237
7	Only a minimum amount of detailed data should be included in financial statements	.051	.133	.693	.018	-.078
11	Information about management and owners should not be included in financial statements	-.148	.041	.613	-.106	-.044
9	Market values should be generally used instead of historical costs	.155	-.005	.127	.822	-.061
5	Market values are generally less relevant than historic costs	.178	.067	.180	-.726	-.136
1	Profits and assets should be valued downwards in case of doubt.	.081	.071	-.036	.002	.660
16	Professional accountants should maintain high standards of ethical conduct	-.014	.116	-.099	.018	.662
13	In times of rising prices, LIFO instead of FIFO should be used in calculation as estimates	.300	.034	.366	.031	.333
	Factor labels	Uniformity	Professionalism	Secrecy	Conservatism in disclosure	Conservatism in measurement

Rotated component matrix (a) extraction method: principal component analysis. Rotation method: Varimax with Kaiser Normalization. Rotation converged in seven iterations

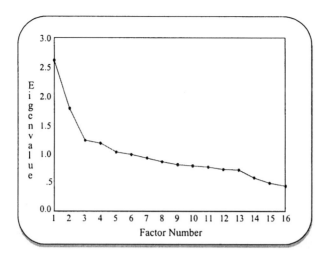

Figure 3 Factor scree plot.

more readily related to Gray's values and the matters discussed in the literature review.

In Table 7, all loadings greater than 30% are highlighted. Given the sample sizes, it is reasonable to claim these are both statistically significant and practically significant, explaining at least 10% of the relevant variables' total variance (Hair, Anderson, Tatham, & Black, 1998). All but two of the questionnaire items (variables) can be identified with the factors in Table 7 according to the standard approach of allocating the variables, that is, moving along each row of the table and identifying the item with the factor on which it has the highest absolute loading. The two exceptions to this rule are shown shaded. It is apparent that in the alternative primary allocation of these items to Factors 1 and 5, respectively, (i) it makes greater sense in terms of Gray's theory; (ii) the differences in the communalities between the standard and alternative factor assignments are small and probably statistically insignificant (less than 3%), and, in addition, (iii) under some other methods of extracting and rotating the factors (e.g., the image method with an oblique rotation), the items are factored using the standard approach precisely in this manner. It is probably unnecessary to focus too much attention on this point, in any case, because the highlighted loadings relating to Items 2, 3, 13, and 15 that appear in more than one factor provide information about how they might be interpreted in each factor on which they load. They also give insight into how either the underlying theory or survey instrument might be improved.

As can be seen, under this interpretation, Factor 1 attracts both the uniformity items and S_1, the transparency aspect of secrecy. Factor 2 attracts P_1, the first three of the questionnaire items intended to relate to

197

professionalism. Factor 3 attracts S_2, the level-of-detail aspect of secrecy; Factor 4 attracts the disclosure aspect of conservatism, C_2; and Factor 5 attracts the measurement aspect of conservatism, C_1, along with Item 16, the remaining element of the intended professionalism construct dealing with ethics.

With respect to Gray's theory, it may be noted that the items representing uniformity invariably load highly on the same factor and only sometimes does an item also load significantly on another factor. Due to Factor 1 attracting S_1, however, it is not clear that the tag of uniformity is necessarily a good description of this factor. There is, for example, a marginally significant loading of Item 13 onto Factor 1. This item split from the others in a confirmatory factor analysis and may not be important. Its presence might, for instance, be due to a problem with respondents' interpretations of the technical nature of the item (regarding the use of LIFO to value inventories). On the other hand, it could conceivably relate to the belief that LIFO produces a more accurate measure of profit in times of rising prices. The factoring patterns in Column 1 of Table 7 could therefore suggest a general concern with the transparent provision of reliable (accurate, comparable, and objective) information.

The uniformity items factor clearly as a separate group in the New Zealand data without attracting S_1. In the Indian data, the uniformity factor fragments into U_2, with Item 10 combining with Item 3, a component of secrecy. Both user-preparer groups collect the uniformity items under a single factor heading, except for Item 2.[9] Due to reasonably persistent factoring of three of the four uniformity items and the tentative nature of the results at this point in the research process, it is probably safe to continue to refer to Factor 1 as "uniformity," but with this term being understood in the extended sense that it possibly encompasses the aspects of reliability and transparency.

The P_1 subset of the professionalism items strongly group together under Factor 2 heading under nearly all extraction methods and in the country and user–preparer subsets of the data. It seems appropriate, therefore, to use the label professionalism for this factor. This factor usually fails to attract Item 16, however, so it is reasonable to conclude that the statement about ethical standards in the questionnaire instrument is not linked to the construct of professionalism in the minds of the respondents.

Factor 3, as well as attracting S_2, also contains a significant, negative loading from Item 3, relating to the transparency aspect of secrecy, and a significant, positive loading from Item 13, which was meant to represent a measurement aspect of conservatism. The elements of S_2 consistently factor across extraction methods and in the subsamples referred to above. The dominance of S_2 and the marginal appearance of Item 3 might be reasonably claimed to provide the justification for labeling this factor "secrecy." However, Item 3 factored separately from S_2 in a confirmatory analysis, perhaps suggesting multidimensionality in this construct. The remaining secrecy item, Item 15, loads insignificantly on this factor (with a communality of less than 5%), but in the expected direction. Item 15 (management forecasts should be included in financial statements) loaded significantly onto three factors, suggesting a relationship of the proposition both with the extended construct of uniformity described above and the disclosure aspect of conservatism, described below.

Factors 4 and 5 contain items representing the separate disclosure and measurement aspects of conservatism, as conceptualized in Section 2. The measurement aspect C_2 loaded onto a single factor without fragmentation under all extraction methods and rotations and in the subsamples. The just more-than-marginal loading of Item 15 relating to the inclusion of management forecasts in financial statements could be interpreted as an expression of conservatism with respect to the disclosure of information, as opposed to a desire for secrecy. It therefore seems appropriate to give Factor 4 the name of "conservatism in disclosure."

It is probably reasonable at this juncture to also label Factor 5 as an aspect of conservatism. Item 1 loads quite significantly on Factor 5 and not significantly on any other factor. Furthermore, there is a significant loading of Item 13, the other component of C_1, on this factor. Factor 5 quite strongly attracts Item 16, the proposition that accountants should maintain high standards of ethical conduct and there is a sense in which that could be held to represent conservatism, especially if the reading of the statement is conditioned upon ethical conduct being interpreted by respondents as following cautious measurement practices with respect to profit. The attraction of Item 2, under the standard method of allocating items to factors, could be explained in the same manner, that is, the statement in Item 2 that "depreciation rules should be set externally for separate groups of assets" might be interpreted as embodying a cautious approach to accounting measurement. The evidence for this interpretation of Factor 5 is not as strong as it is in the case of the other factors, however, and the cluster analysis reported below confirms that the need to treat the interpretation tentatively. Nevertheless, because the Factor 5 pattern is observable under most factoring methods and rotations in the Indian and preparer subsets of the data (but less so in the New Zealand and user subsets), the label "conservatism in measurement" for this factor seems to be as reasonable as any alternatives evident at this time.[10]

4.3 Cluster analysis

Cluster analysis was conducted to triangulate the results of the factor analysis reported in the preceding subsection. It is possible that cluster analyses might, by using different metrics and assumptions to those used in factor analysis, give different results and perhaps shed light on some of the points

Rescaled Distance

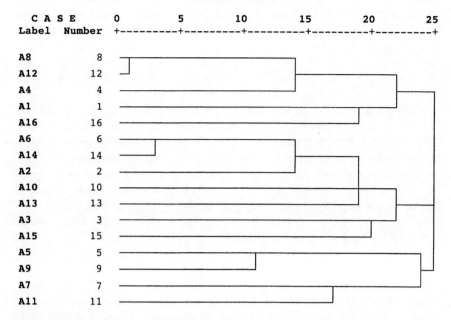

Figure 4 Dendrogram using complete linkage.

of interpretation arising from the latter. This section follows the approach to cluster analysis of Aldenderfer and Blashfield (1984).

Of the approaches to cluster analysis, the hierarchical method was adopted. Given the purpose of the research, the distance measure used was the absolute value of the Pearson correlation coefficient. The dendrogram presented in Fig. 4 uses the furthest neighbor method of clustering and gives results consistent with the factor analysis. Reading down from the top, Elements 4, 8, and 12 constitute P_1, the professionalism factor. Elements 1 and 16 are two of the items loading on what was called the conservatism in measurement factor in Section 4.2. Elements 6, 14, 2, and 10 are the key items defining the uniformity factor, based upon the original conceptualization of that accounting value. That cluster captures Element 13, a component of C_1 (the measurement aspect of conservatism in the theoretical analysis), which presents a stronger impression of the relationship of that item with the uniformity construct than did the factor analysis (although this was marginally significant, see Table 7). Next, Elements 3 and 15 are the items making up S_1, the transparency aspect of secrecy; Elements 5 and 9 constitute C_2, the disclosure aspect of conservatism; and Elements 7 and 11 are S_2, the level of detail aspect of secrecy.

The dendrogram offers some evidence of the originally expected relationship between the ethical aspect of professionalism and the other items intended to define that construct. This connection appeared to be absent from the factor analysis. In contrast, the cluster on P_1 and the relationship between S_1 and uniformity (both the U_1 and U_2 aspects) closely reflect the results of the factor analysis. The disclosure aspect of conservatism (C_2) seems to be more clearly linked to S_2 than in the factor analysis and what was labeled as the conservatism in measurement factor is absent from the cluster analysis. This warrants the caution expressed in labeling Factor 5 in the preceding subsection. Nevertheless, despite minor differences, the overall picture presented by the cluster analysis is consistent with the factor analysis. Both give some support to Gray's theory of accounting subcultural values.

5. Conclusions, limitations, and future research

This paper reports the first attempt to operationalize and empirically measure Gray's accounting values. It represents one way of assessing the usefulness of the Hofstede–Gray framework approach to evaluating the cultural relevance hypothesis in accounting. Gray's accounting value constructs were operationalized as 16 items in an accounting value survey questionnaire on the basis of theoretical considerations, with four items representing each of Gray's four accounting values. The questionnaire was used to survey a large sample of users and preparers of financial statements in India and New Zealand in 1995–1996.

The responses to the survey were analyzed using the reliability, factor, and cluster analyses. The originally envisaged construct of professionalism emerges most clearly as a coherent operational accounting value construct. The elements of the uniformity construct seem to attract aspects of secrecy, as originally conceptualized, and indicate that the uniformity construct might be contained within a broader accounting value construct. The secrecy construct also emerged, although less strongly than in the case of either professionalism or uniformity. Conservatism appears to split into two parts, possibly related to the two theoretical subdimensions of disclosure and measurement. There are a number of significant limitations relating to the research framework and method that require these conclusions to be interpreted cautiously, however.

The research question underlying this paper is, "Are Gray's accounting subcultural values valid empirical constructs?" An a priori strategy was adopted to answer this question. Questionnaire items were developed based upon theoretical, rather than empirical, considerations. This approach can be defended as being an appropriate way to attempt to answer the research question because it is *capable* of testing the validity of Gray's theoretical constructs. If the responses had divided nicely into four factors and clusters, with a clear interpretation consistent with Gray's theory, for example, this would have been confirming evidence for the existence of accounting values as useful empirical constructs while, if there had been no pattern in the responses at all, it would have cast doubt on their veracity. In the event, the reliability scores were lower than would have been hoped. The factor analysis did not produce four factors, but five, and the cluster analysis produced three large clusters rather than four, although it appears to be possible to interpret the results from both latter types of analysis in the context of Gray's original values.

One problem with the approach taken to instrument development in this paper, however, is that it could bias the results in favor of Gray's theory. There was no attempt to look for the existence of other accounting values, for example. The factor analysis reported in the paper explains only about 50% of the variation in the data. This suggests that there could be other, as yet unrecognized, accounting value dimensions. An alternative, more empirical approach to questionnaire design would be appropriate to investigate this possibility.

A specific issue that arises using the theoretical approach adopted here is the difficulty of clearly identifying the constructs of interest with particular questionnaire item statements. For example, the statement that "Market values should be used instead of historic costs" could have several meanings in the context of conservatism. Support for this statement could depend upon whether market values are greater or less than historic costs or it could relate to the relative reliabilities of the measurement of market values and actual costs. The assumed information set, upon which judgments of this sort are conditioned, introduces ambiguity into the responses that may obscure the factor and cluster analyses. The reality of accounting systems, especially in an increasingly globalized environment, is that they are not directly determined by cultural values. The state of development of capital markets, the influence of tax laws, an so forth, are conditioning factors that sometimes reinforce, sometimes obscure, the impact of cultural values on accounting practice. Future research should try to take explicit account of the impact of such factors so that it may have greater relevance to practical policy making.[11]

There is also, of course, the general question of the ability of questionnaire surveys to reveal subtle, cultural traits. It is assumed that the questionnaire responses were truthful and meaningful, and that reported attitudes, perceptions, beliefs, and values have significance for the respondents in terms of social action. The reliability of the responses can be gauged to some extent from the consistency of the responses to particular questionnaire items. For example, the factor analysis produced signs on the significant loadings (e.g., with respect to Items 5 and 9) that give some confidence that they make sense and are consistent with basic, prior expectations.

It is also assumed that the responses to the questionnaire items reflect substantive constructs rather than reactions to linguistic cues. The deliberate spreading of what were intended to be items associated with the same underlying construct was an attempt to reduce the risk of the latter effect. In addition, the explicit linking of the types of questionnaire items and their motivation to underlying theories concerning the relationships between accounting values and accounting practices was designed to enhance the substantive import of the individual items. However, the lack of specificity in the theoretical analysis and the questionnaire can easily lead to ambiguity of a type that Gray had not envisioned. It is acknowledged that different instruments may be developed that better elicit Gray's (and possibly other) accounting values.

With regard to the factor analysis, the process of assigning meaningful labels to a group of items forming a factor necessarily involves judgment. This study, as with most factor analysis, is open to the criticism that others interpreting the factor analysis results might assign different labels to factors or interpret factor loadings differently. The labeling of the factors has been guided by the literature relating to the Hofstede–Gray framework, results from reliability, factor, and cluster analyses, and the questions hypothesized to operationalize the constructs. Until such time that other primary data (preferably with as great a coverage of different countries as possible) prove otherwise, however, the conclusions presented here may provide a starting point for further AVS research.

The discussion of the interpretation of the factors above suggests three important lessons for future AVS research. These relate to (i) the problems involved in dealing with the orthogonality of the factors and questionnaire items; (ii) the possibility that as yet unrecognized additional accounting value constructs exist and the potential difficulties that may be caused for analysis by the existence of subdimensions in some of the factors; and (iii) the fact that the quantitative approach to researching the impact of culture on accounting can be potentially useful.

With respect to Point (i) in the design stage of the research, it was thought that the orthogonality of Gray's accounting values concepts might prove to be problematic when analyzing the respondents' returned questionnaires. Previous theoretical research had identified the possibility of overlap in these concepts. However, the results of the analysis were not sufficiently strongly indicative in either direction to determine if this is likely to be a problem. Orthogonal and oblique rotations of the factors did not produce significantly different results, suggesting that the natural factors are reasonably robust and independent of one another. Four of the 16 questionnaire items did load onto more than one factor, but it is not clear that this is a serious problem, or even necessarily undesirable in exploratory research. The design of more orthogonal survey items in future AVS type studies, however, should be informed by the experience reported here.

With respect to Point (ii), it was also anticipated that some of the accounting value constructs might be multidimensional. Those values with the most obvious a priori multidimensionality, however, had the highest reliability scores. There was some evidence in the subsamples of the existence of subdimensions but, apart from the dividing of the conservatism construct, it did not seem to be a strong feature of the total data set. This may have been a consequence of the simplicity of the survey instrument (which was deliberate) which resulted with not being able to capture the multidimensional aspects of professionalism and uniformity sufficiently well. For example, uniformity potentially has a time versus company and measurement versus disclosure subdimensions, giving at least four subdimensions. If this fact is empirically significant, it would require more questionnaire items than were used in the version of the AVS, on which the results of this paper are based, to identify these subdimensions of accounting values. Again, this supports the need for a more extended, empirically based AVS.

With respect to Point (iii), it does seem that whatever the correct choice of labels for the factors revealed in the factor analysis are, systematic, quantifiable patterns do emerge from the data and are worthy of further investigation. This remains the case even after taking into account the many limitations of the study, such as the small size of the pilot study and the inability to gauge the effect of any nonresponse bias. It is probably a point that pertains to a more important issue than whether one particular theory about the identity of accounting subcultural dimensions is confirmed by research. The test of the usefulness of an approach to research is whether it leads to new and interesting information, including new questions. This study raises a number of new and interesting questions concerning the identity and nature of accounting's cultural dimensions that would not necessarily be so clearly identified by other more qualitative approaches to the subject. Given the viewpoint that is sometimes expressed in the literature about the impossibility of gaining knowledge about cultural matters by quantitative means, this point is not without significance.

The AVS needs to be developed to address the limitations and weaknesses of design noted here and to be applied across different countries and samples of users and preparers. Such studies would contribute to the development of a repository of accounting values data for research and would help to address the current problems of lack of data associated with researching the cultural relevance hypothesis. This study aimed to provide primary data on an issue about which there is little empirical evidence. Subject to the provisos discussed, the study found some support for Gray's accounting value constructs. The development and administration of the AVS provides a potential operational foundation for improving the application of the Hofstede–Gray framework in cross-cultural studies and will, we hope, raise the debate about the cultural relevance hypothesis in the accounting literature to one based upon a more empirical approach.

Acknowledgements

The authors would like to acknowledge the advice and helpful suggestions received from the two referees of this paper; the Editor, A. Rashad

Abdel-khalik; Alan MacGregor, Markus Milne, Paul Pillai, and Reg Matthews; and participants in the annual conference of the AAANZ in Cairns, Australia.

Notes

1 Hofstede's dimensions of value have come under increasing scrutiny and criticism for a number of reasons. A recent critical appraisal of Hofstede's theory is Baskerville (2003).

2 This aspect was also discussed by Gray (1988, pp. 11–12).

3 The survey is part of a larger ongoing program of research concerned with operationalizing and testing the Hofestede–Gray framework.

4 Hofstede's original IBM study of work-related values included dozens of questions. The VSM developed for later use contains four questionnaire items per dimension. See Hofstede (1980, 1994, 1997).

5 The generalisation of the results of the study nevertheless may be limited by the fact that India and New Zealand appear to differ significantly only on power distance in Hofstede (1980).

6 The sampling process was "restricted" in the case of Indian bank loan officers in the sense that lists of such officers were only available for two banks at the time of the survey. Questionnaires were mailed out to officers in both banks, and, when the responses proved insufficient in number, questionnaires were also sent to officers in the 90 banks listed in the Yellow Pages of the Bombay Telephone Directory. The returned questionnaires from these sources made up the total responses in this group.

7 The development of standards for survey design and implementation in the context of cross-national research is still in its infancy (see Japec, 2001; Lynn & Clarke, 2001).

8 The authors are not aware of a test of significance for changes in Cronbach alpha scores resulting from dropping particular items.

9 The results by country and by user–preparer group are available from the authors on request.

10 Apart from the two instances relating to Item 13 in Factor 1 and Item 3 in Factor 3, confirmatory factor analysis showed no other evidence of multidimensionality in the constructs described in the text.

11 The authors are grateful to an anonymous reviewer for the discussion in this and other paragraphs in the conclusion.

Appendix A. The AVS

Without taking into account the recommendations of your own professional organisation to what extent do you believe the following practices are desirable? To what extent would you agree or disagree with each of the following statements. Please indicate your preference on the *equally spaced 7 point scale* from strongly agree to strongly disagree.

	Strongly agree					Strongly disagree	
1. Profits and assets should be valued downwards in case of doubt.	1	2	3	4	5	6	7
2. Depreciation rules should be set externally, specifically for separate groups of assets.	1	2	3	4	5	6	7
3. Financial statements should be available to the general public rather than just to shareholders and managers.	1	2	3	4	5	6	7
4. Accounting profession should be self-regulated.	1	2	3	4	5	6	7
5. Market values are generally less relevant than historic costs.	1	2	3	4	5	6	7
6. Financial statements of all companies should have standardised formats.	1	2	3	4	5	6	7
7. Only a minimum amount of detailed data should be included in financial statements.	1	2	3	4	5	6	7
8. Professional accountants are the best judges of how to measure a firm's financial position and performance.	1	2	3	4	5	6	7
9. Market values should be generally used instead of historic costs.	1	2	3	4	5	6	7
10. Accounting policies once chosen should not be changed.	1	2	3	4	5	6	7
11. Information about management and owners should not be included in financial statements.	1	2	3	4	5	6	7
12. Professional accountants are the best judges of what to disclose in financial statements.	1	2	3	4	5	6	7
13. In times of rising prices LIFO instead of FIFO should be used in calculations as estimates.	1	2	3	4	5	6	7
14. The level of detailed standardisation in financial statements should be increased.	1	2	3	4	5	6	7
15. Management forecasts should be included in financial statements.	1	2	3	4	5	6	7
16. Professional accountants should maintain high standards of ethical conduct.	1	2	3	4	5	6	7

References

Aldenderfer, M. S., & Blashfield, R. K. (1984). *Cluster analysis*. Beverly Hills: Sage.

Amat, O., Blake, J., Wraith, P., & Oliveras, E. (1999). *Dimensions of national culture and the accounting environment—The Spanish case*. Department of Economics and Business, Universitat Pompeu Fabra.

Arnold, D. F., Bernardi, R. A., & Neidermeyer, P. E. (2001). The association between European materiality estimates and client integrity, national culture and litigation. *The International Journal of Accounting, 36*(4), 459–483.

Arpan, J. S., & Radebaugh, L. H. (1985). *International accounting and multinational enterprises*. New York: Wiley.

Aswasthi, V. N., Chow, C. W., & Wu, A. (2001). Cross-cultural differences in the behavioral consequences of imposing performance evaluation and reward systems: An experimental investigation. *The International Journal of Accounting, 36*(3), 291–309.

Backstrom, C. H., & Hursch, G. (1963). Survey research. (1st ed.). Chicago: Northwestern University Press.

Barrett, M. E. (1976). Financial reporting practices: Disclosure and comprehensiveness in an international setting. *Journal of Accounting Research*, 10–26.

Baskerville, R. (2003). Hofstede never studied culture. *Accounting, Organizations and Society, 28*(1), 1–14.

Baydoun, N., & Willett, R. J. (1995, March). Cultural relevance of western accounting systems to developing countries. *Abacus*, 67–91.

Beeny, J. H. (1975). *European financial reporting*. West Germany: Institute of Chartered Accountants in England and Wales.

Beeny, J. H. (1976). *European financial reporting*. France: Institute of Chartered Accountants of England and Wales.

Belkaoui, A. R. (1990). *Judgement in international accounting*. France: Quorum Books.

Belkaoui, A. R. (1995). *The linguistic shaping of accounting*. Quorum Books.

Bhimani, A. (1999). Mapping methodological frontiers in cross-national management control research. *Accounting, Organizations and Society, 6*(5), 413–440.

Buzby, S. L. (1979). Selected items of information and their disclosure in annual reports. *The Accounting Review, XLIX*(3), 423–435.

Chanchani, S., & MacGregor, S. (1999). A synthesis of cultural studies in accounting. *Journal of Accounting Literature, 18*, 1–30.

Choi, F., & Mueller, G. (1984). *International accounting*. Englewood Cliffs, New Jersey: Prentice-Hall.

Chow, C. W., Shields, M. D., & Wu, A. (1999). The importance of national culture in the design of and preference on management controls for multi-national operations. *Accounting, Organizations and Society, 24*(5), 441–461.

Chow, L. M., Chau, G. K., & Gray, S. J. (1995). Accounting reforms in China: Cultural constraints on implementation and development. *Accounting and Business Research, 26*(1), 29–49.

Chow, W., Deng, F. J., & Ho, J. L. (2000). The openness of knowledge sharing within organizations: A comparative study in the United States and the People's Republic of China. *Journal of Management Accounting Research, 12*, 65–95 (Sarasota).

Cooke, T. E. (1993, Autumn). The impact of accounting principles on profits: The US versus Japan. *Accounting and Business Research, 23*(92), 460–477 (London).

Dyball, M. C., & Valcarcel, L. J. (1999). The rational and traditional: The regulation of accounting in the Philippines. *Accounting Auditing & Accountability Journal, 12*(3), 303–327 (Bradford).

Eddie, I. A. (1991). Asia pacific cultural values and accounting systems. *Asia Pacific International Management Forum, 16*(3), 22–30.

Farrell, B. J., & Cobbin, D. M. (2001, July). Global harmonization of the professional behaviour of accountants. *Business Ethics*, 257–266.

Fechner, H. E., & Kilgore, A. (1994). The influence of cultural factors on accounting practice. *International Journal of Accounting, 29*, 265–277.

Gerhardy, P. (1990). An evaluation of the role of culture in the development of accounting principles in West Germany. *Accounting and Finance Research Paper. 90/2*. South Australia: Flinders University.

Gray, S. J. (1980, Spring). The impact of international accounting differences from a security analysis perspective: Some European evidence. *Journal of Accounting Research*, 64–76.

Gray, S. J. (1988). Towards a theory of cultural influence on the development of accounting systems internationally. *Abacus*, 1–15.

Gray, S. J., & Coenenberg, A. G. (Eds.) (1984). *EEC accounting harmonization: Implementation and impact of the fourth directive*. Amsterdam, New York: North Holland.

Hair, J. E., Anderson, R. E., Tatham, R. L., & Black, W. C. (1998). *Multivariate data analysis* (5th ed.). Upper Saddle River, New Jersey: Prentice-Hall.

Harrison, G. L., & McKinnon, J. L. (1999). Cross-cultural research in management control systems design: A review of the current state. *Accounting, Organizations and Society*, *24*(5), 483–506.

Harrison, P. D., Chow, C. W., Wu, A., & Harrell, A. M. (1999). A cross-cultural investigation of managers' project evaluation decisions. *Behavioral Research in Accounting*, *11*, 143–160.

Hofstede, G. (1980). *Cultures consequences*. Beverly Hills: Sage.

Hofstede, G. (1983). National cultures in four dimensions: A research-based theory of cultural differences among nations. *International Studies of Management & Organization*, *13*(1,2), 46–75.

Hofstede, G. (1994, Manual). *Value module survey*. Maastritch, The Netherlands: Institute for Research on Intercultural Cooperation.

Hofstede, G. (1997). *Cultures and organizations: Software of the mind*. (Revised ed.). New York: McGraw-Hill.

Hofstede, G. (2001). *Culture's consequences: Comparing values, behaviors, institutions and organizations across nations* (2nd ed.). Thousand Oaks, California: Sage Publications.

Holzer, H. P. (Ed.) (1984). *International accounting*. New York: Harper and Row.

Jaggi, B. L. (1975). The impact of the cultural environment on financial disclosures. *International Journal of Accounting*, 75–84.

Jaggi, B. L., & Low, P. Y. (2000). Impact of culture, market forces, and legal system on financial disclosures. *The International Journal of Accounting*, *35*(4), 495–519.

Japec, L. (Ed.) (2001). *Survey quality: Proceedings of the international conference on survey quality. Stockhold. May 2001*. Stockholm: Statistics Sweden.

Jones, S., Romano, C., & Smymios, K. S. (1995, Spring). An evaluation of the decision usefulness of cash flow statements by Australian reporting entities. *Business Research*, *25*(98), 115–129.

Kaiser, H. F. (1974). An index of factorial simplicity. *Psychometrika*, *39*, 31–36.

Lanis, R. (2001). *The influence of culture on corporate disclosure: An inquiry into and rectification of the methodological defects of the culture/CRS models in prior research* PhD Dissertation, University of Newcastle. Newcastle. Australia.

Lau, C. M., & Buckland, C. (2000). Budget emphasis, participation, task difficulty and performance: The effect of diversity within culture. *Accounting and Business Research*, *31*(1), 37–55.

Lynn, B. E. (1999). Culture and intellectual capital management: A key factor in successful ICM implementation. *International Journal of Technology Management*, *18*(5–8), 590–603.

Lynn, P., & Clarke, P. (2001). Separating refusal bias and non-contact bias: Evidence from UK national surveys. *Working papers of the Institute for Social and Economic Research* (pp. 1–29). Colchester: University of Essex (Paper 2001–24).

Meek, G., Roberts, C. B., & Gray, S. J. (1995). Factors influencing voluntary annual report disclosures by U.S., U.K. and continental European multinational corporations. *Journal of International Business Studies*, *26*(3), 555–572.

Nestle, D. (2001). Evaluation of a communication skills course: Cultural relevance of the patient-centered interview in a Hong Kong Chinese setting. *Medical Teacher*, *23*(2), 212–214.

Nobes, C. (1992). *International classification of financial reporting*. London, New York: Routledge.

Nobes, C. (1998, September). Towards a general model of the reasons for international differences in financial reporting. *Abacus, 34*(2), 162–188.

Nobes, C., & Parker, R. H. (Eds.) (1995). *Comparative international accounting*. New York: Prentice-Hall.

Nunnally, J. C. (1978). *Psychometric theory*. New York: Penguin.

O'Connor, N., 1995. *The influence of national culture on the use of performance evaluation systems in Singapore and South Korea*. PhD thesis. Faculty of Business and Hotel Management, Griffith University. Australia.

Perera, H. (1989). Towards a framework to analyse the impact of culture on accounting. *International Journal of Accounting, 24*, 42–56.

Perera, M. H. B., & Mathews, M. R. (1990). The cultural relativity of accounting and international patterns of social accounting. *Advances in International Accounting, 3*, 215–251.

Radebaugh, L., & Gray, S. J. (1993). *International accounting and multinational enterprises* (3rd ed.). New York: Wiley.

Radebaugh, L., & Gray, S. J. (2000). *International accounting and multinational enterprises* (5th ed.). New York: Wiley.

Roberts, C. B., & Salter, S. B. (1999, Summer). Attitudes towards uniform accounting: Cultural or economic phenomena? *Journal of International Financial Management and Accounting, 10*(2), 121–142.

Salter, S. B., & Niswander, F. (1995). Cultural influence on the development of accounting systems internationally: A test of Gray's (1988) theory. *Journal of International Business Studies* (Second Quarter) 379–397.

Schultz, J. J., & Lopez, T. J. (2001). The impact of national influence on accounting estimates: Implication for international accounting standard-setters. *The International Journal of Accounting, 36*(3), 271–290.

Sekaran, U. (1992). *Research methods for business* (2nd ed.). New York: Wiley.

Sterling, R. R. (1967, December). Conservatism: The fundamental principle of valuation in traditional accounting. *Abacus*, 109–132.

Taylor, P., & Turley, S. (1986). *The regulation of accounting*. Oxford, New York: Blackwell.

Tsui, J. S. L. (2001). The impact of culture on the relationship between budgetary participation, management accounting systems and managerial performance: An analysis of Chinese and Western managers. *The International Journal of Accounting, 2*(36), 125–146.

Ticehurst, G., & Veal, A. J. (2000). *Business research methods: A managerial approach*. Melbourne: Pearson Education.

Watts, R. L. (1977, April). Corporate financial statements: A product of the market and political processes. *Australian Journal of Management*, 53–75.

Weetman, P., & Gray, S. J. (1991, Autumn). A comparative international analysis of the impact of accounting principles on profits: The USA versus the UK, Sweden and the Netherlands. *Accounting and Business Research, 21*(84), 363–380.

Willett, R. J., Nishimura, A., & Baydoun, N. (1997). Reflections on the relationship between culture and accounting in the Asia-Pacific region. In N. Baydoun, A. Nishimura, & R. J. Willett (Eds.), *Accounting in the Asia Pacific Region* (pp. 400–26).

8

EXTERNAL ENVIRONMENT, CULTURE, AND ACCOUNTING PRACTICE

A preliminary test of a general model of international accounting development

Timothy S. Doupnik and Stephen B. Salter

Source: *International Journal of Accounting* 30(3) (1995): 189–207.

Abstract

Previous theoretical frameworks of accounting development and change are synthesized in a general model of accounting system development. The general model is then subjected to a preliminary empirical test of its explanatory power by examining the relationship between countries' accounting practices and a set of environmental factors and cultural dimensions hypothesized as relevant elements of the model. The results lend support for the general model and provide insight into the importance of various factors in explaining existing accounting diversity worldwide.

A considerable amount of literature has been written with regard to classification and explanation of the diversity of accounting practice across countries. This literature has emphasized the description of similarities and differences in accounting systems around the world. Despite the volume of literature, it is disappointing that, at the end of an extensive review, Wallace and Gernon[1] conclude that international accounting scholars lack theories and their research efforts lack rigor. This paper reports the results of a study which attempts to address these concerns.

The objectives of this study are twofold. First, the various attempts in the literature to develop a theoretical model of accounting development are synthesized to form a general model of international accounting development. The model describes a country's accounting development as a complex interaction among external environment, institutional structure, and culture. The second objective is to test whether relationships exist between accounting practice and elements of the model across a broad range of countries. This study introduces the use of hierarchical cluster analysis and canonical correlation analysis as tools for examining those relationships.

An understanding of how external environment, institutional structure, and cultural factors affect cross-national accounting diversity can be useful in efforts to reduce that diversity and enhance the comparability of accounting information worldwide. Empirical evidence on the relative importance of the different elements of the model can provide information as to where comparability efforts need to be intensified and also can provide insight as to the feasibility of reducing cross-national differences. If differences in accounting practice are significantly affected by national differences in institutional structure or culture, for example, then, to the extent that these model elements do not change (or change very slowly) over time, achieving comparability of accounting across countries might be extremely difficult.

This study represents a first step in examining empirically the inter-relationship between environment, institutional structure, culture, and accounting. The results suggest that all three elements contribute to accounting diversity, but that on a global level institutional structure is of greatest importance.

Prior research

The major questions that have been examined in international comparative financial accounting research are:

(1) What differences and similarities exist across national accounting systems (classification studies)?
(2) What factors explain these differences and similarities (environmental factors studies)?

Concerning both questions there has been a limited attempt to develop theories to explain how various factors affect national accounting systems.

Classification studies

A number of studies have attempted to classify countries by accounting practices either inductively[2] or deductively.[3] The inductive studies primarily rely on factor analysis of survey data on financial reporting practices collected by Price Waterhouse.[4] The primary result of these studies has been to establish on an ongoing basis the continued diversity of financial reporting practices across countries.

The deductive studies have used deductive reasoning and personal knowledge of countries' accounting to develop classifications of accounting systems. These studies do not attempt to develop a formal theory but rather to arrive at an accurate description of what the world appears to be.

Environmental factors studies

The earliest attempts to explain cross-national differences in accounting consist of lists of environmental factors explaining often undefined differences in financial reporting practices.[5] An extension of this approach is contained in a comprehensive framework which attempts to incorporate the Farmer and Richman model of business environments into an accounting context.[6] This model does not specify the weight of the factors influencing the accounting system or the level at which the influence is applied.

Classification/environmental factors studies

A number of inductive classification studies[7] have attempted to use subsets of environmental variables to predict clusters of countries with similar accounting practices. These research efforts are useful in that they empirically establish some connection between the environment and accounting practices. These studies do not provide or test a theoretical framework which explains how environmental factors affect cross-national accounting diversity.

Theoretical frameworks of account development

Schweikart[8] attempted to develop a theory of international accounting within the general framework of contingency theory. In his financial accounting model, the environment (education, economic, political, social, etc.) is seen as an external contingency on institutional structure (e.g., corporations, stock exchanges, and regulatory agencies) and decision makers (e.g., investors and lenders). The environment provides the types of institutions and these institutions, within a nation's cultural framework (availability filter), provide information to the public for decision-making purposes. Changes in the external environment may change the decision environment which causes decision-makers to put pressure on the institutional structure to provide more relevant information.

Harrison and McKinnon[9] developed a framework which attempts to explain the process of change in a society's accounting system. Change is analyzed in terms of four major elements: intrusive events, intra-systems activity, trans-systems activity, and cultural environment.

Within the model, accounting system change is the product of both the intrusion of events and the continuous interactions among the accounting system and its neighboring systems. Change occurs as a specific system identifies an intrusion, chooses to deal with that intrusion, and produces a series of response events based on its perception of suitable reactions. The response events occur after the subject systems and neighbouring system have made clear to each other what needs to be done and have determined a culturally appropriate way of achieving these objectives.

Robson[10] hypothesizes and demonstrates that the process of accounting change involves translating accounting needs into a form that permits discourse with other systems. This process, by moving accounting issues into the wider social, political, and economic realm, allows accounting to assess its role, select options for change, and, in turn, influence societal decisions. The ability to translate accounting to wider issues appears to be a cultural one.

Gray[11] extended Hofstede's[12] model of societal culture patterns to develop a model of culture, societal values, and the accounting subculture. In Hofstede's model, societal values (culture) are determined by environmental factors (geographic, economic, demographic, etc.) modified by external influences (forces of nature, trade, conquest, etc.). Societal values, in turn, have institutional consequences in the form of legal system, political system, nature of capital markets, and so on. Gray extends this model to propose that the value systems or attitudes of accountants (accounting values) are related to and derived from societal values, and these accounting values, along with the institutional structure, affect the accounting system.

A general model of accounting development

A synthesis of the various frameworks discussed above leads to a general model of accounting system development as presented in Exhibit 1. There are three elements which appear to determine a nation's accounting development: (1) the *external environment*, which affects both a society's culture and its institutional structure and provides external stimuli (intrusive events) that initiate change; (2) *cultural values*, which affect the institutional structure, and which govern the interactions between components of the institutional structure in evaluating suitable responses to external stimuli; and (3) the *institutional structure* within which responses are made. The importance of these three elements is echoed by Hopwood who notes that

> rather than being isolated and thereby a more influenceable technical phenomenon, accounting is now recognized as being something shaped by cultures, institutional configurations and socio-historical circumstances of the specific societies in which it emerged.[13]

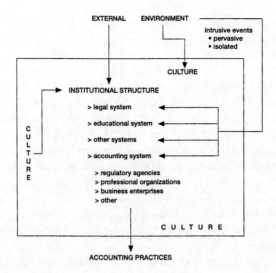

Exhibit 1 A general model of accounting development.

In an international context, these elements vary across national borders and therefore can be expected to lead to differences in accounting systems across countries.

Although culture appears to be depicted in the model as being wholly extraneous to the institutional structure, this is not the case. Culture permeates the various systems that constitute the institutional structure, impacting on accounting practice through norms and values held by members of the accounting system and norms and values held by members of other systems with which the accounting system interacts. Among other things these norms and values influence the importance (weighting) attached to intrusive events as they disrupt individual systems. This model is based on the following propositions:

(1) There exists in every country an institutional structure comprised of various systems (accounting, legal, educational, etc.).

(2) The accounting system, in turn, is comprised of various subsystems (regulatory agencies, professional organizations, corporations, etc.). The accounting practices followed within a country derive from the accounting system.

(3) A society's institutional structure, including the accounting system, is determined by the external environment and cultural norms and values.

(4) A society's cultural norms and values, in turn, are influenced by the external environment.

(5) The external environment creates intrusive events which act as stimuli for action by the institutional structure. Each intrusion is evaluated by a

214

member or members of the set of systems within society. Cultural norms and values affect the importance attached to a particular intrusive event.

(6) If an intrusive event relevant to accounting is not initially sourced within the accounting system it will be transmitted to the accounting system by a neighbouring system.

(7) The accounting subsystems interact to develop a response to the intrusive event. Cultural norms and values affect the interaction among the various subsystems.

(8) The accounting system does not act in a vacuum but interacts with other systems in developing culturally appropriate responses to intrusive events. Culture affects the interaction among the various systems.

(9) Intrusive events are conceptualized in two categories: (i) pervasive intrusions, such as colonization, EC Directives, inflation, and change from a planned to a market economy, which require extensive changes in the financial reporting system; and (ii) isolated intrusions, such as foreign currency fluctuations, banking scandals, and rising health care costs, which require changes in individual reporting practices only.

These propositions lead to a number of interesting avenues of research, including examination of such questions as:

(1) How does the external environment affect the institutional structure, especially the accounting component?

(2) How does culture affect the institutional structure, especially the accounting component?

(3) With which neighboring systems does the accounting system interact, in what manner, and how does culture affect this interaction?

(4) How does culture affect the interaction among the subsystems within the accounting system?

(5) How does culture affect the weight attached to a specific intrusive event?

(6) What are the past intrusive events (either pervasive or isolated) that are embodied in current accounting practice?

Case studies of individual countries would appear to be a fruitful method to address these questions.

Before embarking on research to address such questions, however, it is necessary to test whether the model is generally valid in a cross-national context. This implies testing whether there exists a relationship between the external environment and accounting practice, between the institutional structure and accounting practice, and between cultural values and accounting practice across a broad range of countries. A logical hypothesis to be developed from the model is that if the external environment, institutional structure, and/or cultural norms and values differ across countries, then it is likely that existing accounting practices will differ across countries as well.

The corollary is that countries with similar environments and cultures should have similar accounting practices. The remainder of this paper reports on a study designed to address this general research question.

A preliminary test of the general model

To test the general model, it is necessary to identify elements of the external environment likely to affect accounting either through their impact on the institutional structure or through intrusive events and identify the cultural values that shape the institutional structure and guide the interaction of the elements within the structure.

External environment

In terms of the model, the external environment encompasses everything in society other than the institutional structure that society has devised to regulate itself and the cultural norms and values shared by members of society. Thus, the external environment encompasses diverse influences, such as economic conditions, geography, colonization, climate, technology, disease, relationships with other societies, and past history.

The external environment is seen as influencing a nation's accounting system in two ways: indirectly through its impact on the institutional structure and directly through the emanation of intrusive events which disrupt the accounting or neighboring systems. Some aspects of the external environment do not affect accounting or do so in such an indirect manner that the link is no longer discernible. This would appear to be true for such factors as geography and climate.

Some environmental factors may influence accounting only indirectly through their impact on those systems within the institutional structure with which the accounting system interacts. It may be no longer possible to identify these factors. For example, the type of legal system used within a country might be the result of historical factors, relations with other countries, colonization, and so on. To test the proposition that the external environment affects accounting indirectly, it becomes necessary to examine whether the form of the institutional system (which is a result of indeterminable external influences) affects accounting practice.

Other environmental factors may influence accounting both directly and indirectly. For example, a country's level of economic development is likely to have an impact on the institutional structure within that country and at the same time be the source of ongoing intrusive events which elicit response from the accounting system.

Finally, there are environmental factors that might influence accounting directly (intrusive events) without affecting the institutional structure. Examples might be inflation or the collapse of the system of fixed exchange rates.

Numerous environmental factors that influence accounting practice have been hypothesized in the literature.[14] In a review of this literature, Meek and Saudagaran[15] indicate that there is general agreement (without empirical support) that the following environmental factors influence accounting:

(1) legal system;
(2) nature of the relationship between business enterprises and providers of capital;
(3) tax laws;
(4) inflation levels; and
(5) political and economic ties.

The current study examines six factors; the first four enumerated above plus:

(5) level of education; and
(6) level of economic development.

These last two factors were originally suggested by Mueller[16] in an accounting context.

The number of factors examined in this study was limited to six to ensure a reasonable ratio of observations to independent variables in subsequent statistical testing. The factor "political and economic ties" was not examined because of difficulty in developing an objective, meaningful scale usable in testing.

Legal system

The legal system is a part of the institutional framework with which the accounting system is very likely to interact. Legal system (code vs. common law) influences the way in which accounting rules are promulgated (legislated vs. non-legislated), which in turn could influence the nature of the rules themselves.[17] To test the relationship between legal system (LEGAL) and accounting, countries are coded on a binary scale according to a classification provided by David and Brierley.[18]

Relationship between business and providers of capital

Meek and Saudagaran[19] indicate that this factor relates to sources of financing, whether the group of capital providers is large and the level of development and sophistication of capital markets. These factors can be viewed as elements of the institutional structure with which the accounting system interacts, as well as intrusive events to which the accounting system must react.

A strong equity market with a diverse group of shareholders has generally been viewed as conducive to the production of sophisticated information. When banks dominate as a source of financing, accounting assumes a creditor protection orientation and disclosure levels are lower.

To test the relationship between this variable and accounting, market capitalization as a percentage of GNP (MC) and trading volume as a percentage of market capitalization (TVOMC) were determined for each country. Data on mean level of market capitalization and trading volume were gathered from the International Finance Corporation's *Emerging Stock Markets Factbook*. GNP data were obtained from the World Bank's *World Development Report* and the International Monetary Fund's *International Financial Statistics*.

Tax laws

In many countries, tax laws effectively determine accounting practice by requiring companies to book revenues and expenses in order to claim them for tax purposes.[20] In other countries, tax accounting and financial accounting are separate. In countries in which a strong link between taxation and accounting exists, companies are likely to adopt very conservative accounting practices so as to minimize their tax liabilities. This is likely to be especially true in countries with relatively high rates of taxation. Taxation, in general, can be seen as an intrusion on the accounting system with a potentially significant impact on accounting practice.

To test whether taxation is an intrusive event that has significantly impacted international accounting, this study examines the relationship between marginal tax rates (MTAX) and accounting practice. Data on corporate tax rates were obtained from Price Waterhouse's *Corporate Taxes: A Worldwide Summary*.

Inflation

Inflation has been one of the most intrusive economic challenges since the Great Depression. Inflation (INF) was included in the study by determining the mean annual rate of inflation over the period 1980–1987 from data provided in *World Development Report* and *International Financial Statistics*.

Level of education

It is often suggested that the level of education in a country or in its accounting profession affects accounting practice.[21] Level of education can be seen as an intrusion on the accounting system as accounting practices are developed within the constraints of the educational environment. The hypothesis is that a simple educational environment prevents development of sophisticated accounting practices. With regard to managerial accounting information, Schweikart[22] found that a stronger educational environment was associated with less relevance for formal reports and more relevance for informal reports. In this study, the percentage of the population with tertiary education as reported in the United Nations' *UNESCO Statistical Yearbook* or the International Labor Organization's *Yearbook of ILO Statistics* was used to measure a country's level of education (EDUC).

Level of economic development

Mueller[23] suggested that stage of economic development, type of economy, and growth pattern of an economy can exert an impact on a country's accounting practices. The stage of development affects the type of business transactions conducted in a country and the type of economy determines which transactions are more prevalent, each of which is an intrusion on the accounting system. Cooke and Wallace[24] have found that a simple dichotomous variable based on level of economic development (developed/ underdeveloped) absorbs the explanatory power of several economic variables considered jointly in explaining differences in countries' accounting systems. For this study, a country's level of development (LDEV) was scored on a binary scale (developed/underdeveloped) based upon classifications provided in *World Development Report*.

Culture

Culture can been defined as "the collective programming of the mind which distinguishes the members of one group or category of people from another."[25] While it affects many levels of society, it is assumed to exist primarily at a regional or national level.

Based upon an extensive cross-national survey, Hofstede[26] identified four underlying dimensions of societal value along which countries can be positioned: individualism, power distance, uncertainty avoidance, and masculinity.

Gray[27] suggests that these cultural dimensions may be useful in explaining international differences in accounting practices and develops two hypotheses which posit a directional relationship between financial reporting practices and culture. These are:

> The higher a country ranks in terms of uncertainty avoidance and the lower it ranks in terms of individualism and masculinity then the more likely it is to rank highly in terms of conservatism.

The higher a country ranks in terms of uncertainty avoidance and power distance and the lower it ranks in terms of individualism and masculinity then the more likely it is to rank highly in terms of secrecy.[28]

Conservatism is defined as a cautious approach to income measurement and secrecy as a preference for the disclosure of business information only to those closely involved with the business.

To test the relationship between culture and accounting practice proposed in the general model, culture is operationalized along Hofstede's four dimensions: individualism (INDIV), power distance (POWER), uncertainty avoidance (UNCERT), and masculinity (MASC). Scores for these variables were obtained from Hofstede.[29] Regional scores for West Africa, East Africa, and the Arab world were applied to those countries included in the study from those geographic areas.

Accounting practices

To examine the relationship between accounting and the independent variables identified above, a practitioner survey was conducted to obtain data on accounting practices in a broad range of countries. A survey approach was used, because it allows data to be gathered on a broader range of both disclosure and measurement practices than is possible using annual reports or international accounting summaries.

Based upon reviews by an expert panel of accounting practitioners, academicians, and financial analysts, 100 accounting issues (55 disclosure and 45 measurement items) were selected for inclusion in the survey. To facilitate input into statistical analysis, respondents were asked to indicate the percentage of companies in their country following a particular practice. To avoid the criticism of subjectivity, multiple respondents within the public accounting profession were contacted in each country with interjudge consistency used as the criterion for inclusion of respondents and countries in the database. Only those countries for which at least two responses that were not significantly different were obtained were included in the study. The resultant database contains information from 174 respondents in 50 countries on the utilization of 100 accounting practices as at January 1, 1990.

To develop a measure of national accounting practice that can be used as a dependent variable in a statistical analysis, the raw data on 100 accounting practices were input into cluster analysis. A country's membership in a particular cluster was used as the dependent variable in a test of the relationship between the independent variables and accounting practice. Because Nobes[30] suggests a multi-level structure to accounting diversity, hierarchical cluster analysis was used as the tool for developing the dependent variable.

Algorithm selection, heuristics for determining optimal solutions, and validation techniques as detailed in Punj and Stewart[11] were employed.

Results

Cluster analysis

Significant solutions were determined by examining pseudo F statistics for peaks and pseudo t^2 statistics for breaks or rapid drops in value. The strongest solution occurs at two clusters with weaker solutions at six and nine clusters. The hierarchy and cluster membership is presented in Exhibit 2. The clusters emerged as broadly consistent with previous inductive literature, especially Nobes.[32] For example, at the nine cluster level, only three countries are classified differently from Nobes' classification of 14 developed countries.[33]

The two cluster solution shown in Exhibit 2 is broadly consistent with the two "classes" of accounting system hypothesized in Nobes. Accordingly, cluster A1 is labeled "micro-based" and cluster A2 is labeled "macro-uniform" per Nobes (1983). Significant differences (at the 0.05 level) in mean score between clusters A1 and A2 exist for 65 out of 100 financial reporting issues.

The hierarchical nature of the cluster solutions suggests that there might be environmental factors and cultural dimensions of universal importance which cause national accounting systems to fall into one of two major classes. There then appear to be factors of secondary and tertiary importance which cause the two major classes of accounting to subdivide creating the six and nine cluster solutions.

For descriptive purposes only, financial reporting practices were categorized as measurement or disclosure and mean scores were computed for each cluster. High scores indicate relatively complex, less-conservative measurement practices and relatively high disclosure. Exhibit 3, which presents a plot of the scores at the two and nine cluster levels, suggests a strong inverse relationship between level of disclosure and conservatism.

Canonical correlation analysis

Countries coded on a 0,1 scale as being non-member/member of a particular cluster served as dependent variables. The independent variables consisted of country scores on the six environmental factors and the four cultural variables described earlier. Because the dependent and several independent variables in this study were non-metric, canonical correlation analysis (Cancorr) was used to examine the relationships among them. In Cancorr, linear combinations (canonical variates) are derived for each of a set of independent and dependent variables so that the correlation between the

Country	Number of Clusters		
	Two	Six	Nine
Japan		B6	C9
Germany		B5	C8
Finland Sweden		B4	C7
Egypt Saudi Arabia Belgium UAE Liberia Thailand Panama	A2 M a c r o	B3	C6
Portugal Spain Colombia Italy Korea Denmark Norway France	u n i f o r m		C5
Argentina Mexico Brazil Chile		B2	C4
Costa Rica			C3
Malaysia S. Africa Zimbabwe Hong Kong Singapore Namibia Ireland United Kingdom Zambia Australia Papua N. Guinea New Zealand Trinidad Nigeria Sri Lanka Botswana Jamaica Philippines Taiwan Netherlands Neth. Antilles Luxembourg	A1 M i c r o b a s e d	B1	C2
Bermuda Israel Canada United States			C1

Exhibit 2 Results of hierarchical cluster analysis.

222

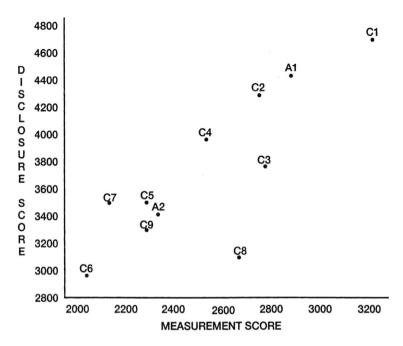

Exhibit 3 Plot of disclosure and measurement scores by cluster.

two variates is maximized. A number of pairs of variates (canonical functions) are extracted. Each canonical function provides insight into which independent variables are associated with the various stages in the development of the hierarchy of accounting systems.

Three criteria were used in deciding which canonical functions to interpret: (1) statistical significance of the squared canonical correlation, (2) magnitude of the canonical correlation, and (3) a redundancy index analogous to R^2.[34] Cross loadings were used to interpret the canonical variates. Cross loadings directly correlate the original dependent variables with the independent canonical variate and, when squared, indicate the total percentage of variation in group membership explained by each independent variate. The relative power of each independent variable within the independent variate is contained in the canonical loadings on that variate. Loadings of 0.40 or greater were used in interpreting the canonical variate of the independent variables. Separate Cancorr solutions were developed for the two, six, and nine cluster solutions.

Two cluster solution

Using the two cluster solution to define the dependent variable, one canonical function was significant at $\alpha = 0.05$. The canonical correlation coefficient

Table 1 Canonical structure at the two cluster level.

A. Cross loadings on variates of significant functions
  Correlations between the clusters of countries and the canonical variates of the independent variables

	Cluster	FUNC1
Macro-based	A1	0.9158
Macro-uniform	A2	−0.9158

B. Canonical loadings on variates on significant functions
  Correlations between the independent variables and their canonical variates

	FUNC1
LEGAL	−0.9271
EDUC	0.0100
INF	−0.2227
LDEV	0.0765
MTAX	−0.0410
MC	0.5316
TVOMC	0.1914
UNCERT	−0.6664
POWER	−0.1610
INDIV	0.2110
MASC	0.2664

was 0.9163. The redundancy index was 0.8388, which indicates that the independent variate explained 83.88 percent of the variance in the country clusters.

Panel A in Table 1 shows that the cross loadings for the dependent variables A1 (micro-based cluster) and A2 (macro-uniform cluster) were 0.9158 and −0.9158, respectively, indicating that the independent variate explains approximately 83 percent of the variance for both clusters of countries. The independent variate FUNC1 was, dominated by LEGAL (−0.9271), with significant loadings on UNCERT (−0.6664), and MC (0.5316). Given the signs of the cross loadings and the coding scheme used for the independent variables, cluster A1 countries can be characterized as being predominantly common law countries with a lower score on the uncertainty avoidance dimension of culture and higher market capitalization.

Referring to Exhibit 3 it can be seen that cluster A1 has a higher level of disclosure which is consistent with a lower level of uncertainty avoidance and greater reliance on equity investors as providers of capital. Cluster A1 also has a higher measurement score, consistent with Gray's hypothesis that low uncertainty avoidance groups tend to be less conservative.

Six cluster solution

The Cancorr solution at the six cluster level explains the breakup of the macro-uniform group, with the separation of Sweden/Finland (B4), Germany (B5), Japan (B6), and a Latin American (B2) cluster from a Core Macro group (B3). Three canonical functions are significant at $\alpha = 05$. The canonical correlations of these three functions are 0.9216, 0.8028, and 0.6982, respectively. The redundancy indices are 0.2229, 0.1242, and 0.0878. The independent variates cumulatively explain 43.5 percent of the variance in the country clusters.

Panel A in Table 2 shows the cross loadings for the dependent variable. The first function (FUNC1) discriminates between the micro-based group of countries (B1) and the various macro-uniform groups (B2–B6). As in the two cluster solution, the significant independent variables on FUNC1 are LEGAL, UNCERT, and MC.

Table 2 Canonical structure at the six cluster level.
A. Cross loadings on variates on significant functions
    Correlations between the clusters of countries and the canonical variates of the independent variables

	Cluster	*FUNC1*	*FUNC2*	*FUNC3*
Micro-based	B1	0.9049	0.1214	0.0053
Latin American	B2	−0.3901	0.6358	0.2363
Core Macro	B3	−0.5947	−0.2855	−0.2348
Sweden/Finland	B4	−0.0897	−0.1571	−0.3137
Germany	B5	−0.0138	−0.3012	0.0981
Japan	B6	−0.0663	−0.3562	0.5550

B. Canonical loadings on significant variates
    Correlations between the independent variables and their canonical variates

	FUNC1	*FUNC2*	*FUNC3*
LEGAL	−0.9033	−0.1506	0.0220
EDUC	0.0187	0.0642	0.0047
INF	−0.3074	0.6935	0.3097
LDEV	0.1664	−0.5064	−0.0748
MTAX	0.0272	−0.3437	0.1792
MC	0.5689	−0.2238	0.4290
TVOMC	0.2380	−0.1262	0.3216
UNCERT	−0.6929	0.0400	0.3718
POWER	−0.2092	0.0905	0.0486
INDIV	0.2666	−0.2470	−0.1582
MASC	0.2767	−0.1680	0.7514

The second function (FUNC2) appears to discriminate the Latin American group (B2) from the other macro-uniform clusters. The independent variables with significant loadings on FUNC2 are, INF (0. 6935) and LDEV (−0.5064). This indicates that the Latin American group of countries generally has higher inflation and a lower level of economic development than the other macro-uniform groups.

The third significant canonical function (FUNC3) primarily appears to discriminate Japan (B6) from the other macro-uniform groups especially B4 (Sweden/Finland). The independent variate was dominated by MASC (0.7514) and MC (0.4290), indicating that Japan has a higher level of masculinity and higher level of market capitalization than the other macro groups. This result is somewhat unexpected as Gray associates higher masculinity with higher disclosure and less conservatism. Yet, Exhibit 3 shows that Japan (C9) has a lower measurement and lower disclosure score than most of the other macro-uniform clusters (C3–C8).

Nine cluster solution

Four canonical functions are significant at the nine cluster level. The canonical correlation coefficients were 0.9311, 0.8671, 0.7695, and 0.7086, respectively. The redundancy index was 0.1206 for Function 1, 0.0961 for Function 2, 0.0713 for Function 3, and 0.0643 for Function 4, indicating that the independent variates cumulatively explained 34.2 percent of the variance in the country clusters.

The cross loadings in Table 3 (Panel A) show that FUNC 1 discriminates between the micro-based clusters, C1 and C2, and the macro-uniform clusters. The loadings on the independent variate were once again dominated by the variables LEGAL, UNCERT, and MC.

The second function appears to separate Latin America (C4) from the other macro-uniform clusters much as occurred in the six cluster solution. The significant independent variables in this second function are again INF and LDEV.

The third function discriminates Japan (C9) from the other macro-uniform groups as was the case in the six cluster solution. Once again, the significant independent variables on FUNC3 are MASC and MC.

The fourth function primarily distinguishes cluster C6 from the Latin American group (C4). The significant independent variables on FUNC4 are EDUC, INF, and Power. Thus, cluster C6 has a lower level of tertiary education, lower inflation and highest power distance than the Latin America group. Exhibit 3 shows that clusters C6 and C4 represent opposite poles within the macro-uniform class of accounting systems.

While not significant at normal levels ($\alpha = 0.14$), FUNC5 explains a further 5 percent of the overall variance in country clusters and helps explain the separation of the Sweden/Finland (C7) group from the other

Table 3 Canonical structure at the nine cluster level.
A. Cross loadings on variates of significant function correlations between the cluster of countries and the canonical variates of the independent variables

	Cluster	FUNC1	FUNC2	FUNC3	FUNC4	FUNC5
USA/Canada	C1	0.4875	−0.1116	−0.3258	0.3258	0.2671
British	C2	0.6414	0.3181	0.2308	−0.2565	−0.1878
Costa Rica	C3	−0.1713	0.0837	−0.3266	0.0270	0.0960
Latin American	C4	−0.3839	0.4951	0.2157	0.4480	−0.0468
European	C5	−0.3290	−0.4583	−0.0874	0.0366	−0.0771
Arab/Hybrid	C6	−0.3754	0.1487	−0.2158	−0.3822	0.2391
Sweden/Finland	C7	−0.0637	−0.2940	−0.1114	0.0402	−0.4467
Germany	C8	0.0367	−0.3147	0.1787	0.2200	0.0995
Japan	C9	−0.0717	−0.2854	0.4802	−0.0879	0.2595

B. Canonical loadings on significant variates
  Correlations between the independent variables and their canonical variates

	FUNC1	FUNC2	FUNC3	FUNC4	FUNC5
LEGAL	−0.8689	−0.2950	0.0092	0.1632	−0.0299
EDUC	0.1507	−0.1999	−0.2797	0.6010	0.1740
INF	−0.3410	0.5073	0.2419	0.6738	−0.1224
LDEV	0.2774	−0.6613	0.0071	0.2075	−0.0935
MTAX	0.0776	−0.4641	0.2650	0.1885	−0.1751
MC	0.5084	−0.8865	0.5367	−0.2350	−0.0840
TVOMC	0.2673	−0.1389	0.3480	0.3774	0.1287
UNCERT	−0.6315	−0.0917	−0.0229	0.2876	0.5325
POWER	−0.3054	0.3977	0.1675	−0.4610	0.1857
MASC	0.2487	0.1020	0.6115	−0.0458	0.6526
INDIV	0.3471	−0.3341	−0.0352	0.2423	−0.1278

macro-uniform groups. The significant independent variables on FUNC5 are cultural (UNCERT and MASC). Sweden and Finland are low masculinity, low uncertainty avoidance countries. Exhibit 3 shows that group C7 (Sweden/Finland) has the second lowest measurement score but has a relatively high level of disclosure which is consistent with low uncertainty avoidance. The key issues of disclosure are social with Sweden/Finland exhibiting a propensity to provide pension and shareholder disclosures. Disclosure of this type of information would appear to be consistent with a low-masculinity society.

The overall explanatory power at the nine cluster level can be seen by examining the squared multiple correlations provided in Table 4. For example, Panel A shows that the first five canonical functions explain 66.7 percent of the variance in cluster C2 (British). These five functions explain more than 30 percent of the variance in seven of the nine clusters.

Table 4 Squared cross loadings on significant variates nine cluster level.

A. Squared multiple correlation between the clusters of countries ad the first five canonical variates of the independent variables

	Cluster	1	2	3	4	5
USA/Canada	C1	0.2376	0.2501	0.3562	0.4624	0.5337
British	C2	0.4114	0.5126	0.5658	0.6316	0.6669
Costa Rica	C3	0.0293	0.0363	0.1430	0.1437	0.1529
Latin American	C4	0.1474	0.3925	0.4391	0.6398	0.6420
European	C5	0.1083	0.3183	0.3260	0.3273	0.3332
Arab/Hybrid	C6	0.1409	0.1630	0.2096	0.3557	0.4129
Sweden/Finland	C7	0.0041	0.0905	0.1029	0.1045	0.3041
Germany	C8	0.0013	0.1004	0.1323	0.1807	0.1906
Japan	C9	0.0051	0.0866	0.3172	0.3249	0.3922

B. Squared multiple correlations between the independent variables and the first five canonical variates of the clusters of countries

	1	2	3	4	5
LEGAL	0.6546	0.7200	0.7200	0.7334	0.7338
EDUC	0.0197	0.0497	0.0960	0.2774	0.2900
INF	0.1008	0.2943	0.3290	0.5569	0.5632
LDEV	0.0667	0.3955	0.3956	0.4172	0.4208
MTAX	0.0052	0.1672	0.2087	0.2266	0.2394
MC	0.2241	0.2297	0.4003	0.4291	0.4310
TVOMC	0.0620	0.0765	0.1482	0.2197	0.2266
UNCERT	0.3458	0.3521	0.3524	0.3939	0.5124
POWER	0.0809	0.1998	0.2161	0.3228	0.3372
MASC	0.0536	0.615	0.2829	0.2804	0.4618
INDIV	0.1045	0.1884	0.1891	0.2186	0.2254

Panel B shows that the independent variables with the greatest explanatory power after five functions are: legal system (LEGAL), level of inflation (INF), uncertainty avoidance (UNCERT), masculinity (MASC), market capitalization (MC), and level of economic development (LDEV).

Summary and conclusions

This study presented and tested a model of accounting development in which accounting practice is hypothesized as being the result of the complex interaction among a society's external environment, cultural norms and values, and institutional structures. Variables related to each of the three elements of the model were found to have significant explanatory power in discriminating across countries. Thus, the results lend support for the general model.

The analysis was not helpful in explaining some of the emergent clusters, most notably Germany. Assuming the model's general validity, there are obviously other environmental factors and cultural dimensions that explain the complete range of international accounting diversity.

Perhaps the most important finding of this study is the emergence of two major classes of accounting systems whose country members differ significantly on the basis of type of legal system. If differences between these two classes of accounting are rooted in differences in institutional structure, the power that intrusive events might have to cause change in accounting practice is likely to be mitigated and comparability of accounting across classes might be extremely difficult to achieve.

In attempting to reduce differences between these two classes of accounting system, the immediate relevant task might be to understand better how a country's legal system and accounting system relate to one another. The answer to this and other questions exploring the interrelationship between institutional structure, culture, external environment, and accounting might prove fruitful in understanding and ultimately reducing accounting diversity worldwide.

References

1. Wallace, R. S. O. and H. Gernon, "Frameworks for International Comparative Financial Accounting." *Journal of Accounting Literature* (1991), 209–264.
2. DaCosta, R. C., J. C. Bourgeois, and W. M. Lawson, "A Classification of International Financial Accounting Practices." *International Journal of Accounting Education and Research* (Spring 1978), 73–85; Frank, W., "An Empirical Analysis of International Accounting Principles." *Journal of Accounting Research* (Autumn) 1979, 593–605; Nair, R. and W. Frank, "The Impact of Disclosure and Measurement Practices on International Accounting Classifications." *Accounting Review* (July 1980), 426–450; Doupnik, T. S., "Evidence of International Harmonization of Financial Reporting." *International Journal of Accounting Education and Research* (Fall 1987), 47–67; Goodrich, P. S., "Cross-national Financial Accounting Linkages: An Empirical Political Analysis." *British Accounting Review* (1986), 42–60.
3. Mueller, G. G., "Accounting Principles Generally Accepted in the United States Versus Those Generally Accepted Elsewhere." *International Journal of Accounting Education and Research* (Spring 1968), 91–103; Seidler, L. J., International Accounting: The Ultimate Theory Course." *Accounting Review* (October 1967), 775–781; American Accounting Association, "Report of the 1975–76 Committee on International Accounting Operations and Education." *Accounting Review* (Suppl. 1977), 65–132; Al Najjar, F. "Standarization in accounting practices: A Comparative International Study." *International Journal of Accounting Education and Research* (Spring 1986), 161–176; Nobes, C. W., "A Judgemental International Classification of Financial Reporting Practices." *Journal of Business Finance and Accounting* (Spring 1983), 1–19.

4. Price Waterhouse International, *Accounting Principles and Reporting practices: A survey in 38 countries* (London: Price Waterhouse International, 1973); *Accounting Principles and Reporting Practices: A survey in 46 countries* (London: Price Waterhouse International, 1975); *International Survey of Accounting Principles and Reporting Practices* (London: Price Waterhouse International, 1979).

5. Mueller, G. G. (1968); AAA, 1977.

6. Radebaugh, L. H., "Environmental Factors Influencing the Development of Accounting Objectives, Standards and Practices in Peru." *International Journal of Accounting Education and Research* (Fall 1975), 39–56.

7. DaCosta *et al.*, 1978; Frank, 1979; Nair and Frank, 1980; Goodrich, 1986.

8. Schweikart, J. A., "Contingency Theory as a Framework for Research in *International Accounting.*" *International Journal of Accounting Education and Research* (Fall 1985), 89–98.

9. Harrison, G. L. and J. L. McKinnon, "Culture and Accounting Change: A New Perspective on Corporate Reporting Regulation and Accounting Policy Formulation." *Accounting, Organizations and Society* (No. 3, 1986), 233–256.

10. Robson, K., "On the Arenas of Accounting Change: The Process of Translation." *Accouting Organizations and Society* (No. 5/6, 1991), 547–570.

11. Gray, S. J., "Towards a Theory of Cultural Influence on the Development of Accounting Systems Internationally." Abacus (March 1988), 1–15.

12. Hofstede, G., *Culture's Consequences: International Differences in Work Related Values.* (Beverly Hill: Sage Publications, 1980).

13. Hopwood, A., "The Future of Accounting Harmonization in the Community." *European Accounting* (1991), 12–21.

14. See, for example, Mueller, 1968; AAA, 1977; Radebaugh, 1975.

15. Meek, G. and S. Saudagaran, "A Survey of Research on Financial Reporting in a Transnational Context." *Journal of Accounting Literature* (1990), 145–182.

16. Mueller (1968).

17. Meek and Saudagaran (1990), 9.

18. David, R. and J. Brierley, *Major Legal Systems in the World Today*. (London: Stevens, 1985).

19. Meek and Saudagaran (1990), 9–10.

20. Ibid., p. 10.

21. Mueller (1968); Radebaugh (1975); and AAA (1977).

22. Schweikart, J. A., "The Relevance of Managerial Accounting Information: A Multinational Analysis." *Accounting, Organizations and Society* (No. 6, 1986), 541–554.

23. Mueller (1968).

24. Cooke, T. E. and R. S. O. Wallace, "Financial Disclosure Regulation and its Environment: Review and Further Analysis." *Journal of Accounting and Public Policy* (Summer 1990), 79–110.

25. Hofstede, G., *Cultures and Organizations: Software of the Mind.* (London: McGraw-Hill, 1991), 5.

26. Hofstede (1980).

27. Gray (1988).

28. Ibid., 10–11.

30. Nobes (1983).

31. Punj, G. and D. W. Stewart, "Cluster Analysis in Marketing Research: Review and Suggestions for Application." *Journal of Marketing Research* (May 1983), 134–148.
32. Nobes (1983).
33. The misclassified countries are Belgium, Japan and the Netherlands.
34. See Hair, J. F., R. E. Anderson, and R. L. Tatham, *Multivariate Data Analysis with Readings* (New York: McMillan, 1987), 194, 199–200, 249 for heuristics used to interpret results of canonical correlation analysis.

9

TOWARDS A GENERAL MODEL OF THE REASONS FOR INTERNATIONAL DIFFERENCES IN FINANCIAL REPORTING

Christopher Nobes

Source: *Abacus* 34(2) (1998): 162–87.

The article first examines the existing modelling literature, which contains a large number of suggested reasons for international differences in accounting. After examining terminological problems, a preliminary parsimonious model is developed to explain the initial split of accounting systems into two classes. The term 'accounting system' is used here to mean the financial reporting practices used by an enterprise. A country might exhibit the use of several such systems in any one year or over time. Consequently, it should be systems and not countries that are classified. The model proposes a two-way classification using two variables: the strengths of equity markets and the degree of cultural dominance. Implications for classifiers and rule-makers are suggested.

Introduction and previous modelling

Many reasons have been suggested in the literature for international differences in financial reporting. Some authors state that they are merely listing plausible reasons; few provide precise hypotheses or tests of them, as noted by Meek and Saudagaran (1990). Wallace and Gernon (1991) complain about the lack of theory in international comparative accounting. This article seeks to address this.

The literature (e.g., Choi and Mueller, 1992, ch. 2; Radebaugh and Gray, 1993, ch. 3; Belkaoui, 1995, ch. 2; Nobes and Parker, 1995, ch. 1) offers a large number of possible reasons for international differences (see Table 1) but no general theory linking the factors. Schweikart (1985) and Harrison and McKinnon (1986) provide some elements of a general theory, without

Table 1 Reasons previously proposed for international accounting differences.

1   Nature of business ownership and financing system
2   Colonial inheritance
3   Invasions
4   Taxation
5   Inflation
6   Level of education
7   Age and size of accountancy profession
8   Stage of economic development
9   Legal systems
10 Culture
11 History
12 Geography
13 Language
14 Influence of theory
15 Political systems, social climate
16 Religion
17 Accidents

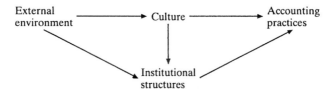

Figure 1 A simplification of DS's model of development.
Source: Adapted from Doupnik and Salter (1995), exhibit 1.

specifying which factors are major explanatory variables for accounting practices. Two somewhat similar theoretical models of the reasons for accounting differences are those of Gray (1988) and of Doupnik and Salter (1995; hereafter DS). Gray suggests a model based on cultural factors, as examined later. DS provide a synthesis of previous discussions, leading to a framework, which is simplified here as in Figure 1 so that an alternative can be proposed later. One difficulty emerging from Figure 1 is that four of DS's ten variables (see Table 2) are cultural (based on Gray) and six are institutional, but culture is seen as giving rise to the institutions. This suggests the possibility of double counting. A related difficulty with DS is that there is no attempt to connect their six institutional factors to see whether they might cause each other. In particular, it is suggested later that four of the six (taxation, inflation, level of education and stage of economic development) are not necessary. DS thus have provided a mix of theories, not a general theory.

Table 2 DS's independent variables.

Cultural	Institutional
Individualism	Legal system
Power distance	Capital market
Uncertainty avoidance	Tax
Masculinity	Inflation levels
	Level of education
	Level of economic development

A number of terminological issues are raised by studying this literature. These need to be addressed before attempting to develop a general model.

Some terminological issues

One of the problems of identifying reasons for differences, and perhaps then classifying accounting systems, is a lack of clarity about what is being examined or classified. This article discusses accounting *practices*, using 'accounting' to mean published financial reporting. In some jurisdictions, the *rules* of financial reporting may be identical, or very similar, to the practices, but sometimes a company may depart from rules or may have to make choices in the absence of rules. The Price Waterhouse data, used by many researchers,[1] seem to contain a mix of *de facto* and *de jure* aspects 'in a perplexing way' (Rahman *et al.*, 1996).

Another difficulty concerns the word 'system' (Roberts, 1995). DS use it to cover such things as regulatory agencies. Others (e.g., Nair and Frank, 1980) have concentrated on a corpus of accounting rules or practices. This article follows the latter route, that is, an 'accounting system' is a set of practices used in a published annual report. Although this is a narrow definition, these practices will reflect the wider context in which they operate.

Another issue is whether to separate disclosure from measurement practices. Nair and Frank (1980) show that this can be important. Nobes (1983) looks at measurement practices only. DS acknowledge the distinction but add the categories together. It seems appropriate to include the presence or absence of certain key disclosures (e.g., earnings per share, cash flow statements) as elements of a system, and this is discussed later.

A further issue is to determine whose accounting practices are being examined. The Price Waterhouse data seem, in practice, to have reported on companies audited by Price Waterhouse (see Nobes, 1981). DS (p. 198) specify the measurement and disclosure practices of 'companies', which is vague, particularly for disclosure practices. Nobes (1983, p. 5) chose the measurement practices of 'public companies', which the context suggests meant those with securities which are traded publicly.

A related point is that all the researchers look at classifications of *countries* by their accounting environments or systems. Roberts (1995) highlighted this problem, noting that a country could have more than one system, for example, one system for companies with publicly traded securities, and another for small private companies.[2] Similarly, some large public companies may adopt very different practices from what is 'normal' for most large companies in the country. This is becoming especially obvious in continental Europe, with the use of U.S. rules or International Accounting Standards (IAS) by some very large companies. Therefore, it may be useful to refer to a country's 'dominant accounting system', which might be defined as that used by enterprises encompassing the majority[3] of the country's economic activity. Hereafter, references to a country's 'system' should be taken to mean its dominant system.

In some countries, the law requires or commercial pressures dictate that a large number of companies use the same system. For example, in the U.K., most provisions of the Companies Act 1985 and of accounting standards apply to all companies. In other countries, a particular accounting system might be legally or commercially imposed on a small minority of companies, as in the U.S. where 'generally accepted accounting principles' are legally imposed on only that small proportion of companies registered with the Securities and Exchange Commission. In both these rather different cases, there is still clearly a dominant system as defined above.

Nevertheless, as there can be more than one system in a country it would be more useful to specify accounting systems, and then to note that particular companies in particular countries at particular dates are using them. Of course, for labelling purposes, it might be useful to refer, for example, to the system used in 1998 by U.S. public companies. With labels, it will then be possible to identify separate influences on, and to show separate places in the classification for, for example, 'normal' German public companies in 1998, compared to the group accounts of such companies as Daimler-Benz, Deutsche Bank and Bayer in 1998.

Also, a country's accounting system may change dramatically over time, for example, as a result of economic or political revolutions (c.f. China, Russia, Poland, etc.). Less dramatically, accounting in a country can change quite significantly as a result of new laws (e.g., Spain from the late 1980s as a consequence of EC Directives).[4]

Lastly, companies in two countries (e.g., the U.K. and Ireland) can use extremely similar accounting practices (i.e., perhaps the same 'system'). In a similar manner to the characteristics of human individuals, the detailed elements of a company's accounting practices can differ so much that the number of different sets of practices is effectively infinite. Nevertheless, it is useful for some purposes to recognize that humans all belong to the same species. The individual members of the species are all different but have certain features in common. By analogy, a certain degree of variation among company practices may be allowed without having to abandon the idea that the companies are all using the same system.

An initial statement of a general model

The proposal here, which will be explained more fully later, is that the major reason for international differences in financial reporting is different purposes for that reporting.

Financing systems

In particular, at a country level, it is suggested that the financing system is relevant in determining the purpose of financial reporting. Zysman (1983) distinguishes between three types of financing system: (a) *capital market based*, in which prices are established in competitive markets; (b) *credit-based system: governmental*, in which resources are administered by the government; and (c) *credit-based system: financial institutions*, in which banks and other financial institutions are dominant.

Zysman suggested that the U.K. and the U.S.A. have a type (a) system; France and Japan a type (b) system; and Germany a type (c) system. According to Zysman, in all systems companies rely considerably on their own profits for capital but their external sources of funds differ. Where external long-term finance is important, securities are the main source in the capital market system. In such countries, there is a wide range of capital instruments and of financial institutions, and the latter have an arm's-length relationship with companies. Investors change their holdings through the secondary securities markets, which are large. In credit-based systems, the capital market is smaller, so companies are more reliant on whoever grants credit. This usually means banks, whether under the influence of governments or not. Cable (1985) examined the importance of banks in the German economic system. In this system, investors will find it more difficult to adjust their holdings, so they may be more interested in long-run control of the management.

For the purposes of this article, a development of the Zysman classification is proposed, as in Table 3. For this, the concept of 'insider' and 'outsider' financiers needs to be developed. This idea of insiders and outsiders, which

Table 3 Financing systems.

	Strong credit	Strong equity
Insiders dominant	I	III
Outsiders dominant	II	IV

has its roots in the finance literature, has been used before for accounting purposes (e.g., see Nobes, 1988, p. 31), and to discuss contrasting corporate governance systems (e.g., Franks and Mayer, 1992; Kenway, 1994). 'Outsiders' are not members of the board of directors and do not have a privileged relationship with the company (e.g., such as that enjoyed by a company's banker who is also a major shareholder). They include both private individual shareholders and some institutions. For example, insurance companies and unit trusts normally have widely diversified portfolios, so that any particular holding does not constitute a large proportion of a company's capital. Therefore, such institutions should perhaps be counted as outsiders. By contrast, 'insiders' such as governments, banks, families and other companies are all likely to have close, long-term relationships with their investees. This will involve the private provision of timely and frequent accounting information.

Both of Zysman's credit-based systems fall into category I of Table 3. Category II (a credit-based system with a large amount of listed debt with outsider owners) is plausible but uncommon. A possible example is discussed near the end of this subsection. Category III is an equity-based system where most shares are owned by insiders. In Japan, for example, there are large numbers of listed companies and a large equity market capitalisation, but the shares are extensively owned by banks and other companies (Nobes and Parker, 1995, p. 9 and ch. 13).

Category IV systems involve important equity markets with large numbers of outsider shareholders. In these systems there will be a demand for public disclosure and for external audit because most providers of finance have no involvement in management and no private access to financial information. This is the classic setting of most of the finance literature (e.g., Jensen and Meckling, 1976; Beaver, 1989). More recently, a connection between more disclosure and lower cost of equity capital has been examined in such a context (Botosan, 1997). Pursuing this line, this article suggests that the key issue for financial reporting is the existence or otherwise of such Category IV financing. Ways of measuring this are proposed below.

In a particular country, there may be elements of several of these four systems. For example, small companies are unlikely to be financed by a Category IV system in any country. However, for the moment, let us assume that the economic activity in any country is dominated by one particular financing system. The hypothesis predicting a correlation between the style of corporate financing and the type of accounting system is that the rule-makers for, and the preparers of, financial reports in equity-outsider (Category IV) countries are largely concerned with the outside users. The conceptual frameworks used by the rule-makers of the U.S., the U.K., Australia and the IASC[5] make it clear that this is so. In particular, they state that they are concerned with reporting financial performance and enabling the prediction of future cash flows for relatively sophisticated outside users of financial statements of large companies. By contrast, credit-based countries (mostly Category I) will be more concerned with the protection of creditors and therefore with the prudent calculation of distributable profit. Their financiers (insiders) will not need externally audited, published reports. This difference of purpose will lead to differences in accounting practices. The less common categories (II and III) will be discussed later.

Empirical researchers would need to establish relevant measures to distinguish the categories (as done, for example, by La Porta *et al.*, 1997). These might include the number of domestic listed companies in a country (or this deflated by size of population), the equity market capitalization (or this deflated by GDP), and the proportion of shares held by 'outsiders'. Although the boundary between the types of financing system may sometimes be unclear (as in many of the classifications in social science, languages, law or, even, biology), the contrast between a strong equity-outsider system and other systems should be clear enough, as the Appendix demonstrates for some countries.

Financial reporting systems

It is proposed that financial reporting systems should be divided initially into two classes, for the moment labelled as A and B. Class A corresponds to what some have called Anglo-Saxon accounting and Class B to continental European. To assist researchers in measuring a system, some core features of the two systems are suggested in Table 4. For example, systems of Class A will share all, or a large proportion of, the practices shown for that class. Clear examples of actual systems exhibiting *all* of the features exist.[6]

Table 4 Examples of features of the two accounting classes.

Feature	Class A	Class B
Provisions for depreciation and pensions	Accounting practice differs from tax rules	Accounting practice follows tax rules
Long-term contracts	Percentage of completion method	Completed contract method
Unsettled currency gains	Taken to income	Deferred or not recognised
Legal reserves	Not found	Required
Profit and loss format	Expenses recorded by function (e.g., cost of sales)	Expenses recorded by nature (e.g., total wages)
Cash flow statements	Required	Not required, found only sporadically
Earnings per share disclosure	Required by listed companies	Not required, found only sporadically

It is proposed that, for developed countries,[7] the extent that a particular country is associated with Class A or Class B accounting is predictable on the basis of its position with respect to financing systems. If the present accounting system was developed in the past, then reference to the past importance of financing systems will be relevant. Strong equity-outsider markets (Category IV) lead to Class A systems; otherwise Class B systems prevail.

Even if a particular country is traditionally associated with weak equity markets and therefore Class B accounting, the country might change. For example, China has been changing in the direction of a strong equity-outsider market and Class A accounting (Chow *et al.*, 1995). However, the accounting might remain stuck in the past for legal or other reasons of inertia. Nevertheless, in some countries, certain companies might be especially commercially affected. They might adopt Class A accounting by using flexibility in the national rules, by breaking national rules, or by producing two sets of financial statements. Some German examples of these routes can be given. Bayer's consolidated financial statements (for 1994 onwards) have used non-typical German rules, that are different from those used in its parent's statements, in order to comply with International Accounting Standards (IAS). Further, officials of the Ministry of Finance have announced that departure from German rules would be 'tolerated' for such group accounts.[8] In the case of Deutsche Bank (e.g., for 1995), two full sets of financial statements were produced, under German rules and IAS, respectively.

A related issue is that, as noted earlier, there are two aspects of financial reporting which can be separated: measurement and disclosure (e.g., Nair and Frank, 1980). Table 4 contains examples of both aspects. As explained below, the measurement issues seem to be driven by the equity/creditor split, and the disclosure issues by the outsider/insider split. The equity/creditor split leads to different kinds of *objectives* for financial reporting. As suggested earlier, systems serving equity markets are required to provide relevant information on performance and the assessment of future cash flows in order to help with the making of financial decisions. Systems in a creditor environment are required to calculate prudent and reliable distributable (and taxable) profit. By contrast, the outsider/insider split leads to different *amounts* of information: where outsiders are important, there is a demand for more published financial reporting.

It has been assumed here that equity financing systems are normally those which are associated with large numbers of outsiders, so that Class A systems are an amalgam of equity and outsider features. However, if there were countries (Category II of Table 3) with large markets for listed debt but not for listed equities, then one might expect a financial reporting system with the high disclosures of Class A but the measurement rules of Class B. Perhaps the closest example of a system with Class B measurement rules but high disclosures is the German system for listed companies.[9] Germany does indeed have an unusually large market in listed debt.[10]

This way of distinguishing between the forces acting on measurement and those acting on disclosure may help to resolve the difficulties of a cultural explanation as discussed by Baydoun and Willett (1995, pp. 82–8).

Category III (equity-insider) financing would not produce Class A accounting because published financial reporting is unimportant. The main financiers may be interested in performance and cash flows but they have access to private 'management' information.

Colonial inheritance

Some countries are affected by very strong external cultural influences, perhaps due to their small size or underdeveloped state or former colonial status. Such culturally dominated countries are likely to be using an accounting system based on that of the influential country even if this seems inappropriate to their current commercial needs (Hove, 1986).

Colonial inheritance (Factor 2 in Table 1) is probably the major explanatory factor for the general system of financial reporting in many countries outside Europe (Briston, 1978). It is easy to predict how accounting will work in Gambia (British) compared to neighbouring Senegal (French).[11] The same general point applies to Singapore (Briston and Foo, 1990) or Australia (Miller, 1994). Colonial inheritance extends of course to legal systems and to other background and cultural factors, not just to direct imports of accounting (Parker, 1989). Allied to this are the effects of substantial investment from another country, which may lead to accountants and accounting migrating together with the capital.

Another influence is invasions (Factor 3) which may lead to major influence on accounting, as is the case with Japanese,[12] French,[13] and German[14] accounting. However, when the invader retires, any foreign accounting can be gradually removed if it does not suit the country: Japan closed down its Securities and Exchange Commission when the Americans left, whereas France retained its accounting plan in order to aid reconstruction after World War II (Standish, 1990).

Why other factors may be less useful

If the above conclusions are accepted (i.e., that a general two-class model of financial reporting systems can be built which rests on only the importance of financing systems and colonial inheritance), then most of the seventeen factors listed in Table 1 seem unnecessary as explanatory independent variables, at least for the initial two-class classification. This section explains why, starting with DS's factors.

Tax

Previous writers (e.g., Nobes, 1983) have not been helpful by listing tax as one of the major causes of accounting differences. These writers have, in effect, suggested that Class A accounting systems are not dominated by tax rules whereas Class B systems are; and therefore, that the tax difference is one of the reasons for the difference in accounting systems. However, the disconnection of tax from accounting in Class A systems may be seen as a *result* of the existence of a competing purpose for accounting rather than the major cause of international accounting differences. Lamb *et al.* (1995) look at this in detail, concluding that:

1. Rules for the determination of the taxable profit of businesses will be important in all countries (assuming that taxation of profit is significant).
2. Without some major competing purpose for accounting for which tax rules are unsuitable, tax rules made by governments will therefore tend to dominate accounting, so that tax practices and accounting practices are the same (as in Class B).
3. In some countries (or for some companies), there is the major competing purpose of supplying financial reports to equity-outsider markets (for which tax rules are unsuitable). In this case, for many accounting topics, there will be two sets of accounting rules (and practices): tax rules and financial reporting rules (as in Class A).

Consequently, the tax variable is not needed to explain the difference between Class A and Class B systems. Nevertheless, for those systems where tax and accounting are closely linked (Class B), international differences in tax rules do create international accounting differences. However, these are detailed differences *within* a class of accounting systems which all share the major feature of being dominated by tax rules, which is one of the distinguishing marks of the class.

There is a further important connection here. The equity/credit split in financing, as discussed earlier, coincides with the proposed equity-user/tax-user split: accounting systems designed to serve creditors are systems dominated by tax rules. This is because the calculation of the legally distributable profit (to protect creditors) and the calculation of taxable profit are both issues in which governments are interested. The calculation of legally distributable profit is a different purpose from the calculation of taxable profit but it is not 'competing' in the sense of requiring a different set of rules because both calculations benefit from precision in the rules[15] and from the minimization of the use of judgment,[16] which is not the case for the estimation of cash flows.

Incidentally, DS follow previous writers and suggest that, 'In many countries, tax laws effectively determine accounting practice' (p. 196). However, they then find that tax is not a useful independent variable in explaining accounting differences. It is argued above that tax is not an independent variable for the main classificatory split. DS failed to find even a correlation, probably because they mis-specified the tax variable by using the marginal rate of corporate income taxes. This measure seems inappropriate for several reasons. First, tax rates change dramatically over time, without any obvious effect on accounting (e.g., the top U.S. rate fell from 46 per cent to 34 per cent in 1987; the main rate in the U.K. rose in 1973 from 40 per cent to 52 per cent, and then fell to 33 per cent in 1991). Second, many systems have more than one marginal rate (e.g., in Germany in 1995, 45 per cent for retained profit but 30 per cent for distributed profit; and, in the U.K., 33 per cent for large companies but 25 per cent for small). Third, the tax burden depends greatly on the definition of taxable income not just on the tax rate. More importantly, in countries with a small connection between tax and accounting (typical of Class A), the tax rate will have little effect on accounting; and in countries with a close connection (typical of Class B), the effect of tax on accounting will be in the same direction and probably almost as strong whether the rate is 30 per cent or 50 per cent. For all these reasons, the level of the marginal rate of tax will not help to predict the financial reporting system.

Level of education

DS's variable here is the percentage of population with tertiary education. It is hard to see how one could explain the major accounting differences on this basis. Can one explain the large accounting differences between, on the one hand, the U.K., the U.S. and the Netherlands (where Class A dominates) and, on the other hand, France, Germany and Italy (where Class B dominates) on the basis of the rather similar levels of tertiary education? Again, can one explain the remarkable similarities between accounting in Malawi, Nigeria and Zimbabwe (Class A countries) and the U.K. (also Class A) on the basis of the rather different levels of tertiary education? Instead there seems to be a connection with the 'colonial inheritance' point, as discussed earlier and as taken up again in the 'level of economic development' point below. Thus it is not surprising that the education variable did not help DS. Previous suggestions related to this factor (e.g., Radebaugh, 1975) seem, more plausibly, to involve the comparison of developed with less developed countries.

Different levels of professional accounting education might be relevant (Shoenthal, 1989), perhaps especially in developing countries (e.g., Parry and Grove, 1990). However, Nobes (1992) casts doubt upon the relevance of this type of factor for classification. To the extent that this is not another issue related to developed versus developing countries, differences in professional education might be covered by Factor 8 in Table 1 (age and size of

242

accountancy profession) and may be a *result* of accounting differences rather than their cause.

Level of economic development

It is suggested that the key issue here is not the influence of the stage of economic development on financial reporting (as chosen by DS). Gernon and Wallace (1995, p. 64) agree that there is 'no conclusive evidence' about the relationship. The problem is that, while many African countries with a low level of development have accounting systems rather like the U.K.'s, some have completely different accounting systems rather like that in France. By contrast, the U.K. or the Netherlands have a rather similar level of economic development to that of Germany or Italy but completely different accounting systems.

It would seem plausible to argue that, if accounting systems were indigenously created in all countries, then they would develop differently in developed and undeveloped economies. However, it is suggested that this point is largely overridden by the proposition that developing countries are likely to be using an accounting system invented elsewhere. Perhaps the system has been forced on them, or they have borrowed it. Either way, it is usually possible to predict accounting in such countries by looking at the source of the external influences. Therefore, the level of development is not the key predictor for the split between Class A and Class B. Cooke and Wallace (1990) seem to support the distinction between developed and developing countries when it comes to the influence of various environmental factors on accounting.

Legal systems

For developed Western countries and for many others (e.g., Japan, South America and most of Africa), it is possible to split countries neatly into codified legal systems and common law systems (David and Brierley, 1985). As DS note, this is of great relevance to the regulatory system for accounting. However, there is a high degree of correlation between equity-outsider financing systems and common law countries, and between credit-insider systems and codified law.[17] On the whole, therefore, the same groupings would result from using a legal system variable rather than from using a financing system variable, as DS find. This again suggests the possibility of double counting. The exception of the Netherlands, which raises further doubts about using the legal variable for accounting classification, is explained below.

For culturally dominated countries, both the legal and accounting systems are likely to have been imported from the same place, so the correlation between these two variables is unsurprising. Both factors can be explained by the colonial influence factor, so the legal factor is not needed. For other countries, there may be aspects of the common law system which predispose a country towards the creation of strong equity-outsider systems (La Porta *et al.*, 1997), but going that far back in the causal chain is not necessary for the present model. For present purposes, it may be more useful to specify the legal variable as the regulatory system for accounting rather than the more general legal system. The variable would be measured by locating the source of the most detailed accounting regulations. A 0/1 variable would contrast (i) rules made by professional accountants, company directors, independent bodies, stock exchanges and equity market regulators, and (ii) rules made by tax authorities, government ministries (other than those concerned primarily with listed companies) and legal bureaucrats.

Once more, it could be argued that this version of the legal variable is not independent but is dependent on the financing variable. In strong equity-outsider systems, commercial pressure gives the strongest power over financial reporting to group (i) because, since the financial reporting for the equity/ outsiders uses separate rules from tax rules, there is no need for group (ii) to control them. In particular, many of the disclosures (e.g., consolidated financial reports, cash flow statements, segmental reporting, interim reporting) are not relevant for tax or distribution purposes in most jurisdictions. Financial institutions and large companies are sufficiently powerful to persuade group (ii) to allow financial reporting to respond to commercial needs. In common law countries, the importance of group (i) creates no problems of jurisprudence because non-governmental regulation is commonplace. In the rare case of a codified law country with a strong equity market (e.g., the Netherlands), the regulatory system for financial reporting can still give prominence to group (i) although this creates tensions (Zeff *et al.*, 1992). In all systems, group (ii) retains full control over tax rules.

Inflation levels

Another factor included by DS is the rate of inflation and, once more, previous writers have not been helpful here. For example, although Nobes (1983) did not include inflation as a key variable, Nobes and Parker (1995, p. 19) suggested that 'Without reference to this factor, it would not be possible to explain accounting differences in countries severely affected by it'. However, on reflection, the more important issue is illustrated by other points that they make in the same section:

1. 'accountants in the English-speaking world have proved remarkably immune to inflation when it comes to taking decisive action';
2. 'in several South American countries, the most obvious feature . . . is the use of methods of general price-level adjustment';

3. 'the fact that it was *governments* which responded to inflation in France, Spain, Italy and Greece . . . is symptomatic of the regulation of accounting in these countries'.

In other words, any accounting system would have to respond at some level of inflation sustained for a certain length of time.[18] The key points are who responds and how they respond. The nature of these responses to inflation is a good indicator of the regulatory system for accounting. In countries where Class A accounting is dominant, professional accountants respond; in countries where Class B accounting is dominant, governments respond within the framework of the tax system.[19] Differential inflation does not cause the difference between Class A and Class B acounting, the regulators typical to the two classes respond differently to it. However, as with some other factors, differential inflation response may lead to differences between the systems *within* Class A or *within* Class B.

Culture

Culture (defined by Hofstede as 'the collective programming of the mind') is clearly a plausible cause of accounting differences as proposed by Gray's (1988) application of Hofstede's (1980) theory. DS's four culture variables (see Table 2) were drawn from Hofstede. However, the attempt to use cultural variables entails large problems (Gernon and Wallace, 1995, pp. 85, 90, 91). Baydoun and Willett (1995, p. 69) also suggest that the mechanisms of the effects are not obvious, and: 'such is the nature of the concepts involved and the state of the available evidence that it is questionable whether Gray's adaptation of Hofstede's theory can in fact be empirically validated in the usual scientific sense' (p. 72).

For the purposes of this article, one can agree with Gray that culture can at least be seen as one of the background factors leading to more direct causes of accounting differences (such as the financing system). Culture may be of more direct help when examining other issues, for example, differences in the behaviour of auditors (Soeters and Schreuder, 1988). It will also be useful later to divide countries into culturally self-sufficient and culturally dominated. As noted in the previous section, the latter countries (e.g., colonies or former colonies) might be expected to adopt practices from other countries. In this sense, culture might indeed overwhelm other factors for certain countries.

Broad factors

Others of the seventeen factors of Table 1, not proposed by DS but elsewhere in the literature, are too wide to be useful and can be accommodated within more specific factors. On these grounds, history and geography (Factors 11 and 12) can be removed. In a sense, 'history' explains everything, but this is not helpful unless it is known which part of history. For example, colonial history and the history of the corporate financing system are likely to be particularly relevant, so other factors can cover this.

'Geography' is also too broad a factor to be useful. It seems unlikely that the physical nature of a country has a major effect on its dominant class of accounting. for example, the Netherlands and Belgium have very different accounting, although they are similar in physical environment. By contrast, the U.K. and Australia have similar accounting although they are dramatically different in climate, terrain and type of agriculture. A country's location may be relevant for other factors (such as colonial inheritance and invasions) or for certain aspects of its financial history (such as the fact that maritime countries may tend to develop certain types of trading or markets). However, the relevant aspects of geography should be picked up by other factors. In the meantime, one merely notes that location seems to be overwhelmed by other factors in the sense that New Zealand has rather similar accounting to the distant U.K.; and the Netherlands has very different accounting from its neighbours, Germany and Belgium.

Covariation

Other factors may involve covariation rather than causation. For example, the fact that many English-speaking countries have similar accounting practices is probably not caused by their shared language (Factor 13): the language was inherited with the accounting or with other factors which affect accounting. Language similarities may contribute to the strength of cultural dominance, and language differences may slow down the transfer of accounting technology. However, these points do not make language a key independent variable.

Theory

Theory (Factor 14), in the form of an explicit or implicit underlying framework, is certainly of relevance in some countries.[20] However, there are always competing theories (as examined for accounting by Watts and Zimmerman, 1979). It is suggested here that the degree of acceptance of particular accounting theories within a country *depends upon* other factors, such as the strength of equity markets and the regulatory system.

Results rather than causes

Some factors above have been seen as more results than causes of the major accounting differences. Similarly, the age and size of the accountancy professions (Factor 7) differ substantially around the world,[21] but this is likely to be the *result* of different accounting systems. For example, the comparatively small size of the German auditing profession seems to result from the comparatively small number of audited companies, which in turn results from comparative weakness of equity markets.

Factors more relevant outside the developed world

Certain other factors might not discriminate between developed Western countries, on which most classifications have concentrated. For example, political systems (Factor 15), religion (Factor 16) and stage of economic development (Factor 8) are probably sufficiently homogeneous in these countries that they do not have major explanatory power. They might well be relevant for a broader study, and at levels of classification below the two major classes. For example, religion may have an effect on accounting in some countries (Gambling and Abdel-Karim, 1991; Hamid *et al.*, 1993). Of course, religion and culture may be closely related.

Accidents

Close examination of accidents (Factor 17) will generally reveal their causes. However, certainly at the level of detailed accounting practices within a class, 'accident' may be a useful summary explanation. For example, some of the largest differences between U.S. and U.K. accounting (LIFO, deferred tax and goodwill) could be said to have accidental causes.[22] However, it is not necessary to resort to 'accidents' as an explanation of the difference between Class A and Class B accounting. It is suggested that the model which is restated in more detail below is powerful enough without this feature. In the end the validity of this claim is an empirical matter.

Summary on excluded factors

Many of the factors which have been examined in this section may be contributory causes to accounting differences or may be *associated* with accounting differences. However, it has been suggested that each can be eliminated as a major reason for the differences identified at the first split of accounting systems into two classes. At lower levels in a classification, many of these factors may be useful explanations of relatively small differences between systems. Further, some of the factors, certainly 'culture', help to explain the different types of capital markets which, according to proposals here, do explain the major groupings.

The proposed model

The proposed model consists of a number of linked constructs which will be expressed as propositions. Part of the model can be expressed in simplified

| External environment | $\longrightarrow$ | Culture, including institutional structures | $\longrightarrow$ | Strength of equity-outsider system | $\longrightarrow$ | Class of accounting |

Figure 2 Simplified model of reasons for international accounting differences.

form as in Figure 2, which amends DS's proposal (summarised in Figure 1). The variables needed have been introduced in the text above, but now need to be marshalled.

The first variable is the type of country culture and the second is the strength of the equity-outsider financing system. This article assumes that some cultures lead to strong equity-outsider markets, and others do not. However, this is an issue for economists and others and is not examined in detail here. The point of departure for the constructs and hypotheses explained below is the second variable: the nature of the equity markets. Suggestions have been made here about how empirical researchers could measure this variable, perhaps leading to a 0/1 (weak or strong equity-outsider market) classification.

A further variable is the type of company. For most companies (insider companies), a controlling stake is in the hands of a small number of owners. For a comparatively few companies (outsider companies), control is widely spread amongst a large number of 'outsider' equity-holders. Countries with strong equity-outsider systems generally have a large number of outsider companies which may comprise most of a country's GNP, but other countries may also have a few of these companies.

The fourth variable is the country's degree of cultural self-sufficiency. As discussed earlier, some countries have strong indigenous cultures whereas others have imported cultures which are still dominated or heavily influenced from outside. This dichotomy will be expressed by using the labels CS (for culturally self-sufficient) and CD (for culturally dominated). Researchers might wish to measure this in various ways, for example by the number of decades since a country gained political independence from another. Many developing countries are CD and many developed countries are CS, but there are exceptions. Again, the boundaries between CS and CD are unclear, but researchers should have little difficulty in classifying many countries. Concentration should be placed on aspects of business culture in cases where this may give a different answer from other aspects of culture.

The final variable is the type of financial reporting system (or, in short, 'accounting system') introduced earlier as Class A or Class B. Again, preliminary suggestions have been made about how researchers might measure and classify systems in this way.

The theoretical constructs which link these variables can now be brought together. It is relevant here to repeat the point that more than one accounting system can be used in any particular country at any one time or over time.

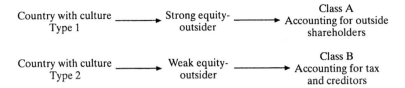

Figure 3 Application of Figure 2 to culturally sufficient countries.

The model can be expressed in terms of propositions, which are then explained and illustrated:

P1: The dominant accounting system in a CS country with a strong equity-outsider system is Class A.

P2: The dominant accounting system in a CS country with a weak (or no) equity-outsider system is Class B.

P3: A CD country has an accounting system imported from its dominating country, irrespective of the strength of the CD country's equity-outsider system.

P4: As a country establishes a strong equity-outsider market, its accounting system moves from Class B to Class A.

P5: Outsider companies in countries with weak equity-outsider markets will move to Class A accounting.

The analysis can begin with culturally self-sufficient (CS) countries (Propositions P1 and P2 above), as illustrated in Figure 3. For these countries, it is suggested that the class of the dominant accounting system will depend upon the strength of the equity-outsider market (or on its strength in the past, if there is inertia). Strong equity-outsider systems will lead to Class A accounting (see Table 4), whereas others will lead to Class B accounting. As explained earlier, the term 'dominant accounting system' is used to refer to the type used by enterprises representing the majority of a country's economic activity. For example, small unlisted enterprises in strong equity market countries might not practise Class A accounting or indeed any financial reporting at all.

Propositions P3 to P5 are now examined. Proposition P3 is that, in culturally dominated (CD) countries, accounting systems are imported. Sometimes a CD country will also have had time to develop the style of equity market associated with the culture. Therein, Propositions P1 or P2 will hold as in CS countries. However, sometimes a CD country may have imported its culture and its accounting system without establishing the related equity market. In this case the accounting system will seem inappropriate for the strength of the equity-outsider financing system. Proposition P4 is that, if either a CS or a CD country with a traditionally weak equity market

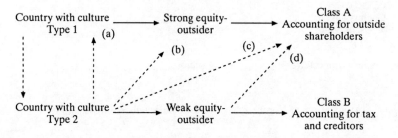

Figure 4 A proposed model of reasons for international accounting differences.

gradually develops a strong equity-outsider system, a change of accounting towards Class A will follow. Also (P5), in a country with weak equity-outsider markets, there may be *some* 'outsider companies' (as defined earlier). Commercial pressure will lead these companies towards Class A accounting, even if the dominant system in the country is Class B. For such a company, there will be rewards in terms of lower cost of capital[23] from the production of Class A statements, particularly if there is an international market in the company's shares. If legal constraints hinder movement towards Class A accounting, then the company can use extra disclosures or supplementary statements.

Figure 4 shows some aspects of these constructs. The continuous arrows are those from Figure 3. Dotted arrows (a) and (c) concern aspects of Proposition P3. Arrow (b) relates to Proposition P4, and Arrow (d) Proposition P5. Some illustrations are:

1 (Arrow a) New Zealand is a CD country with wholesale importation of British culture and institutions (Type 1), including a strong equity-outsider system and Class A accounting. Whether the Class A accounting results from the equity market or from direct cultural pressure is not important to the model; it probably arises from both.

2 (Arrow b) China is a country without a strong equity-outsider tradition but which seems to be moving towards such a system. Class A accounting is following (Davidson *et al.*, 1995).

3 (Arrow c) Malawi is a CD country with very weak equity markets[24] but where the accountancy profession has adopted Class A accounting, consistent with its colonial inheritance from the U.K.

4 (Arrow d) The Deutsche Bank, Bayer and Nestlé are companies from countries with traditionally weak equity markets. These companies are now interested in world equity-outsider markets, so they are adopting[25] Class A accounting for their group accounts.

Implications for classification

Discussions about the reasons for international differences in financial reporting are clearly related to the topic of classification of financial reporting 'systems'. Some implications of the above suggestions for classification researchers are examined here.

Before Darwin, the Linnaean classification was drawn up on the 'intrinsic' basis of observations about the 'essential' differences in the characteristics of species. Later, genetic and inheritance ('extrinsic') issues became the normal basis for classification, but largely came to the same conclusions. In accounting, one may also see both intrinsic and extrinsic classifications (Roberts, 1995), which may lead to similar conclusions. For example, one can extrinsically trace modern U.K. and modern New Zealand accounting back to a common ancestor; and one can intrinsically note many similarities in the accounting systems currently used. However, it is proposed here to discuss the classifications based on intrinsic factors. For this reason, the term 'species', to which Roberts (1995) objected, will be omitted.

It is not proposed here to re-work previous classifications but to suggest implications of the above conclusions for future classification work. Taking the classification by Nobes (1983), some improvements can be suggested, as shown in Figure 5. The two classes are shown, much as in the earlier classification, but the labels are sharper, following Propositions P1 and P2 above. The bottom level of classification is now a 'system' not a country. This accommodates P5 above. In order to make the classification easier to use, the systems could be labelled (e.g., U.S. GAAP). The classification in Figure 5 is by no means complete, for it merely seeks to illustrate the type of amendments proposed for future classifiers.

Below each system, there are examples of users of the system. This accommodates the points made earlier about the meaning of the term 'dominant accounting system'. For instance, U.S. GAAP is used by SEC-registered companies but not by all U.S. companies. Similarly, some Japanese companies are allowed to follow U.S. GAAP for their group accounts for both U.S. and Japanese purposes. As another instance, the 'standard German' system is that used by German companies for individual company accounts and, by most of them, for group accounts. However, several German listed companies are now publishing group accounts in accordance with International Accounting Standards, either by carefully choosing unusual German options (e.g., Bayer for 1994) or by producing two sets of group accounts (e.g., Deutsche Bank for 1995).

Proposition P3 would be relevant for the inclusion of developing countries in a classification. The fourth proposition could be used to predict which countries would move their dominant systems towards Class A in the classification.

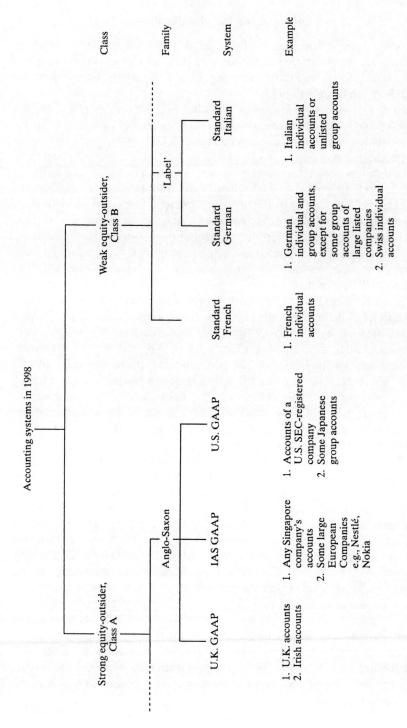

Figure 5 Extract from proposed scheme for classification.

Policy implications for rule-makers

The import and export of accounting technology (Parker, 1989) seems to be accelerating as a result of globalization and the formation of economic blocs such as the European Economic Area and the North American Free Trade Area. Also, the World Bank has funded advice for China on reforming its accounting; the British Foreign Office for Romania; the European Union for Russia; and so on. This section examines some implications of the article's earlier sections for standard-setters and other rule-makers.

In a CD country, the rule-makers should note that the country's accounting system is likely to have been imported and may not be appropriate for the main purpose of accounting. For example, in a developing country with imported Class A accounting but with few or no listed companies, the paraphernalia of Class A (e.g., extensive disclosure, consolidation, external audit) may be an expensive luxury. Resources might be better spent on establishing a reliable and uniform bookkeeping system, partly for the purpose of improving the collection of tax.

A similar point applies to many former communist countries, where the introduction of Class A accounting for a large proportion of enterprises might be inappropriate. However, for some such countries (perhaps China) where an impression has been created that the population and the government seem keen on moving to an equity-outsider system, the introduction of Class A might be appropriate, at least for large or listed companies.

In CS countries with a credit-insider system, again the rule-makers should think carefully before a generalized introduction of Class A. For example, it is not at all clear that the benefits of Class A would exceed its cost for the bulk of German companies. It is also not clear that there would be much benefit in any improved ability to compare corner grocery shops in Stuttgart with those in Sydney. However, German rule-makers should ask themselves (and are doing so) whether they should assist the large German companies who are being forced by commercial pressures towards Class A. One approach would be exemption from normal German rules for the preparation of consolidated financial statements by such companies.

There is another policy question for governments whose countries do not have equity-outsider financing systems but who wish to encourage them. Would the imposition of a Class A financial reporting system encourage a change in financing system? The thrust of this article is that the financial reporting *follows* from the financing system. This is reminiscent of the debate in the literature about the relationship between double-entry bookkeeping and the rise of capitalism (e.g., Sombart, 1924; Yamey, 1949; Yamey, 1964; Winjum, 1971). The weight of argument seems to rest with those who believe that double entry follows business developments rather than leading them. None of this proves that developments in accounting cannot assist in economic development. However, the *imposition* of Class A might be inappropriate, particularly if done for unlisted companies or within a detailed and slow-moving legal system, given that an important feature of Class A accounting is that it can adapt to commercial circumstances. It might be better to concentrate on making Class A *available* by removing any legal or economic barriers to its usage and by subsidizing education.

In CS countries with equity-outsider financing systems and Class A accounting, the rule-makers should ask whether the full panoply of Class A is necessary for smaller companies or whether a separate financial reporting system should be allowed for them. This issue has largely been resolved in the U.S.A., as discussed earlier, and recent moves in the U.K. have exempted some smaller companies from audit and from the disclosure rules of several standards.[26]

The International Accounting Standards Committee (IASC) does not impose its rules on any enterprises; it merely makes them available to companies or regulators. However, some regulators impose IASs on some or most enterprises in their countries.[27] Also, the World Bank requires its borrowers to use IASs. The IASC should consider whether it could make available some additional 'system' which might be more suitable for financial reporting by unlisted companies.

Summary

This article proposes a general model of the reasons for international differences in accounting practices. Instead of dozens of potential independent variables, it proposes two explanatory factors for the first split of accounting systems into classes. For culturally self-sufficient countries, it is suggested that the class of the predominant accounting system depends on the strength of the equity-outsider market. For culturally dominated countries, the class of the accounting system is determined by the cultural influence. However, sometimes an equity-outsider market may gradually develop, or certain companies may be interested in foreign equity markets. This will lead to the development of the appropriate accounting, and it is one of the reasons for the existence of more than one class of accounting in one country.

Many other factors, which had been suggested previously as reasons for accounting differences, result from or are linked to the equity market. Some factors are perhaps reasons for the differences in equity markets, but are too unclear to measure with any precision. A general theory previously proposed by Doupnik and Salter (1995) mixed several of these factors and mis-specified some of them.

Some improvements to the classification of accounting systems have been suggested, incorporating the idea that it is accounting practice systems, not countries, that should be classified. Some implications for rule-makers are suggested, warning against inappropriate transfers of technology.

Acknowledgements

The author is grateful for helpful comments on earlier drafts from Michael Page, Bob Parker, Alan Roberts and Autar Singh, and from the editor and the referees of this journal.

Notes

1 For example, Da Costa *et al.* (1978); Frank (1979); Nair and Frank (1980).
2 I am grateful to my colleague, Autar Singh, for discussions that clarified my thoughts on this.
3 Researchers would have to decide whether to start from the smallest enterprise or from the largest. Presumably, it would make sense to start from the largest, since this would involve far fewer enterprises, and since the small enterprises would not be publishing any financial reports in most countries.
4 See, for example, Gonzalo and Gallizo (1992), ch. 3.
5 Statements of Financial Accounting Concepts of the FASB, particularly SFAC 1, *Objectives*; the similar chapter 1 of the ASB's draft *Statement of Principles; Statements of Accounting Concepts* of Australia; and the IASC's *Framework for the Preparation and Presentation of Financial Statements*, para. 15.
6 For example, Australia, the U.S. and the U.K. exhibit *all* the features of Class A, whereas the dominant systems in France, Germany and Italy exhibit *all* the features of Class B (although a few consolidated statements use a different system and depart from some aspects). Most items in Table 4 are covered by the relevant country chapters of Nobes and Parker (1995) or, for example, see Scheid and Walton (1992) for France, or Gordon and Gray (1994) for the UK.
7 The idea of 'developed' or 'culturally self-sufficient' is examined further later.
8 Herr Biener of the German Finance Ministry announced this at the board meeting of the International Accounting Standards Committee in Amsterdam in May 1996. In 1998, German law changed in order specifically to allow this.
9 This feature of German accounting was highlighted by Nair and Frank (1980), who prepared separate classifications based on measurement and disclosure practices.
10 For example, in 1993, the number of listed bonds in Germany was 13,309, whereas the number in France was 2,516 and in the U.K. 2,725 (data from *European Stock Exchange Statistics*, Annual Report, 1993).
11 An unpublished PhD thesis by Charles Elad (University of Glasgow, 1993) shows the colonial influences clearly.
12 Japan's SEC, its structure of Securities Laws and its stock market owe much to U.S. influence during the occupation following World War II.
13 The distinguishing feature of French accounting, the *plan comptable*, was first adopted in France while under German occupation (Standish, 1995).
14 The German accounting plan, though copied in France, was abolished by the occupying Western powers after World War II. A version survived in the communist East Germany until reunification.

15 For example, in both the U.K. and Germany (typical Class A and Class B countries, respectively), there are large numbers of legal cases on the determination of taxable income and some on the determination of distributable income, but there are few or none on the determination of consolidated accounting profit (i.e., cases where there is no tax motivation).

16 In the U.K., and recently in the U.S. with SFAS 115, certain assets are revalued above historical cost; and unsettled profits are taken to income (e.g., on long-term contracts and on foreign currency monetary balances). None of this is possible under German law.

17 This is examined in Nobes and Parker (1995, ch. 1).

18 From observation of Anglo-Saxon countries, it seems that inflation of above 10 per cent for several years will cause a response (e.g., in the U.K. in the early 1950s or early 1970s), and the same applies to some continental European countries in the 1970s (Tweedie and Whittington, 1984).

19 For example, many South American countries respond with compulsory government-controlled systems of general price level adjusted accounting, whereas English-speaking countries responded with rules written by the profession (although there was government involvement) which required some supplementary disclosures (Tweedie and Whittington, 1984).

20 For example, the Netherlands is often said to have been influenced by the current value theories of Limperg and the German business economist Schmidt (Zeff et al., 1992; Clarke and Dean, 1990).

21 For example, see Table 1.1 in Nobes and Parker (1995).

22 This is examined by Nobes (1996), where it is suggested that timing is a key factor. For example, the U.S. requirement to amortize goodwill was introduced earlier than U.K. standard setting on this issue, when goodwill was far less significant.

23 It is argued that equity investors and lenders will be persuaded to provide funds at lower returns to companies using more accepted, familiar and transparent financial reporting (see Botosan, 1997).

24 These issues are discussed by Nobes (1996).

25 For example, Bayer adopted international accounting standards (IASs) for its group accounts for 1994, and Deutsche Bank produce supplementary IAS group accounts for 1995. Nestlé published IAS group accounts.

26 In 1994, the audit requirement was removed or reduced for private companies with turnover under ≤350,000. The Accounting Standards Board published an exposure draft for a Financial Reporting Standard for Smaller Entities in 1996.

27 This is approximately the position for Singapore, Hong Kong, and many other Commonwealth countries.

Appendix

This appendix contains an example (relating to 1995) of the measures that could be used to distinguish between strong equity markets and others. The data in Table A relate to the eight largest economies in Europe, which are probably all CS countries.

In order to identify a Category IV financing system, it would also be necessary to establish that strong equity markets (e.g., U.K. and Netherlands) had a high level of 'outsiders'. This could be done using statistics of ownership of shares (e.g., Federation of European Stock Exchanges, 1993).

Table A Equity market measures.

	Domestic equity market capitalization/GDP	Domestic listed companies per million of population
U.K.	1.34	30.2
Netherlands	0.99	14.4
Sweden	0.76	24.4
Belgium	0.50	14.3
France	0.40	12.4
Spain	0.36	9.3
Germany	0.31	8.4
Italy	0.18	4.3

Sources: *European Stock Exchange Statistics, Annual Report 1995*, Federation of European Stock Exchanges; and *Pocket World in Figures 1995*, The Economist.

References

Baydoun, N., and R. Willett, 'Cultural Relevance of Western Accounting Systems to Developing Countries', *Abacus*, March 1995.

Beaver, W. H., *Financial Reporting: An Accounting Revolution*, Prentice-Hall, 1989.

Belkaoui, A., *International Accounting*, Quorum, 1995.

Botosan, C. A., 'Disclosure Level and the Cost of Equity Capital', *Accounting Review*, July 1997.

Briston, R. J., 'The Evolution of Accounting in Developing Countries', *International Journal of Accounting*, Fall 1978.

Briston, R. J., and Foo See Liang, 'The Evolution of Corporate Reporting in Singapore', *Research in Third World Accounting*, Vol. 1, 1990.

Cable, J., 'Capital Market Information and Industrial Performance: The Role of West German Banks', *Economic Journal*, March 1985.

Choi, F. D. S., and G. G. Mueller, *International Accounting*, Prentice-Hall, 1992.

Chow, L. M., G. K. Chau and S. J. Gray, 'Accounting Reforms in China: Cultural Constraints on Implementation and Development', *Accounting and Business Research*, Vol. 26, No. 1, 1995.

Clarke, F. L., and G. W. Dean, *Contributions of Limpberg and Schmidt to the Replacement Cost Debate in the 1920s*, Garland, 1990.

Cooke, T. E., and R. S. O. Wallace, 'Financial Regulation and its Environment: A Review and Further Analysis', *Journal of Accounting and Public Policy*, Summer 1990.

Da Costa, R. C., J. C. Bourgeois and W. M. Lawson, 'A Classification of International Financial Accounting Practices', *International Journal of Accounting*, Spring 1978.

David, R., and J. E. C. Brierley, *Major Legal Systems in the World Today*, Stephens, 1985.

Davidson, R. A., A. M. G. Gelardi and F. Li, 'Analysis of the Conceptual Framework of China's New Accounting System', *Accounting Horizons*, March 1995.

Doupnik, T. S., and S. B. Salter, 'External Environment, Culture, and Accounting Practice: A Preliminary Test of a General Model of International Accounting Development', *International Journal of Accounting*, No. 3, 1995.

Federation of European Stock Exchanges, *Share Ownership Structure in Europe*, 1993.

Frank, W. G., 'An Empirical Analysis of International Accounting Principles', *Journal of Accounting Research*, Autumn 1979.

Franks, J., and C. Mayer, 'Corporate Control: A Synthesis of the International Evidence', working paper of London Business School and University of Warwick, 1992.

Gambling, T., and R. A. A. Abdel-Karim, *Business and Accounting Ethics in Islam*, Mansell, 1991.

Gernon, H., and R. S. O. Wallace, 'International Accounting Research: A Review of its Ecology, Contending Theories and Methodologies', *Journal of Accounting Literature*, Vol. 14, 1995.

Gonzalo, J. A., and J. L. Gallizo, *European Financial Reporting: Spain*, Routledge, 1992.

Gordon, P. D., and S. J. Gray, *European Financial Reporting: United Kingdom*, Routledge, 1994.

Gray, S. J., 'Towards a Theory of Cultural Influence on the Development of Accounting Systems Internationally', *Abacus*, March 1988.

Hamid, S. R., R. Craig and F. L. Clarke, 'Religion: A Confounding Cultural Element in the International Harmonization of Accounting?', *Abacus*, September 1993.

Harrison, G. L., and J. L. McKinnon, 'Culture and Accounting Change: A New Perspective on Corporate Reporting Regulation and Accounting Policy Formulation', *Accounting, Organizations and Society*, No. 3, 1986.

Hofstede, G., *Culture's Consequences: International Differences in Work-Related Values*, Stage Publications, 1980.

Hove, M. R., 'Accounting Practice in Developing Countries: Colonialism's Legacy of Inappropriate Technologies', *International Journal of Accounting*, Fall 1986.

Jensen, M. C., and W. H. Meckling, 'Theory of the Firm: Managerial Behavior, Agency Costs and Ownership Structure', *Journal of Financial Economics*, October 1976.

Kenway, P., 'The Concentration of Ownership and its Implications for Corporate Governance in the Czech Republic', University of Reading, Discussion Papers in Economics, Series A, No. 288, 1994.

Lamb, M., C. W. Nobes and A. D. Roberts, 'The Influence of Taxation on Accounting: International Variations', Reading University Discussion Papers, 1995.

La Porta, R., F. Lopez-de-Silanes, A. Shleifer and R. W. Vishny, 'Legal Determinants of External Finance', *Journal of Finance*, July 1997.

Meek, G., and S. Saudagaran, 'A Survey of Research on Financial Reporting in a Transnational Context', *Journal of Accounting Literature*, No. 9, 1990.

Miller, M. C., 'Australia', in T. E. Cooke and R. H. Parker (eds), *Financial Reporting in the West Pacific Rim*, Routledge, 1994.

Nair, R. D., and W. G. Frank, 'The Impact of Disclosure and Measurement Practices on International Accounting Classifications', *Accounting Review*, July 1980.

Nobes, C. W., 'An Empirical Analysis of International Accounting Principles: A Comment', *Journal of Accounting Research*, Spring 1981.

——, 'A Judgmental International Classification of Financial Reporting Practices', *Journal of Business Finance and Accounting*, Spring 1983.

——, Ch. 1 in C. W. Nobes and R. H. Parker (eds), *Issues in Multinational Accounting*, Philip Allan, 1988.

——, 'Classification of Accounting Using Competencies as a Discriminating Variable: A Comment', *Journal of Business Finance and Accounting*, January 1992.

——, 'Corporate Financing and its Effect on European Accounting Differences', Reading University Discussion Papers, 1995.

——, *Compliance with International Standards*, UNCTAD, 1996.

Nobes, C. W., and R. H. Parker (eds), *Comparative International Accounting*, Prentice-Hall, 1995.

Parker, R. H., 'Importing and Exporting Accounting: The British Experience', in A. G. Hopwood (ed.), *International Pressures for Accounting Change*, Prentice-Hall, 1989.

Parry, M., and R. Grove, 'Does Training More Accountants Raise the Standards of Accounting in Third World Countries? A Study of Bangladesh', *Research in Third World Accounting*, Vol. 1, 1990.

Radebaugh, L. H., 'Environmental Factors Influencing the Development of Accounting Objectives, Standards and Practices in Peru', *International Journal of Accounting*, Fall 1975.

Radebaugh, L. H., and S. Gray, *International and Multinational Enterprises*, Wiley, 1993.

Rahman, A., H. Perera and S. Ganeshanandam, 'Measurement of Formal Harmonization in Accounting: An Exploratory Study', *Accounting and Business Research*, Autumn 1996.

Roberts, A. D., 'The Very Idea of Classification in International Accounting', *Accounting, Organizations and Society*, Vol. 20, Nos 7/8, 1995.

Scheid, J.-C., and P. Walton, *European Financial Reporting: France*, Routledge, 1992.

Schweikart, J. A., 'Contingency Theory as a Framework for Research in International Accounting', *International Journal of Accounting*, Fall 1985.

Shoenthal, E., 'Classification of Accounting Systems Using Competencies as a Discriminating Variable: A Great Britain–United States Study', *Journal of Business Finance and Accounting*, Autumn 1989.

Soeters, J., and H. Schreuder, 'The Interaction between National and Organizational Cultures in Accounting Firms', *Accounting, Organizations and Society*, Vol. 13, No. 1, 1988.

Sombart, W., *Der Moderne Kapitalismus*, 6th edn, Duncker & Humblot, Vol. 2.1, 1924.

Standish, P. E. M., 'Origins of the *plan comptable général*: A Study in Cultural Intrusion and Reaction', *Accounting and Business Research*, Autumn 1990.

——, 'Financial Reporting in France', Ch. 11 in C. W. Nobes and R. H. Parker (eds), *Comparative International Accounting*, Prentice-Hall, 1995.

Tweedie, D. P., and G. Whittington, *The Debate on Inflation Accounting*, Cambridge University Press, 1984.

Wallace, R. S. O., and H. Gernon, 'Frameworks for International Comparative Financial Accounting', *Journal of Accounting Literature*, Vol. 10, 1991.

Watts, R., and J. Zimmerman, 'The Demand for and Supply of Accounting Theories: The Market for Excuses', *Accounting Review*, April 1979.

Winjum, J. O., 'Accounting and the Rise of Capitalism: An Accountant's View', *Journal of Accounting Research*, Vol. 9, 1971.

Yamey, B. S., 'Scientific Bookkeeping and the Rise of Capitalism', *Economic History Review*, 2nd ser, Vol. 1, 1949.

——, 'Accounting and the Rise of Capitalism: Some Further Notes on a Theme by Sombart', *Journal of Accounting Research*, II, 1964.

Zeff, S. A., F. van der Wel and K. Camfferman, *Company Financial Reporting: A Historical and Comparative Study of the Dutch Regulatory Process*, North-Holland, 1992.

Zysman, J., *Government, Markets and Growth: Financial Systems and the Politics of Industrial Change*, Cornell University Press, 1983.

10

THE EVOLUTION OF ACCOUNTING IN DEVELOPING COUNTRIES

Richard J. Briston

Source: *International Journal of Accounting* (Fall 1978): 105–20.

Nature of western accounting

In his text *Accountancy and Economic Development Policy,* Adolf Enthoven[1] argues that

> Accounting covers the entire administration or management of information for all socioeconomic activities and conditions in the micro and macro economic sector, covering internal and external needs of various groups. It may be classified in broad terms as: (i) the development of economic facts — based on real world phenomena — involving measurements and their further appraisal and supply — in the form of costs and benefits — to enable effective evaluations and decisions about activities and the allocation of resources; and (ii) the communication of the results of evaluations and decisions made for present and prospective purposes. Such an orientation involves greater focus of micro and macro managerial decision making and economic planning and control content, rather than on the micro entity accountability or stewardship content. ... The broader scope as we conceive it makes the separation between micro and macro accounting somewhat artificial as the two show a high degree of coordination and unity. Micro data are used for macro accounting, while the latter is used for evaluation and decisions at the enterprise and governmental accounting level. Consequently, our concept is far broader than the scope of the traditional micro entity and its quantification, recording and verification of largely historical financial events.

In his broader definition of accountancy, Enthoven defines three major areas: enterprise accounting (including financial accounting, management accounting, and auditing), government accounting (including financial recording, budgeting, and taxation) and social accounting (including national income accounts, flow of funds statements, balance of payments accounts, and so forth), and he stresses the need to integrate all of these areas into a single accounting framework. To this end, he advocates the adoption of uniform accounting techniques arguing that the improved comparability and integration at all levels of accounting far outweigh the possible disadvantages of inflexibility and unwieldiness, especially as these disadvantages may be guarded against in the construction of the system.

Whether or not Enthoven is too ambitious in his definition of the role of accountancy, it is clear that accountancy in the United Kingdom and the United States does not begin to satisfy this role, primarily because it has been distorted by historical factors with the result that it has concentrated almost entirely upon the enterprise sector, and even there the emphasis has been upon financial accounting and auditing to the virtual exclusion of management accounting. An analysis of U.K. and U.S. accounting and auditing standards demonstrates that they are concerned only with the problems of corporate reporting and of auditing annual statements, while the information needs of managers, of the government administration sector, and of government planners are not regarded as the concern of the accountant. Admittedly there are specialized professional bodies which observe these sectors,[2] but there is no professional body which considers accountancy from a broad, integrative viewpoint. This bias of the accounting profession is probably attributable to its growth resulting from the U.K. auditing and reporting requirements of the Companies Acts during the nineteenth century,[3] as a consequence of which accountants worked and were trained in the fields of financial reporting and auditing. At that stage, management accounting was very much in its infancy, and its subsequent evolution was distorted by the bias towards the provision of information for the annual report rather than with a concern for the needs of managers for decision-making purposes.[4] This bias has dominated the accounting profession to the present in those cases where it continues to apply nineteenth century concepts of valuation, income measurement, and stewardship at a time when the nature and role of companies have been completely transformed. While it should be admitted that the current response of the accounting profession to the problems posed by inflation has demonstrated an admirable speed of reaction, this response has still involved the retention of many traditional — though outmoded — concepts, and it has still been undertaken within the straitjacket of the corporate report. So long as the profession is given a monopoly of auditing with fees therefor estimated in the United Kingdom at between £300m. and £500m.,[5] this bias is likely to continue regardless of the economic value of this work. In effect, then, in the United Kingdom the accounting system was established to meet the perceived needs of mid-nineteenth century capitalism, but it was created in a rigid and self-perpetuating structure which has proved resistant to the changing needs of the economy. Certainly if an accountancy system were to be designed from "scratch" to meet the current informational requirements of the economy, it would take a very different form in both the private and the public sectors from that currently operated. Unfortunately, however, due to the vast rewards offered to accountants by the current system, there is little chance of fundamental reform except from without.

As emphasized above, the current U.K. accounting system is barely adequate for meeting the external reporting needs of the private sector, and it is completely inadequate in the fields of public sector accounting,[6] economic planning, and the definition and measurement of efficiency — fields incidentally which have long since overtaken reporting to investors as the main concerns of modern economics.

The spread of western accounting

In spite of the virtual irrelevance of U.K. and, by inference, U.S. accounting to the modern economic environment, this system not only continues to thrive in most developed countries but is also gradually being established in a predominant position in many developing countries. In a number of countries, of course, the British influence is very long standing, and almost all of the colonial territories in which any substantial degree of industrial development took place under British rule will have had imposed upon them a British Companies Act with the usual reporting and auditing requirements. At the same time, the status of professional accountant could be attained only by admission to one of the British professional bodies and as a result, both the certified and the cost and management accountants obtained a large number of members and students.

Once a reporting system and a nucleus of an accounting profession have been established in this way, it becomes very difficult to modify the system, for those who operate it have a vested interest in its perpetuation, partly because of the high rewards which it provides and partly because they are not prepared to admit that what they studied and practiced under the colonial regime is now possibly irrelevant. Furthermore, the British system tends to be extended because after independence, the small nucleus of qualified accountants will often create a monopolistic and elitist professional body which is virtually a carbon copy of the Institute of Chartered Accountants and which has a similar examination and training structure and an identical emphasis upon private-sector auditing. Even where a local accounting organization is not established, the British professional bodies still have enormous influence because membership therein provides ready access to senior accountancy posts not only in one's own country, but also, and more important, in a wide range of overseas countries. As such, their membership conveys many of the advantages of a passport.[7]

A good example of the outright adoption of the colonial system is provided by the evolution of accountancy in Nigeria.[8] The Institute of Chartered Accountants of Nigeria was established in 1965; by 1974 it had 760 members. Most of these were admitted to membership on the basis of an overseas qualification, generally that of certified accountant or cost and management accountant. After January 1, 1980, admission to the institute will be obtained only on the basis of the institute's own examinations which are to be monitored by the Association of Certified Accountants, followed by a period of approved service.

At present three universities and five technical colleges provide courses in accounting, but there is a serious shortage of staff, and pass rates are very low. The bulk of accountancy training is based on British correspondence courses and is aimed at the qualifications of British professional bodies. At the postexperience and postgraduate levels, there is virtually no training available. Those accountants available tend to be concentrated in the private sector, which is governed by a Companies Act derived from the U.K. 1948 Act; the areas of government accounting and national accounting have attracted very few accountants. In summary, the situation is similar to that in many of the countries which have adopted British methods and likewise suffer from many defects attributable to that adoption:

1. An accounting profession which is biased towards British attitudes. This implies examinations which concentrate upon legal and professional subjects, often in a British rather than in a native form, the use of the articles system, a dominant emphasis upon auditing, and an abhorrence of subprofessional grades of accountants.
2. Financial control of the private sector based upon accounting concepts laid down by the U.K. Companies Acts, which may have been relevant to a British capitalist system one hundred years ago, but are hardly calculated to provide the information necessary for government regulation of industry in a newly independent developing country.
3. A complete lack of interest on the part of most accountants in the problems of providing information within the spheres of government administration and economic planning. This deficiency is especially crucial when the major part of the industrial sector has been nationalized or the government has a controlling interest therein.

The major criticism of the evolution of accountancy in Nigeria and other countries which have adopted the colonial system almost entirely is that due to a mixture of habit, inertia, and vested interests; these countries have adopted accounting principles and systems of accountancy training which originally evolved to meet the needs of U.K. capitalism a century ago. These principles and systems have already been shown to be of dubious relevance for the present-day U.K. economy, and they are, therefore, most unlikely to be appropriate for the entirely different social and economic environments of the developing world. Instead of blindly embracing the colonial system, developing countries should concentrate upon an assessment of their information needs in the enterprise, government, and national accounting sectors and should seek to establish training programs to produce the staff for the provision and use of that information.

Although it could be argued that some irrelevant accountancy training is better than none at all, the influence of the U.K. accountancy bodies upon developing countries is, on balance, highly detrimental. Not only does it bias the accountancy system of the economy towards private sector auditing, but it also places demands upon the scarce educational resources of the country, for courses in U.K. taxation, company law, executorship, and so on, for students whose main aim is either to work as private sector accountants or to leave the country altogether. These distortions have been exacerbated by the nature of British aid which has attempted to improve the quality of accountancy in developing countries by sponsoring students for U.K. professional qualifications. As an example, it was recommended that accountancy in the Seychelles should be encouraged by financing the training of a few students to become certified accountants.[9] Even if the students returned to the Seychelles after qualifying, they would probably hinder the development of a relevant accounting system in that country by many years. Instead of being encouraged in this way, accountants in developing countries should be positively discouraged from membership in U.K. professional bodies, for these bodies make no concessions to overseas students and insist upon a set of knowledge which is largely peculiar to U.K. practice and almost certainly irrelevant and possibly harmful if applied in the wrong context.

Quite apart from the direct influence of the U.K. professional bodies, there are many other potent factors which are encouraging the spread of U.K. and U.S. accounting concepts. In the first place, most of the major multinationals have been based in the United Kingdom or the United States, and these have adopted the accounting systems of the home country for their overseas subsidiaries and have trained local staff in those systems. Furthermore, almost all of the large international firms of accountants are American or British, and these have also trained local accountants to service the audits of multinational companies according to American and British concepts. Another factor has been the insistence by the World Bank and other international financial institutions upon the use of an international firm of accountants to audit many of the projects which they finance.[10] Overseas aid has been another major contributory factor. This has often taken the form of exchanges of staff, provision of scholarships for local students, and grants of textbooks. The fact that so much aid has been provided by English-speaking countries has strongly influenced teachers towards British, American, Canadian, and Australian concepts.[11] Finally, the spread of English as a second language in many countries has meant that British and American accounting texts and trainers are being used in many developing countries. This strong trend toward a British and American approach has been resisted in certain situations. In some countries, for instance, particularly those with a strong French influence, there has been a loyalty towards the French "plan comptable," a variation of which has been designed for the Organisation Commune Africaine Malgache et Mauritienne (OCAM) countries.[12] Nevertheless, the British and American influence has been extremely strong as evidenced by the example of Indonesia.[13]

Until World War II, the accountancy profession in Indonesia was controlled by the Dutch, and Indonesians could only become registered accountants by qualifying as members of the Dutch Institute. Only five had succeeded in qualifying by that date. Even after independence was gained in 1949, Dutch accountants continued to dominate, and it was not until 1955 that accountancy courses were begun in the University of Indonesia, and then under Dutch professors. At the same time, the government passed the Accountants Act which provided that henceforth only those who completed a university sarjana course (involving a minimum of five years) followed by a three-year period of government service could become registered accountants. The Indonesian Institute of Accountants, which evolved as a result of this Act, now has about 1,000 members, of whom about 800 work for the government, and there is an annual increase of about 100 to 150. Estimates of the actual number of accountants needed range from 5,000 to 10,000, which certainly does not seem to be an over-estimate for a country with a population of 130,000,000.

Since 1960, other universities have introduced courses in accountancy, and at present six of them offer sarjana courses in accounting. Most of these are given within departments of economics, and student demand has followed the U.K. pattern of moving from economic theory through business economics to accounting, though staff shortages have hindered expansion. It is doubtful whether there is a single full-time academic in the field of accounting in the entire country, a phenomenon largely attributable to the low level of academic salaries and the favorable job opportunities for accountants. Most universities attempt to overcome this shortage by employing students who have passed the first stage of the degree course to teach those at lower levels.

The basic training and educational system was clearly modeled upon that of the Netherlands with the five-year master's degree rather than the bachelor's level being regarded as the basic degree and with a period of practical training additionally required. Such a system is clearly too inflexible to provide the swift expansion of trained accountants which the economy clearly needs because due to the high failure rate of students, the average period for qualification is about ten years; unfortunately due to the vested interests involved, there is little hope of any material modification of the system. The Ministry of Education, which is responsible for the universities, is most unlikely to agree to the removal of a university degree as a prerequisite for registration, the Ministry of Finance is certain to be unwilling to relax the requirement of government service, providing as it does guaranteed personnel, and the members of the Institute of Accountants are probably not unhappy with a system which limits the number of accountants in the private sector.

Despite the structural inflexibility of the system, enormous philosophical changes have taken place within it, involving the almost total substitution of American for Dutch accounting principles. As a result of the factors mentioned earlier, such as multinationals, international firms of accountants, U.S. aid, and the language factor, university courses are now biased strongly toward American texts, and courses are structured with much more emphasis upon finance and management as opposed to administration and economic theory. At the same time, the Institute of Accountants has adopted a set of accounting and auditing standards virtually identical to those of the American Institute.[14]

As a consequence of this evolution, the Indonesian profession is Dutch in its qualification structure, but the training (which is exclusively undertaken in universities) and philosophy are American. Neither, however, is in the least relevant to the needs of Indonesia, a country with no companies acts, no capital market, a massive public sector, and an economic and cultural environment totally dissimilar to that of the Netherlands or of the United States. Notwithstanding its substantial irrelevance, western accounting continues to influence developing countries, and the avenues of this influence seem likely to grow.

The problems of modifying U.K./U.S. accounting systems

Certain countries which originally inherited a colonial system have since changed their style of government and their economic philosophy and have deliberately reconstructed their accounting system to make it more relevant to their needs. Thus, a study on the future training of accountants in Sri Lanka published in December 1973 found that the previous system of education and training based almost exactly upon that of the British chartered accountant was inadequate for their needs and proposed instead a much more flexible and relevant system.[15]

The basic premises of the report were as follows.

1. Accounting is primarily concerned with the collection, analysis, and evaluation of information for the purpose of decision making in the process of control of limited resources by entrepreneurs and management at various levels.
2. Accounting is primarily a service function, and its development and progress must be related to the economic, social, and organization forms. Considering the economic context in Sri Lanka today, the following features must be specially noted.
    a. The increase in controls on the economy exercised by the state showing a tendency towards a centrally planned economy;
    b. The rapid and sudden growth of large-scale government enterprises;
    c. The rapid development of the state-owned and state-controlled sectors; and
    d. Decentralization of the operation of economic programs through rural and village-level organizations such as local authorities, co-operative societies, district development councils, and so forth.
3. The consequential demand for information over a very wide area and the necessity to design, install, and implement information systems to cater to these needs.

The committee therefore held the opinion that the new plans for training, apart from increasing the number of accountants, must also satisfy the following needs prevailing at the moment:

1. The need for accountants who can present information lucidly to decision makers, taking into account the needs of the country in the present context;
2. The need for able financial managers and advisors who can appreciate the problems of the country; and
3. The need for accountants who are imaginative organizers able to undertake the problems of management arising in the overnight creation of large-scale undertakings and also small-scale decentralized management units.

In particular, it was recommended that (a)

There should be a change in the approach to the subject of education and training of accountants. Accounting should be treated as a control and management function based on collection, analysis and evaluation of information. The approach through auditing alone does not give the student a grasp of the purpose, functions and the nature of accounting,

and (b)

268

> In the present schemes of lectures and examinations, negligible place is given to the study of accounting systems, procedures and financial management. General understanding of all these aspects should be part of the basic training of accountants: they should not be treated as subjects for specialisation.

The point was made that

> Experience under articles is heavily biased towards the legal and statutory audit. This approach does not give adequate recognition to accounting as a control function. Experience is centered generally on the techniques of bookkeeping and preparation of accounts which is no doubt important. But this concentration could result in a warped attitude to the subject on the part of the student.

The alternative system which has been adopted has many admirable features. In particular, it provides for a licentiate level of qualification which is a very effective way of motivating accounting technicians, and it also requires a period of planned training as opposed to articles. Further improvements are the use of case studies and compulsory attendance at seminars, but not at lectures.

On the other hand, the new examination structure is rather disappointing and appears to be a rehash of the traditional accounting subjects rather than a fundamental reassessment of the subjects in which a qualified accountant should be skilled. As a result, although the criticisms leveled at the old system were both warranted and praiseworthy, the new plan does not appear at first sight to have incorporated a sufficient remedy, and its designers have probably been too greatly influenced by the traditional approach.

The disappointing remedy prescribed in Sri Lanka following such a farsighted analysis of the disease is largely attributable to deep-seated British influence exercised directly through underlying commercial attitudes and through the cadre of U.K.-qualified professional accountants in that country. The low status given to government accounting in the United Kingdom has been transmitted to other countries in the British sphere of influence and has further encouraged the dominance of private sector auditing, making it more difficult for the government sector to control the structure and the duties of the accounting profession.

Even where there has been virtually no development of local accountants prior to independence, it is still difficult to avoid British influence. Tanzania,[16] for example, had very few indigenous accountants on attaining independence and has therefore been in a strong position to establish a relevant accounting system which would meet national needs. The economy is centrally planned and dominated by the public sector. The importance of a satisfactory accounting system was quickly appreciated and a study of manpower requirements for fulfilling the accountancy requirements of the economy was made. A professional structure, established and regulated by the government, was designed not only to encourage the training of the requisite accountants, but also to provide motivation by recognizing status at all professional levels. Thus, the same professional body incorporated technicians (accounts assistants), semiprofessionals (assistant accountants), and professional accountants with advancement based upon examination and training requirements.

The Tanzanian approach has much to commend it, first for the scientific assessment of manpower requirements, and secondly for the structure given to the professional body which has enormous advantages over the British system because the one body incorporates all areas of accounting, both public and private sector and both managerial and financial accounting, and all levels of attainment. This is a welcome change from the fragmentation in the United Kingdom with regard to both specialization and status. Nevertheless, it proved impossible to avoid British influence, for not only did the educational and examination content stress British professional subjects (though with at least the addition of project evaluation and political economics), but also British professional bodies were called upon to monitor the system with the result that the pass rate in the higher-level examinations has been abysmally low.

Towards the establishment of a relevant system

So far no developing country has been able to construct a system of accounting designed primarily to meet its own information needs. In all cases, the external pressures referred to earlier have been too great, and western influences have dominated both education and practice. These external pressures are increasing, and there is no indication that they are likely to be reversed. Even the United Nations in its guidelines of information for monitoring the activities of multinationals[17] has produced a mish-mash composed of extracts from the U.K. Companies Acts and the U.S. SEC reporting requirements, which are self-admittedly inappropriate for the control of multinationals by local governments. The proposals by the Organization for Economic Cooperation and Development (OECD) on the same subject are not better. The introduction of international accounting standards is, on the surface, fairly innocuous, for the standards themselves, being lowest common denominators of practice in western countries, are highly permissive. Nevertheless, the enthusiasm of accountancy bodies from developing countries for joining the International Accounting Standards Committee suggests that these standards may influence the direction of accounting in those countries.

However, it is imperative that instead of pressing for international accounting standards, the profession should pause to consider the nature of accounting. If accounting is seen in Enthoven's broad definition as opposed to being a system of producing audited accounts for a declining body of uninterested investors, then it should be highly responsive to the social and economic environment and an analysis of this response in different types of environment must enhance the study of accounting. For this reason, it may not be entirely perverse to suggest that the industrialized countries have as much to learn from the developing countries in the field of accounting as the latter have to learn from them. Accountancy has not evolved in the industrialized world as an absolute science but as a response to economic and social factors. If this is not realized, there is a serious danger that accountants will continue to propound techniques which evolved under circumstances which no longer exist and which are irrelevant or even positively harmful in the current situation. A comparative study of the evolution of accounting under different environments should provide important lessons regarding the true nature of accounting and the extent to which it is possible to separate the fundamental truths from the historical accidents. Such a study cannot be undertaken by a small group of academics, for its is necessary to spend considerable time in a country before comprehending the full relationship between the accounting system and the environment in which it evolved, and consequently very little work has been done in this field. However, a valuable start could be made if academics and professional accountants who spend any length of time in an overseas country were to publish their views on the development of accounting there. On the basis of case studies of this sort, the subject of comparative accounting could begin to evolve on a worldwide context as opposed to the predominantly western bias which it has so far received.

Nevertheless, although the appropriate accountancy system for each country will depend upon a wide variety of historical, political, economic, and social factors, there seem to be certain standard questions which should be posed in the construction of such a system. For this purpose, accounting is regarded as the collection and communication of information for making and controlling the implementation of economic decisions in both the public and the private sector.

In the first place, it is necessary to decide what information is relevant for economic decisions at both the micro and macro level. At the micro level, it is necessary to decide what the relevant costs and revenues are. To what extent should current costs, opportunity costs, replacement costs, social costs, benefits, and so on be taken into account? What use should be made of sensitivity analysis? Should a feasibility study be required by law for all major projects? Should this feasibility study be made subject to independent audit? If so, should this be carried out by an internal auditor, a private external auditor, or a government auditor? At the macro level, what are the objectives of the government and what information is necessary to devise plans for the attainment of those objectives? What rules are necessary to ensure that the private sector provides the necessary information in an easily accessible fashion? Does information need to be submitted to the government on foreign exchange transactions, investment plans, projected imports and exports, profits (if so, how defined), social costs and benefits, and such? Which accountancy system will permit this information to be collected in the most efficient and best-integrated fashion? How are the decisions of multinationals to be monitored? Should these be controlled through formal concession agreements? If so, what right of access is the government to be given to obtain information to ensure that the agreement is being adhered to? Should the government have the right to monitor investment plans and feasibility studies therefor?

As far as the implementation and control of decisions are concerned, the structure of financial reporting and auditing must be determined. Are the results of decisions to be recorded on a traditional historical cost basis, or should there be a real attempt to measure performance against the criteria adopted at the time of the decision? What financial reporting requirements should be established for both internal and external reporting? What measurement criteria should be adopted for these reports and to whom should they be made available? What should be the respective roles of the internal auditor, the external auditor, and the government auditor in the audit of these reports, and should the audit itself consider managerial and social factors? How should the implementation of public sector decisions be monitored? Should this be left to government auditors or to external auditors, and in either case, how is their independence to be assured?

These are only a few questions which need to be answered. Very few of them have ever been asked in the United Kingdom and then in a sporadic and unintegrated fashion. As a result, the overall accountancy system is in a state of chaos with private sector accounts prepared by accountants being quite unsuitable for national accounts prepared by statisticians and economists. Similarly, national economic planning with which accountants are not involved at all is conducted in complete isolation from private-sector accounting information whether forward looking or backward looking. The main concern of professional accountants appears to be the preparation and audit of private-sector financial accounting data, and most other constituents of the national financial information system are left to economists, statisticians, corporate planners, operational researchers, and so on. However, instead of recognizing the inadequacies of the U.K./U.S. system and attempting to make it more relevant and integrated, U.K. and U.S. accountants are gradually imposing that outmoded system upon developing countries. On the contrary, developing countries must create their own system before this adverse influence has reached an irreversible stage.

In light of the information which a country deems desirable, it is necessary to consider the manpower needs. This will involve an estimate of the accountants required at various levels of expertise and an assessment of the educational resources that will be called upon. It will also be necessary to decide upon the professional structure which should be granted to accountants. It seems probable that at least a three-tier structure should be created involving a technical, an intermediate, and a senior grade with automatic progression between grades subject to examination and experience requirements. The education should ultimately cover the whole range of the national financial information system including its philosophy, objectives, and technical construction, and specialization should only be built into this broad comprehension, perhaps at the technical level. As such, the examination system will contain a great deal of economics, both micro and macro, and quantitative methods and will exclude much of the traditional accounting syllabus, particularly in the areas of law and private-sector financial reporting.

Due to lack of trained personnel, it will normally be impossible to establish the new system immediately, and there will need to be a rather long transitional period. To alleviate this problem, it may be possible to adapt an existing uniform accounting system, either in major industries or for the economy as a whole. The United Nations Industrial Development Organization (UNIDO) is already offering a training and implementation package based upon the OCAM plan comptable, and the experience of Peru suggests that this plan can provide at least a quick improvement in the quality of national statistics. The great advantage of such plans is that they permit relatively unskilled personnel to be trained quickly to provide a flow of basic financial data, and as such they provide a good foundation for the transitional period to a more relevant, tailor-made system. On the other hand, they are strongly biased toward western accounting, and there is also the fear that once in operation, they will become inflexible and self-perpetuating. They should never be seen as an end in themselves but as a step forward on the long path to the appropriate system, which itself, of course, must be subject to modification as national priorities and information needs change.

In conclusion, each country has its own political, social, economic, and cultural characteristics, and it is highly probable that the goals and thus the information needs of the managers of the economy will differ from one country to another. As a consequence, each country should be encouraged not to standardize the structure and specifications of its information system, but to create a system appropriate to its own needs. At present the worldwide tendency is in an exactly opposite direction. The International Accounting Standards Committee, the United Nations, and OECD, together with the other influences referred to earlier, are all attempting to standardize international private-sector financial reporting. In itself, this is relatively unimportant, for it influences only a small and tangential part of the overall national accounting function. Unfortunately, it is being presented by all involved, and with the active support of the professional bodies in most countries, as being the predominant goal of accountancy and as such, it is widening the chasm between accountants and economists and making it more unlikely that a satisfactory information system for national economic planning and control will ever be attainable. Even if it is, it will be achieved, sadly, in spite of the accountancy profession rather than with its encouragement and guidance.

Notes

1 A. J. H. Enthoven, *Accountancy and Economic Development Policy* (Amsterdam: North-Holland Publishing, 1973), pp. 112–13.
2 For example, in the United Kingdom, the Institute of Cost and Management Accountants is mainly concerned with management accounting, and the Chartered Institute of Public Finance and Accounting is primarily involved with public-sector accountants.
3 See H. C. Edey and Prot Panitpakdi, "British Company Accounting and the Law 1944–1900" in *Studies in the History of Accounting*, ed. A. C. Littleton and B. S. Yamey (London: Sweet and Maxwell, 1956).
4 See Sidney Pollard, *The Genesis of Modern Management* (Harmondsworth: Penguin Books, 1968), pp. 245–90.
5 See R. J. Briston and R. Perks, "The External Auditor — His Role and Cost to Society," *Accountancy* (November 1977): 48–52; and D. Fanning, "How Slow Are the Auditors in Britain?" *Accountancy* (August 1978): 44–48.
6 See various reports of the Expenditure Committee, the Committee on Nationalized Industries, the Public Accounts Committee, and various committees of inquiry such as that into the affairs of the Crown Agents.
7 Most of the arguments in the above section and many of those in succeeding sections are based upon evidence collected verbally either at meetings in various developing countries or in conversation with overseas students attending the short course for developing countries organized at Strathclyde University.
8 Most of the material in this section is based upon discussions with Nigerians and upon A. J. H. Enthoven, *Accountancy Systems in Third World Economies* (Amsterdam: North-Holland Publishing, 1977), pp. 201–7.
9 This assertion is based upon an unpublished report made available to the author.
10 This assertion is based upon conversations with World Bank officials and with members of relevant ministries in various developing countries. It has also been supported by local representatives of major international firms with whom the author had interviews in developing countries.
11 Among the links which the author has personally encountered are those between U.K. and Ghanaian and Nigerian universities, between U.S. and Indonesian and Chilean universities, and between Canadian and Kenyan universities. There are, of course, innumerable such links throughout the world.
12 See *OCAM General Accounting Plan* published in English by the Joint Organization of African, Malagasy, and Mauitian states, 1973.
13 This section is based upon two unpublished reports by the author, "Finance and Accountancy Training in Indonesia" (with E. Newbiggins), January 1974, and "Report on a Visit to Indonesia to Advise on Accountancy Training," July/ August 1974. The reports were prepared for the Overseas Development Ministry. They were circulated by the Council for Technical Education and Training for Overseas Countries, London.

14 Indonesian Accounting and Auditing Standards, *Prinsip-Prinsip Akuntansi* (Jakarta: IAAS, 1973), and *Norma-Norma Pemeriksaan Akuntan* (Jakarta: IAAS, 1973).

15 "Report of the Future Training of Accountants Committee." See also, "Report of the Committee on Duties, Responsibilities and Standards of Professional Accountants and Auditors to the Public Accounts Committee," Sessional Paper No. XI, 1974.

16 This section is based partly upon A. J. H. Enthoven, "An Evaluation of Accountancy Systems, Developments and Requirements in Africa" (a Ford Foundation-sponsored study), pp. 8–34, and upon a conversation with Tanzanian government officials and the external moderator of the new examination system.

17 *International Standards of Accounting and Reporting for Transnational Corporations* (New York: United Nations, 1977).

11

CULTURAL RELEVANCE OF WESTERN ACCOUNTING SYSTEMS TO DEVELOPING COUNTRIES

Nabil Baydoun and Roger Willett

Source: *Abacus* 31(1) (1995): 67–92.

It has been suggested recently that the accounting systems used in developing countries may be irrelevant to their needs because they originate in Western countries with different cultural values. The accounting literature on this point, however, is vague in its assessment of exactly what aspects of Western accounting systems fail to meet the test of relevance. Furthermore, it is not clear whether the differences between the needs of users in various countries are differences in kind or only differences in degree. This article analyses these issues by introducing technical considerations in addition to the behavioural ones usually discussed and by separating out problems of accounting *measurement* from problems of accounting *disclosure*. This distinction is used to argue that it is the specific disclosure rules of particular calculations inherent in Western accounting systems rather than the transaction cost database that are most likely to fail to satisfy the needs of users in developing countries. The effect of the importation of the French Unified Accounting System to Lebanon is examined and an amended version of the Hofstede–Gray cultural accounting framework is used to clarify the concept of cultural relevance.

In recent years increasing attention has been paid to the cultural dimension of accounting (Gray, 1988; Tay and Parker, 1990; Hamid *et al.*, 1993).

AlHashim and Arpan (1992) argued that the needs of users are influenced by environmental factors specific to the locality in which their decisions are made. Similarly, according to Perera (1989a), accounting practices evolve to suit the circumstances of a particular society at a particular time. However, many developing countries have adopted accounting systems from Europe and North America (Briston, 1978). Consequently it is difficult to judge the validity of these arguments directly. A number of studies have been carried out to assess the impact of Western accounting systems on individual developing countries (e.g., Briston and Liang, 1990; Briston and Wallace, 1990; Parry and Grove, 1990) and others have undertaken comparative analysis of two or more developing countries (e.g., AICPA, 1964, 1975; Briston, 1990). Consensus is lacking as to the accounting system that would best suit each country, but there does seem to be general agreement that Western accounting systems are deficient to some extent in meeting the requirements of users in developing countries.

The existing literature is rather vague in its assessment of what aspects of Western accounting systems fail to meet the test of relevance to developing nations' needs. For example, is it the case that the recording and analysis of costs through the double entry bookkeeping system is at fault or is there some less fundamental defect in the system, such as the need for a change in some of the regulations regarding the specific items to be disclosed in annual financial statements? One of the main theoretical paradigms which has been used to address the question of the relevance of Western accounting systems to developing nations is due to Hofstede (1980) and Gray (1988). This article discusses the application of Hofstede–Gray theory in these circumstances. The theory is illustrated by examining the use of the French Unified Accounting System (UAS) in Lebanon. It is argued that although Gray's 'dimensions' may possibly help us to understand how social factors affect the technology of accounting, certain purely technical aspects of accounting which are also pertinent to the question of cultural relevance should be considered more formally. The analysis depends upon appreciating that the measurement–disclosure distinction recognized by Gray and others in the literature on harmonization and the cultural impact of accounting (e.g., Fechner and Kilgore, 1994) brings with it a certain amount of information about what is most likely to be influenced by cultural context. This extension of the Hofstede–Gray theory is used to argue that the specific disclosure rules of particular calculations inherent in Western accounting systems rather than the transaction cost database are most likely to fail to satisfy the needs of users in developing countries. Due to the limited nature of the evidence currently available, the generality of the analysis is limited. In return, however, it allows relationships between some aspects of culture and items of financial information to be discussed more specifically.

Developing countries and Hofstede–Gray theory

The description 'developing country' refers to a country falling within the rather vague definition used by Wallace (1990): a country in the midstream of economic development.[1] Developing countries possess a monetary economy, some parts of the social and economic infrastructure of developed countries (Makdisi, 1977; Perera, 1989b) and, in particular, accounting systems. Since one of the functions of accounting systems, presumably, is to serve some purpose (FASB, 1978) it is natural to ask whether the accounting systems adopted by developing countries are most suitable for those countries.

An answer to this question either requires a piecemeal, case-by-case judgment on what elements constitute an appropriate accounting system for a specific developing country, region or cultural group, or it requires a theory of what is relevant to the needs of users in developing countries. The theory which has so far found the most favour in this regard is due to Hofstede (1980) and Gray (1988). Hofstede's is a theory from the literature of cross-cultural psychology and is not concerned with accounting per se. Gray's is an extension of Hofstede's theory which attempts to understand some of the mechanisms through which cultural variables might impact on the correct design of accounting technology. The remainder of this section describes this composite theory in detail.

Hofstede (1987) defined 'culture' as a collective programming process by a society which distinguishes the belief systems of its members from other societies. Four characteristics of culture were specified: symbols, heroes, rituals and values. The last (which is relevant here) is the most difficult to change, according to Hofstede, and he suggested that differences in institutional behaviour can be explained by differences in four dimensions of value. These are: large versus small Power Distance; strong versus weak Uncertainty Avoidance; Individualism versus Collectivism; and Masculinity versus Femininity. All of these dimensions are assumed to be ordinally measurable. Power Distance depends upon the extent to which members of society accept the unequal distribution of power within institutions and society generally. Uncertainty Avoidance is reflected in the extent to which ambiguous situations are tolerated and the extent to which institutions insist on conformity. Individualism refers to the relationship of members of society to their families vis-à-vis other societal units. Cultures are more individualistic to the extent that the self and immediate family claim priority over the interests of broader social groupings such as the firm and the state. Masculinity implies strongly differentiated sex roles and stresses material success in competitive societies.[2]

It seems plausible to suggest the existence of an effect by culture on accounting practices (e.g., Burchell *et al.*, 1980, p. 19; Meyer, 1986) but the mechanisms by which such an effect might be transmitted are not immediately

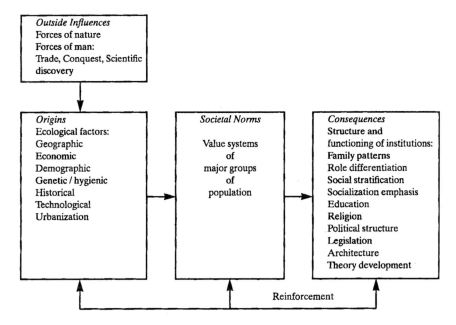

Figure 1 Hofstede's framework.
Source: Hofstede (1980).

obvious. Hofstede's framework is shown in Figure 1. Societies are influenced by different underlying technological and environmental factors and consequently develop different societal values. These in turn effect institutional processes including, presumably, information needs about those processes. This appears to be the basic argument supporting the contention that each culture should develop its own accounting system to serve its own distinct requirements.

Gray attempted to use Hofstede's theoretical framework to explain more specifically the effect of cultural values on accounting practices. Gray related four accounting variables to Hofstede's dimensions: Professionalism, Uniformity, Conservatism and Secrecy. Basically to use Gray's framework one must be able to determine, by some means, whether an accounting system scores high or low on each of the dimensions. Then, Gray hypothesized, the relationship between his accounting values and Hofstede's cultural values is as shown in Table 1. The specific areas of practice which these variables are supposed to affect is shown in Figure 2, reproduced from Radebaugh and Gray (1993), and described originally by Gray as those of authority, measurement and disclosure. Gray would expect a high value for Individualism in a society to be associated with the willing exercise of individual judgment and thus, the reasoning goes, relatively influential professional

Table 1 Relationships between Gray's accounting dimensions and Hofstede's cultural dimensions.

Cultural Values (Hofstede)	Accounting values (Gray)			
	Professionalism	Uniformity	Conservatism	Secrecy
Power Distance	−	+	?	+
Uncertainty Avoidance	−	+	+	+
Individualism	+	−	−	−
Masculinity	?	?	−	−

Note: '+' indicates a direct relationship between the relevant variables; '−' indicates an inverse relationship. Question marks indicate that the nature of the relationship is indeterminate.

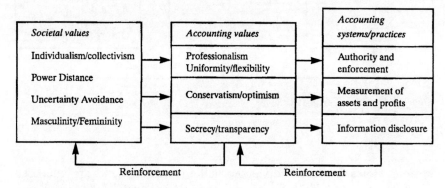

Figure 2 Gray's accounting dimensions and measurement and disclosure.
Source: Radebaugh and Gray (1993).

accounting bodies. High Individualism similarly implies a suspicion of Uniform or Secretive disclosure practices and a Conservative calculation rule like the lower of cost and market value might be expected to be less popular on the basis that undue pessimism is associated with Conservatism. The interpretation of Gray's variables will be discussed in more detail throughout this paper.

A number of studies have been carried out at the theoretical level utilizing the Hofstede–Gray framework. For example, Perera (1989a) applied the approach to developing countries generally and Gerhardy (1990) to the specific case of West Germany.[3] To our knowledge, however, the theory has yet to be empirically tested. Indeed such is the nature of the concepts involved and the state of the available evidence that it is questionable whether Gray's adaptation of Hofstede's theory can in fact be empirically validated in the usual scientific sense.

The problem of substantiating the Hofstede–Gray theory is particularly acute in the context of understanding the relevance of accounting practices to the needs of developing countries. Widely differing accounting practices have evolved in the EEC and other Western countries, as has been highlighted by recent attempts at harmonization. These differences can be explained in terms of local, cultural conditions (Pratt and Behr, 1987; Schreuder, 1987) and a number of environmental factors (Nair and Frank, 1980; Goodrich, 1982; Nobes, 1983). If such clear differences have evolved among relatively similar developed economic systems it is quite possible that had accounting systems evolved independently in developing countries they would have had a rather different form from any we now witness in present day Europe. However, most accounting systems used in developing countries have been directly imported from the West through a variety of channels: by colonialism in the past (Engleman, 1962; Heatly, 1979); and through Western multinational companies (Seidler, 1969), the influence of local professional associations (usually founded originally by Western counterpart organizations) and aid and loan agencies from the industrialized nations in the present (Heatly, 1979). The consequence of this transmission of technology is that it *may* have once been relevant to the information needs of the colonisers and *may* today be relevant to the information needs of the managers of multinational companies, Western governments and the International Monetary Fund.[4] However the process of importation makes it extremely difficult to determine in a straightforward, positive fashion, by simple correspondence of the theory with the facts, whether Western technology is relevant to the current needs of developing societies. Due to the interference in what would otherwise have been the natural evolution of financial information requirements there are no uncontaminated examples of modern accounting practices in developing countries. Consequently great care has to be taken in using data from developing countries to draw inferences about relevance on the basis of the Hofstede–Gray framework. Probably the best that can be achieved presently is to adopt the Hofstede–Gray framework as an implied definition of cultural relevance and apply it to specific cases to see if the results of such an enterprise are consistent with the available evidence. This method is applied to the case of Lebanon in the next section.

The case of Lebanon and the French UAS

The French UAS

In order to apply the Hofstede–Gray schema to analyse the relevance of the UAS in both France and Lebanon it is necessary to examine the latter's attributes with respect to the accounting value dimensions. There is a difficulty of interpretation with this exercise in that Gray's values are defined in terms of social dispositions rather than the attributes of financial reports.

The theoretical significance of this matter will be taken up later. In the meantime Gray's dimensions will be informally analysed as if they were attributes of the UAS itself.

Descriptions of the French accounting system lead one to conclude that Professionalism, under Gray's definitions, is low and that Uniformity is high (e.g., AlHashim and Arpan, 1992).[5] The reasons for the present pattern of French accounting practices appear to be largely historical (Nobes and Parker, 1991). Since then there has been a long tradition of accounting legislation in France. The *Code Napoleon*, for example, was a forerunner of much Continental accounting regulation and the present UAS is a modern version of the 1947 *Plan Comptable Général*.[6] The basic form of these accounts developed out of the belief on the part of successive French governments that a national uniform system would both help to promote a more equitable distribution of wealth through a more effective taxation policy (Scott, 1970) and would also benefit the national economy through a more informed planning strategy (Holzer, 1984). The necessary involvement of the French government in the creation of this grand design, together with a strong legislative influence on company disclosure practices, has resulted in a system of accounting in which the exercise of Professional judgment is substantially reduced in order to achieve higher Uniformity of practice.

Gray's definition of conservatism (1988, p. 8) is similar to Chambers' (1966) interpretation of it as a deliberate downward bias or 'pessimism' in accounting estimates. This emphasises a statistical aspect of accounting measurement which is likely to be context specific and the effects of which will be seen mainly in the choice of valuation method and income determination. It is usually accepted from the earlier work of Gray (1980) and others (e.g., Nobes and Parker, 1991) that the UAS, like German accounting, is inherently more conservative than Anglo-American systems in this respect. For example, depreciation policies are determined strictly in accordance with taxation law and rather large portions of annual profit (5 per cent) have to be set aside to a statutory reserve until the latter reaches a level of 10 per cent of the issued share capital. Again, the reason behind this practice appears to be historical and culturally specific: the dominant position of banking institutions and government in the ownership structure of French companies (Nobes, 1989).

Gray's fourth accounting dimension of Secrecy relates to an issue of disclosure: the extent to which accounting information about the firm finds its way into the hands of third parties. The evidence strongly supports the belief that the UAS provides less information to third parties and hence is considerably more Secretive than the accounting disclosures required of their British and American counterparts (Barrett, 1980). The position of investors seems to be particularly affected in this regard (Scott, 1970). The reason for the appearance of this trait in the UAS is presumably similar to the causes of Conservatism, that is, the close control of companies by government and large financial institutions which have powers of access to the information they require.

The UAS was developed by the French and therefore it is to be expected that correlations would be observed between Hofstede's cultural dimensions and Gray's accounting dimensions in the directions described in Table 1 if Gray's theory of relevance is valid. If either Perera's or Hofstede's data on cultural values is used (Perera, 1989a, p. 53; Hofstede, 1980, pp. 92–152), this is the case for the first three cultural dimensions, namely Power Distance, Uncertainty Avoidance and Masculinity. Power Distance and Uncertainty Avoidance in France are both relatively high compared to most other democratic European and Anglo-Saxon countries.[7] Masculinity is on the low side of the international average for France, particularly when the organizational role aspect of the concept is applied to perceived differences between the sexes at the expert strata of management, that is, the level at which accounting information might be thought to be especially relevant (Hofstede, 1980, p. 281). However, the pattern of Individualism in French society appears to run in the opposite direction to the way predicted by Gray. The comparison of French cultural values with Gray's accounting values may thus indicate that, in this regard, the UAS fails to meet the needs of French accounts users. Alternatively it may be that this cultural dimension is not appropriate to the question being asked, or that Gray's theory is invalid.

For the reasons given in the preceding section, one possible use of Gray's theory as applied to developing countries is as a definition of relevance. In this context it is instructive to apply the definition to the case of Lebanon, to see if the result leads to conclusions which appear to be sensible in the light of what we know about Lebanese history, environment and culture.

Historical, environmental and cultural background of Lebanon

Lebanon is a relatively small country with limited natural resources. It is densely populated with about three and a half million people occupying only 10,452 square kilometres of the Levant. The country's strategic position on the Eastern Mediterranean seaboard has assured the region and its surrounding area of the role of an important trading centre since ancient times.[8] Following World War I in 1920, the Allied Supreme Council granted France a mandatory authority over Lebanon. The components of this new state consisted of Arabic-speaking people, both Muslim and Christian, and had been part of the Ottoman Empire since 1518. Despite the long period of Turkish rule there is little evidence of Turkish influence in the everyday life of the Lebanon today.[9] Lebanon was a French colony until 1943 and French troops remained in the country until 1946. During the period of French occupation the Lebanese Pound was tied to the French Franc, which had the effect of exporting the economic problems of France during the years of the Great Depression (Badrud-Din, 1984). In the first thirty years following World War II Lebanon experienced a period of relative economic prosperity with an annual average GDP growth rate of approximately 6 per cent.

Since 1975 Lebanon has been subjected to a crippling civil war. The main economic effect of this and the more general conflict in the Middle East in recent years has been significant levels of inflation and destabilization of the economy (Baydoun and Gray, 1990). The civil war has reduced the level of commerce and virtually eliminated a once-healthy tourist industry (Saidi, 1986). Lebanon's limited manufacturing industry, which has also been badly affected by the war, is light, modern (e.g., food processing) and depends heavily upon imported raw materials (Badrud-Din, 1984). The country exports mainly food and tobacco products to the Arab market. The industrial sector now consists mainly of small firms owned and operated chiefly by private interests with little government involvement. A trend towards greater privatization has continued despite the present conflict (Labaki, 1991).

The influence of the French style of life is clearly visible in Lebanon today, especially among the Maronite community. The French period led to the establishment of schools, hospitals and other institutions which acted as vehicles for the transmission and assimilation of French culture (Bucheiry, 1991). Strong trading relations between France and Lebanon still exist, French law is deeply embedded in Lebanon's constitution and French is the official second language (Gordon, 1983). Most importantly, the French government sponsored the transfer of the French UAS to Lebanon in 1983 and it has since been adopted by all Lebanese firms.[10] Nevertheless, despite the strong French influence in Lebanon there exist significant environmental and cultural differences between the two countries today, some of which may affect the relevance of the UAS to Lebanese user needs.

Unlike the case of France, no direct assessments of Lebanon's four cultural dimensions are publicly available. However, Hofstede (1991) provides data on a group of Arab countries including Lebanon and this can be used as the starting point for the analysis. Hofstede's values for the Arab countries compared to France are shown in Table 2. As can be observed, as a group the Arab countries exhibit higher Power Distance and Masculinity and lower Individualism and Uncertainty Avoidance than France.

There are a number of reasons, however, why these scores are unlikely to reflect Lebanese cultural values. The group of countries Hofstede described as 'Arab' consists of Egypt, Iraq, Kuwait, Libya, Saudi Arabia and the United Arab Emirates as well as Lebanon. Included in this sample are countries belonging to the Gulf region, North Africa and the Mediterranean, areas of great cultural diversity with representatives from among the richest (e.g., Kuwait) and poorest of nations (e.g., Egypt) on a per capita GNP basis. Furthermore the effects of colonization on individuals within this group are likely to have been diverse since Saudi Arabia was never colonized directly; Egypt, Iraq and Kuwait were colonized or influenced less

Table 2 Hofstede's Arab countries cultural values scores compared to those of France.

	Arab countries	*France*
Power Distance		
Score rank	7	15/16
Score	80	68
Reference page (Hofstede, 1991)	26	26
Individualism		
Score rank	26/27	10/11
Score	38	71
Reference page	53	53
Masculinity		
Score Rank	23	35/36
Score	53	43
Reference page	84	84
Uncertainty Avoidance		
Score rank	27	10/15
Score	68	86
Reference page	113	113

Source: Hofstede (1991).

directly by the British; Libya by the Italians; and Lebanon by the French. Given these factors we might expect considerable variability on some of the dimension scores by the countries within the group.

Since the Arab countries score is an aggregate it acts as a measure of location for the scaled values for each individual country in the group. This enables us to estimate very roughly how Lebanon's cultural values stand in relation to these 'average' measures and thus to the values of the cultural dimensions of France. In the assessment of Lebanon's cultural values which follows, the analysis relies upon a triangulation of Hofstede's data with impressionistic emic data and with observations of some of the institutional processes, which, according to Hofstede's theory, are consequences of cultural values.[11] It also serves to raise the question of the extent to which it is sensible to ask questions about *the* culture of Lebanon, since there may be several cultures seeking to coexist within the same Lebanese geographical boundary. This point is returned to in the concluding discussions.

Power distance   The Arab countries as a group ranked seventh out of fifty national groupings with a score of 80 compared to a ranking of fifteenth and a score of 68 for France (see Table 2). Consideration of Lebanese institutional arrangements and general norms suggest that, comparatively with the other Arab countries in Hofstede's group, Lebanon's Power Distance score would be below the aggregate score of 80.

Lebanon possesses a written constitution originally based upon the French model which was introduced in 1926 and which established a parliamentary democracy (Gordon, 1983; Salem, 1991). The constitution has been amended several times since then, the last time being in 1990. It guarantees certain fundamental rights of the individual, including 'respect for public liberties, especially the freedom of opinion and belief' (Salem, 1991). The political intention behind the clauses in the preamble to the latest amendment of the constitution and in particular the *mithaq al-aysh al-mushtarak*[12] may be interpreted as an attempt to lower the level of Power Distance in Lebanese society.

Most of the effects of the recent civil war have tended to further reduce Power Distance. Indeed, the war may be interpreted as evidence of the rejection of inequalities in the power structure implicit in the pre-1975 political system. The powers of the Maronite president, for example, have been substantially curtailed in the amended constitution. The former executive powers of the president have now been ceded to a Council of Ministers, thus establishing a more non-French, collegial political decision making apparatus. The Lebanese presidential office, as modified by the recent constitutional changes, now has a ceremonial role more reminiscent of Ireland, Germany and Israel (all of which score low on the Power Distance scale) than of France.[13]

At the level of individual organizations as well as at the lower, non-ministerial levels of political institutions, the proposed aboliton of the 'six to five' employment policy which requires the appointment of six Christians for every five Muslims (including Druze) seeks to redress a perceived imbalance between the different religious groups (Article 95, Salem, 1991; Soffer, 1986; Faour, 1991). These movements toward more equal power distribution in Lebanese society are typical of changes in the political and social structure which have occurred since the 1970s and reflect a current system of values which strongly rejects the distribution of power imposed by the French (Fawaz, 1991).

On Hofstede's scale, a high reading of Power Distance depends upon two basic characteristics both being present: one is that significant inequalities in the distribution of power exist; the other is that members of society accept the inequalities. Given the present difficult circumstances in Lebanon, the extent of the first characteristic is difficult to gauge although, by comparison with the Arab grouping, the basis of Lebanese power-sharing structures appears to be in a state of transition towards a more egalitarian template. The absence of the second characteristic, however, is clear: as evidenced by the current conflicts and recent changes in the constitution the *acceptance* of inequality between at least some of the important groupings in Lebanese society is low.

These institutional characteristics of Lebanese society suggest that, if the Lebanese power distance value is greater than the moderate position of

France it is probably much closer to the French value than the average 'Arab countries' score of 80 would indicate. A more moderate score on the Power Distance scale is also suggested by consideration of the family, school and workplace norms described by Hofstede (1991, p. 37). The norms which characterize Lebanese communities are fairly evenly distributed between those associated with small and large Power Distances. For example, while parents teach children obedience and children are expected to treat parents with respect, there is also a belief that inequalities among people should be minimized and that subordinates should be consulted. Furthermore, decentralization is one of the main characteristics of Lebanese history in stark contrast to, say, the position in Egypt (e.g., Khalaf, 1987). This reasoning suggests that the Lebanese value for Power Distance probably falls into the middle range.

Uncertainty avoidance   Hofstede's Uncertainty Avoidance score for the Arab countries of 68, with a ranking of twenty-seventh, is low in comparison with France, which scored 86 and was ranked tenth equal in the study. The traits exhibited by Lebanon suggest a relatively low level of Uncertainty Avoidance compared to the other countries in the Arab group, which implies that this value is relatively weak in Lebanese society compared to France's quite high score.

This trait is particularly well illustrated in Lebanon by a strongly free-enterprise economy. The Lebanese region has old commercial and trading traditions and economic growth, past and present, has been mainly due to the investment of private capital (Labaki, 1991). Government economic policies have, in fact, long been based upon the implicit objective of allowing the private sector to lead economic expansion, sometimes with the encouragement of large investment and tax incentives for both home and foreign investors (Gordon, 1983). This is unlike most other Arab countries and is representative of a more free-market philosophy than that which would be found in many European countries, particularly France. Uncertainty is a normal feature of life. There is no unemployment benefit in Lebanon and health is mostly privately funded (Kuvian, 1982). Although the state makes free education available at both elementary and higher levels, 70 per cent of Lebanese nevertheless chose private education (McDowall, 1986).

The general norms of Lebanon are mostly on the weak Uncertainty side: the Lebanese are, for instance, comfortable in ambiguous situations with unfamiliar risks and are motivated by achievement (Hofstede, 1991, p. 125). While some norms are indicative of stronger Uncertainty Avoidance (e.g., the display of aggression at appropriate times is socially acceptable) they are relatively few compared to those reflecting weak Uncertainty Avoidance. The key differences in politics and ideas between Lebanon and the typical Arab country in Hofstede's data also point in the same direction. Citizen protest is more acceptable and Lebanon is more regional and international, with stronger human rights traditions (Hofstede, 1991, p. 134). The institutional facts of life in Lebanon, therefore, as well as some strong cultural characteristics, impose a greater tolerance of Uncertainty on Lebanese society than in the other Arab countries in Hofstede's sample, and thus its Uncertainty index must be low relative to that of France.

Individualism The Arab countries score low on Individualism (scoring 38 and ranked equal twenty-sixth) compared to France (scoring 71 and ranked equal tenth). However, many traits on the continuum of Individualism run parallel to those of Uncertainty Avoidance and suggest that Individualism in Lebanese society is considerably higher than in other Arab countries.

Interference in private life by the organs of state is relatively low, for example. There are low levels of taxation (Torbey, 1986) and there are absolutely no controls over foreign exchange (Badrud-Din, 1984). The Lebanese family is the strongest social unit, dominating economic and political life at the expense of affection for non-family and state organizations and cutting across the boundaries of wealth and education (McDowall, 1986), something which Hofstede describes as 'fragmented collectivism'. Individualism and private property rights are, in fact, basic principles which are now enshrined in the written constitution (pp. 122–6, Salem, 1991), which itself embodies a long-running, free-market oriented philosophy.[14]

The written constitution guarantees individual liberties in specific ways. For example, Article 9 of the amended 1990 constitution pledges absolute freedom of conscience (Salem, 1991). The toleration of individualism has led over a number of years to Lebanon being seen as a refuge for asylum seekers (Gordon, 1983, p. 41) and it is a country traditionally renowned for its free press (Salem, 1991, p. 166). There is not a single government-owned newspaper and, since 1980, no state involvement in the television services (Kuvian, 1982). A further manifestation of the Lebanese tolerance for free thinking can be found in the content of the typical syllabi of political and economic studies in the higher education system. For example, commercial subjects studied at the Lebanese University include both Western capitalist economic theory as well as the theories of Communism and Third World developing economies (Centre for Lebanese Studies, 1991). Foreign languages such as English and French are also more important than usual among Middle Eastern countries (Badrud-Din, 1984). Private educational institutions enjoy almost complete autonomy (*Middle East and North Africa Yearbook*, 1992, p. 675). This liberal style of education is considered so fundamental that it was singled out for special mention in the 1990 amendment to the constitution (Salem, 1991). Lebanon thus possesses many of the characteristics of freedom taken for granted in Western societies and also, perhaps, places greater emphasis on individual self-reliance than would usually be expected in modern welfare-state capitalist societies.

The norms of Lebanese society are predominantly Individualistic (Hofstede, 1991, p. 67): people focus on the nuclear family, identity is based on the individual and employee–employer relationships are based upon mutual advantage; and the politics and ideas of Lebanon are overwhelmingly individualistic in contrast to the typical Arab country; people have a right to privacy, a personal opinion, equality under the law and so on. Lebanon's value for Individualism would lie well above the score for the composite of the Arab countries and probably lies along with France in the high individualism category.

Masculinity Hofstede's data on Masculinity placed the Arab country group in the middle range of the index with a score of 53 and ranked twenty-third. France lies toward the more Feminine end of the scale with a score of 43 and ranked equal thirty-fifth with Iran. As is typical of the Arab group as a whole, the role of the sexes is typically more clearly differentiated than it is in the West. This may be due to family size, which is larger than it is in Europe.[15] Male children are more highly valued than female children (Khalaf, 1987) and, given the biological imperative, the number of women available to enter the workforce is severely curtailed. Historically, the number of women actually in the workforce is relatively low, particularly in higher management positions.[16] Within the Arab group, Lebanon is probably among the most strongly masculine societies. The war has tended to emphasize gender differences. Women do not serve in the Lebanese Army, for example. War by its very nature emphasises toughness and male assertiveness. Moreover, the armed forces as organizations usually have what Hofstede (1980, p. 261) refers to as Masculine goals.

The typical modern role model reinforced by literature such as that of Barakat (1974), Pound (1986) and Mahfouz (1989) and by the free-market economic environment is of a self-reliant, competitive male with strong family loyalties and a woman whose main duty is still that of a housewife and mother. The general norms of Lebanese society (Hofstede, 1991, p. 96) are overwhelmingly masculine, the dominant values in society being material success and progress with men being assertive and women tender. These characteristics and those relating to politics and ideas (such as the importance of economic growth, Hofstede, 1991, p. 103) place Lebanon toward the higher end of the Masculinity scale, on the other side of the Arab countries away from France.

Information mismatch in the Lebanese UAS

This analysis of Lebanese society in terms of Hofstede's cultural values has, of necessity, been brief and selective. Lebanese society has undergone substantial changes in recent years in the characteristics described and will presumably continue to do so in the future. Aspects such as Power Distance have noticeably changed in the last two decades and not all influences point in the expected direction. It might be expected, for example, that war may increase Power Distance in certain ways (Hofstede, 1980, Chapter 8). Again, religion is a key factor in the Middle East but it is often difficult to gauge its effect on cultural values. One might argue that the Muslim faith professed by a substantial number of the Lebanese population is a force towards egalitarianism and against Power Distance. The *zakat* (taxation) and the *mirath* (inheritance) laws, for instance, are based upon a principle of equal distribution of wealth (Gambling and Abdel-Karim, 1991). On the other hand, the strong hierarchical structure of some of the religious sects in Lebanon might be argued to lead in the opposite direction.

These considerations make it necessary to handle the available evidence with a great deal of care and only to infer that which is relatively obvious. In this case the evidence is sufficiently clear for a reasonably strong conclusion to be drawn about the relative positions of Lebanon and France on the Power Distance and Individualism scales. There appears to be sufficient cause, however, for concluding that Uncertainty Avoidance is low compared to France's high score and that Lebanon's Masculinity value is high compared to France. On this basis, using the definition of cultural relevance implied by Table 1, it would appear that Lebanon's requirements are for less Uniformity, Conservatism and Secrecy in financial reporting practices. This conclusion may possibly strike the reader as a reasonable result based upon the general impression one receives of the Lebanese environment. However, this is some way from determining what specific information would be more relevant to Lebanese users. To achieve more definite recommendations it is necessary to extend the Hofstede Gray Theory further by explicitly considering the nature of the basic technical accounting dimensions of measurement and disclosure.

Measurement and disclosure

The charge that Western accounting systems fail to serve users in developing countries is often stated in a vague manner and a part of the function of a theory like Gray's is to make this sort of claim more precise. As shown in the previous section, it probably does go some way to achieving this objective, but does it go far enough? To claim that more or less Uniformity, Conservatism and Secrecy are desirable or to be expected in a Lebanese accounting system does not reveal the detailed structural relationships through which cultural predispositions are translated into definite policy recommendations on the detailed physical appearance of accounting reports.

As was shown in Figure 2, Gray's theory attempts to link his accounting values to specific attributes of accounting practice in the form of authority, enforcement, measurement and disclosure. The first two of this latter group are seen as being distinct from the last two in that the former are influenced by the values of Professionalism and Uniformity and represent characeristics of the social and political framework in which the activity of accounting takes place, while the latter are influenced by Conservatism and Secrecy and represent what and how financial information is reported to users. Both of these issues are clearly of important theoretical and practical interest, but the first is of an entirely different character from the second. The linkages between cultural values and the authority and enforcement characteristics found in the arrangements developed by society to organize its accounting activities are a direct application of Hofstede's theory that cultural values will impact on the forms institutions take and the processes they use. On the other hand, the linkages between cultural values and the physical attributes of financial reports (i.e., what they look like, what they contain and how much information they contain, etc.) is an entirely different type of question because it demands assessing the impact of the social dimension of accounting on the technical.

One of the problems with using Gray's theory to address either issue is that it is not entirely clear whether, to the extent that they are meant to be cultural attributes of social groups rather than physical attributes of the technology of accounting, his accounting values serve any useful purpose as intervening explanatory variables between Hofstede's basic cultural dimensions and the characteristics one might expect to find in accounting practice. All of Gray's accounting values are defined in terms of preferences for particular courses of action rather than in terms of apparent attributes of financial statements, such as the qualitative characteristics described in the FASB's Conceptual Framework project (FASB, 1980). Professionalism, for example, appears from Gray's description to refer to the disposition either of individual accountants to use judgments rather than mechanically follow pre-imposed rules, or possibly of professional bodies to prefer self-regulation as opposed to regulation by the State. Uniformity as defined by Gray (1988, p. 8) really appears to be little more than an inverse quality to Professionalism although there is clearly another sense (which may have been what Gray implicitly intended it to take) in which Uniformity could also be interpreted as the physical attribute of an accounting system (e.g., the extent to which the financial reports of one accounting entity are physically similar to those of other accounting entities).

The treatment of Professionalism and Uniformity by Gray is consistent with the framework described in Figure 2. These values are argued to influence authority and enforcement aspects of accounting systems, which are part of the social and political structure of accounting rather than the technical processes of accounting. Nevertheless, the need for such supposed relationships is far from obvious. For example, Uncertainty Avoidance supposedly has the relationship to Professionalism and Uniformity shown in Table 1 and the latter also supposedly relate to Authority in the way shown in Figure 2. However, given the very close connections between Uncertainty Avoidance and 'concepts of authority' in Hofstede's original theory (1991, pp. 120–3), these linkages appear to be superfluous.

Gray's discussion of the other two accounting value concepts, Conservatism and Secrecy, in relation to the issues of measurement and disclosure suggest that they would be expected to be more influential in determining the technical nature of accounting. This raises the question of whether such an interpretation is tenable. In the first place, it is not self-evident that the social characteristic of Secrecy is any more important in the determination of financial statement attributes than is the social attribute of Uniformity. A trait of high Secrecy in a culture, for instance, may mean that financial reports are less likely to contain certain types of information than in other, less secretive societies. However a high Uniformity score might be expected to directly influence the uniformity with which financial statements of differing entities are prepared, something about which Secrecy apparently would have little to say. Consequently the justification for choosing the particular linkages suggested in Figure 2 is unclear. In the second place, there are obvious questions of interest in understanding the possible forms which financial reports might take which do not seem, at least at a superficial level, to be formally addressed at all in Gray's theory. For instance, under what circumstances might a Statement of Value Added be more culturally relevant than a Profit and Loss Account? Consequently, Gray's theory seems, on the one hand, to overlook some important accounting effects of culture, and on the other hand, to say less than it could about some important aspects of the form and content of financial statements.

It is probably unrealistic to expect to be able to obtain complete agreement on a full and comprehensive theory of the form and exact content of corporate reports. Nevertheless, at least some part of the difficulty in applying Gray's theory and variants of it such as Mathews and Perera (1993) to providing answers to more specific questions about the form and content of financial statements lies in the need to consider certain basic characteristics of accounting technology itself. It seems a lot of thought has been given to the behavioural aspects of accounting but an insufficient amount has been given to the effect of limitations on the influence of cultural factors imposed by the tehnical dimension of accounting. Culture does exert an influence on the technology of accounting but it does so differentially, affecting some parts strongly, other parts less so and certain parts hardly at all. Consideration of why this is so, therefore, is an essential exercise in any attempt to determine the type of financial statements (as opposed to the forms of social and political organization) which are culturally relevant to a society.

The conventional wisdom in the literature holds that the relevance of accounting numbers depends upon some perceived purpose such as decision usefulness or accountability (Gray et al., 1988). Cultural differences may lead to many specific differences in the requirements of users for accounting information but it is likely that users in developing and developed societies also have many information requirements in common. Therefore, are those who argue that Western accounting systems are irrelevant to the needs of developing countries (Briston, 1978; Perera, 1989b; Samuels and Oliga, 1982; Wallace, 1990) suggesting that transaction costs should not be recorded and analysed into economic activities? Or are they simply arguing that the detail and type of information about calculations which are disclosed in Western financial statements should be amended in some way to accommodate differing cultural perspectives?

The first suggestion is extremely radical. Without careful recording of the effects of transactions on activities it is difficult to see how it would be possible for developing countries to enjoy the benefits obtainable from economic analysis. Where independent evolution has taken place, developing countries seem to attach the same significance as do developed countries to the analysis of economic activities through the recording of transactions by systems of bookkeeping (Hayashi, 1989);[17] although developing societies differ in the level of complexity of the events that take place, the transactions these events generate and the variety of decision needs accounting information has to serve.

The second, weaker suggestion, that patterns of disclosure should be adjusted but that basic measurement processes should be left intact, seems more plausible and in fact has a certain theoretical significance in the context of the distinction made between measurement and disclosure issues in accounting noted by a number of writers (Solomons, 1983; Sterling, 1987; Willett, 1987).[18] The main features of this distinction are illustrated in the hierarchy shown in Figure 3.

Measurement issues split into two main types: *fundamental* measurements which involve the direct assignment of a number to an object or event by a relatively objective procedure; and indirect or *derived* measurements which usually involve a calculation based upon fundamental measurements. In accounting, the assignment of debt values to transactions is an example of a fundamental measurement while the profit figure (which includes calculations like the depreciation adjustment) is an example of a derived measurement. The common characteristic of both types of measurement is that they represent observed properties of something in the real world.[19] Disclosure issues are, in contrast, not issues of representational faithfulness at all but of whether anybody wants the information concerned — even if it is properly measured. Relevance does not determine whether an accounting measurement is valid but it does determine, with some degree of probability, whether it is or ought to be disclosed in a set of financial statements. Consequently, the major significance of the concepts of cultural values and cultural relevance is likely to be in terms of their effect on practices which have more to do with disclosure than measurement.

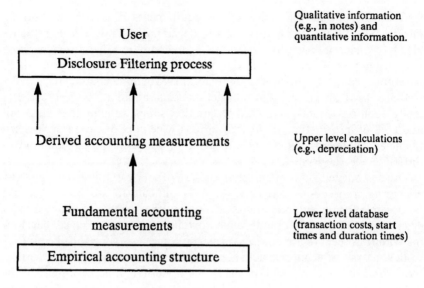

Figure 3 Levels of measurement and disclosure in accounting.

The distinction between measurement and disclosure is, however, not entirely black and white in this context. The framework outlined in Figure 3 identifies the levels at which accounting information is more likely to be open to the charge of cultural irrelevance. The lowest, most fundamental level activity cost measurements (e.g., the cost of inventories and fixed assets) rely much more on purely technological relationships than do the higher levels, and consequently are less affected by social and cultural differences. Higher level, derived measurements such as depreciation calculations and market values, in contrast, are decision-specific statistics and more likely to become irrelevant to user needs if arbitrarily transferred across cultural boundaries. Finally, at the interface between measurements and user, the disclosure filtering mechanisms are by definition culturally determined and it is at this level particularly, the *disclosure* level, that Western accounting practices are most likely to be irrelevant to user needs in developing countries.

This analysis suggests that the subject matter which forms the basis of *any* disclosed financial information is relatively fixed. Essentially, this basis consists of an activity analysis of a defined subset of the population of invoice costs, the subset chosen depending upon whether the accounting is actual cost or current value. Asset analysis requires at least the three main financial reports of position statement, income statement and funds statement to fully account for the data base in aggregate (Hodgson *et al.*, 1993). However, precisely how much of the information contained in the chosen basis is disclosed to users is very much determined by factors such

Table 3 Relationships between Gray's reinterpreted dimensions, qualitive characteristics and the form and content of corporate reports.

Accounting dimensions — technical aspects	Qualitative characteristics relating to disclosure	Examples of issues relating to the form and content of corporate reports
Uniformity		
	Uniform content and presentation:	
	Consistency	Standardized accounts
	Comparability	Accounting policies
	Quality of Information:	
	Timeliness	Normal publication date
	Materiality	Cost versus market values
Conservatism	Objectivity	Cash flow accounting
	Verifiablity	Lower of cost and market
Secrecy	Reliability	
	Neutrality	
	Substance over form	
	Amount of information:	Extent of disaggregated data:
	Accountability	Number of items disclosed
	Decision usefulness	Group accounts
		Supplementary statements

as the cultural forces discussed here. This is what makes it theoretically useful to try to more formally relate the *qualitative characteristics* of financial statements to Hofstede's cultural values via the intervening social attributes suggested by Gray. By extending Gray's framework in this way, it may be possible to explain more formally some of the important, overt characteristics of financial reports. In fact, by grouping the commonly cited qualitative characteristics of financial statements (Mathews and Perera, 1993) in the way decribed in Table 3, it appears that a suitable, technical, reinterpretation of Gray's values of Uniformity, Conservatism and Secrecy can satisfactorily accommodate many of those characteristics in so far as they are pertinent to matters of disclosure. Furthermore, since the reinterpreted concepts can be expected to have the same relationships with Hofstede's cultural values as the original concepts, the amendment allows the Hofstede–Gray framework to be extended to more specific policy prescriptions in a straightforward manner.

Table 3 suggests some relationships between the technical, disclosure characteristics of financial reports, Gray's three concepts of Uniformity, Conservatism and Secrecy and some examples of the manner in which the qualitative characteristics are manifested in the form and content of published accounts. Uniformity as a technical characteristic of financial statements is interpreted as encompassing the two qualities of consistency and comparability, each in different ways relevant to the question of apparent uniformity of accounting policies over time and uniformity of presentation of accounting information between accounting entities. Conservatism and Secrecy overlap in their effects on the remaining qualitative characteristics. Conservatism is pertinent to the *quality* of disclosed information and is thus associated with such physical characteristics as objectivity, verifiability, reliability, neutrality and substance over form. They determine such specific issues of the form and content of financial reports as the communication of historic cost versus current value accounting and the use of rules such as 'lower of cost and market'. These characteristics may, if scaled in the appropriate manner, be expected to be correlated in the same way with underlying cultural values, as is Gray's original concept of Conservatism. Gray's original Secrecy concept can be similarly related in a consistent manner both to the quality characteristics and to the *amount* of information in financial reports, the latter being manifested in such traits as the number of items disclosed and the extent to which aggregated data is disclosed in contrast to disaggregated data. This allows the possibility of bringing into the analysis the attributes of accountability and decision usefulness. These notions are concerned with patterns of disclosure such as user focus and the nature of the accounting entity,[20] matters which are not clearly addressed in Gray's original analysis.

In the case of Lebanon the relationships shown in Table 3 suggest a number of policy prescriptions which are more specific than those determined at the close of the discussion in the previous section. Assuming that cultural relevance is or should be a factor in determining the form of financial statements, we would expect Lebanese financial statements to be less uniform across time and between entities, to contain more market value information and provide more items of disaggregated information. Normal publication dates should be relatively flexible and there should be less call for conservative valuation rules such as lower of cost and market.

It would appear that these and other similar prescriptions implied by Table 3 cannot be tested directly at present. Since 1983 all Lebanese firms have been required to follow the UAS and this system has not yet been modified to accommodate any cultural differences between France and Lebanon. If the Hofstede–Gray theory is to amount to anything more than a statement of what some theorists believe to be the cultural relevance of accounting information, however, our analysis suggests that modifications along the lines described above either will or should take place in Lebanese accounting in the future.

Conclusion

This article has discussed the issue of the relevance of Western accounting to developing societies. The difficulty with much of the existing literature in this area is that it is not clear exactly what aspects of Western accounting systems are irrelevant to the needs of users in developing countries and it is not always obvious what the term 'relevance' means. The analysis was based on Hofstede's (1980, 1991) characterization of cultural values and Gray's (1988) accounting-value hypotheses were used to define the notion of 'relevance of an accounting system'. These were used to analyse the relevance of the French UAS to the Lebanon. It was argued that although the Hofstede–Gray framework does appear to provide a structure within which to examine issues of the cultural relevance of accounting systems, insufficient notice has been taken of important technical aspects of accounting technology. In particular it was suggested that the charge of irrelevance aimed at an accounting system applied to a developing society was most likely to be substantiated against disclosure rules rather than against the underlying fundamental recording systems upon which most accounting information is based. This led to an extension of the Hofstede–Gray theory which redefined the concepts of Uniformity, Conservatism and Secrecy in terms of the physical characteristics of financial statements.

As in many areas in accounting research, great care has to be taken in pursuing analysis of this kind. Interesting insights into fundamental accounting issues can be revealed but there are also significant qualifications, two of which deserve special mention. One qualification is the delicate juxtaposition of the positive and the normative in analysis of this kind. It was stated earlier that in order to descriptively test a theory of cultural relevance like Gray's it is necessary, from a strictly logical point of view, to already have in one's possession a definition of cultural relevance. Unfortunately, in the context of cultural analysis we do not have such a definition. The usual 'decision usefulness' definitions in the literature will not do, for example, because they focus on the level of the individual and this does not necessarily translate in a simple manner to the macro-social, cultural level. Therefore, in the absence of an independent definition there is a danger that testing hypotheses relating cultural values to accounting characteristics will degenerate into circular reasoning. The analysis in this paper attempted to avoid this mistake by taking Gray's hypotheses as a tentative implied definition of cultural relevance and to then use it to see if the results produce reasonable conclusions in the light of the available evidence. This is clearly not a strong scientific methodology but it is internally consistent and non-trivial in the sense that, should the evidence for instance turn out to never or only infrequently synchronize with Gray's concept of cultural relevance, then it would surely eventually be discarded in favour of something else. Given the paucity of culturally uncontaminated evidence in the case of studying the accounting practices of developing countries, this means that the possibility of convincingly accepting or rejecting the Hofstede–Gray theory in this context is likely to be a long and arduous process based upon carefully examining those elements of practice which have evolved distinctly within such societies.

A second qualification relating to the Hofstede–Gray framework lies in the scope of its application. Hofstede places great importance on the fact that his cultural values relate to the characteristics of nations and that it is meaningful to reason at this level, despite the many differences which exist within subcultures at the many levels of society. To apply this thesis to the question of the relevance of accounting information is a significant departure from the normal way in which this concept is normally discussed in the modern literature. Virtually all analysis of this matter takes as its reference point the needs of a relatively homogeneous group of users (e.g., shareholders, creditors, investors, trade unionists, etc.). The focus in the cultural relevance literature is different from this mainstream approach to the issue of usefulness. It is uncertain whether it will eventually lead to similar conclusions, or even whether it will ultimately be possible to reconcile the two approaches. In the context of Lebanon, this is especially obvious. It contains a number of important religious groups which have significantly distinct subcultural characteristics, some of which may run counter to the apparent national cultural values. In Lebanon the question of the Islamic community is a case in point. Under Islam the social order is closer to collectivism and the rights of private ownership are ultimately subordinate to Allah. Consequently, the forms of presentation and disclosure which are most applicable to a moderately individualistic society may not be so relevant to the kind of accountability required by the Islamic *Shari'a*. The issue of the extent to which Hofstede's concepts are applicable to the analysis of more specific social groups is an open question at the present time.

It would be interesting to apply the kind of analysis used in this paper to other developing societies. Perhaps further research will reveal patterns of relevance common to developing nations. One of the main problems for research in this area is access to data. Most of the data we have used is in the public domain. Pertinent data of this type, which has the advantage of helping to build a general picture, is often less easy to acquire in the case of developing countries than in the case of developed countries. Direct data from questionnaires is also less easy to acquire in developing countries. Nevertheless, given that the position of the Lebanon makes it more difficult to obtain usable data than in most countries, this should not be an insurmountable problem.

Acknowledgements

The authors gratefully acknowledge the helpful comments of Alan MacGregor, Rob Gray, Hector Perera, Ng Su-May, Jill McKinnon and members of staff in the Department of Accountancy at Otago University.

Notes

1 As Wallace (p. 3) states, developing countries are typically African, Asian, South American, Middle Eastern and South Pacific which were decolonized by the

European powers in the 1950s and in which there is often a sizeable section of the population who would be considered poor by Western standards. This definition ties in reasonably well to those used in the statistical analysis of economic development (e.g., World Bank, 1991). Osmanczyk (1985) is a useful reference for the United Nations definitions of developing and developed countries.

2 These dimensions seem to be independent of one another according to Hofstede (1980) and were the outcome of a factor analysis of the questionnaire responses of a large sample of IBM employees in over forty countries. Hofstede claimed that his values relate to three cultural dimensions identified in anthropological research and sociological theory. These are relationship to authority, the concept of the self and gender role differentiation (Parsons and Shils, 1951; Inkeles and Levinson, 1969). It is important to understand that Hofstede's cultural values are to be interpreted as social attributes of collections of people, not as psychological attributes of individuals (Hofstede, 1991, Chapter 1). Hofstede (1991) discusses a possible fifth dimension extracted from a study of Chinese cultural values which appears to be independent of the four dimensions discussed in this paper and relates to the degree to which people take a short-term view or a long-term view of life. This has some possibly interesting implications for certain accounting issues such as cash flow versus accrual accounting. However, due to the fact that it is not yet clear how Gray's framework would accommodate this additional value, and also to the absence of data with respect to Lebanon on this issue at the present time, the 'Confucian' dimension is not incorporated into the analysis.

3 At the theoretical level with respect to developing countries in general, Perera traced the societal values inherent in Power Distance, Uncertainty Avoidance, Individuality and Masculinity together with institutional characteristics such as the legal system, capital markets, education and professional associations back to underlying ecological, economic, historic and technological factors.

4 It may not, of course. Some would argue that the present form of Western financial statements fails even to satisfy the needs of Western users (e.g., see Briston, 1978). As Hopwood states: 'It is just not true that current or past practice necessarily reflect desirable practice' (1974, p. 166).

5 Professionalism, in this context, refers to the extent to which individual accountants have the discretion to depart from detailed rules and guidelines in measurement and disclosure issues (Gray, 1988; Perera, 1989a). It is not always clear in the literature that 'professionalism' is an attribute of an accounting system rather than an attribute of the cultural environment. For example, it is unclear how 'self-regulation' as a defining characteristic of professionalism is a quality that one might expect to find in an accounting system instead of a quality that is exhibited by professional organizations within a particular society. In fact, solely in the context of accounting systems, 'uniformity' often appears to simply be the inverse attribute of 'professionalism'.

6 The basis of the *Plan Comptable* actually seems to have been laid down by the occupying German authorities in World War II. More details of the French UAS may be found in Baydoun and Gray (1990).

7 This has been attributed to the preference of the French for highly centralized bureaucratic structures, a trait which seems to be a stable and accepted characteristic of French society over a long period of time and to be exhibited in political and economic hierarchies at all levels (Most, 1984).

8 This is the land in which the Phoenicians once dwelt and is part of what was once referred to as 'Asia Minor', an area colonized in turn by Persians, Greeks, Romans, Arabs and Turks among others.

9 Apart from some elements in the Lebanese vocabulary, the typical Lebanese menu, dress and some family relationships.

10 A grant of 500,000 French Francs was given by the French government to finance the transfer (personal interview in 1990 with A. Mattar, Chairman of the Technical Affairs Committee, Lebanese Association of Certified and Public Accountants).

11 Hofstede's values have certain consequences for the institutional arrangements societies develop. Hofstede's theory therefore justifies our making inferences about cultural values on the basis of observed patterns of institutional behaviour. From a mechanistic point of view, group decision making processes which manifest themselves in institutional actions are presumably determined with some degree of probability by the common norms held by individuals who collectively constitute the relevant organization.

12 Literally, 'communal coexistence'. This principle reaffirms the interconfessional amity between Muslims and Christians which in principle has existed since the inception of the Lebanese state.

13 See Article 17 of the 1990 Lebanese Constitution (translated in Salem, 1991).

14 It should be noted that, in respect of Individualism, Lebanese society is considerably less clannish than other countries in the Middle East (Khalaf, 1987).

15 Official demographic statistics about Lebanon appear to be virtually impossible to obtain (Faour, 1991). Our information in this respect is based upon personal estimates of family sizes in Lebanon.

16 The participation rate of Lebanese males in the workforce in 1975 was 42.1 per cent and that of Lebanese females was 9.6 per cent. This compares to male and female rates of 55.6 per cent and 29.3 per cent respecively in France for the same year (International Labour Office, 1978). No official statistics are available after 1975 for Lebanon on this matter.

17 Both Japan ('Daifuku-cho') and the Islamic word, *before Paciolo*, independently developed bookkeeping systems of this sort according to Hayashi (1989, p. 8).

18 In particular, in the conceptual framework literature the distinction between representational faithfulness and relevance (Sterling, 1987) is similar to that between measurement and disclosure, as is the distinction between the political and technical dimensions of accounting, in the standard setting literature (Solomons, 1983). There also appears to be a growing awareness of the significance of this distinction in the recent literature on cultural values (e.g., Fechner and Kilgore, 1993) and on harmonization (e.g., van der Tas, 1988).

19 See Hines (1988) for an unusual discussion of the doctrine of realism as applied to accountancy. Details of the argument that issues of measurement must logically be considered prior to issues of disclosure can be found in Willett (1987, 1991).

20 In the sense that the greater the extent of the accounting entity (e.g., a group entity) and the wider the focus of the accounts in terms of users, the greater is the potential amount of information disclosed.

References

AlHashim, D., and J. Arpan, *International Dimension of Accounting*, 3rd edn, PWS-Kent Publishing Co., 1992.

American Institute of Certified Public Accountants, *Professional Accounting in Twenty-Five Countries*, AICPA, 1964.

——, *Professional Accounting in Thirty Countries*, AICPA, 1975.

Badrud-Din, A. A., *The Bank of Lebanon: Central Banking in a Financial Centre and Entrepot*, Frances Pinter, 1984.

Barakat, H., *Days of Dust*, The Mediana University Press International, 1974.

Barrett, M. E., 'Financial Reporting Practices: Disclosure and Comprehensiveness in an International Setting', *Journal of Accounting Research*, Spring 1980.

Baydoun, N., and R. Gray, 'Financial Accounting and Reporting in The Lebanon: An Exploratory Study of Accounting in Hyperinflationary Conditions', *Research in Third World Accounting*, Vol. 1, 1990.

Briston, R. J., 'The Evolution of Accounting in Developing Countries', *International Journal of Accounting Education and Research*, Fall 1978.

——, 'Accounting in Developing Countries: Indonesia and the Solomon Islands as Case Studies for Regional Cooperation', *Research in Third World Accounting*, Vol. 1, 1990.

Briston, R. J., and F. S. Liang, 'The Evolution of Corporate Reporting in Singapore', *Research in Third World Accounting*, Vol. 1, 1990.

Briston, R. J., and R. S. O. Wallace, 'Accounting Education and Corporate Disclosure Regulations in Tanzania', *Research in Third World Accounting*, Vol. 1, 1990.

Bucheiry, M., *Beirut's Role in the Political Economy of the French Mandate: 1919–39*, Centre for Lebanese Studies, Oxford, 1991.

Burchell, S., C. Clubb, A. Hopwood, J. Hughes and J. Nahapiet, 'The Roles of Accounting in Organizations and Society', *Accounting, Organization and Society*, Vol. 5, No. 1, 1980.

Chambers, R. J., *Accounting, Evaluation and Economic Behavior*, Prentice-Hall, 1966.

Engleman, K., 'Accounting Problems in Developing Countries', *Journal of Accountancy*, January 1962. *Europa World Yearbook*, Vol. 1, Europa Publication, 1992.

Faour, M., 'The Demography of Lebanon: A Reappraisal', *Middle Eastern Studies*, October 1991.

Fawaz, T. L., *Merchants and Migrants in Nineteenth-Century Beirut*, Harvard University Press, 1983.

——, *State and Society in Lebanon*, The Centre for Lebanese Studies and Tufts University, 1991.

Fechner, H. E., and A. Kilgore, 'The Influence of Cultural Factors on Accounting Practice', *The International Journal of Accounting Education and Research*, Vol. 29, No. 3, 1994.

Financial Accounting Standards Board, SFAC 1, *Objectives of Financial Reporting by Business Enterprises*, FASB, 1978.

——, Statement of Financial Accounting Concepts No. 3, *Qualitative Characteristics of Accounting Information*, FASB, 1980.

Gambling, T., and R. A. A. Abdel-Karim, *Business and Accounting Ethics in Islam*, Mansell, 1991.

Gerhardy, P. G., *An Evaluation of the Role of Culture in the Development of Accounting Principles in West Germany*, Accounting and Finance Research Paper 90/2, The Flinders University of South Australia, 1990.

Goodrich, P. S., 'A Typology of International Accounting Principles and Policies', *British Accounting Review*, Spring 1982.

Gordon, C. D., *The Republic of Lebanon: Nation in Jeopardy*, Westview Press, 1983.

Gray, R., D. Owen and K. Maunders, 'Corporate Social Reporting: Emerging Trends in Accountability and the Social Contract', *Accounting Auditing and Accountability*, Vol. 1, No. 1, 1988.

Gray, S. J., 'The Impact of International Accounting Differences from a Security Analysis Perspective: Some European Evidence', *Journal of Accounting Research*, Spring 1980.

——, 'Towards a Theory of Cultural Influence on the Development of Accounting Systems Internationally', *Abacus*, March 1988.

Hamid, S. R., R. Craig and F. L. Clarke, 'Religion: A Confounding Cultural Element in the International Harmonization of Accounting?', *Abacus*, September 1993.

Hayashi, T., *On Islamic Accounting: Its Future Impact on Western Accounting*, The Institute of Middle Eastern Studies, The International University of Japan, Working papers series, No. 18, 1989.

Heatly, R., *Poverty and Power*, Zed Press, 1979.

Hines, D. R., 'Financial Accounting: In Communicating Reality, We Construct Reality', *Accounting, Organization and Society*, No. 3, 1988.

Hodgson, A., J. Okunev and R. J. Willett, 'Accounting for Intangibles: A Theoretical Perspective', *Accounting and Business Research*, Spring 1993.

Hofstede, G., *Culture's Consequences: International Differences in Work-Related Values*, Sage Publications, 1980.

——, 'The Cultural Context of Accounting', in B. E. Cushing (ed.), *Accounting and Culture*, American Accounting Association, 1987.

——, *Cultures and Organisations: Software of the Mind*, McGraw-Hill, 1991.

Holzer, H. P. (ed.), *International Accounting*, Harper and Row, 1984.

Hopwood, A., 'Accounting and Human Behavior', *Accountancy Age Books*, Haymarket Publishing Limited, 1974.

Inkeles, A., and D. J. Levinson, 'National Character: The Study of Modal Personality and Sociocultural Systems', in G. Lindsey and E. Aronson (eds), *Handbook of Social Psychology*, 2nd edn, Vol. 4, Addison-Wesley, 1969.

International Labour Office, *Yearbook of labour statistics*, ILO, 1978.

Khalaf, S., *Lebanon's Predicament*, Columbia University Press, 1987.

Kuvian, G. T., *Encyclopedia of the Third World*, Vol. 2, Mansell, 1982.

Labaki, B., 'The Challenge of Socioeconomic Reconstruction', in Fawaz, L. (ed.), *State and Society in Lebanon*, The Centre for Lebanese Studies and Tufts University, 1991.

Mahfouz, N., *Palace Walk*, W. M. Hutchins and O. E. Kenny (trans.), Doubleday, 1989.

Makdisi, S., *Financial Policy and Economic Growth: The Lebanese Experience*, Columbia University Press, 1977.

Mathews, M. R. and M. H. B. Perera, *Accounting Theory and Development*, 2nd edn, Nelson, 1993.

McDowall, D., *Lebanon: A Conflict of Minorities*, The Minority Rights Group, London, Report No. 61, 1986.

Meyer, J. W., 'Social Environments and Organizational Accounting', *Accounting, Organizations and Society*, Vol. 11, No. 4/5, 1986.

Middle East and North Africa Yearbook, Europa Publication, 1992.

Most, K. S., 'Accounting in France', in H. P. Holzer (ed.), *International Accounting*, Harper and Row, 1984.

Nair, R. D., and W. G. Frank, 'The Impact of Disclosure Measurement Practices on International Accounting Classifications', *Accounting Review*, July 1980.

Nobes, C., 'A Judgemental International Classification of Financial Reporting Practices', *Journal of Business, Finance and Accounting*, Spring 1983.

——, *Interpreting European Financial Statements: Towards 1992*, Butterworth, 1989.

Nobes, C., and R. Parker, *Comparative International Accounting*, Prentice-Hall, 1991.

Osmanczyk, E. J., *The Encyclopedia of the United Nations and International Agreements*, Taylor and Francis, 1985.

Parry, M., and R. Grove, 'Does Training More Accountants Raise the Standards of Accounting in Third World Countries? A study of Bangladesh', *Research in Third World Accounting*, Vol. 1, 1990.

Parsons, T., and E. A. Shils, *Toward a General Theory of Action*, Harvard University Press, 1951.

Perera, H., 'Towards a Framework to Analyze the Impact of Culture on Accounting', *International Journal of Accounting*, Vol. 24, 1989a.

——, 'Accounting in Developing Countries: A Case for Localised Uniformity', *British Accounting Review*, June 1989b.

Pound, S. O., *Arabic and Persian Poems*, The National Poetry Foundation, University of Maine at Orono, 1986.

Pratt, J., and G. Behr, 'Environmental Factors, Transaction Costs, and External Reporting: A Cross-National Comparison', *International Journal of Accounting Education and Research*, Spring 1987.

Radebaugh, L. H., and S. J. Gray, *International Accounting and Multinational Enterprises*, Wiley, 1993.

Saidi, N., *Economic Consequences of the War in Lebanon*, Centre for Lebanese Studies, Oxford, 1986.

Salem, P., 'The New Constitution of Lebanon and the Taif Agreement', *The Beirut Review*, Spring 1991.

Samuels, J. M., and J. C. Oliga, 'Accounting Standards in Developing Countries', *International Journal of Accounting Education and Research*, Fall 1982.

Schreuder, H., 'Accounting Research, Practice and Culture: A European Perspective', in B. E. Cushing (ed.), *Accounting and Culture*, American Accounting Association, 1987.

Scott, G. M., *Accounting and Developing Nations*, University of Washington Graduate School of Business Administration, 1970.

Seidler, L. J., 'Nationalism and the International Transfer of Accounting Skills', *International Journal of Accounting Education and Research*, Fall 1969.

Soffer, A., 'Lebanon — Where Demography is the Core of Politics and Life', *Middle Eastern Studies*, April 1986.

Solomons, D., 'The Political Implication of Accounting and Accounting Standard Setting', *Accounting and Business Research*, Spring 1983.

Sterling, R. R., *An Essay on Recognition*, Accounting and Finance Foundation within the University of Sydney, 1987.

Tay, J. S. W., and R. H. Parker, 'Measuring International Harmonization and Standardisation', *Abacus*, March 1990.

Torbey, J., *Income Taxation in Lebanon* (in Arabic), Dar-Annahar, 1986.

Van der Tas, L. G., 'Measuring Harmonization of Financial Reporting Practice', *Accounting and Business Research* Vol. 18, No. 70, 1988.

Wallace, R. S. O., 'Accounting in Developing Countries', *Research in Third World Accounting*, Vol. 1, 1990.

Willett, R. J., 'An Axiomatic Theory of Accounting Measurement', *Accounting and Business Research*, Spring 1987.

——, 'The Measurement Theoretic and Statistical Foundations of the Transactions Theory of Accounting Numbers', *Proceedings of AAANZ*, 1991.

World Bank, *World Development Report*, International Bank for Reconstruction and Development, 1991.

Part 3

CLASSIFICATION

12

SOME VARIATIONS IN ACCOUNTING PRACTICE IN ENGLAND, FRANCE, GERMANY AND THE UNITED STATES

Henry Rand Hatfield

Source: *Journal of Accounting Research* (Autumn 1966): 169–82.

Henry Rand Hatfield (1866–1945) was a pioneer in collegiate accounting education in the United States. He received a Ph.D. in political economy and political science in 1897 from the University of Chicago, and in 1898 joined the Chicago faculty. He became the first dean of the College of Commerce and Administration at the University of Chicago in 1902 and offered an accounting course in 1901–02 and 1902–03, based in part on a three-month tour of Colleges of Commerce in France and Germany in 1899–1900, where, at the University of Leipzig, he met and became influenced by Johann Friedrich Schär. In 1904, he moved to the University of California, beginning a long tenure in the College of Commerce as associate professor, then, professor of accounting.

In 1911, the American Association of Public Accountants (predecessor of the American Institute of Certified Public Accountants) held its annual convention in San Francisco, and Hatfield was asked to present a paper. Unlike most of his contemporaries, Hatfield eschewed the dogmatic approach in favor of critical surveys of what legal and accounting authorities had written. He chose as his topic the accounting practices in England, France, Germany, and the United States, evidently believing that the collective wisdom of practitioners and writers in these countries might profitably be used as authoritative guidance in the United States. In 1911, the accounting literature in this country was small indeed.

Hatfield discovered Simon's treatise during his European trip in 1899–1900, and it is probable that he found the identically titled work by Rehm shortly after it was published, in 1903. Since he was unable to be present for the A.A.P.A. meeting, the paper was read by another. It has never been published

307

or referred to in the accounting literature, and was recently found, together with several other unpublished papers, in Hatfield's files at the University of California, Berkeley. In point of chronology, the paper is Hatfield's first article-length manuscript on accounting which survives. It followed publication of his *Modern Accounting* by two years, antedated "An Historical Defense of Bookkeeping" by thirteen, and was one of Hatfield's few literary efforts during the fifteen-year period between these two better-known works. In the context of the currently expanding interest in international accounting, the paper represents a rare source of insight into comparative accounting practices 55 years ago. It is reproduced with permission from the Hatfield Papers, Schools of Business Administration, University of California, Berkeley.—STEPHEN A. ZEFF

To make such a comparison as is called for by the title of this paper implies first of all, exact knowledge as to what is the accounting practice of any particular country. But who can with confidence describe even the practice of American railways in regard to showing sinking fund transaction. One road differs from another in this respect and who can say which represents the best, or even the typical American practice? Or, in American practice, what is meant by the term "Reserve Fund," or what rate of depreciation is the customary one? So vague is accounting terminology, so unsettled is accounting practice, so unhampered are the idiosyncracies of accountants that it would take a high degree of assurance for one to assert that he knew the rules of accounting practice, even in his own country.

The same difficulty is found in studying the methods in vogue in foreign countries. In some of them there is a little less self-initiative, in some respects there may be a greater uniformity, but it is indeed difficult to determine whether some peculiar form met in foreign accounts is typical of differences between foreign and American methods, or whether it represents merely such a particular variation as might as well be found by comparing different American accounts.

Furthermore it is to be recognized that foreign and American accounting methods are, at heart, one. Accounting in all the modern world has developed from the same simple beginnings. Paciolo's *Tractatus*, either in the original or in translations or adaptations, spread through all Europe, and everywhere is the basis upon which modern accounting rests. One speaks in accounting literature of Italian, of American, of German bookkeeping. But Italian bookkeeping is not at all limited to Italy, American bookkeeping, at least as the term is used abroad, did not even originate in America, and German bookkeeping differs only in unessential details from the other systems.

308

Recognizing then fully the difficulty, or even the impossibility, of adequately discussing the subject, it may still be possible to bring forward a few points in which differences are found and to compare some variations in the accounting methods prevalent in the several countries.

The first point on which one can with some confidence speak, is that in European countries, there has, at least to the present time, been a more definite effort made to regulate accounting practice by direct legislation. On this point the United States, in very recent years, has made some marked progress, of which the most noteworthy step has been the minute regulations prescribed by the Interstate Commerce Commission. But in general, accounting has been neglected, perhaps not altogether to its injury, by legislation. But in Europe, especially on the continent, bookkeeping methods, like so many other industrial activities, have been distinctly regulated by the government. Thus, it is almost universally the custom in countries all around the world to prescribe by law that merchants, as well as corporations, must keep accounts. Except in the Spanish-speaking countries, it is not distinctly specified that books must be kept in double entry, but the provision found in German law that the books must be kept according to the principles of *"ordnungsmässige"* bookkeeping, and the law, common to the other European countries, that the accounts must include a balance sheet and a statement of profit and loss, are by some thought to imply, that at least so far as concerns corporations, the keeping of double-entry books is not merely a matter of common practice, but is as well an obligation under the law.

German law provides further that the books of account must be bound with consecutively numbered pages, free from lacunae, erasures and alterations.[1] England makes no such requirement. France[2] and other continental countries, however, have similar requirements so far as relates to consecutive numbering and uninterrupted records. In France, Belgium and Switzerland, but not in Germany, there is provision for having the main books of accounts inspected and viséed by a public official, who certifies that the book is the recognized account book and that it contains such a number of pages. This provision, it is interesting to note, goes back almost unchanged to the very beginning of bookkeeping, the method being fully described in the seventh chapter of Paciolo's treatise.

The provisions relating to the use of bound books, with consecutive and uninterrupted records, and even those providing for the authentification of books of accounts have, perhaps not necessarily, had an impeding effect on the introduction of loose leaf forms in bookkeeping, although even in Europe this modern improvement is growing somewhat in favor.

The next step in the regulation of bookkeeping is the specifications as to the particular books which are to be kept, or the specific accounts which are to be framed. Almost all countries, with the exception of Germany, England and the United States, distinctly provide that there must at least be kept a chronologically arranged book of original entry called a journal or day-book. This may be kept in approved double entry form, but generally that is not specifically required, and it may follow the model of the old *memorial* current in the very beginning of bookkeeping. Of the more than twenty-five countries having such a provision, almost all follow rather slavishly the provision of the French Code, which, indeed, has set the standard for most of the continental regulation of accounting practice. The Code reads in part "Every merchant is bound to keep a day-book (*livre journal*) which shall exhibit, day by day, the debts due to or payable by him, his business transactions, and negotiations, the acceptance or endorsement of bills, and generally all that he receives or pays on any account whatever, and that shall show month by month, the sums used for the expenses of his household; the above being irrespective of other books generally used in business, but which are not obligatory."[3]

This provision, says Stern, on the face requires that every transaction should be entered in a single book. But this insistence on a single book of original entry, honored though it may be by the doctrine first laid down by Paciolo, and confirmed by *Ordonnance of 1673*, from which the Code has borrowed freely, is but seldom observed in actual French practice.[4] The absurdity of attempting to conduct modern books, on the model which served well enough in the primitive conditions of the 15th century, has been formally objected to by French accountants, whose official congress demanded a modification of this article of the Code. But so far the change demanded has not been made.

In addition to the daybook, almost every nation except the United States requires that an annual inventory be prepared. The provisions in this respect are almost identical; an annual balance sheet also is required in some thirty countries, in most of which the requirement applying to individual traders as well as to corporations.

Less uniform are the requirements in reference to the form of the balance sheet, and the conditions of its publication. Legislation has generally contented itself with prescribing a balance sheet, without laying down rules as to the form in which it shall be made out. Indeed, when the question was distinctly raised by the French commission of 1902 it was finally decided that the better policy was merely to demand publicity without prescribing forms. Similar action was taken in Belgium. But a somewhat close approximation to a uniform balance sheet is found in the well-known model located in Table A of the English Company's Act of 1862. While this form has been somewhat followed by accountants, it was never compulsory, and in the revision of 1906 it was dropped from the Table. It is not necessary to dwell upon the peculiar nature of this commonly accepted English form, for the divergence which it shows from the practice of other countries, in placing the liabilities on the left side, has been commented upon, favorably or unfavorably by every writer on accounting. Nor is it necessary to emphasize the peculiarities of another form of balance sheet used in England, the so-called double account balance sheet, applicable to parliamentary companies and familiar in the reports of English railroads. The separation in such balance sheets of the capital assets and liabilities from the other accounts has been much criticized and has led to some perhaps unnecessary inferences as to the treatment of a decline in value of the fixed plant. The double account form is almost unknown outside of England, the only instances of its use in this country which I have noticed, being found in the accounts of the Atchison, Topeka & Santa Fe Railway and in those of the Mexican International Railroad. Except, however, in the implications drawn from the form, and the effect which it may have had, in leading the English accountants to disregard losses of fixed capital, the variation between the double account balance sheet and the conventional form is of very little significance.

In this country the legal provisions in regard to balance sheets are few and generally limited in character. Massachusetts has indeed published a model balance sheet, and specific forms are required of national banks and of railroads. In the latter, as laid down by the Interstate Commerce Commission, there is a greater amount of detail and a more strenuous effort to secure a scientific and intelligible exposé of the status of the company, than is attempted by the legislation, or attained by the ordinary practices of any other country. So much may not be said of the form prescribed for national banks, yet even these compare favorably with the statements published by either the Bank of France or the Bank of England. The former being rather confused in arrangement and the latter woefully deficient in details.

Another rather important variation rests upon the principle of German law that the balance sheet is in large part designed to indicate the amount of profit available for dividend. In England, and probably also in the United States, the balance sheet seems designed rather to assure the interested creditor of the solvency of the concern. This is particularly true in case of banks in this country where neither in the balance sheet nor in any other published statement is there any indication whatever of the earnings of the bank. But the German balance sheet must show not merely the balance of the undivided profits, but by law must, and in practice actually does, exhibit the net earnings of the year; and within the limits of the balance sheet itself is indicated the proposed allocation of profits, so much to reserve, so much as tantième to directors, so much as dividends, and so much carried over to the new account. A balance sheet thus prepared does not exhibit the exact status of affairs after the final adjusting entries have been made, so it is not unusual to offer two balance sheets, one indicating total net profits with an indication of their proposed allocation, the other showing the condition of the accounts after such a distribution shall have been made.

Of greater moment in the comparison of usage in the different countries is the fact that in orderliness and clearness of statement the balance sheets prepared in England and on the continent do not rank as highly as those prepared by the leading corporations in this country. In some respects foreign balance sheets may be more accurate, and they may excel in some minor detail mentioned below, but so far as the grouping of items, the arrangement so as to make an easy comparison of related categories, e.g., the familiar juxtaposition of Current Assets and Current Liabilities, American balance sheets are superior to those of England, France or Germany.

Further difference in legal regulation is found in regard to the publication of the balance sheets of corporations. In both Germany and France the balance sheet must be presented to the stockholders at their annual meeting, in England limited companies must file an annual balance sheet with the registrar. While not absolutely required to send copies to the several shareholders, yet Table A and most of the articles adopted by companies do provide for submitting the balance sheet to the annual meeting, and as well for sending them to the registered members. Belgium, though in general copying closely the French Code, goes further in requiring that the annual balance sheet shall not merely be accessible before the annual meeting but shall be sent together with the profit and loss statement to the shareholders and afterwards published. In this country, with rare exceptions, there is no legal requirement for securing publicity of the balance sheet. In part this lack of legal requirement is remedied by the rules of the New York Stock Exchange.

One other general requirement in Germany and France is in contrast to the practice in England and the United States. In the former countries (as is indeed true of most continental countries) the directors must furnish to the shareholders a profit and loss account as well as the balance sheet. It is true that in this country the railroads are compelled to publish an income and profit and loss account, and both here and in England many companies, not required by law, do publish similar statements. But it is evident that there is no general requirement of American companies to make public a profit and loss account. This is most strikingly brought into contrast in the statements published by banks. Detailed though they are, there is never any indication even of the net profits of the year. Sometimes this may be estimated by comparing the balance of surplus and undivided profits of two years and adding the dividends paid in the meantime. But this is indirect, unsatisfactory, and often misleading. In marked contrast are the statements of German banks. These regularly exhibit not merely the balance of the income but also the separate items entering into it, showing as credits, for instance exchange account, interest, commissions on securities, commission on coupons, rental of building; and on the debit side, general expenses, depreciation on inventory, depreciation on accounts current, etc. The leading English banks less satisfactorily exhibit the gross profits and the expenses of the business, or, in other cases merely the net profits, together with unusual charges, and the allocation of the profits, but without indicating the various sources from which the several items of gain have accrued. One may search in vain for information regarding American banks similar to that furnished in Europe. This seems curious when one reflects on the details furnished by American railroads. Doubtless it would seem undesirable to the bankers of this country to furnish such information, on the ground that it might excite competition. Yet there seems no logical reason why the information regarding the operation of banks should not be as minute as that published by the railroads. The banks, perhaps even more than the railroads, perform a public function, for the issuing of currency is historically an attribute of sovereignty, while from time immemorial furnishing transportation has been a private industry. In other respects the regulation of banks, the restriction on their business, the supervision of their activities, has been more marked than is the case with railways. But in no instance, not even during the life of either of the great monopolistic Banks of the United States, has there been any publication of the profits earned by the banks.

We have considered the divergent attitude of the laws in the leading nations regarding accounting forms and procedure. While certain differences have been noted, it should be borne in mind that custom varies less than the laws. Thus while one country may require double entry bookkeeping and another have no such requirement, yet in practice both will alike use that system of accounting. But in some cases a substantive difference in practice exists. Probably the most striking of these differences in actual practice are those already alluded to, *viz.*, in the continental countries there is a more widespread publication of the details of profit and loss, and in America there is considerable superiority in orderly arrangement of the fundamental statement, the balance sheet.

Turning now from the question of form to the more vital point of substance some differences in accounting practice may be noticed, most of which depend on legal enactment, but some of which have arisen merely from business custom.

The vital question in all accounting is the value which is to be placed on existing assets. That being determined, almost every other question is decided, although, in some cases, there may arise a question as to whether an excess of assets is available for distribution as dividends. Yet in both English and American law there has been almost no attention given to the question of valuation. England does, it is true, require in the Companies Acts that the accounts shall be "full and fair" or "a true and correct" view of the status of the company, and in the United States there is, as well, obligation that accounts rendered shall be correct. But as to what is correct, as to what principles should be observed in estimating values, our statutes are generally silent, and the dicta of the courts have been conflicting, confusing, and often irrational. In this respect Germany excels the other countries in definiteness and in comprehensiveness of legislation, some of the laws applying to all corporations, while in other countries, as is particularly true of Switzerland, and to some extent the United States, the rules that are laid down apply only to a particular class of corporations, the railroads. In Germany the general rule is that all assets and debts are to be set down at the value which they possess at the time of the balance sheet. This is to be interpreted, however, in the light of the following provisions: 1. Securities and commodities which have a publicly quoted price are to be listed at that price when it is below the cost price. But when the quoted price exceeds the cost price the latter is to prevail. 2. Other articles are not to be valued above their cost price. 3. Fixed assets may be valued at cost irrespective of change in market price, regard, however, being had to depreciation. 4. Costs of organization and administration are not to be listed as assets.[5] No other country has laws of general application attempting to regulate these matters.

Some of the more important kinds of assets may be briefly considered in respect to actual practice. All accountants incline to the view that fixed assets are to be carried at an unchanged price, save as influenced by depreciation in their use value.

In all countries custom has sanctioned the carrying of plant purchased by securities at the par value of the securities thus issued. Abuse in this matter has probably been greater in the United States than in other countries, although recent events in England seem to furnish a counterpart for almost any abuse on this side of the ocean. But while Germany has been more conservative in this respect, as is clearly indicated by the quoted price of industrial securities, many of which command a premium, yet even in that country it is apparently not merely customary, but even obligatory to list such purchases at the par value of the securities issued, this being true even when the stock is clearly issued at a discount.[6] On the other hand there is a growing tendency in this country to prevent an overvaluation of plant in this fashion, as is clearly indicated in the restrictive regulations of the various public service commissions and of the Interstate Commerce Commission. France, however, does not always permit the construction account of a railroad to show all of the actual cost, for if that exceeds the amount authorized by the state, the excess, although an actual capital expenditure, must appear as a charge against revenue.[7] A curious custom has, however, arisen in Germany. Where it is estimated that a plant will cost a given sum and securities are issued to that amount, any saving in cost of construction is treated not as diminishing the value of the plant, but as creating a surplus. This absurdity which would be universally condemned in this country, was not only customary in earlier days, but even received the sanction of the Prussian ministry.[8] A somewhat similar variation is found in cases where German corporations have provided by capital issues not only for the cost of construction of the plant but for a sum to be used as actual working capital. By a stupid misuse of terms in the Code[9] it has been considered necessary to show such a sum as a reserve on the credit side of the balance sheet necessitating either listing the plant at the full amount of the capital stock, only part of which was invested therein, or inserting some purely fictitious and arbitrary asset. Somewhat reversed is the position regarding contributions made to the company by promoters or other interested persons. In this country these are generally credited as if constituting a surplus, perhaps under the misleading title of "working capital." But while this too has been done in many cases in Germany, it is held to be counter to the law, and the Swiss law even explicitly states that "the cost of construction and equipment covered by subventions *à fonds perdu* may not be charged to construction account." This attitude, while perhaps convenient as a rule affecting the price at which a railroad is to be taken over by the state, is not in essence a correct method of valuing the plant, and is, furthermore, contrary to both practice and legal interpretation in England and America.

German custom seems to be steadfastly opposed to marking up the value of the fixed assets, even as an offset to a previous excessive depreciation. Simon states that, in many thousand balance sheets examined by him, he finds no case where fixed assets have been thus marked up. But such an action is justified in England, and is not unknown in American practice, as for instance by the Excelsior Water and Mining Company, in which instance the action was subsequently sanctioned by the Supreme Court of California.

Closely allied to the problem of valuing assets is that of depreciation. On this matter both the law and the practice of the continental countries is in advance of England. Still more do they transcend American accounting practice, for until the recent rulings of the Interstate Commerce Commission, which are still fragmentary and inconsistent, there was almost no clear expression, in statute book or court decision, of the necessity of depreciation. Moreover, practice as shown in corporation accounts was as unsatisfactory as the laws. The provisions of the German Code, already cited, definitely prescribe depreciation, and an examination of published balance sheets shows that depreciation is reckoned by almost every German company, including banks as well as industrial corporations. In contrast with the rules of the Interstate Commerce Commission, the Prussian railways require provision for renewal, not only of all equipment, but also for ties and rails. In this country, depreciation is likely to be dependent on large profits, and to be omitted in lean years. In Germany even when there is a net loss, the companies almost invariably show a depreciation charge.[10] But even in Germany there is apt to be greater liberality when profits are high; and such a procedure in Switzerland is even sanctioned by law.

In England, depreciation is less consistent. Some, as Sakolski, have claimed that the "double account balance sheet does not permit the writing-off of depreciation and abandoned assets acquired through capital expenditure."[11]

In practice it is doubtless true that the loss of capital assets has generally been ignored in English balance sheets. But it should be noted that even in the decision given in the case which has been most relied on as justifying the disregard of capital losses, Justice Lindley was careful to state: "It is obvious that capital lost must not appear in the accounts as still existing intact; the accounts must show the truth and not be misleading or fraudulent."[12] The double account form of balance sheet certainly encourages the neglect of depreciation; that it either practically or legally compels such neglect is surely to be questioned.

The treatment of plant discarded because of obsolescence resembles depreciation. In the United States, companies such as street railways and water companies have frequently failed to take any recognition of the outgrown pipes or of the antiquated equipment discarded for newer models. Thus the Census Bureau openly criticizes the failure to charge off the capital lost by the replacement of horse and cable, by electric roads. This criticism doubtless conforms to advanced professional opinion, but corporation practice has lagged somewhat behind. But in France abandoned property of railways is generally charged off.[13] In Germany, however, the custom is similar to that in this country, the abandoned portions, as well as the new, being included in the assets. A distinction, however, is drawn between property displaced by innovations, or improvements, and that destroyed by use or accident. Thus an old station, though torn down to give place to a new one, the temporary structure used during the alterations, and the new station are, with Simon's approval,[14] all included in the assets of a German railroad. But a building which accidentally fell down must be charged off. Surely this furnishes a proper stimulus to provide fit accommodations without waiting until the old structure actually falls on the patrons' heads; and might with some reason be recommended to certain American railroads. In England, custom and authority are divided on the proper treatment of superseded plant,[15] but Swiss law requires writing-off all abandoned plant.[16]

The listing of securities whose market price has declined, at the original cost less only the proper amortization, is in this country generally discountenanced, especially so in the case of banks and insurance companies. In Germany the question is somewhat uncertain, for while law prescribes that listed securities be taken at the quoted price when that is below cost, it also provides that assets for permanent holding may be valued at cost irrespective of market price. Accordingly, the bank for Oriental Railways holds its railroad securities at cost despite shrinkage, agreeing therein with the English decision in the case of the Commercial and General Trust. But despite this decision English banks at the present time quite generally take account of the present low price of British consols. Thus at the last annual meeting of the Capital and Counties Bank, $500,000 was taken from the reserve and $200,000 from the year's profit in order to mark the consols down to 80, the directors calling attention to the fact that in 1910, thirty-two of the leading banks had written-off more than $10,000,000 to cover the decline in the market value of securities held by them. But French companies go far in considering securities as permanent rather than circulating assets, government securities being generally maintained at cost despite subsequent decline in market price.[17]

Organization expenses are in Germany specifically excluded from the list of assets. As a consequence the promoter generally pays such out of his own pocket, taking the stock at par, and then places the stock with the ultimate holders at a premium sufficient to reimburse his outlay. But the law, inconsistently, does not prohibit the inclusion of organization expenses as part of the cost of construction, drawing the line only at showing them openly in the balance sheet. A differentiation is further made between expenses of establishing the company and those of organizing the plant. France allows organization expenses among the assets but requires a rapid amortization. But in practice French companies often include in organization expenses items which do not properly belong there.[18] In England and the United States the inclusion of organization expenses in the cost of plant is common, with less uniformity in regard to writing-off such items.

Interest paid during the period of construction somewhat resembles the costs of organization. It is practically universal to allow such payments to be counted among the costs of construction and hence to appear among the permanent assets, and even in this country such treatment has been specifically allowed by the Interstate Commerce Commission. But in both England and Germany a further step is taken which is not permitted in France or in the United States. While dividends are not ordinarily permissible where there are no profits, and the contract to pay a fixed dividend is not binding, yet in both English and German law[19] there is provision made allowing, in certain circumstances, interest in lieu of dividends, to be paid to shareholders during the period of construction. Such payments, as is interest on bonds, are added to the cost of construction. The practice of England and Germany is logically consistent, for it admits that the real cost of a completed plant includes not merely the immediate payments for construction, but, as well, reimbursement for capital necessarily idle during a long period of time. If the purpose of accounting is to determine a real cost upon which a fair return is to be allowed by rate regulation, there can surely be no ground for regarding the accidental circumstance under which the capital is secured. The objection to the logical method is a precautionary one. Its purpose is to oppose the dangerous tendency to show an unrealized gain by the simple process of marking-up assets.

Goodwill is probably more overvalued in this country than abroad, and its writing-off is relatively infrequent. In Germany, however, it is not uncommon for prosperous industrial companies to write-off their goodwill in periods running from three to fifteen years. English companies, like

American, are less inclined to write-off goodwill, and in this are supported by the courts and by many accounting authorities.

England took the advanced step in 1889, in the now famous decision in the Lee case, that exploitation of wasting assets, such as a mine, need not be regarded in determining profits available for dividends. In the United States the same view has been authoritatively accepted, at least by the courts, and France goes even further in not permitting the writing-off of such assets.[20] But Germany clings to the older view and requires that as exploitation proceeds, the exhaustion be shown, and only the net profits may legally be divided.

Discount on securities issued in England, France and Germany is customarily placed elsewhere than in profit and loss. In the accounts of German railways it either appears as a permanent asset not being amortized, or is added to the construction account. German industrials sometimes treat discount as a permanent asset, sometimes write it off in arbitrary instalments, with a more recent tendency to charge off at once against surplus. In this country it is recognized that a regular amortization is most legitimate, but in many instances it is more rigorously treated.

Premium on stock is variously treated. In England it is perfectly legal to use such premium to pay dividends, and this is occasionally done. But in Germany corporations may not do so.[21] France agrees with England in regarding premiums as available for dividends. But in all these countries alike, conservative custom looks askance at increasing profits by including premiums therein.

It is a delicate task to attempt to characterize the accounting systems of the different countries or to make comparisons which might seem invidious. It is, however, obvious, that Germany and France, with greater definiteness, attempt to regulate accounting procedure by statutory provisions, France being more particular in the details of bookkeeping form, Germany being much more definite in the enunciation of certain important accounting principles. On the other hand, England, where, with few exceptions concerning forms for particular enterprises, rules for accounting procedure are not enacted, does require that all company accounts shall be audited, the auditors to be appointed in the interest of the shareholders and to report to the annual meeting.

In this country we have been accustomed to look to England rather than to the continent for accounting inspiration. When one attends a gathering of public accountants, his first thought is that he has been transported to England, his second, after his ears catch the pleasing "burr", that he is north of the Tweed. Our system of certifying public accountants is based on English models, and the examination questions are frequently cribbed from those set in London. The works of Pixley, and Dicksee, of Mathewson, of Garcke and Fells, of Lisle, and Dawson are standard authorities. Yet at one time Pixley himself stated that the standard of bookkeeping among commercial people is far higher on the continent of Europe than in the United Kingdom.[22]

Continental bookkeeping is more methodical, more cumbrous, more tenacious of inherited forms than British, and much more so than American. Time must indeed hang heavy on the hands of the continental bookkeeper, if one is to judge by the elaborateness of entry, the duplication of records, the time-consuming methods of closing books.

The more advanced work in accounting in Germany and France, if one is to judge at all by published treatises, has generally been done by jurists, as for instance Rehm and Simon in Germany, Rousseau and Bastide in France, and enters into minute discussion of the verbal niceties of the law. But in England the best work has been done by chartered accountants, and bears particularly on the work and the responsibilities of the auditor. In England, moreover, cost accounting appeared earlier and has been more scientific than on the continent.

And as to America? Here is to be found accounting almost unregulated either by statutes or by courts. No authority recognized, almost every abuse apparently sanctioned by the practice of prominent if not always reputable concerns. Yet throughout all there is an exhibition of American adaptability and inventiveness. So successful have American accountants been in devising forms suited to the desired ends that on the continent any bookkeeping device recognized as having peculiar merit and originality is, irrespective of its actual origin, apt to be called "American" bookkeeping.[23] Particularly advanced has been the development, in the United States, of cost accounting, and this may properly be spoken of as the great characteristic contribution which the present generation has made to the science of accounting. As on the continent one looks to jurists, and in England to chartered accountants, in this country it is perhaps to engineers that one looks for the greatest stimulus and inspiration in accounting progress; for in large part the development of cost accounting is due to the initiative of engineers, although the public accountant has greatly contributed to its development.

In education for accountants the United States has its peculiar field. Here has preeminently flourished the business college. Once the object of deserved ridicule because of crudeness and superficiality, it has spread a knowledge of bookkeeping throughout the country, and, while doing this, has raised its own standard, almost without assistance from professional organizations or higher educational institutions. More recently have appeared colleges of commerce and technical schools for training the public accountant. Founded though these are on European models, and in some instances, perhaps, at first harmed by too slavish an imitation, they are, I believe, superior in their particular field to their foreign prototypes. Under their influence there is appearing a new literature of accounting, and the dreary and apparently interminable succession of bookkeeping texts, for long all that appeared in this country, has been broken by the appearance of such scientific treatises as those of Sprague and of Cole.

The new activity in regard to the examination and certification of public accountants is a new powerful force in the development of accounting methods, as is the work of the American Association and of its subordinate state organization. And finally the recent action of the Interstate Commerce Commission, and of the various Public Utility Commissions, and the necessity of more exact accounting as a basis for income and corporation taxes, and for regulation of railroad rates and of monopoly charges, give earnest that America will soon, if it does not already, hold chief place as the exponent of exact and scientific methods of accounting.

Acknowledgements

This paper was prepared for presentation before the annual meeting of the American Association of Public Accountants, at San Francisco, on September 20, 1911. The author having been absent on leave at the time, the paper was read by George R. Webster, of the California State Society of Certified Public Accountants. As far as is known, it has never been published or circulated generally. The original manuscript has been slightly edited, to correct mispellings, to improve punctuation, to implement the author's own pencilled alterations (where intelligible), and to bring older spellings into agreement with current practice.

Notes

1 *D. H. G. B.* § 43.
2 *Code de Commerce*, Article 10.
3 Article 8.
4 R. Stern, *Buchhaltungs Lexikon* (1904), 275.
5 *D. H. G. B.*, Article 40.
6 H. V. Simon, *Die Bilanzen der Aktiengesellschaften* (1899), 376; H. Rehm, *Die Bilanzen der Aktiengesellschaften* (1903), 706.
7 Sakolski, in *Quarterly Journal of Economics*, XXIV, 493.
8 Simon, *op. cit.*, 121, 37.
9 *D. H. G. B.*, 261, 5.
10 See annual statements published in Neumann's, *Tabellen.*
11 *Quarterly Journal of Economics*, XXIV, 481.
12 L. R. [1894] 2 Ch. 267.
13 Sakolski, *op. cit.*, p. 494.
14 *Die Bilanzen der Aktiengesellschaften*, 372.
15 *Cf.* the interesting decision in *Cox v. Edinburgh and District Tramways Co. Lim.*, 6 S. L. T. 63.
16 Law 27 Mar. 1896 Art 6.

17 Simon, *op. cit.*, 332.
18 *Bulletin de l'Institut International de Statistique*, XIV, 2, p. 173.
19 *Companies* (*Consolidation*) *Act*, 1908, Sec. 91; *D. H. G. B.*, 215.
20 Simon, *op. cit.*, 381.
21 *D. H. G. B.*, 262.2.
22 *Accountant*, XVI, 135.
23 C. P. Kheil, *Ueber amerikanische Buchhaltung*.

13

ACCOUNTING PRINCIPLES GENERALLY ACCEPTED IN THE UNITED STATES VERSUS THOSE GENERALLY ACCEPTED ELSEWHERE

G. G. Mueller

Source: *International Journal of Accounting* 3(1) (1968): 91–103.

Substantial evidence exists to support the claim that material differences characterize generally-accepted accounting principles as applied in various countries.[1] While these differences are significant for a number of individual concepts and practices, they should not obscure the equally important observation that there are also a great many similarities between the generally-accepted accounting principles of different countries. The differences, however, are the source of frequent and substantive problems in accounting practice.

With a steadily increasing volume of international business and investments, national differences in accounting principles have a growing impact. From a practical point of view, these national differences cause difficulties in at least these areas:

1. Reporting for international subsidiaries whose financial statements are to be consolidated or combined with United States parent-company statements.
2. Reporting for international subsidiaries which lie beyond the consolidation or combination requirements — separate reports being required by the United States parent company.
3. Reporting for independent companies located in countries other than the United States where the statements are for local use and a standard United States form of opinion is to be furnished.

4. Reporting for independent companies in countries outside the United States where the statements and the opinions are likely to be read and used in the United States, *e.g.*, for SEC filings, use by bankers, and possible acquisitions or general publication in English to stockholders residing in the United States.

This paper has as its main purpose the empirical evaluation of the complexities of varying accounting principles among different countries. While it is recognized that conceptual considerations are only one aspect of the over-all problem, a better perspective should be possible by limiting the focus of the discussion.

Economic and business environments differ among various countries

Experience and observation tell us that the business environment normally varies from one country to the next. Indeed, some parts of an overall business environment may well differ between individual regions of a single country. On the other hand, there are instances where two or more countries have essentially the same environmental conditions. This reduces to the proposition that the dimensions of a business environment are primarily economic in nature whereas borders of a country are drawn because of political factors. Thus, political boundaries are not necessarily the only or the best lines of distinction for differing business environments.

What separates one business environment from another? Primarily, there are four marks of separation:

1. States of economic development — A highly developed economy provides an environment different from an undeveloped economy. In an African country, workers at a plant had to walk three hours twice each day to get to and from work. An AID program provided them with bicycles, after which they quit work. Possession of a bicycle was the sole motive for their accepting employment in the first place.
2. Stages of business complexity — Business needs as well as business output are functions of business complexity. An example of this is that West Germany in a recent year imported approximately DM 600 million (net) of industrial know-how in the form of Research and Development services outside Germany.
3. Shades of political persuasion — Political tendencies clearly affect business environments. Among the better known international examples are the expropriations of private property by central governments in South America and the Near and Far East. Forms of social legislation also affect business environments directly.

4. Reliance on some particular system of law — Differences between common law and code law are widely known. There are other differences as well. Detailed companies legislation may inhibit or protect business, as the case may be. The United States has rather stringent unfair trade and antitrust laws. The legal systems of some European countries tolerate market share agreements and cartel arrangements.

Using principally these four elements of differentiation, a quick analysis of business environments existing in different countries can be undertaken. This yields, in the author's opinion, ten distinct sets of business environments. Each differs from all others in at least one important respect. The ten are:

1. United States/Canada/The Netherlands — There is a minimum of commercial or companies legislation in this environment. Industry is highly developed; currencies are relatively stable. A strong orientation to business innovation exists. Many companies with widespread international business interests are headquartered in these countries.
2. British Commonwealth (Excluding Canada) — Comparable companies legislation exists in all Commonwealth countries and administrative procedures and social order reflect strong ties to the mother country. There exists an intertwining of currencies through the so-called "sterling block" arrangement. Business is highly developed but often quite traditional.
3. Germany/Japan — Rapid economic growth has occurred since World War II. Influences stemming from various United States military and administrative operations have caused considerable imitation of many facets of the United States practices, often by grafting United States procedures to various local traditions. The appearance of a new class of professional business managers is observable. Relative political, social, and currency stability exists.
4. Continental Europe (Excluding Germany, The Netherlands and Scandinavia) — Private business lacks significant government support Private property and the profit motive are not necessarily in the center of economic and business orientation. Some national economic planning exists. Political swings from far right to far left, and vice versa, have a long history in this environment. Limited reservoirs of economic resources are available.
5. Scandinavia — Here we have developed economies, but characteristically slow rates of economic and business growth. Governments tend toward social legislation. Companies acts regulate business. Relative stability of population numbers is the rule. Currencies are quite stable. Several business innovations (especially in consumer goods) originated in Scandinavia. Personal characteristics and outlooks are quite similar in all five Scandinavian countries.

6. Israel/Mexico — These are the only two countries with substantial success in fairly rapid economic development. Trends of a shift to more reliance on private enterprise are beginning to appear; however, there is still a significant government presence in business. Political and monetary stability seem to be increasing. Some specialization in business and the professions is taking place. The general population apparently has a strong desire for higher standards of living.

7. South America[2] — Many instances are present of significant economic underdevelopment along with social and educational underdevelopment. The business base is narrow. Agricultural and military interests are strong and often dominate governments. There is considerable reliance on export/import trade. Currencies are generally soft. Populations are increasing heavily.

8. The Developing Nations of the Near and Far East[2] — Modern concepts and ethics of business have predominantly Western origins. These concepts and ethics often clash with the basic oriental cultures. Business in the developing nations of the Orient largely means trade only. There is severe underdevelopment on most measures, coupled with vast population numbers. Political scenes and currencies are most shaky. Major economic advances are probably impossible without substantial assistance from the industrialized countries.

9. Africa (Excluding South Africa)[2] — Most of the African continent is still in the early stages of independent civilization and thus little or no native business environment presently exists. There are significant natural and human resources. Business is likely to assume a major role and responsibility in the development of African nations.

10. Communist Nations — The complete control by central governments removes these countries from any further interest for the purpose of this article.

The above categorization suggests that each country does not necessarily have a separate and distinct environment for its business. It also suggests a manageable way of viewing the existing differences.

One additional general observation on business environments seems worthwhile. In the ten categories listed above, little likelihood of change may be expected in the near future. Of course, details and specifics constantly change in the economic surroundings of business. But the overall philosophy and character that distinguish the ten separate cases seem rather well established, perhaps for as long as a quarter of a century. Therefore, relative stability appears to be one of the properties of different business environments. This means two things: (1) business concepts and practices, including accounting concepts and practices, do not necessarily require rapid changes if they are based on environmental conditions, and

(2) business environments are probably more difficult to change than is sometimes assumed.

Accounting and the economic/business environment

In society, accounting performs a service function. This function is put in jeopardy unless accounting remains, above all, practically useful. Thus, it must respond to the ever-changing needs of society and must reflect the social, political, legal, and economic conditions within which it operates. Its meaningfulness depends upon its ability to mirror these conditions.

The history of accounting and accountants reveals the changes which accounting consistently undergoes. At one time accounting was little more than a recording system for certain banking services and tax collection plans. Later it responded with double-entry bookkeeping procedures to meet the needs of trading ventures. The industrialization and division of labor made possible cost and management-type accounting. The advent of modern corporation stimulated periodic financial reporting and auditing. Most recently, accounting has revealed a greater social awareness by assuming public-interest responsibilities together with the providing of decision information for the larger public-securities markets and management-consulting functions. Accounting is clearly concerned with its environment. Its developmental processes are often compared with that of common law.

From an environmental point of view, various developments in society affect accounting. What else would have caused, for instance, the very serious preoccupation of United States accountants with the needs of United States security analysts? Similar influences are present in recent U.S. efforts concerning lessor and lessee accounting, accounting for business combinations, and the wholesale extension of accounting to international business problems.

But accounting also affects its environment. Many economic resources are allocated to specific business uses on the basis of relevant accounting information. In some measure, national economic policies are formulated on the contents or message of corporate financial statements, and unions often base wage demands on similar information. Rate cases of regulated companies are based primarily on accounting data, and so are most anti-trust cases initiated by governmental agencies. Therefore, accounting both reflects environmental conditions and influences them.

Dudley E. Browne touches on the relationship of accounting to its environment in his review of *Corporate Financial Reporting in a Competitive Economy*, by Herman W. Bevis:

> The financial accounting and reporting of any corporation are subject to a variety of external influences. A larger number of common approaches to accounting and reporting problems can be found in

a given industry or other relatively homogeneous group of corporations than in all of industry, but the internal relationship of its operations and programs with external influences will continue to make each corporation different from every other.

The necessity that corporate financial accounting and reporting be sufficiently unrestricted to respond readily to change should be kept in mind . . . the principle of full and fair disclosure must remain the keystone of successful corporation-stockholder and corporate-society relationships.[3]

The issue of different accounting principles

If we accept that (1) economic and business environments are not the same in all countries, and (2) a close interrelationship exists between economic and business environments and accounting, it follows that a single set of generally-accepted accounting principles cannot be useful and meaningful in all situations. This conclusion admits the possibility of some honest and well-founded differences in accounting principles that find general acceptance in certain national or geographic-area circumstances.

Let us postulate for a moment that accounting principles generally accepted in the United States were enforced in all countries of the free world. This would create an international uniformity which would have some intellectual appeal and would ease many problems in international accounting practice and international financial reporting.

At the same time, such uniformity would lack meaning. It would have to assume that business conditions are the same in all parts of the free world and that the same stage of professional, social, and economic development has been reached everywhere. This is certainly not the case. In fact, enforced international uniformity on the basis of United States accounting principles alone would probably lead to misinformation or inaccurate results in many instances. The same types of calamity which have characterized so many U.S. foreign aid problems in the past would result.

Nevertheless, the issue of international differences in accounting principles does not resolve itself into a complete laissez-faire approach. A strong theoretical argument can be made for consistency of generally-accepted accounting principles between those countries or geographic areas where economic and business environments are substantially similar. In other words, from a theoretical viewpoint, generally-accepted principles in the United States should be the same as those in Canada, but may differ in some respects from those used in South America or Pakistan or India. The business and economic environments of the United States and Canada are very similar; the respective environments of the United States and India are very dissimilar.

Environmental circumstances and appropriate accounting principles

Reference to environmental conditions is subjective. It is not possible, therefore, to develop a conclusive list of those circumstances which permit or require differing accounting principles from one country or area to the next, but some of the circumstances affecting the determination of appropriate accounting principles in an international framework can be identified. Such circumstances include:

1. Relative stability of the currency of account — If a currency is quite stable over time, historical cost accounting is generally indicated Significant currency instability calls for some form of price index adjustment, with the form of adjustments depending largely on the type of indexes available and reliable.

2. Degree of legislative business interference — Tax legislation may require the application of certain accounting principles. This is the case in Sweden where some tax allowances must be entered in the accounts before they can be claimed for tax purposes; this is also the situation for LIFO inventory valuations in the United States.

   Furthermore, varying social security laws may affect accounting principles. Severance pay requirements in several South American countries illustrate this.

3. Nature of business ownership — Widespread public ownership of corporate securities generally requires different financial reporting and disclosure principles from those applicable to predominantly family or bank-owned corporate equities. This is in essence a difference because public and closely held companies do not need to capitalize small stock distributions at market value whereas publicly held companies do.

4. Level of sophistication of business management — Highly refined accounting principles have no place in an environment where they are misunderstood and misused. A technical report on cost variances is meaningless unless the reader understands cost accounting well. A sources and uses of funds statement should not be prepared unless it can be read competently.

5. Differences in size and complexity of business firms — Self-insurance may be acceptable for a very large firm where it is obviously not for a smaller firm. Similarly, a large firm mounting an extensive advertising campaign directed at a specific market or season may be justified in deferring part of the resultant expenditure, whereas smaller programs in smaller firms may need to be expensed directly.

   Comparable conclusions apply to complexity. Heavy and regular Research and Development outlays by a United States corporation may require accounting recognition, especially when long-range projects are involved. Incidental development costs of a firm producing only oil additives in Mexico normally have no such requirement.

6. Speed of business innovations — Business combinations became popular in Europe only a few years ago. Before that, European countries had little need of accounting principles and practices for this type of business event. Very small stock distributions occur most generally in the United States. Again, this produces differences in accounting principles. Equipment leasing is not practiced in a number of countries with the consequent absence of a need for lease accounting principles.

7. Presence of specific accounting legislation — Companies acts containing accounting provisions are found in many countries. While these acts change over time (for example, there were new acts recently in both Germany and the United Kingdom), their stipulations must be observed when in force and legally binding. The German act requires setting aside certain earnings as a "legal reserve." It also stipulates when and how consolidated financial statements are to be prepared. The British act defines how the term "reserve" is to be used in accounting. Many other examples of this type exist.

8. Stage of economic development — A one-crop agricultural economy needs accounting principles different from a United States-type economy. In the former, for instance, there is probably relatively little dependence on credit and long-term business contracts. Thus, sophisticated accrual accounting is out of place and essentially cash accounting is needed.

9. Type of economy involved — National economies vary in nature. Some are purely agricultural, while others depend heavily on the exploitation of natural resources (oil in the Near East, gold and diamonds in South Africa, copper in Chile, etc.). Some economies rely mainly on trade and institutions (Switzerland, Lebanon), whereas still others are highly diversified and touch on a great variety of economic and business activities. These are reasons for different principles regarding consolidations, accretion or discovery of natural resources, and inventory methods, among others.

10. Growing pattern of an economy — Companies and industries grow, stabilize, or decline. The same applies to national economies. If growth and expansion are typical, the capitalization of certain deferred charges is more feasible than under stable or declining conditions. Stable conditions intensify competition for existing markets, requiring restrictive credit and inventory methods. Declining conditions may indicate write-offs and adjustments not warranted in other situations.

11. Status of professional education and organization — In the absence of organized accounting professionalism and native sources of accounting authority, principles from other areas or countries may be needed to fill

existing voids. The process of adaptation, however, will be unsuccessful unless it allows for circumstantial factors of the type identified here.

12. General levels of education and tool processes facilitating accounting — Statistical methods in accounting and auditing cannot be used successfully where little or no knowledge of statistics and mathematics exists. Computer principles are not needed in the absence of working EDP installations. The French general accounting plan has enjoyed wide acceptance in France because it is easily understood and readily usable by those with average levels of education and without sophisticated accounting training.

The reader will recognize that several of the factors listed above may apply to a national situation as well as the international scene. This is not surprising since national variations in accounting concepts and practices are increasingly analyzed in terms of their respective environmental backgrounds, particularly in the United States. A relationship seems to exist between accounting flexibility within a country and among countries or areas. The topic of such a possible relationship, however, falls beyond the scope of this paper.

Some examples

As a limited test of the applicability of the list of environmental circumstances referred to in the preceding section, several different accounting principles are related to this list in order to evaluate at least some of the underlying environmental relationships. A complete diagnosis of this type would be a substantial undertaking and is not attempted here.

Different circumstances resulting in different accounting principles

Investments in marketable securities are generally carried at the lower of cost or market, stock exchange quotations being used as indications of "market." A different principle needs application where no national stock exchange exists, for example, in Guatemala.

Severance payments are normally at the option of the employer and thus are customarily expensed at the time of payment. If severance payments of material amounts are required by law, however, they should be accrued in some fashion before actual severance occurs.

In the United States, owners' equity is recorded, classified, and reported as to source. Interest in dividend potential is one reason for this. It results in basic distinctions between contributed capital, retained earnings, and capital from other sources.

On the other hand, a single owners' equity principle of legal capital dominates accounting in some European countries, *e.g.*, Germany. This is based on a balance-sheet accounting orientation to creditor protection.

330

Similar circumstances resulting in (largely unexplained) different accounting principles

The circumstances of inventory valuation are highly similar in the United States and the United Kingdom. In the lower of cost or market test, "market" means essentially replacement value in the United States and net realizable future sales value in the United Kingdom.

Despite close similarities of circumstances, deferred income tax "liabilities" are generally recognized in the United States and only sparingly recognized in Canada. Deferred tax accounting is not a generally-accepted accounting principle in Canada.

Accounting terminology varies internationally to a considerable degree without good reason. United States and United Kingdom usage of the terms "reserve" and "provision" differs, French use of the term "depreciation" differs from that in other European countries, and "goodwill" means nearly all things to all people. This is largely unexplainable.

Change in accounting principles

For the time being, meaningful international uniformity of generally-accepted accounting principles should have full regard for differences existing in the environments in which accounting operates. While complete differentiation for each politically recognized country is undesirable and unwarranted, fundamentally different conditions between different countries or areas conceptually call for separate recognition.

Assuming that this can be achieved, a most important mandate of accounting is to respond to any changes in environmental conditions as soon as they occur. Accounting can actually further the cause of change since it has, as we have seen, some influence on its environment in addition to reacting to its environment. Therefore, identification with desirable efforts toward change, and quick and full response to accomplished change are probably the primary leverage factors available to accounting in resolving justifiable international differences in generally-accepted accounting principles.

Three practical examples illustrate the force of change in accounting. First, the revised German companies law enacted in 1965 contains several financial disclosure provisions which are definitely patterned after United States SEC requirements. As Germany moves closer to a corporate business society that has much in common with the United States business society, tested SEC-type legislation would seem to be a valid response to the changes occurring.

Second, more comprehensive general financial-disclosure requirements are in evidence in the United Kingdom via the widely discussed 1964 London Stock Exchange memorandum as well as the recent new companies legislation. For some time the Swiss business press has carried repeated strong appeals for greater disclosure in the financial statements of Swiss companies. These and similar admonitions for wider general disclosures seem to be a consequence of widening securities markets in the countries concerned. Here again, an environmental condition has changed and accounting should respond.

Third, there is a notable increase in consolidated financial reporting on the part of larger corporations in countries outside of North America. In many instances, consolidated financial statements are presented even though applicable laws do not require such presentations. The cause of this move toward greater use of consolidated financial reports undoubtedly lies in the ever growing extent of inter-corporate investments and the steady growth of portfolio investments beyond the domicile countries of respective investors. The companies affected may have changed somewhat, but the far greater change has occurred in the environment of their operations.

In summary, a particular responsibility which accounting has in relation to change seems to exist. Awareness of this responsibility and concentrated efforts in connection with it are theoretically the most effective ways in which accounting principles between countries can be brought into greater harmony.

Conclusions

The three main conclusions of this paper are:

1. *United States generally-accepted accounting principles should not be enforced arbitrarily in other countries.* There is a theoretical incompatibility between the economic and business environments prevailing in different countries and an arbitrary imposition of any single set of generally-accepted accounting principles would run counter to environmental differences which exist.

   Only where environments are alike or similar can meaningful results be achieved by the use of a particular single body of accounting principles. At the same time, the overall theoretical framework of accounting itself needs to be general and permit analysis in terms of applicable environmental circumstances.

2. *Complete international diversity of accounting principles is undesirable and unnecessary.* The author has attempted to define ten different areas in which comparable environmental conditions exist and which therefore would gain from a particular approach to generally-accepted accounting principles. The ten-fold classification is highly subjective; nevertheless, it demonstrates a frame of reference with regard to limited international diversity of accounting principles.

Free international exchange and cooperation with regard to accounting principles would avoid unnecessary duplications in accounting research and provide the latest accounting knowhow for application when conditions demand it.

3. *Accounting is dynamic and operates in an atmosphere of change.* Even though the basic character of a given business environment seems slow to change, the continuing evolution of the accounting discipline affords means toward more international harmony in generally-accepted accounting principles. Efforts to change unnecessary international diversities in accounting in response to changing economic and business conditions appear to hold greater promise, in theory, than legislation or another form of enforcement of dictated international accounting uniformity.

Acknowledgements

Support from the Price Waterhouse Foundation for the preparation of this article is gratefully acknowledged.

Notes

1 For instance, *Professional Accounting in 25 Countries* (American Institute of Certified Public Accountants, 1964).
2 These areas are obviously treated very generally; exceptions exist for a few given countries.
3 Dudley E. Browne, *Financial Executive*, January 1966, p. 50.

14

THE IMPACT OF DISCLOSURE AND MEASUREMENT PRACTICES ON INTERNATIONAL ACCOUNTING CLASSIFICATIONS

R. D. Nair and Werner G. Frank

Source: *Accounting Review* 55(3) (1980): 426–50.

Abstract

This article examines whether the classification of countries into groups based on their accounting practices is the same whether measurement or disclosure practices are used to do the grouping. Data from the Price Waterhouse & Co. survey relating to these two subsets of accounting practices for 38 countries in 1973 and 46 countries in 1975 formed the data base. The groupings yielded by analyzing disclosure practices were found to be different from groupings based on measurement practices. A further analysis was then done to determine whether the same underlying environmental variables (such as the structure of the economy and trading affiliations of each country) were associated with the two groupings. It was found that although economic variables were related to the groupings, the specific variables most closely related to each subset were different. Because of these differences, it may be more difficult for policy makers to achieve harmonization of accounting practices than was previously realized.

Several attempts have been made to classify countries into groups based on the accounting practices that they follow. Examples of such efforts include Previts [1975], Seidler [1967], Buckley [1974], Mueller [1967, 1968], and Frank [1979]. In all of these studies, accounting practices were treated as a single group and no attempt was made to determine whether the clustering of countries was dependent on the composition of the set of accounting practices under study.

One important way of disaggregating accounting practices into two sub-sets is to distinguish whether they deal with disclosure or with measurement practices. The importance of this distinction in the United States can be seen by referring to the report of the American Institute of Certified Public Accountants' Committee on Generally Accepted Accounting Principles for Smaller and/or Closely Held Businesses ["Report," 1976]. The committee recommended that measurement principles should apply to all businesses regardless of their size or number of shareholders, while, on the other hand, the applicability of disclosure principles should vary depending on a number of factors and should not be required in all circumstances. A similar dichotomy has also served as a basis for distinguishing between the roles of the Securities and Exchange Commission and the Financial Accounting Standards Board (FASB), with the former concerning itself with disclosure practices and the latter with measurement practices. Beaver [1978] notes that the current jurisdictional controversy between these two bodies is the result of each encroaching on the other's role.

This article reports the results of a study which groups countries first by their measurement practices, and then by their disclosure practices. We also attempted to find whether different economic and cultural variables were associated with each subset of practices. It was found that the two subsets yield very different results. The number of groupings, the alignment of countries, and the underlying environmental variables associated with the practices were all different between the two subsets. The next section describes and compares the groupings of countries on each subset for 1973 and then this comparison is repeated for 1975. Section II describes and compares the environmental variables most closely associated with each subset of practices, while Section III points out the limitations of the analyses. Section IV presents the conclusions of the study and its implications for policy making.

I. Country groupings

The reasons why we expected measurement and disclosure practices to yield different country groupings were as follows. As noted above, disclosure and measurement practices sometimes fall in the province of two different rule-making bodies. Besides the United States, this disclosure/measurement regulatory dichotomy can also be observed in the United Kingdom, as pointed out by Benston [1975]. The administration of the Companies Acts of 1948 and 1967 which govern disclosure is largely the responsibility of the Department of Trade and Industry while measurement practices are addressed mainly by the Accounting Standards Committee. Second, measurement practices sometimes may have application over a wider range of business enterprises than disclosure practices, as is the case, for example, with respect to reporting segmented and earnings per share data in the United States. Third, the criteria brought to bear in the choice of measurement practices may be different from those used in choosing among disclosure practices. While factors such as relevance, verifiability, and objectivity may be important in the choice of the former, cost considerations in preparing the data may predominate in the choice of the latter. Finally, some may argue that given efficient capital markets, those disclosure practices dealing with format are much less substantive than most measurement practices. If this last line of argument is followed, one would expect disclosure practices to exhibit more diversity and yield more country groupings than measurement practices.

A. Data

The data for this part of the analysis consisted of the results of two surveys conducted by the accounting firm of Price Waterhouse & Co. on accounting principles and reporting practices. In 1973, the survey covered 233 principles and practices in 38 countries. The 1975 survey constitutes a richer data source, with eight countries being added and 264 principles and practices being covered. The eight new countries were Bermuda, Denmark, Greece, Iran, Malaysia, Nigeria, Norway, and Zaire. The 164 practices reported on in 1975 included all but 22 of the practices reported on in 1973. The samplings of countries in both years have a bias towards Western Hemisphere countries—a not unimportant group in their own right. Also, while the 1973 survey had six categories (Required, Majority, About Half, Minority, No Application, and Not Permitted), the 1975 survey added a seventh category: Not Found in Practice. The categories were numerically coded in this research as follows:

Survey Category	Numerical Code (Percentage Usage)
Required	100%
Majority	75%
About Half	50%
Minority	25%
Not Found in Practice	0% (not used in 1973)
Not Permitted	0%
No Application	0%

The reason for the percentage coding was to permit input of the data into a factor analysis program. The possibility of measurement error being introduced into the analysis by this transformation is taken up in Section III.

The principles and practices for both years were classified as either measurement practices or disclosure practices independently by the two

336

researchers. The criterion used for the classification was the following. If the application of a specific practice would result in the recording of a different value in a given account, then it was classified as a measurement practice. If it did not, or if the practice dealt explicitly with disclosure, then it was classified as a disclosure practice. For example, Item 12 from the 1975 survey deals with whether "A note is appended to historical cost financial statements, disclosing the effects of price level changes." This item was classified as a disclosure practice. On the other hand, Item 13 from the same survey asks whether "In preparing current purchasing power financial statements, a general price-level index is used and not an index or indices which measure the level of particular goods or services." Since this item measures how the figures appearing in the statements are determined, it was classified as a measurement practice. In most cases, the choice was clear-cut. In a few cases (not exceeding 15 in either year), different classifications initially were made by the two researchers. These were then resolved by mutual discussion until a consensus emerged. This procedure resulted in the following classification:

Year/Classification[1]	Disclosure	Measurement
1973 (38 countries)	86 practices	147 practices
1975 (46 countries)	102 practices	162 practices

The data from the 1973 and 1975 surveys were used as inputs into a factor analysis program. There were two objectives of the factor analysis procedure. One was to see whether the groupings yielded by the two subsets of data for each year were the same, or whether the disaggregation of accounting practices into disclosure and measurement subsets caused the composition of groups to change. The second objective was to use the groupings obtained with the 1975 subsets as inputs into a discriminant analysis. In this second step of the overall analysis, we wanted to see whether the same economic, social, and cultural variables would predict the membership of countries in the different accounting groups. The remainder of this section describes the results of applying the factor analysis procedure four times (two years of data × two subsets of practices). Section II describes the results of the discriminant analysis.

B. 1973 analysis:

1. Measurement practices

Percentage data on the extent of acceptance of the 147 practices in 38 countries were used as 147 observations in a factor analysis based on a correlation matrix to identify common patterns among the 38 countries. Factor analysis is a statistical technique which uses a measure of similarity between variables, such as the coefficient of correlation, to search for variables which are like each other and collapses these variables into more compact groups or factors. The strength with which each of the original variables is associated with these new basic variables or factors is measured by a statistic called factor loading. A statistic called the eigenvalue helps determine the number of factors to be extracted, while the percentage of the variance in the original data which is accounted for by the extracted factors is a measure of the overall success of the factoring procedure. Using the usual criterion that only those factors whose eigenvalues exceeded 1.0 would be considered, five factors were identified. Each factor represents a different common pattern of acceptance of measurement practices. These five factors accounted for approximately 71 percent of the variance in the data. To provide an intuitive interpretation of the groups, the factor matrix was rotated using a varimax rotation procedure. This procedure associates the various individual variables or countries in the strongest way possible with a single factor. A complete listing of the loadings of the countries on the rotated factors is given in Table 1. Each country was assigned to the factor on which it had the highest loading. The countries within each group or factor are those which are quite similar to each other in terms of accounting practices and quite different from the countries which are members of other groups or factors. As can be seen no country had its highest loading on the fifth factor, and no logical grouping appears to exist for the countries with relatively high loadings on that factor. That factor is, therefore, not used in the subsequent analysis. The remaining four factors yield the following groupings of the 38 countries:

Group I	Group II	Group III	Group IV
Australia	Argentina	Belgium	Canada
Bahamas	Bolivia	France	Japan
Fiji	Brazil	Germany	Mexico
Jamaica	Chile	Italy	Panama
Kenya	Colombia	Spain	Philippines
Netherlands	Ethiopia	Sweden	United States
New Zealand	India	Switzerland	
Pakistan	Paraguay	Venezuela	
Republic of Ireland	Peru		
Rhodesia	Uruguay		
Singapore			
South Africa			
Trinidad & Tobago			
United Kingdom			

By noting the overall composition of each group and the alignment of countries, the following intuitively appealing characterizations can be made:

Table 1 Rotated factor matrix based on measurement practices.
(1973 survey data)

Variable/Factor	1	2	3	4	5
1 Argentina	.154	.814	.130	.144	−.013
2 Australia	.664	.115	.237	.235	.592
3 Bahamas	.662	.228	.101	.410	.051
4 Belgium	.329	.355	.726	−.004	.100
5 Bolivia	.085	.845	.187	.080	.169
6 Brazil	.215	.674	.249	−.074	−.094
7 Canada	.535	.057	.199	.627	.050
8 Chile	.249	.662	.250	.129	−.008
9 Colombia	.210	.500	.406	.384	.329
10 Ethiopia	.419	.438	.286	.246	.259
11 Fiji	.653	.138	.253	.255	.577
12 France	.316	.247	.650	.150	.059
13 Germany	.339	.213	.619	.484	.070
14 India	.402	.496	.470	.108	.184
15 Italy	.041	.302	.676	.290	.073
16 Jamaica	.731	.275	.293	.179	.250
17 Japan	.339	.337	.475	.476	.040
18 Kenya	.647	.225	.321	.262	.173
19 Mexico	.301	.309	.241	.561	.128
20 Netherlands	.690	.146	.241	.363	−.213
21 New Zealand	.643	.143	.263	.273	.587
22 Pakistan	.492	.472	.331	.075	.285
23 Panama	.313	.393	.316	.436	.270
24 Paraguay	.114	.717	.261	.214	.107
25 Peru	.084	.843	.187	.084	.177
26 Philippines	.426	.247	.207	.712	.183
27 Republic of Ireland	.815	.176	.207	.140	.170
28 Rhodesia	.739	.234	.277	.199	.092
29 Singapore	.765	.327	.139	.127	.086
30 South Africa	.765	.160	.136	.289	.205
31 Spain	.299	.433	.600	−.052	.121
32 Sweden	.423	.294	.609	.121	.055
33 Switzerland	.373	.145	.571	.291	.034
34 Trinidad & Tobago	.761	.223	.274	.205	.081
35 United Kingdom	.784	.026	.233	.231	−.052
36 United States	.328	.018	.049	.831	.068
37 Uruguay	.202	.696	.189	.196	−.067
38 Venezuela	.133	.462	.606	.151	.251

(Highest factor loading for each country is underlined)

Group I: British Commonwealth model
Group II: Latin American model
Group III: Continental European model
Group IV: United States model

A comparison of these groupings with those obtained by Frank [1979] when he used all 233 principles from the same period reveals little difference. The number of factors stays the same as does the general overall composition and character of each group. Five countries—Ethiopia, Pakistan, Colombia, Netherlands, and Germany—do change group membership, but some of these shifts are understandable since in three of the five cases the loadings on the two groups are approximately equal.

2. Disclosure practices

A similar factor analytic procedure was applied to the 86 observations on reporting practices in the same 38 countries for 1973. The same criteria for extracting and rotating factors were used. Seven factors, *i.e.*, country groupings, were identified, accounting for 73.2 percent of the total variance in the data. A complete listing of the loadings of the countries on the rotated factors is given in Table 2. Each country again was assigned to the factor on which it had the highest loading. The seven factors yield the following groupings of the 38 countries. (Factors 6 and 7 both yield separate single-country "groups", but this treatment seems valid since each country's loading on its individual factor is much greater than its loading on any other factor.)

Group I	Group II	Group III	Group IV	Group V	Group VI	Group VII
Australia	Bolivia	Belgium	Canada	Argentina	Sweden	Switzerland
Bahamas	Germany	Brazil	Mexico	Chile		
Fiji	India	Colombia	Netherlands	Ethiopia		
Jamaica	Japan	France	Panama	Uruguay		
Kenya	Pakistan	Italy	Philippines			
New Zealand	Peru	Paraguay	United States			
Republic of Ireland		Spain				
Rhodesia		Venezuela				
Singapore						
South Africa						
Trinidad & Tobago						
United Kingdom						

Comparing these results with the groupings obtained in the previous section reveals that the clusterings of countries can change depending upon the subset of accounting practices used. The impact, however, is different on the various groups. For example, the British Commonwealth group (Group I) and the United States group (Group IV) are basically unchanged in character and composition between the two comparisons. The countries

340

Table 2 Rotated factor matrix based on disclosure practices.
(1973 survey data)

Variable/Factor	1	2	3	4	5	6	7
1 Argentina	.210	.444	.320	.266	.473	.363	.047
2 Australia	.867	.091	.142	.183	.173	.067	.078
3 Bahamas	.473	.275	.161	.444	.055	−.264	−.089
4 Belgium	.392	.152	.616	.063	.087	.127	.083
5 Bolivia	.227	.731	.382	.169	.250	.071	−.117
6 Brazil	.130	.217	.763	−.147	.271	−.003	−.081
7 Canada	.431	.319	−.016	.697	.014	−.024	−.148
8 Chile	.164	.377	.232	.148	.537	.284	−.118
9 Colombia	−.028	.354	.699	.047	−.064	.160	.077
10 Ethiopia	.373	.313	.028	.042	.602	.012	−.061
11 Fiji	.817	.120	.213	.260	.196	.007	.007
12 France	.083	.108	.724	−.168	−.140	.332	−.047
13 Germany	.208	.768	.070	.196	−.025	.054	.240
14 India	.435	.681	.196	.181	.123	.150	.086
15 Italy	.081	.043	.646	.220	.024	−.141	.457
16 Jamaica	.790	.438	.133	.120	.136	−.015	.062
17 Japan	.078	.673	.282	.249	.192	.089	.150
18 Kenya	.711	.341	.041	.065	.327	.089	.259
19 Mexico	.271	.389	.167	.522	.353	−.062	−.060
20 Netherlands	.384	.090	−.026	.672	.081	.111	.290
21 New Zealand	.855	.204	.168	.145	.205	.050	.189
22 Pakistan	.397	.640	.077	.231	.210	.231	.191
23 Panama	.143	.288	.217	.480	.380	3.12	.017
24 Paraguay	.076	.226	.639	.057	.331	.302	−.066
25 Peru	.125	.711	.339	.237	.224	.083	−.108
26 Philippines	.194	.189	.173	.639	.183	.434	.210
27 Republic of Ireland	.794	.014	.131	.206	−.110	−.140	−.177
28 Rhodesia	.749	.165	.112	.116	.221	.219	.299
29 Singapore	.670	.266	−.001	.027	.026	.404	.022
30 South Africa	.643	.237	−.036	.106	.023	.477	.125
31 Spain	.166	−.055	.786	.095	.276	−.154	.070
32 Sweden	.175	.173	.288	.136	.118	.649	.028
33 Switzerland	.284	.204	.207	.035	−.138	.073	.695
34 Trinidad & Tobago	.568	.508	.145	.234	.263	.067	.216
35 United Kingdom	.659	−.097	−.049	.280	−.187	.368	−.182
36 United States	.151	.416	−.065	.741	−.167	0.90	.010
37 Uruguay	.091	.061	.414	−.203	.732	−.017	.005
38 Venezuela	−.024	.228	.708	.265	.226	.025	.238

which are affected by the differences between reporting and measurement practices are the Latin American and Continental European countries. The previously identified Latin American model disintegrates, with Bolivia and Peru joining Germany and Japan in a grouping (Group II) which has no ready intuitive identification; Argentina, Chile, and Uruguay break off to form a predominantly "South" Latin American group (Group V), while

Table 3 Transformation matrix.
Disclosure and measurement groupings for 1973

Measurement Groups	Disclosure Groups						
	I	*II*	*III*	*IV*	*V*	*VI*	*VIII*
I	.95046	.01836	−.24363	.09157	.03178	.15910	−.02553
II	.00219	.51636	.42280	.07120	.57897	.15573	−.20126
III	−.15747	−.00932	.69828	−.13866	−.20452	.40454	.42632
IV	−.24282	.38358	−.11821	.81579	.00990	.04072	.07050
V	.44992	.12042	.12218	−.10335	.13736	−.12002	.01576

Brazil, Colombia, and Paraguay join a group of European countries (Group III). Similarly, in the previously identified Continental European model, a group of Central and Southern European countries—Belgium, France, Italy, and Spain—join with the above-mentioned Latin American countries, while Germany, Sweden, and Switzerland, on the other hand, go in different directions. The groupings obtained here do not lend themselves to an intuitive basis for differentiation, and it is difficult to characterize these groups.

The difference in the factor structures between those obtained for measurement practices and those obtained for disclosure practices were quantified by the transformation analysis procedures suggested by Rummel [1970]. This is a method for comparing the structures of factor matrices yielded by two different factor analyses. The method yields a transformation matrix, the elements of which can be interpreted as regression coefficients. The coefficients give the best prediction of each factor of one factor matrix in terms of each factor of the second matrix. The transformation matrix is given in Table 3, with factors from the analysis of measurement practices as the rows and the factors from the analysis of disclosure practices as the columns. The U.K. group (Group I in both) and to a slightly lesser extent the U.S. group (Group IV in both) are similarly delineated in both factor analyses. The latter shows some similarity with Group II from the disclosure practices, perhaps because of the shift of Japan. Observing the elements for the rows dealing with the Latin American group (Group II) and the Continental European group (Group III) it can be seen that both lose their clearcut distinctiveness and the outlines of both groups become blurred as each becomes positively associated with two or more groups on the disclosure dimension. These observations tend to bolster the conclusions drawn earlier about the lack of cohesiveness in the Latin American and Continental European groups when disclosure practices are considered.

Rummel also suggests the computation of an index of deviation for each variable, *i.e.*, country. This index would measure the overall (factor loading) similarity of a country from one factor analysis to the next. The index is zero if a country has identical loadings on all factors in both factor analyses.

A level of 0.1 was arbitrarily picked as the level at which a change in factor loadings would be studied to identify outliers. (The average index was 0.17 and the range was from 0.02 to 0.36.) Using this criterion, all but 11 countries had significant shifts in their overall factor loadings between the two factor matrices. The 11 which did not shift significantly in overall factor loadings were: Argentina, Australia, Belgium, Chile, Fiji, Jamaica, Mexico, New Zealand, Rhodesia, United States, and Venezuela. These countries exhibit the greatest stability between the two sets of practices. The fact that most countries registered a shift in loadings between the factor analyses of the two sets of practices again confirms that the groupings achieved are quite different.

C. 1975 analysis

The above analyses which had been performed with the data from the 1973 Price Waterhouse survey were all replicated using data from the 1975 survey.

1. Measurement practices

The 162 practices relating to measurement in the 46 countries surveyed in 1975 were analyzed using the same criteria as before for the extraction and rotation of factors. Six factors accounting for approximately 72 percent of the variance were isolated and a complete listing of the loadings of the 46 countries is given in Table 4. For the purpose of grouping, each country was assigned to the factor on which it loaded the highest. Since no country loaded highest on the sixth factor, it was ignored in the subsequent analysis. The remaining five factors yielded the following groups (including a single-country "group"):

Group I	Group II	Group III	Group IV	Group V
Australia	Argentina	Belgium	Bermuda*	Chile
Bahamas	Bolivia	Denmark*	Canada	
Fiji	Brazil	France	Japan	
Iran*	Colombia	Germany	Mexico	
Jamaica	Ethiopia	Norway*	Philippines	
Malaysia*	Greece*	Sweden	United States	
Netherlands	India	Switzerland	Venezuela	
New Zeland	Italy	Zaire*		
Nigeria*	Pakistan			
Republic of Ireland	Panama			
Rhodesia	Paraguay			
Singapore	Peru			
South Africa	Spain			
Trinidad & Tobago	Uruguay			
United Kingdom				

* Countries not included in the 1973 survey.

Table 4 Rotated factor matrix based on measurement practices.
(1975 survey data)

		1	2	3	4	5	6
1	Argentina	.125	.735	.085	.193	.465	.132
2	Australia	.785	.136	.204	.260	.136	.378
3	Bahamas	.603	.344	.053	.438	−.134	−.010
4	Belgium	.293	.408	.648	.124	.053	−.208
5	Bermuda	.485	.169	.241	.650	.115	−.087
6	Bolivia	.145	.851	.106	.122	.173	−.036
7	Brazil	.122	.541	.360	.133	.349	.016
8	Canada	.384	.145	.153	.808	.118	−.025
9	Chile	.242	.292	.308	.035	.632	−.048
10	Colombia	.199	.698	.294	.169	.008	.132
11	Denmark	.385	.212	.558	.166	.300	.084
12	Ethiopia	.467	.628	.231	.069	−.010	−.001
13	Fiji	.756	.171	.222	.274	.124	.397
14	France	.375	.258	.557	.200	.286	.207
15	Germany	.297	.368	.664	.300	.031	−.026
16	Greece	.154	.501	.400	.265	.113	−.387
17	India	.449	.575	.388	.029	.005	−.227
18	Iran	.373	.372	.244	.346	.199	−.294
19	Italy	.158	.565	.420	.238	−.107	−.074
20	Jamaica	.777	.252	.272	.116	.115	−.084
21	Japan	.274	.274	.380	.554	−.037	−.162
22	Kenya	.674	.308	.198	.973	−.038	.052
23	Malaysia	.653	.233	.423	.292	.068	−.102
24	Mexico	.443	.234	.250	.596	.220	−.028
25	Netherlands	.583	.145	.277	.429	.148	−.100
26	New Zealand	.764	.146	.239	.268	.129	.376
27	Nigeria	.628	.442	.242	.281	−.083	−.045
28	Norway	.230	.253	.636	.302	.251	.049
29	Pakistan	.543	.636	.114	.067	−.114	−.159
30	Panama	.326	.589	.162	.339	−.024	.237
31	Paraguay	.138	.824	.187	.125	.087	−.039
32	Peru	.131	.727	.231	.229	.195	−.145
33	Philippines	.403	.385	.186	.575	.168	.149
34	Republic of Ireland	.747	.017	.212	.408	.147	−.114
35	Rhodesia	.765	.247	.174	.238	.214	−.173
36	Singapore	.754	.157	.318	.204	.050	−.030
37	South Africa	.753	.162	.135	.325	.095	−.075
38	Spain	.100	.582	.476	.032	.008	.065
39	Sweden	.404	.232	.623	.160	.209	.049
40	Switzerland	.223	.185	.732	.195	−.007	.163
41	Trinidad & Tobago	.658	.414	.194	.051	.061	−.071
42	United Kingdom	.736	.058	.166	.414	.167	−.112
43	United States	.311	.115	.141	.806	−.047	.180
44	Uruguay	.196	.652	.127	.228	.472	.035
45	Venezuela	.272	.436	.328	.584	.024	−.101
46	Zaire	.272	.450	.516	.188	.080	−.241

A comparison with the measurement grouping obtained in 1973 indicates that the overall composition and character of the groups has remained stable over time. Although the number of groups has changed they can be characterized as follows:

Group I: British Commonwealth model
Group II: Latin American/South European model
Group III: Northern and Central European model
Group IV: United States model
Group V: Chile

Of the 38 countries common to both surveys, the major change between 1973 and 1975 in the measurement groupings is the expansion of the Latin American group. Pakistan (from the British Commonwealth group), Panama (from the United States group), and Italy and Spain (both from the Continental European group) join it, while only Chile leaves it to become its own "group." The only other change is Venezuela, going from the Continental European model to the United States model.

Another point to note is the affiliation of the eight countries included for the first time in the 1975 survey. Most of them are linked with those groups which one would have expected on the basis of Seidler's "spheres-of-influence" classification [1967]. Denmark and Norway are to be found in the North/Central European group, which also includes Sweden. Zaire (formerly the Belgian Congo) is also included in that group, which is not anomalous considering that that group also included Belgium. Nigeria and Malaysia also follow colonial patterns by exhibiting an affiliation with the British Commonwealth model. Greece is associated with the Latin American/South European group, while Iran and Bermuda are linked with the British Commonwealth and United States models, respectively.

2. Disclosure practices

The same factor analytic procedure was applied to the 102 observations on disclosure practices in the 46 countries. The factor analysis yielded eight factors accounting for 73 percent of total variance in the data. A complete listing of the loading of the countries on the rotated factors is given in Table 5. Each country was assigned to the factor on which it had the highest loading. Factor 7 on which no country loaded the highest is ignored in the subsequent analysis. The seven remaining factors yield the following groupings of the 46 countries:

Table 5 Rotated factor matrix based on disclosure practices.
(1975 survey data)

		1	*2*	*3*	*4*	*5*	*6*	*7*	*8*
1	Argentina	.366	.229	.377	.058	.526	.278	.217	−.118
2	Australia	.172	.874	.176	.232	.042	.021	.138	.024
3	Bahamas	.140	.386	.505	.396	−.011	.046	.159	−.154
4	Belgium	.747	.109	−.080	.211	.049	.244	.014	.130
5	Bermuda	.010	.210	.334	.701	.137	.048	.278	.131
6	Bolivia	.775	.222	.228	.061	.212	.039	.211	−.155
7	Brazil	.624	.047	.209	−.023	.226	.193	.354	−.069
8	Canada	.037	.203	.366	.749	.113	.036	.220	.098
9	Chile	.629	.139	.234	.240	.315	.209	.281	.056
10	Colombia	.675	.059	.402	−.024	.146	−.041	−.140	.155
11	Denmark	.217	.252	.108	.198	.147	.693	.165	−.007
12	Ethiopia	.309	.569	.368	−.005	.010	.300	.188	.108
13	Fiji	.238	.832	.214	.266	.021	.022	.079	.044
14	France	.578	.148	.184	.151	−.065	.507	−.228	.058
15	Germany	.089	.147	.603	.036	.238	.306	.159	.207
16	Greece	.694	.129	.083	.044	.065	.050	.025	.041
17	India	.295	.262	.235	.170	.482	.337	.274	.242
18	Iran	.171	.174	.081	.135	.708	.180	−.055	−.051
19	Italy	.506	.029	.253	−.018	.058	.188	−.077	.514
20	Jamaica	.208	.409	.207	.582	.107	.215	.139	.055
21	Japan	.333	.158	.643	.115	.212	.228	.188	.115
22	Kenya	.188	.741	.127	.121	.345	.262	.048	.098
23	Malaysia	.114	.558	.128	.323	.346	.243	−.089	.383
24	Mexico	.256	.370	.531	.301	.279	.093	.106	.166
25	Netherlands	.056	.374	.375	.492	.183	−.092	−.007	.056
26	New Zealand	.175	.876	.155	.254	.039	.126	.070	.093
27	Nigeria	.025	.598	.070	.347	.290	.330	−.060	.227
28	Norway	.287	.072	.191	.123	.161	.567	.459	.175
29	Pakistan	.265	.310	.213	.162	.470	.066	.301	.409
30	Panama	.298	.247	.728	.224	−.027	.003	.129	.037
31	Paraguay	.804	.208	.263	.064	.222	.121	.099	.054
32	Peru	.360	.274	.352	.285	.540	.019	.272	.032
33	Philippines	.156	.182	.591	.251	.479	.021	.038	.214
34	Republic of Ireland	.241	.250	.164	.750	.107	.107	−.180	−.111
35	Rhodesia	.063	.491	.189	.638	.105	.076	.038	.105
36	Singapore	.092	.790	.155	.266	.253	.110	−.151	.042
37	South Africa	.069	.514	.178	.362	.260	.277	.095	−.097
38	Spain	.859	.033	−.038	.021	−.024	.045	−.035	.206
39	Sweden	.192	.112	.142	.094	.188	.754	−.034	.139
40	Switzerland	.303	.290	.272	.129	−.090	.184	.171	.587
41	Trinidad & Tobago	.355	.502	.121	.259	.136	.161	.470	.217
42	United Kingdom	−.011	.295	−.005	.674	.036	.381	−.101	.019
43	United States	.040	.097	.723	.454	.175	.032	−.035	.147
44	Uruguay	.520	.260	.290	.216	.338	.189	.319	−.220
45	Venezuela	.132	.203	.690	.288	.030	.237	−.187	−.020
46	Zaire	.863	.187	.065	.052	.065	.089	.042	.064

Group I	Group II	Group III	Group IV
Belgium	Australia	Bahamas	Bermuda*
Bolivia	Ethiopia	Germany	Canada
Brazil	Fiji	Japan	Jamaica
Chile	Kenya	Mexico	Netherlands
Colombia	Malaysia*	Panama	Republic of Ireland
France	New Zealand	Philippines	Rhodesia
Greece*	Nigeria*	United States	United Kingdom
Paraguay	Singapore	Venezuela	
Spain	South Africa		
Uruguay	Trinidad & Tobago		
Zaire*			

	Group V	Group VI	Group VII
	Argentina	Denmark*	Italy
	India	Norway*	Switzerland
	Iran*	Sweden	
	Pakistan		
	Peru		

* Not included in the 1973 survey.

A comparison of the groupings obtained here with those obtained with the 1975 measurement practices reveals the same lack of clear-cut groups that was observed with the 1973 data. It is apparent that the pattern underlying measurement practices in different countries is quite different from the pattern underlying disclosure practices. It is interesting to note that Chile is not an outlier with respect to disclosure practices as it was with measurement practices. The major point to note in comparing these groupings with the 1975 measurement groupings is the same disintegration of the Continental European model that was observed with the 1973 data. Denmark and Norway, both new to the survey in 1975, join Sweden, which was a single-country "group" in 1973, to form a Scandinavian cluster; France and Belgium (and also Zaire) join the Latin American/South European clustering which was apparent in the 1973 disclosure clusters. Germany, on the other hand, joins Japan as it had in the 1973 clusters, while Italy joins Switzerland as a separate "group."

The other major point to be noted is that while the U.S. group stays largely intact across the two sets of methods, the British Commonwealth cluster splits into two groups. This split was not observed with the 1973 data; it may be speculated that it is the result of the entry of the United Kingdom into the European Common Market during the intervening period. However, in general, there is no clear-cut basis for systematically differentiating between the various groups and offering intuitively appealing characterizations.

Table 6 Transformation matrix.
Disclosure and measurement groupings for 1975

Disclosure Groups	Measurement Groups					
	I	II	III	IV	V	VI
I	.03471	.62300	.33670	.00283	.16781	−.13457
II	.73277	.10673	.04313	−.05188	−.06535	.28554
III	−.01699	.32644	.12510	.58064	−.07843	.21107
IV	.54843	−.15385	.07851	.52763	.18130	−.26455
V	.03742	.43512	−.14613	.06364	.22529	−.29476
VI	.24183	.00069	.63196	.03558	.22162	−.07316
VII	−.13349	.10818	−.08318	−.19601	.15844	.12999
VIII	.12464	−.01960	.52809	.06689	−.37418	−.01581

The lack of agreement between the factor structures can also be seen in the transformation matrix given in Table 6. The rows indicate the factors obtained from the analysis of disclosure practices, while the columns give the factors obtained from the analysis of measurement practices. None of the elements of the matrix is above 0.8, and only one (between the "Eastern Commonwealth" group—group II on disclosure practices and the British Commonwealth group—Group I on measurement practices) is above 0.7. Since 1.0 would indicate congruence of two factors, the results here indicate that the clusters of countries obtained with measurement practices are not similar to the clusters of countries obtained with measurement practices are not similar to the clusters obtained with disclosure practices. Examination of the index of deviation indicated that nine of the 46 countries had significant (index greater than 0.1) shifts in their overall factor loadings. These nine countries were: Argentina, Bahamas, Chile, Ethiopia, Germany, Greece, Japan, Nigeria, and Pakistan.

The preceding analysis answers the first question raised in this study. It shows that the groupings achieved on different subsets of accounting practices are, in fact, different. Also, disclosure practices exhibit greater diversity than the factors obtained from the analysis of measurement practices. In the second part of the analysis, we attempted to see whether different underlying economic and cultural variables were associated with the groupings.

II. Association of economic and cultural variables with groupings

It has long been argued by accountants that accounting is shaped by its environment. APB Statement No. 4 [1970, para. 209] states, "Generally accepted accounting principles change in response to changes in economic and social conditions, to new knowledge and technology, and to demands of users for more serviceable financial information." A similar line of argument can be found in the FASB's Objectives of Financial Reporting by Business Enterprises [1978, para. 9], "Accordingly, the objectives in this Statement are affected by the economic, legal, political, and social environment in the United States." Following this line of reasoning would lead one to believe that countries with similar environments, in the sense of similar economies and cultures, should have similar accounting practices and those with different environments should exhibit differences in accounting practices. As Choi and Mueller [1978, p. 22] state, "If we then accept the proposition that the environments in which accounting operates are not the same in different countries . . . it stands to reason that accounting must necessarily differ from case to case if it is to retain the sharp cutting edge of social utility."

The earlier study by Frank [1979] confirmed that an association between environmental variables and accounting groupings exists. However, it is of interest to investigate whether the environmental variables associated with disclosure practices are different from those associated with measurement practices. For example, one might expect factors such as extent of similarity between legal structures to be more important in the determination of disclosure practices since many disclosure requirements are laid down in laws such as the Securities Acts of 1933 and 1934 in the United States. Similarly, the degree of separation of ownership from management and the overall state of economic development might have an impact more on the determination of disclosure issues as would the degree of public ownership of business enterprises, since disclosure issues become more urgent as ownership is diffused. Similarity in measurement practices, on the other hand, might be affected more by a similar economic experience, such as rapid inflation or the emergence of firms with significant overseas investments. In such cases, we would expect the countries to draw upon each other's experiences in formulating approaches to measuring such economic events.

A. Data

In this, the second step of the analysis, discriminant functions were first constructed using data from 36 countries. Four countries (Bahamas, Bermuda, Malaysia, and Rhodesia) were excluded from this part of the study since the United Nations source for the economic and cultural variables did not provide data for these countries. Six countries (Denmark, Greece, Iran, Nigeria, Norway, and Zaire) were kept as a hold-out sample to test the predictive power of the discriminant functions. These countries were chosen to form the hold-out sample since they were new to the 1975 sample.

349

The major cultural variable used was the country's official language. This variable should capture similarities in legal systems, since colonizing countries usually bequeathed their own legal system and official language to the colonies. Use of English, French, Spanish, Portuguese, German, and Italian was indicated through use of a separate (0, 1) dummy variable for each of these countries.

Eight economic structure variables were included to capture the importance of the degree of industrialization and the state of development. These were: (1) per capita income, (2) private sector consumption relative to gross national product, (3) relative gross capital formation, (4) relative balance of trade (exports less imports), (5) agricultural sector output relative to gross national product, (6) geometric (average) annual growth rate of real gross national product, (7) average annual change in the country's foreign exchange rate for U.S. dollars, and (8) average annual change in consumer prices. Averages were computed over the period 1962–1970 inclusive.

Three bilateral trade variables were constructed for this analysis to capture trading ties between countries: imports, exports, and total trade (imports plus explorts). Two differences exist in terms of how these variables were measured in this study as compared to Frank's earlier study [1979] of 1973 accounting practices. In the earlier study, country A's imports from country B were assumed to be equal to B's exports to A. Because of differences in how duties are assigned, the point in time when warehoused goods are included in the import/export category, etc., the equality mentioned above does not strictly hold. In this study, separate import and export data were gathered and used in constructing the trade variables. Differences due to this alternative measurement procedure are minor.

The major difference in the construction of the trade variables between this and the Frank study [1979] is how the data were summarized for use in the discriminant analysis. In the earlier study, the trade statistics for individual countries were aggregated by country groupings, as determined from the factor analysis. The same country groupings were thus assumed to be known for the dependent variable (country groups with similar accounting principles and reporting practices) and for the independent trade variables. This was not a major concern in that study since the discriminant analysis was used in the earlier study primarily for the descriptive purposes to show the close association between a country's economic and cultural characteristics and the accounting principles and practices it followed. In this study, we use the discriminant functions for prediction, as well as classification, purposes. To make unbiased prediction tests requires that information incorporated in the dependent variable not be used in constructing the independent, explanatory variables. To avoid creating such a bias, we used the Gutman-Lingoes smallest space analysis technique, SSA-I, to construct three sets of six trading blocks, one based on imports, a second based on exports, and a third based on total trade.

Smallest space analysis (SSA) is a technique whose objective is similar to factor analysis, i.e., to reduce a large number of variables into a more compact set. Instead of "loadings" and "factors," this technique yields "coordinates" and "dimensions" which can be interpreted analogously. Each dimension represents a block of countries closely linked to each other through their trading ties. As mentioned above, three sets of six dimensions or trading blocks were identified. The scores or coordinates of each country on each dimension obtained after a varimax rotation procedure similar to factor analysis were then used as additional variables in a stepwise multiple discriminant analysis.

B. Measurement practices

To separate the five groups identified from the 1975 measurement practices, four discriminant functions incorporating 14 variables were developed. These are the variables which are most helpful in distinguishing one group from another. Variables having an F-value of less than 1.0 were excluded from the functions to ensure that each new variable added a significant amount of separation above and beyond the variables already included in the functions. The number of discriminant functions to be used in further analysis was determined by examining the relative percentage of variance explained by each function. The functions themselves can be interpreted like the factors in factor analysis, and clues to the dimension each function represents can be found by looking to the variable whose standardized coefficient has the largest absolute value on that function. The standardized discriminant function coefficients are given in Table 7 along with other summary statistics on the four functions. Table 8 lists the names of the variables entering the analysis.

The first two of these functions represent approximately 92 percent of the discriminatory power, and are significant at the .001 level. All three types of variables—cultural, economic structure, and trading block data play a role in the discriminant functions. The five economic structure variables are: per capita income, private sector consumption, balance of trade, role of the agricultural sector, and the GNP growth rate. The four cultural variables are English, French, German, and Italian. The trade variables include two of the import trading blocks and three of the total trade trading blocks. Based on the absolute value of the standardized discriminant function coefficients, the single most important variable for each of the functions are:

Function 1: French
Function 2: Trading block of Mexico, Peru, Paraguay, Uruguay, Argentina, Bolivia, Brazil, and Chile based on imports
Function 3: Per capita income

Table 7 Statistics and coefficients for discriminant functions.
(Five country-groups based on 1975 measurement practices)

Discriminant Function	Eigenvalue	Relative Percentage of Variance Explained
1	20.28123	72.14
2	5.54915	19.74
3	1.79360	6.38
4	.48847	1.74

Standardized Discriminant Function Coefficients

Variable*	Func. 1	Func. 2	Func. 3	Func. 4
PCINC	−.15783	−.03425	−.70824	−.23241
PVTCOM	.02090	−.42862	−.15204	.28516
BOT	.12204	−.13515	−.40640	−.17116
AGSEC	−.36588	−.22393	.02271	−.30652
GNPGR	.17815	.03300	−.66175	−.04788
IMPORT2	.03758	−.53581	−.38788	−.29477
IMPORT5	−.11883	−.02301	.49665	−.70039
TOTTR2	−.04576	−.11889	.08155	.93717
TOTTR5	.30093	−.06241	−.52312	.50142
TOTTR6	.15269	−.20809	−.43914	−.21185
ENGLISH	.43462	.05506	−.56149	.28497
FRENCH	−.56961	−.06400	−.22521	−.11773
GERM	−.55298	.01100	−.13039	−.04819
ITAL	.03094	−.29792	.00304	−.05797

(Largest Coefficient for each function is underlined)

Centroids of Groups in Reduced Space

	Func. 1	Func. 2	Func. 3	Func. 4
Group 1	.45353	1.08409	.56911	.18319
Group 2	.13371	−.98595	.43719	−.29004
Group 3	−2.33724	.30685	−.32964	.07103
Group 4	.73674	.19949	−1.60335	−.28097
Group 5	.53867	−1.83878	−.67534	3.08613

* See Table 8 for names of variables

Function 4: Trading block of Argentina, Paraguay, and Peru based on total trade.

There are two ways of judging the success of discriminant analysis—first, how well the functions classify the cases which had been used in constructing those functions, and second, and also more importantly, how well it predicts the membership of new cases excluded from the function-building process. Discriminant functions may be outstanding successes by the first

Table 8 List of variables.

PCINC:	per capita income
PVTCOM:	private sector consumption relative to Gross National Product
BOT:	relative balance of trade
AGSEC:	agricultural sector relative to Gross National Product
GNPGR:	geometric annual growth rate of real Gross National Product
IMPORT2:	Trading block of Argentina, Bolivia, Brazil, Chile, Mexico, Paraguay, Peru, and Uruguay
IMPORT5:	Trading block of Denmark, Greece, Iran, and Ireland
EXPORT1:	Trading block of Belgium, France, Italy, Netherlands, Nigeria, Republic of Ireland, South Africa, Spain, United Kingdom, United States, Uruguay, and Zaire
EXPORT2:	Trading block of Argentina, Brazil, Chile, Colombia, Denmark, Panama, Paraguay, Sweden, Trinidad, and Venezuela
EXPORT4:	Trading block of Ethiopia, Japan, Mexico, Peru, and Philippines
EXPORT6:	Trading block of India, Iran, Pakistan, Singapore, and Switzerland
TOTTR2:	Trading block of Brazil, Canada, Chile, Denmark, Colombia, Germany, Norway, and Switzerland
TOTTR5:	Trading block of Argentina, Paraguay, and Peru
TOTTR6:	Trading block of Mexico, Panama, and Trinidad & Tobago
ENGLISH:	Dummy variable for use of the English language
FRENCH:	Dummy variable for use of the French language
GERM:	Dummy variable for use of the German language
ITAL:	Dummy variable for use of the Italian language

test, but may fail the stronger second test. In such instances, as happens in this study, the results of the analysis should be treated with caution and any conclusions that may be drawn are only tentative in nature.

The four functions classified all of the 36 countries used to construct the functions correctly, as shown in Table 9. The predictive results with respect to the six countries in the hold-out sample, which had not been used to construct the discriminant functions, however, were not as impressive. Only three out of the six countries were classified correctly. These were Greece, Nigeria, and Zaire. Denmark (actually in Group III) was classified in Group II; Iran (actually in Group I) was classified in Group IV, and Norway (actually in Group III) was classified in Group I.

C. Disclosure practices

A similar discriminant procedure was run to identify the variables associated with the seven groups present in the 1975 disclosure data. Six discriminant functions incorporating 13 variables were developed. The standardized discriminant function coefficients are given in Table 10 along with other summary statistics on the six functions.

In this case, the first three of these functions are the most important ones since they represent approximately 92 percent of the discriminatory

Table 9 Prediction results—measurement practices.
(Countries used to construct discriminant functions)

| Actual Group | No. of Cases | Predicted Group Membership | | | | |
		Group 1	Group 2	Group 3	Group 4	Group 5
Group 1	11	11	0	0	0	0
		100.0%	0%	0%	0%	0%
Group 2	13	0	13	0	0	0
		0	100.0%	0%	0%	0%
Group 3	5	0	0	5	0	0
		0%	0%	100.0%	0%	0%
Group 4	6	0	0	0	6	0
		0%	0%	0%	100.0%	0%
Group 5	1	0	0	0	0	1
		0%	0%	0%	0%	100.0%

Percentage of "grouped" cases correctly classified: 100.0%

power, and are significant at the .02 level (or better). Again, all three types of variables play a role in the discriminant functions. The four economic structure variables are: per capita income, private sector consumption, balance of trade and the role of the agricultural sector. The two cultural variables are English and German, while the trade variables include four of the export trading blocks and three of the total trade trading blocks.

Based on the absolute value of the standardized discriminant function coefficients, the single most important variable for each of the functions are:

Function 1: English
Function 2: Importance of the agricultural sector
Function 3: Trading block of Mexico, Panama, and Trinidad & Tobago based on total trade
Function 4: Trading block of India, Iran, Pakistan, Singapore, and Switzerland based on exports
Function 5: Germany
Function 6: Trading block of Brazil, Canada, Chile, Colombia, Denmark, Germany, Norway, and Switzerland based on total trade.

It should be noted that none of the variables found to have the greatest association with disclosure clusters had the same dominant position with respect to measurement groups. This result would suggest that measurement and disclosure practices in countries may be determined by different underlying environmental variables. It is difficult, however, to distinguish between the two sets of environmental variables on any conceptual basis. Our *a priori* reasoning had led us to believe that the cultural and economic

Table 10 Statistics and coefficients for discriminant functions.
(Seven country groups based on 1975 disclosure practices)

Discriminant Function	Eigenvalue	Relative Percentage of Variance Explained
1	11.72267	58.12
2	3.99413	19.80
3	2.86354	14.20
4	.76771	3.81
5	.54109	2.68
6	.27982	1.39

Standardized Discriminant Function Coefficients

Variable*	Func. 1	Func. 2	Func. 3	Func. 4	Func. 5	Func. 6
PCINC	.39505	−.28494	−.02571	−.48939	.22529	−.39951
PCTCOM	.21276	.57404	.03531	−.32088	−.30422	−.22466
BOT	−.15062	.15253	−.24851	.17354	.25479	.11367
AGSEC	.58180	−.66993	.33218	.27298	.06118	.32783
EXPORT1	.14490	.25057	.27401	−.44714	−.40396	−.21583
EXPORT2	.67356	−.24167	.31235	.19114	−.18493	−.41792
EXPORT4	.19721	−.22063	−.26943	.12212	.26166	−.26464
EXPORT6	.44322	−.00375	−.09753	.76185	−.08608	−.41329
TOTTR2	−.38305	−.19641	.16900	.13527	−.12939	.91950
TOTTR5	−.06748	.35371	−.25224	.63948	−.08820	−.22954
TOTTR6	−.40387	.24153	−.64160	−.24475	.29130	.07630
ENGLISH	−.77968	.35789	−.02730	.36794	−.31581	−.32416
GERM	.07383	−.21313	−.49613	−.24463	−.82295	0.01277

Centroids of Groups in Reduced Space

	Func. 1	Func. 2	Func. 3	Func. 4	Func. 5	Func. 6
Group 1	.74584	.84687	.40572	−.06867	−.07152	.41290
Group 2	−1.20260	−.69315	.51180	.45512	−.18182	.25944
Group 3	−.20234	−.17771	−1.24025	−.23496	.77264	.09474
Group 4	−.43695	.02123	.53887	−1.22565	−.25167	−.62538
Group 5	.22810	.80079	−.27398	1.16953	−.08310	−.89321
Group 6	2.40021	−3.42810	1.59997	.31260	.92131	−.38827
Group 7	1.45102	−1.56073	−2.66827	−.17208	−2.56927	.22025

* See Table 8 for variable names.

variables might be associated with disclosure practices, while the trading variables might be more important for measurement practices. This, however, does not seem to be the case.

With respect to the classification of countries into similar disclosure groups, the discriminant functions classified all but one of the 36 countries correctly. Thus, the analysis was very successful by the first, weaker test. The exception was Japan, which was actually in Group III but was classified

Table 11 Prediction results—disclosure practices.
(Countries used to construct discriminant functions)

Actual Group	No. of Cases	Predicted Group Membership						
		Group 1	Group 2	Group 3	Group 4	Group 5	Group 6	Group 7
Group 1	10	10 100.0%	0 0%	0 0%	0 0%	0 0%	0 0%	0 0%
Group 2	8	0 0%	8 100.0%	0 0%	0 0%	0 0%	0 0%	0 0%
Group 3	7	0 0%	0 0%	6 85.7%	0 0%	1 14.3%	0 0%	0 0%
Group 4	5	0 0%	0 0%	0 0%	5 100.0%	0 0%	0 0%	0 0%
Group 5	4	0 0%	0 0%	0 0%	0 0%	4 100.0%	0 0%	0 0%
Group 6	1	0 0%	0 0%	0 0%	0 0%	0 0%	1 100.0%	0 0%
Group 7	1	0 0%	0 0%	0 0%	0 0%	0 0%	0 0%	1 100.0%

Percentage of "grouped" cases correctly classified: 97.22%.

in Group V. The classification results are given in Table 11. The predictive results with respect to the six hold-out countries was poor. Only one out of the six, Greece, was classified correctly, reflecting the lack of any clear-cut systematic basis for differentiating between the disclosure groups. Nigeria (Group II) and Denmark (Group VI) were both predicted to belong to Group I; Iran (Group V) and Zaire (Group I) were predicted to belong to Group II and Norway (Group VII) was predicted as a Group III country. Thus, the analysis was quite unsuccessful as judged by this second, stronger, test.

III. Limitations

The analyses described above suffer from several limitations; the purpose of this section is to describe the more prominent of these shortcomings and the steps taken to deal with them. These limitations should be kept in mind when drawing conclusions from this study.

First, the primary data source for this study)—the Price Waterhouse & Co. Survey—may be a source of potential error. In its favor, it should be pointed out that uniform procedures are used worldwide in collecting, compiling, editing, and checking the consistency of the data. Also, the firm tries not to bias the survey in favor of the accounting practices of their own clients but tries to develop an overall consensus about the accounting practices used in presenting financial statements to shareholders in a given country.[2] This process entails the use of considerable judgment when there is diversity of practice within a country. A similar situation arises when there are not many published financial statements in a given country. The last two considerations have an impact on the validity of the data. Another point to be noted is that the companies whose practices are surveyed may not be comparable across countries. For example, the companies whose practices are reported on in the the survey may not all meet the same criteria such as being listed on a stock exchange, or even being publicly held. While these drawbacks of our data source are all quite important, there was no feasible way to make alterations to the published data.

A second possible source of error is the transformation of the original categorical data into percentages which represent the mid-points of intervals, as described above in Section II. To assess the possible error from this source, each factor analysis for 1975 was replicated by SSA using counts of category codes in common between all possible pairs of countries as input. The reason for this replication is that while factor analysis requires that the data be measured on an interval scale, SSA is satisfied with nominally scaled data, a weaker level of measurement. SSA is, therefore, useful in validating the results of factor analysis when, as was done in this study, data which are measured on a scale intermediate between a nominal and interval scale is input into factor analysis. In this analysis, six dimensions were recovered from the original data. Both the disclosure and the measurement analysis yielded a Kruskal stress coefficient value of 0.07. This value is usually interpreted as indicating goodness of fit to the data, much like the R-square statistic in regression analysis. This coefficient can take on values from 0.0 to 1.0 with lower values indicating better fits. A value of .05 is usually considered to indicate a good fit.

As pointed out earlier, SSA yields coordinates and dimensions which can be used to prepare graphic plots of the original variables (i.e., countries) with respect to these dimensions. The degree of similarity between the original variables is revealed by their distances from each other. The results of the analysis are displayed in Figures 1 and 2. For ease in presentation, each country is plotted using only its scores on the first two of the six dimensions. Countries are numbered with the same numerical code used in Table 4, and each group of countries identified in the factor analysis is identified by a Roman numeral. The robustness of the groupings yielded by the factor analysis on the 1975 survey data confirms a similar finding by Frank [1979] with respect to the 1973 survey data. The implication of this finding is that measurement error in coding the data is not a limitation of this analysis.

A third possible source of concern is the lack of predictive power of the discriminant functions, especially those fitted to the disclosure groupings. Several possibilities exist which could account for the weak predictive performance of this set of discriminant functions, other than an inherent lack of distinctiveness of the disclosure groups. The (assumed correct) original assignment of the misclassified countries to common disclosure practices groups could have been in error. We discount this possibility since all of the countries in the hold-out samples had relatively high loadings on only a single factor. A partial explanation might relate to the removal of Denmark and Norway from the set of 42 countries used to form the seven disclosure groups. This transfer reduced the Scandinavian group (Group VI) to a single country, Sweden. The two single-country groups (Groups VI and VII) accordingly show an unrealistic degree of homogeneity, and might account for the misclassification of Denmark and Norway. Another explanation is the "overfitting" of the discriminant function to the sample data occurred. The relatively large number of groups (seven), small number of countries per group (from one to ten), and large number of variables in the discriminant function (13) may have combined to yield an excellent fit to the sample of 36 countries from which the six discriminant functions were constructed, but poor predictive power to new countries not in the original sample of 36. A final possible explanation is that the number of countries (six) on which the prediction tests were made is too small to be representative. Some of these possibilities were pursued further and the discriminant analysis was rerun with (a) changes in the F-level for inclusion of variables in the analysis, (b) an increase in the number of countries in the hold-out sample to a

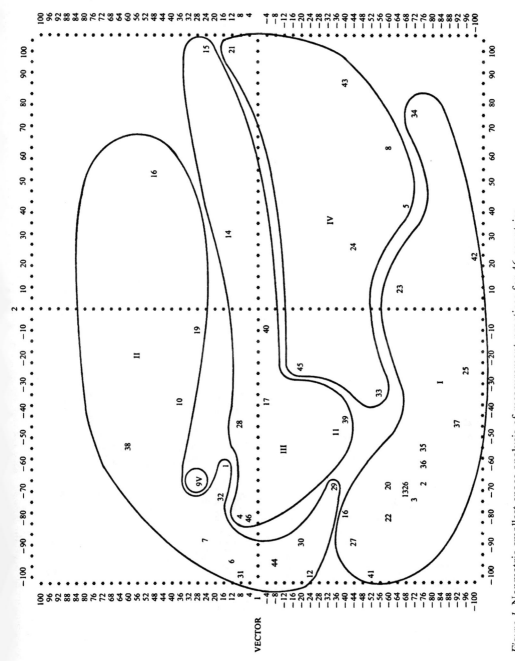

Figure 1 Nonmetric smallest-space-analysis of measurement practices for 46 countries.
(Scores on first two dimensions based on 1975 survey data)

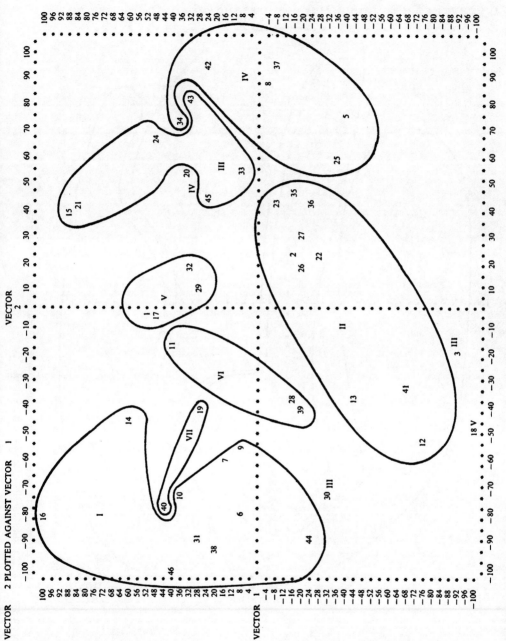

Figure 2 Nonmetric smallest-space-analysis of disclosure practices for 46 countries. (Scores on first two dimensions based on 1975 survey data)

randomly selected set of 14, and use of the remaining 28 to construct the discriminant functions, and (c) a reduction in the number of variables in the analysis to two economic structure variables (per capita income and change in the foreign exchange rate), the six total trade variables, and three language variables (English, French, and German). None of these changes had the effect of improving the predictive power of the discriminant functions or changing their form in any significant way.

The fourth limitation to be kept in mind is the possibility of omitted variables in the discriminant analysis. As pointed out by Benston [1975] and Zeff [1972], a variety of factors can have an impact on the similarities and differences between the accounting principles of countries. Many of them are factors which are difficult to quantify (and hence were excluded from the analysis). These omitted factors include the prospect of governmental intervention in the establishment of accounting standards, the professional and regulatory environment, the existence of a sophisticated and demanding financial press, the prevalence of widespread stock ownership, and the vulnerability of accountants to lawsuits. Also, in Third World countries the presence of U.S.- or U.K.-based multinational firms may be a powerful homogenizing influence.

IV. Summary and conclusions

This study attempted to determine whether the classification of countries suggested by various authors applies equally well to the measurement and disclosure subsets of accounting practices. Observations on both the disclosure and measurement practices in 1973 for a sample of 38 countries were factor-analyzed, and the resulting factor structures for disclosure and measurement were compared. The environmental variables most closely associated with each set of groupings were determined by discriminant analysis. The analyses were then replicated for the same two subsets of practices using 1975 data on the measurement and disclosure practices for 46 countries. It was found that the number of groupings, the character and composition of each group, and even the underlying environmental variables most closely associated with the practices were quite different between the two subsets of accounting practices.

The major implication of these findings is that the groupings of countries and the classification schemes offered by authors such as Seidler [1967] and Frank [1979] may have only limited validity. The clearcut distinctions that they propose are found to apply primarily to the measurement subset of practices. The disclosure practices do not seem to conform to any such conceptual classification schemes. They present a picture of greater diversity where the boundary lines between different groups become blurred and indistinct. A less direct implication is that greater care needs to be exercised in cross-country comparisons. Since the affiliation of a given country with others is dependent upon the set of accounting practices selected, the validity of cross-country comparisons depends upon the nature of the practice on which the comparison is made. For example, the financial statements of Belgian and Swiss firms are much more comparable on the measurement subset than on the disclosure subset.

Both the earlier Frank [1979] research and this study have established a clear association between economic and cultural variables and accounting groupings. The next step in this line of research would be to establish empirically a direction of causation with a longitudinal study of a sample of countries over a sufficiently long period of time. The objective would be to see whether, as economic structure and trade and cultural affiliations change over time, they are accompanied by a change in accounting affiliations. Another direction that research could take is that of using the methodology presented in the first part of the study, factor analysis, as a tool for evaluating the success of harmonization measures. A decreasing number of groups over time would be an indicator of success in reducing the diversity of accounting practices. This kind of research could further help policy makers by isolating the specific practices which cause the most difference between groups of countries. For instance, the differences between groups may be caused by differences in a small set of practices such as those dealing with inflation. The attention of policy makers attempting to harmonize accounting practices could then be directed toward these practices.

Since this research was largely aimed at empirically assessing the validity of international classifications proposed repeatedly in the accounting literature rather than researching specific issues of policy alternatives, it is difficult to make definite policy prescriptions. This task is complicated further by the fact that the basic thrust of our empirical results is that the situation is more complex than has generally been assumed by accountants and may not be amenable to easy manipulations by policy makers. The findings do suggest that policy-making bodies concerned with the harmonization of international accounting standards should concern themselves with reducing diversity in disclosure practices, since it it is with respect to them that the greatest dispersion exists. Our findings, however, tend to confirm the conclusions drawn by Frank [1979] that underlying environmental variables are closely associated with the groupings obtained from accounting practices. The implications of this are that reaching the goal of harmonization may be difficult because, given the above association, countries may be reluctant to make a change in accounting practices so long as the underlying environmental variables are significantly different. If this is the case, then the issuance of authoritative standards by policy-making bodies may be a less effective force for harmonization of accounting practices than is the growing commonality of world-wide economic interests.

Notes

1 The list of practices falling into each group for each year is available from the authors.
2 Details on the procedures used to collect, process, and check the consistency of the survey data were obtained from Alan D. Stickler of Price Waterhouse & Co., Toronto.

References

Accounting Principles Board (APB) (1970), "Basic Concepts and Accounting Principles Underlying Financial Statements of Business Enterprises," *Statement No. 4* (AICPA, 1970).

Beaver, W. H. (1978), "Current Trends in Corporate Disclosure," *Journal of Accountancy* (January 1978), pp. 44–52.

Benston, G. J. (1975), "Accounting Standards in the United States and the United Kingdom: Their Nature, Causes and Consequences," *Vanderbilt Law Review* (January 1975), pp. 235–68.

Buckley, J. W. and M. H. Buckley (1974), *The Accounting Profession* (Melville, 1974).

Choi, F. D. S. and G. G. Mueller (1978), *An Introduction to Multinational Accounting* (Prentice-Hall, 1978).

Financial Accounting Standards Board (FASB) (1978), "Objectives of Financial Reporting by Business Enterprises," *Statement of Financial Accounting Concepts No. 1* (FASB, 1978).

Frank, W. G. (1979), "An Empirical Analysis of International Accounting Practices," *Journal of Accounting Research* (Autumn 1979).

Mueller, G. G. (1967), *International Accounting* (Macmillan Company, 1967).

——, "Accounting Principles Generally Accepted in the United States Versus Those Generally Accepted Elsewhere," *The International Journal of Accounting Education and Research* (Spring 1968), pp. 91–103.

Previts, G. J. (1975), "On The Subject of Methodology and Models of International Accountancy," *The International Journal of Accounting Education and Research* (Spring 1975), pp. 1–12.

Price Waterhouse International, *Accounting Principles and Reporting Practices* (Price Waterhouse, 1973).

——, *Accounting Principles and Reporting Practices* (Price Waterhouse, 1975).

"Report of the Committee on Generally Accepted Accounting Principles for Smaller and/or Closely Held Businesses," *Journal of Accountancy* (October 1976), pp. 116–20.

Rummel, R. J. (1970), *Applied Factor Analysis* (Northwestern University Press, 1970).

Seidler, L. J. (1967), "International Accounting—The Ultimate Theory Course," THE ACCOUNTING REVIEW (October 1967), pp. 775–81.

Zeff, S. A. (1972), *Forging Accounting Principles in Five Countries: A History and an Analysis of Trends* (Stipes Publishing Company, 1972).

15

AN EMPIRICAL ANALYSIS OF INTERNATIONAL ACCOUNTING PRINCIPLES

A comment

C. W. Nobes

Source: *Journal of Accounting Research* 19(1) (1981): 268–70.

In a recent article in this *Journal*, Frank uses data from the 1973 Price Waterhouse survey of financial accounting practices to classify countries' accounting systems into groups.[1] While the methodology seems more satisfactory and the results greatly more reasonable than those reported elsewhere using the same data,[2] neither Frank nor other researchers have investigated the reliability of these data and how appropriate they are for their statistical analyses.

I believe that the data may be questionable on three counts. First, they may contain some straightforward mistakes. These are illustrated in table 1. The easiest answers for me to check are those for the United Kingdom in the 1976 survey. Note that if such answers can be wrong for this country, would it be reasonable to rely on similar answers for Bolivia?

Second, some of the answers, although either strictly or conditionally true are misleading, particularly to a computer. Table 2 gives examples of this. The survey's impression that U.K. or U.S. accounting is as conservative as German accounting and more conservative than French accounting is surely misleading. The table hides the fact that German or French conservatism is of a wholly different order than Anglo-Saxon prudence.[3] Regarding the "clear profit figure," anyone acquainted with continental European financial statements knows of the greater difficulty in arriving at a figure for, say, profit after corporation tax but before extraordinary items, transfers to reserves, and payment of dividends. Moreover, in Germany, the "contrived" nature of the profit is well known.

Table 1 Survey Answers for the United Kingdom.

	Number and Score	
Practice	*1973*	*1976*
A. "Land is shown separately from other fixed assets." *Comment:* It is normally not separated from buildings.	77, Required	40, Required
B. "Cost of inventories is determined by *FIFO*."		93, Required
"Cost of inventories is determined by Weighted Average."		95, Not permitted
"Cost of inventories is determined by Retail Inventory." *Comment: SSAP 9* specifically allows all three (appendix, paras. 11–14).		98, Not permitted
C. There are several examples where U.K. practice is said to differ from Irish practice in 1976, even though the countries used identical Standards on the subject, e.g., 205.		
D. "Leases are capitalized by the lessee." *Comment:* This was not the case in 1973 or 1976; a forthcoming exposure draft calling for this is expected to meet criticism.	178, Majority	47, Majority

Table 2 1973 Survey Answers.

	Country and Score*			
PW *Practice*	*U.S.*	*U.K.*	*France*	*West Germany*
11. Conservatism applies	5	5	4	5
201. Clear profit figure	2	5	5	5
14. Consolidated statements *only*	4	1	2	1
15. Consolidated + parent statements	1	5	2	5
16. Parent statements *only*	1	1	4	1
49. *EPS* disclosed	5	5	2	1
50. *EPS* on outstanding shares	1	5	4	1
51. *EPS* on shares and equivalents	5	1	1	1

* 1 = not permitted or not found; 2 = minority practice; 3 = followed by half of the companies; 4 = majority practice; 5 = required.

Thirdly, the questions were not chosen for the purpose for which Frank and others used them. This may be illustrated by the consolidation questions in table 2 (14, 15, and 16). The most revealing of these is 16, but when all three are put into a computer with equal weight, confusion must result. Similarly, the important answers to question 49 will be diluted by 50 and 51. Finally, discriminating questions whether the accounting is designed to present a "fair" view, and about whether one finds income smoothing, secret reserves, tax-based depreciation, etc. are missing entirely. It is natural to try to avoid subjectivity in the selection of data, but the refusal to select here means that one is left with the subjective choice of several busy *PW* staff who had a different purpose in mind than do researchers who might use the data.

These problems appear not to be too serious for Frank's analysis, mainly because his results are so appealing. Whatever errors exist are probably minor and unsystematic. The one bias I personally fear is that the differences between the U.K. and the U.S. are comparatively exaggerated because of their familiarity to the question compilers who come from these countries. For example, in both the da Costa *et al.* and the Frank results, the classification of the U.S. with Germany and not with the U.K. seems to run heavily counter to experience in using sets of published financial statements.

I think that any future researchers who intend to use *PW* or similar data should first investigate these possible data problems or at least acknowledge them in their publications.

Notes

1 Werner G. Frank, "An Empirical Analysis of International Accounting Principles," *Journal of Accounting Research* (Autumn 1979): 593–605; Price Waterhouse and Co., *Accounting Principles and Practices: A Survey in 38 Countries* (New York, 1973).
2 R. C. da Costa, J. C. Bourgeois, and W. M. Lawson, "A Classification of International Financial Accounting Practices," *International Journal of Accounting* (Spring 1978).
3 See G. G. Mueller, *International Accounting* (New York: Macmillan, 1967), pt. 1; J. H. Benny, *European Financial Reporting, West Germany* (London: Institute of Chartered Accountants in England and Wales, 1975), chaps. 3 and 4; J. H. Benny, *European Financial Reporting, France* (London: Institute of Chartered Accountants in England and Wales, 1976), chaps. 6–8; C. W. Nobes, "Why International Accounting Is Important," *The Accountant* (September 1977): 277–78, 312–14; and M. Lafferty, *Accounting in Europe* (Cambridge: Woodhead-Faulkner, 1975), pp. 8–21, 50–64.

16

A JUDGEMENTAL INTERNATIONAL CLASSIFICATION OF FINANCIAL REPORTING PRACTICES

C. W. Nobes

Source: *Journal of Business Finance and Accounting* 10(1) (1983): 1–19.

Much recent work and published material has concerned the classification of countries into groups by their financial reporting practices. The purpose of classification has been discussed in that material (cited below) and elsewhere (AAA, 1977). Briefly, it is seen as a fundamental step in an organised and scientific study of a population; as a method to "sharpen description and analysis" (AAA, 1977, p.97), to reveal underlying structures, and to predict the behaviour of a member of the population; and as a tool to assist in the analysis of the need for, means towards and progress of harmonisation.

The aim here is to examine the recent papers and their weaknesses, and to propose an alternative approach. After a brief survey of these papers, they are examined in greater detail by looking at the data and methodology they used. The alternative approach of this paper is proposed in the third section, which includes a detailed statement of the problem tackled. It waits until then, because the other papers surveyed have not defined the problem in such detail or with exactly the same scope.

A brief survey of recent work

International classification in accounting had been discussed many times before the late 1970s, for example by Hatfield in 1911 (Hatfield, 1966) and Mueller (1967). However, from the late 1970s, a series of papers (e.g. da

Table 1 Four-group "measurement" classification (Nair and Frank).

Group I	Group II	Group III	Group IV
Australia	Argentina	Belgium	Canada
Bahamas	Bolivia	France	Japan
Fiji	Brazil	Germany	Mexico
Jamaica	Chile	Italy	Panama
Kenya	Colombia	Spain	Philippines
Netherlands	Ethiopia	Sweden	United States
New Zealand	India	Switzerland	
Pakistan	Paraguay	Venezuela	
Republic of Ireland	Peru		
Rhodesia	Uruguay		
Singapore			
South Africa			
Trinidad and Tobago			
United Kingdom			

Source: Nair and Frank, 1980, p.429.

Costa *et al.*, 1978; Frank, 1979; Nair and Frank, 1980; and Goodrich, 1982) have reported on a "scientific" approach to classification, which has moved away from the earlier "subjective" studies.

These recent studies have used data on differences in practices between countries provided in the surveys of Price Waterhouse (1973, 1975 and 1979). These data have been subjected to factor analysis in order to identify important discriminating variables, and then a clustering technique has been used. This results in a number of groupings of countries: from two to six groups depending on the researchers and the survey they were using (Table 1 shows such a grouping). The intention is to produce groups of countries whose accounting characteristics are more similar to those of other members of the same group than to those of members of another group. In the case of Nair and Frank (1980), the accounting practices were split into those relating to accounting measurements and those relating to disclosure, and then two separate analyses were performed. In addition, Frank (1979) and Nair and Frank (1980) investigated whether their groupings correspond with differences in underlying environmental variables.

The data and the general methodology for this are discussed and criticised in the next section; the detailed statistical techniques, which are neither criticised nor used in this paper, are explained in the original papers.

Criticism of data and methodology

The data

Doubts have been expressed elsewhere on the use of the Price Waterhouse data for the purpose of classification (Nobes, 1981). Four types of problem with the 1973 data were noted: (i) straightforward mistakes, (ii) misleading answers, (iii) swamping of important questions by trivial ones, and (iv) exaggeration of the differences between the USA and the UK because of the familiarity of these countries (and thus their differences) to the compilers of the survey questions. The examples from the 1973 survey will not be repeated here, but a few errors in the 1979 survey will be mentioned.

Taking consolidation practices as an example, the survey reports that, for practice 209 ("consolidated statements . . . . are prepared for the shareholders") the answer is "required" in France. The reason given for this is that the *Commission des Opérations de Bourse* (COB) "requires" consolidation. However, as the Annual Report of COB shows, only 305 listed companies published consolidated balance sheets and profit and loss accounts in 1979 (289 in 1978). This is less than half of the listed companies, and a very much smaller proportion of "enterprises which issue their statements to the general public" about which the survey is said to be (Price Waterhouse, 1979, p.5). Further, one wonders whether consolidation practices in Fiji, Malaysia or Trinidad are really correctly understood by suggestions in various survey practices that Standard No.3 of the IASC is being followed.

These examples could be replicated many times over. They suggest that, at some points, the surveys report not on actual practices but on what practices might be if non-mandatory rules were obeyed or on what Price Waterhouse partners might like practices to be. This and the other types of error may suggest that the data are unsatisfactory for the purpose of classification. At the very least, it calls for substantial caution when interpreting the results.

The methodology

All the researchers cited above use cluster analysis on the Price Waterhouse data, and appear to consider that this may be superior to previous subjective classifications. Nair and Frank state that their research is:

> aimed at empirically assessing the validity of international classifications proposed repeatedly in the accounting literature.
>
> (p.449)

369

This version of "empiricism" may be challenged. It does not directly test a particular hypothetical classification. It classifies a mass of data which was not collected with this purpose in mind. The use of this approach leads one set of researchers (da Costa et al., 1978, p.79) to conclude that the country least like the UK group is the USA. That is, accounting in Uruguay or Ethiopia is more like accounting in the UK than accounting in the USA is. While this may be a statistically sound result from the Price Waterhouse data, it is clearly a very inaccurate representation of the real world (Mueller, 1967; and Carsberg and Eastergard, 1981). By itself such a result is of interest, but the researchers, who were generating an hypothesis from doubtful data rather than testing one,[1] fell into the trap of taking their results seriously. This led them to the conclusion that a group of countries containing France, West Germany, Belgium and Italy among many others:

> follows the lead of the United States in dissociating themselves from practice common to the British Model.

However, it seems highly unlikely that the makers of the detailed and rigid company and tax laws that govern accounting in such countries bear in mind either that they should follow the USA or that they should dissociate themselves from the UK when legislating. The differences between the USA and continental European countries are great, and also suggest that there is no accidental or subconscious "following" of the former by the latter (Mueller, 1967; Macharzina, 1981; and Parker, 1981).

A further illustration of the unlikely results that may be obtained by these so-called "empirical" methods is the classification by Goodrich (1982) which suggests that accounting in the USA is more similar to that in Peru or Bolivia than it is to accounting in the UK (from which US accounting developed); and that Australia is in the same group as Japan and Colombia but in a different group from New Zealand and the UK, which have very similar accounting to Australia (Standish, 1981).

The problem that these two examples illustrate stems from the use of data which contains errors and which was not designed for the purpose in hand. In order to seek a way out of these difficulties, it may be useful to draw an analogy with classification in other disciplines. There have been many attempts in law, economics and politics (e.g. Kagan, 1955; David and Brierley, 1978; Neuberger and Duffy, 1976; Gregory and Stuart, 1980; Finer, 1970; and Shils, 1966). However, these have been simple compared to the recent accounting attempts. Turning to the Linnaean biological system for an analogy may be more useful. To the extent that subjectivity and empiricism can be counterposed, the life scientists use a large measure of the former. Exactly which criteria to use for classification of living things, and which weights to give them are matters of judgement.

Judgement is needed to avoid such classifications as Plato's of man as a featherless biped.[2] In fact, man is now seen to be much more closely related to most quadrupeds, and to dolphins which appear to have no feet at all. Aristotle saw this latter distinction. He referred to homologues, where organs similar in structure play different roles (e.g. human feet and dolphins' flippers), and to analogues where similar functions are performed by quite different organs (e.g. birds' wings and bees' wings). It is the homologues which indicate nearness.

David and Brierley (1978, p.19) make a similar point when discussing the classification of legal systems:

> When endeavouring to determine the families into which different laws can be grouped, it is preferable to take into consideration these constant elements rather than the less stable rules found in the law at any given moment . . . . The classification of laws into families should not be made on the basis of the similarity or dissimilarity of any particular legal rules, important as they may be; this is . . . . inappropriate when highlighting what is truly significant in the characteristics of a given system of law.

Looking in more detail at the Linnaean biological classification, one notes that, when classifying plants or animals, biologists largely ignore the most obvious characteristics. That is, they do not carry out factor analysis on animals by weight, colour, number of legs, nature of body covering, length of life, etc. This would merely lead to a classification of those data. It would put men with ostriches, dolphins with sharks, bats with owls, and so on. In fact, by concentrating on a subjective model which involves underlying (but less obvious) characteristics, biologists classify men, dolphins and bats more closely with each other than with any of the other three types of animal. It is then found that behaviour, intelligence, reproduction and ancestry begin to fit with the classification. The biological scientists, then, use a classification which is evolutionary and concentrates on underlying fundamental variables.

The analogy with classification in accounting seems clear. The danger with "empirical" classifications is that one merely classifies the Price Waterhouse data, which concentrate on differences which may be ephemeral and superficial (and which may not be correctly recorded). The need is apparent for a model based on the evolution of accounting practices and upon variables which have caused differences in them. This needs to be checked against carefully measured "structural" practices.

A hypothetical classification

Thus, it would be possible to criticise previous classifications for (i) lack of precision in the definition of what is to be classified, (ii) lack of a model to compare the statistical results with, (iii) lack of hierarchy which would add more subtlety to the portrayal of the size of differences between countries, and (iv) lack of judgement in the choice of "important" discriminating features. Can these problems be remedied?

(i) Definition

The purpose of the present research is to classify countries by the financial reporting practices of *public companies*. The countries chosen as a population are those of the *developed Western world;* the reporting practices will be those concerned with *measurement and valuation*. The date of the classification is *1980*, before the enactments in EEC countries of the Fourth Directive on Company Law.

It is public companies whose financial statements are generally available, and whose practices can be most easily discovered. It is the international differences in reporting between such companies which are of interest to shareholders, creditors, auditing firms, taxation authorities, managements and harmonizing agencies (like the International Accounting Standards Committee or the EEC Commission) (Mason, 1978, ch.5). It is really only in developed Western countries that public companies exist in large numbers. It has been mentioned above that the Price Waterhouse data seem to suffer from the difficulties of holding this factor constant across their very broad coverage.

Measurement and vaulation practices have been chosen because these determine the size of the figures for profit, capital, total assets, liquidity and so on. Nair and Frank (1980, pp.426 and 428) point out that it is useful to separate measurement from disclosure practices.[3] The present research deals with the former only; the latter would require an additional paper.

(ii) and (iii) A model with a hierarchy

The hypothetical classification shown as Table 2 was drawn up in 1979 and first published in 1980;[4] it has been slightly amended since then. It is based on the evolution of accounting, and the suggestions of many academics interested in comparative accounting.[4] Some explanatory variables for differences in measurement practices were also borne in mind when drawing up this proposed classification; for example, the importance of the influence of law or of economics.[5] Some descriptions are included at the branching points in Table 2. The proposed classification which results from consideration of these background factors is designed as a "prediction" of how countries will be grouped together on consideration of their measurement practices. The testing of this is the main subject of the rest of this paper.

Table 2 A hypothetical classification of financial reporting measurement practices in developed western countries in 1980.

CLASS	Developed Western Countries
SUB-CLASS	Micro-based / Macro-Uniform
FAMILY	Business Economics, Theory — Business practice, Pragmatic, British origin (UK Influence, US Influence) — Continental: Tax, Legal / Government — Government, Economics
SPECIES	Netherlands — Australia NZ UK Ireland Canada USA — Italy France Belgium Spain W. Germany Japan Sweden

The number of countries is kept to 14,[6] but all these are developed Western nations; they are all included in the Price Waterhouse Surveys and thus in the results of the above researchers; and they include all the countries identified as "vital" by Mason (1978, ch.6) for the purposes of international harmonization.

Previous classifications have contained separate groups (e.g. Table 1) but no hierarchy which would indicate the comparative distances between the groups. It may well be reasonable to classify the UK and the USA in different groups, but it might be useful to demonstrate that these two groups are closely linked compared to, say, continental European countries.

The classification in Table 2 contains a hierarchy which borrows its labels from biology.

(iv) Discriminating features

An attempt has been made to isolate those features of a county's accounting which may constitute long-run fundamental differences between countries. The exercise was made possible by having reduced the scope to 14 countries with public companies. A programme of visits, interviews and reading relating to these countries was carried out. The result was a selection of nine factors which unlike the factors of most of the researchers above, are overt and thus available for inspection, criticism and amendment (see Table 3).

These factors are designed to operate for developed Western countries, which share certain economic features. Thus, if one wished to include developing countries or Eastern bloc countries, it would be necessary to

Table 3 Factors for differentiation.

Factor No. and Abbreviation	Factor Name
1 (USER)	Type of users of the published accounts of the listed companies
2 (LAW)	Degree to which law or standards prescribe in deatil, and exclude judgement
3 (TAX)	Importance of tax rules in measurement
4 (PRU)	Conservatism/prudence (e.g. valuation of buildings, stocks, debtors)
5 (HC)	Strictness of application of historic cost (in the historic cost accounts)
6 (RC)	Susceptibility to replacement cost adjustments in main or supplementary accounts.
7 (CONS)	Consolidation
8 (PROV)	Ability to be generous with provisions (as opposed to reserves) and to smooth income
9 (UNI)	Uniformity between companies in application of rules

include other discriminating factors, like degree of development of economy or nature of economic systems. Incidentally, such a process might not be sensible because there are few or no public companies in these other countries, so one would have to classify something other than published financial reporting.

Also, the nine factors do not include consideration of, for example, whether on "a sale by a parent company to its partly owned subsidiary, profit is eliminated only to the extent of the parent's interest" or whether "deferred taxes are provided on timing differences resulting from intercompany transactions." These are Practices 222 and 224 of the Price Waterhouse Survey (1979). They are perfectly legitimate for the purpose of the Survey but they (and 40 or so other consolidation practices) are trivial in comparison to Practice 210 on whether or not a country's companies present consolidated financial statements. However, in the "empirical" research using the Survey, all 40 practices were given equal weight.[7]

It is not straightforward to separate out measurement practices from explanatory variables. However, it is clear that at least the first two factors in Table 3 are examples of the latter. Other factors are less clear. For example, the "taxation" factor could be taken as a factor explaining differences, or, by scoring this factor on the basis of whether particular valuations are affected by tax rules, it could be seen as a measurement practice. All the factors except the first two have been taken in this latter sense, and scored using examples of practices.

This difficulty is shared by all the studies mentioned in the first section of this paper, where a number of characteristics like "conservatism" or "tax effects" were included. In this case, two separate exercises are carried out. First, factors 1, 2 and 3 are analysed as explanatory variables; then, factors 3 to 9 are analysed as measurement practices. Before this can be done, the nine factors must be measured for each of the 14 countries.

The testing

Scoring

The basis of scoring countries on factors is shown in the "morphology" of Table 4. The scores are set out in Table 5. The scoring was done on the basis of an extensive programme of reading, followed by visits to a great majority of the countries included. References for the accounting practices of countries are included in an Appendix. The author will be pleased to supply a detailed justification of the scoring on request.

The scale 0 to 3 was chosen on the grounds that it compromised between a smaller scale, which would have restricted differentiation, and a larger scale, which would have exaggerated the fineness with which judgement is possible. It is clear that one problem is the implied assumption of linearity.

Table 4 Morphology based on table 3.

Factor	0	1	2	3
1 USER)	banks, revenue		institutions	individuals
2 (LAW)	detailed prescription			lack of prescriptions, much room for judgement
3 (TAX)*	nearly all figs. determined			no figures determined
4 (PRU)**	heavy conservatism			dominance of accruals
5 (HC)	no exceptions			many exceptions
6 (RC)	no susceptibility	small experimentation	supplementary	used, considered for all
7 (CONS)	rare consolidation	some consolidation	domestic subsids	all subsids + assocs
8 (PROV)	considerable flexibility			no room for smoothing
9 (UNI)	compulsory accounting plan			no standardised format, rules or definitions

* Scoring on this factor (see Table 5) is carried out using particular valuation practices affected by taxation, i.e. depreciation, bad debt provisions, the valuation of buildings and the establishment of provisions for risks, contingencies, etc.
** Scoring on this factor is based on particular practices, i.e. the prevalance of provisions in the valuation of stocks and debtors, and the strength of rules against capitalisation of certain expenses.

Table 5 Scoring based on table 4.

	Australia	Belgium	Canada	France	Germany	Italy	Japan	Netherlands	New Zealand	R. of Ireland	Spain	Sweden	UK	USA
1 (USER)	3	1	3	1	0	1	0	2	3	2	1	0	2	3
2 (LAW)	3	1	2	1	0	1	1	3	3	2	1	1	2	1
3 (TAX)	3	0	3	0	0	1	0	3	3	3	1	0	3	2
4 (PRU)	2	0	2	0	0	0	0	3	2	2	0	0	2	2
5 (HC)	2	1	1	1	0	0	0	3	2	3	1	0	3	1
6 (RC)	2	1	2	1	0	0	0	3	2	2	0	1	2	2
7 (CONS)	3	1	3	1	2	0	1	3	3	3	0	2	3	3
8 (PROV)	2	1	2	1	1	1	0	2	2	2	1	0	2	3
9 (UNI)	3	0	3	0	1	2	1	3	3	3	0	1	3	3

However, it is also a problem with all the previous research, and the results in the following figures may be seen to be so clear that some other reasonable assumption would not alter the classification seriously.

It may also be noted that the "direction" of the factors could be altered, that is that Factor 4 might have "heavy conservatism" with a score of "3" (see Table 4). This is dealt with by concentrating on differences or roots of squared differences, as seen below.

A further matter to consider is what weights the factors should have. The implication in all the previous research reviewed and reported here is that all practices have equal weight. This procedure is continued here, but the analysis is repeated With three of the factors being given double weight to see if the results are sensitive to such adjustments.

Finally, one might be criticised for adding different factors together as though they were measured in the same units. This is connected with the weighting problem. All previous researchers had to do this addition, which perhaps may not be so serious when dealing with the *differences* in scores, and in the light of the clear results which follow.

Analysts of results

The final stage is to analyse these figures in order to produce a classification. Several methods are attempted.

(i) Totalling

A simple analysis is merely to total the scores. This ignores the non-linearity of the scoring system, and assumes that none of the factors is "back to front". However, the extremely clean split of the countries into two groups (as in Table 6) may reduce concern about these problems. The high-scoring countries correspond with the "micro" group of Table 2, and the low-scoring countries with the "macro" group. This split is clear both for the explanatory variables and for the measurement practices. Having established that the two point in the same direction, the rest of the analysis will proceed with measurement practices only, as it is these which are to be classified.

(ii) Totalling differences

A somewhat more sophisticated approach is to calculate the sum of the differences on the factors, taking all possible pairs of countries. For example, using the scored morphology of Table 5, one might find the difference in the scores of Australia and Belgium on Factor 3 and add this to the difference on Factor 4, and so on. This would give a matrix of differences as shown in Table 7, The difference in scores for the pair Australia-Belgium is seen to be "13".

Table 6 Totals from Table 5.

	Practices	*Explanatory*
Netherlands	20	8
United Kingdom	18	7
Ireland	18	7
Australia	17	9
New Zealand	17	9
Canada	16	8
United States	16	6
France	4	2
Italy	4	3
Belgium	4	2
Sweden	4	1
W. Germany	4	0
Spain	3	3
Japan	2	1

Table 7 Matrix of total differences between countries.

	Aus	*Bel*	*Can*	*Fra*	*Ger*	*Ita*	*Jap*	*NL*	*NZ*	*Ire*	*Spa*	*Swe*	*UK*	*USA*
Aus	0													
Bel	13	0												
Can	1	12	0											
Fra	13	0	12	0										
Ger	13	4	12	4	0									
Ita	13	6	12	6	4	0								
Jap	15	4	14	4	2	4	0							
NL	3	16	4	16	16	16	18	0						
NZ	0	13	1	13	13	13	15	3	0					
Ire	1	14	2	14	14	14	16	2	1	0				
Spa	14	3	13	3	5	3	5	17	14	15	0			
Swe	13	4	12	4	2	6	2	16	13	14	7	0		
UK	1	14	2	14	14	14	16	2	1	0	15	14	0	
USA	3	12	2	12	12	12	14	6	3	4	13	12	4	0

This technique may be preferable to the simple totals of Table 6. First, it avoids the need to ensure that all the factors have been placed in the correct "direction". When concentrating on differences, it would not matter if, say, factor 4 had scored "heavy conservatism" as "3" and "dominance of accruals" as "0", Secondly, concentrating on differences reveals that countries with similar total scores in Table 6 may nevertheless be significantly different from each other. For example, Italy and France have identical total scores in Table 6, but these totals have somewhat different causes. Thus Italy and France are differentiated in Table 7.

Table 8 Groups of countries from Table 7.

"Micro"	Netherlands UK, Ireland, Australia, New Zealand, Canada USA, Canada
"Macro"	France, Belgium, Spain Italy Germany, Japan, Sweden

By inspection of the information in Table 7, particularly by focusing on one country at a time by listing out the differences between it and each other country, groupings as in Table 8 may be prepared. Again, the simple classification which results seems to fit with Table 2.

(iii) Squaring the differences

One may also calculate similar information involving the totals of the squares of differences and the roots of the totals of the squares of differences. This data presents a similar picture to Table 7, and thus the remarks in the previous section apply to it.

(iv) Clustering

The next approach is to use this output (in this case, the roots of the squared differences) in a systematic way to produce clusters. A computer program designed to do this was used.[8] This starts with the two countries which are nearest to each other (in this case, Belgium and France, which have identical scores). Next. it identifies another set of two or more similar countries. That is, in this case, Australia and New Zealand, which are closer together than Belgium plus France plus x. Thus, there are now twelve clusters: Australia plus New Zealand; Belgium plus France; and ten clusters of one country each. This process continues, culminating in a "two cluster solution" which, in this case, has the same groups as Tables 6, 8 and 2.

Interesting information may be obtained by noting which countries are classified last. Italy is the last to fall into the "macro" group. This seems very reasonable. Italy has seen dramatic changes in accounting in the last few years;[9] most of these have been excluded from the 1980 scoring process, but the fact that they have occurred suggests that the country must have been different from its "macro" neighbours *before* they occurred. The USA is the last to be included in the "micro" group; this seems reasonable for a group which starts off clustering around Australia and New Zealand.

379

Table 9 Four-group clustering.

1	2	3	4
Australia	Netherlands	Belgium	Germany
Canada	Ireland	France	Japan
New Zealand	UK	Italy	Sweden
USA		Spain	

The four-group cluster is shown as Table 9.[10] This seems plausible, but it illustrates one of the problems of clustering. The data used here for clustering do not suggest that Australia is more like the USA than the UK (see Table 7). However, Table 9 does suggest this. The confusion arises because the USA is the last "micro" country to fall into a group, and it is easier for the program to get the USA into group 1 of Table 9 than to get the whole of group 2 into group 1 instead. The "problem" arises because Australia-plus-New Zealand and UK-plus-Ireland set themselves up as groups in the early stages of clustering. Once the clusters have thus been "seeded", they tend to grow and resist combination with other clusters. If the clustering process were seeded around the USA and the UK, slightly different groups would emerge. Indeed, a group consisting of Australia, New Zealand, Ireland and the UK has a considerably smaller "total internal difference" than the group: Australia, Canada, New Zealand and the USA.[11] However, the groupings are very stable even if factors 3, 4 and 5 are given double weighting or if Australia, Ireland and Belgium (which have identical scores to New Zealand, the UK and France, respectively, and thus seed immediate clusters) are omitted.

Conclusion

The scoring and testing process reported on above seems to support the hypothetical classification presented as Table 2, which was drawn up nearly two years before that process. The split between the two "classes" is very clear in Table 6. The further split into subclasses and then families is best supported by Table 8, which draws on Table 7.

It may be noted that the classification of Nair and Frank (1980) as shown in Table 1 is also quite closely consistent with Table 2 for the relevant countries; the main difference being that the "macro" group has not been split up. However, this should probably not be seen as support for Table 2 nor for "empirical" classification using the Price Waterhouse data, because most of the other "empirical" results reported in the first part of this paper are quite different from Table 2 and from Nair and Frank's results.

Thus, this paper has proposed a classification based on evolution and "general knowledge" of background factors. This has been tested by selecting factors which are thought to be long-run and "structural", and by scoring these on the basis of detailed investigation in particular countries. Such a process of hypothesis, followed by selection and analysis of data specifically designed to test it, might be claimed to be *more* scientific and reliable than research which generates hypotheses from data which may be unreliable and unsuitable for such a purpose.

Acknowledgements

The author wishes to express his gratitude for the comments of R. H. Parker, I. C. Stewart and an anonymous referee on earlier drafts of this paper. (Paper received March 1982, revised August 1982).

Notes

1 See Armstrong (1967) for a powerful exposition of the pitfalls of factor analysis used without a theoretical framework.
2 There is a useful discussion of this problem under "Cassifcation, Biological" in *Encyclopaedia Britannica*, 15th edn. vol.4, pp.683–694. Also, see Knight (1981).
3 It is convincingly suggested that measurement practices and disclosure practices produce different classifications. Thus, to combine them would cause "interference". To study dislosure practices would involve a separate and additional research programme. The author regards the classification of measurement practices as the more difficult, useful and interesting task.
4 The author is particularly grateful to R. H. Parker for comments on the first draft of the hypothesis. It was first presented at the AUTA conference, Loughborough, April 1980, when useful suggestions were received. It has also been discussed at Staff Seminars at Monash University University of Tasmania, University of New South Wales and the Australian National University. It was published in a tentative way in Nobes and Parker (1981, p.213).
5 The causal relationships cannot easily be proved, but many may be fairly easily demonstrated to be plausible. For example, see Nobes and Parker (1981, pp.3–6).
6 The countries were chosen as those with whose accounting the author was already familiar, or those which were "vital" and with whose accounting the author made himself familiar. It is hoped that this may be regarded as reasonable coverage of the developed Western world.
7 The da Costa, *et al.* (1978) work omitted some factors, because they were "uniform" across countries. It is not possible to tell which factors they refer to.
8 The programs used were "clustering by nearest neighbour" and "clustering by furthest neighbour" (see, K. V. Mardia, J. T. Kent and J. M. Bibby, *Multivariate Analysis*, Academic Press, London, 1979, pp.369–375).
9 The taxation system in Italy was reformed as from 1.1.1974. This reduced the arbitrariness of tax assessments by limiting the power of inspectors. It has resulted in the partial freeing of financial accounting from tax accounting; e.g. the greater use of the accruals convention and "fairness". In June 1974 the Stock Exchange body *(Commissione Nazionale per le Società e la Borsa)* was formed. In March 1975 a presidential decree required listed companies to have a more extensive audit (effective date: 1982 onwards). These will be carried out mainly by Anglo-American audit firms using new Accounting Standards issued by the professional accounting body from 1979. These have a strong Anglo-American flavour.

10 This grouping was produced using a computer program "clustering by furthest neighbour" with the roots of the squared differences of the data in Table 5.

11 "Total internal difference" merely sums the differences on each pair of countries, using the differences in Table 7. For Australia, New Zealand, Ireland and the UK, the total internal difference is 4; for the alternative group, as in Table 9, the difference is 10.

Appendix
References for accounting in some countries considered in the text

France: Mueller (1967), pp.103–108.
Beeny (1976).
Nobes and Parker (1981), ch.4.
Choi and Mueller (1978), chs.2 and 6.

West Germany: Mueller (1967), ch.4.
Beeny (1975).
Macharzina (1981).
Choi and Mueller (1978), chs.2 and pp.191–192.

Netherlands: Mueller (1967), ch.2.
Muis (1975).
Klaassen (1980).
Nobes and Parker (1981), ch.6.
Choi and Mueller (1978), ch.2 and pp.195–196.
Beeny and Chastney (1978).

United States: Carsberg and Eastergard (1981).
Choi and Mueller (1978), ch.2.
Mueller (1967), ch.3.
Benston (1976).
Zeff (1972).

Canada: Carsberg and Eastergard (1981), pp.275, 281.
Zeff (1972).

Sweden: Choi and Mueller (1978), pp.25, 38–40, 113, 114, 218, 219.
Johansson (1965).
Mueller (1967), pp.27–30, 95–96, 108–109, 229.
Price Waterhouse (1979) on consolidation and equity method.

Japan: Ohno et al. (1975).
Dale (1979).
Katsuyama (1976).
Ballon et al. (1975), chs.10 to 15.

Italy: Stillwell (1976).

Belgium: Pauwells and Flower (forthcoming).

Spain: McRossin (1975).
Forrester (1981).
Donaghy and Laidler (1982).

References

American Accounting Association (1977), Report of the Committee on International Accounting Operations and Education, *Accounting Review Supplement,* (1977), pp.65–132.

Armstrong, J. S. (1967), "Derivation of Theory by Means of Factor Analysis", *American Statistician,* (December 1967), pp.17–21.

Ballon, *et al.* (1976), *Financial Reporting in Japan* (Kodansha Int. Ltd., 1976).

Beeny, J. H. (1975), *European Financial Reporting – 1* (ICAEW, 1975).

—— (1976), *European Financial Reporting – 11* (ICAEW, 1976).

—— and J. C. Chastney (1978), *European Financial Reporting – 4* (JCAEW, 1978), London.

Benston, G. J. (1976), "Public (US) Compared to Private (UK) Regulation of Corporate Financial Disclosure", *Accounting Review* (July 1976).

Carsberg, B. and A. Easterguard (1981), "Financial Reporting in North America" in (Nobes and Parker, 1981).

Choi, F. D. S. and G. G. Mueller (1978), *An Introduction to Multinational Accounting* (Prentice Hall, 1978).

da Costa, R. C., J. C. Bourgeois and W. M. Lawson (1978), "A Classification of International Financial Accounting Practices", *International Journal of Accounting* (Spring 1978), pp.73–85.

Dale, B. (1979), "Accounting in Japan", *Australian Accountant* (April 1979).

David, R. and J. E. C. Brierley (1978), *Major Legal Systems in the World Today* (Stevens, 1978).

Donaghy, P. J. and J. Laidler (1982), *European Fnancial Reporting – 5* (ICAEW, 1982).

Finer, S. E. (1970), *Comparative Government* (Penguin, 1970), p45.

Forrester, D. A. R. (ed.) (1981), *Spanish Accounting in the Past and Present,* (Strathclyde Convergencies, University of Strathclyde, 1981), ch.3.

Frank, W. G. (1979), "An Empirical Analysis of International Accounting Principles", *Journal of Accounting Research* (Autumn 1979), pp.593–605.

Goodrich, P. S. (1982), "A Typology of International Accounting Principles and Policies", *AUTA Review* (1982).

Gregory, P. R. and R. C. Stuart (1980), *Comparative Government* (Praeger, 1980).

Hatfield, H. R. (1966), "Some Variations in Accounting Practices in England, France, Germany and the US", *Journal of Accounting Research* (Autumn 1966).

Johansson, S. (1965), "An Appraisal of the Swedish System of Investment Reserves", *International Journal of Accounting* (Fall 1965).

Kagan, K. K. (1955), *Three Great Systems of Jurisprudence* (Stevens, 1955).

Katsuyama, S. (1976), "Recent Problems of the Financial Accounting System in Japan", *International Journal of Accounting* (Fall 1976).

Klaassen, J. (1980), "An Accounting Court: The Impact of the Enterprise Chamber on Financial Reporting in the Netherlands", *Accounting Review* (April 1980).

Macharzina, K. (1981), "Financial Reporting in West Germany" in (Nobes and Parker, 1981).

Mason, A. K. (1978), The Development of International Reporting Standards (ICRA, 1978).

McRossin, F. M. (1975), "Spain – Country at the Crossroads", *Accountant's Magazine* (February 1975).

Mueller, G. G. (1967), *International Accounting* (Macmillan, 1967), Part 1.

Muis, J. (1975), "Current Value Accounting in the Netherlands: Fact or Fiction?", *Accountant's Magazine* (November 1975).

Nair, R. D. and W. G. Frank (1980), "The Impact of Disclosure and Measurement Practices on International Accounting Classification", *Accounting Review* (July 1980), pp.426–449.

Neuberger, E. and W. Duffy (1976), *Comparative Economic Systems*, (Allyn and Bacon, 1976) chs.6 to 9.

Nobes, C. W. (1981), "An Empirical Analysis of International Accounting Principles: A Comment", *Journal of Accounting Research* (Spring 1981), pp.268–270.

—— and R. H. Parker (1981), *Comparative International Accounting* (Philip Allan, 1981).

Ohno, *et al.* (1975), "Recent Changes in Accounting Standards in Japan", *International Journal of Accounting* (Fall 1975).

Parker, R. H. (1981), "Financial Reporting in France" in (Nobes and Parker, 1981).

Pauwells, P. A. and J. F. Flower (forthcoming), *European Financial Reporting – 6* (ICAEW, forthcoming).

Price Waterhouse (1973), *Accounting Principles and Reporting Practices* (Price Waterhouse, 1973).

—— (1975), *Accounting Principles and Reporting Practices* (P.W. 1975).

—— (1979), *International Survey of Accounting Principles and Reporting Practices*, (Butterworths, 1979).

Shils, E. (1966), *Political Development in the New States*, (Mouton, 1966).

Standish, P. E. M. (1981), "Financial Reporting in Britain and Australia" in (Nobes and Parker, 1981).

Stillwell, M. (1976), *European Financial Reporting – 3. Italy* (ICAEW, 1976), p.49.

Zeff, S. A. (1978), "The Rise of Economic Consequences", *Journal of Accountancy* (December 1978).

Part 4

MEASURING STANDARDISATION

17

MEASURING HARMONISATION OF FINANCIAL REPORTING PRACTICE

Leo G. van der Tas

Source: *Accounting and Business Research* 18(70) (1988): 157–69.

Abstract

Many organisations are currently engaged in the process of national and international harmonisation of financial reporting. This paper examines the nature of the harmonisation problem and the possibility of developing a method to quantify the degree of harmony of financial reporting practice. This quantification can be useful in determining problem areas where the degree of harmony is low, and the impact of standards on financial reporting harmony and spontaneous harmonisation, i.e. harmonisation that cannot be attributed to laws, standards or guidelines. Standard setters might use the method to set goals in respect of the required degree of harmony when issuing a standard, guideline or opinion.

Introduction

Many national and international organisations, such as the Accounting Standards Committee, the Financial Accounting Standards Board (FASB), the International Accounting Standards Committee (IASC) and the European Community (EC), and also governments, are currently engaged in the process of national and international harmonisation of financial reporting. They issue guidelines, standards and laws aiming, among other things, at the harmonisation of financial reporting practice. However, it is not always clear what harmonisation is and how to measure the impact that these organisations have on the degree of harmony.

This paper tries to quantify degrees of harmonisation. First, a framework will be developed to define harmonisation, identify the various harmonisation objects and state the object to be measured. Subsequently a method will be developed that quantifies the degree of harmony of financial reporting practice for each item in the annual accounts. This method can be used by the organisations mentioned above to identify problem areas requiring harmonisation. Second, it is possible with the aid of this method to determine when and to what extent harmonisation has taken place. Third, the method can be used to measure what impact the above-mentioned organisations have on the harmonisation of financial reporting practice by attributing changes in the degree of harmony to three factors:

1. the introduction or amendment of mandatory provisions;
2. the introduction or amendment of non-mandatory provisions;
3. spontaneous harmonisation, for example as a consequence of developments abroad or evolution of practice.

Definition of harmonisation

Financial reporting is a communication process. A company translates the events that influence its financial position and affairs into its financial report so as to provide users with information about its financial position and affairs. The translation process is based upon the company's accounting policies. As part of these policies, a company decides whether to translate a particular event in its financial report (the decision between alternative degrees of disclosure) and which accounting method to apply (the choice between alternative methods of valuation, profit determination, consolidation and presentation). For example, the company must decide whether to provide segmental information and forecasts, and whether to use historical cost or current value.

When formulating an accounting policy the company's choice between alternative degrees of disclosure and alternative accounting methods is restricted by standards. Standards will be defined as any financial reporting rule published by either the government or a private standard setting body. These standards can refer either to the degree of disclosure or to the accounting method to be applied.

Harmonisation is a coordination, a tuning of two or more objects. Users are confronted with several financial reports. It would be useful for them if these financial reports were more in harmony. Therefore, financial reports are a target of harmonisation. One way to harmonise financial reports is by formulating standards, thus setting limits to the difference between financial reports. Standards are not only a means of achieving the harmonisation of financial reports. They are also an object of harmonisation themselves. Companies, notably multinationals, are confronted with differing and sometimes conflicting national standards. For them harmonisation of standards is presumed to be useful.

Harmonisation of financial reports will be called *material harmonisation* while harmonisation of standards will be called *formal harmonisation*. This paper is confined to material harmonisation. When measuring the degree of material harmony it is possible to determine the impact of standards and formal harmonisation on material harmonisation. Since they limit the company's choice between alternatives, standards lead towards harmonisation. Formal harmonisation is not only an end in itself but also a means of accomplishing material harmonisation by coordinating the national standards. However, formal harmonisation may be accompanied by disharmonisation if the coordination of standards leads to more options for companies in one country. It should also be noted that material harmonisation can take place without being initiated by standard setting. This will be referred to as spontaneous harmonisation. The harmonisation of financial reports or standards can refer either to the degree of disclosure or to the accounting method to be applied. Harmonisation of the extent of disclosure will be called *disclosure harmonisation*, while harmonisation of the applied accounting methods will be called *measurement harmonisation*. This paper is confined to measurement harmonisation.

Thus, this paper is concerned with the harmonisation of financial reports in respect of the accounting method applied (material measurement harmonisation), which implies an increase in the degree of comparability of financial reports. Two financial reports are comparable in respect of one specific event if under the same circumstances this event is accounted for in the same way in both reports or if multiple reporting takes place. Multiple reporting means that a company gives additional information based on an accounting method other than its primary accounting method. There are three forms of multiple reporting:

1. A company provides two financial reports, each based on a different accounting method.
2. A company provides one financial report with two sets of annual accounts based on two different accounting methods.
3. A company provides one financial report with one set of annual accounts, but gives additional information so that the primary accounts can be transformed into secondary accounts based on another accounting method. For example, a company defers research and development (R&D) costs and writes them off in subsequent years. In order to make the accounts comparable with the accounts of a company which writes off R&D costs immediately, this company gives additional information, specifically the level of R&D costs deferred and the level of R&D costs written off in the current year.

In conclusion we reach the following definition:

Material measurement harmonisation is an increase in the degree of comparability and means that more companies in the same circumstances apply the same accounting method to an event or give additional information in such a way that the financial reports of more companies can be made comparable.

The words 'comparability' and 'harmony' will be used as synonyms for 'material measurement harmony'.

Another problem to be addressed is the question of when circumstances are the same. A distinction can be made between the circumstances of the company itself and the circumstances in which an event to be accounted for occurs. In the first case, the nature of the firm is involved. Taking a narrow point of view one could state that every firm operates under unique circumstances, and that consequently each firm can set up its financial reports in the way it thinks is best in line with these unique circumstances. Taking a broader point of view, companies can be grouped into categories of the same industry or the same product groups. However, most of the organisations engaged in the process of harmonisation of financial reporting use an even coarser division. In general, only companies in a limited number of sectors (such as banking and insurance) are thought to be in a position which is so special that separate provisions are necessary. This latter view is taken in this paper.

In the second case, the nature of the event is involved. We should guard against unlike events being accounted for in the same way simply for the sake of harmonisation. For example, it might be argued that the choice of depreciation method should not be imposed on the companies. This choice depends upon the situation within the company, such as the expected useful lifetime of the asset and the production process.

Measurement methods

National harmonisation

In this section a method is developed to measure the degree of comparability for each item in the financial reports, based upon the number of financial reports which are comparable in respect of an item: for example, acquisitions of fixed assets, treatment of foreign currencies. It is presumed here that two financial reports are either comparable or not comparable in respect of one item. Thus, there is no gradation in comparability when only one item is taken into account. First, a method is developed without taking multiple reporting into account. Subsequently this method is modified to make allowance for multiple reporting.

Comparability increases when the result of the choice that companies make between alternative accounting methods becomes concentrated on one or on only a limited number of accounting methods, even where the number of available methods remains the same. Thus, comparability can be considered as an increase in the degree of consensus concerning the choice between the alternative methods of accounting for an item in financial reports. Kirkpatrick (1985) suggests that a reduction in the number of alternative accounting practices contributes to harmonisation. However, the degree of harmony depends not only on the number of alternative accounting methods used, but also on the extent to which each method is applied.

The increase in the degree of consensus can be forced or stimulated, or it may be spontaneous. In the first case mandatory provisions prescribe or forbid one or more accounting methods. In the second case non-mandatory guidelines recommend or discourage the application of one or more accounting methods. In the third case the increase of the degree of consensus cannot be attributed to the introduction or amendment of mandatory or non-mandatory provisions. This spontaneous harmonisation may be caused by developments in theory, experimentation or developments in other countries.

Harmony should not be seen as synonymous with rigid uniformity. As stated in the preceding section, one should take account of differences in circumstances. The companies included in the sample to which the method is applied should be chosen carefully. They should be operating under like circumstances. It is also possible to apply the method only to companies operating in a specific industry.

Statistical methods have been developed to measure the degree of concentration. One of these concentration indices is the Herfindahl index (Theil, 1973, pp. 42–43), which is calculated by weighting the relative frequencies of the alternative opinions against each other. This means that high relative frequencies have a higher weighting than low relative frequencies. As a consequence, the Herfindahl index (H index) rises when the methods of the parties involved concentrate more on one or only a limited number of alternative methods. In this context the frequency of a method means the number of parties choosing this particular method. The relative frequency is the number of parties choosing this particular method divided by the total number of parties.

An example may serve to illustrate the H index. A particular item can be accounted for by two different methods, A and B. Fifty companies from a group of 100 companies apply method A in period 1. The other 50 apply method B. In period 2, 70 companies apply method A and 30 companies method B. In period 3 the ratio is 90:10. The relative frequencies and the H index derived from these data are given below:

Period	Method A	B	H Index
1	0.5	0.5	$0.5^2 + 0.5^2 = 0.5$
2	0.7	0.3	$0.7^2 + 0.3^2 = 0.58$
3	0.9	0.1	$0.9^2 + 0.1^2 = 0.82$

This is only a trivial example but it clearly shows that the H index increased, indicating an increase in the concentration of opinions and a growth in the degree of consensus. Thus, in this case the degree of harmony rose, which means that harmonisation took place. This method can also be applied in cases involving more than two different methods. The formula of the Herfindahl index is:

$$H = \sum_{i=1}^{n} p_i^2 \tag{1}$$

where:

H = Herfindahl index.
n = number of alternative accounting methods.
p_i = the relative frequency of accounting method i.

The H index fluctuates between 0 (no harmony, with an infinite number of alternative methods all with the same frequency) and 1 (all companies using the same method). The movements of this index indicate the degree of (dis-) harmonisation. The number of different opinions is, in this case, the number of accounting methods applied in practice. However, if all theoretically possible accounting methods are taken into account, this leads to the same H value because the H index does not change when accounting methods with a frequency of 0 are added.

The Herfindahl index is only one of many concentration measures. The advantage of this method is that it is simple but on the other hand gives more information than the rough method of taking as a measure the relative frequency of the accounting method most applied by the examined companies or the sum of the relative frequencies of the two or three accounting methods most applied, especially when many alternative accounting methods are applied. If only two accounting methods are differentiated as is the case in the simple illustration above, the rough method of only taking into account the relative frequency of the accounting method most applied leads to the same conclusion as the application of the H index. But if more than two alternative accounting methods can be distinguished the H index is a more refined method of measuring harmony/harmonisation. The following examples illustrate the application possibilities of the Herfindahl index.

Example I. Deferred tax in the UK

In the *Survey of Published Accounts* (ICAEW, 1968–1981) the following ways of presenting deferred tax were found:

1. As a separate heading or grouped with deferred liabilities.
2. Grouped with current liabilities.
3. Grouped with reserves.
4. As a deduction from assets less current liabilities.
5. Not identifiable in balance sheet, but transfer shown in profit and loss account.

The following regulations relate to how deferred tax should be presented in the balance sheet:

Companies Act 1967: not as a reserve.
Recommendation N27 of the ICAEW, July 1968: not as a reserve, nor as a current liability.
Exposure Draft 11, May 1973: not as a reserve, nor as a current asset or current liability.
SSAP 11, August 1975: same as ED 11.
Exposure Draft 19, May 1977: not as a reserve, but presentation as a current asset or current liability is allowed again.
SSAP 15, October 1978: same as ED 19.
Companies Act 1981: as a provision.

As can be seen, method III was rejected in 1967. Method II was rejected in 1968, but allowed again in 1977 (proposal) and 1978 (definitive).

Table 1 shows the application frequencies of these five methods in the period from 1968 to 1980. The ICAEW Surveys in respect of deferred tax only covered this period, so one cannot examine the impact of the

Table 1 Frequencies and, in brackets, relative frequencies of deferred tax methods.

			Method				*H*
Period	*I*	*II*	*III*	*IV*	*V*	*Total*	*Index*
1968	161 (0.809)	6 (0.03)	6 (0.03)	26 (0.131)	— (—)	199	0.673
1969	169 (0.849)	3 (0.015)	4 (0.02)	23 (0.116)	— (—)	199	0.735
1970	176 (0.871)	3 (0.015)	2 (0.01)	20 (0.099)	1 (0.005)	202	0.769
1971	205 (0.833)	3 (0.012)	8 (0.033)	29 (0.118)	1 (0.004)	246	0.709
1972	241 (0.92)	— (—)	4 (0.015)	17 (0.065)	— (—)	262	0.851
1973	248 (0.915)	1 (0.004)	2 (0.007)	20 (0.074)	— (—)	271	0.843
1974	254 (0.907)	— (—)	1 (0.004)	25 (0.089)	— (—)	280	0.831
1975	266 (0.908)	— (—)	— (—)	27 (0.092)	— (—)	293	0.833
1976	275 (0.945)	— (—)	— (—)	16 (0.055)	— (—)	291	0.896
1977	252 (0.962)	2 (0.008)	1 (0.004)	7 (0.027)	— (—)	262	0.926
1978	237 (1)	— (—)	— (—)	— (—)	— (—)	237	1
1979	239 (0.992)	2 (0.008)	— (—)	— (—)	— (—)	241	0.984
1980	213 (0.943)	13 (0.058)	— (—)	— (—)	— (—)	226	0.892

Source: *Survey of Published Accounts*, Institute of Chartered Accountants in England and Wales.

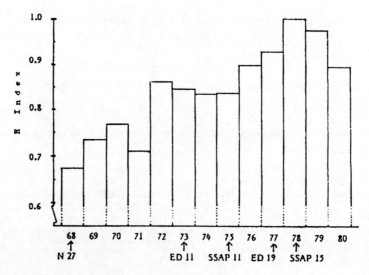

Figure 1 H Index for deferred tax in the UK.

Companies Act 1967, of N 27 or of the Companies Act 1981. This table also contains the relative frequencies and the H indices. Figure 1 is a graph of the fluctuations of the H index and the periods in which the provisions concerning deferred tax mentioned above were issued.

The figure shows a gradually rising trend until 1978, indicating an increase in the degree of harmony. In 1971 the H index shows a fall which cannot be explained here. In 1978 the rising trend changed into a declining one. This was caused by the fact that SSAP 15 (October 1978) gave companies more freedom in the presentation of deferred tax by allowing them to be presented as a current asset of current liability.

The following conclusions can be drawn from this example:

• The H index of the presentation of Deferred Tax shows a gradual increase in the 1968–1978 period which cannot be attributed to the introduction or amendment of mandatory or non-mandatory provisions. In other words, spontaneous harmonisation took place.
• The impact of the introduction or amendment of provisions can be measured by the H index (see, for example, the change after SSAP 15 was introduced).

Example II. Accounting for the WIR (Investment Tax Credit) in the Netherlands

In 1978 an investment stimulation plan was introduced. This involved an investment tax credit (WIR), comparable to the investment tax credit in the United States before it was abolished by the Tax Reform Act in 1986. There are three ways of accounting for the WIR:

1. The credit is recognised directly in the Profit and Loss Account or in Equity in the year it is awarded (flow-through method).
2. The credit is deducted from the investment, thus leading to lower depreciation in subsequent years (deduction method).
3. The credit is charged to an equalisation account on the credit side of the balance sheet and expensed during subsequent years (equalisation method).

In 1983 the Dutch Council for Annual Reporting (Raad voor de Jaarverslaggeving, 1983) issued a draft guideline stating its preferrence for methods 2 and 3.

Table 2 contains the application frequencies of these three methods for the surveyed companies in the period 1978 to 1984. In the same table the relative frequencies and the H indices are given. In Figure 2 fluctuations

Table 2 Frequencies and, in brackets, relative frequencies of WIR methods.

Period	Method 1	Method 2	Method 3	Total	H Index
1978	5 (0.062)	21 (0.259)	55 (0.679)	81	0.532
1979	3 (0.032)	19 (0.204)	71 (0.763)	93	0.625
1980	1 (0.011)	17 (0.181)	76 (0.809)	94	0.687
1981	1 (0.011)	15 (0.158)	79 (0.832)	95	0.717
1982	1 (0.011)	13 (0.139)	80 (0.851)	94	0.744
1983	2 (0.017)	15 (0.13)	98 (0.852)	115	0.743
1984	2 (0.017)	14 (0.121)	100 (0.862)	116	0.758

Sources: 1978–1982: Beckman (1980) and Noordzij (1984); 1983–1984: Van der Tas (1986).

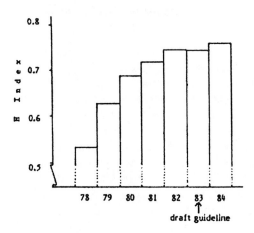

Figure 2 H Index for the WIR in the Netherlands.

Table 3 Frequencies and, in brackets, relative frequencies of ITC methods.

Period	Method 1	Method 2	Total	H Index
1965	226 (0.787)	61 (0.213)	287	0.665
1967	257 (0.793)	67 (0.207)	324	0.672
1968	290 (0.815)	66 (0.185)	356	0.698
1969	300 (0.831)	61 (0.169)	361	0.719
1970	245 (0.819)	54 (0.181)	299	0.704
1971	329 (0.801)	82 (0.199)	411	0.681
1972	489 (0.864)	77 (0.136)	566	0.765
1973	496 (0.864)	78 (0.136)	574	0.765
1974	504 (0.875)	72 (0.125)	576	0.781
1975	518 (0.896)	60 (0.104)	578	0.814
1976	502 (0.869)	76 (0.131)	578	0.772
1977	504 (0.871)	75 (0.129)	579	0.775
1978	521 (0.88)	71 (0.12)	592	0.789
1979	529 (0.888)	67 (0.112)	596	0.801
1980	528 (0.887)	67 (0.113)	595	0.8
1981	531 (0.895)	62 (0.105)	593	0.813
1982	537 (0.909)	54 (0.091)	591	0.834
1983	541 (0.915)	50 (0.085)	591	0.844
1984	543 (0.919)	48 (0.081)	591	0.851

Source: *Accounting Trends and Techniques.*

in the H index are plotted and the period in which the draft guideline was issued is indicated. The figure shows clearly a strong increase in the H index. The draft guideline had a slight impact on the degree of harmony at the very time when the process of harmonisation stopped.

Example III. Accounting for the Investment Tax Credit (ITC) in the US

In *Accounting Trends and Techniques* (AICPA, various years) two different methods were found to account for the ITC:

1. Flow-through method, comparable to method 1 in Example II;
2. Deferral method, comparable to methods 2 and 3 in Example II.

Table 3 gives the application frequencies of the two methods in the 1965–1982 period based on data from *Accounting Trends and Techniques*. In Figure 3 the H index is plotted against time. The degree of harmony clearly rose during this period. More and more companies applied the flow-through method, even though the Accounting Principles Board (APB) had rejected this method in 1962 (Opinion 2) and, after Congress over-rode this Opinion, had allowed but discouraged the method in 1964 (Opinion 4).

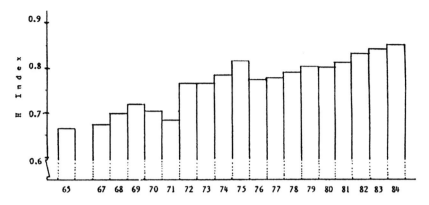

Figure 3 H Index for the ITC in the US.

Example IV. The WIR equalisation account in the Netherlands

If a company applies the equalisation method (method 3 in Example II), the WIR equalisation account can be presented in five ways:

1. As a current liability;
2. As a non-current liability or as a provision;
3. As part of the reserves;
4. As a separate item between debt and equity (deferred income);
5. As a separate deduction from fixed assets.

In a 1983 draft guideline the Council for Annual Reporting discouraged presentation as part of the reserves or as a provision. In 1984 the EC Fourth Directive was implemented in Book 2 of the Dutch Civil Code as a new Title 8. This makes it clear that a WIR equalisation account cannot be presented as a provision.

Table 4 shows the application frequencies of these five methods in the examined financial reports. In Figure 4 the fluctuations of the H index are plotted, showing a slight increase from 1978 to 1983 and a big increase in 1984, caused by the new legislation.

Multiple reporting

The advantage of the H index is that it is simple and easy to calculate. However, a disadvantage is its inability to take account of multiple reporting, because each company can only be assigned to one of the alternative accounting methods. Here a method will be developed which does take multiple reporting into account.

The degree of comparability of financial reports in a country can be measured by relating the number of 'compatible' pairs of companies to the

397

Table 4 Frequencies and, in brackets, relative frequencies of the WIR equalisation account.

Period	1	2	Method 3	4	5	Total	H Index
1978	2 (0.036)	30 (0.546)	1 (0.018)	22 (0.4)	— (—)	55	0.459
1979	2 (0.028)	35 (0.493)	2 (0.028)	32 (0.451)	— (—)	71	0.448
1980	1 (0.013)	37 (0.487)	2 (0.026)	36 (0.474)	— (—)	76	0.462
1981	1 (0.013)	36 (0.456)	2 (0.025)	40 (0.506)	— (—)	79	0.465
1982	— (—)	30 (0.375)	1 (0.013)	49 (0.613)	— (—)	80	0.516
1983	— (—)	35 (0.358)	— (—)	61 (0.617)	2 (0.025)	98	0.51
1984	— (—)	10 (0.107)	— (—)	88 (0.869)	2 (0.024)	100	0.767

Sources: 1978–1982: Beckman (1980) and Noordzij (1984); 1983–1984: Van der Tas (1986).

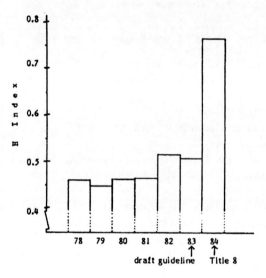

Figure 4 H Index for the WIR equalisation account in the Netherlands.

number of pairings possible. The financial reports of two companies are compatible if both companies apply the same accounting method or if one or both of the companies give additional information to enable comparison. For example, if there are three companies (A, B and C), the total number of comparisons is three, namely between A and B, between A and C and between B and C. Suppose company A applies accounting method I and the other two companies apply method II. In this case the degree of harmony is 1/3, i.e. the number of compatible pairs (one, namely B and C), divided by the total number of comparisons (three). In the next period company B gives information based on both method I and method II. In that case the number of compatible pairs is two (A and B, and B with C). So the degree of harmony has increased from 1/3 to 2/3.

Table 5 Frequencies of valuation methods, and C Index.

Period	A	B	C	Method D	E	F	G	H	Total	C Index
1976	73	26	0	2	7	2	1	0	111	0.633
1977	71	29	0	2	7	1	1	0	111	0.611
1978	63	29	0	3	14	2	1	0	112	0.634
1979	59	30	0	3	17	2	1	0	112	0.644
1980	56	30	0	3	20	2	1	0	112	0.659
1981	55	30	0	3	21	2	1	0	112	0.664
1982	54	31	0	3	21	2	1	0	112	0.660
1983	53	30	0	3	23	2	1	0	112	0.674
1984	46	20	0	2	41	1	0	1	111	0.811
1985	46	19	0	2	43	1	0	1	112	0.821

A. historical cost
B. current value
C. land at current value, buildings at historical cost
D. land at historcal cost, buildings at current value
E. both A and B
F. both A and C ⎤
G. both B and D ⎬ by way of additional information in the notes
H. both A, B and D ⎦

The result is an index, ranging from 0 to 1, which we will call the C index. If the number of examined financial reports is large and no multiple reporting takes place, the C index approximately equals the H index discussed above. The advantage of the C index, however, is its ability to take account of multiple reporting. The derivation of the formula of the C index is shown in Appendix 1. The same applies to the proof of the statement that the C index and the H index are approximately equal when a large number of companies is examined and no multiple reporting takes place. An example of the application of the C index follows.

Example V. Valuation of land and buildings in the Netherlands

Both historical cost and current value are allowed as valuation methods for land and buildings. Many companies, when applying one of these methods, provide additional information based upon the other. Table 5 shows the findings of an examination of how many companies listed on the Amsterdam Stock Exchange provide additional information on the value of land and buildings based upon the method not used in the main financial statements. The fluctuations in the C index are shown in Figure 5.

The increase in the C index in 1984 was caused by the new Title 8 of the Dutch Civil Code which encouraged companies applying historical cost to give additional information about the current value of these assets.

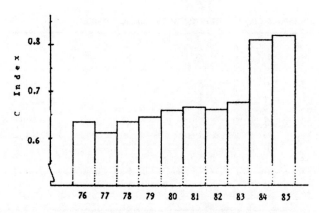

Figure 5 C Index of valuation methods in the Netherlands.

International harmonisation

There are two ways of looking at international material harmonisation. From the first point of view international harmony is the degree of comparability of financial reports of companies irrespective of the country in which they are established. This could be the point of view of an international investor who wants to compare financial reports irrespective of the home country of the companies. From the second point of view international harmonisation takes place when there is a convergence of opinions in two or more countries on the way in which a specific item should be accounted for. This could be the point of view of a standard setting body that wants to know what differences exist between the countries in respect of the way in which a particular item is accounted for.

From the first point of view international harmony is measured in the same way as national harmony, except that the area of examination consists of more than one country. The two indices developed above can be applied accordingly. However, it should be borne in mind that, in this case, countries with many companies have a larger weighting than countries with fewer companies. From the second point of view the degree of international material harmony indicates the degree to which the companies in one country apply the same or only a limited number of alternative accounting methods, compared to the companies in another country. It can be measured in the following way. If the companies in two countries apply the same method to a large extent this means that the relative frequencies with which this method is applied in the two countries reinforce each other. So we can measure the degree of international material harmony by multiplying the relative application frequency of a method in country A by the relative application frequency of the same method in country B and subsequently by adding the results of all alternative methods. This sum will be called the I index.

400

As an example of the use of the I index, assume that the relative frequencies of the alternative accounting methods 1 and 2 in countries A and B are as follows:

	Country		
Time 1:	A	B	I index
Method 1	1	0	$1 \times 0 + 0 \times 1 = \underline{0}$
2	0	1	
Time 2:			
Method 1	0.6	0.3	$0.6 \times 0.3 + 0.4 \times 0.7 = 0.46$
2	0.4	0.7	

The result is an index ranging from 0 to 1, indicating the degree of international material harmony. The formula of the I index is:

$$I = \sum_{i=1}^{n}(f_i^1 \times f_i^2) \tag{2}$$

where

f_i^1 = the relative application frequency of method i in country 1.
n = the number of alternative accounting methods.

Example VI. I index for the ITC in the US and the Netherlands

In the previous section, we saw an increasing application of the flow-through method in the US, while in the Netherlands the deferral method received greater support. The frequencies and relative frequencies in the USA and the Netherlands as well as the I indices are given in Table 6, which shows that the degree of international harmony decreased, while the two countries concentrated on a different method. They moved in opposite directions.

Table 6 I Index for ITC.

Period	Netherlands		US		I Index
	deferral	flow-through	deferral	flow-through	
1978	0.938	0.062	0.12	0.88	0.167
1979	0.968	0.032	0.112	0.888	0.137
1980	0.989	0.011	0.113	0.887	0.122
1981	0.989	0.011	0.105	0.895	0.113
1982	0.989	0.011	0.091	0.909	0.1
1983	0.983	0.017	0.085	0.915	0.099
1984	0.983	0.017	0.081	0.919	0.095

The I index for 1978, for example, is calculated as: $0.938 \times 0.12 + 0.062 \times 0.88 = 0.167$

This method is also applicable to more than two countries. In that case, however, a correction factor should be built in, as otherwise the I index would be very unequally distributed over the interval 0 to 1. The resulting formula and the statistical motivation for the correction factor can be found in Appendix 2.

Application possibilities

The potential applications of such a quantification of the degree of material measurement harmony/comparability are:

1. It gives an indication of the degree of harmony in respect of the accounting treatment of a specific item at a particular moment.
2. Fluctuations in the degree of harmony indicate when and to what extent harmonisation has taken place.
3. Fluctuations in the degree of harmony can be attributed to:
   - the introduction or amendment of mandatory provisions concerning financial reporting;
   - the introduction or amendment of non-mandatory provisions concerning financial reporting;
   - spontaneous harmonisation caused, for example, by developments in accounting theory or developments abroad.
4. It can be used to identify problem areas in financial reporting; these are the items with a low degree of harmony.
5. Organisations concerned with the harmonisation of financial reporting might use the measurement method to set goals in respect of the desired degree of harmony for a certain item in the financial report. In that case the degree of harmony achieved by a standard or by harmonisation of standards can be compared with the goal being pursued.

As mentioned earlier, comparability of financial reporting is related to the circumstances of the reporting companies as well as to the circumstances under which an event to be accounted for takes place. Harmonisation should not lead to unlike circumstances being accounted for in the same way. This means that, when applying the developed measurement methods, the sample of companies to be examined should be chosen carefully. What exactly is meant by 'like curcumstances' is open to discussion but is independent of the measurement method. It influences only the sample of companies to be examined.

The problem of like circumstances also has an impact on the question of whether there is any purpose in calculating the degree of harmony in respect of a specific item. For example, the choice of the depreciation period depends on the specific circumstances within the company such as the production process and the expected useful lifetime of the assets. Thus, calculating the degree of harmony in respect of the depreciation period applied to specific assets is of hardly any use.

A practical problem is that it is not always possible to determine the way in which a company has chosen to account for an item, for example because of insufficient explanation. Moreover it can prove difficult to determine whether a company did not account for a particular item because it was not applicable or because the company opted not to take the item into account. For example if a company presents no deferred tax in its balance sheet, there are two possibilities:

- there is no deferred tax; or
- there is deferred tax, but the company applied the flow-through method, which does not take deferred tax into account.

These practical problems may hamper the application of the described measurement methods.

However, there is a third limitation of a more fundamental character. The measurement indices presuppose that the differences between the alternative accounting methods are of about the same size. If three alternative methods are distinguished (A, B and C) the measurement indices presuppose that the magnitude of the differences between A and B, B and C and between B and C are about the same. This is not always true, as we saw in Examples II and III concerning accounting for the ITC. The difference between the flow-through method and the other two methods is larger than the difference between the deduction method and the equalisation method. This problem arises at the time when the alternative accounting methods are distinguished, even before collecting the data. This might impose a limitation on judging the degree of material harmony. On this subject, three remarks should be made here:

- It was assumed that financial reports are not comparable if they are each based on a different accounting principle, regardless of the extent of the difference between the methods. Two financial reports are either comparable or not; there is no gradation in comparability when only one item is taken into account.
- The most important advantage of the described methods is the possibility of quantifying the degree of harmonisation. This means that *fluctuations* in the degree of harmony are more important than the level of harmony. Thus, once a particular classification of alternative accounting methods is chosen, the problem of unequal differences is of minor importance. In any case it is possible to determine whether and when (dis-) harmonisation took place. Only the determination of the extent to which harmonisation took place might cause some difficulties.

- A solution to the problem of unequal differences between the alternative accounting methods could be found by applying a more sophisticated measurement method that weights the differences between the alternative accounting methods. Further research should determine how this could be realised.

Conclusion

In this paper there is an attempt to identify ways of quantifying the degree of harmony in financial reporting practice. First, it was concluded that harmonisation is a process whereas harmony is a state. Harmonisation is an increase in the degree of harmony. Subsequently, a distinction was made between formal and material harmonisation. *Formal harmonisation* is harmonisation of the provisions concerning financial reporting. *Material harmonisation* is harmonisation of financial reporting practice itself. A second distinction was made between *disclosure harmonisation* (harmonisation of the extent of information disclosure) and *measurement harmonisation* (harmonisation of the nature of information disclosed). This paper is confined to material measurement harmony, which is an increase in the degree of comparability of financial reporting practice. More specifically:

> Material measurement harmonisation means that more companies in the same circumstances apply the same accounting method to an event or give additional information in such a way that the financial reports of more companies can be made comparable.

Based on this definition, a statistical concentration index was used to develop a method that quantifies the degree of comparability (the H index). This method could not, however, take account of multiple reporting (supplying information based on more than one accounting method). So the next step was to develop a method that could take account of multiple reporting (the C index). These two methods can be used to measure national comparability. They can also be used to measure international comparability from the point of view of an international investor or creditor but are less suited for measuring international comparability from the point of view of an international standard setter, for which a third method was described which is more suitable (the I index).

These methods were illustrated by applying them to some items in financial reporting, with the conclusions that it is possible to quantify the degree of harmony and harmonisation of financial reporting. It also proved possible to measure the influence of mandatory and non-mandatory provisions concerning financial reporting and the degree of spontaneous harmonisation.

404

Organisations engaged in the process of harmonisation of financial reporting might use the developed measurement methods to set goals in respect of the degree of harmony of a particular item in financial reporting. In this way the realised degree of harmony can be compared with the desired degree of harmony in order to evaluate the impact of a specific standard, guideline or law.

Acknowledgements

This paper is a revision of one presented at the Ninth Annual Congress of the European Accounting Association in Stockholm, March 1986. The author would like to thank Professors M. A. van Hoepen and F. Krens for their valuable comments on a previous draft.

Appendix 1. Formula for the C index

The C index divides the number of compatible pairs of financial reports by the total number of possible comparisons. The number of pairs of financial reports out of a sample of n financial reports is:

$$0.5 \times (n^2 - n). \tag{3}$$

Two financial reports are comparable if they are based on the same accounting method. This means that, if no multiple reporting takes place, the total number of financial reports must be subdivided into classes of financial reports with the same accounting method in respect of a specific item. *Within* these classes it is possible to compare the financial reports. However it is not possible to make comparisons *between* financial reports in different classes. The number of possible comparisons within such a class is $0.5 \ (a_i^2 - a_i)$ where a_i is the number of financial reports within this class. This means that the total number of compatible pairs is:

$$0.5(a_1^2 - a_1) + 0.5(a_2^2 - a_2) + \ldots + 0.5(a_i^2 - a_i)$$

where

   a_i = the number of companies applying accounting method i.
   i = the number of alternative accounting methods.

This sum must be divided by the total number of possible comparisons. So the formula for the C index is:

$$C = \frac{0.5(a_1^2 - a_1) + 0.5(a_2^2 - a_2) + \ldots + 0.5(a_i^2 - a_i)}{0.5(n^2 - n)} = \frac{\left(\sum_{t=1}^{i} a_1^2\right) - n}{n^2 - n} \tag{4}$$

405

where:

a_i = the number of companies applying accounting method i.
i = the number of alternative accounting methods.
n = the total number of companies.

Applying the formula to the example in the sub-section 'Multiple Reporting' in the situation without multiple reporting gives the following result:

$$C = \frac{1^2 + 2^2 - 3}{3^2 - 3} = 1/3$$

It is possible to relate the C index to the H index, because the latter can be stated as:

$$\frac{\sum_{i=1}^{i} a_i^2}{n^2} \tag{6}$$

So

$$C = \frac{H \times n^2 - n}{n^2 - n} = \frac{H - 1/n}{1 - 1/n} \tag{7}$$

When n reaches infinity: $C = H$.

If a financial report provides information based on more than one accounting method (multiple reporting), this financial report has to be subdivided into more than one class of financial reports. However, this means that the comparison between two financial reports which both supply information based on the same two or more accounting methods is counted double, triple or more because the comparison is counted in more than one class of financial reports. To avoid this double counting the number of comparisons between two financial reports based on the same two or more accounting methods should be deducted. The result is that the total number of compatible pairs is the same as described above in the case of no multiple reporting, except that a deduction is made to avoid double counting (analogous to Mood, Graybill and Boes, 1974, p. 24):

$$0.5 \sum_{j=1}^{i} (a_j^2 - a_j) - 0.5 \left(\sum_{j=1}^{i-1} \sum_{k=f+1}^{i} (a_{jk}^2 - a_{jk}) + \sum_{j=1}^{i-2} \sum_{i=j+1}^{i-1} \sum_{l=k+1}^{i} (a_{jki}^2 - a_{jkl}) \ldots \right.$$

$$\left. + (-1)^{i+1} \sum \ldots \sum (a_{j\ldots}^2 - a_{j\ldots}) \right)$$

where $a_{jkl\ldots}$ is the number of companies supplying information based on accounting methods j, k, l, et cetera and j, k and l are parameters fluctuating between 1 and i. This sum must be divided by the total number of possible comparisons ($0.5(n^2 - n)$). The result is:

$$\sum_{j=1}^{i}(a_j^2 - a_j) - \sum\sum_{j<k}(a_{jk}^2 - a_{jk}) + \sum\sum\sum_{j<k<l}(a_{jkl}^2 - a_{jkl}) - \dots$$

$$C = \frac{+ (-1)^{i+1}\sum \dots \sum (a_{j\dots}^2 - a_{j\dots})}{n^2 - n} \tag{8}$$

Applying this formula to the earlier example with multiple reporting gives:

$$C = \frac{2^2 - 2 + 2^2 - 2 - 0}{3^2 - 3} = 2/3$$

Appendix 2: The I index in the case of more than two countries

On p. 165 above the situation was described where two countries were compared. The I index is also applicable when more than two countries are compared. However, in this case the I index becomes very small because a large number of fractions are multiplied. This leads to a very unequal distribution of the I index over the interval $0 - 1$.

To improve the possible application of the I index a correction factor should be built in, perhaps as follows. Where all accounting methods are applied with the same relative frequencies in every country, the addition of another similar country only leads to a small change in the I index. For example:

	Country A	Country B	
Method I	0.5	0.5	$I = 0.5 \times 0.5 + 0.5 \times 0.5$
Method II	0.5	0.5	$= \underline{0.5}$

After the addition of country C (where half of the companies apply method I and the rest apply method II) the calculation of the uncorrected I index leads to:

	Country A	Country B	Country C	
Method I	0.5	0.5	0.5	$I = 0.5 \times 0.5 \times 0.5 + 0.5 \times 0.5 \times 0.5 = \underline{0.25}$
Method II	0.5	0.5	0.5	

The I Index with correction factor is: $I^x = I^{1/(m-1)}$ where $m = $ the number of examined countries. In the example above the corrected I index would be: $I^x = 0.25^{1/2} = 0.5$. The addition of country C does not therefore lead to a change in the corrected I index.

The general formula of the I index is as follows:

$$I^x = \left(\sum_{i=1}^{n}(f_i^1 \times f_i^2 x \dots x f_i^m)\right)^{1/(m-1)} \tag{9}$$

where

f_i = relative frequency of method i in country m.
m = number of countries.
n = number of alternative accounting methods.

References

AICPA, *Accounting Trends and Techniques*, annual publication.

Beckman, H. (1980), *Verwerking van WIR-premies, voorontwerp van Beschouwingen en de praktijk van de jaarverslaggeving*, Rapport 8014/Acc, Centrum voor Bedrijfseconomisch Onderzoek, Erasmus Universiteit, Rotterdam.

ICAEW, *Survey of Published Accounts*, editions 1968 to 1981, Institute of Chartered Accountants in England and Wales.

Kirkpatrick, J. L. (1985), *Proceedings of the OECD Congress on Harmonization of Accounting Standards*, Paris, April 1985.

Mood, A. M., F. A. Graybill and D. C. Boes (1974), *Introduction to the Theory of Statistics*, Tokyo.

Noordzij, M. W. (1984), *De verwerking van WIR-premies in de jaarrekening van 100 ondernemingen over de periode 1979 tot en met 1982*, Centrum voor Bedrijfseconomisch Onderzoek, Erasmus Universiteit, Rotterdam.

Raad voor de Jaarverslaggeving (1983), *Ontwerp-richtlijn 'Voorzieningen voor latente belastingen'*.

Theil, H. (1973), *Statistical Decomposition Analyses*, Amsterdam.

Van der Tas, L. G. (1986), 'Belastingen naar de winst'. *Jaar in/Jaar uit*, J. Dijksma (ed.), Groningen.

18

MEASURING INTERNATIONAL HARMONIZATION AND STANDARDIZATION

J. S. W. Tay and R. H. Parker

Source: *Abacus* 26(1) (1990): 71–88.

This paper analyses six recent studies dealing with the measurement of international harmonization of financial reporting. Methodological issues and problems relating to the definition and operationalization of terms, sources of data, statistical methods and causation are discussed, and an alternative methodology for measuring harmonization suggested.

The purpose of this paper is to discuss the problems involved in the measurement of the concepts of 'harmonization' and 'standardization'. We do so by analysing six recent empirical attempts to measure those concepts in the context of international accounting. These harmonization measurement studies may differ from studies which appraise the extent of disclosure in company accounts (e.g., Singhvi and Desai, 1971; Buzby, 1974; Barrett, 1976). Such disclosure studies are ultimately concerned with the quality of information contained in company accounts. Harmonization measurement studies are, more simply, concerned with the similarity or otherwise of accounting practices and regulations. Table 1 summarizes the six studies in terms of their objectives, the data sources used, the countries surveyed, their general methodology, the statistical methods employed, and their main conclusions. These studies used different data sources and methodologies and, perhaps unsurprisingly, arrived at somewhat different conclusions.

409

Table 1 Measurement studies surveyed.

	Nair and Frank (1981)	Evans and Taylor (1982)	McKinnon and Janell (1984)	Doupnik and Taylor (1985)	Nobes (1987b)	van der Tas (1988)
Objectives	To assess the success of 'formal' harmonization efforts by the IASC	'To determine the impact of IASC standards on the financial reporting in member nations' (p. 119)	To analyse the direct and indirect influence of the IASC on accounting standards and requirements	To assess conformity of Western European countries to a 'basic core of accounting practice' (p. 27), and changes in conformity over time	To test the hypothesis that U.S. and U.K. companies do not obey IASC standards	To quantify harmony, determine when and to what extent harmonization has taken place, and the impact of standard-setting bodies
Countries surveyed	37 countries common to the 3 PW surveys	France, Japan, U.K., U.S. and West Germany	64 countries covered by the 1979 PW survey	16 Western European countries	The U.K. and the U.S.	The Netherlands, the U.K. and the U.S.
Scope	IASs 1–10	IASs 2–4, 6 and 7	IASs 3 and 4, ED 11 (IAS21)	IASs 1–8	IASs 3, 4 and 22 (U.S.) and IASs 9, 14 and 19 (U.K.)	Accounting for deferred tax and investment tax credit; valuation of land and buildings
Data sources	PW surveys 1973, 1975 and 1979	9–10 financial reports from each country surveyed, for the period 1975–88	PW 1979 survey	PW 1979 survey and own questionnaire	Published 1985 accounts for separate random samples of listed companies	National surveys
Methodology	Changes in the distribution of countries among requirement categories tested for significance with Friedman's ANOVA	Reports examined for evidence of compliance with IASs. Results given as percentage compliance rates per country for each year	Descriptive analysis of accounting regulations of IASC members. Discussion of IASC influence on ASC and FASB statements on foreign exchange translation	Response categories weighted. Average scores calculated for regions and countries. Nonparametric tests used to differentiate regions and groups	Differences of content or timing identified between national standards and IASs. Compliance rates inspected for signs of obedience to IASs	3 indices developed to measure harmony and comparability, used for different countries. Changes in values related to legal and professional regulation
Main conclusions	'the period of the IASC's existence has coincided with a growing harmonization of accounting standards' (p. 77)	'the IASC has had very little impact on the accounting practices of the countries surveyed' (p. 126)	'the IASC has not succeeded in changing existing standards or setting new standards' (p. 33)	'much diversity continues...to exist among the countries of Western Europe' (p. 33)	that 'IASs are not obeyed may be accepted' (p. 13)	'it is possible to measure the influence of mandatory and non-mandatory provisions' (p. 167)

Some terminological distinctions

Both 'harmonization' and 'standardization' are used rather loosely in accounting practice and in the literature. This paper therefore begins with an attempt to clarify the distinction between them, and the related concepts of 'harmony' and 'uniformity'. The suggested terminology is intended for both national and international contexts. The use of the term 'harmonization' is not restricted to the latter.

Harmonization and standardization

Harmonization (a *process*) is a movement away from total diversity of practice. Harmony (a *state*) is therefore indicated by a 'clustering' of companies around one or a few of the available methods. Standardization (a process) is a movement towards uniformity (a state). It includes the clustering associated with harmony, and reduction in the number of available methods. (As it is difficult to measure a process, the six studies have tried to measure harmony or uniformity at different points in time.) Harmony and uniformity are therefore not dichotomous. The former is any point on the continuum between the two states of total diversity and uniformity, excluding these extreme states, as illustrated in Figure 1.

Regulation and practice

Harmonization, harmony, standardization and uniformity exist at the levels of concepts, principles, regulations and practice. This paper is concerned with the last two, which have the most immediate impact on company accounts. In this context, both states and processes may be either *de jure* or *de facto*. The former refers to harmony or uniformity of accounting regulations (which may be contained in the law and/or professional accounting standards). The latter refers to the actual practices of companies.

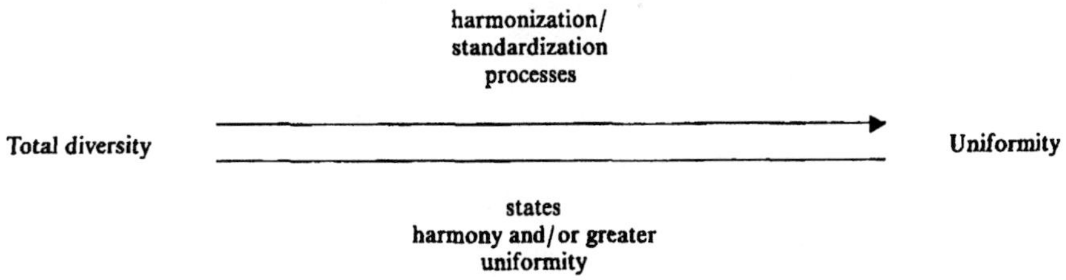

harmonization/
standardization
processes

Total diversity ⟶ Uniformity

states
harmony and/or greater
uniformity

Figure 1 Harmonization and standardization

411

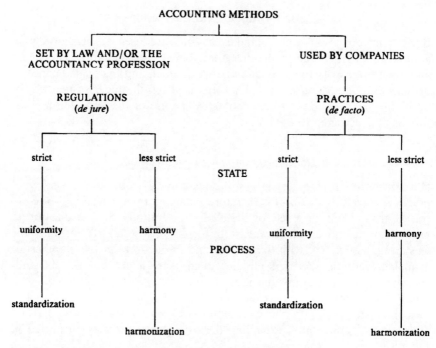

Figure 2 Terminology of harmonization and standardization.

Strict and less strict regulation

Accounting regulations may be strict or less strict in three different senses. First, a regulation may apply to all companies (strict) or only to some companies (less strict). Second, a regulation may be contained in the law (strict) or in a professional accounting standard (less strict). Compliance with a legal regulation may be expected to be higher than compliance with a standard. Third, a regulation may contain a precise definition (strict) or a discretionary one (less strict). All three senses of the terms 'strict' and 'less strict' imply that the former is associated with uniformity, the latter with harmony.

There are thus eight concepts in all (see Figure 2), which can be illustrated by a simple example, drawn from segment reporting. A regulation (contained in a companies act, a national accounting plan or an accounting standard) prescribes the disclosure of sales by strictly defined geographical areas. This represents *de jure* uniformity at a point in time, and *de jure* standardization over a period of time. *De facto* uniformity and *de facto* standardization would exist if all relevant companies actually disclosed sales as required, by strictly defined geographical areas. (Uniformity and standardization can exist *de facto* with or without concurrent *de jure* uniformity and standardization, as it may be in the interest of all companies to make such disclosures even if there are no formal regulations.) If, however, regulation or practice result in disclosure of sales by geographical areas which are not strictly defined but left to the discretion of the company, the result is *de jure* harmony, *de jure* harmonization, *de facto* harmony and *de facto* harmonization respectively.

Taking account of both the desirability of international comparability of financial statements, and the operational difficulties involved in measuring processes rather than states, the most suitable concept for measurement appears to be *de facto* harmonization, in the form of studies of *de facto* harmony over time.

Compliance with regulations

Accounting regulations may be expressed in various ways — in statute law and/or through professional standards, through a regulatory body or through self-generated standards of acceptable practice (GAAP). In many countries, accounting regulations originate from a combination of these sources.

Non-compliance with accounting regulations from different sources has different consequences. Compliance with a legal regulation is compulsory, and non-compliance has legally defined repercussions — for example, the directors of the company may be fined or even imprisoned. Non-compliance with a professional accounting standard with exactly the same requirement may have no such legal consequences, so that compliance is of a more voluntary nature. For example, compliance with the requirements of the European Community (E.C.) Directives, once they have been enacted into the relevant national legislation, falls into the first category, while compliance with International Accounting Standards (IASs) issued by the International Accounting Standards Committee (IASC) falls into the second.

Professional accounting standards are also endowed with varying degrees of authority in different countries. A standard

> can range from one that is legally enforced (e.g., Canada), to one that is usually obeyed and is binding on auditors (e.g., U.K.), to one that is persuasive (e.g., the Netherlands), to one that is unimportant (e.g., domestic pronouncement of the accountancy body in West Germany), to one that is largely unknown to companies or auditors.
>
> (Nobes, 1987b, pp. 78–9)

Even where compliance with standards is legally required, companies may not comply if it is perceived that the consequences of non-compliance are not serious. This may be demonstrated by comparing the Australian situation with that in the U.S. In Australia, companies are required to comply with standards approved by the Accounting Standards Review Board. Compliance is monitored by the Corporate Affairs Commission of each state. It has not been clearly shown what these commissions have the power (or the will) to do to non-complying companies. In the U.S., the SEC has the power, and the will, to refuse to register financial statements.

Both legal and professional regulations may apply to all companies, or only to a certain specified sub-set of companies, such as publicly listed companies. Thus, when seeking to measure compliance, the different types of regulations, and the different types of companies to which they relate, must be distinguished.

In the sections which follow, the distinctions which have been made here are used to indicate more clearly what each study has tried to measure and whether or not concepts have been confused. Attention is also drawn to what researchers have *not* tried to measure.

Measurement studies reviewed

In terms of Figure 2, the studies may be categorized as follows:

1. Nair and Frank (NF; 1981): *de jure* uniformity in three different periods. The study used survey data based on accounting requirements.
2. Evans and Taylor (ET; 1982): *de facto* uniformity over a six-year period. The accounts of companies were examined for compliance with certain IASs.
3. McKinnon and Janell (MJ; 1984): *de jure* uniformity. This is a non-statistical analysis of the IASC's influence on accounting standards in various countries.
4. Doupnik and Taylor (DT; 1985): *de jure* uniformity in two different years. Accounting requirements in various countries were ranked in terms of compliance with IASs.
5. Nobes (N; 1987b): *de facto* uniformity. Accounts of companies were examined for compliance with certain IASs.
6. van der Tas (VDT; 1988): *de facto* harmony over periods of time. The study developed a cardinal measurement method, which was used on national survey data of company reporting practices.

It must be noted that NF, ET and DT all believed that they were measuring *de facto* harmonization. However, this was not the case. NF and DT assumed erroneously that the accounting requirements provided by their data sources were strictly adhered to. All three studies defined harmonization in terms which actually defined standardization. These problems are discussed in later sections of this paper.

414

To summarize, despite the authors' claims to the contrary, two of the six studies are concerned with states: MJ (*de jure* uniformity) and N (*de facto* uniformity). The other four are concerned with the processes of harmonization and standardization, represented by studies of harmony and uniformity at different points in time. Of the eight concepts outlined in Figure 2, it appears that only five have been covered by the six studies: *de jure* uniformity (MJ); *de jure* standardization (NF, DT); *de facto* uniformity (N); *de facto* standardization (ET); and *de facto* harmonization (VDT). There has not been any comprehensive measurement study of the concept of *de facto* harmonization. Thus, evaluations of the work of the IASC and the E.C. in achieving greater comparability of financial statements produced by companies in different countries have been incomplete.

Problems arising

Several important questions arise in relation to the measurement of harmony, harmonization, uniformity and standardization:

1. What data sources should be used?
2. How should the concepts be operationalized?
3. What statistical methods should be used?
4. How can changes in accounting practice due to compliance with a standard be distinguished from changes due to other reasons?

Each of these questions is discussed below, in the context of the six studies surveyed.

Possible data sources

The six studies under review made use of three types of data sources: international or multi-country surveys (NF, DT and MJ), original financial statements (ET and N), and national surveys (VDT). The choice of data source has important repercussions for the overall research design, as there are advantages and difficulties involved with using each of them.

Surveys

The international surveys used were those prepared by Price Waterhouse International (hereafter referred to as 'the PW surveys'), reflecting reporting requirements in 1973, 1975 and 1979 in a varying number of countries. The national surveys used by VDT were those published by the professional accounting bodies in the U.S., the U.K. and the Netherlands. A list of international and national surveys available is given in Appendix A.

There are obvious advantages involved in using survey data, whether national or international — someone else has already done all the difficult and tedious work of collecting the data, which relate to a large number of countries and/or companies, cover a wide range of accounting topics and are available in a language which the researcher can understand (the PW surveys, for example, are available in five major languages). However, the difficulties involved with using survey material are also well known, and perhaps best summarized by Nobes (1981).

Probably the main difficulty involved with using surveys is the appropriateness (and hence the validity) of the data collected. Often, the questions were not asked for the purposes to which researchers subsequently put them. In the PW surveys, respondents were asked to fit their country's requirements in relation to an accounting practice into one of several categories, ranging from Required to Not Permitted. However, both these extreme categories imply the same degree of *uniformity*. Moreover, all the questions may not be of the same relative importance in capturing the variable in which the researcher is interested.

Survey data may not be provided in the way in which the researcher needs them. This is a particular problem when using data from more than one survey. NF found that only 37 countries and 131 accounting practices were common to the three PW surveys, and that the response categories had changed over time (pp. 66–7). It would obviously be even more difficult to compare data from surveys carried out by different organizations.

Furthermore, surveys (especially international surveys) may not contain sufficient detail. The PW survey (1979) contains a warning to this effect:

> given the necessity for a brief description of a principle or practice, it is not possible to indicate variations that may be of importance in a particular country. The reader is therefore cautioned against drawing too precise an interpretation on specific matters or in relation to specific countries.
>
> (p. 3)

Survey data may also be unreliable. Nobes (1981) has pointed out several inaccuracies in the 1979 PW survey, relating to the responses given about practice in the U.K. (p. 268). It is probable that there were similar inaccuracies involved in the responses given for other countries; inaccuracies which the researcher may not be aware of through unfamiliarity with different accounting systems.

Such unfamiliarity may also lead researchers to misinterpret survey data. Both NF and DT assumed that practices which are categorized as Required or Recommended in countries are complied with by all relevant companies. This assumption may be due to the authority of FASB standards for SEC-listed companies in the U.S. However, it ignores the 'hierarchy of sources' (i.e., different sources of regulations have differing degrees of authority in different countries).

A copy of the DT questionnaire (kindly provided by Doupnik) showed that, in all cases, the source of regulations for various accounting practices in France was an IAS. However, although IASs are recommended by the *Commission des Operations de Bourse* (COB), they are not uniformly practised, even by listed companies. COB data quoted by Nobes (1987b) 'show that only about half of even the listed French companies prepared consolidated accounts (as required by IAS3) in 1979' (p. 78). However, the assumption that regulations are complied with led to DT's conclusions that France was in complete compliance with the requirements of IASs 1–8 in 1979.

The possibility of similar misinterpretation is lessened in a more recent international survey carried out by Gray, Campbell and Shaw (1984; hereafter referred to as 'the Gray survey'), in conjunction with Deloitte Haskins & Sells. This gives information on the (estimated) level of compliance as well as requirements for 1982. A comparison of the 1979 PW survey and the Gray survey is contained in Appendix B.

The researcher must also consider the sample of companies and/or countries involved in each survey. At least ten IASC member countries are excluded from the 1979 PW survey, and there is no information on the type of companies (either by size or by industry) whose reporting practices are assessed. The Netherlands is noticeably absent from the Gray survey, although it is revealed that the sample consists of about fifty large companies in developed countries, and twenty large companies in less developed or smaller countries (Gray *et al.*, 1984, p. 4). It is obviously important for researchers to be aware of the sample on which their data are based, as this could affect the suitability of the data for their particular research purposes. Both NF and MJ, who used PW survey data, expressed reservations about the data (NF, p. 65; MJ, p. 22); whereas neither DT (who used the 1979 PW survey) nor VDT (who used three national surveys) gave any evidence of having considered the shortcomings of their data sources and the effects which these might have on their conclusions.

One final drawback with using survey data is that there is a time-lag between the publication of the survey and the period surveyed. In some cases this is not a problem: the 1979 PW survey, published in 1980, is based 'on the position at January 1, 1979, in all cases' (PW, 1979, p. 7); the Gray survey, published in 1984, is based on 'relevant current pronouncements as at 1 January 1982' (Gray *et al.*, 1984, p. 3). Some national surveys (e.g., France) may relate to financial statements issued either two or even three years earlier. Moreover, there may also be a small time-lag between the date at which requirements were current and the period to which the surveyed financial statements relate (Gray *et al.*, 1984, pp. 3–4).

National surveys are generally more detailed and more reliable than international surveys, simply because their scope is smaller. However, they are not carried out in many countries, or may only be produced sporadically. Moreover, the bases on which each national survey is compiled may render comparisons between countries difficult and even invalid. Finally, they may not be available in a language which the researcher can understand.

Financial statements

The use of financial statements is not without its own difficulties. While the data are 'raw' and may be manipulated in any way the researcher wishes, the collection of these data is often a tedious, time-consuming process. This may be a problem especially if the researcher wishes to obtain reports from countries other than his or her own. First, companies in that country may not be in the practice of sending their annual reports to anyone apart from their shareholders. Second, the reports may not be available in a language which the researcher can understand (translation is sometimes difficult, and always expensive). Third, even when, say, English-language versions are available, other problems may arise (McLeay, 1988). These may be either abridged (one has only to compare the English and French versions of the annual reports of some French companies to appreciate this), or the financial statements may be restated on bases other than those used in the original statements. Campbell (1985) points out that in Japan, for example, some companies produce 'convenience translations' which 'may include additional disclosure items that are not required by Japanese GAAP, and may reclassify some financial statements into a form that is more familiar to non-Japanese readers' (p. 153). Thus, while such translations may provide useful insights for the researcher, 'they do not provide a completely accurate picture of financial reporting in Japan' (p. 154). N used original statements of U.S. and U.K. companies, which presented no language problems. However, ET used Japanese, French and German reports, of which 'all the Japanese and part of the French and West German statements were English-language versions' (p. 121). It is therefore possible that their data are either incomplete, or presented in a different form from the original statements.

The choice of countries and/or companies sampled is also important when using financial statements. ET was the only study of the six which used such a sample, but little attempt was made to justify their choice:

> The countries selected . . . are France, Japan, the United Kingdom, the United States and West Germany. All these nations are founding members of the IASC . . . the published financial statements of a sample of corporations in each country were examined . . . in

general, nine or ten financial statements were examined in each country.

(pp. 120–1)

However, there are four other founding members of the IASC, and the inclusion of one more of them, the Netherlands, would have enabled ET to justify the countries selected as being those identified as 'vital countries' by Mason (1978). Moreover, an examination of the companies surveyed (ET, pp. 127–8) does not give any evidence that they have been matched. Given the shortcomings of the sample, it is therefore surprising that the authors extended their results to conclude that 'the IASC has had very little impact on the accounting practices of countries involved' (ET, p. 126).

Operational definitions

The operationalization of the concepts of harmony, harmonization, uniformity and standardization is necessarily linked with the type of data used. NF, MJ and DT used the PW survey, where regulations were categorized as Required, Recommended, etc. (see Appendix B). This has two effects on operationalization. First, it is assumed that companies comply 100 per cent with the requirements, whatever they might be. As pointed out above, this is a somewhat naive assumption. Second, harmonization is viewed in terms of movements of countries from category to category. NF 'looked for those practices on which more than half of the thirty-seven countries [common to the three PW surveys] . . . were to be found in either the Required or Not Permitted categories by 1979' (p. 68). This is perhaps too strict a definition of harmonization, as the categories selected imply uniformity rather than harmony. More appropriately, harmonization would merely involve looking for changes, over the period surveyed, in the *clustering* of companies within any of the categories, that is, whether *more* countries were grouped into particular categories at the end of the period than at the beginning.

DT assigned 'weights' to the PW categories, and assessed the level of harmony by calculating weighted average scores. The use of weights implies that there is some quantifiable relationship among the response categories. For example Majority Practice, weighted as 3, represents three times more harmony than Rarely or Not Found, which is weighted as 1. This implication was strengthened in their analysis by frequent references to percentage changes in the weighted average scores over time. However, such relationships would be difficult to support, given the form of the PW data.

The other three studies used sources which give actual compliance rates, although VDT's rates are based on national surveys, while those of N and ET are based on samples of financial statements. Harmony was a function of the observed compliance rate, with a higher rate indicating a greater degree of harmony. However, one could argue that compliance with strictly defined disclosure requirements is more an indication of uniformity than of harmony.

Statistical methods

The six studies used three different statistical methods to measure harmonization and standardization. These may be broadly described as descriptive statistics, nonparametric statistics and indices.

Descriptive statistics

This was the simplest and the most common method employed (used by ET, MJ and N), involving the calculation of the number or percentage of companies within the sample which complied with specified regulations. The size of the percentage described the degree of uniformity.

These studies fall short of providing useful insight into the overall degree of harmony, either among countries or across time. ET showed the level of compliance per country, per year, but there was no summary of the overall level of compliance for any one country over the period surveyed, or of compliance among the group of countries for any particular year. MJ summarized the requirements of IASC member countries in relation to IAS4 (p. 24), but were unable, given the non-quantitative nature of their analysis, to comment on the level of uniformity involved. N's results were shown in terms of both the numbers and percentages of companies displaying different levels of disclosure. This was extrapolated to apply to the populations of large U. S. and U. K. corporations from which the two random samples were drawn. However, given the emphasis on compliance with very narrowly defined IAS requirements, the result does not reflect general standardization of accounting practice so much as uniformity of compliance with these IAS requirements.

Nonparametric statistics

NF and DT employed PW survey data, which place countries into requirement categories. These categories may be regarded as ordinal in nature, except that the extreme categories (Required and Not Permitted) imply the same degree of uniformity.

NF assigned ranks to the survey categories, and tested changes in these rankings with Friedman's ANOVA (appropriate 'when the data from k matched samples are in at least an ordinal scale', Siegel, 1956, p. 166). Of the five response categories (NF, p. 67), it is obvious that movements from 3 (Minority Practice) to 2 (Predominant Practice) to 1 (Required Practice) would indicate increasing uniformity, as would movements from 3 to 4 (No

Application), and from 3 to 5 (Not Permitted). (What movements from 4 to 5 would indicate is not clear.) In a small example (p. 69), it is not apparent that this fact has been appreciated. For country A, increasing harmonization is shown as a movement from 1 to 3; for B, the same movement is given the opposite ranking. It is possible that this inconsistency affected the analysis, as the Friedman ANOVA test is based on the simple idea that 'under Ho [i.e. the three matched samples have been drawn from the same population] the mean ranks of the various columns would be about equal' (Siegel, 1956, p. 168). Thus the actual *numbers* assigned by NF to indicate varying degrees of harmonization would affect the analysis.

DT assigned weights to the PW categories, calculated weighted average scores for countries, ranked the scores, and tested these rankings for significant changes. The Kruskal–Wallis test was applied to data from five regions differentiated by DT, to ascertain whether they could be said to have been drawn from different populations (see Siegel, 1956, p. 184). (However, DT had no statistical basis for differentiating these five regions, which appear to have been rather arbitrarily drawn.) The Mann–Whitney U test, which shows 'whether two independent groups have been drawn from the same population' (Siegel, 1956, p. 116), was used to see if there was a significant difference between the mean scores of the E.C. and non-E. C. groups of countries.

These two studies show that nonparametric statistics may be useful in testing for evidence of harmony when data are ordinal in nature. However, they also show that the concept must be properly defined and operationalized, and data properly interpreted and appropriately categorized.

Indices

VDT's study is based on the calculation of three indices, the H-index, the I index and the C index. The first two are used for calculating national and international harmony. The third calculates comparability of accounts when different accounting methods are used but sufficient information is provided to show the effect of using alternative methods.

The H-index, from which the I index is developed, is one of many measures developed by industrial economists to quantify industrial concentration. Its use in the context of financial reporting harmonization implies an analogy between accounting harmonization and industrial concentration. The validity of this analogy is worthy of some discussion.

Industrial concentration deals with measuring actual market structures in relation to the two extremes of monopoly and perfect competition. The former is a situation in which one firm generates all the sales in a particular market. The accounting counterpart of this would be a situation in which one strictly defined accounting method is used by all companies, that is, there is *uniformity* in accounting practice. Perfect competition could be regarded as a situation in which every company was free to use a different accounting method. This may be difficult to envisage for accounting for a particular item within a set of financial statements, but it is something which is possible for the financial statements as a whole — very few companies use identical combinations of accounting methods in producing their financial statements. The 'real world' of accounting lies somewhere between these two extremes, that is, there is some degree of uniformity in some areas. Harmony is thus the counterpart of imperfect competition.

This analogy has intuitive appeal, but may be difficult to operationalize. In measuring industrial concentration, the variables measured are the number of firms, and their market share, share of labour or capital employed, or share of valueadded. Industrial economists complain that it is difficult to ascertain how many firms there are in a particular industry. In accounting harmonization, the relevant variables would be the number of accounting methods, and the number of companies using each method. The following questions would have to be answered: How many accounting methods are there for any particular topic? Should we consider only the ones which are allowed by law or professional standards, or should we include all methods which are used? Do we know what all the methods actually in use are? How do we identify the companies which are affected by accounting for this particular topic?

Such questions may be satisfactorily answered in relation to *samples* of companies. The results obtained can then be generalized if the sample used is representative of a certain type of company.

Different methods of calculating concentration are described and compared in a comprehensive survey by Curry and George (1983), who discuss in detail the five most widely used methods: the concentration ratio (CR); the Herfindahl index (VDT's H-index); entropy/relative entropy; the variance of logarithms; and the Hannah-Kay index, which is a generalized v ersion of the Herfindahl index). Curry and George also provide a useful worked example, showing how different measurement methods give different results for industries with different structures (p. 212). Although they conclude that

> the literature which considers the mathematical properties of concentration measures has not resolved the question of which is the best measure to use . . . [and] the complexity of business life is such that in practice it is unlikely that there is one concentration measure which will clearly be superior in all circumstances.
>
> (p. 215)

this does not detract from the approach suggested by VDT. The use of a concentration index seems to be a useful way to evaluate the level of harmony, and track movements in harmonization over time.

The main problem with concentration indices is that no significance tests have been devised to indicate how trivial or significant (statistically) variations in index values are.

Causes of changes in compliance

Causation poses a difficult problem in the social and management sciences, because of the inability to conduct controlled laboratory experiments. However, it is easier to show causation between legal regulations and the use of accounting methods and/or the disclosure of certain information, than between professional regulations and accounting practices. This is because compliance with legal regulations is compulsory, whereas compliance with professional regulations is not, and it is thus often assumed that compliance with the former is greater than compliance with the latter. Taking the example of consolidation accounting in France again, the proportion of companies producing consolidated accounts will rise now that the Seventh Directive has been partially implemented in France.

Five of the six studies surveyed examined compliance with IASC standards, which are not mandatory. VDT alone looked at legal regulations as a possible explanation for some observed changes in practice. All six studies looked for direct links between IASC activities and accounting practices. MJ and N also pointed out that the IASC may also have indirect influence on practice.

NF's conclusion reflects the difficulty of establishing direct causation:

> The period of the IASC's existence has *coincided* with a growing harmonization of accounting standards. This association between the two is *strengthened* by the fact that many of the topics on which the IASC has issued pronouncements are those on which the authors observe harmonization.
>
> (NF, p. 77, emphasis added)

However, this conclusion, cautious as it is, does not appear to be fully supported by NF's results. The study identified 37 countries and 131 accounting practices common to the three PW surveys, and 49 practices which showed evidence of harmonization as defined in the study. These 49 practices were tested for statistically significant changes in the distribution of ranked groupings over the time period, and 29 practices showed changes significant at the 5% level. These 29 practices were then related to the requirements of IASs 1–10, and formed the basis of NF's conclusion. However, this does not take into account the 102 practices for which there was no evidence of harmonization as defined by the study, nor how these practices relate to the ten IASs. NF's conclusion would be more defensible if it had been based on a study of the changes in the distribution of country groupings over all the 131 common practices (or at least all of those which related to the relevant IASs).

MJ postulate that even the degree of compliance observed may be due to reasons other than the conscious desire to comply with IASs. For example, 'France, which credits the IASC standard [on depreciation], is actually strictly governed by its uniform *Plan Comptable'* (p. 24); similarly, the fact that Japanese companies now practice equity accounting on a wider scale than before is 'not in response to IAS No. 3 but to new securities legislation' (p. 26). Their conclusion is that 'the IASC has not succeeded in changing existing standards or setting new standards' (p. 32).

However, MJ's analysis leads to the comment that the IASC is

> most effective when it has been able to obtain endorsements for its opinions by parties having greater enforcement powers ... [it] lobbies to have its standards considered by the FASB and the ASC, and its power to influence EEC law directives is considerable.
>
> (pp. 32–3)

Similarly, N's results suggest that, while IASs 'are not generally obeyed ... there is some doubt [that] IASs have no direct impact' (p. 13)

VDT graphs fluctuations in the H-index over time (VDT, pp. 161–4). These indicate a rising trend in the level of harmony, as measured by the H-index, with year-to-year fluctuations. Some of these fluctuations are ascribed to particular events (e.g., p. 163, the effect of new legislation on the presentation of the investment tax credit equalization account in the Netherlands); but others appear to have no particular cause (e.g., p. 160, the presentation of deferred taxation in the U. K. in 1971). The analysis shows that, while it may be possible to measure the degree of harmony, it is difficult to distinguish trend movements from random movements. It also reflects our view that little is known about causation.

An alternative approach to harmonization measurement

Based on the discussion above, the following approach to measuring harmonization is suggested.

First, if harmonization activities are the result of concern about the comparability of accounts produced by companies from different countries, then a measurement study should focus on actual reporting practices rather than regulations, that is, on *de facto* rather than *de jure* harmonization.

Second, actual reporting practices may be assessed most accurately from annual accounts, or detailed surveys of such accounts. Thus the appropriate data sources would be published accounts, or national surveys based on samples of company accounts (if the companies in the sample are appropriate to the research objective), rather than surveys of legal and professional accounting regulation.

Third, given the sources suggested, data on proportions of companies using different accounting methods can be obtained. An operational definition of harmony could then take the form of comparing the observed distribution of companies among different methods with either a random distribution or some expected distribution. A suitable proxy for the former could be a uniform/equal/rectangular distribution, that is, a distribution in which equal numbers of companies would be expected to use each of the available alternatives. (This would represent no preference for, or bias towards, any one available method.) Evidence of harmony would then be the existence of a significant difference between the observed and expected distributions, as measured by some appropriate significance test, for example, chi-square.

Finally, the level of harmony could be quantified by using a concentration index, preferably one describing the entire distribution, rather than just a portion of it. Comparison of levels of harmony over different periods would yield evidence of harmonization or disharmonization.

Summary

This paper has shown that insufficient research has been undertaken to date on the measurement of harmonization and standardization of financial reporting. The concepts involved have not been clearly defined, and this may explain the evidence of confusion in the methodology of some studies, and the inconsistent results between studies.

Two important points have emerged from this review: first, that none of the six studies reviewed involved a comprehensive measure of *de facto* harmonization, that is, the increasing comparability of financial statement produced by companies. This is a somewhat surprising result, as comparability would appear to be the *raison d'être* of harmonization activities.

Second, the studies suggest two useful measurement approaches — the use of concentration indices, which may be applied to cardinal data; and the use of nonparametric tests when data are only ordinal. Both approaches have been incorporated in a suggested methodology for measuring *de facto* harmony.

Acknowledgements

The authors acknowledge the helpful comments of C. W. Nobes, R. S. O. Wallace and the anonymous referees of earlier versions of this paper. One of the earlier versions was presented at the Tenth Congress of the European Accounting Association, London, March 1987.

Appendix A
Possible data sources

International surveys

Gray, S. J., L. G. Campbell and J. C. Shaw, *International Financial Reporting: A Comparative Survey of Accounting Requirements and Practices in 30 Countries*, Macmillan, 1984.

OECD, *Accounting Practices in OECD Member Countries*, OECD, 1980.

Price Waterhouse International, *Survey of Accounting Principles and Reporting Practices in 38 Countries*, The Institute of Chartered Accountants in England and Wales, 1973.

——, *A Survey in 46 Countries: Accounting Principles and Reporting Practices*, The Institute of Chartered Accountants in England and Wales, 1975.

——, *International Survey of Accounting Principles and Reporting Practices*, Butterworths, 1979.

SGV, *Comparative Accounting Practices in ASEAN*, Sycip, Gorres, Velayo and Co., 1984.

National surveys

Australia: *Australian Financial Reporting*, based on 120 public companies. First survey published in 1972. Several surveys since, carried out by the Australian Accounting Research Foundation. Most recent based on 1980 accounts. No further surveys planned.

Canada: *Financial Reporting in Canada*, published bi-annually by the Canadian Institute of Chartered Accountants since 1955. Sixteenth edition (1985) relates to 1983 and 1984 accounts of 325 public companies; 1981 and 1982 data are also included.

France: *Les Rapports Annuels des Sociétés Françaises*, published bi-annually by l'Ordre des Experts Comptables et des Comptables Agréés. Based on a sample of 150 large French companies. Available in French only.

India: *Precedents in Published Accounts*, published by the Institute of Chartered Accountants of India in 1981. Relates to the 1979 accounts of 202 public and private-sector companies. Available in English.

Netherlands: *Onderzoek Jaarverslaggeving*, published by the Nederlands Instituut van Registeraccountants, based on the accounts of 120 companies. Editions relate to accounts published one to two years before. Available in Dutch only.

New Zealand: *New Zealand Company Financial Reporting*, published in 1982 and 1984 with financial support from universities. The latter contains information on annual reports of the 100 largest NZ companies for 1979, 1982 and 1983.

Sweden: *Survey of Accounting Practices*, most recently published in 1985 by the Swedish Institute of Authorised Public Accountants. Based on 100 companies listed on the Stockholm Stock Exchange, with year-ends between 1/3/83 and 29/2/84. Four earlier editions. English translations are available.

United Kingdom: *Financial Reporting* (called *Survey of Published Accounts* until the 1983 edition), published annually since 1970 by the Institute of Chartered Accountants in England and Wales. Editions relate to annual reports issued in the previous year, by a sample of 200 large and medium listed companies, and 100 large unlisted companies.

United States: *Accounting Trends and Techniques*, published annually by the American Institute of Certified Public Accountants since 1944. Covers 600 industrial and merchandising companies, about 90% of which are SEC-listed.

Appendix B
The 1979 PW and Gray surveys compared

	1979 PW	*Gray*
Publication date	1980	1984
Based on position at	1/1/79	1/1/82
Available in	English, French German, Spanish and Italian	English
No. of countries covered	64	30
No. of propositions/questions	267	430
Response categories	*Requirements*	*Requirements*
	Required	Required
	Insisted upon	Recommended
	Predominant practice	Permitted
	Minority practice	
	Rarely or not found	
	Not accepted	
	Not permitted	Not permitted
		Practice
		A 91–100%
		B 76–90%
		C 51–75%
		D 26–50%
		E 11–25%
		F 1–10%

References

Barrett, M. E., 'Financial Reporting Practices: Disclosure and Comprehensiveness in an International Setting', *Journal of Accounting Research*, Spring 1976.

Buzby, S. L., 'Selected Items of Information and their Disclosure in Annual Reports', *The Accounting Review*, July 1974.

Campbell, L. G., 'Financial Reporting in Japan', in C. W. Nobes and R. H. Parker (eds), *Comparative International Accounting*, Philip Allan, 1985.

Curry, B., and K. D. George, 'Industrial Concentration: A Survey', *Journal of Industrial Economics*, March 1983.

Doupnik, S., and M. E. Taylor, 'An Empirical Investigation of the Observance of IASC Standards in Western Europe', *Management International Review*, Spring 1985.

Evans, T. G., and M. E. Taylor, '"Bottom-line Compliance" with the IASC: A Comparative Analysis', *International Journal of Accounting*, Fall 1982.

Gray, S. J., S. G. Campbell and J. C. Shaw, *International Financial Reporting: A Comparative Survey of Accounting Requirements and Practices in 30 Countries*, Macmillan, 1984.

McKinnon, S. M., and P. Janell, 'The International Accounting Standards Committee: A Performance Evaluation', *International Journal of Accounting*, Spring 1984.

McLeay, S., 'International Financial Analysis', in C. W. Nobes and R. H. Parker (eds), *Issues in Multinational Accounting*, Philip Allan, 1988.

Mason, A. K., *The Development of International Financial Reporting Standards*, International Centre for Research in Accounting, Lancaster University, 1978.

Nair, R. D., and W. G. Frank, 'The Harmonization of International Accounting Standards', *International Journal of Accounting*, Fall 1981.

Nobes, C. W., 'An Empirical Analysis of International Accounting Principles: A Comment', *Journal of Accounting Research*, Spring 1981.

——, 'Compliance by U.K. and U.S. Corporations with IASC Standards', paper presented at the Tenth Congress of the European Accounting Association, London, March 1987a.

——, 'An Empirical Investigation of the Observance of IASC Standards in Western Europe: A Comment', *Management International Review*, Winter 1987b.

Price Waterhouse International, *Survey of Accounting Principles and Reporting Practices in 38 countries* Institute of Chartered Accountants in England and Wales, 1973.

——, *A Survey in 46 Countries: Accounting Principles and Reporting Practices*, Institute of Chartered Accountants in England and Wales 1975.

——, *International Survey of Accounting Principles and Reporting Practices*, Butterworths, 1979.

Siegel, S., *Nonparametric Statistics for the Behavioral Sciences*, McGraw-Hill, 1956.

Singhvi, S. S., and H. B. Desai, 'An Empirical Analysis of the Quality of Corporate Financial Disclosure', *The Accounting Review*, January 1971.

van der Tas, L. G., 'Measuring Harmonisation of Financial Reporting Practice', *Accounting and Business Research*, Spring 1988.

19

MEASURING INTERNATIONAL HARMONIZATION AND STANDARDIZATION

A comment

Leo G. van der Tas

Source: *Abacus* 28(2) (1992): 211–16.

In the March 1990 issue of this journal Tay and Parker (T&P) compared six studies in the field of international accounting. According to T&P, each of those studies deals with the measurement of international harmonization of financial reporting and they evaluate the advantages and disadvantages of those studies. Moreover, T&P suggest an alternative methodology for measuring harmonization. This comment is a reaction to the definitions and methodology applied and the suggested alternative method for measuring harmonization of financial reporting.

Although there is increasing interest in international accounting, little research has been done in the field of the measurement of (international) harmonization. That is why contributions like that of T&P are very important.

Studies examined

First of all, only two of the six studies T&P refer to are really trying to measure harmonization (Nair & Frank, 1981, and van der Tas, 1988). The other four are measuring the degree of compliance with or observance of the standards of the International Accounting Standards Committee (IASC). Although T&P argue that Evans and Taylor (1982) and Doupnik and Taylor (1985) believed they were measuring de facto harmonization, the articles of Evans and Taylor and Doupnik and Taylor provide no evidence of the fact that they did believe so. This makes a comparison of both categories of studies less appropriate. International harmonization on the one hand and compliance or observance with IASs on the other are related in the sense that setting international standards may further harmonization. But they are two very different phenomena.

1. When an IAS allows different methods to be applied and companies apply these different methods, compliance with the IAS may be high, but because different methods are applied, the degree of harmony may be low.
2. If all or a large number of companies apply the same method, the degree of harmony is high. The degree of compliance with IASs, however, may be low when that method is not allowed by the IAS. A comparable situation existed when APB-Opinion 2 on accounting for the Investment Tax Credit (ITC) in the United States of America prescribed the deferral method, but most of the companies applied the flow-through method (compliance is low, the degree of harmony is high).

One could argue that the first problem will be reduced after the adoption of IASC's Exposure Draft 32 on comparability (1989) and the related Statement of Intent (IASC, 1990) because the number of options offered by IASs will be reduced, but it will increase the second problem. That is, the degree of observance of or compliance with IASs is a poor proxy for the degree of harmony.

Definitions

I agree with T&P that a distinction must be made between harmonization of financial reporting regulation (defined by T&P as '*de jure* harmonization') and harmonization of accounting practice ('*de facto* harmonization'). I also agree that harmony and uniformity are states while (dis)harmonization is a process which reflects a decrease/ an increase in the degree of harmony. Both distinctions were made in my earlier article (van der Tas, 1988). However, the distinction between standardization (strict rules) and harmonization (less strict rules) is less appropriate. What T&P are probably trying to say is that before we are able to measure harmonization, we will first have to define the level of detail at which we want to measure harmony. For example, when accounting for deferred taxation, a distinction can be made between the application of the tax payable method and the deferral method. We can measure the degree of harmony concerning the choice companies make between these two alternatives. This implies a low level of detail. However, we can also increase the level of detail at which we measure the degree of harmony when we distinguish between alternative types of the deferral method: net-of-tax method versus separate deferred taxes; liability versus deferred method; and partial versus comprehensive method. At this

430

level of detail the companies' choice between two methods changes into a choice between nine methods and we measure the degree of harmony concerning the choice companies make between these nine alternative methods.

Therefore, instead of a distinction between harmonization and standardization we can speak of different levels of detail at which to measure the degree of harmony. The choice of the level of detail is at the discretion of the researcher and determined by the purposes of the study.

The distinction between measurement harmony and disclosure harmony is very important when seeking to measure harmonization. Measurement harmonization is concerned with the choice between alternative measurement methods. Disclosure harmonization is concerned with the amount and detail of information supplied in the financial report. To clarify the importance of this distinction we will consider the goals of harmonization. *De facto* measurement harmonization is aimed at an improvement in the comparability of financial reporting. To facilitate comparability, it is important that companies operating in comparable circumstances make the same choice between alternative accounting methods. This would eliminate one of the disturbing aspects causing differences between the figures in a financial report not originating from performance differences. But is it important that companies make the same choice in disclosure issues? Does the fact that one company is disclosing particular information while the other is not cause any problem? *De facto* disclosure harmonization is aimed at the disclosure of specified information with a specified degree of detail, which is regarded as the minimum required for all financial reports. In order to conform with this minimum disclosure, we will have to distinguish between items which form part of the minimum information to be disclosed and other items. In respect of items which belong to the minimum information, the degree of harmony increases when the percentage of companies disclosing that information increases. To assess *de facto* disclosure harmonization in respect of other items, the degree to which that information is disclosed is of no interest. If the degree of *de facto* disclosure harmony was measured the same way as *de facto* measurement harmonization, namely as the extent to which companies make the same choice between alternatives, harmony would increase when, instead of 60 per cent, 80 per cent of the companies do *not* disclose information concerning a particular item. This is a rather strange interpretation of *de facto* disclosure harmonization. Still this would be the outcome of T&P's method if they applied it to measure disclosure harmony.

Also in respect of *de jure* harmony, the distinction between measurement and disclosure harmony is important. Apart from improving *de facto* measurement harmony, one of the aims of measuring *de jure* harmony is the avoidance or removal of obstacles such as conflicting or substantially different standards. In disclosure issues, standards may differ substantially but will seldom conflict, because few standards will prohibit companies from disclosing particular information in the financial report. Differing from measurement issues, in *de jure* disclosure harmonization the introduction of minimum standards is important.

The conclusion reached from the argument presented above is that it is not possible to develop one method for measuring both *de jure* harmony and *de facto* harmony. Differing methods must be developed for measurement and disclosure issues respectively. T&P argue (pp. 84–5) that measurement studies should focus on actual reporting practices rather than regulation, that is, on *de facto* rather than *de jure* harmonization. These are, however, two different phenomena, each pursuing different goals.

Suggested method of measuring harmonization

As pointed out above, only two of the studies in T&P's analysis provide methods for measuring harmonization. One of these studies (Nair and Frank, 1981) claims to be measuring *de jure* harmonization, both disclosure and measurement. Their idea is to classify countries into five categories with respect to each accounting method or disclosure issue. These five categories are: required (application of this accounting method or the disclosure of this particular information respectively is required in this country); predominant practice; minority practice; no application; not permitted.

According to Nair and Frank, the movement toward harmonization is defined as movement in the direction taken by a majority of countries toward requiring (or prohibiting) a given accounting practice. The Nair and Frank method is, however, not appropriate to measure either *de jure* measurement harmony/harmonization or *de jure* disclosure harmony/ harmonization. Apart from the terminology and data problems already brought forward by T&P, their method mixes up accounting regulation and accounting practice. The five categories incorporate both regulation (required, not permitted) and practice (predominant practice, minority practice and no application) which implies that neither *de jure* harmony, nor *de facto* harmony is measured. Moreover, in disclosure issues they do not distinguish between items which can be considered part of the minimum information to be disclosed and other items. Furthermore, as far as *de jure* measurement harmony is concerned, their measurement harmony approach is incorrect. They start by looking at a particular measurement method, while the starting point for measuring measurement harmony should be a particular sort of transaction or event to be accounted for by alternative measurement methods. If, for example, all countries prohibit measurement method A, their conclusion would be that the degree of *de jure* measurement harmony is high. However, the degree of *de jure* measurement harmony may be very low, for example, when that sort of transaction must be accounted for by method B in country I, by method C in country II and by method D in country III. So we may conclude that the Nair and Frank method is inappropriate for *de jure* measurement harmony and is only applicable to measuring *de jure* disclosure harmony when it is modified.

The second study providing methods to measure harmony/harmonization is my earlier study (1988). I provide two methods to measure the degree of *de facto* measurement harmony, namely the H index and the C index. The H index is calculated as the square of the relative frequencies of each of the alternative measurement methods for a particular sort of transaction or event, applied by companies. In this way a concentration of the companies on one or only a few alternative measurement methods leads to a higher H index, indicating an increase in the degree of harmony. The criticism of T&P upon the H index concerns the fact that this index is a concentration index for which no significance tests have been derived to indicate how trivial or significant (statistically) variations in index values are. This is indeed a problem. Unfortunately T&P do not discuss the other *de facto* measurement harmony method (C index) because this index does not suffer from this problem, as shown below.

The C index is not a concentration index. It is a ratio, calculated as the number of comparable pairs of financial reports divided by the total number of pairs of financial reports. So there is no problem in applying the usual statistical significance tests. We are even able to apply regression analysis. The advantages of the C index are that:

1. The C index is able to include the effect on the degree of *de facto* measurement harmony of multiple reporting and the disclosure of additional information in the notes on the accounts enabling the reader to reconcile the financial report into a report based upon an alternative measurement method.
2. Movements in the C index can be tested for their significance and can be correlated with movements in explaining variables such as the introduction of a standard.

The alternative to the measurement harmonization approach suggested by T&P (p. 85) involves the following:

> [First] . . . data on proportions of companies using different accounting methods can be obtained . . . [Second,] . . . the observed distribution of companies among different methods . . . [is compared] . . . with either a random distribution or some expected distribution. A suitable proxy for the former could be a uniform/equal/rectangular distribution, that is, a distribution in which equal numbers of companies would be expected to use each of the available alternatives. (This would represent no preference for, or bias towards, any one available method.) Evidence of harmony would then be the existence of a significant difference between the observed and expected

distributions, as measured by some appropriate significance test, for example, chi-square. [Finally,] the level of harmony could then be quantified by using a concentration index, preferably one describing the entire distribution, rather than just a portion of it. Comparison of level of harmony over different periods would yield evidence of harmonization or disharmonization.

Unfortunately T&P did not illustrate their method and, by its description, it seems rather complicated and leaves some questions unanswered, such as what significance test and what concentration measure to apply and how to apply the method in disclosure issues. Moreover, the significance test included in their method is not used to test the significance of movements in the degree of harmony, as one would expect when looking at their criticism of the H index, but it is directed towards the significance of the degree of harmony itself. The significance of movements in the degree of harmony is not tested by their method either. That is, their method suffers from the same problem they raised against the H index.

Further disadvantages of the methodology of T&P are that it is not able to include the impact of multiple reporting or additional information in the notes on the accounts on the degree of *de facto* measurement harmony, because each financial report can only be allocated to one alternative measurement method.

The conclusion reached is that the methodology of Tay and Parker is certainly not a better method to measure *de facto* measurement harmony than the C index, and may even be worse.

References

Doupnik, S., and M. E. Taylor, 'An Empirical Investigation of the Observance of IASC Standards in Western Europe', *Management International Review*, Spring 1985.

Evans, T. G., and M. E. Taylor, '"Bottom-Line Compliance" with the IASC: A Comparative Analysis', *International Journal of Accounting*, Fall 1982.

International Accounting Standards Committee, *Exposure Draft 32: Comparability of Financial Statements*, London, January 1989.

——, Statement of Intent: *Comparability of Financial Statements*, London, 1990.

Nair, R. D., and W. G. Frank, 'The Harmonization of International Accounting Standards, 1973–1979', *International Journal of Accounting*, Fall 1981.

Tay, J. S. W., and R. H. Parker, 'Measuring International Harmonization and Standardization', *Abacus*, March 1990.

van der Tas, L. G., 'Measuring Harmonisation of Financial Reporting Practice', *Accounting and Business Research*, Spring 1988.

20

MEASURING INTERNATIONAL HARMONIZATION AND STANDARDIZATION: A REPLY

J. S. W. Tay and R. H. Parker

Source: *Abacus* 28(2) (1992): 217–20.

Van der Tas' comment (1992) on our article (Tay and Parker, 1990) is greatly appreciated for two reasons: first, as he points out, and as evidenced by our article, there is little research in the field of measuring international harmonization and standardization; second, because his original paper (van der Tas, 1988) was instrumental in beginning our evaluation of different measurement approaches.

We consider our article a preliminary examination of the issues involved in the measurement of harmonization and standardization. It did not include an example of the measurement approach we proposed, as we did not have what we had suggested were the necessary data, nor had we concluded which (if any) of the available concentration measures and tests of statistical significance to apply. These issues have been addressed in a more comprehensive work (Tay, 1989), and will be dealt with below.

Studies examined

Measuring harmonization

Only two of the six studies we reviewed contained the word 'harmonization' in their title, and explicitly cited harmonization measurement as a formal objective. In the four other studies, however, compliance with IASC standards was more or less explicitly linked with harmonization, indicating, to our minds, that the authors of those studies had assumed that greater compliance with IASC standards would be equivalent to greater harmony of financial reporting.

Compliance with IASC standards and harmonization

We recognize, as does van der Tas, the difference between the two phenomena of compliance with IASC standards and accounting harmonization, hence the distinction we drew between *de jure* and *de facto* harmonization. The point which was made was that some of the authors of these studies appeared not to be aware of this difference.

Definitions

Standardization and harmonization

Van der Tas' point about differing levels of detail at which harmony may be measured is interesting, and conceptually important. However, it is not what we meant when discussing the differences between standardization and harmonization. The former we associated with regulation applying to all companies, legal regulation and/or regulation containing precise definitions; the latter with regulation affecting only certain subsets of companies, professional regulation and regulation containing discretionary definitions. In short, the concept of standardization appears to us to be associated with reduction or exclusion of choice; harmonization with a degree of flexibility and some choice.

Measuring measurement and disclosure harmonization

One of our first statements about harmonization measurement was that it is simply concerned 'with the similarity or otherwise of accounting practices and regulations' (p. 71). We followed this with a general definition of harmony as 'a "clustering" of companies around one or a few of the available [accounting] methods' (p. 73). This implies that pure harmonization is, in a sense, value neutral, that is, not concerned with whether suitable or unsuitable accounting methods are being used, or more or less information is being disclosed. If one accepts this premise, then the same measure can be applied to measurement and disclosure harmony. Otherwise, we agree with van der Tas that strange results can be obtained in relation to disclosure harmony. However, incorporating some notion of more suitable accounting methods or higher levels of disclosure (such as the 'minimum information to be disclosed' suggested by van der Tas) will inevitably introduce value judgment — and subjectivity — to the measurement process. It will also, in our opinion, necessitate the use of a separate measure.

436

De jure *and* de facto *harmony*

The measurement of *de jure* harmony was not explicitly addressed in our article, as our main concern was (and remains) with *de facto* harmony. We appreciate van der Tas' point about the different aims of *de jure* harmonization, although we do not agree with it completely. However, the measurement of *de jure* harmonization does not appear to us a very useful exercise in itself, if the ultimate concern of harmonization is to increase the comparability of financial reporting. In fact, focusing on *de facto* harmony when regulation changes would help to indicate the closeness (or otherwise) of the link between *de jure* and *de facto* harmonization. This would be important in terms of evaluating the effectiveness of, for example, the harmonization efforts of the IASC and the EC.

Suggested method of measuring harmonization

Application

The methodology we proposed has since been applied in more or less the manner suggested (Tay, 1989). Briefly:

1. Data on accounting methods and disclosure levels were obtained from the financial statements of listed companies from five different countries.
2. For each accounting method or disclosure item, companies were grouped according to the practice followed.
3. The chi-square test was used to assess the significance of the actual degree of harmony demonstrated by the grouping, compared with a rectangular distribution.
4. Harmony was quantified using two different concentration measures — the H-index suggested by van der Tas, and the entropy measure (E) — in three different forms (absolute, numbers-equivalent and relative measures).
5. Improvements in the level of disclosure and superiority of accounting method were quantified using a disclosure index.
6. The effects of disclosure of information and accounting methods on comparability were quantified by calculating the C index.
7. Changes in the values of H, E, C and the disclosure index were tested for statistical significance by using nonparametric tests.

Problems encountered with harmony measures

A general problem associated with using concentration measures to quantify harmony stems from their implicit weighting of clustering (c) of companies around one or two of a number of available alternatives, against the number (n) of those available alternatives. Intuitively, harmony should increase when c increases, and decrease when n increases. However, it is difficult to predict how a particular harmony measure will react when both c and n change at the same time, and in different directions.

A survey of common concentration measures suggested by the relevant literature suggested that the Herfindahl index (H) and the entropy measure (E) would be the best measures to test. In application, the latter proved to be unsatisfactory in two instances: first, it could not be calculated when the companies in the sample failed to use one of the available accounting methods; second, values of the relative E measure sometimes conflicted with values for the absolute and numbers-equivalent forms of E. H therefore proved to be a more reliable measure of harmonization, and appeared to be most meaningful in its numbers-equivalent form.

Problem with the comparability measure

The C-index value is affected by changes in either similarity of accounting methods used (i.e., harmony) or disclosure or both. Once again, there was a general problem of assessing how the index weights changes in harmony against changes in disclosure, which occur at the same time.

Statistical significance of the degree of harmony and harmonization

We believe that assessing the significance of the existing degree of harmony (compared to no preference or bias in favour of any one method) is an important part of measuring harmonization. For a start, it could indicate to standard-setters areas in which the existing situation is satisfactory. Also, given the lack of significance tests for the various measures used, comparing the significance of the degree of harmony at different points in time appears to be an acceptable substitute for evaluating the significance of harmonization. While van der Tas asserts that 'there is no problem in applying the usual statistical significance tests' to C, as it is not a concentration measure, he throws no light on exactly what tests he is referring to. It is our belief that more work should be conducted on the distribution of the measures used, and the distribution of companies among alternative accounting methods and levels of disclosure, and it is in these areas that our future efforts will be focused.

References

Tay, J. S. W., 'Corporate Financial Reporting: Regulatory Systems and Comparability', PhD thesis, University of Exeter, June 1989.

Tay, J. S. W., and R. H. Parker, 'Measuring International Harmonization and Standardization', *Abacus*, March 1990.

van der Tas, L. G., 'Measuring Harmonization of Financial Reporting Practice', *Accounting and Business Research*, Spring 1988.

——, 'Measuring International Harmonization and Standardization — a Comment', *Abacus*, September 1992.

21

A STATISTICAL MODEL OF INTERNATIONAL ACCOUNTING HARMONIZATION

Simon Archer, Pascale Delvaille and Stuart McLeay

Source: *Abacus* 32(1) (1996): 1–29.

This article shows how the difference between the observed frequencies of accounting policy choice and the outcome of a random policy choice, where each available method has an equal chance of being selected, may be fully explained with a statistical model. The process of harmonization is described in a way that identifies departures from equiprobable accounting policy choice as either: (a) the systematic effects of harmonization, or (b) the effects of systematic divergence from international harmony where the frequency of adoption of differing accounting methods varies across countries, or (c) the effects of company-specific accounting policy choices.

The understanding of *harmony* that underlies previous attempts to measure harmonization is such that, with respect to a particular financial statement item, a situation of maximum harmony is reached when all companies in all countries use the same accounting method. From the standpoint of modelling the harmonization process, however, a different concept of harmony may be more useful. In this article, therefore, we posit a state of *distributional harmony* in which, other things being equal, the expected distribution of accounting policy choices is the same in each country. In this theoretical state, the odds of selecting a given accounting method from those available for a particular financial statement item are identical for each country. A major advantage of this benchmark is that it provides a basis for distinguishing between two possibly conflicting components of the international harmonization process: between-country harmonization and within-country standardization.

A hierarchy of nested statistical models is then used to describe accounting policy choices made by companies with an international shareholding and registered in Europe, where the European Union has been involved in a program of accounting harmonization. The accounting policies analysed in depth in this article comprise the treatment of goodwill and accounting for deferred taxation. The results are compared with the comparability index method used previously in harmonization research studies.

Introduction

The literature on the measurement of international accounting harmonization has focused almost exclusively on the use of index measures. In the first published paper on this subject, van der Tas (1988) considered a concentration index approach (the H index), derived from the Hirschman–Herfindal index of industrial concentration, before developing his own comparability index (the C index). We have discussed the mathematics of the comparability index elsewhere (Archer, Delvaille and McLeay 1995), and some further reference to the C index will also be made below. The aim of this article, however, is to present a method of modelling statistically the process of international accounting harmonization which, we believe, provides a richer insight into that process than the use of index measures.

The possibility of a statistical modelling approach is hinted at by Tay and Parker (1990, p. 85), in the context of a discussion in *Abacus* concerning the measurement of harmonization (see Tay and Parker, 1990, 1992; van der Tas, 1992a, 1992b, 1992c). They suggest that the level of harmony in the accounting practices adopted by companies in different countries may be assessed for a particular financial statement item by comparing 'the observed distribution of companies between different methods with either a random distribution or some expected distribution', and that a suitable representation of a random distribution could be 'a distribution in which equal numbers of companies would be expected to use each of the available alternatives'. Given this approach, Tay and Parker propose that 'evidence of harmony would then be the existence of a significant difference between the observed and expected distributions, as measured by some appropriate significance test, for example chi-square'.

In this article, we show how the difference between the observed frequencies of accounting policy choices and the outcome of a process of random choice can be fully explained by means of a statistical model. In so doing, we describe harmonization in a way that allows us to identify those departures from random, or equiprobable,[1] accounting policy choice which are associated with either national standardization or international harmonization, or which are company-specific.

The notion of harmony, as normally understood in the literature, is such that the process of harmonization will lead to a situation of maximum harmony with respect to a particular financial statement item when all companies in all countries use the same accounting method. This notion ignores the possibility that companies may be subject to different circumstances

441

which arguably justify the use of correspondingly different accounting methods in respect of that item.[2] The approach envisaged in this article is based on the assumption that different commercial circumstances do indeed motivate the choice of different accounting methods. This implies an alternative notion of international harmony. According to this notion, a state of international harmony exists when, other things being equal, the odds of selecting a given accounting method are identical in each country. Hence, our statistical modelling approach incorporates a theoretical state of affairs which may be termed *distributional harmony*, and which allows measurement of the extent to which distributions of accounting policy choices are similar between countries.

We develop these ideas in the context of a hierarchy of nested statistical models based on logistic Poisson regression. These provide a description of (a) systematic effects of harmonization, (b) systematic divergence from a state of international harmony, and (c) non-systematic accounting policy choices made by individual companies.

The method is illustrated by an analysis of corporate accounting policy choices carried out during the period subsequent to the original empirical study (van der Tas, 1988) which prompted the debate in *Abacus*. The accounting policies analysed in depth here are the treatment of goodwill and accounting for deferred taxation. The companies in our sample are based in Belgium, France, Germany, Ireland, the Netherlands and the U.K., where the process of harmonization in the European Union is likely to have had an effect, and also Sweden and Switzerland where the accounting practices of multinational companies have been influenced by the EU directives. The particular companies in the sample are interlisted within Europe and are likely to be the focus of attention of financial analysts carrying out international comparisons.

In this article, we also reconcile our results with the indexation approach proposed by van der Tas (1988) and extended in Archer *et al.* (1995), and for this purpose we separate the comparability index, or C index, into two components relating to the within-country (intra-national) effects of domestic standardization and the between-country (inter-national) effects of harmonization. We show that the expected values from our model of harmonization, a model in which there are no country-specific or companyspecific accounting policy choices, yield the same C index value overall as the observed data, and that it is the within-country and between-country components of the index which reflect the divergence from harmony caused by differing national standards and company-specific policy choices.

Statistical modelling of harmonization

Using a numerical example, this section develops the idea of a hierarchical sequence of statistical models to describe the harmonization process. A

Table 1 An illustration of policy choices in two periods.

Method	Year k = 1				Year k = 2				Combined			
	j = 1	j = 2	j = 3	Total	j = 1	j = 2	j = 3	Total	j = 1	j = 2	j = 3	Total
Country												
i = 1	51	61	38	150	19	169	12	200	70	230	50	350
i = 2	99	89	112	300	41	311	48	400	140	400	160	700
Total	150	150	150	450	60	480	60	600	210	630	210	1050

three-dimensional array in Table 1 shows for each year the number of companies in each country selecting each accounting method, cross-classified in this case for two years, two countries and three accounting methods.

We increase the number of companies from 450 in year 1 to 600 in year 2 in order to demonstrate the functioning of the model with respect to such changes. It can be seen that, for the two countries combined, the distribution of accounting policy choices has changed from a uniform distribution in year 1 (33% : 33% : 33%) to a high degree of convergence in year 2 on method 2, the generally accepted practice adopted by 80 per cent of companies. It will be noted, however, that the aggregate frequencies in each of the two periods do not fit the individual *country* subsamples precisely.

The aim of the statistical model is to estimate from the observed patterns of policy choices the extent to which the changes may be attributed to a process of international harmonization rather than to behaviour that is specific to individual countries or companies. In order to develop a sequence of models which describe this kind of data adequately, we may generalize by letting x_{ijk} be the observed number of companies in the *i*th country selecting the *j*th accounting method in the *k*th year, where $i = 1, \ldots, I$ countries; $j = 1, \ldots, J$ methods; and $k = 1, \ldots, K$ years. The marginal totals are summed over the subscripts by replacing the relevant subscript with '+'. Thus, x_{+12} is the total number of companies selecting method $j = 1$ in year $k = 2$. The corresponding notation for the three-dimensional array of observed counts and the relevant marginal totals is set out in Table 2 giving, first, the general notation for an $I \times J \times K$ table and, second, the specific notation for a $2 \times 3 \times 2$ table.

The probability of a count falling in cell (*ijk*) is p_{ijk} and the corresponding expected value will be denoted as m_{ijk}. An estimate $\hat{m}_{ijk}$ of the expected value is obtained by multiplying the grand total x_{+++} by the estimated probability, $\hat{p}_{ijk}$, where the latter is estimated from the relationships between marginal totals that vary depending on the level of the model.

A suitable probability model for count data in the context of multicategory response such as multiple accounting choices is provided by the Poisson distribution. This distribution can take any non-negative integral value and may be used to describe the number of events (i.e., companies making

443

Table 2 $I \times J \times K$ array by country, accounting method and year.

Method	Year k = 1				Year k = 2				Combined			
	j = 1	j = 2	j = 3	Total	j = 1	j = 2	j = 3	Total	j = 1	j = 2	j = 3	Total
Country												
i = 1	x_{ijk}	x_{ijk}	x_{ijk}	x_{i+k}	x_{ijk}	x_{ijk}	x_{ijk}	x_{i+k}	x_{ij+}	x_{ij+}	x_{ij+}	x_{i++}
i = 2	x_{ijk}	x_{ijk}	x_{ijk}	x_{i+k}	x_{ijk}	x_{ijk}	x_{ijk}	x_{i+k}	x_{ij+}	x_{ij+}	x_{ij+}	x_{i++}
Total	x_{+jk}	x_{+jk}	x_{+jk}	x_{++k}	x_{+jk}	x_{+jk}	x_{+jk}	x_{++k}	x_{+j+}	x_{+j+}	x_{+j+}	x_{+++}
Method	Year k = 1				Year k = 2				Combined			
	j = 1	j = 2	j = 3	Total	j = 1	j = 2	j = 3	Total	j = 1	j = 2	j = 3	Total
Country												
i = 1	x_{111}	x_{121}	x_{131}	x_{1+1}	x_{112}	x_{122}	x_{132}	x_{1+2}	x_{11+}	x_{12+}	x_{13+}	x_{1++}
i = 2	x_{211}	x_{221}	x_{231}	x_{2+1}	x_{212}	x_{222}	x_{232}	x_{2+2}	x_{21+}	x_{22+}	x_{23+}	x_{2++}
Total	x_{+11}	x_{+21}	x_{+31}	x_{++1}	x_{+12}	x_{+22}	x_{+32}	x_{++2}	x_{+1+}	x_{+2+}	x_{+3+}	x_{+++}

accounting policy choices) which have occurred in a given period of time or in a given space, although no *a priori* knowledge of the total number of observations is assumed. However, a restriction may be imposed whereby the total sample size is fixed and, if the x_{ijk}s have been generated according to a Poisson sampling scheme, then the conditional distribution is multinomial, with the probability function as given in Bishop *et al.* (1975).[3] Further discussion of the relevant sampling scheme for cross-classified data is to be found in Fienberg (1977) and, with respect to measurements repeated through time, in Lindsey (1993).

When a Poisson-distributed error term is linked to a multinomial logistic regression, we may estimate simultaneously the probabilities, the p_{ijk}s, for the type of cross-classified categorical data dealt with in this article As closed-form solutions are not feasible for all levels of three-way interaction models with multiple responses, the estimation of the expected values, the m_{ijk}s, may be achieved by fitting parameters from a generalized linear model for the complete cross-classification by explanatory variable using iterative proportional fitting (Aitken *et al.*, 1989). In this article, the analysis was carried out using the generalized linear modelling system GLIM4 (Francis *et al.*, 1993).

Model 1: Complete independence

For the model of complete independence, the expected value of accounting policy choices is equal in each cell, regardless of country or year.[4] However, when subsamples are unbalanced because there are different numbers of observations in each country and/or in each year, the model of complete independence has no descriptive validity, and the appropriate model of independence is one which reflects the sampling design, as below.

Model 2: Conditional independence

For a population of company financial disclosures, the number of disclosing companies may vary as a result of population differences between countries and as a result of changes in the population of companies from one time period to another. This may be reflected in sampling design. Furthermore, if non-disclosure is not considered as one of the choices and, as a result, statistical modelling is restricted to accounting policy choices only, this may also cause variation in the country and year subsamples for the reduced set of data. The second model, the model of conditional independence, reflects these constraints imposed by sampling design.

As the model of conditional independence provides estimates of the effects associated with the numbers of observations by country and by year, the components of the model are a country factor (C), a year factor (Y) and the second-order interactions between countries and years $(C.Y)$. The linear model of conditional independence is, therefore, denoted as

$$C + Y + C.Y \text{ (or, more succinctly, } C_*Y)$$

where . represents the interaction between main effects, and $*$ indicates the inclusion of both main effects and interaction effects.[5]

For the example, the two-level country factor measures the relative odds of a company belonging to country 1 or country 2. Given the marginal totals indicated in Table 1 above, the relative odds of a company being in country 1 are $x_{1++}:x_{2++} = 350:700$, or 1:2. Likewise, the two-level year factor is described by the odds ratio $x_{++1}:x_{++2}$ which, using the marginal totals in Table 1, gives the relative odds of an observation falling in year 1 as 450:600, or 3 : 4. From the logistic regression, we obtain each of these parameter estimates as a logit, that is, the logarithm of the relative odds ratio.

Under this model, C_*Y, the estimated probability $\hat{p}_{ijk}$ of a count falling in cell (ijk) is equal to $(x_{i+k}/x_{+++})/J$, where J is the total number of methods.[6] For the model of conditional independence (and all higher-order models), the estimate $\hat{m}_{i+k}$ of the expected marginal count for each country in each year is equal to the observed marginal count x_{i+k}. However, for this model, the estimated marginal count for each method $\hat{m}_{+jk}$ is equal to x_{++k}/J, and not to the observed value. The expected values for the example are given in Table 3.

The model of conditional independence reproduces the situation where the selection of an accounting method for a financial statement item from among the various possible methods is entirely random and where each of the possible methods thus has an equal chance of being used. We refer to this model as being one of *conditional* independence, since the expected number of companies selecting a particular method in a given country in a

Table 3 Expected values under conditional independence.

| Method | Year k = 1 | | | | Year k = 2 | | | | Combined | | | |
	j = 1	j = 2	j = 3	Total	j = 1	j = 2	j = 3	Total	j = 1	j = 2	j = 3	Total
Country												
i = 1	50	50	50	*150*	67	67	67	*200*	117	117	117	*350*
i = 2	100	100	100	*300*	133	133	133	*400*	233	233	233	*700*
Total	150	150	150	*450*	200	200	200	*600*	350	350	350	*1050*

Note: In this table, expected values are rounded to the nearest integer. Furthermore, in this table and those that follow, expected values which are equal to the observed data are given in italics.

given year is conditional only on the total number of companies in that country sample for that year.[7]

We may consider model 2 to be the null model. By adding further terms, we are able to account for systematic effects relating to changes in policy choices. At subsequent levels of the model hierarchy, the increase in the goodness of fit that is achieved is divided through by the number of degrees of freedom lost by adding parameters to the model, thus providing the basis for tests of the usefulness of the additional parameters in the model. The inferential procedures are described in greater detail later in this section.

Model 3: The static model of harmony

A situation of *distributional harmony* may be said to exist when accounting policy frequency distributions are identical across countries. When there is no harmonization between years, these frequency distributions also remain identical across years. That is, if we allow policy choices to depart from equiprobability and to vary overall, but not to depart from this pattern across countries, or from year to year, the resulting model describes the most likely pattern of policy choices in a state where there is an unchanging level of harmony for the period as a whole. This may be achieved by adding the three-level policy factor (P) to the model as a main effect, giving the following:

$$C + Y + P + C.Y \text{ (or } C_*Y + P).$$

As a result of adding policy main effects, the estimates of expected values are distributed over the policy choices in the proportions observed for total policy choices for all years combined, that is x_{+j+}/x_{+++}, a distribution which remains constant for each country and for each year. The expected values from the static model of harmony for the example, which follow the pattern 1:3:1 throughout, are shown in Table 4.

Under this model, the estimated probability $\hat{p}_{ijk}$ of a count falling in cell ijk is equal to $(x_{i+k}/x_{+++}) * x_{+j+}/x_{+++})$. For example, for the first accounting

446

Table 4 Expected values from the static model of harmony.

Method	Year k = 1				Year k = 2				Combined			
	$j = 1$	$j = 2$	$j = 3$	*Total*	$j = 1$	$j = 2$	$j = 3$	*Total*	$j = 1$	$j = 2$	$j = 3$	*Total*
Country												
$i = 1$	30	90	30	*150*	40	120	40	*200*	70	210	70	*350*
$i = 2$	60	180	60	*300*	80	240	80	*400*	140	420	140	*700*
Total	90	270	90	*450*	120	360	120	*600*	210	630	210	*1050*

method in the first country in the first year, our probability estimate $\hat{p}_{111}$ is equal to

$$\frac{x_{1+1}}{x_{+++}} * \frac{x_{+1+}}{x_{+++}} = \frac{150}{1050} * \frac{210}{1050} = \frac{1}{35} = 0.0286$$

and the estimated expected value $\hat{m}_{111}$ is equal to $\hat{p}_{111} * x_{+++} = 30$.

Model 4: The dynamic model of harmonization

If we allow policy choices to vary from year to year, but still not from country to country, the model describes the change in harmony from one period to the next. This is achieved by adding the interaction between years and policy choices ($Y.P$) to the model to give

$$C + Y + P + C.Y + Y.P \text{ (or } C*Y + Y*P).$$

The $Y.P$ interaction terms represent, for each policy, the change from one year to the next in the relative odds of it being selected. These changes are identified in this study as the *harmonization effects*. Hence, this model describes the level of harmony year by year, given the aggregate distribution of policy choices for all countries as observed in each year, and consequently the harmonization effect between years. Thus, if the data are such that the distribution of aggregate policy choices converges on a smaller number of generally accepted methods over time, this increase in harmony will be reflected in the better fit of model 4 (the dynamic model) compared to model 3 (the static model). In this case, the sign of the estimated parameter values for the $Y.P$ interactions between years and policies would be positive. In the case of a reduction in harmony, the sign of the estimated parameter values for those $Y.P$ interaction effects would be negative.

The expected values for the example are shown in Table 5. It can be seen that the estimated expected marginal counts of policy choices by year, $\hat{m}_{+jk}$, are equal to the observed marginals x_{+jk}, which was not the case with the previous model where the distributions were constant over time. Within each country and for each year, the distribution of expected values reflects

Table 5 Expected values from the dynamic model of harmonization.

Method	Year k = 1				Year k = 2				Combined			
	j = 1	j = 2	j = 3	Total	j = 1	j = 2	j = 3	Total	j = 1	j = 2	j = 3	Total
Country												
i = 1	50	50	50	150	20	160	20	200	70	210	70	350
i = 2	100	100	100	300	40	320	40	400	140	420	140	700
Total	150	150	150	450	60	480	60	600	210	630	210	1050

the proportions of total policy choices for each year, and the estimated probability $\hat{p}_{ijk}$ of a count falling in cell ijk is equal to $(x_{i+k}/x_{+++}) * (x_{+jk}/x_{+++})$. For example, the probability estimate $\hat{p}_{111}$ is now equal to

$$\frac{x_{1+1}}{x_{+++}} * \frac{x_{+11}}{x_{++k}} = \frac{150}{1050} * \frac{150}{450} = \frac{1}{21} = 0.0476$$

and the estimated expected value $\hat{m}_{111}$ is equal to $\hat{p}_{111}{}^{*}x_{+++} = 50$.

The paramaterization of model 4 may be compared instructively at this stage with that of the lower-order models 2 and 3 which, given that they contain a subset of its terms, are nested within model 4. The linear logits from each fit are given below and the corresponding exponentiated values are also listed:

	Model 2 (conditional independence)		Model 3 (static harmony)		Model 4 (dynamic harmonization)	
	logits	exponent	logits	exponent	logits	exponent
m_{111}	3.912	50.00	3.402	30.00	3.912	50.00
C2	+0.693	2.00	+0.693	2.00	+0.693	2.00
Y2	+0.288	1.33	+0.288	1.33	−0.916	0.40
C2.Y2	+0.000	1.00	+0.000	1.00	+0.000	1.00
P2			+1.099	3.00	+0.000	1.00
P3			+0.000	1.00	+0.000	1.00
Y2.P2					+2.079	8.00
Y2.P3					+0.000	1.00

As noted, the exponentiated parameter values are relative odds. An example of the computation of the linear predictor and the exponentiated expected value in the case of m_{222} is as follows:

	Model 2		Model 3		Model 4	
	logits	exponent	logits	exponent	logits	exponent
m111	3.912	50.00	3.402	30.00	3.912	50.00
C2	+0.693	*2.00	+0.693	*2.00	+0.693	*2.00
Y2	+0.288	*1.33	+0.288	*1.33	−0.916	*0.40
C2.Y2	+0.000	*1.00	+0.000	*1.00	+0.000	*1.00
P2			+1.099	*3.00	+0.000	*1.00
Y2.P2					+2.079	*8.00
m_{222}	4.893	133.33	5.482	240.00	5.768	320.00

For instance, for model 4, the odds of selecting method 2 rather than method 1 in the first year are evens (the exponent of P2 is equal to 1) while the relative odds of selecting the second method in the second year, as measured by the term Y2.P2, are 8:1

Model 5: The full model

The full second-order interaction model, model 5, allows policy choices to vary systematically from country to country from year to year. By adding the interactions between countries and policy choices (*C.P*), this model accounts for policy choices which depart from the overall pattern and are specific to individual countries. In other words, the increase of goodness of fit is attributable to the extent to which the distribution of national policy preferences differs from their distribution internationally. The components of the full model are

$$C + Y + P + C.Y + Y.P + C.P \text{ (or } C_*Y + Y_*P + C_*P).$$

In this case, the probabilities are estimated using an iterative procedure. All expected marginal counts under model 5 are in agreement with observed marginals, now including $\hat{m}_{ij+} = x_{ij+}$, the sum over the years for each policy choice in each country. Thus, except for random variation attributable to non-systematic policy selection by individual companies, the full model is a perfect description of the data. The expected values for the full model applied to our example are given in Table 6.

Model 5 is treated for all purposes in the following analysis as the full model, with all previous models being nested within it. The degrees of freedom for model 5 therefore provide the index for F-tests, as shown at the end of this description of the model hierarchy. The full model provides a description of systematic accounting policy choice, including effects of international harmonization (*Y.P*) and national standardization (*C.P*), the significance of each being reflected in the parameter estimates.

Table 6 Expected values from the full second-order interaction model.

Method	Year k = 1				Year k = 2				Combined			
	j = 1	j = 2	j = 3	Total	j = 1	j = 2	j = 3	Total	j = 1	j = 2	j = 3	Total
Country												
i = 1	52	61	37	150	18	169	13	200	70	230	50	350
i = 2	98	89	113	300	42	311	47	400	140	400	160	700
Total	150	150	150	450	60	480	60	600	210	630	210	1050

Note: The expected values in this table are rounded to the nearest integer.

Table 7 The sequence of nested harmonization models.

Model hierarchy, main effects and interaction effects	Description of models and effects
1 Grand mean	Model of complete independence
Add: Country$_*$Year	Sample design effects
2 (C_*Y)	Model of conditional independence
Add: Policy	Convergence effects
3 $(C_*Y) + (P)$	Static model of harmony
Add: Year.Policy	Harmonization effects
4 $(C_*Y)+(Y_*P)$	Dynamic model of harmonization
Add: Country.Policy	Divergence effects
5 $(C_*Y)+(Y_*P)+(C_*P)$	Full model
Add: three-way effects	Random company effects
6 (C_*Y_*P)	Saturated model

Model 6: The saturated model

Finally, by adding the three-way interaction effects $(C.Y.P)$, which account for the residual random variation in the previous model, the data are fully saturated. This maximal model has the following structure

$$C + Y + P + C.Y = Y.P + C.P + C.Y.P \text{ (or } C_*Y_*P)$$

and fits expected values without error to the observed values, where $\hat{m}_{ijk} = x_{ijk}$. The sum of errors is therefore zero.[8] There are as many parameters as there are observations, and the degrees of freedom are consequently also zero. The difference between models 5 and 6 is attributable to those policy choices by companies which are not systematic, that is, they are described neither by international harmonization nor by national patterns of accounting policy choice.

The hierarchical sequence of the models is summarised in Table 7.

Measuring goodness of fit

The appropriate measure of goodness of fit for Poisson data is the log likelihood-ratio test statistic, referred to more generally as the deviance and calculated as the difference between the maximized log likelihoods for the fitted and saturated models, multiplied by -2. For the Normal model, the deviance is equal to the residual sum of squares, but in the case of the Poisson model it has an interpretation similar to that of the Pearson goodness of fit statistic (Francis *et al.*, 1993).

The relative goodness of fit of two nested models can be compared by examining the ratio of (a) the change in deviances from two models within the hierarchy divided by the change in degrees of freedom, to (b) the deviance for the full model (which we define as model 5 above, the model

450

which reproduces all marginals exactly) divided by its degrees of freedom. That is, where the deviance of a higher-order model M_H is D_H on v_H degrees of freedom and the deviance of the lower-order model M_L containing a subset of the terms in model M_H is D_L on v_L degrees of freedom, and D_F is the deviance of the full model on v_F degrees of freedom, the ratio $[(D_L - D_H)/(v_L - v_H)]/(D_F/v_F)$ has an F-distribution on $(v_L - v_H)$, (v_F).[9]

A small F-statistic indicates that model M_H and model M_L may not be distinguished, as the residual deviance for the reduced model M_L is not much larger than for model m_H. The F-statistic provides a likelihood ratio test of the hypothesis that the variables added to the model have zero regression coefficients and do not contribute to the regression function, in the first case with respect to the accurate model or, in the case of the alternative test described above, with respect to successive higher-order models.

Non-disclosure

In some cases, a particular item may not be reported in a company's financial statements. A possible explanation may be that there were no transactions of the relevant kind, thus obviating the need for an accounting policy in that area. A further possibility is that there were such transactions but the company chose not to recognize the item for reporting purposes. Another possibility is that the item was reported, while the company provided insufficient information to allow the reader to determine the accounting method used. One explanation of this may be that the company in question considered that it did not need to disclose the accounting method used because it took the view that readers of its financial statements would be able to make an informed default assumption on the basis, for instance, that only one method is permitted by law in the company's country of registration. An alternative explanation is that the company may have decided not to report the method used even though no default assumption was applicable.

In the context of a statistical model, we may wish to treat such a decision process either as stochastic, where there is an element of choice by the company, or as non-stochastic. In the analysis carried out in this article, we were unable to make any default assumptions. Accordingly, we first treat non-disclosure as stochastic by assuming that such non-disclosure is one of the choices available to a company alongside the J accounting methods (i.e., given $J = 3$ methods, there would exist four choices including non-disclosure). We then compare the results of model-fitting under the above assumption with those obtained under the alternative assumption that non-disclosure is not a matter of choice since there had been no relevant transactions for the companies in question. This is achieved by weighting non-disclosures out of the generalized regression, thus restricting the estimation of expected values to the subset of companies selecting one or other of the J accounting methods.

Comparability indices

In this article we also compare our results with the comparability index introduced by van der Tas (1988). The C index is best interpreted as a model of interfirm comparison, as it measures for a single financial statement item the proportion of pairwise comparisons that are feasible given the alternative accounting methods adopted by different companies. Thus, it represents the probability that, for the item in question, two companies selected at random will report financial information that is comparable. Other things being equal, comparability increases when the choices made by companies converge towards a generally accepted method or when the number of accounting methods in use is reduced.

The C index may be constructed for each model from the expected marginal counts in any year k. In this context, the C index would measure the total number of expected pairwise comparisons given a particular model (obtained by summing over the alternative accounting methods the expected numbers of pairwise comparisons in each subset using the same accounting method) expressed as a proportion of the maximum number of pairwise comparisons that would be made if all companies were to use the same accounting method. The expected value of the C index is as follows:

$$\frac{\sum_j (m_{+jk}(m_{+jk} - 1))}{m_{++k}(m_{++k} - 1)}$$

where, for year k, m_{+jk} is the number of companies expected to select the jth method and m_{++k} is the total number of companies.[10]

For a given number of companies and a given number of different accounting methods for a particular financial statement item, the lowest level of comparability exists when the accounting methods are assumed to be selected with equal probability by companies.[11] Thus, the C index estimated from the model of conditional independence (model 2) is a measure of the minimum level of comparability for the sample, which converges each year on the reciprocal of the number of accounting methods, $1/J$, as sample size increases. The C index estimated from the static model of harmony (model 3) also remains constant through time as it measures the level of comparability that would exist in a state of unchanging distributional harmony. In contrast, the index value estimated from the expected values of the dynamic model of harmonization (model 4) varies over time as it measures the effects of harmonization on comparability.

The index values obtained for the example are given in Table 8. It can be seen that the minimum level of comparability with three methods is 33 per cent, the level estimated from the model of conditional independence. This would increase to a constant level of 44 per cent under the static model of harmony, where the distribution of policy choices remains unchanged from

Table 8 Comparability indices.

		Year 1	*Year 2*
Model 2	Conditional independence	33	33
Model 3	Static harmony	44	44
Model 4	Dynamic harmonization	33	66
Model 5	Full model	33	66
Model 6	Observed values	33	66

year to year. Allowing for harmonization, the C index increases from 33 per cent in year 1 to 66 per cent in year 2, as shown in Figure 1.

The C index values obtained from model 4 are equal to those obtained from models 5 and 6 (the full model and the saturated model), as all information required for the C index is accurately estimated by each of these models. It will be recalled that, in the earlier discussion of the sequence of nested models, the expected marginal counts were given as sufficient statistics whose accuracy increased for higher-order models. The equivalence between expected marginals and observed marginals may be summarized as follows:

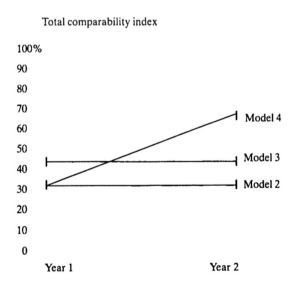

Figure 1 Comparability indices
Key: Model 2 = Minimum comparability (conditional independence): Modal 3 = Harmony (static): Modal 4 = Harmonization (dynamic). Note that the total comparability index values are identical when estimated from the model of harmonization (model 4), the full model (model 5) and the actual data (observed values in the saturated model, model 6).

Expected marginal	*Description of marginal*	*Models where expected marginal equals observed marginal*
m_{+++}	grand total	1,2,3,4,5,6
m_{i++}	counts in the ith country	2,3,4,5,6
m_{++k}	counts in the kth year	2,3,4,5,6
m_{i+k}	counts in the ith country in the kth year	2,3,4,5,6
m_{+j+}	counts of the jth policy choice	3,4,5,6
m_{+jk}	counts of the jth policy choice in the kth year	4,5,6
m_{ij+}	counts of the jth policy choice in the ith country	5,6

It can be seen that the expected number of companies selecting the jth accounting method in the kth year, m_{+jk}, is an accurate estimate in each of the higher-order models 4, 5 and 6.

It follows that the C index is not able to distinguish the within-country effects of national standardization that are allowed for in model 5 from the between-country effects of international harmonization in model 4, a feature of the C index which makes it deficient as a measure of international harmonization. Consequently, we also use in our analysis a within-country index of international comparability and between-country index of international comparability. The latter is a more appropriate index of international harmonization.

The number of pairwise comparisons that may be expected in the ith country amongst companies selecting the jth accounting method in the kth year is $^1\!/\!2 m_{ijk}(m_{ijk} - 1)$. Therefore, the expected total number of such within-country comparisons is given by summing over I countries and J methods. This is maximized for the ith country at $^1\!/\!2 m_{i+k}(m_{i+k} - 1)$ when all companies within that country use the same method. Thus, the within-country index for year k is given by

$$\frac{\sum_i \sum_j (m_{ijk}(m_{ijk} - 1))}{\sum_i (m_{i+k}(m_{i+k} - 1))}$$

Between-country comparability is based on the number of pairwise comparisons that may be expected between companies selecting the jth accounting method but operating in different countries. As the number of companies outside the ith country using the jth accounting method in the kth year is equal to $m_{+jk} - m_{ijk}$, it follows that between-country comparability index for year k may be expressed as

$$\frac{\sum_i \sum_j (m_{ijk}(m_{+jk} - m_{ijk}))}{\sum_i (m_{i+k}(m_{++k} - m_{i+k}))}$$

454

Finally, it should be noted that non-disclosure could influence the C index in a number of ways. If a company does not disclose a particular financial statement item because no such transactions took place, that company's accounts may be compared with those of all other companies, whichever method the other companies have adopted. If a company discloses a financial statement item but not the accounting method (which was referred to earlier as stochastic non-disclosure), comparison will not be possible with the accounts of other companies disclosing the item. In this article, we assume that all non-disclosures fall into the latter category and the comparability indices are calculated accordingly.

The analysis of accounting practices

In this section, we describe how we analysed the accounting practices studied for the purpose of measuring the degree to which harmony existed in 1986/87 and 1990/91 and hence the process of harmonization (i.e., the change in harmony) between those years. For the sample on which our analysis is based, we selected from eight European countries those companies whose shares are traded internationally and which, therefore, are likely to be influenced by international factors, country-specific factors and company-specific factors in the selection of accounting methods. The companies were first selected in 1986 (see Archer, Dufour and McLeay 1989) and, for the purpose of this analysis, the financial statements of the same set of companies were reviewed again for the 1990 calendar year (or for accounting periods over 1990/91). The accounting policies considered are deferred taxation and goodwill, for which a more detailed description of the regulations and practices in each of the countries studied is given in Archer *et al.* (1995). Further discussion of financial reporting practices may be found in detailed studies of the countries involved: Belgium (Lefebvre and Flower, 1994), France (Scheid and Walton, 1992), Germany (Ordelheide and Pfaff, 1994), Ireland (Brennan *et al.*, 1992), the Netherlands (Dijksma and Hoogendoorn, 1993), Sweden (Heurlin and Peterssohn, 1995), Switzerland (Laffournier, 1995) and the United Kingdom (Gordon and Gray, 1994).

Deferred taxation

The cross-classification of methods of tax accounting adopted by eighty-nine companies from eight countries in two separate periods 1986/87 and 1990/91 is set out in Table 9.

Overall, there was a decline in the number of companies using the taxes payable method and an increase in deferred tax accounting, in the cases of both the partial provision method and the full provision method. Nevertheless, non-disclosure remained a serious barrier to comparability.

455

Table 9 Deferred tax cross-classifications.

Netherlands	1986/87 Accounting method						1990/91 Accounting method					
	A	*B*	*C*	*D*	*E*	*Total*	*A*	*B*	*C*	*D*	*E*	*Total*
Belgium	2	0	1	0	1	4	2	1	0	0	1	4
France	0	6	5	1	0	12	0	8	4	0	0	12
Germany	0	2	1	15	4	22	0	4	4	12	2	22
Ireland	0	0	3	0	1	4	1	0	3	0	0	4
Netherlands	0	6	2	4	0	12	0	6	1	4	1	12
Sweden	8	1	0	3	1	13	2	5	1	5	0	13
Switzerland	0	0	0	2	2	4	0	0	3	1	0	4
U.K.	0	0	18	0	0	18	0	0	18	0	0	18
Total	10	15	30	25	9	89	5	24	34	22	4	89

Key: A = Nil provision (taxes payable method); B = Full method; C = Partial method: D = Deferred tax recognized but method unspecified; E = No recognition of deferred tax and it is not known whether or not it is applicable.

A substantial number of companies recognizing deferred tax did not disclose the deferred tax method used and a small number of companies not recognizing deferred tax did not indicate whether or not it was applicable. However, in both cases, the number of companies not disclosing sufficient information decreased.

The statistical analysis was carried out first for companies in all eight countries. Secondly, in order to exclude country–year and country–policy effects which could not add significantly to explanation (due to the small number of observations), it was repeated for a subset that excluded the three smaller subsamples in Belgium, Ireland and Switzerland. The remaining five countries represent 87 per cent of the total sample.

With regard to policy choices, we treated the five categories A to E as stochastic in a first fit of the models and we repeated the procedures treating those companies which did not recognize deferred tax (category E) as nonstochastic. That is, in the latter cases, we assumed that selection was restricted to the four choices A to D.

A notable feature of the analysis reported in Table 10 is the small residual from the full model, attributable to random company effects. This has some influence on the F-tests of changes in goodness of fit with respect to the full model (reported as F_1 in Table 10), as explanations other than company-specific selection of accounting methods account for a high proportion of the deviance.

For the F_1 likelihood ratio test with respect to the full model, harmony (the addition of the policy choice main effect) and national divergence (the addition of the interaction between countries and policies) are both seen to be highly significant, with probabilities of a larger F-value being almost zero. Harmonization effects (the addition of the interaction between years

Table 10 Statistical analysis of deferred tax harmonization.

	Scope of stochastic model							
	All disclosures and non-disclosures				Four main policy choices only			
	Eight countries		Five countries		Eight countries		Five countries	
Models and effects	Deviance	DF	Deviance	DF	Deviance	DF	Deviance	DF
Null model 358.69	79		266.06	49	314.24	63	220.62	39
Country.Year	−60.91	−15	−9.86	−9	−64.71	−15	−7.13	−9
Conditional independence	297.78	64	256.20	40	249.53	48	213.49	30
Policy	−56.19	−4	−63.92	−4	−33.76	−3	−35.91	−3
F_1	*(19.07)*		*(33.38)*		*(16.75)*		*(41.28)*	
p	*(.000)*		*(.000)*		*(.000)*		*(.000)*	
F_2	*(3.49)*		*(2.99)*		*(2.35)*		*(1.82)*	
p	*(.012)*		*(.031)*		*(.085)*		*(.167)*	
Static harmony	241.59	60	192.28	36	215.77	45	177.58	27
Year.Policy	−6.21	−4	−6.23	−4	−4.09	−3	−5.69	−3
F_1	*(2.11)*		*(3.25)*		*(2.03)*		*(6.54)*	
p	*(.107)*		*(.039)*		*(.141)*		*(.007)*	
F_2	*(.369)*		*(.268)*		*(.271)*		*(.265)*	
p	*(.829)*		*(.896)*		*(.846)*		*(.850)*	
Dynamic harmonization	235.38	56	186.05	32	211.68	42	171.89	24
Country.Policy	−214.75	−28	−178.39	−16	−197.57	−21	−168.41	−12
$F_1 = F_2$	*(10.41)*		*(23.29)*		*(14.00)*		*(48.41)*	
p	*(.000)*		*(.000)*		*(.000)*		*(.000)*	
Full model	20.63	28	7.66	16	14.11	21	3.48	12
Random company effects	−20.63	−28	−7.66	−16	−14.11	−21	−3.48	−12

Notes:
1. Classification of policy variable

Treated as stochastic in each analysis:
A = Nil provision, or taxes payable approach
B = Full provision
C = Partial provision
D = Deferred tax recognized but method unspecified

Treated as non-stochastic in the restricted analysis of four main policy choices:
E = No recognition of deferred tax, and it is not known whether or not deferred tax accounting is applicable

2. Countries included in each analysis: France, Germany, Netherlands, Sweden, U.K. Small samples included only in eight-country analysis: Belgium, Ireland, Switzerland.
3. The first F-test, F_1, compares the additional explanatory power of successive models with the random company effects, that is, it compares the reduction in deviance for successive models with the deviance after fitting the full model (model 5). The second F-test, F_2, compares the additional explanatory power of each model with the unexplained variation after fitting that model.

and policies) are significant when the nuisance parameters associated with the small country samples are removed, as the p-value for the five-country analysis is reduced to 0.7 per cent. As recalled above, the F_1 test compares the harmonization effects with the impact of policy choices made by individual companies, of which relatively few are non-systematic. It can be seen that the reduction in deviance attributable to the systematic effects of harmonization is -5.69, compared to -3.48 for the non-systematic effects of company-specific accounting policy choice, suggesting that where companies departed from national preferences during the period investigated, they tended to select accounting policies which led to harmonization.

The F_2 test provides an alternative perspective on deferred tax accounting. Although some harmonization occurred during the period, as shown above, it did not have a significant effect on changing the level of harmony between the two years in question, as little explanatory power was offered by fitting the dynamic model instead of the static model.

Furthermore, a comparison of the model of conditional independence and the static model reveals that there was relatively little harmony when the model fit was restricted to the main policy choices only. The main characteristic of the data is the existence of national differences in deferred tax accounting. However, a stronger case that there is some harmony in tax accounting arises when non-disclosure, a decreasing practice, is treated as stochastic, with the low p-values of 1.2 per cent (eight countries) and 3.1 per cent (five countries) suggesting that the significant impact on harmonization has been greater disclosure.

As shown in Table 11, the parameter estimates obtained for all categories of policy choice when fitting model 4, the dynamic model of harmonization, indicate that there was during the test period a relatively high probability that companies would select the partial method or would choose not to disclose the method of deferred taxation used. The only change of any statistical significance concerns the increase in probability of selecting the full method. These inferences are unchanging under the full eight-country analysis and the restricted analysis of the five larger countries.

However, a further analysis restricted in this case to the EC countries in the sample (i.e., excluding Sweden and Switzerland), also reported in Table 11, reveals that the harmonizing effect with respect to the full method is no longer present to such a marked extent. This is because Swedish companies discontinued the use of the taxes payable method, with most of those disclosing the new policy indicating that the full method had been selected. Thus, we are able to conclude from results that have some statistical significance that an important harmonizing effect (although limited in its extent) had been the change in policy choice by European companies outside the EC at the time to one or other of the more generally accepted practices within the EC.

Table 11 Parameter estimates for deferred tax harmonization.

	All countries		Five largest countries		EC countries	
	Policy effects	Year effects	Policy effects	Year effects	Policy effects	Year effects
A: Nil provision		−0.693 (.881)		−1.386 (.842)		+0.406 (1.14)
B: Full method	+0.406 (.408)	+1.163* (.639)	+0.629 (.437)	+1.814* (.857)	+1.946* (.755)	−0.100 (.977)
C: Partial method	+1.099* (.365)	+0.818 (.602)	+1.179* (.404)	+1.460 (.836)	+2.708* (.729)	−0.406 (.948)
D: Method unspecified	+0.916* (.374)	+0.565 (.621)	+1.056* (.410)	+1.295 (.846)	+2.303* (.741)	−0.629 (.972)
E: Deferred tax not recognized	−0.105 (.459)	−0.118 (.813)	−0.470 (.570)	+0.875 (1.08)	+1.099 (.816)	−0.811 (1.12)

Note: Parameter estimates are reported as log-relatives with respect to Policy A, and are not directly comparable between the full and reduced data sets. The boxed year-policy interaction effects are additive with respect to the main effects outside the box. The estimates are obtained by fitting model 4, the dynamic model of harmonization. The intercept estimate and the country effects are not included in the above table as they do not affect the interpretation of the policy, year and year-policy parameter values. Standard errors of log-adds are given in brackets and significant values are indicated with an asterisk.

Nevertheless, this conclusion must be interpreted in the light of the main explanation arising from the F_2 test relating to the systematic behaviour of companies using methods that are widely adopted nationally but not internationally. All *p*-values reported in Table 10 for the comparison between dynamic harmonization and the full model (the difference being explained by country–policy effects) arc virtually zero.

The conclusions reached above are reflected in the disclosure-adjusted comparability indices presented in Table 12 which have been constructed from the expected values given by each model for the eight-country analysis of all disclosures and non-disclosures. The financial statements of com

Table 12 Deferred taxation comparability indices.

	Within-country comparability		Between-country comparability		Total comparability	
	1986/87	*1990/91*	*1986/87*	*1990/91*	*1986/87*	*1990/91*
Conditional independence	8.51	8.51	12.00	12.00	11.46	11.46
Static harmony	14.96	14.96	18.44	18.44	17.89	17.89
Dynamic harmonization	12.10	18.65	15.47	22.18	14.94	21.63
Full model	35.07	38.09	11.21	18.58	14.94	21.63
Observed values	37.09	37.91	10.84	18.61	14.94	21.63

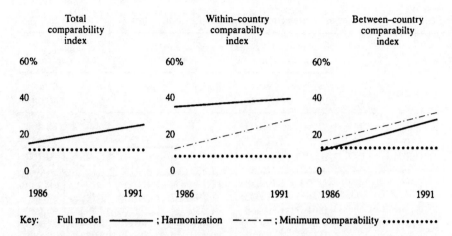

Figure 2 Deferred taxation comparability indices constructed from expected values.

panies falling in categories D (deferred tax method unspecified) and E (not known whether deferred tax accounting is applicable) were treated as non-comparable with regard to deferred tax.

Constant comparability in a state of static harmony stands at 17.89 per cent overall, a low figure attributable in particular to the low levels of disclosure on average over the two periods about the method of deferred taxation used. The increase in disclosure from 1986/87 to 1990/91 and the greater use of deferred taxation brought about an increase in total comparability levels from 14.94 per cent in 1986/87 to 21.63 per cent in 1990/91. As shown earlier in the article, these estimates of the total comparability index are equal under the dynamic model of harmonization, the full model and for the actual data.

Figure 2 shows the index values constructed from the fitted estimates under minimum comparability (model 2), dynamic harmonization (model 4) and the full model (model 5).

The measures of within-country and between-country comparability are greatly influenced by the national clustering of policy choices.[12] For instance, within-country comparability is substantially higher in both years when the expected index values from the full model, which allows for divergent country practices, are compared with those from the model of dynamic harmonization, which assumes distributional harmony. This is because a majority of disclosing companies in France, the Netherlands and Sweden use the full provision method (method B) while all British and Irish companies and the majority of Swiss companies use the partial provision method (method C). In contrast, the divergence from a harmonized state has an opposite effect on the expected between-country index values. For instance, the between-country index in 1990/91 stands at 22.18 per cent given the assumptions of distributional harmony compared to 18.58 per cent given

Table 13 Goodwill cross-classifications.

| | 1986/87 Accounting method | | | | | | 1990/91 Accounting method | | | | | |
	A	B	C	D	E	Total	A	B	C	D	E	Total
Belgium	0	0	0	4	0	4	0	0	0	4	0	4
France	0	1	0	11	0	12	0	1	0	11	0	12
Germany	3	10	2	6	1	22	0	11	0	8	3	22
Ireland	1	2	0	0	1	4	1	2	0	0	1	4
Netherlands	0	12	0	0	0	12	0	9	0	1	2	12
Sweden	1	2	0	10	0	13	0	4	0	9	0	13
Switzerland	0	0	0	2	2	4	0	2	0	2	0	4
U.K.	0	15	0	1	2	18	0	15	0	1	2	18
Total	5	42	2	34	6	89	1	44	0	36	8	89

Key: A = Written off against profit and loss account in the year of acquisition: B = Eliminated against reserves in the year of acquisition; C = Shown as an asset and not amortized: D = Shown as an asset and amortized through the profit and loss account over more than one year: E = Other or unspecified.

the assumptions of systematic divergence from distributional harmony inherent in the full model.

Finally, it may be noted that the non-systematic selection of deferred tax methods by individual companies has a negligible effect on comparability. The expected values of the between-country and within-country comparability indices obtained from the full second-order interaction model are similar to those obtained from the actual data.

Goodwill arising on consolidation

The cross-classification of goodwill accounting methods is given in Table 13. There was little change overall. Two German companies, which in 1986/87 were still using the method formerly adopted in Germany (method C, the capitalization of goodwill without subsequent amortization), abandoned that practice at a later date. We did not consider method C as equiprobable in either period of our study, and we treated the counts under method C as structural zeros for the purposes of stochastic analysis. In addition, we note that non-disclosure was not a serious problem in the case of goodwill.

As previously, the statistical analysis was carried out for companies in all eight countries and also for a subset that might improve explanatory power by excluding the three smaller countries. With regard to policy choices, we first treated choices A, B, D and E as stochastic in the model fitting and then, in a second analysis, we treated as deterministic the behaviour of those companies which did not specify the method used,[13] thus restricting the estimation of fitted values to methods A, B and D. The results are summarized in Table 14.

Table 14 Statistical analysis of goodwill harmonization.

	Scope of stochastic model							
	All disclosures and non-disclosures				Four main policy choices only			
	Eight countries		Five countries		Eight countries		Five countries	
Models and effects	Deviance	DF	Deviance	DF	Deviance	DF	Deviance	DF
Null model	328.16	63	238.29	39	268.74	47	185.30	29
Country.Year	−60.92	−15	−9.87	−9	−58.73	−15	−6.05	−9
Conditional independence	267.24	48	228.42	30	210.01	32	179.25	20
Policy	−126.19	−3	−125.18	−3	−90.00	−2	−87.77	−2
F_1	(63.14)		(111.0)		(91.57)		(146.3)	
p	(.000)		(.000)		(.000)		(.000)	
F_2	(13.42)		(10.91)		(11.25)		(8.64)	
p	(.000)		(.000)		(.000)		(.002)	
Static harmony	141.05	45	103.24	27	120.01	30	91.48	18
Year.Policy	−3.24	−3	−7.19	−3	−3.02	−2	−5.59	−2
F_1	(1.62)		(6.38)		(3.07)		(9.32)	
p	(.215)		(.008)		(.078)		(.008)	
F_2	(.329)		(.599)		(.361)		(.521)	
p	(.804)		(.622)		(.700)		(.604)	
Dynamic harmonization	137.81	42	96.05	24	116.99	28	85.89	16
Country.Policy	−123.82	−21	−91.54	−12	−110.11	−14	−83.49	−8
$F_1 = F_2$	(8.85)		(20.30)		(16.00)		(34.79)	
p	(.000)		(.000)		(.000)		(.000)	
Full model	13.99	21	4.51	12	6.88	14	2.40	8
Random company effects	−13.99	−21	−4.51	−12	−6.88	−14	−2.40	−8

Notes:
1. Classification of policy variable

   Treated as stochastic in each analysis:
   A = Goodwill on consolidation is written off against profit and loss in the year of acquisition
   B = Goodwill on consolidation is eliminated against reserves in the year of acquisition
   D = Goodwill on consolidation is shown as an asset and amortized through the profit and loss account over more than one year

   Treated as structural zero:
   C = Goodwill on consolidation is shown as an asset and not amortized

   Treated as non-stochastic in the restricted analysis of three main policy choices:
   E = Other or unspecified

2. Countries included in each analysis: France, Germany, Netherlands, Sweden, U.K. Small samples included only in eight-country analysis: Belgium, Ireland, Switzerland.
3. The first F-test, F_1, compares the additional explanatory power of successive models with the random company effects, that is, it compares the reduction in deviance for successive models with the deviance after fitting the full model (model 5). The second F-test, F_2, compares the additional explanatory power of each model with the unexplained variation after fitting that model.

As in the case of deferred taxation, the analysis of goodwill accounting choices shows that policy main effects (i.e., static harmony) and country.policy interaction effects (i.e., divergence) account for most of the reduction in deviance in the full and restricted analyses. Accordingly, the F_1 and F_2. tests show that harmony was highly significant and that the nationally systematic behaviour of companies causing divergence from complete harmony was also highly significant.

Overall, there was little evidence that harmony increased during the period, with high p-values arising from the F_2 test which compares the deviances for the static and dynamic models. However, the F_1 test reveals (when calculated for the subset of five countries, thus removing the disturbance effects of the small subsamples) that harmonizing policy choices were significant by comparison with company-specific policy choices, suggesting that where companies departed from national preferences in goodwill accounting during the period investigated, they tended to select accounting policies which led to harmonization.

The parameter estimates obtained from fitting the dynamic model of harmonization confirm that there were no significant changes between 1986/87 and 1990/91 in the probability of selecting between the categories of policy choice. This applies to the analysis of the complete eight-country data set and to the reduced five-country set, and also to a further analysis of the countries in the EC at the time.

Finally, disclosure-adjusted comparability indices were calculated using the expected values from each of the models. For this purpose, the non-comparability of companies in category E (other methods and methods not specified) was assumed.

Constant comparability in a state of static harmony stands at 39.22 per cent overall, a much higher level than in the case of deferred taxation. The near absence of harmonization effects is reflected in the index values given under the dynamic model of harmonization which changed little from 38.33 per cent in 1986/87 to 40.25 per cent in 1990/91 (see Table 16).

Again, within-country comparability is increased by the clustering of policy choices within countries, and between-country comparability is reduced accordingly, as illustrated by the relative positions of the lines representing the full model and the dynamic harmonization model in Figure 3. It can be seen from the cross-classifications in Table 13 that most Dutch and British companies eliminated against reserves, most French and Swedish companies capitalized and then amortized through the profit and loss account, while the choices of German companies were mixed.

Finally, it may be noted that non-systematic choices by individual companies cause a noticeable change in the within-country comparability index based on observed values, which falls from 58.17 per cent in 1986/87 to 53.92 per cent in 1990/91.

Table 15 Parameter estimates for goodwill harmonization.

	All countries		Five largest countries		EC countries	
	Policy effects	Year effects	Policy effects	Year effects	Policy effects	Year effects
A: Written off against profit and loss		−1.386 (1.31)		−8.445 (20.7)		−1.609 (1.29)
B: Eliminated against reserves	+2.303* (.524)	+1.335 (1.14)	+2.303* (.524)	+8.445 (20.7)	+2.128* (.473)	+1.656 (1.11)
C: Asset not amortized	+1.705* (.544)	+1.514 (1.16)	+1.946* (.535)	+8.514 (20.7)	+1.917* (.479)	+1.667 (1.12)
D: Asset amortized through profit and loss	−0.693 (.866)	−5.094 (11.0)	−0.693 (.866)	+0.693 (29.3)	−0.916 (.837)	−5.548 (15.4)
E: Other or unspecified	+0.000 (.707)	+2.079 (1.28)	−0.288 (.764)	+9.292 (20.7)	+0.182 (.605)	+1.897 (1.22)

Note: Parameter estimates are reported as log-relatives with respect to Policy A, and are not directly comparable between the full and reduced data sets. The boxed year-policy interaction effects are additive with respect to the main effects outside the box. The estimates are obtained by fitting model 4, the dynamic model of harmonization. The intercept estimate and the country effects are not included in the above table as they do not affect the interpretation of the policy, year and year-policy parameter values. Standard errors of log-adds are given in brackets and significant values are indicated with an asterisk.

Table 16 Goodwill comparability indices.

	Within-country comparability		Between-country comparability		Total comparability	
	1986/87	1990/91	1986/87	1990/91	1986/87	1990/91
Conditional independence	14.66	14.66	18.75	18.75	18.11	18.11
Static harmony	36.01	36.01	39.82	39.82	39.22	39.22
Dynamic harmonization	35.00	37.17	38.95	40.82	38.33	40.25
Full model	54.87	56.35	35.27	37.26	38.33	40.25
Observed values	58.17	53.92	34.66	37.71	38.33	40.25

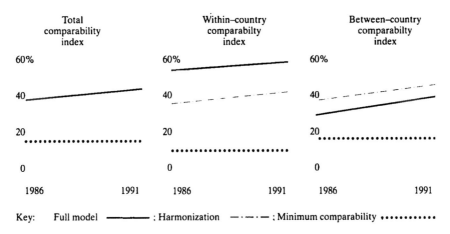

Figure 3 Goodwill comparability indices constructed from expected values.

Conclusions

In this article, we have shown how the measurement of harmonization over time can be analysed by means of a nested hierarchy of log-linear models. This hierarchy of models enables a distinction to be made between two sets of systematic effects: those which account for the level of international harmony (and the change in such levels through time which we have defined as international harmonization); and those systematic effects which account for international disharmony, which may be attributed to national differences in the distribution of accounting policy choices. In addition, the approach used permits the identification of any non-systematic policy choices by companies, that is, choices that are explained by neither international nor national patterns of choice and appear as residual values.

The models were fitted sequentially to the sample data, starting with a null model in which accounting policy choices are assumed to be random and, hence, equiprobable within each subsample for each country in each year. We then introduced the main policy effects, in which the frequencies of the policy choices for the total sample are assigned pro-rata to the country–year subsamples, so that neither the country nor the year affects the probabilities of the subsample policy choices.

The next step was to add the effect of changes in policy choices from year to year, but not from country to country. At this level, the model captures the process of harmonization at the international level, assuming that the distribution of policy choices is identical across countries in a given year but varying from year to year.

The final step was to add the interaction effect between countries and policy choices, to arrive at a full second-order interaction model, thus capturing the extent to which national standardization on different methods detracts from international harmonization. This full model provides a systematic statistical characterization of accounting policy choices, including the effects of both harmonization at the international level and differential standardization at the national level, the significance of each being reflected in its parameter estimates. The differences between the policy choices modelled in this full model and the actual data were the non-systematic or individualistic policy choices at the company level. For the samples considered in this article, such choices were unusual.

It was also shown how the goodness of fit of the model can be measured, and a test of significance for each step up the hierarchy can be applied by estimation of the relevant *F*-statistic.

We applied the hierarchy of models to two areas of accounting policy choice, deferred tax and consolidated goodwill. In each case, the full model was shown to capture the systematic policy choices reflected in the sample data very precisely and to reveal the small extent of harmonization, or change in harmony, during the period. In other words, neither individualistic policy choices, unsystematic in the sense of not being explained by either international harmony or differential national standardization, nor policy choices leading to an increase in the level of harmony, could be said to be common. This can be seen clearly in Figure 4, where the proportion of

Deferred taxation

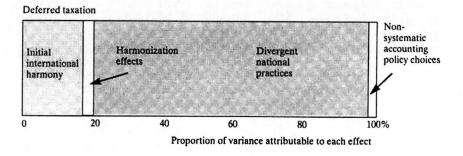

Proportion of variance attributable to each effect

Goodwill

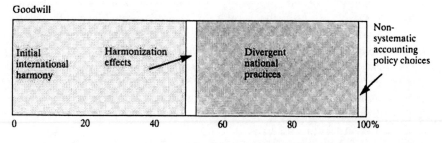

Proportion of variance attributable to each effect

Figure 4 Proportion of statistical variation attributable to each effect.

statistical variation attributable to each effect in the models is shown, based on the statistics reported earlier in Table 10 and Table 14.

However, there was some evidence, when the analysis was restricted to the five largest country subsamples (France, Germany, the Netherlands, Sweden and the U.K.) and the variability attributable to company-specific choices fell even further, that when companies did select policies which were not in line with national practice this tended to have a positive but small harmonizing effect.

Our analysis indicates that, in the two areas of deferred taxation and consolidated goodwill, little progress in harmonization took place between 1986/87 and 1990/91, but that such progress as there was can be attributed to increases in between-country comparability, since the change in within-country comparability was either very small or negative.

The EU Directives have brought about a significant amount of *rapprochement* of national accounting standards in Europe, not just in the member states but also in potential member states and other countries having close links with the EU. However, both deferred taxation and consolidated goodwill are areas where the EU Directives left considerable latitude to member states, and where national standards have continued in some cases to be somewhat flexible.

Acknowledgements

The authors are grateful to Jean-Bruno Dufour and Wolfgang Dick for their research assistance, to the Institute of Chartered Accountants in England and Wales for financial support provided during the first phase of this project and to Groupe ESCP for financial support during the second phase. The authors also wish to acknowledge the useful comments made by participants at the following conferences where an earlier version of the paper was presented: British Accounting Association. April 1994; European Accounting Association, April 1994; University of Wales Gregynog Colloquium. May 1994: Association Française de Comptabilité. June 1994.

Notes

1 If an accounting policy choice is made by selecting an accounting method from those available by means of a random process, then each available method has an equal chance of selection, and the expected distribution of accounting policy choices will be an equiprobable, or uniform, distribution.
2 One fairly obvious set of different circumstances is membership of different industries. Thus, for example, real estate companies might arguably be justified in treating buildings held as investments in a similar way to financial investments rather than as tangible fixed assets subject to systematic depreciation. Similarly, there may also be size effects. For example, smaller oil and gas extraction companies may choose the full cost method of accounting for hydrocarbon reserves, while the larger companies choose the successful efforts method.

3 For a three-dimensional table with observed cell counts x_{ijk}, and $n = x_{+++}$, the probability function for the multinomial model is $\prod ((m_{ijk}/m_{+++})x_{ijk}) (x_{+++}!/\prod x_{ijk}!)$.

4 In this case, the expected value is the grand mean (the only parameter in the model), where the total number of repeated observations, $\sum x_{ijk}$, is divided by the number of cross-classifications from I policy choices in J countries over K years (for the example, the expected value in each cell would be given by x_{+++}/IJK or $105/(2 \times 3 \times 2)$, which is equal to 8.75).

5 A corresponding algebraic representation of the linear structure is

$$\beta_o + \beta_i^C + \beta_k^Y + \beta_{ik}^{C.Y}$$

with levels $i = 1, \ldots, I$ of the country variable and $k = 1, \ldots, K$ of the year variable, where main effects allow the intercepts to vary and the interaction term allows the slopes to vary for all levels of C and Y. A useful introduction to the structure of generalized linear models is provided in Dobson (1990).

6 With regard to the $C.Y$ interaction effects, the logistic parameter values would differ from 0 (and, accordingly, the exponentiated odds ratios would differ from 1) if there were any differences between countries in the proportionate change in sample size from one period to another. In the case of the above example, for instance, the sample design is fully described by the C and Y main effects, and the $C.Y$ interaction effects are equal to zero.

7 It may be noted that the benchmark of a 'uniform distribution' proposed by Tay and Parker (1990) relies implicitly upon a comparison of observed values with the expected values given by the basic model of conditional independence (model 2). An empirical study by Emenyonu and Gray (1992) bases its chi-square tests on a main effects model which is equivalent to our static model of harmony (model 3). As shown here, these approaches do not distinguish between the systematic effects of international harmony, the systematic effects of nationally generally accepted practices, and the non-systematic choices made by individual companies.

8 In longer repeated measure studies, time (the variable Y) may be treated as continuous. This would add degrees of freedom to the analysis which may more than compensate for the loss in estimating accuracy and, if effective, could provide summary statistics for long-term harmonization effects described by the $Y.P$ interaction — see model 4. It follows that model 6 would not necessarily fully saturate the data, leaving some residual error attributable to the smoothing of harmonization effects to a single slope parameter.

9 The deviance is proportional to a χ^2 variable. It follows under certain general conditions that the difference between deviances is asymptotically χ^2 with degrees of freedom equal to the number of independent parameters that are omitted in fitting the nested model. The ratio of two χ^2s has an F-distribution which is indexed $(v_L - v_H)$, (v_F), as shown in the text.

10 The comparability index assumes that comparison occurs in pairwise combinations. The number of combinations of n companies taken r at a time is given by

$$\binom{n}{r} = \frac{n!}{(n-r)!r!}$$

For n companies, the number of permutations is factorial n, and the number of permutations of n companies taken r at a time is given by $n!/(n-r)!$ This simplifies to the second factorial $n(n-1)$ for pairwise permutations, and, to $^1/_2n(n-1)$ for pairwise combinations.

468

11 For J accounting methods, we may substitute m_{++k}/J for m_{+jk} in this minimum comparability model. It follows that the minimum of the comparability index would be

$$\frac{J\left(\dfrac{m_{++k}}{J}\left(\dfrac{m_{++k}}{J}\right)-1\right)}{m_{++k}(m_{++k}-1)} = \frac{1}{J}\left(\frac{m_{++k}-J}{m_{++k}-1}\right)$$

which tends to $1/J$ as the number of companies m_{++k} increases. Thus, under the model of conditional independence, inter-company comparability is at its minimum level. Even a marginal change in the overall distribution of accounting choices will increase the level of comparability, as there will be a marginal preference for one method over the others.

12 The index values differ for within-country, between-country and total comparability due to sample design and index construction, as shown at the beginning of this article. There is also a differing proportional impact which can be seen in the relative index values from the dynamic harmonization and full models for within-country and between-country indices.

13 This group also includes two companies which each used a different non-standard method. Due to the non-comparability of their financial statements with respect to the treatment of goodwill, these have been classified under E (other or unspecified) together with non-disclosers.

References

Aitken, M. A., D. A. Anderson, B. J. Francis and J. P. Hinde, *Statistical Modelling in GLIM*, Oxford University Press, 1989.

Archer, G. S. H., P. Delvaille and S. J. McLeay, 'The Measurement of Harmonization and the Comparability of Financial Statement Items: Within-Country and Between-Country Effects', *Accounting and Business Research*. Spring 1995.

Archer, G. S. H., J.-B. Dufour and S. J. McLeay, *Audit Reports on the Financial Statements of European Multinational Companies: A Comparative Study*, ICAEW, 1989.

Bishop, Y. M., S. E. Fienberg and P. W. Holland, *Discrete Multivariate Analysis: Theory and Practice*, MIT Press, 1975.

Brennan, N., F. J. O'Brien and A. Pierce, *European Financial Reporting: Ireland*, Routledge, 1992.

Dijksma, J., and M. Hoogendoorn, *European Financial Reporting: The Netherlands*, Routledge, 1993.

Dobson, A. J., *An Introduction to Generalized Linear Models*, Chapman and Hall, 1990.

Emenyonu, E. N., and S. J. Gray. 'European Community Accounting Harmonization: An Empirical Study of Measurement Practices in France, Germany and the United Kingdom', *Accounting and Business Research*, Winter 1992.

Fienberg, S. E., *The Analysis of Cross-Classified Data*, MIT Press, 1977.

Francis, B. J., M. Green and C. D. Payne (eds), *GLIM4: The Statistical System for Generalized Linear Interactive Modelling*, Oxford University Press, 1993.

Gordon, P. D., and S. J. Gray, *European Financial Reporting: The United Kingdom*, Routledge, 1994.

Heurlin, S., and E. Peterssohn, 'Sweden', in D. J. Alexander and G. S. H. Archer (eds), *The European Accounting Guide* (2nd edn), Harcourt Brace, 1995.

Laffournier, B. 'Switzerland', in D. J. Alexander and G. S. H. Archer (eds), *The European Accounting Guide* (2nd edn), Harcourt Brace, 1995.

Lefebvre, C., and J. Flower, *European Financial Reporting: Belgium*, Routledge, 1994.

Lindsey, J. K., *Models for Repeated Measurements*, Oxford University Press, 1993.

Ordelheide, D., and D. Pfaff, *European Financial Reporting: Germany*, Routledge, 1994.

Scheid, J.-C., and P. Walton, *European Financial Reporting: France*, Routledge, 1992.

Tas, L. G. van der, 'Measuring Harmonization of Financial Reporting Practice', *Accounting and Business Research*, Spring 1988.

——, 'Evidence of EC Financial Reporting Practice Harmonization: The Case of Deferred Taxation', *European Accounting Review*, May 1992a.

——, *Harmonization of Financial Reporting*, Datawyse Maastricht, 1992b.

——, 'Measuring International Harmonization and Standardization: A Comment', *Abacus*, September 1992.

Tay, J. S. W., and R. H. Parker, 'Measuring International Harmonization and Standardization', *Abacus*, March 1990.

——, 'Measuring International Harmonization and Standardization: A Reply', *Abacus*, September 1992.

22

AN APPROACH FOR MEASURING THE DEGREE OF COMPARABILITY OF FINANCIAL ACCOUNTING INFORMATION

Vera M. Krisement

Source: *European Accounting Review* 6(3) (1997): 465–85.

Abstract

This contribution sets out to provide an index to measure comparability of financial accounting information concerning specific kinds of transactions or events. It suggests definitions for the terms of comparability of financial accounting information and of accounting method. Requirements are derived from these definitions which must be met by an index of comparability, and entropy is shown to be an appropriate measure fulfilling these requirements. The problem of multiple reporting is dealt with separately. Finally, the measurement concept developed is applied to an example from the FEE report for 1989.

Introduction

Financial accounting is the process of collecting and transforming information about transactions and events affecting the assets and liabilities, the financial position and the performance of an enterprise, and of presenting this information in the annual accounts, the notes thereto, and other supplementary accounts, e.g. a cash flow statement. In particular, the objective of financial accounting is to provide information that is relevant to the economical decisions of external users of the accounts with respect to the enterprise (IASC, 1992: 32).

To be relevant to the decisions of external users, information about an enterprise must be comparable through time and with information about other enterprises (IASC, 1992: 39). Since the preparation and presentation of financial accounts in different countries is determined by different rules and practices (Radebaugh and Gray, 1993: 79–140), the question arises as to the international comparability of financial accounting information. This question is tightly linked to the judgement of the various efforts to harmonize financial accounting.

Examples for harmonization efforts are (i) on the global level the standards of the International Accounting Standards Committee (IASC) (Fleming, 1991; Chandler, 1992) and (ii) on the European level the EC directives (van Hulle, 1992). The result of such efforts is discussed controversially in the literature (Nobes and Parker, 1991: 70–3, 77–9, 84; Choi and Mueller, 1992: 257–61). As a basis for judgement of these efforts, a precise definition of comparability of financial accounting information is needed.

Besides harmonization, multiple reporting is another approach to increase comparability of financial accounting information. Multiple reporting means that information is given on a specified transaction or event applying several alternative accounting methods simultaneously (van der Tas, 1988: 158). For example, the amount of a specific kind of assets may be disclosed both at historical cost and at replacement and market value. In particular, multiple reporting occurs in the case of a domestic enterprise quoted on a foreign stock exchange whereby the obligation arises to prepare supplementary accounts corresponding to the accounting rules required by that stock exchange (Parker, 1991: 124; Choi and Mueller, 1992: 306–17). To assess the results of the multiple reporting approach, a well-defined notion of comparability of financial accounting information has to be presupposed.

In this contribution, a formal definition of comparability of financial accounting information is put forward. Following from this definition, a suggestion is developed to quantify the degree of comparability. Concentration indices used in statistics are shown to be basically appropriate to this measuring problem with entropy, a particular concentration index, meeting all the qualifications required of a measure of comparability. Special problems of measuring comparability arising from multiple reporting are treated in a separate section. In conclusion, the feasibility of the measuring concept put forward is demonstrated, and the results of the present contribution are summarized.

Comparability of financial accounting information

Introductory remarks

To be comparable, all information is required to refer to facts of the same kind. For the problem under consideration, this means that the transactions and events affecting the assets and liabilities, the financial position and the performance of enterprises have to be classified into groups of similar events so that the treatment in financial accounting (or rather the resulting information presented) of transactions or events of the same class may be compared. Valuation of certain fixed or current assets, allocation of depreciable amounts to similar fixed assets or deferral of development cost to future periods are examples of classes of events and their treatment in financial accounting. Classes of transactions or events may be defined taking a broader or a narrower point of view depending on the concrete issue under consideration. In any case, comparability of financial accounting information is dealt with on the level of particular items of the annual accounts and not on the level of the accounts as a whole (van der Tas, 1988; 1992a: 72; 1992b: 418; 1992c: 235–7).

As a matter of principle, information on similar transactions or events are comparable to one another if they represent these transactions or events in the same way, i.e. if they have the same contents. In regard to the comparability of financial accounting information the question arises as to how information about similar transactions or events must be collected, transformed and presented to have the same contents. Obviously, the answer to this question depends on the accounting method(s) applied. Concerning the formal definition of comparability of financial accounting information, a thesis is put forward which shall be discussed in the following, namely: financial accounting informations on similar transactions or events are comparable to one another if they are collected and transformed applying the same accounting methods.

In consequence of this definition, multiple reporting will, as a rule, raise the degree of comparability of financial accounting information (van der Tas, 1988: 158; 1992a: 72; 1992c: 112–3; 199).[1] If for instance an enterprise accounting so far for specified fixed assets at historical cost only is going to disclose henceforth the replacement value of these assets in addition, the accounting information of this enterprise becomes comparable with the corresponding accounting information of other enterprises accounting for similar assets at replacement value only.

The conception of an accounting method

As a prerequisite for discussing the definition of comparability of financial accounting information, the notion of accounting method has to be agreed upon. Since comparability of information is dependent on its contents, the concept of accounting method comprises all methods of collecting and transforming information which influence the contents of the annual accounts.

To begin with, the recognition methods form part of the accounting methods. If events of some distinct kind are recognized in the annual accounts of an enterprise, while another enterprise does not recognize similar events in its accounts, comparability of information referring thereto is impaired. Moreover, methods of valuation and income determination are accounting methods as well (van der Tas, 1992a: 70–1; 1992b: 408; 1992c: 13, 36, 46).

473

Furthermore, the contents of financial accounting information are influenced by the choice between alternative disclosure policies. If information on a specific kind of events may be disclosed separately or combined with information on events of a different kind in a summary item, the latter alternative results in less detailed financial accounting information than the first one. However, if supplementary notes are added which allow breakdown of the summary item, the degree of detail of financial accounting information is not affected by the choice between the two alternatives which, in this case, is a matter of presentation and not of disclosure policy. Therefore, alternatives of disclosure are looked upon as accounting methods, whereas alternative methods of presentation are not.

Depending on which kind of accounting method is under consideration, comparability may be characterized as concerning the recognition, valuation, income determination or disclosure alternatives applied to collect and transform information on specific transactions or events.

Comparability of accounting information subject to environmental conditions

As is shown in the comparative accounting literature, there are numerous more-or-less important differences between national accounting systems (Radebaugh and Gray, 1993: 79–140). Apparently, these differences are caused by different economical, political, social and cultural environmental conditions that influence accounting in each country (Zeff, 1972; Choi and Mueller, 1992: 39–43). Law and taxation system, language, possible inflation etc. may be cited as examples for such environmental conditions (Nobes and Parker, 1991: 11–20; Choi and Mueller, 1992: 40–3). Environmental conditions are tightly linked to the fact that in different countries the various groups of users of external accounting information have differing means to enforce their partially diverging interests (Nobes and Parker, 1991: 12–5).

Considering these various national environmental factors, the question arises as to which accounting methods should be regarded as 'the same' under different environmental conditions according to the definition of comparability of financial accounting information. This question cannot be answered in general but only for special cases. For instance, such a special case is the occurrence of inflation. It makes no sense for an enterprise operating in a hyperinflationary economy to account for its assets at historical cost, since this information has no decision relevance for anyone and therefore does not create comparability with the corresponding financial accounting information of an enterprise in a non-inflationary country accounting for its assets also at historical cost. Comparability would more likely exist if the enterprise in the hyperinflationary country were accounting for its assets at replacement value, since historical cost in a non-inflationary environment may be considered as a replacement value in a special case.

It follows from the foregoing that the degree of comparability of financial accounting information is dependent on the number of alternative accounting methods for collecting and transforming information on a specific kind of transaction or event and on the number of enterprises applying each of these alternatives. Obviously, the highest possible degree of comparability is reached if all enterprises choose the same accounting alternative (or rather if only one accounting method exists, i.e. the choice between accounting alternatives is omitted).

In the following, an approach to quantify the degree of comparability of financial accounting information based on frequencies of application of each accounting alternative will be put forward. To begin with, several requirements following from the definition of comparability are set up which a measure must fulfil to qualify as an index of comparability. Subsequently, a method of measurement is described that complies with these requirements. Problems arising in connection with multiple reporting are deferred for later consideration.

Measuring the degree of comparability by means of the entropy

Requirements to be met by a measure of comparability

Resulting directly from the nature of the measuring problem under consideration, the first requirement to be fulfilled by a measure of comparability (briefly designated as index) reads as follows (by analogy to industrial concentrations: Jacquemin and de Jong, 1977: 42):

> The index sought shall increase or decrease steadily and monotonically with increasing comparability of financial accounting information.

The expression 'with increasing comparability' requires to be considered more closely. If any conceivable situation characterized by the frequencies of application of the alternative accounting methods could *ex ante* be arranged corresponding to its degree of comparability on an ordinal scale, the index sought should just transform the ordinal into an interval scale leaving the order unchanged. Requiring transformation on a ratio scale would not be appropriate (Münzner, 1963: 3–4). Actually, there are many situations which may not *ex ante* be ordered as to their respective degree of comparability. In these cases, the index sought shall allocate figures to the situations allowing them to order on an interval scale (by analogy to industrial concentrations: Paschen, 1969: 30–1; Paschen and Buyse, 1971: 5–6).

475

An inverse measure, i.e. an index increasing with decreasing degree of comparability, may well be suitable for the measuring problem under consideration and is therefore not excluded in the above-mentioned qualification. Furthermore, the index sought is required to be steady. Since proportionally small changes of the frequencies of application of the alternative accounting methods have only small implications on the degree of comparability, they should produce but small variations of the index. In other words, the measure of comparability may not feature points of unsteadiness (by analogy to industrial concentrations: Marfels, 1972: 462).

A second requirement of the index sought is concerned with the number of enterprises studied as to the comparability of their accounting information (by analogy to industrial concentrations: Hall and Tideman, 1967: 163):

> With constant relative frequencies of application of the accounting alternatives given, the index sought shall be independent of the number of enterprises studied as to their collecting and transforming of information about specific transactions or events.

The relative frequency of application of an accounting method is the number of the enterprises applying this accounting method in proportion to the number of all enterprises where the kind of transaction or event under consideration is found. Of course, all the enterprises where a certain kind of transaction or event is found may not be recorded in practice, in which case samples must be taken instead. In that case, the relative frequencies of application refer to the sample size, i.e. the number of enterprises studied where a specified kind of transaction or event is found. Obviously, the measure of comparability should not depend on the sample size, since this would be an arbitrary influence. This is why the second requirement postulates that the index sought be independent of the number of enterprises studied. In other words, the index should depend upon the relative but not upon the absolute frequencies of application of the accounting alternatives.

The third requirement is consideration of the elementary process which causes the degree of comparability to increase (by analogy to industrial concentrations: Curry and George, 1983: 204–7):

> If the relative frequency of application of an accounting method increases to the debit of the lower or equal relative frequency of application of an alternative accounting method, the index sought shall indicate that the degree of comparability of financial accounting information is increasing.

To illustrate this requirement, a specific transaction is considered which may be treated in the annual accounts applying two alternative accounting methods. Comparability of corresponding accounting information is at its maximum (under the assumption of equal environmental conditions) if all enterprises studied, where the transaction under consideration is found, give information about it applying the same accounting method. The degree of comparability decreases with more and more enterprises turning to apply the other accounting alternative. The minimum degree of comparability is reached if each of the two accounting alternatives is applied by exactly half of the enterprises studied. Thus, the third requirement is describing a step on the way from minimum to maximum degree of comparability.

The fourth and last requirement to be met by a measure to quantify comparability results from the necessity of practical applicability (by analogy to industrial concentrations: Marfels, 1971: 143):

The index calculated for the enterprises operating in a larger geographical unit (for example Europe) shall be decomposable additively into the contributions of the enterprises operating in segments (for example countries or groups of countries) forming part of that geographical unit.

If for example the result of harmonization efforts in Europe has to be judged, the degree of comparability would not only be of interest regarding all Europe but also regarding the two groups of countries formed by the member states and the non-members of the EC and regarding each individual European country. If the corresponding values of the index for the countries and the groups of countries can be additively isolated from the index for all Europe, the measuring concept of comparability is simple to handle, and the results produced may be interpreted meaningfully.

Entropy as a qualified comparability measure

Since the degree of comparability of financial accounting information is determined by the number and the relative frequencies of application of alternative accounting methods, concentration indices seem basically to be appropriate for its measurement. Namely, these indices quantify concentration as accumulation of a quantity at single elements of a set of objects (Rosenbluth, 1955: 57, 61; Marfels, 1971: 143; Paschen and Buyse, 1971: 2; Jacquemin and Kumps, 1971: 60). In the case under consideration, the objects are the alternative accounting methods, and the quantity is the relative frequency of application by the enterprises. Concentration indices, in any case, meet the first three of the four requirements for a measure of comparability (Curry and George, 1983: 207–12), but entropy is the only one of the current concentration indices to be also additively decomposable (Hildenbrand and Paschen, 1964; Paschen and Buyse, 1971).

Entropy is computed as follows (Curry and George, 1983: 208):

$$\sum_{i=1}^{N} y_i \cdot \ln\frac{1}{y_i}$$

with i = numeral characterizing the alternative accounting methods to collect and transform information on a specific kind of transaction or event, N = number of existing alternative accounting methods, y_i = relative frequency of application of accounting method i and ln = natural logarithm. In the literature, entropy is calculated using logarithms to different bases (Theil, 1967: 293; Horowitz and Horowitz, 1968: 197; Marfels, 1971: 150). Natural logarithm is choosen here for convenience.

Entropy is an inverse measure of the degree of comparability. Given the number N of alternative accounting methods, the maximum value of entropy, $E = \ln N$, is reached where the degree of comparability is at minimum, i.e. if the frequencies of application are equally distributed among the alternative accounting methods (by analogy to Theil, 1967: 291). If the degree of comparability is at its maximum, which is the case with application concentrated on a single accounting alternative, entropy takes the value $E = 1$ (by analogy to Theil, 1967: 291).

Additive decomposition of entropy

In the following, the additive decomposition of entropy will be described taking as an example the decomposition of the index calculated for the geographical unit of Europe into the contributions from groups of countries (in the following, briefly called regions; e.g. member-states of the EC versus non-members) and from individual European countries. To this end, some symbols have to be introduced:

l = numeral characterizing the individual European countries.

r = numeral characterizing the groups of individual European countries (i.e. the regions).

M_r = set of all countries l belonging to region r.

y_{il} = number of enterprises in country l applying accounting alternative i as a proportionate part of the number of all European enterprises studied (relative frequency of application of accounting method i in country l).

y_i = relative frequency of application of accounting method i in Europe

$= \sum_i y_{il}$

$y_{.l}$ = number of enterprises studied in country l as a proportionate part of the number of all European enterprises studied $= \sum_i y_{.ie}$

478

y_{ir} = number of enterprises in region r applying accounting alternative i as a proportionate part of the number of all European enterprises studied (relative frequency of application of accounting method i in region r)

$$= \sum_{l \in M_r} y_{ie}$$

$y_{.r}$ = number of enterprises in region r as a proportionate part of the number of all European enterprises studied

$$= \sum_{l \in M_r} y_{.l}$$

The additive decomposition of the total amount of entropy, which represents a measure for the comparability of specific accounting information between all European enterprises studied, into contributions from individual European countries and groups of countries (regions) is shown in Figure 1

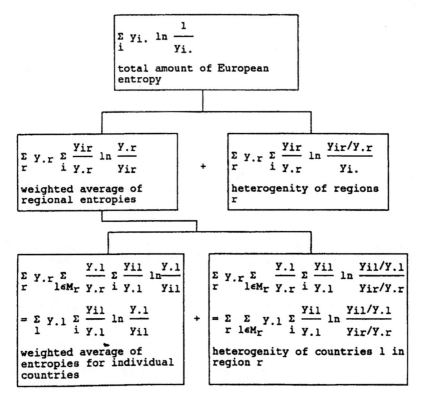

Figure 1 Additive decomposition of entropy into the contributions of individual countries and groups of countries.

(by analogy to Theil, 1967: 295–303). There are two main parts of the decomposition, namely weighted averages of entropies as well as hetero-genities. On the regional level, for each region r the corresponding regional entropy:

$$\sum_i \frac{y_{ir}}{y_{\cdot r}} \cdot \ln \frac{y_{\cdot r}}{y_{ir}}$$

is computed as a measure for the degree of comparability of specified accounting information in that region. The respective weighting factor to calculate the average of regional entropies is equal to $y_{\cdot r}$. The weighted average of the entropies for the individual countries l is computed analogously.

In terms of heterogenity, which shall not be discussed in detail, the distributions of the relative frequencies of application among the alternative accounting methods i in the individual countries, in the regions and in all Europe are compared (by analogy to Theil, 1967: 297–8). The terms of heterogenity can be characterized as correcture terms which may not be interpreted as a constituent of the index indicating the degree of comparability in individual countries or regions. Rather, they are added to the weighted averages of entropies for countries or regions to calculate the total amount of entropy for all Europe. In the special case of the relative frequencies of application being equally distributed among the alternative accounting methods on all geographical levels, the entropies take the same value for all countries, regions and for the whole of Europe, and therefore all hetero-genities become zero. In this case, the degree of comparability of financial accounting information is judged equally on all geographical levels.

Measuring the effects of multiple reporting on the comparability of financial accounting information

The problem of assignment

In the following, the special difficulties of measuring the comparability of financial accounting information at the occurrence of multiple reporting is treated. These difficulties are caused by the so-called assignment problem. This means that the number of enterprises where multiple reporting is found may not be assigned definitely to one of the accounting alternatives applied with multiple reporting (van der Tas, 1988: 163; 1992a: 73; 1992c: 184). Also multiple reporting may not be treated as a separate accounting method with a frequency of application of its own.

Both of the aforementioned procedures would lead to obvious mistakes while measuring comparability. To begin with, assigning the frequency of application of multiple reporting to the frequency of application of an accounting alternative applied thereby would be quite arbitrary. Furthermore,

480

both procedures would cause the degree of comparability to be underesti-
mated for they do not take into consideration that enterprises where multiple
reporting is found are not only mutually comparable, but also with the enterprises applying only one of the accounting alternatives used with multiple
reporting. Moreover, any compromise solution distributing the frequency
of application of multiple reporting among the accounting alternatives
applied thereby would be arbitrary and deficient, too.

Obviously, the effort of measuring comparability of accounting information at the occurrence of multiple reporting by means of entropy seems to
fail because the frequencies of application of diverse accounting methods
needed as input for the index used may not be specified definitely. However, at least for multiple reporting with two accounting alternatives only,
a well-defined situation without multiple reporting may be specified which
is equivalent to the situation with multiple reporting regarding the comparability of accounting information. Thus, the use of entropy would become
possible. To ascertain this equivalent situation, the so-called C-index (van der
Tas, 1988: 163–5, 167–8; 1992a: 74–9; 1992c: 185–8; 199–202) is used which
will be described briefly in the following.

The C-index

The derivation of the C-index is based on the idea that the number of
pairs of enterprises applying the same accounting alternatives respectively
to collect and transform information about like transactions or events be
a measure for the comparability of accounting information. The ratio of
these pairs of enterprises to the maximum possible number of such pairs
of enterprises is computed. This maximum is reached if all enterprises
studied are applying the same accounting method. In the case of two
accounting alternatives existing, the C-index is calculated in the following
way (van der Tas, 1988: 163–4, 167–8; 1992a: 74–9; 1992c: 185–202):

$$C = \frac{a_1 \cdot (a_1 - 1) + a_2 \cdot (a_2 - 1) - a_{12} \cdot (a_{12} - 1)}{m \cdot (m - 1)}$$

with C = C-index, a_1 = number of enterprises applying accounting method 1
(including multiple reporting), a_2 = number of enterprises applying accounting method 2 (including multiple reporting), a_{12} = number of enterprises
applying multiple reporting with accounting methods 1 and 2 simultaneously, and m = total number of enterprises studied with $m = a_1 + a_2 - a_{12}$.

On the grounds of its structure, the C-index is in a position to cope
with the assignment problem. Nevertheless, the C-index may not directly be
used as a measure of comparability, since this index does not meet two of
the requirements raised above. First, the C-index depends on the number
of enterprises studied. For instance, in a situation with two alternative

accounting methods whose relative frequencies of application are $y_1 = 0.6$ and $y_2 = 0.4$ respectively, for $m = 100$ enterprises the absolute frequencies of application and the C-index are $a_1 = 60$, $a_2 = 40$ and $C = 0.516$, whereas for $m = 200$ enterprises $a_1 = 120$, $a_2 = 80$ and $C = 0.51759$. In fact, there is no reason for assuming different degrees of comparability for $m = 100$ and $m = 200$ enterprises.

Furthermore, the C-index is not additively decomposable according to geographical criteria. The decomposition of the C-index for some larger geographical unit into the contributions of the individual countries forming part of that unit results in multiplicative expressions that may not be assigned definitely to the individual countries since these expressions contain products of frequencies of application of an accounting alternative in two different countries.[2]

Thus, the C-index is suited to cope with the problem of assignment but cannot be decomposed additively, while entropy is fulfilling all the requirements that ought to be met by a measure of comparability but fails at the occurrence of multiple reporting. Subsequently, a combination of C-index and entropy shall be put forward that is appropriate to measure the degree of comparability at the occurrence of multiple reporting.

Applying the entropy index to situations with multiple reporting

A situation (characterized by the frequencies of application of the existing accounting alternatives) with multiple reporting can be transformed by means of the C-index into a so-called 'equivalent situation' without multiple reporting so that the degree of comparability can be measured using the entropy. However, the definite determination of an equivalent situation is only possible for multiple reporting with two accounting alternatives. This case shall be investigated, in the first instance, with the aid of a simple example.

To collect and transform information on a specific kind of transaction in the annual accounts, two alternative accounting methods are available. The number of enterprises studied is $m = 100$ whereof $a_1 = 60$ enterprises are applying accounting alternative 1 and $a_2 = 60$, alternative 2, i.e. multiple reporting with both alternatives is found at $a_{12} = 20$ enterprises. In this situation, entropy is not applicable because of the impossibility of assigning the frequency of application a_{12} definitely to one of the two alternatives. Therefore, an equivalent situation is constructed showing the same degree of comparability as the situation described before, but without multiple reporting. To measure the equivalence of the degrees of comparability, the C-index is used as an auxiliary quantity. The value of the C-index for the situation with multiple reporting described above amounts to:

$$C = \frac{a_1 \cdot (a_1 - 1) + a_2 \cdot (a_2 - 1) - a_{12} \cdot (a_{12} - 1)}{m \cdot (m - 1)}$$

$$= \frac{60 \cdot 59 + 60 \cdot 59 - 20 \cdot 19}{100 \cdot 99} = 0.677$$

Now an equivalent situation is sought characterized by two absolute frequencies of application a_1' and a_2' such as to meet the following equations:

$$a_1' + a_2' = m = 100$$

$$\frac{a_1' \cdot (a_1' - 1) + a_2' \cdot (a_2' - 1)}{m \cdot (m - 1)} = 0.677$$

The first of these two equations ensures that effects resulting from a change in the number of enterprises studied are eliminated from the value of the C-index. In the second equation, the value of the C-index for the equivalent situation is specified. From this system of equations, the values of the frequencies of application a_1' and a_2' can be derived as follows:

$$a_1' = + \sqrt{(C - 1) \cdot m \cdot (m - 1)/2 + m^2/4} + m/2$$

$$= + \sqrt{(0.677 - 1) \cdot 100 \cdot (100 - 1)/2 + 100^2/4} + 100/2$$

$$= + 30 + 50$$

$$a_2' = m - a_1'$$
$$= 100 - (+ 30 + 50)$$
$$= 50 + 30$$

Hence, the set of solutions to the system of equations consist of the pairs $a_1' = 80$, $a_2' = 20$ and $a_1' = 20$, $a_2' = 80$. These two pairs of solutions only differ formally from one another, for obviously they show the same degree of comparability which can now be measured by means of entropy:

$$E = 0.8 \cdot \ln \frac{1}{0.8} + 0.2 \cdot \ln \frac{1}{0.2} = 0.5004$$

In any case of multiple reporting with only two accounting alternatives, a definite equivalent situation can be constructed using the formulae for a_1' and a_2' mentioned above. There are always two pairs of solutions $a_1' \geq 0$, $a_2' \geq 0$. In contrast to the example, these solutions as a rule are not integers. However, since the (ficticious) absolute frequencies of application of the equivalent situation must be transformed into relative quantities before computing entropy, this fact does not argue against the suitability of the approach put forward to quantify the degree of comparability of financial accounting information.

As can be shown by means of the general formulae for a'_1 and a'_2, both pairs of solutions feature the same degree of comparability and hence the same value of entropy. Thus, at the occurrence of multiple reporting with only two accounting alternatives an equivalent situation without multiple reporting can be constructed which is well-defined in the sense that exactly one value of entropy may be assigned to it.

The approach put forward in this contribution to solve the assignment problem is to link C-index and entropy so that the advantages of these two measures complement one another while any disadvantages are eliminated. The inability of entropy to cope with the assignment problem is offset by the application of the C-index, whose dependence on the number m of enterprises studied is taken into consideration, by a conditional equation keeping m constant. In addition, the problems arising from the fact that the C-index is not additively decomposable are also solved since by means of the construction of an equivalent situation the additive decomposition of entropy may be exploited in situations with multiple reporting as well.

If comparability of accounting information is to be measured considering several countries whereby multiple reporting is found with two specified accounting alternatives, the equivalent situations and the entropies for the individual countries and for all countries as a whole are determined as follows:

- For each country where multiple reporting is found an equivalent situation and the pertinent entropy are calculated separately, i.e. disregarding the other countries.
- The frequencies of application observed in each individual country are summed up to a total amount for each accounting alternative. From there, an equivalent situation is constructed for all countries as a whole which is taken as a basis for the calculation of the total entropy.

Summing up the application frequencies in the equivalent situations determined for the individual countries and calculating a total entropy would result in an incorrect measurement of the comparability for all countries as a whole, because this procedure would not consider the effects of multiple reporting on the comparability of accounting information from different countries.

If multiple reporting is found not with two but with three or more accounting alternatives an equivalent situation is no longer definitely determinable. C being the value of the C-index of a situation with multiple reporting, an equivalent situation is characterized by the following equations which the (fictitious) absolute frequencies of application a'_i of the n accounting alternatives applied with multiple reporting have to fulfill:

$$\frac{\sum_{i=1}^{n} a_i' \cdot (a_i' - 1)}{m \cdot (m - 1)} = C'$$

$$\sum_{i=1}^{n} a_i' = m$$

For $n \geq 3$ accounting alternatives applied with multiple reporting, this system of equations has an infinite number of solutions, i.e. there is an infinite set of equivalent situations with different values of entropy meeting the equations. However, a conservative estimate of the degree of comparability can be made determining that equivalent situation with maximum value of entropy. Since entropy is an inverse measure, maximum value of entropy corresponds to minimum degree of comparability. By means of electronic data processing, it is quite easy to determine numerically the extreme values of entropies assigned to the equivalent situations (at least in cases of multiple reporting with three accounting alternatives). Besides, the question remains if multiple reporting with more than two accounting alternatives is of importance in practice.

Measuring comparability: an example

In a survey for the year 1989, the Fédération des Experts Comptables Européens (FEE – Federation of European Accountants) has analysed the annual accounts of a total of 441 enterprises from 15 countries (FEE, 1991: 1). Each of these countries is assigned to one of the following three groups, respectively (FEE, 1991: 1):

- The group EC I consists of those EC countries where the application of a legislation transforming the 4th EC directive was mandatory in 1989.
- The group EC II is made of those EC countries where there was no legislation transforming the 4th EC directive to be applied mandatorily in 1989.
- The group Non-EC consists of European countries which were not members of EC in 1989.

The FEE survey treats 12 domains in accounting (FEE, 1991: v–vi). For each of these domains, several individual problems of collecting, transforming and reporting accounting information are discussed enumerating the respective accounting alternatives, and their absolute frequencies of application observed. Hence, the FEE survey is basically appropriate to serve as a data base for applying the concept of measuring comparability of accounting information put forward in the previous sections.

485

The data collected in the FEE survey are not employed there for further calculations. The comments in the survey are restricted to explanations concerning the problems of collecting, transforming and reporting accounting information and the respective alternative accounting methods. Nevertheless, statements are presented which are designated as conclusions drawn from the data collected (FEE, 1991: 5). However, since no reasons are given for these statements, they are hypotheses only. Subsequently, two of these hypotheses (in the following called H 1 and H 2) shall be investigated more closely. In detail, H 1 and H 2 read as follows:

- H 1: Comparing the accounting practice between the country groups EC I, EC II and Non-EC, only minor differences are found.
- H 2: There are major differences between the countries of group EC I regarding the practice of accounting unless the publication and disclosure of information are concerned.

These hypotheses are now tested by considering the recognition of the income effect of foreign currency translation differences. Table 1 shows the data collected in the FEE survey concerning this matter (FEE, 1991: 243, 246, 251) and the calculations needed. In Table 1, for each country, each group of countries and for all countries as a whole, the number of enterprises is given where there is evidence of an income effect resulting from the translation of foreign currency balances and where information is given as to the recognition of this income effect (cf. the line 'number of enterprises').

For each country, each group of countries and for all countries as a whole, the absolute frequencies of application of four recognition alternatives are listed in Table 1. Multiple reporting is not found. From these data, values of entropy are calculated for each country, group of countries and for all countries as a whole. These values of entropy are measures for the degree of comparability of accounting information within the geographical regions for which they are calculated. Within the scope of a more extensive investigation, such calculations may be carried out and compared to one another for several periods of time.

However, this contribution is designed to verify or falsify the two hypotheses H 1 and H 2. To that end, two heterogenities have to be calculated. The heterogenity on the regional level, Het_{total}, has a value of 0.04939459.[3] This amount is a measure of the dissimilarity of the distributions of the application frequencies among the alternative recognition methods in the groups of countries EC I, EC II and Non-EC as well as in all Europe (by analogy to Theil, 1967, 297–8). Computing the ratio V_{total} of Het_{total} to the total entropy E_{total} yields a value of

Table 1 Comparability of accounting information concerning the recognition of the income effect of translation differences in 15 European countries.

	Belgium	Denmark	France	Germany	Greece	Ireland	Luxembourg	Netherlands	UK	EC I
Number of enterprises	12	19	32	43	19	32	9	18	37	221
Recognized:										
all gains and losses	6	17	1	0	1	28	2	16	35	106
realized gains and all losses	6	0	31	43	18	1	6	0	1	106
only realized gains and realized losses	0	2	0	0	0	0	0	0	1	3
other	0	0	0	0	0	3	1	2	0	6
Entropy	0.69314	0.35129	0.13906	0	0.20619	0.44706	0.84868	0.34883	0.24775	0.86107

	EC II	Spain	Italy	Finland	Norway	Sweden	Switzerland	Non-EC	Total
Number of enterprises	18	7	11	3	6	7	6	22	261
Recognized:									
all gains and losses	4	3	1	2	1	0	2	5	115
realized gains and all losses	10	1	9	1	5	3	1	10	126
only realized gains and realized losses	3	2	1	0	0	0	2	2	8
other	1	1	0	0	0	4	1	5	12
Entropy	1.11999	1.27703	0.60016	0.63651	0.45056	0.68290	1.32966	1.24983	0.9109

$$V_{total} = \frac{Het_{total}}{E_{total}} = \frac{0.04939459}{0.96109846} = 5.14\%$$

Now the question arises as to which is the critical share V_{crit} where the hypothesis H 1 is just becoming false. This question is not discussed in the following for this would be beyond the scope of the present contribution which is intended to demonstrate the applicability of the measuring concept put forward. For instance, for $V_{crit} = 10\%$ H 1 would be judged to be correct.

Hypothesis H 2 is tested analogously. The heterogenity $Het_1 = 0.58619315$ is a measure of the dissimilarity of the distributions of the application frequencies among the alternative recognition methods in the countries of group EC I and in EC I as a whole (by analogy to Theil, 1967: 268). Calculating the ratio V_I of Het_I to the value E_I of the entropy for the group of countries EC I yields a share of

$$V_I = \frac{Het_I}{E_I} = \frac{0.58619315}{0.86107907} = 68.08\%$$

For hypothesis H 2 to be verified, the ratio V_I must exceed a critical lower boundary V_{crit}, whose amount will not be discussed in the following for this would be beyond the scope of this paper. For example, H 2 would be correct for $V_{crit} = 40\%$.

The example treated in this section has shown the application of the measuring concept developed previously to a practical problem. However, multiple reporting was excluded from consideration since for most cases of multiple reporting contained in the FEE data the survey does not present enough information to construct equivalent situations. In fact, only the absolute numbers a_i of enterprises applying an alternative accounting method i are given in the survey. If there are more than two accounting alternatives, it is impossible to deduce the absolute numbers a_{ij} of enterprises applying multiple reporting with methods i and j simultaneously. However, the numbers a_{ij} are needed to construct an equivalent situation.

Applying the measuring concept put forward in this contribution to conduct an empirical investigation, a period of several subsequent years should be surveyed so that conclusions as to the development of the degree of comparability can be drawn. Furthermore, statistical problems should be considered such as the critical ranges of acceptance or refusal of a hypothesis with the sample size and level of significance given. It would go far beyond the scope of this contribution to demonstrate these aspects in an extensive empirical example. In any case, collection of a data base which is statistically representative, contains the relevant information to cope with multiple reporting, and covering a period of several years, would be a precondition for further research using the method developed here.

Summary and outlook

Initially the present contribution was concerned with the notions of comparability of financial accounting information as well as of accounting methods. In this connection, the influence of different economical, political, social and other environmental conditions on the comparability of accounting information was taken into consideration. The degree of comparability may be raised by so-called multiple reporting.

Subsequently, requirements to be met by a measure of comparability were derived from the notion of comparability of financial accounting information defined previously. Concentration indices were shown to be basically appropriate to solve the measuring problem discussed. However, entropy is the only one of all current concentration indices to fulfill all the requirements mentioned above; in particular, it is additively decomposable according to geographical criteria.

A special problem for the measurement of the degree of comparability results from the occurrence of multiple reporting and the assignment problem related thereto. In the case of two alternative accounting methods, the problem was solved by constructing an equivalent situation and combining entropy with the so-called C-index. For multiple reporting with more than two accounting alternatives, an approximate solution was suggested.

The applicability of the measuring concept proposed was demonstrated by means of an example from the FEE report for 1989. In particular, the importance of heterogenities in the context of international investigations was shown.

This simple example without multiple reporting reveals the advantages of entropy resulting from its additive decomposition for international investigations of comparability of financial accounting information. For instance, the harmonization effects of the 4th and 7th EC directives in individual EC countries may be quantified by means of entropy and compared with accounting practice in countries not belonging to the EC. Yet, to this end it would be necessary to collect a data base meeting the statistical requirement of a sufficient sample size.

Notes

1 In any case, multiple reporting will never cause the degree of comparability to fall. In fact, comparability is not affected by the occurrence of multiple reporting if all enterprises studied are applying the same alternative accounting method to collect and transform information on a specific kind of transaction or event.

2 Archer *et al.* (1995) present a method to decompose the C-index into a within-country and a between-country component. However, as can be seen by the examples given in this contribution (Archer *et al.*, 1995: 70–1), the within-country and the between-country components do not sum up to the value of the total

index. Hence, the decomposition of the C-index is not an additive one in the sense of this paper.
3 As to the calculation of heterogenities, cf. Figure 1.

References

Archer, S., Delvaille, P. and McLeay, S. (1995) 'The measurement of harmonisation and the comparability of financial statement items: within-country and between-country effects', *Accounting and Business Research*, 25: 67–80.

Chandler, R. A. (1992) 'The international harmonization of accounting: in search of influence', *International Journal of Accounting*, 27: 222–33.

Choi, F. D. S. and Mueller, G. G. (1992) *International Accounting*, 2nd edition. Englewood Cliffs: Prentice-Hall.

Curry, B. and George, K. D. (1983) 'Industrial concentration: a survey', *Journal of Industrial Economics*, 31: 203–55.

Fédération des Experts Comptables Européens (FEE) (1991) *FEE European Survey of Published Accounts 1991*. London: Routledge.

Fleming, P. D. (1991) 'The growing importance of international accounting standards', *Journal of Accountancy*, 172 (9): 100–6.

Hall, M. and Tideman, N. (1967) 'Measures of concentration', *Journal of the American Statistical Association*, 62: 162–8.

Hildenbrand, W. and Paschen, H. (1964) 'Ein axiomatisch begründetes Konzentrationsmaß', *Statistische Informationen, Vierteljahreshefte zur wirtschaftlichen Integration Europas*, 5 (3): 53–61.

Horowitz, A. R. and Horowitz, I. (1968) 'Entropy, Marcov processes and competition in the brewing industry', *Journal of Industrial Economics*, 16: 196–211.

International Accounting Standards Committee (IASC) (1992) *International Accounting Standards 1993 – The Full Text of all International Accounting Standards Extant at 1 January 1993*. London: IASC.

Jacquemin, A. P. and de Jong, H. W. (1977) *European Industrial Organisation*. London and Basingstoke: Macmillan.

Jacquemin, A. P. and Kumps, A.-M. (1971) 'Changes in the size structure of the largest European firms: an entropy measure', *Journal of Industrial Economics*, 19: 59–70.

Marfels, Ch. (1971) 'The consistency of concentration measures: a mathematical evaluation', *Proceedings of the American Statistical Association, Business and Economic Section*, 143–51.

Marfels, Ch. (1972) 'On testing concentration measures', *Zeitschrift für Nationalökonomie*, 32: 461–86.

Münzner, H. (1963) 'Probleme der konzentrationsmessung', *Allgemeines Statistisches Archiv*, 47: 1–9.

Nobes, Ch. W. and Parker, R. H. (1991) 'Introduction, and causes of differences', in Nobes, Ch. W. and Parker, R. H. (eds) *Comparative International Accounting*, 3rd edition. New York: Prentice Hall, pp. 3–22.

Parker, R. H. (1991) 'Financial reporting in the United Kingdom and Australia', in Nobes, Ch. W. and Parker, R. H. (eds) *Comparative International Accounting*, 3rd edition. New York: Prentice Hall, pp 122–58.

Paschen, H. (1969) *Die Messung der Betriebs- und Unternehmenskonzentration.* Freiburg im Breisgau: Rudolf Haufe.

Paschen, H. and Buyse, R. (1971) 'Zur messung der betriebs- und unternehmenskonzentration', *Statistische Hefte*, 12: 2–13.

Radebaugh, L. H. and Gray, S. J. (1993) *International Accounting and Multinational Enterprises.* New York: Wiley.

Rosenbluth, G. (1955) 'Measures of concentration', in *Conference on Business Concentration and Price Policy*, National Bureau of Economic Research, Princeton: NBER, pp. 57–95.

Theil, H. (1967) *Economics and Information Theory.* Amsterdam: North-Holland.

van der Tas, L. G. (1988) 'Measuring harmonisation of financial reporting practice', *Accounting and Business Research*, 18 (70): 157–69.

van der Tas, L. G. (1992a) 'Evidence of EC financial reporting practice harmonization – the case of deferred taxation', *European Accounting Review*, May, 1 (1): 69–104.

van der Tas, L. G. (1992b) 'Harmonisatie van de financiële verslaggeving – Specifiek gericht op de Europese Gemeenschap', *Maandblad voor Accountancy en Bedrijfseconomie*, 66: 407–19.

van der Tas, L. G. (1992c) *Harmonisation of Financial Reporting – With a Special Focus on the European community.* Maastricht: Datawyse.

van Hulle, K. (1992) 'Harmonization of accounting standards – a view from the European Community', *European Accounting Review*, 1 (1) May: 161–72.

Zeff, S. A. (1972) *Forging Accounting Principles in Five Countries: A History and an Analysis of Trends.* Champaign, Illinois: Stipes Publishing.

23

INTERNATIONAL HARMONY MEASURES OF ACCOUNTING POLICY
Comparative statistical properties

Richard D. Morris and R. H. Parker

Source: *Accounting and Business Research* 29(1) (1998): 73–86.

Abstract

Van der Tas's (1988) I index and the between-country C index introduced by Archer *et al.* (1995) are competing measures of international harmony. We present comparative statistical properties of these indices, via a simulation study covering three accounting methods in 10 countries, with uniform, bimodal and unimodal distributions of companies across accounting methods. The indices are also adjusted for non-disclosures using techniques developed by Archer and McLeay (1995) and Archer *et al.* (1995). The I index and the between-country C index are mathematically equivalent in the two-country case even in the presence of non-disclosures. As more countries are compared, the two indices diverge. The means and standard deviations of the I index, with a correction proposed by Archer and McLeay (1995), decrease and there is little skewness or kurtosis. In contrast, as more countries are compared, the between-country C index exhibits more stability in means, lower standard deviations, higher skewness and kurtosis. The between-country C index may be superior to the corrected I index because (i) between-country C index means approximate their 'expected values' (where all observations equal expected values) more closely than do corrected I index means; and (ii) between-country C index means are more stable than corrected I index means where the data come from stable distributions.

1. Introduction

Beginning with van der Tas (1988), a stream of literature[1] has examined national and international harmony[2] of accounting policies using a number

492

of index measures. These measures are van der Tas's H, I and C indices, and two derivatives of the C index—the between-country C index and the within-country C index—identified by Archer *et al.* (1995). The I index and the between-country C index are measures of international harmony. Little is known about their statistical properties as more countries are compared or as the distribution of companies across accounting methods changes. We examine these properties using a simulation study. Techniques to adjust the C index for non-disclosures, suggested by Archer and McLeay (1995) and Archer *et al.* (1995), are extended to the I index.

2. Background to harmony measures

Van der Tas (1988) introduced to the accounting literature precise ways of measuring national and international harmony of accounting policies. National harmony is measured by the H or Herfindahl index, used in industrial concentration studies. H is the sum over accounting methods of their squared frequencies of use within a single country, that is:

$$H = \sum_{i=1}^{k} p_i^2$$

where H = the Herfindahl index
 k = number of alternative accounting methods
 p_i = the relative frequency of accounting method i.

For international comparisons, van der Tas introduced the I index as an analogue of the H index. He defined the I index as:

$$I = \sum_{i=1}^{k} (f_{i1} \, f_{i2} \ldots f_{im})$$

where $f_{i1}, f_{i2}, \ldots f_{im}$ are the relative frequencies of accounting method i in each of m countries and k is the number of alternative accounting methods. Van der Tas's I index is the sum over accounting methods of the product of the relative frequencies of accounting method i in each of m countries.

The I index tends to zero as more countries are compared, since additional relative frequencies will almost always be fractions, resulting in a skewed distribution for I over the range 0–1. To overcome this skewness, van der Tas suggested applying the (m−1)th root as a correction factor:

$$I^* = I^{1/(m-1)}$$

where I* = corrected I index

m = number of countries.

Archer and McLeay (1995) have criticised van der Tas's formulation of the I index. They argue that the correction factor $1/(m-1)$ is not consistent with the I index being an analogue of the H index because $1/(m-1)$ does not equal 2—the exponent in the H index—and is applied to the sum of cross products and not to individual cross products for each accounting method. To ensure that the I index is an analogue of the H index, Archer and McLeay (1995: 4) suggest that the I index be calculated as:

$$I = \sum_{i=1}^{k} (f_{i1} \, f_{i2} \ldots f_{im})^{2/m}$$

where m is the number of countries and k the number of accounting methods as before. Archer and McLeay's I index is the sum across accounting methods of the squared geometric means of the relative frequencies of accounting method i in each of m countries. In the two country case, the exponent equals 1 and the corrected and uncorrected I indices are equivalent.

Van der Tas (1988) also introduced the comparability or C index as a means of dealing with companies using multiple accounting policies for the same issue (e.g. via footnote disclosures), although the index can be employed as an alternative to the H and I indices. The C index is based on combinatorial mathematics and measures the probability that any pair of randomly selected companies adopts the same accounting method. It is the number of company pairs in which each pair uses the same accounting method, summed over accounting methods and divided by the number of possible pairs if all companies used the same accounting method (Archer and McLeay, 1995: 5–6). Pair members can be from the same or different countries. Algebraically, van der Tas's C index is:

$$C = \frac{\sum_{j=1}^{k} (x_j(x_j - 1))}{n(n - 1)}$$

where x_j is the number of companies using accounting method j, k the number of accounting methods, and n the total number of companies.

Van der Tas showed that the H index and his C index were related thus (assuming no multiple reporting):

$$C = \frac{H - 1/n}{1 - 1/n} \quad \text{or} \quad H = \left(\frac{n-1}{n}\right) C + \frac{1}{n}$$

where n is the total number of companies. As $n \to \infty$, $C \to H$. The convergence occurs rapidly for even moderate values of n.

When used to measure international harmony, van der Tas's C index does not distinguish between national and international effects. To correct this deficiency, Archer *et al.* (1995) decomposed van der Tas's C index into a between-country C index and a within-country C index, the former being used for measuring international harmony of accounting policies. The between-country C index is the number of pairs of companies using the same accounting method, where each pair member is from a *different* country, divided by the total number of company pairs if all companies used the same accounting method but each pair member is from a different country. Intuitively, the between-country C index gives the probability that any pair of randomly selected companies, each from a different country, uses the same accounting method. Using Archer *et al.*'s (1995) notation, the between-country C index is:

$$\frac{\sum_i \sum_j x_{ij}(x_{+j} - x_{ij})}{\sum_i x_{i+}(x_{++} - x_{i+})}$$

where x_{ij} is the number of companies in country i using accounting method j, x_{+j} is the total number of companies in all countries using method j, x_{++} is the grand total of companies across countries, and x_{i+} is the number of companies in country i.

The within-country C index is the number of pairs of companies using the same accounting method, where each pair member comes from the *same* country, divided by the sum across countries of the number of company pairs in each country if all companies used the same accounting method. Using Archer *et al.*'s (1995) notation, the within-country C index is:

$$\frac{\sum_i \sum_j x_{ij}(x_{ij} - 1)}{\sum_i x_{i+}(x_{i+} - 1)}$$

To illustrate, Table 1 shows the I indices, with Archer and McLeay's correction, and the between-country C indices for fixed asset valuation in three countries A, B and C. Samples of 50 companies from each country use historical cost, replacement cost, and net realisable value in the numbers shown. Historical cost and replacement cost are equally popular in country A, net realisable value predominates in country B, while the three methods are used evenly in country C. The I index for countries A/B is low because of the non-use of net realisable value in country A and replacement cost in country B. The I indices for A/C and B/C exceed A/B because the three accounting methods are used evenly in country C and boost the I indices for

495

Table 1 Numerical example.

	Country			
	A	B	C	Total
Historical cost	25	5	17	47
Replacement cost	25	0	16	41
Net realisable value	0	45	17	62
Total	50	50	50	150

	A/B	B/C	A/C	A/B/C
Archer and McLeay I index	0.05	0.34	0.33	0.07
Between-country C Index	0.05	0.34	0.33	0.24

Calculations:

Archer & McLeay I index:
A/B: $(25/50 \times 5/50) + (25/50 \times 0/50) + (0/50 \times 45/45) = 0.05$
B/C: $(5/50 \times 17/50) + (0/50 \times 16/50) + (45/50 \times 17/50) = 0.34$
A/C: $(25/50 \times 17/50) + (25/50 \times 16/50) + (0/50 \times 17/50) = 0.33$
A/B/C: $(25/50 \times 5/50 \times 16/50)^{2/3} + (25/50 \times 0/50 \times 16/50)^{2/3} + (0/50 \times 45/50 \times 17/50)^{2/3}$
$= 0.07$

Between-country C index:
A/B: $[25(5) + 25(0) + 0(45)]/(50 \times 50) = .05$
B/C: $[5(17) + 0(16) + 45(17)]/(50 \times 50) = .34$
A/C: $[25(17) + 25(16) + 0(17)]/(50 \times 50) = .33$
A/B/C: $[[25(5) + 25(0) + 0(45)] + [17(25 + 5)] + [16(25 + 0)] + [17(0 + 45)]]/[(50 \times 50) + (50 \times 100)] = 0.24$

A/C and B/C. The between-country C index for each two-country comparison equals its corresponding I index, a point which will be returned to later.

Archer and McLeay (1995: 5, 10–11) argue that the between-country C index is a more robust measure of international harmony than the I index. The I index tends to zero if one or more accounting methods have low frequencies in one country. In particular, the contribution of an accounting method to the I index is zero if that method is not used in one country, even if it is widely used in all other countries. The between-country C index avoids these problems. For example, in Table 1, the three country I index, with Archer and McLeay's correction, is only 0.07, yet the corresponding between-country C index is 0.24, because (as already mentioned) net realisable value and replacement cost are not used in countries A and B respectively, and hence contribute nothing to the I index even though these accounting methods are used by 103 companies (69%) in the total sample.

The between-country C index and the Archer and McLeay-corrected I index are competing measures of international harmony with the between-country C index superior to the corrected I index, if Archer and McLeay's criticisms are accepted. Beyond simple examples like Table 1, little is known of the relationship between these indices as more countries are compared. Also little is known about the indices' sensitivity to variations in the distribution of companies across accounting methods as more countries are compared. Accordingly, further examination of these matters is warranted.

Table 2 contains an algebraic example which shows how the corrected I index and the between-country C index evolve as additional countries are compared. Three accounting methods are used by al, a2 and a3 companies in country A, by bl, b2 and b3 companies in country B and so on for four

Table 2 Index formulae.

Panel 1

	Country A	Country B	Country C	Country D
Method 1	a_1	b_1	c_1	d_1
Method 2	a_2	b_2	c_2	d_2
Method 3	a_3	b_3	c_3	d_3
Total	n_a	n_b	n_c	n_d

Panel 2

Countries I Index with Archer and McLeay's correction

A/B
$$\frac{a_1b_1 + a_2b_2 + a_3b_3}{n_a n_b}$$

A/B/C
$$\frac{(a_1b_1c_1)^{2/3} + (a_2b_2c_2)^{2/3} + (a_3b_3c_3)^{2/3}}{(n_a n_b n_c)^{2/3}}$$

A/B/C/D
$$\frac{(a_1b_1c_1d_1)^{2/4} + (a_2b_2c_2d_2)^{2/4} + (a_3b_3c_3d_3)^{2/4}}{(n_a n_b n_c n_d)^{2/4}}$$

Panel 3

Countries between-country C index

A/B
$$\frac{a_1b_1 + a_2b_2 + a_3b_3}{n_a n_b}$$

A/B/C
$$\frac{a_1b_1 + a_2b_2 + a_3b_3 + c_1(a_1 + b_1) + c_2(a_2 + b_2) + c_3(a_3 + b_3)}{n_a n_b + n_c(n_a + n_b)}$$

A/B/C/D
$$\frac{\begin{array}{c}a_1b_1 + a_2b_2 + a_3b_3 + c_1(a_1 + b_1) + c_2(a_2 + b_2) + c_3(a_3 + b_3) + \\ d_1(a_1 + b_1 + c_1) + d_2(a_2 + b_2 + c_2) + d_3(a_3 + b_3 + c_3)\end{array}}{n_a n_b + n_c(n_a + n_b) + n_d(n_a + n_b + n_c)}$$

countries as shown in panel 1. Applying the formulae described above and rearranging terms, the corrected I index and the between-country C index appear in panels 2 and 3 respectively.

In the two country case, the corrected I index and the between-country C index are identical. The identity can be shown to hold for any number of accounting methods. For more than two countries, the two indices diverge, but each evolves in a systematic pattern. Panel 2 shows that as an additional country D is added to the corrected I index, the marginal change to the numerator is that the number of companies using method i in country D is multiplied by the product of the number of companies using method i in countries A, B and C, while the marginal change to the denominator is that the number of companies in country D is multiplied by the product of the numbers of companies in countries A, B and C. In both numerator and denominator, the exponents equal two divided by the number of countries.

Panel 3 shows that as an additional country D is added to the between-country C index, the marginal change to the numerator is that the number using method i in country D is multiplied by the sum of the numbers using method i in countries A, B and C, while the marginal change to the denominator is that the total number in country D is multiplied by the sum of the totals in other countries. That is, as additional countries are added marginal changes to the indices involve *products*, and a change to the exponents to reflect the number of countries, for the corrected I index and *sums* for the between-country C index.

3. Simulation study

Table 2 does not show the statistical properties of the two indices as more countries are compared. Using a simulation study, we investigate these properties. The study is designed to be similar to Emenyonu and Gray (1992, 1996) and Herrman and Thomas (1995) in sample size, number of accounting methods and number of countries.

Samples of 50 companies were drawn from each of 10 countries, with 250 iterations of the selection process. Within each country, there are three accounting methods covering a particular accounting issue. Companies are assumed to be distributed across accounting methods in three mutually exclusive ways: (a) uniformly[3] so that the probability of companies choosing accounting method i in country m is the same for all i and m; (b) bimodally so that the probability of companies choosing either of two accounting methods—the same two in all countries—is twice that of choosing the third accounting method; (c) unimodally so that the probability of one accounting method being chosen is three times the probability of either of the other methods being chosen.

In the unimodal data set, the dominant accounting method alternates across countries, being the first in countries 1, 4, 7 and 10, the second in countries 2, 5 and 8, and the third in countries 3, 6 and 9. For the uniform data set, there is also a fourth accounting 'method' (dealt with later) representing companies which do not disclose how they account for the particular issue. The expected value of each observation in the uniform data set is 50/4 or 12.5. For the other data sets, companies were assigned to accounting methods using the Poisson distribution with mean values for each dominant accounting method of 20 in the bimodal, and 30 in the unimodal, data set. So expected values of the three accounting methods are 20, 20 and 10 in the bimodal data set and 30 for the dominant accounting method and 10 for each of the other two methods in the unimodal data set.

An important issue is what statistical properties of the corrected I index and the between-country C index to measure. The uniform and the bimodal data sets have stable distributions of companies across accounting methods while the unimodal data set has three different distributions, depending on which accounting method is dominant, the first for countries 1, 4, 7, 10, the second for countries 2, 5, 8 and the third for countries 3, 6, 9. Therefore, it seems reasonable to compare the stability of the I index and the between-country C index across the three data sets. Stability will be measured by examining changes in the means, standard deviations, skewness and kurtosis of each index as more countries are compared. Stability will also be examined by comparing each index's mean with its 'expected value', which is the value of each index where *all* observations in the underlying data set equal their expected values. This comparison is of interest because it indicates how extensively the obtained means have been affected by variability in the data sets.

3.1 Simulation results—the I index

Table 3, panel 1 shows the means, standard deviations, skewness and kurtosis for the I index with Archer and McLeay's correction where the underlying data are uniformly distributed. Panels 2 and 3 show these results for the bimodal and unimodal data sets respectively. In each panel, the final row shows the index's 'expected value'.

For the uniform data set in panel 1, the means and standard deviations for Archer and McLeay's I index[4] both decline, but at a decreasing rate, as more countries are compared. There is no pronounced skewness or kurtosis. Similar results occur for the bimodal data set in panel 2, except that the index is leptokurtic for 7 or more countries. For the unimodal data set in panel 3, the Archer and McLeay I index means decline as more countries are compared, the rate of decline increasing for three, six and nine country comparisons when the three distributions of accounting methods occur in equal numbers. Standard deviations remain steady; there is negative skewness but no pronounced kurtosis.

In panels 1 and 2, the 'expected values' of the Archer and McLeay I index are 0.333 and 0.36 respectively for all countries. However, the obtained

Table 3 Simulation results — the I index with Archer and McLeay's correction.

Panel 1: Uniform data set

Number of countries

	2	3	4	5	6	7	8	9	10
mean	0.329	0.280	0.250	0.226	0.215	0.206	0.197	0.193	0.189
s.d.	0.115	0.093	0.074	0.063	0.056	0.053	0.049	0.045	0.043
skewness	0.097	0.379	0.241	0.296	0.223	0.301	0.283	0.235	0.229
kurtosis	0.199	0.187	0.093	−0.315	0.004	−0.054	0.041	−0.053	0.064
expected value	0.333	0.333	0.333	0.333	0.333	0.333	0.333	0.333	0.333

Panel 2: Bimodal data set

Number of countries

	2	3	4	5	6	7	8	9	10
mean	0.354	0.345	0.339	0.336	0.334	0.332	0.330	0.329	0.328
s.d.	0.033	0.029	0.026	0.024	0.023	0.021	0.020	0.019	0.019
skewness	0.693	0.590	0.376	0.162	−0.103	−0.384	−0.633	−0.383	−0.460
kurtosis	1.461	0.562	0.563	0.494	0.746	2.033	2.472	1.638	1.513
expected value	0.360	0.360	0.360	0.360	0.360	0.360	0.360	0.360	0.360

Panel 3: Unimodal data set

Number of countries

	2	3	4	5	6	7	8	9	10
mean	0.277	0.240	0.240	0.231	0.220	0.220	0.218	0.213	0.212
s.d.	0.038	0.037	0.039	0.032	0.039	0.040	0.036	0.039	0.040
skewness	0.138	−0.428	−0.445	−0.903	−0.822	−1.113	−1.174	−1.079	−1.101
kurtosis	0.195	0.051	0.225	1.006	0.558	1.502	1.473	0.820	0.812
expected value	0.280	0.250	0.259	0.255	0.250	0.252	0.252	0.250	0.251

means fall increasingly below these amounts, by more than two standard deviations for six or more countries (panel 1) or for three or more countries (panel 2). In panel 3, the means also fall by increasing amounts below the corresponding 'expected values', but in each case by less than one standard deviation.

3.2 Simulation results—the between-country C index

Table 4 shows the means, standard deviations, skewness, kurtosis and 'expected values' of the between-country C index for the uniform data set (panel 1), bimodal data set (panel 2) and unimodal data set (panel 3).

Table 4 Simulation results — between-country C index.

Panel 1: Uniform data set

	Number of countries								
	2	3	4	5	6	7	8	9	10
mean	0.329	0.335	0.336	0.333	0.334	0.333	0.333	0.333	0.333
s.d.	0.115	0.074	0.048	0.037	0.03	0.026	0.023	0.021	0.018
skewness	0.097	0.904	1.048	1.027	1.018	1.131	1.311	1.457	1.559
kurtosis	0.199	1.363	1.608	1.656	1.392	1.511	2.269	3.038	3.398
expected value	0.333	0.333	0.333	0.333	0.333	0.333	0.333	0.333	0.333

Panel 2: Bimodal data set

	Number of countries								
	2	3	4	5	6	7	8	9	10
mean	0.354	0.355	0.354	0.354	0.354	0.354	0.354	0.354	0.354
s.d.	0.033	0.026	0.021	0.019	0.017	0.015	0.013	0.013	0.012
skewness	0.693	0.983	0.831	0.788	0.727	0.681	0.502	0.670	0.557
kurtosis	1.461	0.807	0.428	−0.024	−0.047	0.229	−0.236	0.328	−0.111
expected value	0.360	0.360	0.360	0.360	0.360	0.360	0.360	0.360	0.360

Panel 3: Unimodal data set

	Number of countries								
	2	3	4	5	6	7	8	9	10
mean	0.277	0.284	0.309	0.312	0.314	0.319	0.320	0.321	0.324
s.d.	0.038	0.023	0.017	0.010	0.009	0.008	0.006	0.005	0.005
skewness	0.138	−0.241	0.460	0.593	0.804	0.507	0.524	0.324	0.375
kurtosis	0.195	−0.383	0.522	0.906	2.958	0.910	1.164	1.149	0.904
expected value	0.280	0.280	0.307	0.312	0.312	0.318	0.320	0.320	0.323

In panels 1–3, the two country columns are identical to the equivalent columns for the I indices in panels 1–3 of Table 3. As more countries are compared, the mean between-country C index is stable for the uniform and bimodal data sets, but increases steadily for the unimodal data set. In all three panels, the standard deviation declines. As more countries are compared, the index becomes increasingly positively skewed for the uniform data set, and leptokurtic for the uniform and unimodal data sets.

The C index mean values closely track their 'expected values' in panel 1, and fall just below their 'expected values', on average by 0.006 in panel 2. In both cases, the differences are all less than one standard deviation. Interestingly, the 'expected values' for the between-country C index in panels 1 and

2 are constant for all countries and are the same as for the Archer and McLeay I indices in panels 1 and 2 of Table 3. In panel 3 of Table 4, the 'expected value' rises from 0.28 for two countries to 0.323 for 10 countries, and the obtained means closely track above the 'expected values', again by less than one standard deviation in all cases.

The between-country C index means from the simulation always exceed their I index counterparts for three or more country comparisons. Figure 1 shows index means for the uniform data set.

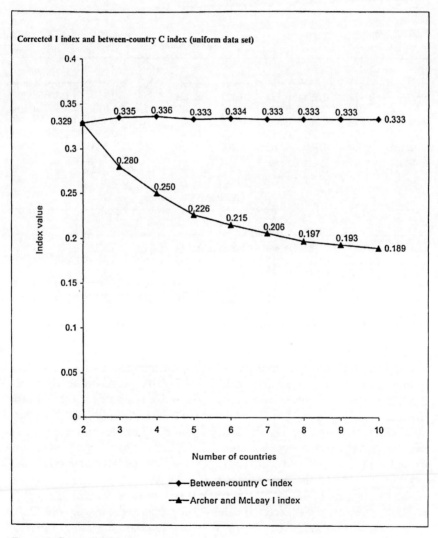

Figure 1 Corrected I index and between-country C index (uniform data set).

4. Adjusting indices for non-disclosures

Failure to disclose the use (or non-use) of a particular accounting method can be a confounding factor in studies of national or international harmony. The impact of non-disclosures increases with their relative frequency. Archer and McLeay (1995) and Archer *et al.* (1995) suggest three alternative ways to handle non-disclosures[5]—they can be omitted from all statistical analyses, treated as not applicable, or treated as if the item exists but is not disclosed. Their suggestions were made in the context of the C index. Treating non-disclosures as not applicable means that each non-disclosing firm is comparable with all other non-disclosers and with every disclosing firm for the item in question. The C index must be adjusted upwards accordingly to give a disclosure-adjusted comparability index. In contrast, if the item exists but is not disclosed, the denominator, but not the numerator, of the C index is adjusted for non-disclosures to give a raw comparability index. For any accounting issue, the disclosure-adjusted C index will usually produce higher scores, and the raw C index lower scores, than the C index calculated by omitting non-disclosures entirely.

Archer and McLeay (1995) define the disclosure-adjusted comparability index as: 'Pairwise comparisons between companies using the same method and with and between (non-disclosing) companies/Maximum pairwise comparisons between all companies'. They define the raw comparability index as: 'Pairwise comparisons between companies using the same method/ Maximum pairwise comparisons between all companies'.

We illustrate their rules with the between-country C index,[6] and extend them to the I index. In an Appendix, we suggest a rule for adjusting the H index for non-disclosures and indicate its relationship to van der Tas's C index.

In the algebraic example in Table 2, let $\phi_a, \ldots, \phi_d$ be the non-disclosers in countries A, .., D respectively. The formulae for disclosure-adjusted and raw between-country C indices for 2, 3 and 4 country comparisons appear in Table 5, panels 1 and 2.

4.1 Simulation results—between-country C index with non-disclosures

For brevity, we restrict our simulation results for the non-disclosure case to the uniform data set. We simulated the disclosure-adjusted C index and the raw C index for two to 10 country comparisons, using the fourth accounting 'method' to represent non-disclosures. The results appear in Table 6, panels 1 and 2.

Like the unadjusted between-country C index in Table 4, both disclosure-adjusted and raw between-country C indices exhibit pronounced stability in their mean values and declining standard deviations as the number of countries compared increases. The disclosure-adjusted index tracks 0.625 and the raw

Table 5 Between-country C index with non-disclosures: formulae.

Panel 1

Countries	Disclosure-adjusted between-country C index

A/B
$$\frac{a_1b_1 + a_2b_2 + a_3b_3 + \varnothing_a n_b + \varnothing_a \varnothing_b}{(n_a + \varnothing_a)(n_b + \varnothing_b)}$$

A/B/C
$$\frac{[a_1b_1 + a_2b_2 + a_3b_3 + c_1(a_1 + b_1) + c_2(a_2 + b_2) + c_3(a_3 + b_3) + \varnothing_a(n_b + n_c) + \varnothing_b(n_a + n_c) + \varnothing_c(n_a + n_b) + \varnothing_a\varnothing_b + \varnothing_c(\varnothing_a + \varnothing_b)]}{[(n_a + \varnothing_a)(n_b + \varnothing_b) + (n_c + \varnothing_c)(n_a + \varnothing_a + n_b + \varnothing_b)]}$$

A/B/C/D
$$\frac{\begin{array}{c}[a_1b_1 + a_2b_2 + a_3b_3 + c_1(a_1 + b_1) + c_2(a_2 + b_2) + c_3(a_3 + b_3) + \\ d_1(a_1 + b_1 + c_1) + d_2(a_2 + b_2 + c_2) + d_3(a_3 + b_3 + c_3) + \varnothing_a(n_b + n_c + n_d) \\ \varnothing_b(n_a + n_c + n_d) + \varnothing_c(n_a + n_b + n_d) + \varnothing_d(n_a + n_b + n_c) + \varnothing_a\varnothing_b \\ + \varnothing_c(\varnothing_a + \varnothing_b) + \varnothing_d(\varnothing_a + \varnothing_b + \varnothing_c)]\end{array}}{\begin{array}{c}[(n_a + \varnothing_a)(n_b + \varnothing_b) + (n_c + \varnothing_c)(n_a + \varnothing_a + n_b + \varnothing_b) \\ + (n_d + \varnothing_d)(n_a + \varnothing_a + n_b + \varnothing_b + n_c + \varnothing_c)]\end{array}}$$

Panel 2

Countries	Raw between-country C index

A/B
$$\frac{a_1b_1 + a_2b_2 + a_3b_3}{(n_a + \varnothing_a)(n_b + \varnothing_b)}$$

A/B/C
$$\frac{a_1b_1 + a_2b_2 + a_3b_3 + c_1(a_1 + b_1) + c_2(a_2 + b_2) + c_3(a_3 + b_3)}{[(n_a + \varnothing_a)(n_b + \varnothing_b)] + [(n_c + \varnothing_c)(n_a + \varnothing_a + n_b + \varnothing_b)]}$$

A/B/C/D
$$\frac{\begin{array}{c}[a_1b_1 + a_2b_2 + a_3b_3 + c_1(a_1 + b_1) + c_2(a_2 + b_2) + c_3(a_3 + b_3) + \\ d_1(a_1 + b_1 + c_1) + d_2(a_2 + b_2 + c_2) + d_3(a_3 + b_3 + c_3)]\end{array}}{\begin{array}{c}[(n_a + \varnothing_a)(n_b + \varnothing_b) + (n_c + \varnothing_c)(n_a + \varnothing_a + n_b + \varnothing_b) \\ + (n_d + \varnothing_d)(n_a + \varnothing_a + n_b + \varnothing_b + n_c + \varnothing_c)]\end{array}}$$

index tracks 0.187, which are their 'expected values' if the number of companies choosing accounting method i (including the non-disclosers) in country m always equalled the expected value of 12.5. Unlike the unadjusted between-country C index, both disclosure-adjusted and raw indices exhibit little skewness and tend to be platykurtic. Comparing Tables 4 and 6, the ranking of the between-country C indices means is (i) disclosure-adjusted; (ii) unadjusted index; (iii) raw index, regardless of the number of countries compared.

4.2 Disclosure-adjusted I index

A disclosure-adjusted I index can be computed by modifying the formula for the unadjusted I index. The number of non-disclosers for country m are added to scores for each accounting method in country m in the numerator of the I index, and are added to the total number of companies in country m in the denominator. It is necessary to deduct a correction factor for double-counting non-disclosers in the numerator, because non-disclosers are added to the frequencies of each accounting method. The severity of

Table 6 Between-country C index with non-disclosures (uniform data set).

Panel 1
Disclosure-adjusted between-country C index

				Number of countries				
2	3	4	5	6	7	8	9	10
mean	0.623	0.632	0.633	0.629	0.627	0.627	0.627	0.626	0.625
s.d.	0.160	0.118	0.097	0.091	0.082	0.072	0.069	0.064	0.062
skewness	−0.489	−0.112	−0.013	0.039	0.068	−0.106	−0.146	−0.125	−0.173
kurtosis	0.051	0.015	−0.384	−0.649	−0.591	−0.442	0.463	−0.313	0.478
expected value	0.625	0.625	0.625	0.625	0.625	0.625	0.625	0.625	0.625

Panel 2
Raw between-country C index

				Number of countries				
2	3	4	5	6	7	8	9	10
mean	0.182	0.187	0.187	0.186	0.187	0.187	0.186	0.186	0.187
s.d.	0.094	0.073	0.058	0.050	0.042	0.038	0.035	0.033	0.032
skewness	0.653	0.560	0.334	0.173	0.177	0.283	0.157	0.215	0.252
kurtosis	0.254	0.324	−0.185	−0.212	−0.285	−0.233	−0.305	−0.372	−0.576
expected value	0.187	0.187	0.187	0.187	0.187	0.187	0.187	0.187	0.187

double-counting increases with the number of accounting methods. The correction factor should reduce the numerator of the I index, be related to the number of accounting methods and the number of countries. For m countries, n accounting methods, the correction factor is $-(n-1)(\prod \phi_m)$. The disclosure-adjusted I index for two countries based on Table 2, panel 1 would be:

$$\frac{[(a_1 + \phi_a)(b_1 + \phi_b) + (a_2 + \phi_a)(b_2 + \phi_b) + (a_3 + \phi_a)(b_3 + \phi_b) - 2(\phi_a \phi_b)]}{(n_a + \phi_a)(n_b + \phi_b)}$$

which simplifies to:

$$\frac{a_1 b_1 + a_2 b_2 + a_3 b_3 + \phi_a n_b + \phi_b n_a + \phi_a \phi_b}{(n_a + \phi_a)(n_b + \phi_b)}$$

and is the same as the two country disclosure-adjusted between-country C index.

Unfortunately, for more than two countries, Archer and McLeay's correction cannot be made to the disclosure-adjusted I index,[7] because the presence of the correction factor for non-disclosers in the numerator violates Archer and McLeay's condition that the I index should be the sum across

Table 7 Raw I index with Archer and McLeay's correction.

Countries	Formulae
A/B	$\dfrac{a_1b_1 + a_2b_2 + a_3b_3}{(n_a + \o_a)(n_b + \o_b)}$
A/B/C	$\dfrac{(a_1b_1c_1)^{2/3} + (a_2b_2c_2)^{2/3} + (a_3b_3c_3)^{2/3}}{[(n_a + \o_a)(n_b + \o_b)(n_c + \o_c)]^{2/3}}$
A/B/C/D	$\dfrac{(a_1b_1c_1d_1)^{2/4} + (a_2b_2c_2d_2)^{2/4} + c(a_3b_3c_3d_3)^{2/4}}{[(n_a + \o_a)(n_b + \o_b)(n_c + \o_c)(n_d + \o_d)]^{2/4}}$

accounting methods of their squared geometric means of the relative frequencies of each accounting method i across m countries. The correction factor is not a geometric mean. Mechanically applying Archer and McLeay's correction to the disclosure-adjusted I index can produce index values greater than 1. Consequently, we do not investigate the disclosure-adjusted I index further.

4.3. Raw I index

By analogy with the raw between-country C index, the raw I index for m countries is the numerator of the unadjusted I index for m countries divided by the product of the number of companies plus non-disclosers in each country $1, 2, \ldots, m$. Using the example from Table 2, the raw I index for 2, 3 and 4 countries, with Archer and McLeay's correction, is shown in Table 7. The index in the two country case is the same as the raw between-country C index.

4.4 Simulation results—the I index with non-disclosures

Table 8 shows simulation results for the raw I index with Archer and McLeay's correction. The means and standard deviations of the raw I index decline as more countries are compared, and there is no pronounced skewness

Table 8 Simulation results: raw I index with Archer and McLeay's correction (uniform data set).

	Number of countries								
	2	3	4	5	6	7	8	9	10
mean	0.182	0.152	0.134	0.120	0.113	0.109	0.103	0.101	0.099
s.d.	0.094	0.075	0.058	0.049	0.042	0.038	0.035	0.033	0.032
skewness	0.653	0.788	0.576	0.627	0.604	0.766	0.675	0.601	0.600
kurtosis	0.254	0.616	0.222	0.295	0.113	0.400	0.503	0.199	0.326
expected value	0.187	0.187	0.187	0.187	0.187	0.187	0.187	0.187	0.187

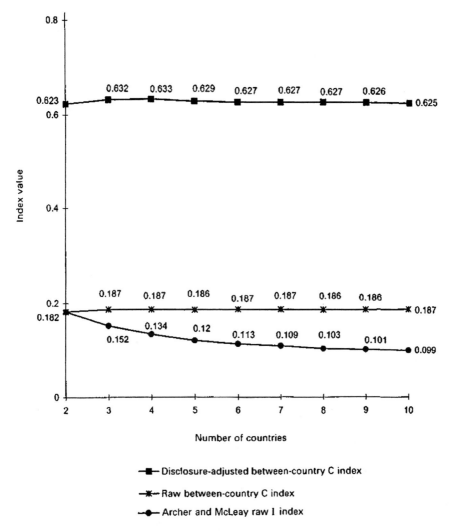

Figure 2 Corrected I index and between-country C index with non-disclosures (uniform data set).

or kurtosis. The means fall increasingly below the constant 'expected value' of 0.187.[8]

Figure 2 shows the means for the disclosure-adjusted and raw between-country C indices and the raw I index with Archer and McLeay's correction. For two-country comparisons the two raw indices are equal. If more than two countries are compared, the ranking of the indices is always (i) disclosure-adjusted between-country C index, (ii) raw between-country C index, (iii) raw between-country I index with Archer and McLeay's correction.

507

5. Discussion

This paper has demonstrated some comparative statistical properties of the I index and the between-country C index. In two country comparisons, the I index and the between-country C index are always equal, even when adjustment is made for non-disclosures. The result holds irrespective of the number of accounting methods in each country and the underlying distribution of companies across accounting methods.

For comparisons involving more than two countries, the corrected I index and the between-country C index diverge. Archer and McLeay's (1995), and not van der Tas's (1988), correction to the I index has been used because it is more consistent with van der Tas's original idea that the I index should be an analogue of the H index. Our simulation results, based on uniformly, bimodally and unimodally distributed data sets show that the means of Archer and McLeay's I index decrease for all data sets as more countries are compared. Standard deviations also fall for the uniform and bimodal data sets. There is pronounced skewness for seven or more countries with the unimodal data set, and pronounced kurtosis in the bimodal data set for seven or more countries, and in the unimodal data set for seven or eight countries. For all data sets, the index means fall increasingly below their 'expected values' (where all observations equal their expected values).

The means of the between-country C index closely approximate their 'expected values' for all country comparisons and usually exceed the corresponding mean I index with Archer and McLeay's correction. The between-country C index's 'expected value' is a constant for the uniform and bimodal data sets and slowly rises for the unimodal data set. Standard deviations fall as the number of countries increases. Skewness and kurtosis vary across data sets but tend to be greater than for the corrected I index as more countries are compared.

For the non-disclosure case, our results are only for the uniform data set. Techniques of dealing with non-disclosures developed by Archer and McLeay (1995) and Archer et al. (1995) for the C index and its derivatives are used. Two variants of the between-country C index are calculated: a disclosure-adjusted version used when non-disclosures are 'not applicable'; and a raw version used when the missing item is applicable to a firm but is not disclosed. Adjusting the between-country C index for non-disclosures tends to shift the mean by a constant, upwards for the disclosure-adjusted, and downwards for the raw, between-country C index. Both adjustments for non-disclosures remove the skewness and kurtosis exhibited by the unadjusted index. The disclosure-adjusted and raw between-country C indices closely track their 'expected values' which are constant for all countries.

We propose disclosure-adjusted and raw versions of the I index (and show in the Appendix the relationship between the H index and van der Tas's C index with non-disclosures). Unfortunately, Archer and McLeay's correction cannot be applied validly to the disclosure-adjusted I index, except in the two-country case. For this reason, the between-country C index is preferable if a disclosure-adjusted index is required. Adjusting for non-disclosures in the case of the raw I index tends to shift its distribution downwards. The means of the raw I index with Archer and McLeay's correction converge on zero as the number of countries increases, and fall increasingly below a constant 'expected value'. Standard deviations also fall and there is no marked skewness or kurtosis.

As Archer and McLeay (1995) noted and our results demonstrate, the assumption made about non-disclosures can have a substantial impact on the resultant harmony measures, especially if the number of non-disclosers is large. Deciding how to handle non-disclosures depends on the underlying facts and requires careful judgement. Using unadjusted indices, that is ignoring non-disclosures, would be reasonable if non-disclosures were relatively infrequent. If non-disclosures are 'not applicable', a dilemma can occur. Usually, the disclosure-adjusted between-country C index should be used. However, if the number of non-disclosers is very much larger than the number of disclosing firms, non-disclosers will dominate the index, which then approaches I and may mask the fact that considerable variation exists among disclosing firms. In that case, ignoring non-disclosures may be preferable in order to bring out variation among the disclosing firms. The raw indices should be used if the accounting policy applies to non-disclosers but they have not disclosed their accounting method.

In short, for the three data sets employed, the between-country C index exhibits more stability, either absolutely or in relation to its 'expected values', than does the corrected I index, even when both indices are adjusted for non-disclosures. The stability of the between-country C index is more consistent with the stability in the uniform and bimodal data sets, which each assigns an unchanging distribution of companies to accounting methods across countries. The unimodal data set is less stable than the other data sets, as the dominant accounting method changes across countries. Yet even here the between-country C index tracks its 'expected values' more closely than does the corrected I index. Where all countries have identical data distributions, it seems counterintuitive that the corrected I index shows decreasing harmony as the number of countries increases. For these reasons, the between-country C index may be superior to the I index.

An implication of the findings is that it would be a mistake to apply identical benchmarks to both indices, for example to say that 'considerable harmony' exists if the value of either index exceeds 0.85. For the same data set, the between-country C index is likely to indicate a higher level of harmony than the Archer and McLeay I index as the number of countries increases. Lower benchmarks should be set for the corrected I index if it is used.

Appendix
The H index and van der Tas's C index with non-disclosures

Let a_1, a_2 and a_3 be three accounting methods in a country,

$n = a_1 + a_2 + a_3$

ϕ = the number of non-disclosers

Disclosure-adjusted H index is:

$$\frac{(a_1 + \phi)^2 + (a_2 + \phi)^2 + (a_3 + \phi)^2 - 2\phi^2}{(n + \phi)^2} = \frac{a_1^2 + a_2^2 + a_3^2 + \phi^2 + 2\phi n}{(n + \phi)^2}$$

An adjustment must be made for double-counting non-disclosers. In any country with n accounting methods and ϕ non-disclosers, the correction for double counting in the numerator is $-(n-1)\phi^2$.

The disclosure-adjusted van der Tas C index[9] is:

$$\frac{0.5[a^1(a^1 - 1) + a^2(a^2 - 1) + a^3(a^3 - 1) + \phi(\phi - 1)] + \phi(a^3 + a^2 + a^3)}{0.5(n + \phi)(n + \phi - 1)}$$

$$= \frac{a_1^2 + a_2^2 + a_3^2 + \phi^2 - (n + \phi) + 2\phi n}{(n + \phi)(n + \phi - 1)}$$

The relationship between the disclosure-adjusted H and van der Tas C indices is:

$$(n + \phi)^2 H = (n + \phi)(n + \phi - 1)C + (n + \phi)$$

$$H = \left(\frac{n + \phi - 1}{n + \phi}\right)C + \frac{1}{n + \phi}$$

The raw H index is

$$\frac{a_1^2 + a_2^2 + a_3^2}{(n + \phi)^2}$$

while the raw van der Tas C index is:

$$\frac{a_1(a_1 - 1) + a_2(a_2 - 1) + a_3(a_3 - 1)}{(n + \phi)(n + \phi - 1)} = \frac{a_1^2 + a_2^2 + a_3^2 - n}{(n + \phi)(n + \phi - 1)}$$

The relationship between the two raw indices is:

$$H = \left(\frac{n + \phi - 1}{n + \phi}\right)C + \frac{n}{(n + \phi)^2}$$

In both disclosure-adjusted and raw cases, the H and C indices converge as $n \to \infty$. If $\phi = 0$, the relationship between H and C becomes that proposed originally by van der Tas (1988) for the unadjusted case, stated earlier.

Notes

1 See for example Emenyonu and Gray (1992, 1996), Hermann and Thomas (1995), Archer and McLeay (1995), Archer *et al.* (1995, 1996).
2 According to Tay and Parker (1990: 73), harmony is a state indicated by a clustering of companies around one or a few available accounting methods, whereas harmonisation is a process of movement away from total diversity of accounting methods. For simplicity we refer only to harmony measures, but our conclusions apply equally to measures of harmonisation. We cover only de facto or material harmony which refers to what companies actually do, rather than de jure or formal harmony which refers to accounting standards and similar regulations. For measures of formal harmony, see Rahman *et al.* (1996).
3 Tay and Parker (1990: 85) suggested the uniform distribution as a benchmark against which to judge actual practices. SPSS for Windows 95 was used to randomly allocate companies to accounting methods in each country. An unavoidable imperfection in the simulation with the uniform distribution is that SPSS gives numbers for each accounting method i in country m which are not whole numbers, but are correct to 14 decimal places. The problem also occurs with other packages such as Excel. It is unlikely that the imperfection biases our results. The problem does not occur with the bimodal and unimodal data sets.
4 By way of comparison, for each data set, the mean of the unadjusted I index declines sharply as the number of countries increases, the mean index for m countries being approximately one third of the mean index for m-1 countries. The standard deviation also declines sharply. The distribution of the index becomes markedly positively skewed and leptokurtic for the uniform and unimodal data sets. These results demonstrate the tendency, noted originally by van der Tas (1988), for the uncorrected I index to tend to zero as more countries are compared. Like Archer and McLeay's correction, van der Tas's correction to the I index arrests the decline in the unadjusted I index. For the uniform data set, the mean I index with van der Tas's correction declines steadily as more countries are compared from 0.329 for 2 countries to 0.287 for 10 countries, and the standard deviation declines. For the bimodal data set, the means for the van der Tas I index increase from 0.354 for 2 countries to 0.378 for 10 countries, and the standard deviation declines. Neither index exhibits pronounced skewness. For the unimodal data set in panel 3, the means for the van der Tas I index fluctuate in a narrow band between 0.270 and 0.287, while the standard deviation declines, and there is no pronounced skewness or kurtosis. In each data set, for three or more countries, the mean van der Tas I index is always greater than the corresponding mean Archer and McLeay I index, which in turn is always greater than the mean unadjusted I index. As more countries are compared, the means of the unadjusted I index converge on the 'expected values'. In contrast, the van der Tas I index, like the Archer and McLeay I index, systematically tracks below its 'expected value'.
5 They also state that sometimes a 'default' assumption may be made whereby non-disclosers can be assumed, from the surrounding circumstances, to use a particular method, such as one required by an accounting standard. In that case, non-disclosers can simply be added to companies disclosing that they do use the method. Archer *et al.* (1996), in their statistical modelling of harmonisation, also treat non-disclosures as if they were a separate accounting method.
6 We thank Stuart McLeay for his assistance in calculating the disclosure-adjusted and raw C indices and their derivatives.
7 Van der Tas's correction can be made to the disclosure-adjusted I index.

8 In contrast, the means and standard deviations for the raw I indices *without* Archer and McLeay's correction, converge on zero as more countries are compared, and the means closely track their 'expected values'. Compared to the unadjusted I index in footnote 4, the rate of convergence for the means is faster for the raw I index. The mean raw I index without Archer and McLeay's correction commences from 0.182 for two countries and the mean for m countries is about 25% of the mean for m-I countries. The raw I index without Archer and McLeay's correction tends to be increasingly positively skewed and leptokurtic as more countries are compared.

9 The number of pairs which can be chosen from n objects is $0.5n(n-1)$. Because van der Tas's C index is the ratio of pairs of comparable companies, the numerator and denominator of the index contains weightings of 0.5 which cancel out and for simplicity have been omitted earlier in the text. The cancellation cannot occur with the disclosure-adjusted van der Tas C index because its numerator contains $\phi(a_1 + a_2 + a_3)$, the number of pairs formed between non-disclosers and all other companies, which does not require a 0.5 weighting. No 0.5 weightings are necessary with between-country C indices because of the condition that each pair member comes from a different country.

References

Archer, S. and McLeay, S. (1995). 'On Measuring the Harmonisation of Accounting Practices'. Paper presented at Workshop on International Accounting, Geneva.

Archer, S., Delvaille, P. and McLeay, S. (1995). 'The measurement of harmonisation and the comparability of financial statement items: within-country and between-country effects'. *Accounting and Business Research*, 25 (Spring): 67–80.

Archer, S., Delvaille, P. and McLeay, S. (1996). 'A statistical model of international accounting harmonization'. *Abacus*, 32 (March): 1–29.

Emenyonu, E. and Gray, S. (1992). 'EC Accounting harmonisation: an empirical study of measurement practices in France, Germany, and the UK'. *Accounting and Business Research*, 23 (Winter): 49–58.

Emenyonu, E. and Gray, S. (1996). 'International accounting harmonization and the major developed stock market countries: an empirical study'. *International Journal of Accounting*, 31 (3) 269–280.

Herrmann, D. and Thomas W. (1995). 'Harmonisation of accounting measurement practices in the European Community'. *Accounting and Business Research* (Autumn): 253–265.

Rahman, A., Perera, P. and Ganeshanandam, S. (1996). 'Measurement of formal harmonisation in accounting: an exploratory study'. *Accounting and Business Research*, 26 (Autumn): 325–339.

Tay, J. S. W. and Parker, R. H. (1990). 'Measuring international harmonization and standardization'. *Abacus*, 26 (March): 71–88.

van der Tas, L. G., (1988). 'Measuring harmonisation of financial reporting practice'. *Accounting and Business Research*, 18 (Spring): 157–169.

24

EVALUATING THE STATISTICAL SIGNIFICANCE OF *DE FACTO* ACCOUNTING HARMONIZATION

A study of European global players

Leandro Cañibano and Araceli Mora

Source: *European Accounting Review* 9(3) (2000): 349–69.

Abstract

Two different forces are involved in the international harmonization of accounting: institutional endeavours to harmonize accounting internationally by developing common accounting rules and reporting standards, and spontaneous efforts by 'global players' to adopt accounting methods that will improve communication with users in other countries. These two developments are proceeding side by side, generally reinforcing one another but occasionally moving independently.

This paper is primarily concerned with the process of harmonization of financial accounting within the European Union. The hypothesis we want to test is that, in spite of the obstacles to the harmonization of regulations in the European Union, there has been greater conformity in recent years in the accounting practices of companies which operate on the international stage. If so, the implications for the harmonization strategies of the international bodies are important.

In this study, we first carry out a critical analysis of previous research on accounting harmonization, summarizing the methods used in empirical studies of *de facto* harmonization and the results obtained. We note that the major deficiency in the index-based methods of measuring harmonization is that no test of significance has been included in prior research. In this paper, we propose a bootstrapping test of the C index as a way of measuring the significance of the change in its value. We consider a sample of eighty-five 'global players' from thirteen countries and we analyse their financial statements with regard to four accounting issues (deferred taxation,

513

goodwill, leasing and foreign currency translation), providing estimates of the significance of *de facto* accounting harmonization for the periods from 1991–2 to 1996–7.

1. Introduction

The free flow of comparable financial information resulting from the harmonization of accounting is a necessary condition for achieving a common market in the European Union. However, the development of global capital markets has created another force for the international harmonization of accounting amongst the companies whose shares are traded on those markets and who have to satisfy the information needs of investors in different countries. This second force, as Thorell and Whittington (1994) point out, is, in one sense, broader, because it extends across the world, but it is, in another sense, narrower, because it is confined substantially to a limited number of international corporations whose securities are traded on global markets.

The European Union strategy with respect to the accounting harmonization of rules has been to use directives, to which all the member states have adapted their legislation. But there appear to be some problems involved in this process. The EU has undoubtedly made progress towards harmonization of accounting law, but the requirements of the EU directives are minimal and do not appear to be sufficient to achieve the desired comparability of financial statements. The inclusion of stricter rules in the directives would not seem to be an acceptable strategy (European Commission, 1995). Regulated international harmonization is difficult to achieve in a business world of cultural, legal, political and economic differences among countries. Now, requiring the use of International Accounting Standards (IASs) for consolidated financial statements would seem to be the strategy adopted by the European Commission (European Commission, 1995). In fact, certain countries (e.g., France, Germany, Italy and Belgium) have already brought their legislation into line with this strategy. However, the use of IASs by 'global players' does not guarantee the comparability of their financial statements because IASs still provide for alternative accounting procedures in some areas.

On the other hand, firms adopting an international competitive strategy are operating in a culture that depends upon global resources. To obtain foreign customers and enhance public image, firms may choose to disclose at least as much as their competitors, which may or may not be 'more' than they are already disclosing in their home country (Thorell and Whittington, 1994). This could be another driving force behind greater comparability that is independent from the institutional efforts previously mentioned.

Therefore, as Meek and Saudagaran (1990) pointed out:

two significant outgrowths of the transnational financial reporting problem are: institutional endeavors to harmonize accounting internationally by developing accounting and reporting standards, and voluntary efforts by MNCs themselves to improve communication with users in other countries. These two developments are proceeding side by side, generally reinforcing one another but occasionally moving independently.

This paper is primarily concerned with the process of harmonization of the financial accounting practices of European 'global players'. The aim of this study is therefore to ascertain whether the level of comparability in practice among 'global players' has increased in recent years, despite the problems and obstacles involved in the harmonization of rules. Accordingly, we wish to test whether there has been such a 'spontaneous harmonization' in recent years among the accounting practices of companies that operate on the international stage, independently from the harmonization of laws. If so, the implications for the harmonization strategies of international bodies are important.

In this study we carry out a critical analysis of previous research on accounting harmonization, summarizing the methods used in empirical studies of *de facto* harmonization and the results obtained. We note that the major deficiency in the index-based methods of measuring harmonization is that no test of significance has been included in prior research. In this paper, we propose a bootstrapping test of the C index as a way of measuring the significance of the change in its value. We consider a sample of 'global players' from thirteen countries, and we analyse their financial statements with regard to four accounting issues which are considered by previous literature as being among the most controversial in terms of comparability (deferred taxation, goodwill, leasing and foreign currency translation). Then, we provide estimates of the significance of *de facto* harmonization for the periods from 1991–2 to 1996–7.

The remainder of this paper is organized as follows: the second section presents the different concepts of accounting harmonization to be found in the international accounting literature. The third section analyses previous empirical research. The fourth section discusses the proposed research methodology, together with data selection, statistical analysis and results. Lastly, the fifth section concludes with an analysis of the results, a summary of the findings and a description of the limitations and implications of the results.

2. The concept of accounting harmonization

We consider it is important to clarify the different uses of the term 'accounting harmonization' in the literature and previous research in order to understand the aim, the proposal of the methodology and the conclusions of this study. First of all, it is important to distinguish between two terms as used in the international accounting context: 'standardization' and 'harmonization'. *Standardization* implies uniform standards in all countries that participate in the effort. *Harmonization*, however, implies a reconciliation of different points of view and permits different requirements in individual countries provided that there is no logical conflict. *Harmonization* is a process, a movement towards *harmony*, which is a state. *Standardization* is also a process, a movement towards *uniformity*, which is also a state (see Tay and Parker, 1990; Nobes and Parker, 2000). *Harmonization* is a more realistic and conciliatory approach and seems more attainable than rigid *standardization*.

As Van der Tas (1988: 157) points out:

> harmonization is a coordination, a tuning of two or more objects. Users are confronted with several financial reports. It would be useful for them if these financial reports were more in harmony. Therefore financial reports are a target of harmonization. One way to harmonize financial reports is to formulate standards, thus setting limits to the difference between financial reports. They are also an object of harmonization themselves.

Accordingly, a distinction can be drawn between two types of harmonization, namely, *'de facto'* or material harmonization and *'de jure'* or formal harmonization. The former refers to the increase in comparability that arises from greater conformity in practices, and the latter to harmonization of regulations. Formal harmonization would normally lead to material harmonization, but this is not necessarily the case. Formal harmonization may be accompanied by disharmonization if the standards allow for more options for companies. At the same time, material harmonization might take place without being increased by formal harmonization. This will be referred to as *spontaneous harmonization*.

Both formal and material harmonization may refer to the degree of disclosure or to the accounting method selected. The former is called *disclosure harmonization* and the latter *measurement harmonization*. Figure 1 illustrates the different meanings of the term harmonization. As Tay and Parker (1990: 75) say,

> taking account of both the desirability of international comparability of financial statements and the operational difficulties involved in measuring processes rather than states, the most suitable concept for measurement appears to be *de facto* harmonization, in the form of studies of *de facto* harmony over time.

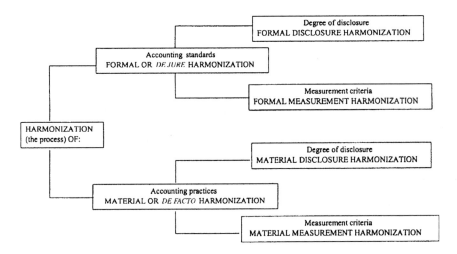

Figure 1 The concept of harmonization.

Following Tay and Parker (1990), for the purposes of this paper, we will focus on ***de facto* measurement harmonization**. It can be said that two financial reports are comparable in respect of one specific event if under the same circumstances this event is accounted for in the same way in both reports or if multiple reporting takes place. Multiple reporting means that a company gives additional information based on an accounting method other than its primary accounting method. *De facto* measurement harmonization is an increase in the degree of comparability and means that more companies in the same circumstances apply the same method to an event or give additional information in such a way that the financial reports of more companies can be made comparable.

The notion of harmony, under these circumstances, is such that the process of harmonization will lead to a situation of maximum harmony with respect to a particular financial statement item when all companies in all countries use the same accounting method. Although, as Herrmann and Thomas (1995) point out, this notion ignores the possibility that companies may be subject to different circumstances which arguably justify the use of correspondingly different accounting methods in respect of that item. For Archer *et al.* (1996), this implies an alternative notion of international harmony. According to this notion, a state of international harmony exists when, all other things being equal, the odds of selecting a given accounting method are identical in each group.

The existence of different notions of material harmony implies, in our opinion, the use of different methods of measuring such harmony depending on the concept used by the researcher in question, as discussed in a later section.

3. Previous literature

In the field of the measurement of harmonization, some researchers have investigated formal harmonization using different statistical methodologies (e.g., Nair and Frank, 1981; Garrod and Sieringhaus, 1995; Rahman *et al.*, 1996; Laínez *et al.*, 1996). But most of the empirical studies have measured *de facto* harmonization or *de facto* harmony at a point in time (e.g., Van der Tas, 1988, 1992a, 1992b; Walton, 1992; Emenyonu and Gray, 1992; Archer *et al.*, 1995, 1996; Herrmann and Thomas, 1995; García-Benau, 1994;[1] Krisement, 1997; Laínez *et al.*, 1997; McLeay *et al.*, 1999; Pierce and Weetman, 2000).

We will now focus our attention on the studies whose main aim has been to evaluate either the *de facto* harmonization process or the state of *de facto* harmony in Europe. In Table 1 representative studies in this field are shown, indicating their objectives, data source, methodology and main conclusions.

According to Rahman *et al.* (1996: 326):

> accounting harmonization studies are very much at an experimental stage, where methodology and analytical techniques are still being proposed and tested on particular samples of accounting issues and countries. Despite similarities in their purpose, they varied in their results. This is attributable to the differences in the issues selected, countries examined and the analytical techniques used.

In this section we briefly analyse the different data sources and methodologies used in the studies shown in Table 1. First, we want to point out that, though most of these authors say they have measured the 'level of harmonization', some of them do not compare two periods of time and, accordingly, they are actually measuring the 'level of harmony' at that date. Only in the cases of Van der Tas (1992a, 1992b), Archer *et al.* (1995, 1996) and McLeay *et al.* (1999) is a measurement of the process carried out.

Data sources

Data instruments or sources of data which can be used in *de facto* harmonization studies are mainly of five types: annual reports, accounting regulations, public databases, questionnaires and laboratory techniques. The choice of data source has important repercussions for the overall research design, since there are advantages and difficulties involved with using each of them. We will focus on the two data sources used in the studies shown in Table 1, survey data and annual accounts.

Table 1 Material harmonization studies.

	Van der Tas (1988)	Van der Tas (1992a, 1992b)	Emenyonu and Gray (1992)	Archer et al. (1995)	Herrmann and Thomas (1995)	Garcia Benau (1994)	Archer et al. (1996)	Krisement (1997)	McLeay et al. (1999)
Objective (European material harmonization or harmony)	*The proposal of a methodology* • C index • Examples of national and international harmonization	*Harmonization* • Deferred taxation	*Harmony* • Inventory valuation • Depreciation • Goodwill • R&D • Fixed assets • Ext. items	*Harmonization* • Deferred taxation • Goodwill	*Harmony* • Fixed asset valuation • Depreciation methods • Goodwill • R&D • Inventories • Foreign currency	*Harmony* • Foreign currency • R&D • Leasing	*Harmonization* • Deferred taxation • Goodwill	*Proposal of a methodology* • Foreign currency as an example	*Proposal of a methodology* • Goodwill as example
Data source	Annual Reports (1978–84) *National* • UK, Netherlands and USA *International* • USA and Netherlands	Annual Reports (1978–88) 154 companies • Belgium • Denmark • France • Germany • Greece • Ireland • Luxembourg • UK • Netherlands	Annual Reports (1989) 78 companies • France • Germany • UK	Annual Reports (1986–7 and 1990–2) 89 companies • Belgium • France • Germany • Ireland • Netherlands • Sweden • Switzerland • UK	Annual Reports (1992–3) 20 companies • Belgium • Denmark • France • Germany • Ireland • Netherlands • Portugal • UK	Survey Data (FEE report for 1989) • Belgium • France • Denmark • Germany • Greece • Ireland • Luxembourg • Netherlands • UK	Annual Reports (1986–7 and 1990–1) 89 companies • Belgium • France • Germany • Ireland • Netherlands • Sweden • Switzerland	Survey Data (FEE Report 1989) • Belgium • France • Denmark • Germany • Greece • Ireland • Luxembourg • Netherlands • UK	Annual Reports (1987–93) 286 companies • Austria • Belgium • Denmark • Finland • France • Germany • Ireland • Luxembourg • Netherlands • Spain • Sweden • Switzerland • UK

Table 1 (cont'd)

	Van der Tas (1988)	Van der Tas (1992a, 1992b)	Emenyonu and Gray (1992)	Archer et al. (1995)	Herrmann and Thomas (1995)	Garcia Benau (1994)	Archer et al. (1996)	Krisement (1997)	McLeay et al. (1999)
Methodology	• H index • C index	• C index • Chi-square	• I index	• C index	• I index • Adjusted I index • Chi-square	• I index • Adjusted I index (IC) • Chi-square	• Nested hierarchy of log-linear models	• V ratio (heterogeneity+ entropy)	• Nested statistical models
Main conclusions	C index is a good method for measuring harmony	The degree of harmony increases considering the 'notes to the accounts' for individual and consolidated accounts. Positive impact of Fourth Directive on individual accounts and no significant impact on consolidated accounts	Relative lack of harmony	C index is an imperfect measure. Little progress in the period. This could be due to small or negative within-country comparability	High level of harmony in • FCT • Inventory value • Depreciation Low level of harmony in • R&D • Fixed assets • Goodwill	Certain progress has been made. FCT has the higher index	Little progress in the period. This could be due to small or negative within-country comparability	Entropy helps to measure harmonization	Harmony does not depend on there being a uniform method but in adopting the same method under the same circumstances. Increase in disharmony in goodwill

There are obvious advantages involved in using questionnaires. As Tay and Parker (1990) say, someone else has already done all the difficult and tedious work of collecting data, which relate to a large number of countries and/or companies, cover a wide range of accounting topics and are available in a language which the researcher can understand. The difficulties with using survey data are well summarized by Nobes (1981). The validity of data, the way the data are presented, inaccuracies which the researcher may not be aware of due to his/her unfamiliarity with different accounting systems and the time lag between publication of the survey and the period surveyed are some of the limitations.

The use of annual reports obviously has great advantages, but also difficulties. It does not have the disadvantages mentioned above, but the collection of data is tedious, companies sometimes do not send the financial information and the reports may not be available in a language the researcher can understand.

Methodologies

Until now, two different methodologies for measuring the level of harmony have been developed: indices and statistical models.

Van der Tas (1988) promotes the idea of **indices**, and meticulously develops the H, C and I indices. The H index from which the I index is developed permits quantification of industrial concentration. Its use in the context of financial reporting harmonization implies an analogy between accounting harmonization and industrial concentration. The idea is that comparability increases when the result of the choice that companies make between alternative accounting methods becomes concentrated on one or only a limited number of methods. The H index adds the square of the relative frequencies of each of the applied methods. But, according to Tay and Parker (1990), this use of the H index 'is worthy of some discussion'. In any case, the main problem of this index is coping with multiple reporting or additional data in the notes regarding the results of alternative measurement methods. Each company (or financial report) must be assigned to one, and only one, alternative measurement method. This problem was solved with the C index developed by Van der Tas (1988). The C index is able to take into account multiple reporting and reconciliation data in the notes to financial statements. Some other adjusted indices based on these two indices have been subsequently developed to try to avoid some of the above limitations. Thus, for example, Krisement (1997) recently proposed a methodology that links the C index and entropy so that, in her opinion, 'the advantages of these two measures complement one another while any disadvantages are eliminated'.

The possibility of using a **statistical modelling approach** was hinted at by Tay and Parker (1990). They suggest that the level of harmony in the accounting practices adopted by companies in different countries may be assessed for a particular financial statement item by comparing 'the observed distribution of companies between different methods with either a random distribution or some expected distribution' and that a suitable representation of a random distribution could be 'a distribution in which equal numbers of companies would be expected to use each of the available alternatives'. Given this approach, Tay and Parker propose the 'evidence of harmony would then be the existence of a significant difference between the observed and expected distributions, as measured by some appropriate significance test, for example chi-square'. Other authors such as Archer *et al.* (1996) developed statistical models which allowed them to measure the level of harmony between countries in a period and the variations in the level of harmony (harmonization) between two periods. McLeay *et al.* (1999) recently developed a new statistical measurement technique. It is important to note that, despite the fact that certain authors used both techniques (indices and statistical models), as alternatives, they are not. The concept of harmonization is different in the two cases. In the case of the statistical model of McLeay *et al.* (1999), these researchers provide a measure of harmonization for which the comparability 'would depend on the use of accounting methods appropriate to a firm's circumstances, and not on the use of the same method by all firms'.

It is important to note that all the methodologies are applied to measure accounting issues separately. Measuring separately gives more refined results because one is able to measure the degree of material measurement harmony for each sort of transaction or event accounted for in the financial report, whereas measuring harmony of the aggregate of all sorts of transactions or events gives only aggregate results, making it difficult to draw policy conclusions on the basis of these measurements. At the same time, measuring harmony of the aggregate of all sorts of transactions or events would require a complete list of the types of transaction and event. It would be very difficult to make an exhaustive list because of the tremendous number of types of transaction and event and of the fact that such a list would change in the course of time. Accordingly, measuring *de facto* measurement harmony separately for each sort of transaction or event is more practical.

Lastly, we want to point out that, in order to measure the 'process of harmonization', most studies compare the value of the indices in the two periods to ascertain whether it has increased, or compare the statistical distribution of the two periods to see if the probability of being a non-random distribution has increased. Until now, only Archer *et al.* (1996) have analysed whether the difference between the two periods is statistically significant using their statistical model approach, but nobody has analysed whether the differences obtained with indices were statistically significant, which is one of the main aims of the present study.

Table 2 Sample of companies.

Company	Country	Company	Country
Abbey PLC	Eire	KNP BT	Netherlands
Accor	France	Kvaerner AS	Norway
Addeco SA	Switzerland	LVMH	France
Akzo Nobel	Netherlands	Man AG	Germany
Alusuissel-Lonza Holding	Switzerland	Movenpick Holding	Switzerland
Arbed SA/Ares Group	Luxembourg	Norsk Hydro	Norway
Asea AB/ABB Group	Sweden	Oce van den Grinten	Netherlands
Astra AB	Sweden	P&C PLC	England
Audiofina SA	Luxembourg	Perkins Foods PLC	England
Bayer AG	Germany	Pernod Ricard SA	France
Benetton Group SA	Italy	Philips NV	Netherlands
Bilspedition Transport &	Sweden	Pilkington PLC	England
Logistics		Pirelli SPA	Italy
Body Shop International	England	PSA Peugeot Citroën SA	France
PLC		Remy Cointreau	France
Bridgen Group PLC	England	Rentokil Initial PLC	England
British Petroleum PLC	England	Repsol	Spain
BSN Groupe	France	Rexam PLC/Bowater PLC	England
Caradon PLC	England	Rio Tinto/RTZ PLC	England
Clondalkin Group PLC	Eire	Royal Dutch Petroleum	Netherlands
CMB Packaging	Belgium	Royal Nedlloyd Group	Netherlands
Compagnie des Machines	France	Royal Pakhoed NV	Netherlands
Bull		RWE AG	Germany
Computer 2000	Germany	Ryan Hotels	Eire
Continental AG	Germany	Saipem SPA	Italy
Daimler Benz AG	Germany	Sandvik	Sweden
Danisco A/S	Denmark	SCA	Sweden
Degussa AG	Germany	Schering AG	Germany
Deutsche Babcock AK	Germany	Shell Trading and	England
Electrolux	Sweden	Transport PLC	
Elf Sanofi	France	Siemens AG	Germany
Elsevier	Netherlands	SKF	Sweden
Emess PLC	England	Société Générale de	Belgium
Endesa	Spain	Belgique	
Ericsson	Sweden	Stora Kopparbergs	Sweden
Esselte	Sweden	Bergslags	
GN Great Nordic	Denmark	Stork NV	Netherlands
Grand Metropolitan	England	Telefonica	Spain
PLC/Guinness		Total SA	France
Great Universal Stores	England	Unilever NV	Netherlands
PLC		Veba AG	Germany
Hafslund Nycomed	Norway	Vew/Vereinigte	Germany
Heineken NV	Netherlands	Elektrizitatswer	
Hunter Douglas NV	Netherlands	Volkswagen AG	Germany
ICI PLC	England	Volvo AB	Sweden
Independent Newspapers	Eire	Wella AG	Germany
PLC		Woodchester Investment	Eire
Jefferson Smurfit Group	Eire	PLC	

4. The empirical analysis

Methodology

The C index

From among the different models for measuring the level of harmonization proposed in previous studies we have selected the C index. Although in some of the studies shown in Table 1 the authors used indices and statistical models as alternatives, as we have already mentioned, they are not. The suitability of each method depends, in our opinion, on the concept of harmonization used and the objectives of the study. As we mentioned before, the use of a statistical model implies a concept of the term 'harmony' that supposes that the distribution of companies between the different alternatives is the same in all countries. On the other hand, the use of an index implies that maximum harmony is reached when all the companies in the sample select the same alternative (or give information to reconcile). For the purpose of this study we consider a sample of companies with very similar characteristics, aiming to test whether they concentrate on certain alternatives regardless of their countries of origin. We assume that 'global players' operate in an international context and the characteristics of the users of their financial statements are similar independently of their national context. Our aim is not then to measure the level of harmony between the countries but the level of harmony of these kind of companies, the 'global players', which are supposed to operate under similar circumstances. For this purpose we have considered the C index as the most suitable method for our analysis. The reason is that it allows us to measure the concentration of companies on one or some alternatives, while a statistical model would be more suitable if we wanted to test the level of harmony between the countries. This would be the case if the sample consisted of companies with a variety of characteristics, and was big enough to obtain significant results for every country. For the same reason, we have not broken down the index in the within-country and between-country comparability indices as other authors have done (see Archer *et al.*, 1995), as we are not interested in measuring the level of harmony between countries but between specific companies, the so-called global players. But, in spite of this, these companies belong to different national regulatory systems, so this could not simply be ignored. Indeed, the results in Tables 3 to 6 are expressed per countries.

We calculate the index in the following way:

$$\text{Total comparability index} = \Sigma(x_{+j} \, (x_{+j} - 1)/x_{++}(x_{++} - 1))$$

where x_{+j} is the number of cases in which the accounting method j is selected. The value of the index would be 1 when all the companies select the same accounting method.

Table 3 Income tax index.

	Period 1991–2						Period 1996–7					
	A1	A2	A3	A4	A5	Total	A1	A2	A3	A4	A5	Total
Belgium	0	2	0	0	0	**2**	0	2	0	0	0	**2**
Denmark	0	1	1	0	0	**2**	0	2	0	0	0	**2**
Ireland	0	0	5	0	1	**6**	0	0	5	0	1	**6**
France	0	7	0	2	0	**9**	0	9	0	0	0	**9**
Germany	8	4	0	2	0	**14**	4	8	0	2	0	**14**
Italy	1	1	1	0	0	**3**	0	3	0	0	0	**3**
Luxembourg	0	0	2	0	0	**2**	0	2	0	0	0	**2**
Netherlands	1	10	0	1	0	**12**	1	10	0	1	0	**12**
Norway	3	0	0	0	0	**3**	0	3	0	0	0	**3**
Spain	0	3	0	0	0	**3**	0	3	0	0	0	**3**
Sweden	8	1	1	1	0	**11**	3	7	1	0	0	**11**
Switzerland	0	1	1	1	0	**3**	0	3	0	0	0	**3**
UK	0	0	14	1	0	**15**	0	1	14	0	0	**15**
Total	**21**	**30**	**25**	**8**	**1**	**85**	**8**	**53**	**20**	**3**	**1**	**85**
Total comparability			**0.27**						**0.41**			

Table 4 Financial leases index.

	Period 1991–2						Period 1996–7					
	A1	A2	A3	A4	A5	Total	A1	A2	A3	A4	A5	Total
Belgium	0	1	0	1	0	**2**	0	1	0	1	0	**2**
Denmark	0	2	0	0	0	**2**	0	2	0	0	0	**2**
Ireland	0	5	1	0	0	**6**	0	5	1	0	0	**6**
France	0	6	3	0	0	**9**	0	8	0	1	0	**9**
Germany	0	1	9	3	1	**14**	0	3	7	4	0	**14**
Italy	0	2	0	0	1	**3**	0	3	0	0	0	**3**
Luxembourg	0	2	0	0	0	**2**	0	2	0	0	0	**2**
Netherlands	0	4	2	6	0	**12**	0	4	1	7	0	**12**
Norway	0	1	0	2	0	**3**	0	2	0	1	0	**3**
Spain	1	0	0	2	0	**3**	1	0	0	2	0	**3**
Sweden	0	1	4	6	0	**11**	0	6	2	4	0	**12**
Switzerland	0	1	1	0	1	**3**	0	1	1	0	1	**3**
UK	0	14	0	1	0	**15**	0	15	0	0	0	**15**
Total	**1**	**40**	**20**	**21**	**3**	**85**	**1**	**52**	**12**	**20**	**1**	**86**
Total comparability			**0.33**						**0.46**			

Table 5 Goodwill index.

	Period 1991–2						Period 1996–7					
	A1	*A2*	*A3*	*A4*	*A5*	*Total*	*A1*	*A2*	*A3*	*A4*	*A5*	*Total*
Belgium	0	0	2	0	0	**2**	0	0	2	0	0	**2**
Denmark	0	1	0	1	0	**2**	0	2	0	0	0	**2**
Ireland	0	4	1	0	2	**7**	0	2	2	0	2	**6**
France	0	0	9	0	0	**9**	0	1	8	0	0	**9**
Germany	2	7	3	1	1	**14**	0	2	8	1	3	**14**
Italy	0	0	1	0	2	**3**	0	0	1	2	0	**3**
Luxembourg	0	0	1	1	0	**2**	0	0	1	1	0	**2**
Netherlands	0	9	0	0	3	**12**	0	8	3	0	1	**12**
Norway	0	0	3	0	0	**3**	0	0	3	0	0	**3**
Spain	0	0	3	0	0	**3**	0	0	3	0	0	**3**
Sweden	2	0	9	0	0	**11**	0	0	11	0	0	**11**
Switzerland	2	0	0	1	0	**3**	0	0	2	1	0	**3**
UK	0	12	1	0	2	**15**	0	11	1	0	3	**15**
Total	**6**	**33**	**33**	**4**	**10**	**86**	**0**	**26**	**45**	**5**	**9**	**85**
Total comparability			**0.31**						**0.38**			

Table 6 Foreign currency index.

	Period 1991–2						Period 1996–7					
	A1	*A2*	*A3*	*A4*	*A5*	*Total*	*A1*	*A2*	*A3*	*A4*	*A5*	*Total*
Belgium	1	0	1	0	0	**2**	1	0	1	0	0	**2**
Denmark	2	0	0	0	0	**2**	2	0	0	0	0	**2**
Ireland	6	0	0	0	0	**6**	6	0	0	0	0	**6**
France	5	0	0	1	3	**9**	8	0	0	1	0	**9**
Germany	2	7	1	1	3	**14**	5	7	0	1	1	**14**
Italy	0	0	0	1	2	**3**	1	1	0	0	1	**3**
Luxembourg	2	0	0	0	0	**2**	2	0	0	0	0	**2**
Netherlands	9	1	1	0	1	**12**	10	0	2	0	0	**12**
Norway	1	0	3	0	0	**4**	2	2	1	0	0	**5**
Spain	1	0	1	2	0	**4**	1	0	2	0	0	**3**
Sweden	5	1	2	1	2	**11**	8	0	1	2	0	**11**
Switzerland	1	0	0	0	2	**3**	1	0	0	0	2	**3**
UK	12	1	0	0	2	**15**	15	0	0	0	0	**15**
Total	**47**	**10**	**9**	**6**	**15**	**87**	**62**	**10**	**7**	**4**	**4**	**87**
Total comparability			**0.34**						**0.53**			

The bootstrapping test and the chi-square test

Having calculated the value of the C index for the four accounting issues (income tax, financial leases, goodwill and foreign currency translation) in the two periods (1991–2 and 1996–7), we analysed whether the change between the two periods was statistically significant by using a simple bootstrapping procedure. No straightforward method has been developed to test the statistical significance of changes in the index until now.

The bootstrapping procedure is a method for estimating the distribution of an estimator or test statistic by resampling one's data. This technique was developed by Efron in 1979 (quoted in Greene, 1997) and has been appearing with increasing frequency in applied econometrics literature. However, as Horowitz (1995) points out, 'the theory of the bootstrap for many semiparametric estimators of interest in econometrics (e.g. single-index models, sample-selection models, partially linear models) is still largely undeveloped'.

We consider that the characteristics of the bootstrapping test could make it an appropriate method if the value of a change in the C index from one period to another is considered significant in order to conclude whether there is (or not) a process of harmonization. Our hypothesis in its null form is:

H_0: The observed change in the value of the index is not different from the changes we obtain with a randomly generated distribution.

If we find that the observed change is unlikely to come from the generated distribution, we conclude that the initial assumption is rejected. The distribution is generated by 1,000 interactions, where the accounting choices are randomly allocated using the binomial distribution, with the number of trials set to the sample size and the probability of success determined by the number of occurrences of that accounting method in the sample. The index is then calculated for each of the 1,000 interactions and 999 changes in the index are subsequently derived. The observed change in the index is then compared with this generated distribution. The probability of the observed change not being greater than zero is given by the rank of the observed change when contrasted with the generated distribution (see Noreen, 1992; Bradley and Tibshirani, 1993).

Besides the previously described methodology for measuring the harmonization process, we have also calculated the chi-square test, but not to ascertain whether there is a significant difference between the countries in one period, as in the case of previous studies, but rather to see whether there is a significant difference in the distribution of companies between alternative accounting methods in the two periods.[2]

In fact, the chi-square test has not been used in previous research to test the significance but it is important to notice that its application in this case has a lot of limitations. One of the assumptions to apply this test is the independence between the two groups (in our case the same sample of companies in two different periods), so the probability of a company to select one alternative in the second period is independent from its selection in the first period. We are aware that it is not easy to assume independence between the two periods when selecting the alternatives, since companies cannot easily shift from one method to another every year. Another limitation to apply the test is the requirement of at least one specific frequency for each of the alternatives.[3] At any rate, and in spite of these limitations, we have considered it could be interesting to compare the results obtained from this further test with those deriving from the bootstrapping test.

The data and the sample

The sample comprises 85 companies[4] from thirteen European countries whose shares are traded internationally ('global players') (see Table 2). The financial statements of the European companies from those countries whose shares were listed in more than one stock exchange market (the national and at least one foreign market) were required by mail. The whole required information was sent by 85 companies which formed the final sample. Therefore there are certain companies that may be global players that are not included in this sample, and there is also a non-response bias relating to companies that did not provide the report requested. This is a common limitation of this kind of study and is quite difficult to solve (see McLeay *et al.*, 1999, for a further description).

We have analysed their financial statements for the accounting periods 1991–2 and 1996–7 to ascertain which alternative is used by each company for each accounting issue we have considered. The selection of this period has been due to several reasons. First, it has not been analysed in prior research. Second, it has been a recent period in which not many changes in the formal harmonization process have occurred, so that it allows us to test our hypothesis of 'spontaneous harmonization'. It is important to note that in the most recent years changes in laws and rules have been undertaken in some European countries to adapt to the new strategy of harmonization for consolidated accounts of the European Commission.

The accounting issues selected are:

- income tax;
- financial leases;
- goodwill;
- foreign currency translation.

The reason for selecting these specific issues is largely that they have all been considered as among the most controversial in terms of comparability.

A very good example of this is the attention that the IASC has given to these issues revising the standards and even the exposure drafts, several times in some cases. Although we could have introduced even more controversial issues, such as asset revaluation and depreciation, among others, we have considered that for the purpose of our analysis these four aspects were sufficient to test our hypothesis and to apply our proposed methodology. For each of these issues we considered five alternatives, as follows:

(a) Income tax

    A1: Nil provision or 'taxes payable' approach.
    A2: Full provision.
    A3: Partial provision.
    A4: Deferred tax recognized but method used not specified.
    A5: No recognition of deferred tax and it is not known whether or not deferred tax accounting is applicable.

(b) Financial leases

    A1: Capitalization as intangible assets.
    A2: Capitalization as tangible fixed assets.
    A3: Non-capitalization.
    A4: The method used and whether it is applicable or not are not specified.
    A5: Capitalization as other assets.

(c) Goodwill

    A1: Credited to income in the year of acquisition.
    A2: Written off against reserves in the year of acquisition.
    A3: Shown as an asset and amortized in more than five years.
    A4: Shown as an asset and amortized in less than five years.
    A5: The method used and whether it is applicable or not are not specified.

(d) Foreign currency translation

For this issue we considered only the accounting treatment of the differences arising from the foreign currency translation of monetary items and transactions in foreign currency, and not that of the differences in the translation of subsidiaries' accounts.

    A1: Exchange gains and losses as income/loss for the year.
    A2: Exchange losses as period expenses and no recognition of unrealized gains.
    A3: Exchange losses as period expenses and unrealized gains deferred.
    A4: No recognition of unrealized exchange differences.
    A5: The method used and whether it is applicable or not are not specified.

Results

In this section we show our results of the selected accounting issues.

The indices

(a) Deferred taxation

The number of companies which select the stated alternatives in each country and the values of the C index for the two periods considered are shown in Table 3. A clear increase can be observed in the value of the total comparability index. The companies clearly concentrate their selection on alternative A2 in 1996–7 (the full provision), due mainly to the large number of companies which depart from the nil-provision approach and to the companies which used a deferred tax method but without specifying which was, although they do know.

(b) Financial leases

The results are shown in Table 4. There is a clear increase in the value of the total index. There is a concentration on the alternative of capitalization as tangible fixed assets in the second period, clearly due to the considerable number of companies which changed from the alternative of non-capitalization (A3) to capitalization as tangible fixed assets (A2). It can be observed that, in this case, the number of companies for which the method used is unknown (A4) is high and does not decrease in the later period considered.

Non-capitalization prevails mainly in German companies, which is normal, taking into account that in the considered period consolidated accounts had to comply with the principles used in individual accounts, which are greatly influenced by tax rules.

(c) Goodwill

The results are shown in Table 5. The increase in the total index is due mainly to the companies which passed from writing off the goodwill in the year of acquisition against income or reserves (alternatives A1 and A2), to the alternative A3, i.e. to amortize the goodwill in more than five years. However, many companies (mainly in the UK and the Netherlands) still use alternative A2 (written off against reserves in the year of acquisition).

(d) Foreign currency translation

The results are shown in Table 6. A large increase in the total index can be observed in this case, due mainly to a concentration on A1 implying the recognition of the realized and unrealized gains and losses in the income statement. This was due mainly to the fact that many companies did not provide any information on the method used in 1991–2, whereas they did in 1996–7. Accordingly, the increase in the index may be due not to a harmonization in the measurement criteria but simply to the disclosure of the method used.

Statistical analysis of the significance

After calculating the value of the indices in the two periods, we used the bootstrapping test to see whether the observed increase in the value of the total index for the four accounting issues is statistically significant. There is not a statistical rule to determine the limits to consider a result as significant. In this case we have to consider that a difference which is between the first ten differences of 1,000 could be regarded as a significant change in the value of the index, and not a random difference. The results are shown in Table 7.

It can be observed that the difference between the two values of the indices we obtained for the two periods could be considered higher than a random difference in all cases. Just as in the case of leasing, the result seems to be less significant but considering the 999 random differences the twenty-third can also be considered, in our opinion, as a non-random difference.

On the other hand, the results of testing the significance of the differences between the indices using the chi-square test are shown in Table 8. It can be observed that the different distribution of companies among the alternatives seems to be statistically significant (at the 0.05% level) in the case of deferred taxation, leasing. In the case of foreign currency translation the results are significant at the 0.1% level, and they are not significant in the case of goodwill. It should be noted that in the case of lease transactions and goodwill the criteria of the frequencies of the chi-square test were not followed

Table 7 Bootstrapping test.

Accounting issue	Total index 1991–2	Total index 1996–7	Bootstrapping ranking out of 1000
Deferred taxation	0.27	0.41	9
Leasing	0.33	0.46	23
Goodwill	0.30	0.38	10
Foreign currency translation	0.34	0.53	1

Table 8 Chi-square test.

Accounting issue	χ^2 test	Significance level
Deferred taxation	15.03	0.004
Leasing	6.10	0.047
Goodwill	4.39	0.222
Foreign currency translation	9.08	0.059

(see note 3). Accordingly, we had to consider only two alternatives in the case of leasing (the most widely used and the others) and three alternatives in the case of goodwill (the two most widely used and the others) and, therefore, the results must be examined with caution.

5. Summary, conclusions and implications

The main objectives of this paper are, on the one hand, to test whether there has been a 'spontaneous harmonization' process in the accounting practices of European 'global players', focusing on certain measurement criteria relating to specific controversial accounting issues. On the other hand, we want to propose a methodology for testing the significance of the results obtained. With these purposes in mind, we have first described the situation of the research in the field of harmonization by making a classification of the studies and a critical analysis of previous studies on material harmonization (their data sources, methodologies and results).

We consider one of the major deficiencies in the index-based methods of measuring harmonization is that no test of significance has been included in previous research. In this paper, we propose a bootstrapping test of the C index as a way of measuring the significance of the change in its value.

For the empirical analysis, we consider a sample of 'global players' from thirteen European countries and analyse their financial statements. Taking into account four accounting issues (deferred taxation, goodwill, leasing and foreign currency translation) we calculate the C index for the periods 1991–2 and 1996–7. Then, besides comparing the value of the index in the two periods for the four accounting issues, we analyse whether there is a statistically significant increase in the level of harmony between the two periods, firstly by analysing the difference in the value of the index using a bootstrapping procedure, and second by using the chi-square test. The main conclusions we obtained from this study can be summarized as follows.

The concept of harmonization used in research is important for knowing which methodology is more suitable to empirical analysis. Indices and statistical models are not alternative methods because the implicit concept of harmonization is different. We consider that the C index is an adequate method for testing our hypothesis and the bootstrapping test seems to be an appropriate way of measuring the significance in the increase in the value of the indices.

In relation to the process of harmonization, previous empirical studies showed there has been an increase in the level of harmony of European accounting practices. Since the end of the 1980s 'global players' seemed to be involved in a process of 'spontaneous' *de facto* measurement harmonization, which was occurring independently from the formal harmonization of accounting standards. In our empirical analysis we have obtained a higher value for the index in the second period and, using the bootstrapping procedure, we have concluded that this increase is significant in all the cases we have considered. So our results corroborate the evidence that this process of spontaneous harmonization of European 'global players' went on in the 1990s.

In our opinion, the implications of this empirical evidence of spontaneous harmonization of 'global players' is that the formal harmonization process carried out by the adaptation of national accounting rules to the EU directives does not seem to be sufficient for the international players. The problems involved in the comparability of financial statements still constitute a barrier in an international context and 'global players' and financial analysts which operate in a global market are pressuring the institutional regulatory bodies, in particular the European Commission.

The implications for regulatory bodies of results of this kind are important. The existence of a *de facto* harmonization process creates pressure to achieve formal harmony, at least for these specific companies whose characteristics make them less easily influenced by specific national factors. In fact, the national regulatory bodies of certain European countries have adopted the strategy of allowing certain companies to use international standards for consolidated accounts following the 'new strategy for international harmonization' of the European Commission (European Commission, 1995). The last Communication of the European Commission (European Commission, 2000) in which the inclusion of IASs in the directives for consolidated accounts of listed companies is proposed, is a good example of the reaction of the institutional bodies to this evidence.

Acknowledgements

The authors are grateful to the Departamento Dirección y Gestión de Empresas (Corporate Management and Administration Department) of Universidad de Almería, where the financial statements were collected, and especially to Professor Bill Rees from Glasgow University and Professor Stuart McLeay from the University of Wales for their help and useful comments. We are also grateful to the participants in the British Accounting Association Congress 1999 and the European Accounting Association Congress 1999 and to the two anonymous reviewers for their effort and their comments and suggestions to improve the paper.

This study forms part of a research project financed by the Directorate-General of Higher Education (DGES) of the Spanish Ministry of Education and Culture (PB96–0022) and the project Harmonia (Accounting Harmonisation and Standardisation in Europe: Enforcement, Comparability and Capital Market Effects) financed by the European Commission under the Potential Human Program.

Notes

1 There is an English version of this study in Socías (1996).
2 This test assumes independence between the two groups considered. In the case at hand, the results must be taken with caution because the selection of one accounting alternative in one period could not be considered independent from the selection made in previous years.
3 At least 20% of the alternatives must have a frequency of five and none less than one. In case it does not happen, some of the alternatives must combine in order to comply with the requirement.
4 Although the sample consists of 85 companies, the total number of cases will be higher for some specific issues because certain companies use two alternative accounting methods at the same time.

References

Archer, S., Delvaille, P. and McLeay, S. (1995) 'The measurement of harmonisation and the comparability of financial statement items: within-country and between-country effects', *Accounting and Business Research*, 25(98): 67–80.

Archer, S., Delvaille, P. and McLeay, S. (1996) 'A statistical model of international accounting harmonization', *Abacus*, 32(1): 1–29.

Bradley, E. and Tibshirani, K. J. (1993) *An Introduction to the Bootstrap*. London: Chapman & Hall.

Emenyonu, E. N. and Gray, S. J. (1992) 'EC accounting harmonisation: an empirical study of measurement practices in France, Germany and UK', *Accounting and Business Research*, 23(89): 49–58.

European Commission (1995) 'Accounting harmonisation: a new strategy *vis-à-vis* international harmonisation', COM 95 (508).

European Commission (2000) 'EU financial reporting strategy: the way forward', COM (2000)-359-Final.

García Benau, M. A. (1994) *Armonización de la información financiera en Europa*. Madrid: ICAC.

Garrod, N. and Sieringhaus, I. (1995) 'European Union accounting harmonization: the case of leased assets in the United Kingdom and Germany', *European Accounting Review*, 4(1): 155–64.

Greene, W. H. (1997) *Econometric Analysis*. Englewood Cliffs, NJ: Prentice-Hall.

Herrmann, D. and Thomas, W. (1995) 'Harmonisation of accounting measurement practices in the European Community', *Accounting and Business Research*, 25(100): 253–65.

Horowitz, J. L. (1995) 'Bootstrap methods in econometrics: theory and numerical performance', Paper presented at the 7th World Congress of the Econometric Society, Tokyo, August.

Krisement, V. (1997) 'An approach for measuring the degree of comparability of financial accounting information', *European Accounting Review*, 6(3): 465–85.

Laínez Gadea, J. A., Callao Gastón, S. and Jarne Jarne, J. I. (1996) 'Información exigida por las bolsas de valores: análisis empírico de la armonización internacional', *Revista Española de Financiación y Contabilidad*, 25(86): 35–56.

Laínez Gadea, J. A., Callao Gastón, S. and Jarne Jarne, J. I. (1997) 'Accounting diversity versus international accounting harmonization. Empirical evidence',

Paper presented at the Annual Congress of the European Accounting Association, Graz, April.

McLeay, S., Neal, D. and Tollington, T. (1999) 'International standardization and harmonization: a new measurement technique', *Journal of International Financial Management and Accounting*, 10(1): 42–70.

Meek, G. K. and Saudagaran, S. M. (1990) 'A survey of research of financial reporting in a transnational context', *Journal of Accounting Literature*, 9: 145–82.

Nair, R. D. and Frank, W. G. (1981) 'The harmonization of International Accounting Standards', *International Journal of Accounting*, Fall.

Nobes, C. W. (1981) 'An empirical investigation of international accounting principles: a comment', *Journal of Accounting Research*, Spring: 268–80.

Nobes, C. W. and Parker, R. (2000) *Comparative International Accounting*, 6th edn. London: Financial Times/Prentice-Hall.

Noreen, E. (1992) *Computer Intensive Methods for Testing Hypothesis: An Introduction*. London: John Wiley.

Pierce, A. and Weetman, P. (2000) 'The impact of non-disclosure on measurement of de facto harmonisation: a two country comparison', Paper presented at the 23rd Annual Congress of the European Accounting Association, Munich.

Rahman, A., Perera, H. and Ganeshanandam, S. (1996) 'Measurement of formal harmonisation in accounting: an exploratory study', *Accounting and Business Research*, 26(4): 325–39.

Socías, A. (ed.) (1996) *Readings in Accounting in the European Union*. Palma.

Tay, J. S. W. and Parker, R. H. (1990) 'Measuring international harmonization and standardization', *Abacus*, 26(1): 71–88.

Tay, J. S. W. and Parker, R. H. (1992) 'Measuring international harmonization and standardization: a reply', *Abacus*, 28(2): 217–20.

Thorell, P. and Whittington, G. (1994) 'The harmonization of accounting within the EU: problems, perspectives and strategies', *European Accounting Review* 2: 215–39.

Van der Tas, L. G. (1988) 'Measuring harmonisation of financial reporting practice', *Accounting and Business Research*, 18(70): 157–69.

Van der Tas, L. G. (1992a) 'Evidence of EC financial reporting practice harmonization', *European Accounting Review*, 1(1): 69–104.

Van der Tas, L. G. (1992b) 'Measuring international harmonization and standardization: a comment', *Abacus*, 28(2): 211–16.

Walton, P. (1992) 'Harmonization of accounting in France and Britain: some evidence', *Abacus*, 28(2): 186–99.